Praise for Volume 1

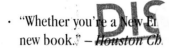 

- "Whether you're a New E..d by [this] intriguing new book." – *Houston Ch*.

- "Lavin makes a strong............................... Patriots are a better organization than they are a team.'" – *New York Times*, Richard Sandomir

- "Lavin has melded together fascinating quotes, statistics, and revelations that keep the reader entranced... A wonderful opportunity to [meet] the players, characters, and team... Lavin's remarkable story provides the recipe for championship stew." – *Boston Phoenix*, Christopher Young

- "Impressive look at what drives the team's success... It doesn't read like some wonkish, academic text." – *Boston Herald*, Greg Gatlin

- "Timely, insightful book." – *(New Orleans) Times-Picayune*, Peter Finney

- "Fascinating." – *Toronto Star*, Dave Perkins

- "Required Reading... If the Colts, Steelers and any other NFL organization would like to get a jump on the Patriots, they should definitely pick up a copy." – *(New Bedford, MA) Standard-Times*, Dan Pires and Steve DeCosta

- "Great book. Having read and enjoyed other football-as-a-metaphor-for-life books... I can say [this] is as comprehensive and well-written a book as you can find on this subject. ...It was his intention to merge his studies of high-performance organizations and his obsession with his favorite team. This he has done most admirably." – *Yahoo! Sports*, Doug Farrar

- "Fascinating read... Gives you a real insight into what goes on in making this franchise what they are. ...I really recommend it." – *Comcast TV's "Sports Pulse,"* Ed Berliner

MANAGEMENT SECRETS
of the
NEW ENGLAND PATRIOTS

MANAGEMENT
SECRETS
of the
NEW ENGLAND
PATRIOTS

Vol 2: Building a High-Performance Organization

James Lavin

Pointer Press

Designed by James Lavin

FIRST EDITION

Book's website: www.PatriotsBook.com
Publisher's website: www.PointerPress.com

Printed in the United States on acid-free paper

Publisher's Cataloging-in-Publication
Lavin, James, 1969-
Management Secrets of the New England Patriots, Vol. 2; Building a High-
Performance Organization / James Lavin
p. cm.
Includes endnotes and index.
ISBN-13: 978-0-9762039-8-8
ISBN-10: 0-9762039-8-7
First edition

1. New England Patriots (Football team).
2. Management–General.
3. Football–General / Professional.

GV956.N36
796.3326   2005907302

08 07 06 05   10 9 8 7 6 5 4 3 2 1

P assion, pride, poise, preparation, perseverance

A ttitude, accountability, aggressiveness, awareness

T eamwork, tenacity, technique, tactics

R esolve, responsibility, resilience, respect

I ntelligence, interdependence, intensity

O rganization, overachieving, optimism

T raining, toughness, togetherness

S elflessness, stamina, sacrifice, self-discipline

TABLE OF CONTENTS

VOLUME 2

MORE PRAISE FOR THE PATRIOTS

"The Patriot Doctrine... shiny jewelry comes to those who play well with others."[1]
  – Dave Boling, The News Tribune

"Based on conversations I've had with qualified executives and coaches around the league, [these Patriots] may be the greatest team ever."[2]
  – Chris Mortensen, ESPN

"They're not the Super Bowl champs for nothing. They are a team. A *team!*"[3]
  – Ed Reed, star safety of the Baltimore Ravens

"There is a team concept in New England, not just from the standpoint of the players but expressed throughout the whole organization. I have developed a feeling in my heart for the way that the Patriots do things, and that is something that I want my name to be tied to for the rest of my life. When people ask me who I played for, I say the New England Patriots."[4]
  – Cornerback Otis Smith, after re-signing for one day in 2005 so he could retire as a Patriot

"We're very lucky to be in a position to have learned a lot from them. You have to be blind to live in New England the last four years and not learn some valuable lessons from what they've accomplished, and how they've accomplished it."[5]
  – Theo Epstein, Boston Red Sox GM, after the Sox won their first World Series since 1918

"[Belichick]'s the model coach and runs the model franchise in the NFL... The job he's done over the last few years may be the best coaching job of all time. He's taken young players and free agents and–even with all the injuries–they don't make mistakes."[6]
  – Jimmy Johnson, multi-Super Bowl champion head coach

"The model coach. The model franchise. The model team. And they stick us in there. It's payback."[7]
  – Oakland Raiders owner Al Davis, unable to contain his gratitude to league schedulers over opening the 2005 season at Foxboro

"We take a lot of criticism in Buffalo like we're the only team that can't beat New England. I don't see anybody beating them, so we have a lot of company."[8]
  – Tom Donohoe, Buffalo Bills general manager

"It's hard to be brief about what Scott [Pioli] and the Patriots have done. 'Impress' is the wrong word. 'Inspired' is a better one."[9]
  – *Cleveland Indians general manager Mark Shapiro*

"36+38+39=Dynasty"
  – *Dunkin' Donuts signs at Super Bowl victory parade*

"When you have that chemistry going, when you have a group working as one, it's hard to beat, and that's what we had. That's what the Patriots have."[10]
  – *Michael Andretti, whose Andretti Green Racing won the IndyCar championship and eight of 16 Honda car races in 2004*

"The Patriots brass is so ahead of the curve. What second-round pick could have possibly given them 1,600 yards and been ridden to a Super Bowl title as Dillon was?"[11]
  – *Todd Christensen, former Oakland Raiders tight end*

"[Belichick] is on top of the pyramid. Is there anyone in the profession today that is performing any more brilliantly than Bill? ...What they do is brilliant in its execution in that it is absolutely fundamentally flawless. [Players] are at the right place at the right time, doing the right things. I have never seen an entire team manage a game as well as the Patriots do."[12]
  – *Baltimore Ravens head coach Brian Billick*

"They play football the way it's supposed to be played. They play a team game. There are no Kobe Bryants on that team. Everybody has one goal, and that's winning. I respect what they do. Look around the league with guys wanting all the stats and publicity. That doesn't happen in New England."[13]
  – *Jason Taylor, Miami Dolphins defensive end*

"I try to read everything I can about them and respect the hell out of the way they've done things."[14]
  – *R.C. Buford, GM of the NBA champion San Antonio Spurs*

"There's no way on God's green earth that New England should be getting away with the current makeup of its secondary. But the defending Super Bowl champs aren't just surviving with spare parts and fill-ins at one of the game's most pivotal segments of the depth chart, they're thriving. ...We may have never seen better use of a regular-season roster than what the Patriots are currently achieving. I'm out of adjectives."[15]
  – *Don Banks, Sports Illustrated*

"How can anybody object to favorably comparing the New England Patriots to any of the great NFL champions?"[16]
  – *Michael Wilbon, Washington Post*

"A model franchise. They've accomplished the building of a very fine stadium in a market that had stadium difficulties for 40 years... and they won [three] Super Bowls."[17]
   – *Kansas City Chiefs owner Lamar Hunt*

"Their big-play players... have made more big plays consistently in critical games really than anybody I can remember."[18]
   – *Indianapolis Colts GM Bill Polian*

"The consistency that [Belichick's] team has displayed over the past three-and-a-half years has been nothing short of amazing. His team wins regardless of injury or whom they are playing... Watching greatness unfold before our eyes is something we all can be thankful for."[19]
   – *Boomer Esiason, NFL analyst and former NFL quarterback*

"The Patriots certainly fall into the [dynasty] category."[20]
   – *Joe Theismann, Super Bowl XVII-winning quarterback*

"Most of the teams in the playoffs beat more losing teams. When [my 2000 St. Louis Rams] won the Super Bowl... 10 or 11 of our wins were against teams that ended up the season with a losing record. If you look at New England... it doesn't matter if it was a winning team or a losing team. They beat them anyway."[21]
   – *Kansas City Chiefs head coach Dick Vermeil*

"I watched that patchwork secondary... [The Patriots] cover up for personnel deficiencies better than any team I've ever seen."[22]
   – *Paul Zimmerman ("Dr. Z"), Sports Illustrated*

"The Patriots have... laid waste to the proverbial level playing field, somehow figuring out parity in a fashion that appears to have escaped their NFL rivals. Moreover, sportswriters and parents have been crying out for exemplars in sport... If we're all lucky, the Pats, with their team-first ethic, have not only won three Super Bowl championships, but have midwived a true revolution in pro sports."[23]
   – *Mark Starr, Newsweek*

"They had a ton of guys who didn't play last year [2004], and it didn't make that much difference."[24]
   – *Indianapolis Colts head coach Tony Dungy*

"The Patriots' level of efficiency should be the envy of every assembly line in the world because each man does his job with precision, craftsmanship and attention to detail. ...They practice [everything] so much that when they do it in a game, it's like they've been doing it their whole lives."[25]
   – *Fox Sports analyst and former NFL lineman Brian Baldinger*

"The Patriots show how to beat the system."[26]
   – Jonathan Rand, KCChiefs.com

"You don't have to have the best players to win a championship. You have to have the best team... The Patriots showed how that works. If you had a skills test and had everybody in the NFL competing, a lot of those Patriots players wouldn't fare well. But when it comes to 11 guys doing what they're supposed to do, playing at a high level each week and not making a lot of mental mistakes, they did that better than anyone."[27]
   – Minnesota Vikings quarterback Daunte Culpepper

"I had a chance to go elsewhere, but after having a conversation with coach Belichick and the other coaches, I realized this is a great group of guys. From the facility to the history of the team, this is a rare opportunity. It's first-class all the way around."[28]
   – New Patriots kick returner/running back Chad Morton

"None of these experts would have made the same [draft] picks... but New England's hoisted too many Super Bowl trophies, won too many big games, and done so with too many overlooked players for anyone to wonder if they know what they're doing. ...Just assume they get it right during the NFL Draft. There's not much historical evidence that they do anything else."[29]
   – Tom E. Curran, Providence Journal

"It's one of those teams that I think everybody looks at, you look at them on paper, and you go, 'We match up pretty well against those guys.' Then you go in there."[30]
   – Pittsburgh Steelers head coach Bill Cowher

"If this is how the Patriots deal with adversity, they may never lose another game... The Patriots are winning against impossible odds."[31]
   – John Clayton, ESPN

"Sports had kind of gotten away from the concept of a team. The leagues seemed to prefer to promote one guy. We've started a new trend. Now you see teams eliminating the 'me' and the 'I.' You heard the Red Sox talk about it. You heard people comparing the [NBA champion] Detroit Pistons to us, because they are a team without stars."[32]
   – Patriots linebacker Willie McGinest

"Even the Yankees have discovered that repeating isn't as easy as it used to be. College basketball hasn't had back-to-back champs since Duke did it in 1991 and '92. ...In today's world, unless you're a quarterback named Tom Brady or a coach named Bill Belichick, you don't repeat in anything."[33]
   – Frank Dascenzo, Herald-Sun

"Congratulations, once again. …It's getting to be old hat here."[34]
  – President Bush, welcoming the Patriots to the Rose Garden for
  the third time in four years

"70% of what I do–how we do things from a personnel standpoint–is the foundation of Bill Belichick. The players we've hit on [in the draft], they matched up with his profile. The ones we missed on didn't fit the description at all."[35]
  – Baltimore Ravens GM Ozzie Newsome, on the value he places on
  notebooks he kept while working with Belichick in Cleveland

"Belichick was getting by with Troy Brown playing nickelback. We know he's a genius, but c'mon."[36]
  – Jeffrey Martin, York Daily Record

"They are the smartest dynasty the NFL has seen. And the calmest. And the most adaptable. And the most humble… The Patriots make fewer mistakes than anyone… Their greatest strength is they have no weakness and their greatest pride is they have no ego."[37]
  – Gary Shelton, St. Petersburg Times

"Just by being here, [I am] a much better player. …Getting a feel for the guys and being around here it is just a totally different feel. It is just a wonderful feeling. I am being honest with you. I feel like I am a rookie all over again, just starting all over with a great organization and great coaches and a great opportunity."[38]
  – David Terrell, former Chicago Bears receiver, one day after
  becoming a Patriot

"I kept asking [Belichick] about discipline, motivation, about team building, about leadership… Thank God for the New England Patriots. They just reconfirm everything we stand for… It's accountability. It's taking care of one another. It's working harder than your opponent."[39]
  – University of Florida football coach Urban Meyer, who seriously
  considered asking Belichick for an autograph when they met

"When the Patriots were figuring out where to display this year's Vince Lombardi Trophy, they should have begun clearing space for next year's, too. Only the Patriots could lose [Charlie Weis, Romeo Crennel, Ty Law, Troy Brown and Tedy Bruschi] and come out better. …Defending world champions shouldn't be allowed to add the talent the Patriots have this offseason. It almost seems unfair."[40]
  – Adam Schefter, NFL.com

"I would have to say [my four years in New England] went pretty well."[41]
  – Romeo Crennel, former Patriots defensive coordinator

"In airports, it's three questions: 'Can I have your autograph?' 'How many touchdowns are you going to throw?' And, 'When are you going to beat New England?'"[42]
– Peyton Manning, Indianapolis Colts quarterback, after shattering the NFL touchdown record with 49

"They've been too good for too long."[43]
– Jon Gruden, Tampa Bay Buccaneers head coach

"Belichick can pick a cornerback off the street and win with him in the lineup three days later."[44]
– Andrew Perloff, Sports Illustrated

"The Patriots could draft six kickers and my little sister and they would still get an 'A' from draft pundits who are terrified to question the genius of Bill Belichick."[45]
– Nat Jackson, Yale Daily News

"When you're deployed, you clutch at a lot of little things. The Patriots were all about team, not individuals, and that's a theme that resonates with the men and women of the armed services."[46]
– John Libby, brigadier general of the National Guard

"How can you not follow him? He's always in the playoffs. You turn the tube on, and there they are."[47]
– New Patriots receiver David Terrell, on whether he–while playing for the Chicago Bears–followed his college quarterback, Tom Brady

"You can feel the confidence in the whole team. It was impressive."[48]
– Kansas City Chiefs linebacker Scott Fujita

"As I surveyed the dysfunctional landscape of sports in recent days, with its flying fists, stun guns, dropping towels and BCS equations, I found myself seeking out the kind of old-school, rock-solid franchise that recalled life before Terrell Owens. I appreciated, once again, the New England Patriots. A team that always seems to avoid notice, but commands admiration. A team not defined by any one individual, but by a collection of individuals with singular purpose."[49]
– Richard Oliver, San Antonio Express-News

"'In Bill We Trust.' …Critical analysis of Patriots moves has disappeared, replaced by a blind obedience to whatever Belichick thinks is the best course of action. (Troy Brown at cornerback? …Um, OK… I guess.) But it is also a literal truth–the Patriots (from the owner on down to the fans) really do believe in Belichick's plan."[50]
– Eric McHugh, The Patriot Ledger (Quincy, MA)

"Who are we to question the New England Patriots? They're winners."
    — Tory Holt, Rams receiver and ESPN guest analyst, during Draft Day coverage

"[The Patriots] knew very well how to work together. In today's era, people celebrate individual accomplishments. But the whole idea of joint operations is bringing our services together as one fighting force–taking into account our individual strengths."[51]
    — Navy admiral Walter Doran, Pacific Fleet commander

"The Patriots made the Chargers look like complete morons for letting Rodney Harrison go, as Harrison has been a beast ever since."[52]
    — Michael Lombardo, Chargers Update

"I've never been around a team like this, where nobody–nobody–ever speaks out."[53]
    — Phil Simms, football analyst and Super Bowl-winning quarterback

"What they do in every facet of the game is unbelievable. In terms of the salary cap, acquiring players, using everything available to them, finding ways to create roles for everyone on their roster in some role, they're way ahead of the curve."[54]
    — Jacksonville Jaguars head coach Jack Del Rio

"If five Super Bowl rings mean anything, [Belichick is] one of the greatest ever."[55]
    — Greg Garber, ESPN football analyst

VOL. 2 OVERVIEW

When I began writing *Management Secrets of the New England Patriots*, I never imagined it might expand to two volumes, let alone a trilogy of more than 1,000 pages. But I have found it impossible to contain the team's inspiring characters, insightful personal philosophies and organizational principles, impressive achievements and instructive lessons within one or even two books without shortchanging you, the reader.

Mark Twain famously apologized that "I didn't have time to write a short letter, so I wrote a long one." I make no such apology. The Patriots are both entertaining and worthy of our extended attention. Patriots players' passion derives from a mindset and lifestyle that can teach us to live more satisfying, fulfilling lives. And Patriots players' professional pride provides a blueprint for designing organizations that harness human hopes to conquer collective challenges. Organizations thrive by dividing group tasks into individual roles and filling each role with an individual whose passionate pursuit of self-actualization aligns with the role he is asked to fulfill. The Patriots have taught me many truths, and I know their story will enlighten and empower you too. I could convey these concepts in fewer pages, but even Mark Twain–who valued brevity–wrote *Huckleberry Finn*, not *Cliff Notes: Huckleberry Finn*. The original, though longer, is a page-turner. For this reason, I share with you the Patriots' story, not just another management textbook.

In Volume 1, I described the astonishing accomplishments of the 2001-2003 Patriots and began sharing their "secrets." Volume 2 is heavy on "secrets," delving deeply into Training, Planning, Collaborating and Motivating. Though these topics sound toast dry, they are essential to any team's success. Volume 3 will break down several more "how" topics (Communicating, Strategizing, etc.) and survey the 2004 and 2005 seasons, including the team's triumph in Super Bowl XXXIX.

Management Secrets analyzes the best football team of the early 21st Century and extracts team-building and leadership principles from an organization as outstanding as any Fortune 500 firm. I decided to write *Management Secrets* not only to celebrate my favorite team but also because Bill Belichick's Patriots can teach organizations everywhere to become "high performance work organizations" whose employees–like Patriots players, coaches and executives–are happier, more engaged with their work, more creative and more productive. As globalization places increasing competitive stress on businesses and workers, who wouldn't want to bolster both labor productivity and job satisfaction? The Patriots' three Super Bowl victories in four seasons demonstrate the benefits of building businesses according to high performance work organization principles.

Such lessons are valuable beyond sports and business. When an organization's mission is as essential as that of the FBI or CIA or FEMA, for example, a dedicated, selfless, mission-driven culture should exist. Leaders should find it easy to fire up employees to perform their jobs with pride and passion because the organization's mission is intrinsically important. Instead, these agencies have been plagued by poor morale and bureaucratic turf wars:

> "The huge failure of the [CIA] to... uncover the 9/11 plot indicates an agency that is demoralized and lacks a unifying *esprit de corps*... Bureaucratic leaders will never get top-level performance from public employees if they rely on individual self-interest... A true leader must... develop a culture of cooperation, trust and pride [where] people believe in the agency, in their work and in their political leadership."[56]

It's perhaps a shame Bill Belichick coached the 2001 New England Patriots to Super Bowl victory rather than run the CIA. It's perhaps a shame he coached the 2002 Patriots rather than serve as Enron CEO. It's perhaps a shame he led the 2003 Patriots to a second world championship rather than run NASA's Space Shuttle program. It's perhaps a shame he led the 2004 Patriots to a third Vince Lombardi Trophy rather than oversee a fair election as Ohio's Secretary of State. And it's perhaps a shame he is coaching the 2005 Patriots rather than running FEMA.

I hope current and future leaders of such organizations will learn from this most successful football program. The world desperately needs to clone Bill Belichick's leadership skills and the professionalism and team spirit of his assistants and players.

TRAINING

"[People] think everything comes easy. They look at professional athletes and think they just woke up one day and rolled out of bed and won all those games. It doesn't work like that."[57]
   – *Tom Brady*

"We tell the players, 'It's not where you start, it's where you finish.' That's what they should be concerned about."[58]
   – *Bill Belichick*

"[His players] respect him, even though he never played the game as well as they do. Because they know that in that head of his, he plays it better than anyone. They want to play it just like he sees it. And more and more each day, they do."[59]
   – *Jonathan Comey, The Standard-Times*

Belichick's Patriots are the General Electric of the NFL. GE is famous for developing talent and for periodically purging its poorest performers. CEO Jack Welch devoted most of his time to training and evaluating GE's executives. And he made GE a true "learning organization" by expanding managerial training, on which GE now spends $1 billion annually.[60]

At a Q&A in a packed auditorium, I asked Welch to comment on the Patriots. A beaming Welch excitedly talked on and on, gushing about the Patriots' outstanding management and how smart Belichick is to prepare replacements at every position, including his coaching positions. Bill Belichick is the NFL's Jack Welch. If Welch had been a football coach's son and Belichick had studied chemistry and gone into plastics, their roles might be reversed.

The biggest difference between the Patriots and many businesses is relentless training. Patriots coaches are obsessed with player development. Each coach spends a good chunk of every day in a cycle of evaluating players' performance and advising players how to improve. Belichick says players are astonished by how much they learn:

"[Our former rookies] didn't know anything, but they thought they did. You can look at them now and say, 'Do you remember a year ago you... thought you knew something about what was going on?' And they are like, 'Man, I am telling you, I had no idea what I didn't know. I wish I knew then what I know now.' It is amazing how much they grow and mature as football players in a year. It is really remarkable. But we laugh about it all the time."[61]

Patriots coaches are such skilled teachers that personnel decisions focus more on a player's "coachability" than his statistics because–no matter how good a college player someone was–an NFL rookie must continue improving to become a good NFL player. The physical superiority of NFL players to college players is obvious, but second-year Giants offensive lineman Chris Snee swears "Physically, it's a step up, but the increase isn't nearly what it is for the mental part of the game."[62] For this reason, Belichick and VP of player personnel Scott Pioli will draft passionate players who posted mediocre college stats due to poor training or poor utilization. But they will not sign players who looked great against college competition but care about the perks of playing in the NFL more than working hard to improve and win football games.

For example, Patriots receiver David Givens was the 253rd of 261 players selected in the 2002 NFL Draft. Givens probably wouldn't have played a day in the NFL if the Patriots hadn't taken a chance on him with the 42nd pick in the seventh and final round. The Patriots saw a kid whose best days lay ahead of him because he was still learning to play wide receiver—after also being a quarterback, running back, and punt returner—and hadn't been thrown enough passes at run-happy Notre Dame to shine. He also needed to become stronger. Patriots coaches knew they could polish Givens' receiving skills because scouts reported he "Has outstanding work habits"[63] and a winning attitude.

The Patriots follow what the Japanese term *kaizen*: a never-ending process of making incremental improvements. If someone at Toyota notices a defect in a car, its root cause is determined and procedures are changed to prevent its recurrence.

The Patriots train and utilize players so well that it has become a recruiting attraction to free agents eager to better themselves. After safety Antuan Edwards chose the Patriots over the Dolphins, Jets, Packers and an unknown team, his agent explained:

> "It wasn't just because of the status of the Patriots organization in the NFL and their dominance over the past few years but also my familiarity with Scott Pioli and Bill Belichick and what they've done for some of my other clients, how they've helped their careers."[64]

The Patriots train so well that they often take players unwanted elsewhere (like Hank Poteat and Randall Gay), plug them into their system and continue winning. After injuries felled both starting cornerbacks early in 2004, reporters repeatedly noted their replacements' inexperience and lowly reputations—with Asante Samuel being drafted in Round 4 and Randall Gay going completely undrafted. Asked about the pressure he felt, Samuel replied with the professional confidence Patriots coaches instill by preparing players so thoroughly:

> "I don't look at it that way, as pressure on myself. I know that I have a job to do, and I am going to work as hard as I can to do the job and do it well. I have confidence in my playing ability, and that is what I'm going to do in practice this week and that is what I will do Sunday, play with confidence."[65]

Because they train so rigorously, Patriots players know they and their teammates will perform well on Sunday. Defensive lineman Warren Sapp gleefully told anyone who would listen how lousy Patriots offensive lineman Russ Hochstein was and how Hochstein's incompetence was about to blow Super Bowl XXXVIII for the Patriots. After Sapp practically called him "Russ Chokestein," Hochstein knew Sapp misjudged him: "I'm confident in myself, and my teammates are confident in me. Otherwise, I wouldn't be in there. I wouldn't be here if I couldn't do it. I believe in that totally."[66] As Belichick said after the 2001 team's Super Bowl win:

> "I've heard people say we don't have three or four guys who could start for the Rams. I don't know if that's true or not. I don't think our players believe that. What's important is what the guys in the locker room think and the kind of confidence they have in themselves and each other."[67]

Developing confidence–but not arrogance or complacency–is essential, Patriots offensive coordinator Charlie Weis says, because "you have no chance of winning if you don't believe you're going to win."[68]

But false confidence is worthless. Every Patriot knows championships cannot be won without hard work and year-round improvement. Asked whether he would lighten the Spring 2004 mini-camp training schedule after Chas Gessner, Bethel Johnson and Asante Samuel all sustained lingering injuries during Spring 2003 mini-camp, Belichick said "no" because "we can't improve by doing nothing. We won't get anyone hurt if we don't do anything, but we've got to progress our program along."[69] With such training, unheralded 4th round cornerback Asante Samuel has become outstanding, so the confidence he expressed before the Super Bowl was absolutely authentic. According to "The Football Scientist," Samuel is near the top of the NFL in almost every category: "7th in completion percentage, tied for 14th in yards per attempt, tied for 3rd in tight/good coverage percentage, and had no blown coverages or burns against him. He was also one of the best on deep routes, finishing 8th."[70] Samuel is outstanding in man-to-man coverage: "He was the key to the Pats defense last year... He's a Pro Bowl candidate this year and I think he has the talent to possibly be the best CB in football."[71] Conversely, on the 2004 season's opening night, the Patriots won a squeaker over the Colts after Indianapolis running back Edgerrin James–who had skipped all four preseason games–fumbled twice. Belichick wondered, "If James had played in preseason, maybe he wouldn't have fumbled."[72]

Training not only improves skills but also educates players about their and their teammates' capabilities, limitations and tendencies. When an entire team trains together passionately, mutual trust and understanding develops, and this builds confidence in each player's mind that, if he focuses on doing his role to the best of his ability, his team will perform well.

Patriots are always talking about how much they trust this teammate and that teammate and how another teammate always comes through in the clutch. Tedy Bruschi says his fellow linebackers have his complete confidence: "I look to my right,

I see Roman Phifer, if I look to my left and I see Ted Johnson–whoever is out there–I believe they will get the job done because they are on the field."[73] After Bruschi decided to sit out the 2005 season following a stroke, Ted Johnson said he had complete confidence in whoever would replace Tedy... though no one yet knew who that would be: "Whoever plays will have a lot demanded of him. He'll know there's pressure to do it right and get it right. The reason he's here–whoever he is–is that management thought highly enough of him to bring him in."[74] Linebacker Rosevelt Colvin says new defensive coordinator Eric "Mangini will do a great job. If he wasn't qualified and wasn't capable, then Bill wouldn't have hired him."[75] Running back Corey Dillon loves being a Patriot because "I'm with guys who can go out there and get the job done... The weight ain't all on me to try to go out there and be Superman, and try to save the day."[76]

Such trust derives from knowing that Patriots coaches always find players who perform well under pressure and from intensively training and practicing together. When newcomers Monty Beisel and Chad Brown were learning in 2005 preseason to play middle linebacker in the Patriots' complex system, Patriots veteran Mike Vrabel admitted, "Are we where Ted [Johnson] and Tedy [Bruschi] and I were? Of course not. But when I came in here in 2001, it's not like I automatically hit it off with those guys. It took time. I had to build a relationship with Willie [McGinest] and Tedy and Ted. They had to learn to trust me."[77] Trust evolves through shared experiences.

The Patriots operate their training program much like a well-run school. They admit only motivated students. They set high performance standards and do not tolerate disruptive slackers. They employ skilled teachers. They offer guidance counseling. And they hand out detailed report cards that inform students about weaknesses they must strengthen. After former Patriots defensive coordinator Romeo Crennel concluded his first training camp as Browns head coach, Cleveland's Terrelle Smith noted, "This was like being in school. You studied, you got tested and then the teachers–the coaches–went over the results with you."[78] Because this analogy is so apt, this chapter is divided into sections covering each of these areas: Students, School, Classroom, Guidance counseling and Report cards.

STUDENTS

"Bill Belichick still seems most at home and satisfied working with young people who really, really want to be good at their job in the game of football. And it's not just players. ...Belichick gave [Eric Mangini and Scott Pioli] time. They've given him everything they could in return."[79]
– *Tom E. Curran, Providence Journal*

In Volume 1, I argued that Bill Belichick could not coach any random collection of NFL players to Super Bowl victories. His Patriots train and prepare with an intensity beyond the tolerance of many NFL players. Being a Patriot requires extraordinary competitiveness and passion for self-improvement. At even the greatest school in the world, learning requires curious, studious students. Realizing this, the Patriots find students who are eager to learn, as Patriots kicker Adam Vinatieri explains: "He brings in players that are blue-collar, hard-working guys that think of the team first. He likes very unselfish guys. He puts a special game plan together and needs guys who will jump head first into the game plan."[80]

Some coaches use human psychology to artificially motivate players. Such coaches–like Bill Parcells–may win many games with troublesome players, but few win championships because psychological manipulation is not as reliable or sustainable as intrinsic motivation. Bill Belichick has zero tolerance for players who can't motivate themselves. I believe this is why *NFL Films'* Steve Sabol said, "If I were starting a team from scratch, I'd want Belichick. If I were rebuilding a team, I'd want Lombardi."[81] Belichick takes players with great attitudes and makes them better football players. Lombardi took talented football players and gave them better attitudes. Belichick's value system meshes with team owner Robert Kraft's. Kraft's only constraint on Belichick is: "Just don't bring thugs or hooligans to New England. If that's what we need to win, then we're out of the business."[82]

It's training, not babysitting

"I will do what anyone tells me to do. If they want me to flip pancakes, I'll flip pancakes. It doesn't matter. I just want to play."[83]
 — *Linebacker Ryan Claridge, 2005 Patriots draftee, on whether he wants to play middle linebacker*

"Just work your butt off. It is all about hard work, and you get what you put into it."[84]
 — *Offensive lineman Nick Kaczur, 2005 Patriots draftee*

"It's been made quite clear. You're no longer on a four-year scholarship program. You're in the NFL, and you have to earn your keep. You have to act like a professional."[85]
 — *Quarterback Matt Cassel, five days after the Patriots drafted him*

"The overall total culture of winning and the personal accountability is probably the biggest difference from other teams."[86]
 — *New Patriot linebacker Chad Brown, a three-time Pro Bowler*

"There's nobody that's above the team. Everybody plays by the same rules. Coach expects of the starting quarterback the same as he expects of a practice squad player: that you come out every day and you give everything you can to the team. And that's what we're all about."[87]
 — *Tom Brady*

Teachers have three distinct roles: educating, grading, and disciplining. Bill Belichick doesn't want his coaches wasting even a second on discipline. When Belichick took over from Pete Carroll, linebacker Ted Johnson said, "You feel like you're walking on eggshells around here again. He's a disciplinarian... Everything is more structured. There's much more accountability."[88] The Patriots rely on self-discipline, not military-style discipline. Explains VP of player personnel Scott Pioli:

> "A, a player has to be selfless. B, they have to be extremely competitive because of the very competitive environment. It takes a lot of discipline. When [we] talk about 'discipline,' it's not about how long their hair is, or how much jewelry they wear. We have certain expectations of guys being in the right place at the right time and doing their job a certain way. That's 'discipline' to us."[89]

When players are smart and motivated and coaches can focus on teaching and scheming rather than daycare, the results are astonishing. Philadelphia Eagles offensive coordinator Brad Childress couldn't believe the film he watched in preparation for Super Bowl XXXIX:

> "It is amazing to me that #51 [Don] Davis can line up and play at the safety position. Then [I] replay the tape thinking that I must have missed that number, that's a 50 [linebacker] number back there playing safety, and he's playing the whole game. ...For those guys to be interchangeable, [coaches] must do a good job of teaching them and teaching them that scheme."[90]

Don Davis–a special teamer and backup linebacker–estimates he played about 200 snaps at safety during 2004. Eugene Wilson is another example. After Wilson played his whole life at cornerback, the Patriots shifted him to safety in Week 2 of the 2003 season because they needed him there. One year and one Super Bowl victory later, Wilson was asked whether he's now a safety: "I'm a football player. Whatever they want we me to play, I'm out there."[91]

Coach coachable players

"Come in and do what Coach asks you to do."[92]
  – *Success formula of Deion Branch, Super Bowl XXXIX MVP*

"He listens. Most rookies, they won't listen. He listens."[93]
  – *Safety Rodney Harrison, on 2004 rookie cornerback Randall Gay, who started many games as an undrafted rookie*

"I just come in, try to keep my mouth shut, and just work hard."[94]
  – *Patriots backup quarterback Chris Redman*

"He's a workhorse. He keeps his mouth shut and does what he's told."[95]
  – *Patriots center Dan Koppen, on rookie guard Logan Mankins*

"I always put myself in the position of second place running for first. The day I get into first place is the day I want to quit the game, because I always feel my game can improve."[96]
    – *Cornerback Ellis Hobbs, 2005 Patriots draftee*

"Wherever the team needs me."[97]
    – *USC star Willie McGinest before the Patriots drafted him, in response to "What position do you want to play?"*

"Weight room. Film room. Trust your coaches."[98]
    – *Tedy Bruschi*

After becoming the Cleveland Browns' new head coach in 2005, former Patriots defensive coordinator Romeo Crennel quickly dumped the entire Browns defensive line, explaining: "As football coaches, you like to think you can coach everybody and anybody, but sometimes you have to recognize that you can't."[99] Patriots coaches are too smart to waste their time on under-motivated players.

Scott Pioli says a player's competitiveness can be measured only through actions, not words: "A lot of people say they care about winning. Not everyone does."[100] Romeo Crennel said his job as Patriots defensive coordinator was easier because "[our players] are professionals. They study in the classroom. They study the opponents. They study the game plan. They want to perform well. They want to win."[101] Players who enjoy being coached improve continuously. The best players obsess over self-improvement and crave advice from coaches and veterans. NBA star Larry Bird arrived before practices to shoot baskets and continued shooting after practices. The Patriots are full of Larry Birds and future coaches.

The Patriots knew Tom Brady possessed outstanding growth potential because they observed him at Michigan learning and teaching his teammates. The *Detroit Free Press* described Brady in 1998 isolating himself in the team lunchroom to complete a worksheet analyzing future opponents' defensive tendencies. Thanks to such analysis, Brady could brag as a college junior, "I don't get confused very often. Very rarely do I not see a certain coverage. I'm pretty much always aware of where the defense is, where they're bringing blitz from, where they're dropping into zone coverage."[102] In the NFL–where defensive schemes are more varied and defenders larger and faster–Brady's greatest asset remains breaking down defenses and attacking their weaknesses because his analytical passion derives from his competitive character. Before Super Bowl XXXIX, Eagles cornerback Sheldon Brown gushed about Brady's preparation: "When you send four [blitzers] weak-side, he recognizes the coverage. He… get[s] rid of the ball to the perfect read. It's just tremendous. …He's 6′5″, and sometimes guys are coming scott-free on blitzes and he still gets the ball off. You can't knock the ball down, and he will stand in there and take a shot."[103] The eternally self-critical Brady of 1998 ("I've improved in some areas, and in some other areas, I've definitely got to get better"[104]) will always be self-critical because he knows hard work is the only path to success: "You never give up, you never fold your tent, and you just keep working harder."[105] If Brady were to win Super Bowls annually from now till retirement, he would probably still have nightmares about his mistakes in 2002 that kept the Patriots out of the playoffs, something he still uses as motivation: "If we don't put [2004] behind us, then [2005] could have the same results as 2002, and we don't look forward to that."[106] He has won two straight Super Bowls but can't stop thinking about a meaningless 2004 defeat in Miami: "I hate that game... You remember that feeling, and you're sick to your stomach. You had everything you wanted, and then you goofed it all up."[107]

Brady also helped his Michigan teammates improve: "I'd like to think that I helped some of the younger guys adapt a little bit more as they went through their first, second or third year of college."[108] A teammate said Brady "acts like a 40-year-old man trapped in a 22-year-old man's body" and couldn't list a single wild thing Brady had ever done: "He's not a real flashy guy. A lot of quarterbacks are real flashy or arrogant. He's really down to earth."[109] Brady also knew in college that coaches coach and players play, so he didn't worry about sharing playing time with Drew Henson and instead fixated on perfecting his performance. He even spoke Belichick's language: "I can only control what I can control."[110] Michigan coach Lloyd Carr admired his quarterback: "There's no finer leader in intercollegiate athletics... He handled a coaching decision in a way that only has enhanced his stature among his teammates and anybody who is involved in Michigan football. He took it in a positive way. He's a tremendous, tremendous guy."[111]

When a player has a great attitude toward self-improvement, you can predict success. The wife of the late Dick Rehbein–Patriots quarterbacks coach until his sudden passing before the 2001 season–recalls, "[Dick] came home one night and said to me, 'Pam, this kid Tom Brady is terrific. He's going to be a household name some day, just like Bledsoe or Montana.'"[112] Former Patriots defensive end Dave Nugent–Brady's housemate early in his pro career–could have made the same prediction:

> "[Patriots quarterbacks] were watching film five hours a day. I was like, 'What could you possibly be watching?' And [Brady] was like, 'When I line up on Sundays and I know why people are lined up against me for a certain reason, it's because of the stuff I'm doing now.' I have a lot more respect for that position just from rooming with him. The stuff he has to learn, the huge books that he brings home and studies–it takes a really smart guy to play that position."[113]

Most Patriots possess Brady-like dedication to their craft and to perpetual self-improvement because the Patriots sign and draft players eager to train constantly. When the Patriots asked rookie Vince Wilfork to quickly learn a new position–nose tackle–Wilfork attacked the challenge with every ounce of energy: "Back in training camp, if I was tired, I couldn't go lay down–I had to learn. It was new to me. I grinded for a long time. I didn't have a clue how to play nose tackle."[114] Wilfork had a strong rookie year, helping his team win another Super Bowl.

Doug Flutie has been a professional quarterback for more than two decades. While playing in three pro leagues and on four NFL teams, Flutie never encountered anything like the Patriots' intensity:

> "It is all business, there's no doubt about it. You're having so much thrown at you, you don't have time to fool around. You don't have time to relax and enjoy it. It's very intense. It's very intense in the meeting room. It's intense when you're on the field because you're thinking. They try and challenge you in everything you do."[115]

Patriots players are, as Scott Pioli puts it, "hardworking, passionate about football, respectful about the game of football, and appreciate football for what the game is and not necessarily the trappings of the game… have their egos in check and are always concerned with doing what we need to do to win, rather than doing a lot of things that pacify our egos."[116] This drives success because:

> "There is a voluminous body of research showing that the best performance on complex or creative tasks… is produced by people motivated by intrinsic interest in the task rather than by contingent rewards. In fact, when employers focus attention on rewards for performance, it is likely to *decrease* performance. …Moreover, high performance–the exhilarating sense of mastery and 'flow'–enhances the value and interest of the task."[117]

When human resources firm Hewitt Associates interviews potential hires, it seeks "SWANs": Smart, Works hard, Achieving, and Nice.[118] Time spent coaching SWANs is far more productive than time wasted coaching ugly ducklings. Belichick's Cleveland Browns proved that talented coaching can be squandered on players who lack the will to reach their full potential. When Belichick was exiled from Cleveland– practically driven to the city limits at gunpoint–all he left behind were heavily discounted "Beavis and Belichick" t-shirts.[119] New defensive coordinator Eric Mangini says Patriots coaches tutor players who seek help but eventually give up on players who fail to learn their assignments: "Everybody has a chance to get it right. Either you don't know or you don't care–both of them are problems. We're here whenever somebody needs us, and we can spend as much time as possible to get it right. Fortunately, we have guys who work hard to get it right."[120]

Belichick brought to New England overlooked players with potential, smarts, and great attitudes, SWANs like offensive lineman Joe Andruzzi, who were eager to learn and improve:

> "I was out of work in 2000 and in Bill's first year he picked me up and gave me a shot. [Otherwise], I probably would have gone back to Green Bay and probably would have gotten into special education, which I studied in college. I just would have started working with kids."[121]

Adaptability to changing circumstances is a key coachability trait Patriots scouts look for. Patriots tight end Christian Fauria says, "Everybody is coachable, and everybody is willing to adapt to different situations."[122] Players won't improve unless they're receptive to advice and inspired by challenges. The Patriots asked Dan Klecko to learn defensive line and fullback before deciding in 2004 to teach him to play linebacker. A year later, the relentless Klecko was still grinding away:

> "To go from never playing the position to the hardest system in the NFL, it was tough. I won't lie, it is tough. But I knew it would take time. I knew it would be a long process, not something where it'd be four preseason games and then that's it. We're still in the middle of it."[123]

Training is also wasted on players who miss games due to non-football distractions. One season after the Redskins used the #5 pick in the entire draft on safety Sean Taylor, Taylor's coach–Hall of Famer Joe Gibbs–spent months begging him to train with his teammates before throwing the throttle into reverse and telling him to stay away after he was charged with felony aggravated assault with a firearm.[124] If convicted, Taylor would spend a minimum of three years in prison. Even if Taylor escapes prison, he doesn't value coaching or personal growth. He ignored his coach for months: "Why was I not here? It was offseason. I could have returned his phone calls, but it was offseason. ...There's places you go."[125] Stories of arrogant, violent players are common throughout the NFL but rare in New England. The football-loving players Belichick's Patriots sign avoid trouble.

The Patriots have not always had football-obsessed players. In 1997, then-Patriots quarterback Drew Bledsoe and offensive lineman Max Lane infamously threw themselves from a rock concert stage into a "mosh pit" (reportedly costing Bledsoe $500,000 after a woman claimed a neck injury[126]) days before a 27-7 spanking by the Tampa Bay Buccaneers in which the Patriots "got run over, splattered, flattened silly."[127] Coach Carroll called the game "pathetic" and "disgusting." The Patriots would have been shut out without a meaningless touchdown pass by backup quarterback Scott Zolak with just seconds to play. Despite playing horribly, Bledsoe insisted "We came out prepared and just got beat. It had nothing to do with the team's preparation."[128] Bledsoe's definition of "preparation" differs from Tom Brady's. Brady would never attend a rock concert during a game week, let alone throw himself off the stage!

Bledsoe also loves dangerous motorcycles and once nearly convinced teammate Ted Johnson to buy a bike, something Johnson was tempted to do before deciding it was too dangerous:

> "Football players are adrenaline junkies. It makes sense that some of the same things you like about football, you'd like about riding a bike. There is some danger involved, and I think that's part of it. It's also a status thing.

We're part of all these shows on cable like 'Orange County Choppers.' There's something edgy and cool about it."[129]

Steelers quarterbacks Ben Roethlisberger and Tommy Maddox both ride motorcycles without helmets. Maddox seems to believe the NFL is a branch of Hell's Angels: "Everybody's had bikes for a long time, and one guy [Cleveland Browns star tight end Kellen Winslow Jr.] wrecks and everybody makes a huge deal out of it. I've got a bike. Everybody rides. One guy's doing tricks in the parking lot and wrecks, and all of a sudden it's a front-page story."[130] Roethlisberger owns five bikes.[131] Top NFL agent Tom Condon admits some of his clients own and may ride motorcycles, despite contracts forbidding it and his warning them of the dangers.

I doubt many current Patriots are riding motorcycles. Linebackers coach Dean Pees rides a Harley, and left tackle Matt Light rides but swears "I'm not out there doing crazy things or popping wheelies... I'm very safe and responsible."[132] Most Patriots, like tight end Benjamin Watson, are too smart and mature: "I'm too scared to get on a motorcycle, so that's something you won't ever see from me. I've seen what can happen to people."[133] Patriots riding motorcycles certainly aren't doing dangerous stunts, as Winslow Jr. was before missing the entire 2005 season due to injuries to internal organs and his knee and a staph infection that caused him to lose over 10% of his body weight. The Patriots sign players who care too much about football, feel too responsible to their teammates and are too smart to risk injuring themselves needlessly off the football field. As Patriots safety Rodney Harrison said before the Super Bowl, "So many [teammates] have sacrificed so much for a long time to get to this point, so you have to commit yourself... to play the biggest game of your life."[134] After Tom Brady told a reporter he went hang gliding and skiing and took motorcycle lessons this offseason, he made sure to add "just kidding,"[135] though that was obvious.

Coachable players are also football-smart. The Patriots don't need astrophysicists or Latin scholars but players who soak up football information and apply it on the field. Belichick describes the search for football intelligence as "watching a player play, talking to his coaches, sometimes talking to his teammates, putting him through a process of what we do and seeing what the retention is and what the conceptual understanding is."[136] Two years after Belichick traded physically talented safety Tebucky Jones to the New Orleans Saints, the bitterly disappointed Saints released Jones. Saints head coach Jim Haslett said, "He doesn't have very good ball skills. He had only one interception with us, and he struggles in space [deciding what to do when there's no one near him]. I don't know why he can't catch a ball. It's the oddest thing I've ever seen."[137] Physical talent is squandered on players who can't translate their knowledge of the playbook and their interpretation of the action on the field into an instant action plan. Belichick knew Jones wasn't absorbing his coaches' training and traded him for greater value.

The astonishing thing is that anyone still trades with Belichick and Pioli. They're like traveling antique experts rummaging through flea markets and yard sales. If they offer you $50 for a piece of junk, snatch the item back and toss it in your safe! If they sign one of your restricted free agents to an offer sheet, match the offer and make the guy a starter! If they want to trade for one of your players, extend his contract!

Patriots defenders' ability to absorb new information was severely tested before Super Bowl XXXIX. Defensive coordinator Romeo Crennel chose to scrap his entire defensive playbook and install a totally new defense specially designed to stop the Eagles. Afterwards, linebacker Tedy Bruschi accurately said, "Unless you got the players, unless you got the brains, unless you got the skill, it's not going to get it done, and we got the skill in this locker room."[138]

Identifying disciplined, focused personnel

"Most of the [activities] that keep the members of our species smiling involve acquiring and exercising skills, doing useful things and doing them well. ...The people I see in their places of work who seem happy are people who are doing their jobs with zest and competence. Do they work well because they are happy? Perhaps, but I also believe that they are happy because they work well; it is called positive feedback."[139]
– *Dr. David Lykken, author of "Happiness"*

"I can't look at you and say how big your heart is [but] if you're committed and love something and have a passion for it, you'll do anything to get it."[140]
– *Patriots safety Rodney Harrison*

Why are Patriots players and coaches so disciplined and focused? The first root cause is that the Patriots admit into their fraternity only players and coaches who love even the "boring" aspects of being a professional football player: lifting weights, scrimmaging, catching passes from ball machines, studying playbooks and film, etc. For such players and coaches, training is rewarding, not a chore, because "the mainstay of any happiness diet is productive effort, developing and exercising skills, doing something that needs doing–that is worth doing–and especially doing it well."[141] New Miami Dolphins head coach Nick Saban says "Belichick told him about the importance of making sure that those around him were as serious about winning as he was."[142] Such players experience "flow" from the very process of striving to improve, not merely from victory. I believe the second source of the team's incredible discipline and focus is that players and coaches who experience "flow" from football derive even more satisfaction by bonding and striving together with like-minded players to overcome challenges.

"Flow"

"When people are in a good mood at work, it builds emotional capital and enhances productivity."[143]
  – *Daniel Goleman, author of "Emotional Intelligence"*

"Recognize what your particular talents are and use them. That's the greatest satisfaction in the world."[144]
  – *Hugh Guthrie, 86-year-old technical advisor at the National Energy Technology Laboratory*

"The only thing that kept me going [after Apple–the company I founded– fired me] was that I loved what I did. You've got to find what you love… The only way to be truly satisfied is to do what you believe is great work. And the only way to do great work is to love what you do. If you haven't found it yet, keep looking. Don't settle."[145]
  – *Steve Jobs, CEO of Apple and Pixar and founder of NeXT*

When the Patriots drafted wide receiver Deion Branch in Round 2 of the 2002 NFL Draft, I was underwhelmed. I hadn't even heard of Anthony "Deion" Branch. The average mock draft predicted Branch would be the fifteenth wide receiver selected and would last until the 4th round, not the 2nd.[146] Bill Belichick was more excited: "We've added a player with an upbeat personality and great attitude toward the game."[147] Huh?!?! "Personality" and "attitude" don't catch touchdown passes, do they? Deion Branch's shiny Super Bowl XXXIX MVP trophy and the free Cadillac XLR he won prove the power of personality and attitude. New 49ers head coach Mike Nolan says he figured this out while defensive coordinator of the free agent-crazed Washington Redskins: "I learned that personnel is about more than a pretty girl who's 6-5, 240 and runs fast. It's hard to have chemistry on a football team that you haven't built on the best character… We'll have that."[148]

Players who love training just keep getting better and better. That's why Scott Pioli says, "We analyze the traits and makeup of individual players. We have specific things we know we are looking for and specific things we know we want to avoid."[149] Patriots safety Rodney Harrison, who tries to stop Branch during practices, says it's impossible because Branch is just too confident and relaxed: "You can't stick him. I try to go up in there and jam him, he's laughing, smiling, having a good time. He has hands like glue, and he's so smart and he's so elusive."[150] Such an enthusiastic, competitive attitude helps a player reach his full physical potential. Branch joins Hall of Famers Lynn Swann and Fred Biletnikoff and future Hall of Famer Jerry Rice as only the fourth receiver named Super Bowl MVP. Branch is also the only receiver ever to catch at least ten passes in consecutive Super Bowls.

Branch's mind is as big a source of his success as his legs and arms. As Belichick says, "You can't separate [talent from mentality]. A kid can have all the talent in the world and not work hard, and that's who he is. If that's what he is, that's what he is. You can't take [his] talent and take somebody else's work ethic and take somebody else's commitment."[151] 2005 Patriots draftee Ellis Hobbs is more succinct: "The talent thing can only take you so far."[152]

Offensive lineman Logan Mankins, the Patriots' 2005 1st-round draftee, could be another Deion Branch because his personality also matches his position. Both men are relentless perfectionists who love their jobs. Mankins possesses an offensive lineman's greatest asset: nastiness. Highlight clips show Mankins knocking defenders on their backs, then knocking them down again as they try to get up… and then hitting them a third time as the whistle blows, just to make a point. Mankins sometimes even steps on an opponent he has just knocked down, perhaps a trait he acquired as a championship cattle-roper while posing with cattle he had roped, winning $10,000 for his troubles. (If you can knock down cattle, how hard can knocking down people be?) Most mock drafts projected Mankins as a 2nd-to-4th-round choice, at best a late 2nd-rounder. So, even expert Patriot-watchers were stunned by Mankins' selection. But Mankins is a rugged competitor who can play guard and serve as an insurance policy at the critical left tackle position, where Matt Light has had no real backup. An injury to Light risks injury to Tom Brady, just as losing one's queen in chess puts one's king in danger. The Patriots valued Mankins more than other teams or "draftniks" because they know his personality and intelligence will help him maximize his potential.

When one worried New England journalist asked Mankins whether he would step on journalists as he does opponents, Mankins replied, "If you fall down, I guess." But he swears "I'm a nice guy. It's just when I put on the pads, I get nasty."[153] Mankins quickly earned Matt Light's seal of approval: "He's getting the majority of reps there at left guard, and he's really jelled well with everyone. The guy knows his offense and he's studied and worked hard. He's in a good position to go out and play good football."[154]

The Patriots adore Dr. Jekyll and Mr. Hyde types like Mankins—sweethearts off the field, monsters on. Listen to Patriots nose tackle Vince Wilfork's high school coach: "A lot of big kids… don't have the tenacity or meanness [and] aren't going out there to tear somebody's head off. With Vince, you could push his button and he would explode. We had a lot of sit downs and talks."[155] Wilfork says "I hate quarterbacks… It's my job to hate quarterbacks." His high school coach concurs:

> "We told everybody not to hit the quarterback [during practice]. Sure enough, Vince comes through—because nobody could really block him—and just kills the quarterback. I jumped all over him. But he goes back and kills him again. I said, 'Vince, I'm telling you to cut it out. Don't do it again.' So he did it again and we were ready to come to blows. I was just hoping the other coaches would make it look good and hold me back."[156]

Off the football field, however, Wilfork was always a role model:

"He wasn't out screwing around with other kids. It was school, football, home… His parents made sure he was doing the right thing, that he was staying clean, that he was humble and respected everyone. He never got in fights at school and never disrespected a teacher. He was always smiling and goofing around. He didn't care about hanging out with all the stud athletes. My offensive coordinator used to say that the team fed off Vince–not his play, but his attitude."[157]

With a devilish grin, Belichick says of Mankins, "It's a lot easier to try and tone them down than to [push] them in the other direction. I think he's got a good playing style. He's tough, he's aggressive, he's a good finisher." The Patriots love nasty because great football players love to hit. The Patriots sign only running backs and wide receivers who block well, and no defense loves hitting more than the Patriots'.

Former offensive coordinator Charlie Weis' love of nasty won over Chris Zorich, who had publicly criticized his alma mater–Notre Dame–for firing head football coach Tyrone Willingham before hiring Weis. After Zorich's initial talk with Weis, Zorich was so thrilled he volunteered to help Weis: "All of a sudden, you have a coach talking to you about having mean and nasty players again, and I kind of got excited."[158] Many of the defensive backs the Patriots have drafted, most recently James Sanders in 2005, idolize safety Ronnie Lott, who is famous (or infamous, depending on whether you play defense or offense) for his brutal hitting. But Sanders is a monster only on the field. After the Patriots drafted Sanders, a Fresno State Bulldogs fan wrote, "I am happy to see good things happen for Sanders because he really seems like a good guy."[159] Another 2005 draftee, Ryan Claridge, is a great guy off the football field but too competitive not to pretend to be nasty: "I was like 242 pounds. I was playing [college tennis] against guys that were 140 pounds. If one of those guys told me the shot that I hit was out and I thought it was in, I would come over to the net and tell him I needed to talk to him. He'd say the shot was in. I got all the calls."[160]

Many sources of happiness–including money and promotions–generate only fleeting bursts of happiness, much like drinking a mug of coffee provides only temporary stimulation. We become habituated to wealth or power just as we become habituated to caffeine and need–over time–to drink more and more until we can't function normally without our morning carafe. There are, however, certain activities that can genuinely make people happy on a continuing basis:

> "[Truly happy] individuals lead vigorous lives, are open to a variety of experiences, keep on learning until the day they die, and have strong ties and commitments to other people and to the environment in which they live. They enjoy whatever they do, even if tedious or difficult; they are hardly ever bored, and they can take in stride anything that comes their way. Perhaps their greatest strength is that they are *in control of their lives*."[161]

Psychologists say "humans have a strong effectance motivation, a desire to impact our environment, to make things happen in predictable ways, to control events… Productive activity is one of the most dependable sources of human happiness."[162] The Patriots organization enables players intensely devoted to football to translate their passion into personal growth and collective achievement. To such players, this never-ending process of individual and team struggle is richly rewarding, whether or not it produces trophies and awards.

The Patriots locker room is full of perfectionists who never become satisfied or complacent. They are strivers and fighters who revel in pushing themselves to their limits… and then pushing even harder. Listen to Tom Brady: "I had the worst temper when I was little. I could never stand to lose in anything. I kicked through glass windows and threw video game controllers at TVs and broke more tennis rackets than I could count. It got to where nobody ever wanted to play with me. You never really grow out of it, I guess."[163] After joining the Patriots in 2005, receiver David Terrell quickly learned that the Patriots hand out no medals for "extra" effort: "You're expected to do your job and expected to do it to the highest of your ability. Not just average. Not just 'All right, you ran the route right.' No. It has to be done at 110 percent of your ability. It makes everyone better when everyone is pushing you like that."[164] Asked after his new Notre Dame team's first spring practice whether he was thrilled to have finally attained his dream of becoming a head coach, former Patriots offensive coordinator Charlie Weis replied, "I'm actually sick to my stomach because I always expect better."[165]

Dr. Mihaly Csikszentmihalyi, the psychologist who discovered and researched "flow," explains it as follows:

> "The best moments in our lives are not the passive, receptive, relaxing times [but] when a person's body or mind is stretched to its limits in a voluntary effort to accomplish something difficult and worthwhile… so involved in [that] activity that nothing else seems to matter."[166]

His study of "flow" experiences (a.k.a. "peak experiences" or "optimal experiences") found eight elements in each of the many flow experiences he studied across a broad range of activities:

1. Reasonable chance of completing task, given sufficient effort
2. Ability to concentrate on task
3. Clear goals
4. Rapid feedback
5. Involvement in task so deep and satisfying that other concerns and thoughts fade from consciousness
6. Sense of being in control
7. Absorption in task leads to loss of concern for self
8. Absorption in task leads time to pass without notice[167]

Patriots offensive lineman Joe Andruzzi does not use the term "flow" but appears to say the Patriots experience it regularly. Andruzzi says players always focus on the task at hand and often lose track of the bigger picture: "You're in a groove. You keep on going week in and week-out, one game at a time. We've done it the last few years now and you just keep on going. You make it that one game at a time. When you win the Super Bowl, even last year or 2001, it's almost like we've got another game the next week."[168]

Every great company is full of employees experiencing "flow," deeply and passionately engrossed in trying to achieve company goals. Such employees feel their work is important to customers and appreciated by their bosses and colleagues. White-collar professional employees hold no monopoly on "flow" experiences. Shopping at Wegmans supermarkets, for example, is fun because Wegmans offers one-stop shopping, exciting sights and smells and knowledgeable, enthusiastic employees who love educating shoppers and making each customer's visit special. Wegmans employees are empowered to take any action to ensure that each customer enjoys the Wegmans shopping experience. Employees are offered generous training, college scholarships, and even company-sponsored trips abroad to study the foods they sell, and they enjoy the creative challenge of sharing their knowledge to help shoppers. Wegmans places special importance on job applicants' potential for "flow" experiences: "'Just about everybody in the store has some genuine interest in food,' says Jeff Burris, who runs the wine shop at Wegmans' Dulles, Va., store. In fact, Wegmans has been known to reject perfectly capable job candidates who lack a passion for it."[169] To build a great company, hire only employees with great "'flow' potential." "Flow potential" predicts how intensely and passionately someone will pour him- or herself into a particular job. Belichick knows this, advising students: "Do something you love to do. Go where your passion is… I feel like I haven't worked a day in my life."[170]

Emotional bonding

"[Vince Lombardi] truly believed in the love that holds a football team together, a love built on the sacrifice of ego and individuality to a loftier common purpose. Lombardi didn't build his teams; he fused them."[171]
– *Ken Hartnett, who interviewed Lombardi three seasons for AP*

"Being with friends provides the most positive experiences. …The importance of friendships on well-being is difficult to overestimate. The quality of life improves immensely when there is at least one other person who is willing to listen to our troubles and to support us emotionally."[172]
– *Dr. Mihaly Csikszentmihalyi, "Finding Flow"*

"Everybody around here's a good person, and they expect that out of you."[173]
– *2005 Patriots draftee Andy Stokes*

"Men who are high in emotional intelligence are socially poised, outgoing and cheerful… They have a noticeable capacity for commitment to people or causes, for taking responsibility, and for having an ethical outlook; they are sympathetic and caring in their relationships. Their emotional life is rich, but appropriate; they are comfortable with themselves, others, and the social universe they live in."[174]
   – Daniel Goleman, "Emotional Intelligence"

Rosevelt Colvin and Matt Light, who played together at Purdue, "sometimes sing duets before practice."[175] Troy Brown enjoys dancing in the locker room. On many football teams, this might be attacked as sissy behavior. If Patriots joke about duets or dancing, they do so only in good fun. Patriots players get a kick out of their teammates' quirks and judge one another only on their job performance.

In schools around America, kids who study hard are teased as "geeks," "nerds," "dorks," "teachers pets" and "losers." Imagine how much better our children would learn if students looked up to their teachers and their hard-working classmates (as they do in China, for example). One secret to the Patriots' success is that locker room respect is granted in proportion to effort and contribution. After joining the Patriots, backup quarterback Chris Redman was asked if he felt a special bond with Deion Branch, who played at Louisville after Redman. He answered, "Deion is a great guy, he's one of those guys who goes out of his way to make sure he says 'hi' to you. …But these guys, you could have a connection with anyone as long as you do your job right."[176]

In the Patriots locker room, what matters is not being "cool" or funny or telling stories. What matters is absorbing coaching and doing your job. Tom Brady says no one cares that Troy Brown was an 8th-round draft pick: "There is no other guy in our locker room that has the respect that Troy has. For 12 years he has done everything the coaches have asked… He's one of the first guys in there in the morning and always doing extra work. This year everyone saw what he's been doing playing different positions… He's been a captain ever since I've been here. He's irreplaceable."[177] When the locker room shares a value system, that belief system becomes self-reinforcing and players feel close to one another.

Patriots linebacker Willie McGinest says "We see everybody as family. And we have a team full of guys who… would rather win and everybody get the spotlight and everybody enjoy it… It's more like a family atmosphere [than other teams]… You need to have that bond with them, you need to have that camaraderie, you need to understand each other so when you're on the field everything comes naturally."[178] People who report having at least five close (non-family) friends are twice as likely to consider themselves "very happy" as those who report having fewer than five close friends.[179] Being a Patriot gives you a large family: "It's definitely a family. We have family squabbles and everything. We've been together for so long that we know what buttons to push with each guy. It's a tight group, we know we have each other's backs."[180]

Cooperation ("task cohesion") is a prerequisite of success in team sports and other group-based activities. Friendship ("social cohesion") is not essential but is beneficial. Many studies have shown that: 1) "Social cohesion" fosters "task cohesion"; and, 2) "Task cohesion" fosters success that–in turn–boosts "social cohesion."[181] As Daniel Goleman says, "Leadership is getting work done well through other people, and laughing together is one of the best ways to do that."[182]

Cooperation provides advantage even in "individual" sports. Venus and Serena Williams helped each other rise to the top of women's tennis. Even auto racers competing for a single prize benefit from cooperation. An article comparing the Andretti Green Racing "team" with the Patriots quotes the star driver saying, "When one of my teammates wins a race, I feel part of it," notes the team is "notorious for pulling pranks [on one another]," and quotes another team driver saying he values the advice, encouragement, and competition he receives from his fellow drivers: "We've got four guys that get along very well that push one another very hard, and we're all at different stages in our career, so we can help one another. Those three helped me develop very quickly."[183] Although driving a car around a race track seems an intrinsically individualistic pursuit, teamwork makes each driver better than he would be on his own, and the drivers enjoy belonging to the team.

Succeeding on one's own merits generates a thrilling, esteem-boosting "flow" sensation. Belonging to and contributing to a successful team heightens the "flow" feeling because the experience is shared with others who have struggled and, eventually, triumphed with you.

People who bond tightly–united by a team banner or a shared goal or belief system–feel empowered and ennobled by their membership in an exclusive club of like-minded people. Membership can be a powerful, cult-like experience. Examples flood the mind: Churches. Yale's Skull & Bones Society. Hitler's SS. Harley-Davidson owners. Terror groups like Hezbollah and Al Qaeda. Though many famous cult-like groups are infamous for evil acts, organizations that forge strong bonds with members and between members are not inherently good or bad. Many successful businesses, for example, began as collaborations between innovative friends: Walter Hewlett and David Packard were friends at Stanford years before they founded HP; Steve Jobs, Steve Wozniak and Ron Wayne worked together at Atari before founding Apple Computer. And emotional bonding has helped many sports teams win. Many human beings are attracted to–and often derive great satisfaction from belonging to and serving in–organizations they believe give their lives greater meaning. There would not exist thousands of cults and religions[184] unless belonging to an organization larger than you were something many found enjoyable.

Men can form especially tight bonds, whence the term "male bonding." Decades after a war, many war veterans still feel closer to one another than to even their spouses or children. After winning Super Bowl XXXVI, Patriots center/guard Damien Woody sounded like an old war vet:

> "Nobody believed in us. Nobody. No matter what we did, they weren't buying we were for real. That brings a team together. That creates something that only we can understand. All I know is it took us winning the Super Bowl for people to finally say, 'Hey, maybe those Patriots *are* pretty good.'"[185]

Male bonding is a huge factor in many workplaces and a presumptive underlying cause of the "glass ceiling" women often confront. A survey of 950 top executives found that female executives judged "exclusion from informal networks" a huge barrier to their advancement.[186] (Male and female genomes, brain structure and behavior have all been scientifically demonstrated to differ, and I believe this is why Google uncovers more than four times as many references to "male bonding" as to "female bonding."[187])

Religiosity is often described as a pleasant—even euphoric—feeling of being simultaneously small and part of something greater and more wonderful. Being a high-functioning cog in a high-functioning machine that achieves great things cogs could never achieve individually generates joyful, rapturous feelings. Scientists believe human genes evolved over millions of years in an environment that rewarded cohesive groups of nomadic humans who communicated and cooperated to out-compete and outfight their main rivals: neighboring nomadic bands of humans. Groups that collaborated well thrived while groups that collaborated poorly were out-competed for scarce resources or even slaughtered. In such an environment, scientists believe, groups composed of individuals whose genes encouraged effective coordination out-competed and outfought less coordinated rival groups. Groups whose members had a higher proportion of genes nudging individuals to enjoy working with others in their "in group" tended to out-compete groups with a lower proportion of "unselfish" genes. (The frequency of wars and genocides in modern history suggests that "us" vs. "them" thinking has always shaped human interactions and that we are each predisposed to perceive the world in such terms. The role of warfare in shaping humanity also explains why we lock up or put to death people who kill "us" but applaud as patriots those who kill "them" in times of war.)

Today, selfish genes coexist with cooperative genes because selfish individuals who belonged to successful groups reproduced—thus passing their genes into the future—rather successfully. The eternal tension between cooperation and selfishness is reflected in the modern gene pool and in the range of personalities in society. Some people are more selfish than others. The Patriots seek players who enjoy collaborating to out-compete their rivals, and this conscious selection of unselfish players facilitates male bonding and helps the team succeed.

The Patriots' company culture arises, in part, because the Patriots sign players who enjoy training with teammates. I can actually substantiate this claim with data from Jonathan Niednagel, who runs BrainTypes.com and consults to professional sports teams regarding personality. The Jung-Myers-Briggs personality framework (or "Myers-Briggs Type Indicator") has four dimensions: 1) Extroversion/Introversion; 2) Sensing/iNtuition; 3) Thinking/Feeling; and, 4) Judging/Perceiving. I created the following chart to give a sense of what these four dimensions represent:

Extraversion: Externally-focused, interpersonally engaged, community-oriented, stimulated by others' company, seeking leadership roles, experientially-driven	Introversion: Self-focused, thought-driven, internally-motivated, energized by ideas
Sensing: Sense-driven, concrete, present-oriented, "what is"	iNtuitive: Abstract thinking (patterns, meanings, possibilities and relationships), future-focused, "what could be"
Thinking: Logical, objective, cause-and-effect	Feeling: Emotional, value, gut-driven
Judging: Organized, planned, careful, meticulous, scheduled, destination-focused	Perceiving: Spontaneous, flexible, unscheduled, exploratory, living for the moment, journey-focused

There are 16 possible combinations of these four personality dimensions (such as "ESTP" and "INFJ"). Niednagel categorizes each player he studies into one of these 16 types and has categorized seven Patriots players: Tedy Bruschi - ESFP; Willie McGinest - ESFP; Rodney Harrison - ENTP; Tom Brady - ENFP; Corey Dillon - ENTP; Deion Branch - ENFP; Adam Vinatieri - ENTP.[188] It is no coincidence that every Patriot is both "Extroverted" and "Perceiving." Since roughly 24.1% of the population is E--P,[189] the odds that all seven Patriots tested would be of this type by chance is $(24.1\%)^7$ or 0.0047% or 4.7 in 100,000. The Patriots look for community-oriented players (Extroverted) who are adaptable and enjoy the day-by-day training process (Perceiving). Patriots players' "E--P" personalities cause them to enjoy training together because they energize each other (Extroversion) and perceive training as fun games and challenges that help them continually improve (Perceiving) rather than a series of tasks and hurdles designed to win a Super Bowl (Judging). A group of "E--P"s enjoy playfully pushing one another and striving to succeed for one another. And, because they're "journey-focused," they take full advantage of each day, seldom daydreaming about the future.

Smart organizations develop a vision for employees' skills and personalities. What works for the Patriots may not work for another organization. Multinationals and innovation-driven firms place great value on diversity. What matters is that an organization's workforce is collectively capable of achieving the organization's goals. The CEO of SAB–which rescued once-faltering Miller Brewing and also owns Peroni, Pilsner Urquell and South African Breweries–says, "We've always believed in deep analysis of our people. We use psychometrics in hiring and in major promotions to see if people fit in our culture. We prize intellectual rigor and emotional engagement."[190] All organizations should seek cultural fit and emotional engagement.

The Patriots' communitarianism is especially obvious from the way Patriots veterans treat rookies, especially undrafted rookies unlikely to make an NFL roster. New Patriot defensive lineman Mike Wright–the only rookie free agent to make the final 2005 roster–credits the player he edged out: "Rodney Bailey was very helpful, giving me advice. All the linemen have been really good. Everybody's unbelievable around here. You're a free agent rookie, you'd think they'd brush you off. But they try to help you. They figure if they can help you, you could help the team."[191] Even rookies cut during training camp invariably say they were treated marvelously and enjoyed their time in Foxboro. After getting cut after a year with the team, P.K. Sam said, "I learned a lot here, and I don't know if I could sum it up in a couple of sentences. [New England] definitely prepared me to handle everything thrown at me in the NFL. There are some great guys on this team, and they've been good to me."[192] This suggests that Patriots scouts follow the insightful advice of Raytheon CEO Bill Swanson:

> "Watch out for those with situational value systems–people who turn the charm on and off depending on the status of the person with whom they're interacting. Those people may be good actors, but they don't become good leaders. There's a consistency in leadership that's greater than mere situational awareness."[193]

Players are coaches too

"I told [rookie cornerback Randall Gay] from the start to ask me anything about anything."[194]
– *Patriots cornerback Asante Samuel*

"Coach is looking for smart guys who have played in [his system], leaders who say, 'Get into the books.'"[195]
– *Patriots safety Lawyer Milloy, 2002*

"I sat down on the plane and talked to so many different guys, telling them, 'This is what to expect.' I talked to Rabih Abdullah and some of the newer guys. ...I even told a guy, 'Don't wear yourself out in pre-game when we go out on the field because once you come back in from pre-game, you have to sit in the locker room for an hour, so pace yourself.'"[196]
– *Patriots safety Rodney Harrison*

"Troy Brown goes and teaches the receivers a lot of things about our offense... I can do the same."[197]
– *Tom Brady*

"Brady's always one of those guys that goes out of his way. If I have a question, he'll answer it and answer it in detail."[198]
 – *Rookie quarterback Matt Cassel*

"I'll help some guys out. I know what Coach Belichick's pet peeves are. I'll be like, 'Why don't you make sure you get this right. You [can] screw everything else up, just don't screw this one thing up and you'll be OK.'"[199]
 – *Patriots linebacker Ted Johnson*

"I just try to pass on some of the stuff that was taught to me as a younger player, such as not getting too excited before the game."[200]
 – *Patriots linebacker Willie McGinest*

The Patriots believe "too many chefs" spoil the soup only if chefs selfishly insist on bossing others around, something New England's locker room does not tolerate. When chefs set egos aside and collaborate, they can make a world-class soup. Safety Rodney Harrison says he wants to be on a team of master chefs: "You have to have a bunch of guys that are willing to be leaders."[201] Linebacker Ted Johnson agrees: "You can't have enough good leaders in the locker room."[202] The Patriots draft and sign only leaders.

The key lies in Belichick's definition of "leadership," which has nothing to do with calling the shots or dominating others: "Leadership is about one word on the New England Patriots... attitude. If a player comes to work with a team attitude and he's well prepared and he's worked hard, that's what leadership is. And everybody who... brings a good attitude shows tremendous leadership."[203] "We talk about 'attitude,' not 'leadership.' That's the energy inside the team."[204] Leadership is "giving for the good of the team... Leadership leads to teamwork, which is the understanding of a common goal and a common commitment–people that are all committed to the same thing and to each other."[205] Linebacker Willie McGinest exemplifies that spirit. He says, "I had to be a team guy. The people surrounding me growing up didn't give me a choice" and "If you start complaining about your own situation, what kind of leader are you?"[206]

Receiver David Terrell said during 2005 training camp that Patriots constantly critique one another's performances in a helpful manner:

"You learn something from all the guys. Some of the guys sit on your breaks, some of them don't. Some of them play high, some of them play low... You learn a whole lot from [different defenders'] different techniques, how they play you, because no one is alike. After we run a route [in practice], we come back and talk, and they might be coaching me 'Dave, when you're breaking down, break down this way, not that way.' It's anything to make you better."[207]

Patriots linebacker Ted Johnson says, "We never want to have a compromised effort from our buddies. Whatever [a player's] role... [he] is going to feel the pressure of his teammates."[208]

Running back Kory Chapman credits Corey Dillon with improving his play: "I've learned a lot from playing behind Corey. One of the main things is that you never stop running and try to stay as low as possible."[209] Staying low is smart football physics. The lower your shoulder pads when you hit an opponent, the better your leverage and the better your chance of continuing forward rather than being stood up or knocked backwards. As Chapman was running for 113 yards on 15 carries and blocking brilliantly for his Cologne Centurions in an NFL Europe game, the broadcasters credited Patriots defenders:

> "The broadcast crew just discussed [Chapman's] work on the Practice Squad last season where Bruschi & Co. used to get on him to finish the run, giving him plenty of bumps and bruises on Wednesday and Thursday. It paid off if his running today is any indication. He's moving people backward, always picking up an extra yard or two after contact."[210]

#1 receiver Deion Branch calls Troy Brown his "big brother" because he gives such "great guidance."[211]

Rookies don't need to prove anything to earn veterans' attention. If the Patriots brain trust thinks enough of a player to bring him to training camp, that player is immediately treated like a full member of the team. Several weeks after joining the Patriots, receiver Bam Childress said, "As a rookie, you feel the veterans would put you off to the side, but that's not the way it is here. Everyone was helping us out. I was getting tips from Rodney Harrison. Any time you're getting tips from a Pro Bowl safety, you listen. You welcome any help you can get."[212] Rookie lineman Nick Kaczur agrees: "The linemen here really help you out tremendously. No one's selfish. If you have a question, any one of them will be glad to answer it for you. That makes everything a lot easier."[213]

Belichick expects veterans to share their knowledge and praises those who do: "[Christian Fauria] has been an outstanding team leader. I think he's done a great job with our younger tight ends–Dan Graham [and] Ben Watson."[214] Players Belichick signs generally enjoy mentoring and are generous with their time and advice. Such players enjoy helping their team prepare, not just helping themselves prepare.

Every time the Patriots release a veteran, a young player at the same position tells reporters how much he learned from his recently-departed teammate. A 2005 victim of the Patriots' constant quest for veterans willing to train their younger replacements is nose tackle Keith Traylor. Three months after helping the Patriots win another Super Bowl, Traylor was released and Ethan Kelley stepped up to reporters' microphones to utter the completely expected words of appreciation: "He kind of showed me the ropes. He's a veteran. He's been in the league a long time and had a wealth of knowledge. For me to not tap into that would not be wise or smart."[215] Before Super Bowl XXXIX, Traylor told reporters that training his replacements was in his job description: "They also asked me to help the young d-linemen move forward and get better. They just wanted me to be a good [role model] in the locker room, and I think I've done what they asked."[216]

Not all players are so selfless. The Buffalo Bills lost two players upset over their lack of playing time. The Bills traded running back Travis Henry to the Tennessee Titans because "We were prepared to keep Travis, but he made it pretty clear that he was not coming back."[217] They also wanted to retain Drew Bledsoe as their veteran backup and mentor to young 1st-round draft pick J.P. Losman. General manager Tom Donahoe talked himself blue pitching his vision—and the example of Jerome Bettis accepting a backup role in Pittsburgh that helped the Steelers reach the 2004 AFC Championship Game—to Bledsoe and his agent only to be spurned. Bledsoe saw himself only as a starting quarterback and refused to accept mentoring a young gun: "When I had the conversation with Mike and first found out the direction they were going to go was with J.P., I was beside myself. It was a shock to me, no question. I was very disappointed. Very angry. All those things."[218] After signing with the Dallas Cowboys, Bledsoe demonstrated his concern for self over team and teammates: "I can't wait to go home and… get rid of all the old gear from the other team."[219]

Patriots also help one another out of selfishness because they want to win. After the Patriots traded a 3rd-round pick for cornerback Duane Starks—who started for the Super Bowl XXXV-champion 2000 Baltimore Ravens—and signed former Steelers starter Chad Scott, Patriots cornerback Randall Gay embraced the newcomers trying to steal his job: "This is a competition league. Everybody's competing all the time. We knew they were going to bring in some good corners. We expected that, and that's what we wanted."[220] After training with his new teammates, Starks himself became excited too: "All the guys out here are doing a great job. They're focused. They're working hard. And they want to start, each and every one of us. Basically, we just have to go out each day and compete."[221] David Terrell explains the Patriots' mindset:

> "The guys make sure you know that there's such a high level of intensity to win here. Everybody is on the same page, and everyone wants the same thing out of the next guy beside him. However they can help me, they will. The team pretty much police themselves, all the guys on the team. I just love this type of environment."[222]

Tedy Bruschi elaborates: "You need good players around you… I need Ty Warren and Richard Seymour out there keeping the blockers off of me. You have to realize that you can't do it all yourself."[223] Indeed, defenses are designed to funnel running backs to the middle linebacker. If Bruschi's teammates fail to prevent an offensive lineman from blocking him, Bruschi doesn't make the tackle. If Bruschi's teammates fail to force the running back toward him, Bruschi can't make the tackle. Linebacker Ted Johnson says peer pressure to optimize collective performance is intense:

> "There's a company culture, there's an expectation of winning. It's not only expected from our coaching staff and management but from the players that are here year in and year out. Peer pressure… On this team, there's a tremendous amount of peer pressure to play to your ability and to work hard and to buy into the system. That, to me, is what makes it work."[224]

Patriots players and coaches are so indoctrinated with team-oriented clichés that they even think in clichés. When wide receiver David Givens says "We practice pretty hard [because] practice makes perfect,"[225] he means it. Since everyone throughout the organization is quickly infected with this selfless, professional work ethic, the Patriots' locker room culture is like a wave propelling players–including newcomers–to improve.

After the Patriots made receiver P.K. Sam the youngest player drafted in the 2004 NFL Draft, Sam was not nearly as professional as his teammates, and his team wound up suspending him. During his second training camp, Sam credited fellow receiver Deion Branch with helping him improve his mindset: "I've been hanging with Deion, and he's helped me out a lot. I did have some maturing to do, and I think I did a lot over the last year–over the offseason."[226]

In 2004, Patriots safety Rodney Harrison helped teammates improve out of necessity. The Patriots secondary sustained so many injuries that "it was one of the biggest challenges of my career, trying to communicate with these guys and be patient and establish a relationship with Asante Samuel… and communicating with a wide receiver who played cornerback [Troy Brown]. It's been tough trying to hold these guys together."[227] After star cornerback Ty Law broke his foot, Harrison said, "I was a nervous wreck, and I was calling Ty saying, 'Hey, when are you going to be back?'"[228] How did Rodney do? As impressive as his All Pro-worthy 2004 performance on the playing field was (though he narrowly missed out on All Pro honors because his cheap-shot reputation lost him votes), Harrison was equally impressive as the defensive secondary's mother hen. Safety Eugene Wilson–who has won two Super Bowls in his two NFL seasons while playing alongside Rodney–says:

> "Rodney, he's one of those guys who's not going to let you do anything less than what he knows you're capable of. If he sees you slacking off–like maybe you won't go up to hit a guy or something like that–he'll get on your head right away. We had some young players in there this year, and I was surprised to see Rodney just go get up in their face because they didn't go jump on the pile like him, like a wild man. Rodney, he expects the best out of everybody. He gets the intensity out of everybody."[229]

Cornerback Randall Gay—an undrafted rookie who started many games, including all three playoff victories—testified:

> "Rodney is the glue of our secondary. When injuries started happening, he was the one who stepped up and got us younger guys together. He has more experience than all of us together. He knew what to expect all the time. Right after Ty got hurt he came to me and told me that I was the starter and that he expected me to play like a starter. Every day at practice he comes to me with the same approach like I need to be ready; making sure that I don't relax and making sure that I am always focused. It has been like that since training camp where he has been pushing me since day one to make sure I listened to him. He would always tell me that, 'If you want to stay here, you need to listen to me.' He said that he knew what I needed to do to stay around. I have been listening to him, and now I am starting in the Super Bowl."[230]

Cornerback Asante Samuel swears "[Rodney] leads in every way possible... by example... with words [and] with his actions on and off the field."[231] Safety Guss Scott agrees: "His aggressiveness, knowledge of the game... everything. From practice even, he sprints out [saying] 'Hey young man, I should never beat you out here on the field.' Stuff like that just makes you a better player. You treat every play like it's your last."[232] Harrison says his mentees kid him respectfully:

> "My job as the elder spokesperson back there in the secondary is just really to help those guys out. They always joke with me and call me 'Old Man' ... but it's just a matter of me trying to set that example on and off the field every time, challenging these guys, making sure that we get the most out of them. It's tough sometimes dealing with young guys because sometimes they have a sense of 'We know it all.' But our young guys—I've been fortunate to play with these guys and they listen, they're humble guys and they work every day to get better."[233]

A final reason Patriots veterans help their teammates—even during training camp before some are cut—is that Belichick emphasizes that he does not keep a specific number of players at any position: "It's not going to be between a corner and a safety. It will be between a safety and a linebacker, or a corner and a wide receiver, or a safety and a running back. Those numbers will be relative to the overall value those players have on the team. That will be up to them to create. Part of that will be ability to do certain things. Part of that will be versatility to do multiple things."[234] If you're great on special teams, for example, that gives you an edge. Belichick's insistence that players aren't competing with their position-mates calms rivalrous competition among players playing the same position and reduces guilt when one player survives but his friends get cut.

SCHOOL

"You don't get a lot of time to relax when you go to work at 7 a.m. and get home at 9 p.m. …With the Patriots, it's a lot easier to work there because everybody works there. It's expected."[235]
— *2005 Patriots draftee Andy Stokes*

"Coach Belichick is very meticulous. Every hour of your day was planned for you. It's a little more laid-back for the players here [in Washington]."[236]
— *Former Patriots wide receiver David Patten, explaining that his new coach–Hall of Famer Joe Gibbs–is more lax on his Redskins*

"There is a rhythm to how you approach the week and the game."[237]
— *Patriots linebacker Ted Johnson*

Bill Belichick never wants–or allows–a player to wonder, "What should I be doing?" Each player's objectives are clear, and each player's schedule is structured to help him improve in important areas daily. Players' days at Gillette Stadium are as scripted as the offense's opening drive each Sunday: "You come here the first day and you start learning real fast how it is around the Patriots. It's pretty disciplined here. They like things done their way."[238] For example, Patriots linebacker Tedy Bruschi says he knows what to do each day of the week:

"Early in the week I try to make it as physical as I can for myself. Weight room and padded practices and extra work in the training room to get rid of the aches and pains early in the week, and as I'm doing that, I'm doing film study. As the week progresses you sort of trail off on the physical aspect of it, we go out in shells and don't hit on Fridays, and sort of lighten up on the workouts. …Saturday… you enjoy with your family because you've done all the preparation and you want to get your mind right because you don't want to get too fired up… When Sunday comes, you have to put it all together."[239]

An effective leader: 1) Enables and motivates employees to develop their talents and use them to contribute to organizational success; and, 2) Promotes a culture that trusts individuals to perform their jobs with minimal distraction and holds individuals responsible for results. Former Giants quarterback and CBS analyst Phil Simms believes Bill Belichick sets up his assistant coaches to succeed by creating an environment where they can focus on teaching, not babysitting or cheerleading:

"Their job and how productive they can be really is related to what environment the head coach sets up for them. So if the head coach takes care of the overall discipline of the team and puts an agenda out there that is really conducive to letting the assistant coaches maximize their talents, then the head coach has done his job. He's made the team better by creating a better atmosphere for his assistants, who now can accomplish what they want to accomplish when teaching their players."[240]

New Patriot linebacker Chad Brown says the Patriots are utterly unlike his previous NFL teams: "There's no sleeping in the meetings. There's no, 'I'll get that later.' Each detail is attended to. Each player, when he steps on the field—more so than any other team I've ever been on—knows what's expected and has prepared at practice."[241]

People learn best by focusing on a few objectives. Telling someone to learn twenty things will cause them to drift aimlessly from task to task, accomplish nothing, become frustrated and perhaps escape frustration by procrastinating. Bill Belichick ensures that every Patriot knows at every minute where he should be, what he should be trying to accomplish, and why it's important that he accomplish it. For example, Troy Brown never had to guess whether to prepare for offense, defense or special teams:

"I come in in the mornings and ask Bill what meeting he wants me in. [If] he tells me to go to offense, I go to offense. [If] he tells me to go to defense, I go to defense. And if I have a little [extra] time in there I just kind of go in with [secondary coach] Eric Mangini and get some more film work, and get some more calls on defense, and where I need to be on defense. I go... after practice and watch some more film with them. Like I said, I spend more time at the stadium than I have in my whole career."[242]

To avoid cognitive overload, the Patriots also try to simplify each week's game plan. Patriots linebacker Willie McGinest says, "He makes it simple for us. He gives us like two or three things that we must do to win. We concentrate on those two or three things and we do them right, nine times out of ten, we'll win the game."[243] For example, during a 2001 game against the St. Louis Rams, Belichick shouted at his players on the sidelines, "Slants and in-cuts. That's the game!"[244] Sure enough, two Rams receivers criss-crossed in the middle of the field ("Proehl and Bruce almost collided. Bruce, in fact, was ducking to avoid Proehl and didn't see the pass."[245]) and Patriots defensive back Terrell Buckley—who had camped out where Belichick had told him to—made the interception and returned it 52 yards for a touchdown.

By explicitly scheduling all activities, Patriots coaches prioritize tasks to maximize productivity. Long before training camp begins, coaches plan what they intend to accomplish each day:

"You lay out a format, you figure out basically how you want to approach the start of the regular season and your opportunities in training camp to practice and improve your team. Every day is an opportunity to do something, whether it's to rest, whether it's to lift weights, whether it's to have meetings, whether it's to practice once, twice. You have to make some adjustments along the way, but you try to have the basic outline of what you're going to try to do."[246]

Eliminate employee distractions

"I was taken aback by [my] visit because of what they offer here, the way they take care of their players... I've never been to a place where they provide breakfast and lunch for you in the offseason workout program."[247]
   – *2005 Patriots free agent signee Tim Dwight*

"My goal was to work those kids so hard, they'd be too tired to do anything else."[248]
   – *Don Norford, who coached young Willie McGinest through high school*

"[Preparing well] is just a matter of pacing yourself, making sure you are mentally and physically grounded, and that you are not wearing yourself out. That you are doing all of the things off the field and in your personal life correctly. You are not out partying and drinking and doing all of the other crazy things."[249]
   – *Patriots safety Rodney Harrison*

In 1982, the New England Patriots used the #1 pick in the NFL Draft on University of Texas defensive end Ken Sims. Sims had just won the 1981 Lombardi Award, which "goes annually to the college football lineman—offense or defense—who, in addition to outstanding performance and ability, best exemplifies the discipline of Vince Lombardi."[250] The Patriots failed to tap into the discipline that won Sims the Lombardi Award:

"When I first got to the pros, I didn't keep it real. My ego got the best of me. It took me a year to realize it was a job and to put my hard hat on. Those are the principles I live by today. I was the guy opening up the bar tab and paying for everyone's drinks at the end of the night."[251]

Expected to be the savior of the Patriots franchise, Sims had a decent eight-year career but achieved far less than he was capable of. If Bill Belichick drafted a Ken Sims today, Sims would be a standout because today's Patriots would keep Sims in the gym and the film room and out of bars.

In "Students," we saw that the Patriots acquire competitive, football-loving players, knowing that those who enjoy and take pride in their work strive harder and derive great satisfaction from work itself and from the success it eventually wins. Patriots players and coaches are "trapped" in a positive feedback loop (Passion + desire --> Effort --> Success --> Pride + job satisfaction --> Passion + desire). In this section, we discuss how the Patriots avoid disrupting this positive feedback loop by avoiding distractions. The Patriots organization works hard to prevent anyone from being seduced by non-work diversions, such as parties, drugs or motorcycles. The fewer distractions employees confront, the harder they work and the more likely success is. Smart organizations minimize employee distractions to amplify the positive feedback loop relating success, job satisfaction, and employee effort.

Avoid non-football distractions

"One of the biggest challenges in the NFL is the multiple paternity suits."[252]
– *Kevin Elko, sports psychologist to some NFL teams*

"You really have to be emotionally stable and have a good support system away from the NFL."[253]
– *2005 Patriots draft choice Andy Stokes*

The Patriots work hard to keep players out of trouble. Belichick regularly warns players that "We all make a lot of mistakes as we go through life. Don't make the big ones. Take care of yourself and your own personal health. It can all end in a second with one stupid decision, and we've seen that happen too many times."[254]

The Patriots sign players who value "football, family and faith" in part because such players stay out of trouble. Trouble keeps players off the football field and lowers on-field performance. Less than a decade ago, former NFL player Tim Green wrote, "Show me an NFL team on a Friday night and I'll show you ten empty kegs of beer… The whole NFL experience is like an endless fraternity party."[255] Some NFL teams resemble the ultimate macho fraternities with the toughest initiation rites, the coolest parties and the sexiest groupies. If "sex, drugs and rock-and-roll" defines the rock star life, "sex, drugs and football" is a lifestyle available to NFL players and attractive to more than a few. Even Troy Brown fell into that trap early in his Patriots career:

> "I was thinking that since I was in the NFL for a year, I was good to go. I went home, hung out with my friends and was drinking and partying and not really working out as much as I should have. I came back and things didn't go the way I wanted [them] to go, and [Parcells] cut me. From that point on, I said if I had the chance to get back in there I wouldn't let it happen again."[256]

Brown now shares his cautionary tale with young teammates so Bill Belichick doesn't have to cut players to lance their swollen heads. The only player Parcells or Belichick ever tolerated trouble from was Hall of Famer Lawrence Taylor, whose off-field problems never hurt his team, only himself. Teams whose players don't succumb to dangerous temptations are competitively advantaged.

Peer pressure intensifies Patriots players' natural caution about engaging in risky behaviors. Patriots know that part of their job is staying out of trouble, and most do so. The only trouble Patriots running back Corey Dillon now gets into, for example, is cramping his hand from his Madden NFL videogame addiction: "Corey does that all the time. He wakes up playing Madden. He plays Madden… before the game [and] on his day off."[257] (I presume Dillon enjoys pretending he's Corey Dillon. Perhaps he wanted to be traded to the Patriots because his Madden team is now much stronger?)

Belichick regularly warns players to stay out of trouble by bringing to their attention every report of an NFL player who has landed in trouble.[258] Belichick's awareness of the importance of off-field activities has grown as he has matured: "I've learned a lot of things in the past 10 years. One thing is to be a little less involved in the football on the field and a little more involved with the team off the field."[259]

300 Google employees ride a Google bus to work each day. The buses shorten employees' commuting time (because the bus travels in the carpool lane), convert time wasted driving into productive time (because buses offer free wireless Internet access) and eliminate a major source of non-work-related stress (because riders relax rather than fight traffic). Google also provides bikes, running trails, massages, washing machines, doctor visits and free tasty meals—like grilled petite New York sirloin with Creole spices. Amgen, Electronic Arts, Merck, Microsoft, Nike and Pixar also smartly provide employees with facilities and perks that simplify their lives and save them time.

The Patriots do the same. Doug Flutie appreciates that chefs provide good meals for Patriots players so "guys can be here all day working out, preparing."[260] New Patriots tight end Andy Stokes was instantly impressed because "Everything is so state of the art. They already did my laundry for me and got it back to me before my next practice."[261]

As Cleveland Browns head coach, Bill Belichick kept the young Scott Pioli engaged in football by treating him as his $14,000/year slave:

> "I was waking up every day, going to work for the Cleveland Browns... from before sun up until well after sun down... It was actually an advantage. It's not like I had the distractions. I couldn't go out and do anything. I couldn't have a social life because I couldn't afford to have a social life. And that was fine because it just meant I'd continue to work and get better."[262]

The Patriots also help players focus by delineating their responsibilities and reminding them to trust their teammates and coaches on everything else. When Bill Belichick suspended receiver Terry Glenn during the 2001 season, he instructed players not to waste brain cycles worrying or feeling guilty about something beyond their control: "This is my job, to make decisions. Don't worry about my job. Your job is to focus and play the best you can."[263]

Avoid pre-game distractions

Another way to deliver players from evil is by leading them not into game-week temptation. Before Super Bowl XXXVI, the Rams—favored by two touchdowns over the Patriots—acted as if they had already won the game and were merely preparing to accept their trophy. Belichick made clear the Patriots would do any partying after the game:

> "While Rams coach Mike Martz allowed his players to roam Bourbon Street, leaving them curfew-free until Friday night, Belichick instituted a midnight bed check beginning on Tuesday. He sold his players on the notion that a sloppy Wednesday practice could cause irreparable harm. St. Louis players, on the other hand, said their Wednesday practice was mistake-filled and disjointed."[264]

The Patriots not only did bedroom checks but even checked out of their hotel and moved to an unknown location to ensure players' privacy. If the team's location is known and accessible, opponents can play dirty tricks, such as calling hotel rooms in the middle of the night. The Patriots wanted no surprises.

Also, the moment the Patriots earned the right to play in that Super Bowl, coaches began preaching the importance of staying focused on the game rather than getting caught up in pre-game hoopla. Defensive coach Pepper Johnson wrote:

> "[Defensive lineman] Bobby Hamilton took one of my [Super Bowl] rings and walked it all around the airport and said, 'This is what it's all about.' ... Some guys it's their first Super Bowl, so they want to go out and party, and I'm trying to tell them about that one week of sacrifice. Believe me, it's worth it. You don't need to worry about enjoying the festivities before the game. That's for your family and your friends. You have the rest of your life. This Sunday will change your life forever, and you just need to make this sacrifice."[265]

The Patriots didn't grow complacent when they returned to the Super Bowl two years later. Said tight end Christian Fauria, "This is my big chance. I'll be buckling down. No excuses. I don't want any visions in my head when I'm 40 about what I should have done."[266]

Before their third Super Bowl victory, the Patriots exiled themselves to a secluded hotel, avoiding Jacksonville except during required media sessions and the game itself. The Patriots also displayed their expertise at ignoring and delegating potential distractions, such as handing out tickets to friends and family. The team urged players to handle all potential distractions during the first pre-Super Bowl week: "It's a headache for a couple of days. You... take care of everything before you come down. That's the biggest key: to get it all under control before you come down so you have focus for the week of the game."[267] Tom Brady says the 2004 team was more focused than the 2001 team:

> "It was very hectic [before Super Bowl XXXVI]. It was [just] a week to prepare, and sometimes you did get caught up in the fact that there were other things going on. Not that you were out there partying or anything, but you were dealing with things you probably didn't need to deal with. Whereas

I think for us now, and I think for many of the guys that have been here before, you put it on other people and let everyone [else] have the fun this week. For us, we realize our fun comes after this game."[268]

Eliminating distractions allowed Brady "to hole up in my room as best as I can around here, and not do a whole lot other than focus on the task at hand," which included "watch[ing] every snap on defense [the Eagles] have all year [and] evaluating the players."[269] Unlike many NFL players who would complain about missing Super Bowl festivities, Patriots players embrace being cut off from the outside world. Special teams captain Larry Izzo called it "a positive that we are kind of isolated a little bit... I think this location is very pretty, and it's in good location for us being able to focus."[270] Receiver David Givens agreed "It's a good spot for a Super Bowl because the guys can't get too distracted... because there isn't a lot to do."[271]

While Patriots players *prepared* to win Super Bowl XXXIX, the Philadelphia Eagles *wanted* to win and *hoped* to win. Eagles cornerback Lito Sheppard said, "Guys are gonna enjoy their time down here. ...We just have to come out and enjoy ourselves while we're here."[272] Linebacker Jeremiah Trotter told reporters, "We are having a blast."[273] Linebacker Mark Simoneau: "Yesterday was pretty wild and crazy. We are here to play a game, but we are here to also enjoy the Super Bowl and the event itself."[274] Eagles players weren't out partying till 3:00 a.m., but they weren't holed up in their rooms–like Brady–either. Head coach Andy Reid gave his players "a lot of time off"[275]–including all dinners and evenings–and long leashes: "I am going to take the positive approach and say that I trust my guys are going to do the right thing. ...We do have a curfew [but] it will still give them plenty of time to enjoy themselves at the different events and enjoy the Super Bowl experience."[276]

For Patriots players, winning the game meant *everything*. For Eagles players, the game was *important*. Eagles safety Brian Dawkins said, "We have a good time, but when it's time to focus, when we come to practice, when we come to meetings, we are here to do a certain job."[277] Eagles defensive tackle Corey Simon said the same: "We're going to enjoy [the trip]. But, we're still here to take care of business... We're not just here to enjoy Jacksonville."[278] The Eagles were intentionally not obsessed with the game: "[The Patriots] can look at the hype... and they can bury it... We're going to enjoy it. We're going to stay loose."[279] Eagles center Hank Fraley said, "You can't be too serious or too tight. ...Our locker room is real loose."[280]

For the Patriots, work is play and this was a pure, serious business trip, as Willie McGinest explained:

> "You've got a lot of mature guys on this team, veterans... that understand how important this game is, how important all the preparation is. The off-season workouts, and [training] camp and everything that we put into this year to get to this point. To go out and just throw it all away partying and hanging out and doing a lot of different things would be stupid."[281]

Linebacker Tedy Bruschi urged teammates to use every precious minute: "Have your playbook next to you. Make sure [you're using] all the free time you have on the bus and that you're watching some extra film."[282] Brady too: "We shouldn't waste any time doing anything that won't help us win the game."[283]

Eagles players talked about Sunday's *game*. Patriots told reporters how critical the week's *practices* and *study* would be. Offensive lineman Joe Andruzzi, for example, said "[Eagles defenders] are going to try to come out and split us up [break through the offensive line]… We have to prepare like we usually do. As an offensive line, we have to go out as a group and get the best [simulated] looks we can at practice."[284] Fellow lineman Matt Light said, "If you're going to bust your tail every offseason and do all that work in the preseason, you might as well go all the way and not let up."[285] That week's preparation was critical because coaches had designed a new defense just for the Super Bowl. Tedy Bruschi said players were cramming to learn it: "Today's practice was a lot of fun. We are getting our adjustments down. We are starting to feel the game plan and guys started turning it loose… The defense was communicating more today than we have been the last few practices. But usually when you get the game plan it takes a couple of practices."[286] Asked about Super Bowl week, Troy Brown said, "You have to get your film time in. You have to get your studying in and practice well. It is like a regular week, except much more detailed."[287] Defensive end Jarvis Green later said, "It really felt like a regular game. As far as the week of practice, Coach Belichick treated it like a regular game. We still practiced the same."[288]

As they conserved energy late in the week, some Patriots spent quiet time with family. But receiver Deion Branch was careful not to let his uncles rile him up: "I'll just spend time with my family. Not with my uncles, though. They always get me worked up about the game. They start talking about the game, and that's not what you want to do."[289] Before the 2005 opener, Branch said "hype is for the fans. As players we have to [focus on game preparation]."[290]

I doubt the Patriots regret working all week, but I suspect–after losing– some Eagles regret not studying and preparing a little harder. Could the Eagles have closed the three-point gap with more thorough preparation? We'll never know.

Avoid post-career worries

The Patriots encourage players to live financially responsible lives because "One recent study… found that 78 percent of NFL players are unemployed, bankrupt or divorced within two years of playing their last game."[291] Defensive lineman Jarvis Green works part time–and sometimes full time during the offseason–on administrative tasks at Rolls-Royce Naval Marine because "Coach Belichick always says when you have a lot of free time and money, that's when trouble comes. I'm keeping busy."[292] Green says, "Hopefully I'll play 10 years, maybe 14. But if not, this is my backup plan."[293] For two offseasons at Rolls Royce, "I did after-market stuff… e-mailing customers or talking to them on the phone, customers in China, Australia and Japan, but my main focus was like a project manager, overseeing a project, getting all the materials out to the foundry, things like that."[294] After signing a five-year contract extension potentially worth $18 million, Green should be set for life if he saves his money, as I am sure he will.

Patriot linebacker Matt Chatham did an internship at *Esquire* magazine in hopes of becoming a columnist. 14-year NFL defensive lineman Anthony Pleasant lived frugally and saved $300,000 after taxes from each of his last few seasons' $1 million salary. While finishing his career with the Patriots, Pleasant was preparing to work in construction after retirement for perhaps $60,000 a year: "If you can get a job that pays you benefits as well as [health] insurance, you won't drain all your investments. Football has been a steppingstone to get ahead in life… a job, not a career."[295]

Offensive lineman Matt Light is also careful with his money: "I try to save as much as possible. When we get the next deal done, I'm going to try and save well more than half of my bonus."[296] I doubt he had much trouble. Spending $4.5 million of his $9 million in bonuses would have required ingenuity.

The award for most creative post-Patriots career aspiration goes to rookie defensive lineman Marquise Hill who did a college internship in a coroner's office to bolster his dream of running his own funeral home because "Everybody's got to go. Might as well send them off the right way."[297] Hill grew up around death in a rough New Orleans neighborhood where multiple homicide weeks were common and even Hill's cousin was killed by gunfire. Hill says of working with dead bodies, "It's nothing I'm afraid of. It's the ones living you have to be afraid of."[298]

Rodney Harrison wins—by a landslide—the award for most ironic post-Patriots career aspiration. The player who has paid the most fines in the history of the NFL and been voted the NFL's dirtiest player by his peers has been interning to become an NFL official! Players in NFL Europe appreciate the irony: "I made a couple of pass interference [calls] and I called one illegal hit to the facemask and some of the guys [were saying], 'Hey, Rodney, that's the way you play.'"[299]

Willie McGinest founded "55 Entertainment" in 1998. He is a record producer and served as executive producer of a horror movie. He also has hosted and produced many hours of *NFL Network* coverage.

Patriots special teams player Je'Rod Cherry, who has a master's degree from University of California, knows that "if you're not one of the multi-million dollar players, you can't retire,"[300] so he has investigated restaurant franchising options and considered teaching or earning a Ph.D. because:

"[Football] can't last forever. You have to have yourself prepared for the next stage. What I tell people is to stay true to yourself and not let this be part of your identity and totally define who you are. If you do, you can't walk away from it. Then you're stuck. You're not playing and then asking 'What is the meaning of life?'"[301]

Cherry's dedication to laying the groundwork for a post-football career has paid off. He has a standing offer to join a Boston-based wealth management company.

Avoid rookie distractions

The Patriots recognize that rookies' newfound fame and fortune creates temptations and dangers. In 2000, "Belichick [told sportswriters] that the largest problem facing young players today is the time and money they have in their first couple of years in the pros, a major change from collegiate years."[302] Rookies need special support and advice to stay focused on their work. The team warns players about common dangers facing NFL rookies, especially the trouble their new celebrity and wealth attract.

Patriots rookies are required to report to Foxboro a week before veterans. They receive mentoring from veterans and coaches, like Willie McGinest who doles out advice to younger players: "If you don't take care of your body and you don't work hard, two things are going to happen: you are going to break down or you're not going to have a job."[303]

The Patriots also bring in outsiders to speak with rookies and share their wisdom and perspective on life. For example, 1960 Heisman Trophy winner Joe Bellino, who played for Navy when Belichick's father coached there, has spoken with the past three cohorts of Patriot rookies.[304]

The Patriots require younger players to live at training camp, while veterans like fullback Fred McCrary can go home once a week: "[Belichick] made training camp bearable last year, especially for the veterans like myself. If it was your seventh year or more, you only had to stay in the hotel for like six days and then you could stay at home as a veteran. That was pretty cool."[305]

All rookies receive a presentation on community and media relations from Patriots director of media relations Stacey James, who warns them "as much time and effort you put into the game on Sunday, take that preparation and also apply it to this other responsibility you have with the media"[306] because cameras and reporters lurk everywhere, seeking to stir up controversy.

New players are strongly encouraged to live near Gillette Stadium, in the sleepy suburb of Foxboro, rather than surrounded by the excitement and lures of Boston.

After the first snowfall of 2004, "Belichick joked that the team held "a little driving seminar this morning for some of our southern members of the team who haven't seen [snow], let alone driven in it."[307]

Belichick and Pioli have managed to quickly sign their rookies so rookies can focus on preparation. In 2005, the Patriots were easily the first team to sign all their draft picks and did so before training camp. In 2004, 2nd-round draft pick Marquise Hill signed his contract before any other 1st- or 2nd-rounder, and Vince Wilfork was just the second 1st-round draft pick to agree to a contract. Deion Branch was a rare exception but missed the rookie reporting deadline by just hours.[308] Prior to 2004, the only Belichick-era rookie who missed significant time for contractual reasons was running back J.R. Redmond in 2000. In 2004, two draftees—Cedric Cobbs and Guss Scott—signed the day after camp opened, and one—Benjamin Watson—held out for several weeks before firing his agent, who had refused to consider letting Watson sign a six-year contract the Patriots insisted on. Watson signed after an 18-day holdout during which, he said, "I was trying to remember the plays in my mind, trying to go over stuff in my mind, but we're not allowed to take the playbook with us, away from here, for security reasons."[309]

Helping new players learn their way around Boston also helps them focus.

But perhaps the biggest factor helping rookies is great expectations. In many football programs, rookies feel like unwanted stepchildren. In New England, veterans embrace rookies, and coaches expect rookies to contribute in Year 1. Patriots center Dan Koppen says rookies suffer from thick playbooks, not hazing:

> "I don't think [we] linemen treat them as, *per se*, they're rookies. We don't make them carry pads and make them do stupid crap. We try and keep everybody into the game and feel like they're a part of the team and encourage them, just like they played here for five years."[310]

Veterans do cut rookies' hair in grotesque ways, but everyone has a fun time with it.

Avoid media troubles

Bill Belichick helps players avoid media trouble by offering helpful suggestions about topics to avoid, ways of phrasing or evading topics, etc. Some reporters are on fishing expeditions for juicy quotations and are not beneath goading players into getting angry or flustered or baiting them into saying too much by appealing to their pride, jealousy or other emotional hot-buttons. Some players—having been burned by unscrupulous or sloppy writers—fight the media, often with unpleasant consequences. Linebacker Ted Johnson says his teammates are too well coached and too aware of reporters' tricks to say controversial things:

> "I know it is hard to try to find a story. You all want somebody to say something outrageous or out of line. When you have been around long enough, the older guys on this team make the new guys know better. And quite frankly, we have a head coach who knows better. We are in a market where it is easy to lose focus and make a mountain out of a mole hill. No offense to the Boston media."[311]

When asked to compare the Patriots with the Bengals, Corey Dillon now politely refuses to say negative things about Cincinnati and often says how much he enjoyed certain aspects of his time there. I believe Dillon began learning from Belichick the moment they met: "He basically told me that he didn't care what happened in the past. All he cares about is what's happening now and in the future. That's something that just stuck with me. I thought about it, and he's right. It really doesn't matter what happened."[312] Realizing the pointlessness of dwelling on the past makes it easier to refrain from making impolitic statements out of bitterness. Dillon had an adversarial relationship with the Cincinnati media similar to Belichick's in Cleveland. Dillon has gotten on well with the New England media, perhaps partly because he adopted some of Belichick's media methods: "In the past, I really didn't want to do some of the media stuff, and I think that irritated some people... I just said to myself that I was going to try to keep that friction away and do whatever was asked of me."[313] In my Volume 3 chapter "Communicating," I will explain in detail how Belichick teaches players to give the media what they need without surrendering secrets or feeding upcoming opponents emotional ammunition.

Provide help avoiding and healing injuries

"The organization does a good job of bringing people in to help you with whatever you need: muscle tissue rehab, massage therapists, extra trainers, extra stretching people and nutritionists. There's just a bunch things that help us play and stay stronger."[314]
– *Patriots linebacker Willie McGinest*

Aches and pains obviously hamper performance, so the team provides many options for players to feel better. Tedy Bruschi says "acupuncture, a massage, things like that [can help] get yourself ready, and the treatment room is good also."[315] Linebacker Roman Phifer says the team will provide anything that might benefit players: "Whatever we need from Coach Belichick or the organization, they supply for us. If it's more protein in our diet that we need to be successful, this organization is willing to provide a nutritionist for us."[316]

Roman Phifer and Willie McGinest are older players who have remained relatively healthy late in their careers. Older Patriots work even harder to ensure they eat and train properly. Corey Dillon takes advantage of the many health maintenance options the Patriots provide: "I definitely do things differently than I used to–almost everything. Just how I train, how I eat, how I rest. I'm not that young stud anymore. I'm an old stud. I have to do the extras."[317] Like what?

"I've got a daily routine: work out, eat right, come out here, and just work your tail off and try to be the best you can be. That's been my motto from Day 1. I do a lot of stretching. A lot of cold tub. It works. The chiropractor works. I get a massage every two days, and it really helps. Earlier in my career, I never got into stuff like that, but now that I'm a little older, I take it seriously. I stay on my routine."[318]

By taking care of their bodies, tight end Christian Fauria says hopefully, Patriots veterans are "like a fine wine, getting better with age."[319]

Of course, it's even better to avoid injuries. Ten-year veteran linebacker Ted Johnson is another "old stud," which is why he was proud to play in every game in 2004: "That was big for me… That was a big accomplishment, just to stay healthy for the entire season… For me to put together a healthy year because I've done it about three years… It's really nice."[320]

Many injuries are unavoidable, but the Patriots do whatever they can to avoid avoidable injuries. When Romeo Crennel took over the Cleveland Browns, he brought with him the use of thigh pads and knee pads, something many Browns had not been using.[321] He also brought the Patriots' innovative schedule of alternating single and double training sessions that Browns tight end Aaron Shea credits with preventing training camp injuries:

> "The 2-to-1 practice schedule really helps your body. I think that's why we had [fewer] hamstring problems this year. In the past, our bodies never got to rest enough. You never lost that soreness because the practices just kept coming at you. And with the extra time off we had, we got to lift more, so I think we'll be stronger. Before, we were practicing so much that we didn't have time to lift. So what happened was that you started to lose all the strength you had worked so hard to build up during the offseason."[322]

But the Patriots haven't been too successful at avoiding injuries. Since the 1985 season, only four Super Bowl champs have won despite starters missing more than 40 games: the 1991 Redskins (41 games lost), the 1994 49ers (44 games lost), the 2003 Patriots (87 games lost) and the 2004 Patriots (55 games lost).[323]

Provide tools and training opportunities

"Five or six years ago, the facilities were depleted. The stadium was in poor shape. The weight room, the offices, you name it, were all substandard in the NFL or even any decent college program. That's all been upgraded tremendously."[324]
– *Bill Belichick*

"We needed [a new stadium] to stay competitive. If we couldn't do it, then I might as well have sold the team."[325]
– *Patriots owner Bob Kraft*

In the years before Robert Kraft purchased the Patriots, the team was lousy. One factor was the poor training facilities and unpleasant environment. Many players stayed home during the offseason because they had superior training facilities at their college gym or even their home. This has changed under Kraft and Belichick. Quarterback Doug Flutie, who played for the Patriots from 1987 to 1989, raved after rejoining the team in 2005: "It's first class. With the new facility, it's night and day from when we were back at Foxboro Stadium."[326] Now, due to Gillette Stadium's superior facilities and welcoming atmosphere, Tom Brady says most Patriots enjoy working out in Foxboro:

> "We don't mind being here. We are hanging out in the locker room with our pads on, playing backgammon and dominoes. Guys are hanging out in the treatment room and screwing around on the computers. It has become a place not only for work, but all your buddies are here, too."[327]

Seeing more of each other helps players push one another, both through macho competition and friendly encouragement. The old facilities were so poor that the Patriots held training camp from 1976 till recently not in Foxboro but at Bryant College in Smithfield, RI, where players didn't enjoy living in dull dorm rooms with little to break up the monotony of practices:

> "[Patriots COO and Sr. VP Andy] Wasynczuk reiterated that the main advantage of the move will lie in the ability to best prepare a football team for the upcoming season. Beds will be placed in areas of the service level for players to nap during down time, the players will have a lounge area to relax and play video games and players will also have the option of returning to the local hotel in which they will be staying if there is sufficient time between meetings and practices."[328]

Before the Patriots built their indoor training bubble, poor weather ruined practices and caused unnecessary injuries:

> "We were talking today about how much higher quality our practices are than when we had the other indoor facility or when the field was outdoors and we still had wet balls and turf. We felt we got a lot done this morning and the facility helps a lot. Rehabbing guys get quality work in, they're not cold, they're not slipping and they're able to rehab and work areas they need to work."[329]

Before the new facilities, days were wasted both before and after each training camp while equipment was crated up and moved the 25 miles between Foxboro and training camp. Meeting rooms were cramped. And practicing without well-lit fields forced the Patriots to squeeze in morning and afternoon practices during daylight without mid-day training meetings to point out morning mistakes for players to correct that afternoon. After moving to Foxboro, the team was no longer held hostage by dusk, so coaches changed the schedule to train only after coaches could teach players to fix problems identified during the previous training session.

In short, the new facilities upgraded the team's ability to train:

"Playing in [Foxboro Stadium] a couple of years ago and the facilities we had, it was a miracle that we got to the Super Bowl then. Now we come into this great facility [Gillette Stadium] with great practice fields, the meeting rooms are great, the cafeteria, and the locker room. That allows us to prepare better and worry less about the things that we shouldn't be worrying about, like warm water. We can come in and get proper treatment so we can be ready to play. That allows the coach to spend more time with us in the meeting rooms."[330]

Also, in 2000, Belichick's Patriots began using cutting-edge technology to study opponents, something that helps coaches and players prepare more efficiently:

"One of [Belichick's] defensive assistants, Brian Daboll, helps chart every play of an upcoming opponent. The plays are mapped out on half sheets of paper and the coach pages through them all. He can also go on his laptop and retrieve any play he wants. He can click a button and see everything Kansas City has done in the red zone. Or how many post patterns the team has run on third and 7."[331]

Set clear expectations

"[Players] know how they need to train and what things they need to be ready and prepared to do this year."[332]
 – Bill Belichick

"A cornerback's got one job: cover the man."[333]
 – Bill Belichick

"We expect [non-starters] to go in and play because they practice every day too, just like we do, because we are a team. If Tom Brady went down, we expect Rohan Davey, or whoever that next quarterback might be, to go in there and take us to the Promised Land. …Whoever goes down, we expect you to step in."[334]
 – Former Patriots cornerback Ty Law

"You either do [your job] or somebody else does it."[335]
 – Bill Belichick

According to Bill Belichick, "We say two things about a receiver. The guy's got two jobs: get open and catch the ball."[336] If so, Patriots receiver Deion Branch is performing spectacularly because KC Joyner–who analyzes every play of every NFL game and compiles unique statistics on each player–reports, "Two things Deion Branch did better than any other [NFL] receiver [in 2004]? He got open and caught passes… If Branch stays healthy, he'll be a Pro Bowler in 2005."[337] Joyner's statistics say Branch caught 69.9% of passes thrown to him, best in the entire NFL. Hines Ward was second, with 66.2%. Most famous receivers caught between 40% and 60% of passes thrown to them. The Patriots' clear expectations have helped Branch become one of the NFL's best receivers.

After a season in which Deion Branch was the NFL's most reliable pass-catcher and won the Super Bowl MVP trophy, Branch managed to find new goals for 2005 training camp: "I'm going to have to block better this season... I want to improve on everything. Running better routes, better hand-eye coordination, blocking better, and staying healthy."[338]

Pre-Belichick, Patriots linebacker Ted Johnson played mainly on intuition. Post-Belichick, Johnson's responsibilities are spelled out clearly:

> "I played my position a little differently then... You have to be able to disengage and use good technique and make plays. That's what I think I do pretty well. I was [more reckless] because of the schemes at the time. It was simpler schematically where I could just go and I didn't have to think about things as much. Now you've really got to be thinking out there. 'Where am I lined up on this play?' I've got to get my defense lined up and make the right call."[339]

New Patriots linebacker Chad Brown is a three-time Pro Bowler but has never before been told what to do in every situation. He has often freelanced. Not in New England:

> "[The Patriots] attempt to have a definite answer for everything the [opposing] offense does. Sometimes in the past [in Pittsburgh and Seattle] we just said, 'Well, hopefully they won't run that [play]' or 'That's just going to be a tough play for us.' They don't say that here. There's an answer for everything. It's my job to learn that answer so I can be prepared for everything."[340]

On the offensive side too, receiver David Terrell learned quickly that "Tom [Brady] wants you to be where you are supposed to be when you are supposed to be there. If you're not there, you want to be accountable."[341] Clear expectations trickle down. Brady himself says, "with Charlie [Weis]... you always knew... what his expectations were."[342]

Why do clear expectations matter? According to the book *Flow in Sports*—whose conclusions Belichick clearly embraces–players, to perform optimally, need to know precisely what is expected of them in any situation: "Having clear goals for all the components of performance ensures you are paying attention to the relevant cues–and only to them."[343]

Belichick told *New England Institute of Technology* graduates: "You guys go to work every day, and that's what the Patriots are all about."[344] But hard work is useful only if channeled in productive directions. Digging a deep hole is hard work but completely unproductive. Patriots strive ingloriously to improve in specific areas because–as Belichick makes certain his players believe–"there are always things on your team that you can address and improve."[345] Winning back-to-back championships doesn't mean you know everything or will win again.

To ensure players' effort is maximally productive, progress is tracked against clear objectives and metrics. For example, Patriots stay in shape year-round because they know they must pass a tough conditioning test in July to participate in training camp and will be shamed–and possibly cut–if they fail. Are players studying hard enough? Belichick's yardstick is whether every player knows what every player is supposed to do in every situation. Anything less than complete understanding of everyone's responsibilities and objectives in every situation is insufficient.

When Tom Brady arrived in New England as a 6th-round pick in 2000, he hadn't been able to hold down the starting job at Michigan and had a small frame, relatively weak arm and zero speed. Belichick advised Brady to strengthen his body, improve his mechanics (esp. his footwork and arm motion), familiarize himself with every nuance of the Patriots playbook and study endless film on opposing defenses. Brady threw himself into these tasks, became the starter a year later and won the Super Bowl that same season. According to Belichick, "nobody worked harder on this football team than Tom Brady, nobody. He made himself into a player, believe me, by not just showing up for the offseason stuff. He showed up and he worked his butt off."[346] The guidance that Belichick, offensive coordinator Charlie Weis and other coaches provided Brady was as important as Brady's dedication. What produced a Super Bowl MVP was a combination of the staff's superb guidance and direction and Brady's dedication to self-improvement. Brady still lacks the NFL's strongest arm, but Eagles defensive coordinator Jim Johnson says Brady's accuracy is a lethal weapon: "He's got a good touch on [passes to] his receivers downfield. He's very consistent and doesn't overthrow many receivers."[347]

After winning his second Super Bowl MVP trophy, Brady set offseason growth objectives: 1) Reducing his fumbles (13 in 2003) by improving his hand strength, grip on the ball and awareness of pressure; 2) Learning to handle his expanded audible (i.e., last-second play-changing) responsibilities; and, 3) Avoiding interceptions (12 in 2003). Brady also added another ten pounds of muscle in his never-ending quest to transform himself from Beaver Cleaver into Arnold Schwarzenegger: "There was lots of just getting in the weight room. I wanted to get my legs stronger and be better conditioned."[348] After all that preparation, Brady had a great training camp where he, amazingly, did not throw a single interception the first week and threw just two "picks" during the first three weeks. In Week 1 against the Colts, he threw for 335 yards and three touchdowns. In 2004, he cut his fumbles in half (to just 7). He threw two more interceptions (14) but also threw five more touchdowns (28) than in 2003 (23). His yards-per-attempt leapt from 6.87 in 2003 to 7.79.

Patriots coaches cleverly motivate players who had superb rookie seasons by warning that teams are studying them and will attempt to exploit their weaknesses:

"As the rookie season goes on, teams do a better job of really attacking the weaknesses of the players as they have seen them play. Going into the second year, there's more of that. Everybody has a way that they think they can beat (second year players) and they will be more specifically inclined to run those types of plays rather than ones he was naturally good at. Going into the offseason, we talk to them about that. The position coaches do a good job of... (making) them aware of what the attack points are."[349]

After starting 15 of 16 games at safety and helping his new team win a Super Bowl as a rookie, Eugene Wilson didn't coast into 2004. He earned AFC Defensive Player of the Month honors for September after intercepting two passes, forcing a fumble, recovering a fumble, and tackling twelve opponents in just eight quarters of play (because the team played only twice that September).

Veterans motivate themselves by looking over their medical charts and over their shoulders. Linebacker Willie McGinest says, "As you get older, you have to train harder. You have to do a lot of extra work to keep up with the young guys."[350]

Every Patriot always knows what coaches expect him to do to lift his performance. For example, several Patriots participated in NFL Europe in spring 2004 because coaches told them getting game experience was a priority. Patriots practice squad player Jamil Soriano:

"I knew... going into the offseason what I needed to work on. And a big part of that was to get some game experience. You can't really work on game experience, obviously, in practice because there is no real way to simulate it. I think that was definitely one of the main things they wanted to see me get. It's something that I needed to get psychologically so I could feel comfortable or see if I could play at this next level."[351]

In Europe, Soriano followed Belichick's constant-improvement mantra: "I try to eliminate at least one mistake from the previous week and try to get a little bit better each week."[352]

Backup quarterback Rohan Davey also played in NFL Europe to practice good habits. Patriots coaches didn't pat Davey on his back and say, "Go have fun!" They handed him a list of objectives:

"If it's a five-step drop, hit five and let it go. If it's a three-step drop, hit three and let it go. Don't hold the football on the three-step drop. It's things like that. Recognizing coverages, recognizing rotations–all the little things that you don't get when you are the backup."[353]

Davey's European goals included the seemingly mundane but actually important issue of foot placement:

"One thing we really emphasized... was getting my left toe pointed at my target. That sounds easy, but the past couple of years, when you're trying to learn the offense, trying to learn where to go with the football, thinking on the run, it's harder for you when you're dropping back and making a last-second decision on where to go. I'm at the stage now in my development where I know where to go with the football, so it's easier for me to point my toe at the target. ...[Before, I] got away with [bad mechanics] because I had a live arm. Whatever I missed in footwork I made up for by letting it rip."[354]

Another goal on Davey's list was tossing the ball away rather than risking interceptions because "I try to make a play on every play, and that can be my downfall."[355] "My mistakes come on trying to squeeze balls in little spots because I have so much confidence in my arm. Throwing it away is a good play sometimes... I still haven't grasped it fully, I want to make a play on every play."[356]

Explain what you want and why you want it

"[Romeo Crennel] will get people in the organization to buy into what he's trying to accomplish. He knows how to deliver his message. He makes you understand where he's coming from."[357]
– *Patriots nose tackle Keith Traylor*

"[Coaches] have meant everything to me. They taught me so much stuff and made me do extra work every day in the film room and after practice, just making sure that we knew what to do to be ready."[358]
– *Undrafted cornerback Randall Gay, who became a rookie starter*

"The first thing we let guys know when they come here is, 'It's not about you. It's about the team. We're spokes on a wheel.' Everyone understands that. And if they don't, they learn real quick."[359]
– *Patriots linebacker Willie McGinest*

The Patriots never tell players what to do without explaining why. 13th-year NFL linebacker–and first-year Patriot–Chad Brown says the "why" helps him understand and remember the "what": "Learning the defense is consuming all my thoughts. It is amazing [in its complexity] at first, but when you get inside and see the philosophy of it, it makes sense."[360]

The Patriots explain what they expect and why so clearly that even short-term Patriots grow tremendously. Former practice squad receiver Jamin Elliott raves about his Patriots experience:

"I learned how to be the ultimate team player up in New England. You have to sacrifice yourself in everything you do; whether it's going on special teams... or giving a look to the first-team defense. The coaching staff emphasizes a total team effort, and you have to give everything for the team to win."[361]

Defensive lineman Vince Wilfork was challenged by the complexity of his playbook because the team expects him to know *what* to do on a particular play, *why* the team is doing what it's doing and *where* his teammates will be: "There's a lot thrown at us, a lot of plays and a lot of explanations about why we run certain defenses. I have to know my job and what the guy next to me is doing."[362]

Here's an example of Belichick describing some keys to effective cut blocking. Even if you have no idea what cut blocking is, after just a few sentences from Belichick, you will understand what it is, when to use it, and how to avoid being victimized by it:

> "If the defender is coming toward you aggressively, then the cut block is a good block. If the guy is standing there, then there really isn't anything to cut. I am definitely not a fan of lying on the ground and hoping they trip over you. That is not a cut block. That is a give-up block. But if you are running at me hard and I go at your legs, it is going to be hard for you to get your balance and get through. Now, if you are just standing there and I go low at you, you just [step back] a little bit and push me down with your hands or whatever and be able to play it. So, a lot of it is being able to read the tempo of the defender."[363]

Here's an example of Tom Brady learning what is desired and why:

> "[Belichick] gets on me for stuff… like throwing the ball to the running backs. … [Belichick] wants [the ball] in a specific spot. He doesn't want it in his facemask, he wants it one foot in front of his numbers. He wants to make it easy for the running back."[364]

After former Patriots offensive coordinator Charlie Weis took over at Notre Dame, players quickly learned that they must "not only …know the details and the rules of the new system but also the philosophy."[365] And Weis teaches them: "He doesn't just teach you your position and what you're supposed to do. He teaches you philosophies. When you can understand the philosophy of the offense and the philosophy of each play, it can help you better understand why you need to do certain things."[366] Even Ron Powlus, former Notre Dame quarterback and acting quarterbacks coach, was astonished by the clarity of Weis' tutorial to players on making hot reads and sight adjustments in response to what an opponent is doing: "That was the simplest I think I've ever heard–through college, NFL, everything– going through hots and sight-adjusts and having someone explain it."[367]

Patriots coaches expect players to grasp the logic underlying their playbook because deep understanding allows the quarterback or middle linebacker to change a play at the last moment–whenever a "multiple call" lets players audible from one option to another–and to adjust smartly as a play unfolds:

> "[Linebacker Mike Vrabel]'s a very smart football player, and he understands everything pretty much conceptually that he would want to do.

Not just what his assignment is but what the overall purpose of the defense is. What the strengths are, what the weaknesses are and why you would want to be in one defense as opposed to another when you have multiple calls."[368]

Because Patriots players truly believe–as defensive tackle Ty Warren says–that "The better you understand something, the better you should perform,"[369] they study intensely.

Keep it lively

"I consider myself a little more shy–kind of the jokester, sit-in-the-back-of-the-room-and-goof-around type of person."[370]
– *Tom Brady*

"We're professional around you all [reporters], but we're jokers. We're jokers in the meeting rooms. We're a bunch of clowns sometimes, and [defensive coordinator] Romeo [Crennel] has been the glue for all of us."[371]
– *Tedy Bruschi*

"I played seven different positions. I like all seven positions. It should help me stay around a while. I even played fullback at 300 pounds. Us fat guys like to run, too."[372]
– *Patriots offensive lineman Russ Hochstein*

Many athletes lump training sessions together with Brussel sprouts, appendectomies and root canals as "necessary evils." Allen Iverson–whose Philadelphia 76ers have, not coincidentally, never won a championship–sees training as an unnecessary evil: "It's just practice. Nobody cares about practice, man."

Properly organized, however, training can be fun. Training is more fun with those you enjoy being around and when organized as a series of competitive games and small challenges. After joining the Patriots, running back Corey Dillon immediately loved his new team for the intensity of its training:

"Right off the bat, [I noticed] the way that they prepared and worked hard in the weight room and conditioned. I was like 'this is going to be something special.' Everybody just works hard. That's something I hadn't experienced before... Everybody is pushing the next man to get better."[373]

Russ Hochstein says his fellow Patriots offensive linemen enjoy training together each offseason:

"I'll do a regimen that the strength staff put together for me. Actually, the whole [offensive] line will work out together. We work out as a group, and we have a lot of fun doing that. We push each other. It's up to [the strength coaches] what specifics we do."[374]

Ty Warren says the same of the Patriots' defensive linemen: "We have real good competition in the [defensive line] group. It's intense sometimes, and that's how we have fun. Whenever we do an agility drill, or a vertical jump or something like that, we go at it."[375] Former Ravens quarterback Chris Redman feels the Patriots push each other harder than his Ravens teammates did:

> "I like the way these guys work here with [strength & conditioning coach] Mike Woicik and the weight program. They push us hard, and it almost feels like that college atmosphere again for me as far as pushing yourself in the offseason to get better, rather than just maintain."[376]

Soon after joining the Patriots, receiver David Terrell spontaneously mentioned how much he enjoyed strength and conditioning training with his new team: "I like [New England]. I like it a lot. All the guys are cool, from [strength coach] Mike Woicik in the weight room to [assistant strength coach] Harold [Nash] to Coach Belichick on down to the players. It's a lot of fun for me."[377] Woicik consciously tries to make it a team-building experience:

> "It's not just about getting in shape, as important as that is. It's about camaraderie and getting to know your teammates. It's being around your position coaches and getting to know your system. A lot of guys can do it on their own, but there's something about doing it in the environment with your teammates. You're doing it with the guys you're going to be working with all year."[378]

How about meetings? Boring, right? Tom Brady says offensive coordinator Charlie Weis "is a great motivator [who] really enjoys the coaching and is fun to be around."[379] Brady even sounds jealous of all the fun in the defensive team meetings:

> "Listening to the defensive players and the kind of respect they have for [defensive coordinator Romeo Crennel], I can see what kind of coach he really is. Their meeting room is right next to ours, and you can always hear them laughing and joking and really getting into it and hear Romeo over there having a great time."[380]

Patriots coaches give plays memorable names–like the names of players or television shows–to motivate players and help them remember plays. The Patriots' all-out blitz is called "Typhoon." It's hard to forget plays with names like "Exxon," "Buffalo," "Ghost," "Illinois" and "Zorro." Romeo Crennel explains, "When you're trying to come up with words for things, sometimes if a player's nickname is 'Wildcat,' and you use 'Wildcat,' that gets his attention... Whether it's the player's nickname or the player's school... it makes it easier for them to remember."[381]

Patriots coaches hold players' interest throughout the two-week build-up to a Super Bowl by installing the game plan gradually, instead of giving them the full monty at the start of Week 1. Asked the Monday before Super Bowl XXXIX whether he would play tight end on the Patriots' goal-line plays, linebacker Mike Vrabel explained, "We haven't put the package in. We won't do that until later on in the week."[382] Defensive coordinator Romeo Crennel says this is an intentional strategy to motivate them and keep their mind from worrying about the game rather than their preparation for the game:

> "We try to hold back some of our installation so that it's not all in, it doesn't get boring or old to them. We give them a couple of new things while we're [in Jacksonville] this week so they have to concentrate and [learn] that as the game gets closer. There are one or two things that we're gonna give you that you've got to concentrate on, that you've got to work at to get right. That's one way of controlling all the anxiety and all of that intensity."[383]

Patriots special teams coordinator Brad Seely echoes Crennel: "You don't want guys to hear the same things six times before they play because they won't listen [to] five of the six. You don't want them to get stale. You want to keep them interested, so you add some new things along the way."[384] (Giving players just basic plays for the first week of preparation also provides two tactical advantages: 1) Time for coaches to intensively study their opponent on film before finalizing the game plan; and, 2) The opportunity to pit the simulated opponent defense (or offense) against the Patriots' base offense (or defense), which is more informative than against complicated blitz schemes, etc.)

Patriots players enjoy their coaches constantly challenging them. The more a player knows, the more coaches expect him to learn. If a player masters a position, coaches teach him another to increase his value and flexibility. Linebacker Mike Vrabel enjoys the challenge of playing multiple positions in the Patriot's complex system for the same reason many enjoy *The New York Times Crossword Puzzle*: "It's certainly fun. It's certainly challenging to know [so many different positions in our defense]."[385] Teaching a linebacker to play tight end is no gimmick. Since linebacker Vrabel learned to morph into tight end Vrabel, he has caught touchdown passes in consecutive Super Bowls. Without checking my facts, I can confidently state Vrabel is the only linebacker in NFL history with touchdown receptions in back-to-back Super Bowls. He has five touchdown catches as a Patriots tight end, something that drives his fellow linebackers nuts: "Oh they hate it. They hate it. They absolutely hate it. I always joke that when we take the Super Bowl pictures I'm going to try and sneak in and show up at the tight end picture just to piss them off a little bit."[386] Because the Patriots' defensive pre-snap movement shuffles players like cards in a deck, a player like Willie McGinest may line up as a linebacker and become a defensive end before the ball is snapped. With such mental and physical challenges, not even the smartest, most experienced players can coast. Doug Flutie, a professional quarterback since 1984, says he's struggling to keep up, despite 21 years of professional experience: "It's hard work, that's the bottom line... You can get away with a little more on other teams. Letting things slide and all that. You let things slide here, you're going to be so far behind that you won't have time to catch up."[387]

As hard as the Patriots worked the week preceding Super Bowl XXXIX, they also stayed loose. *3 Games to Glory III* shows assistant coach Pepper Johnson preparing to throw a football at full speed at a Patriot player (whose face and number were not visible). As Johnson prepares to fire, onlookers are shouting "Bust his face open!" and "Bust it!" After the dejected player fails to catch the ball, onlookers whoop and holler and jump around. Trying to catch high-speed footballs seems an inherently unpleasant drill, but to Patriots, it combines the thrill of bungee jumping and skydiving with the danger of dueling and jousting. Players love laughing at a teammate when a ball bounces off him. And it happens to be a great drill for learning to catch passes.

Players also energize one another. New linebacker Monty Beisel says of safety Rodney Harrison "the way he gets out there and plays the game, it's uplifting to everybody."[388] Tom Brady agrees Harrison electrifies every practice:

> "The way he plays on Sunday is the way he practices on Wednesday, Thursday, and Friday. It's funny because when you're on his side of the ball, you love playing with him on Sunday, but you hate playing against him on Wednesday, Thursday, and Friday, just like everybody else does. Rodney's so fierce and feisty, he's such a competitor that you get into it with him all the time…He can ruin a practice for an offense. He likes to do the scout team stuff. You don't see a lot of people that like to do it, but he'll line up at corner and play scout team, and try to intercept every ball. Then he'll intercept it and he'll dance and he'll throw the ball up. We'll get done with practice and be like, 'Damn, we messed up three plays,' and [realize] Rodney's in the middle of all three. I kept wondering why guys from other teams just hate playing against him—and that's without him hitting us [during practices]—but that's just what he brings."[389]

Belichick is not boisterous like Harrison but also keeps things lively with his deadpan, sardonic humor. Receiver Deion Branch says Belichick has a future on *Comedy Central*: "He is funny… He is a great guy. He is funny with us and laid back."[390] Punter Josh Miller agrees but warns against confusing humor with lack of professional dedication: "He has a very dry sense of humor and makes us laugh all the time. But, at the same time, if you don't do what he brought you in to do, you are out of here."[391]

Charlie Weis brought the joy of training to Notre Dame. Irish alum and Oakland Raiders star Tim Brown was pumped up after serving as a celebrity coach during a glorified scrimmage: "This is probably one of the bigger thrills I've had in a long time. I had a ball. It almost makes me think about coaching… I never thought that I would enjoy being on the sidelines like that. It was a blast for me."[392]

Tease one another

The Patriots enjoy constantly kidding one other. Doing so is fun and keeps everyone's ego in check. The bigger a player's public reputation, the more he gets teased. So Tom Brady is the biggest target, and receiver Deion Branch eagerly rips into him: "He can't sing. He can't dance. And I think his touchdown celebration is crazy. Did you see him slam me last year in the endzone in the Super Bowl?"[393] After the Patriots won their second Super Bowl, linebacker Ted Johnson wanted to know "Is there going to be a statue of [Tom Brady] in downtown Boston?"[394] (Not an absurd question, given that Brady pulls hats low to obscure his face in public and says "I've had guys telling me to kiss their girlfriends. I don't know what to say to that. That's not me."[395]) Locker room legend says Brady has as many backgammon victories as Super Bowl wins; former backup QB Damon Huard adds for good measure, "And when I kick his ass, he throws the board on the floor."[396] (That's utterly believable, given that—when Brady was competing for the starting job at University of Michigan—"I couldn't sleep. I'd be up at 2:30 in the morning checking the weather to see how windy it was going to be because I knew I was going to be throwing."[397]) Players whine about having to serve as Brady's bodyguards. After Brady was invited to the White House and appeared on national television during a State of the Union speech, linebacker Willie McGinest started calling him "Little Bush," a zinger because most of Brady's relatives are Democrats.[398] Soon after he appeared in a Gap ad, players decorated the training room with copies. After a *Saturday Night Live* skit in his undies, Brady's locker turned into a Christmas tree with underwear ornaments. In mid-August 2005, reporters—worried because Brady had thrown scarcely a pass for ten days—asked players how Brady looked in his return to practice; safety Rodney Harrison dodged the question by twisting it around: "He's ugly. That's how he looked. Real ugly. He was just his skinny, old, frail self."[399]

Though outgunned, Brady tries to fight back. He teases Mike Vrabel about his Super Bowl touchdown: "Every time we get in the huddle, Mike [says] 'Don't forget about your boy.' I started throwing it, and his eyes got about that wide. He's like, 'You're throwing it!' After he caught it, he didn't know what to do. He had an interception dance, but he didn't have a touchdown dance."[400]

After Ty Law limped 65 yards for a touchdown to cement a 2003 win over Tennessee, Willie McGinest was more impressed with Law's acting ability than his playing prowess, implying the limp was cheap melodrama: "I think he should have gotten an Oscar for that."[401] Defensive lineman Richard Seymour—who regularly battles left guard Matt Light during practices—jokes that Light's greatest strength is that "He talks well."[402] Star running back Corey Dillon is permanently saddled with his former team's joke-inspiring reputation: "This is my first experience being in a Super Bowl, so I get a lot of jokes… I get a lot of Cincinnati [Bengals] jokes. They think they are funny, and I get quite a few from the guys."[403] Deion Branch says the receivers have great fun practicing against receiver-turned-defensive back Troy

Brown: "We beat him up a lot at practice. We have fun in practice and at the same time Troy wants to get better. We go hard and have fun."[404] After backup linebacker Matt Chatham demolished star running back Corey Dillon during a blitz pickup drill, Chatham joked about the invisible hierarchy separating starters and backups: "I did check to see if Mr. Kraft and Mr. Pioli were around, just [to] make sure I still had a job."[405]

Players even make fun of owner Robert Kraft. Several days after Russian president Vladimir Putin walked off with Kraft's third Super Bowl ring, Kraft issued a statement saying that he "gave" Putin his ring, but–on film–it sure appeared that Putin pocketed Kraft's ring and refused to return it. Patriots linebacker Ted Johnson poked fun by correcting a reporter who asked him about his three Super Bowl rings: "Well, I've got [just] two now. Putin's got my third one. So I lost one to Putin."[406] Johnson explained he wasn't worried about teasing Kraft because

> "Mr. Kraft–he's got a great sense of humor, so he's not immune to a little ribbing. And I think I'm entitled to dish a little bit of that out, and we'll have a good laugh about it. Hopefully, he struck a nice deal while he was there. I hope it was worth it. Hopefully, his paper business is increased because of it."[407]

Linebacker Tully Banta-Cain followed Johnson's lead. Banta-Cain–the butt of many jokes after embarrassingly leaving his 2003 ring in a mall bathroom–said, "It was good to hear that I wasn't the only one who had ring issues. It kind of took the pressure off me a little bit."[408] The one player with any immunity is Richard Seymour. After missing eight days of 2005 training camp due to a financial holdout, Seymour should have been the butt of many jokes. But linebacker Rosevelt Colvin hurled no jokes at perhaps the NFL's best defensive lineman because "He's a big guy, 300 pounds. I was just, 'How you doing. Good to see you. Let's get busy.'"[409]

Train when trainees are alert

Instead of holding two practices a day and then cramming in film-and-teaching sessions at night, the Patriots in training camp 2004 switched from daily two-a-days to alternating days between double and single sessions. One reason was to ensure players were alert enough during film sessions to learn rather than fall asleep. After determining that regular two-a-days exhaust players, Belichick decided that working players less brutally could produce better results:

> "The players have been on the field for five-and-a-half/six hours during the day, and it is getting later at night, their attention span with the coaches is–at that point–[faltering]. So, the quality of it just wasn't as good... You have 24 hours in a day, you are using them to eat, sleep and get ready for football in one form or another. We just feel like this is a more productive use of our time."[410]

Reducing the frequency of training camp practice sessions and holding a classroom session after each practice didn't prevent the 2004 Patriots from winning another Super Bowl.

Maintain continuity

"I have to get better from the last time I stepped on the field. Looking at film, there are a lot of things I could have done a lot better. I know I'll be better this year because I know [the defense] in and out. I'm starting to understand the whole defense, not just my position."[411]
– *Patriots nose tackle Vince Wilfork, working hard in May*

"I only went to college for 2½ years, but I think I know the meaning of the word 'voluntary.'"[412]
– *Indianapolis Colts running back Edgerrin James, explaining why he trained on his own, not with his team, in the 2001 offseason*

Unlike many teams that allow new coordinators to install new playbooks, new vocabulary, new philosophies and new hand signals, the Patriots maintain continuity by changing players and coaches but never ripping up their playbook or system. Coaches and players must fit into the system, not vice versa. This prevents unlearning: "You can really build year-to-year on the things that you learn. You never go backwards in our system. When new players come in, they have to learn the system, but… it's that much easier to teach it."[413]

American children spend the first month of each school year re-learning what they learned in the final months of the previous school year because students forget (or "unlearn") every summer. Not the Patriots. Patriot Jake Schifino says that in the so-called "offseason," "There's a lot of competition among us to see who is the strongest, who jumped the highest, who is the fastest. We're working hard. It's intense."[414]

CLASSROOM

"I have to work really hard at it. And I enjoy working. I enjoy the classroom. I enjoy the off-season program."[415]
– *Tom Brady*

"The only thing we can control is the next practice… What's happened in the past, and what could be going on in the future, really is irrelevant."[416]
– *Bill Belichick*

To Patriots players, Gillette Stadium is more Attica than Aruba. Training begins before dawn and ends long after dusk. Life is regimented: "We know we're going to be in the meeting room in the morning, and we'll find out where we are going for that day."[417] And coaches create a sense of urgency on every play of every practice. During scrimmages, players aren't just running around hitting each other. Coaches tell them "It's 3rd-and-8 with 1:12 left from our 18 yard line" and they're expected to know exactly what to do. Before each practice, coaches script every situation and drill they will put players through. One training camp observer reports "It's well structured. There's not a second wasted."[418] Film study is a different form of pressure. Coaches grill players: "What defense is that?" "What should the left cornerback be doing?" "Why did the weakside linebacker lose containment on this reverse?" "What mistake did the right tackle just make?" Active participation is demanded. And poor performance leads to "detention": benching in that week's game.

Months after arriving in New England following four disappointing seasons as a Chicago Bear, receiver David Terrell so loved the Patriots atmosphere ("happy to be here... very excited... a lot of fun"[419]) that he desperately wanted to make the team's final roster and "do my job to the best of my abilities."[420] "My fear factor is back... a sense of urgency and a sense of not wanting to let people down in any way. That makes you work a lot harder."[421] His fear was well-founded; he didn't survive the final cut-down.

Players who thrive as Patriots are like Kevin Bacon's character in "Animal House" who says "Thank you, sir. May I have another?" each time Neidermayer paddles his behind in a sadistic fraternity initiation rite... except Patriots paddle their own behinds, knowing continual improvement is the only path to NFL success.

Coaches must love teaching

"We'll teach, teach, teach, teach, teach."[422]
   – *Woody Hayes, Ohio State coach with 238-72-10 career record*

"They say that some players are like gym rat players. Well, Belichick was like a gym rat coach–and he still is. When he was with the Giants, he just enjoyed sitting around and talking football. If you ever got away from talking football, he would just go right back to it."[423]
   – *John Madden, Super Bowl-winning coach and NFL analyst*

"The coaching staff is molding us the right way."[424]
   – *Patriots defensive lineman Ty Warren*

"We've learned a lot of football from [Belichick] because he's always teaching us something new, and there's lessons learned from different situations."
   – *Patriots receiver Troy Brown*

Though some suggest Belichick conjured up victory in Super Bowl XXXVI with X's and O's, tactics alone will never win any team a Vince Lombardi Trophy.

Jealous of the Patriots' success, NFL teams are rushing to add "3-4" defenses to their playbooks to copy the Patriots' "multiple" defensive looks, in which the Patriots switch–seemingly effortlessly–between "3-4" and "4-3" fronts before the ball is snapped. But Carolina Panthers offensive coordinator Dan Henning cautions that having a "3-4" in their repertoire does not make the Patriots defense successful. Henning says Patriots coaches are superbly knowledgeable about the radically different blocking techniques and tactics required to maximize the effectiveness of a "3-4" and a "4-3." Henning says Patriots defensive coordinator "Romeo [Crennel] is a superb two-gap teacher. Everyone doesn't have his 23 years of experience teaching the system. Just because you line up in a defense doesn't mean you're going to be successful."[425]

The same is true of the Patriots offense. Offensive coordinator Charlie Weis' passion for teaching made quite an impression on receiver Freddie Mitchell when he came out of college: "My first favorite guy coming into the NFL and the only guy I can remember from the [spring scouting] combine was Charlie Weis. I loved what he was all about. He gave me his card and said, 'Call me personally and I'll tell you what you need to do to get better.' I remember thinking, 'Damn. I want to play for the Patriots.'"[426] Don't wait by your phone, Freddie.

As an undergraduate at Notre Dame, Weis studied speech and drama, preparing for what he hoped would be a career in sports journalism. He later taught high school English for six years and, while coaching at South Carolina for four years, earned a master's degree in education. At the high school level, Weis was asked to coach the basketball team and coached them to a championship. He won a New Jersey high school football championship. He even coached a successful fencing team. Weis' acting and teaching skills are extremely valuable coaching assets.

Weis' Notre Dame players are astonished by their new coach's ability to explain complex strategy simply: "Coach Weis knows the game in and out and not only does he know it like that, but he can simplify it for us. It makes it easy for us to learn, and makes it easy for everybody."[427] Another agreed Weis is a master teacher: "He knows the ins and outs and everything, and he knows the best way to teach it."[428] Unsurprisingly, NFL players at whatever position Weis has coached have had great seasons:

Year(s)	Weis' job	Performance
1993-1994	Patriots' tight ends coach	Charlie Weis helped Ben Coates become the best tight end in football in 1993 and 1994: 1991: 10 catches, 95 yards (1 TD) [without Weis] 1992: 20 catches, 171 yards (3 TDs) [without Weis] 1993: 53 catches, 659 yards (8 TDs) [with Weis] 1994: 96 catches, 1,174 yards (7 TDs) [with Weis] Coates' 1,174 yards and 96 catches in 1994 remain his career highs. 96 catches remains the NFL record for tight ends.

1995	Patriots' running backs coach	As a rookie, Curtis Martin ran for 1,487 yards (4.0 yards/carry) and 14 touchdowns. Receiving, he gained another 261 yards and scored another touchdown.
1996	Patriots' receivers coach	As a rookie, Terry Glenn broke the NFL rookie receptions record with 90 catches for 1,132 yards and six touchdowns. Glenn has subsequently had only one season (1999) remotely comparable to his rookie season.
1997	Jets' wide receivers coach	Keyshawn Johnson gained 844 yards in 1996 and 874 yards in 2000. The three middle years, under Weis' tutelage, Johnson gained 963, 1,131, and 1,170 yards.
1998-1999	Jets' offensive coordinator	Statistically, the Jets' passing attack was stronger in the Weis years (1997-1999) than in 1996 or 2000. The major difference is far fewer interceptions, something receivers help with by running better routes and knocking down passes they can't catch: 1996: 6.2 yards per pass, 22 TDs, 30 INTs (8 more INTs) 1997: 6.3 yards per pass, 20 TDs, 10 INTs (10 more TDs) 1998: 7.6 yards per pass, 33 TDs, 13 INTs (20 more TDs) 1999: 6.3 yards per pass, 22 TDs, 16 INTs (6 more TDs) 2000: 6.3 yards per pass, 23 TDs, 29 INTs (6 more INTs)
2000-2004	Patriots' offensive coordinator	Three Super Bowl championships in five seasons. Developed 6th-round draft pick into two-time Super Bowl MVP quarterback.

Part of Bill Belichick's brilliance is surrounding himself with staffers who teach well. Charlie Weis is but one example. Belichick's assistants are in demand. After the 2003 season, the Patriots lost three assistants: 1) Outside linebackers coach Rob Ryan (son of legendary NFL coach Buddy Ryan) became the Oakland Raiders' defensive coordinator after Patriots defensive backs coach Eric Mangini turned down the same job;[429] 2) The New York Giants hired quarterbacks coach John Hufnagel as their offensive coordinator; and, 3) The Buffalo Bills hired Steve Szabo as their defensive backs coach. After the 2004 season, coordinators Weis and Crennel were hired as head coaches. Crennel brought Patriots assistant offensive line coach Jeff Davidson with him to Cleveland and promoted him to offensive line coach. Despite losing six assistants in two years, it could have been worse. Eric Mangini turned down defensive coordinator offers—each for more money—from Cleveland and Miami, and Scott Pioli spurned a very lucrative general manager offer from Seattle. Competitors have obviously noticed that Bill Belichick hires detail-obsessed assistants and trains them to provide players with advice and coaching that helps them perform better.

Mike Woicik

Perhaps the most overlooked element in the Patriots' success is strength and conditioning coach Mike Woicik, who shows players how best to develop football muscles. If you believe likely Hall of Fame Cowboys receiver Michael Irvin, Woicik was the engine powering the Cowboys' dynasty, which won three Super Bowls under two different head coaches during Woicik's years in Dallas (1990-1996). Remember Emmitt Smith in his prime? Remember dominating Dallas linemen like Charles Haley, Nate Newton, Kevin Gogan, Leon Lett, Erik Williams, Mark Stepnoski, Russell Maryland, and Jay Novacek? They used Woicik's Soviet-style training methods, especially "plyometrics," which develops short bursts of explosive power. Traditional weight lifting is smooth, with steady ups and downs. Conversely, plyometrics pushes muscles rapidly through their entire cycle of expansion and contraction. An example is your pectoral (chest) muscles during a series of rapid push-ups, each lifting you high enough off the ground to clap your hands together. After each clap, your chest falls rapidly toward the floor and your pectorals expand (lengthen). If you immediately push hard enough to propel your body back into the air, your pecs contract (shorten) rapidly.

Many football challenges require brief bursts of tremendous power. The key to plyometrics' astonishing results on the football field (and in other sports requiring quick power bursts) is that muscles that rapidly contract-and-expand become optimized for power bursts. Doing many clap push-ups in rapid succession keeps your pecs expanding and contracting and trains them to push harder in a short burst than the same number of push-ups done slowly would. Clap push-ups prepare an offensive lineman to punch at a defensive lineman's chest and knock him backwards... or a cornerback to shove a receiver trying to get off the line of scrimmage, something Belichick's defense is famous for. A pass rusher powering pas the offensive line toward the quarterback is another example, as Patriots linebacker Roosevelt Colvin explains: "Man, if I didn't have to do [Belichick's annual conditioning drill], I'd be good. I don't like running for distance. Give me 5 yards to get around the corner and get to the quarterback. That's all the running distance I need."[430] Other plyometrics exercises—some involving repeated jumps high into the air (which lengthen leg muscles) and landings (which shorten the same muscles)—optimize leg muscles to dash off the line of scrimmage or leap high to catch passes.

The Cowboys dynasty fizzled after Woicik's firing (after he chewed out coach Barry Switzer for allowing kicker Chris Boniol to kick a record-tying seventh field goal in a 21-0 game instead of kneeling on the ball to end the game). In 1996, former NFL player Tim Green dedicated a book chapter to Woicik titled "The Most Valuable Man in the NFL." Green called Woicik "more important to the Cowboys organization than... Deion Sanders."[431] In it, Green quotes former Cowboys coach Jimmy Johnson saying in 1994, "If I do ever get back into coaching, the first phone call I make after I get the job will be to Mike."[432] Bill Belichick—who eats football books for breakfast–undoubtedly read Green's book and remembered Johnson's advice in 2000, signing Woicik immediately after becoming the Patriots' head coach. Woicik has now collected an astonishing six Super Bowl rings since 1990, better than even Belichick himself!

Direct proof of Woicik's effectiveness is players' rapid improvement while training under him. Tim Green played college football at Syracuse and credits Woicik–then Syracuse's strength coach–for his finishing second on the all-time NCAA sack list and being drafted in Round 1 of the NFL Draft. And David Patten–who once failed to catch on with the Edmonton Eskimos–has become so explosive as a Patriot that his ability to separate from defenders[433] convinced the Washington Redskins to give him a $3.5 million signing bonus, a $13 million 5-year contract and a starting job.

Adapt curriculum to students' ability

"You have to have enough [complexity in your schemes] so you can counter your opponent but keep it simple enough so your players can execute. You don't want to give [players] too much [to learn], but you don't want to be predictable, either. So that's where you are constantly finding that balance."[434]
– *Bill Belichick*

Having spent 13 years in public schools plus four years in college and eight in graduate school, I know some teachers assign far too much material while others assign far too little. Several teachers assigned so much required reading that I thought it would be impossible to read everything, even if I neglected all my other courses. But some classes were so simple I stopped bothering to attend lectures. The Patriots put real thought into how much they ask players to learn. And they are aware of the tradeoffs. Excessive complexity causes confusion and mistakes. Insufficient complexity allows opponents to exploit your predictability.

The Patriots playbook uses modularity to provide almost unlimited tactical flexibility with a minimum of complexity. Plays are constructed using building blocks, just as children can build most any shape they desire by connecting individual Legos. The "shorthand" description of a Patriots play is quite long. Each portion of the description describes a module of the play. The first module describes the base formation. The next tells a running back where to line up. The third describes pre-snap motion: who moves, where to move and what to do (block or run a pass pattern). The fourth sets the blocking scheme. Another may tell the two- or three-receiver combination on the left side of the field what they should each do: which pattern to run to what distance against which type of coverage. Another may tell the receiver(s) on the opposite side what to do. Another may signal the quarterback will drop back seven steps (instead of three or five) with the intent of throwing deep.

Coaches can mix-and-match modules to create a vast number of potential plays while requiring players to learn only those modules relevant to whatever position(s) they play. If, for example, there are ten base formations, ten places for the running back to position himself, ten pre-snap motions, ten blocking schemes, ten route combinations for the receivers on the left side of the field and ten route combinations for the receivers on the right side, coaches could call any of 1,000,000 (10·10·10·10·10·10) possible plays. The hypothetical one million plays would require players to learn—at most—sixty (10+10+10+10+10+10) modules. Offensive linemen would need to learn only ten things: the ten blocking schemes.

The playbook is also well-conceived because its plays are not categorized by personnel. There's not one chunk of playbook for two tight end plays and another for four wide receiver plays. Every play has five offensive linemen, a quarterback and one player each at the "F," "H," "X," "Y" and "Z" positions. Normally, "F" and "H" are running backs, "Y" a tight end and "X" and "Z" receivers, but not necessarily. Two "tight ends" may be on the field but one—playing the "Y" role—lined up as a wide receiver and the other—playing the "F" role—a running back. This allows coaches to call any play with whoever's on the field. Also, some players are able to play multiple roles, which compounds opponents' confusion.

This approach is also brilliant because it makes it hard for opponents to "study the Patriots' playbook." They may *think* they've seen a play before, but it may differ slightly but significantly from what they saw on film. And Patriots players may execute the same exact play differently against different defenses. Some plays, for example, tell a receiver to run one route against press coverage but another if the cornerback plays off the line of scrimmage.

Buffalo Bills defensive backs coach Steve Szabo knew ten-year-old "Billy" Belichick in the early 1960s and served as a Patriots assistant in 2003. Szabo insists Belichick avoids complicated schemes that might confuse players and result in broken defenses and big plays for opposing offenses:

> "Everybody thinks he plays a lot of defenses. It's not true. He's exactly the opposite. He doesn't like a lot of (different) things. He doesn't like a lot of what he calls 'moving parts' because you're apt to make a mistake. If the truth be known, his defensive game plans are very simple. What they rely on is letting the players play and their ability to play techniques perfectly."[435]

Another example of Belichick's desire for simplicity is his reluctance to change schemes to prevent opponents from exploiting inside knowledge of the Patriots acquired through a former Patriots player or coach. In 2004, Belichick feared Szabo would use his knowledge—gained as a Patriots assistant coach in 2003— to help his Buffalo Bills prepare: "It's definitely a concern. Steve is a smart guy. Does he know things about us that other people don't know? Absolutely. He was in all those meetings. He knows what our strategies were."[436] Nevertheless, Belichick didn't overhaul his system because he knew his players have a limited capacity to absorb information: "We could adjust our terminology and we could adjust our signals. That's the game you get into. But the downside of it is you can outsmart–or what I like to call outdumb–yourself. I think there's a [tradeoff] there."[437]

Belichick says you can also "outdumb" yourself guessing what the other team is trying to do: "Sometimes, you get a little too much into that stuff and you're listening to their calls and trying to figure out what they're trying to do–you just better be able to go out there and execute your stuff."[438] "Even if somebody were to walk in here and open up the Buffalo playbook and say 'There it is,' there is only so much you can do with that."[439]

Each week, Belichick spends Sunday evening through Tuesday in the film room studying the team's next opponent and identifying tactics he believes can sway the game in the Patriots' favor, perhaps quickly pressuring a slow quarterback and forcing him to scramble, encircling a fast quarterback to prevent him from scrambling, picking on a slow defensive back by running deep routes or hitting the opponent's fastest receiver after the ball is snapped. Belichick also seeks clues players can look for that predict what their opponent is doing, perhaps that their opponent always passes in the red zone with a particular personnel grouping. On Wednesday, he presents players with a short, punchy tip sheet... bullet points, not *War and Peace*. According to former Patriots guard/center Damien Woody, "[Belichick] tell[s] us the three or four things we needed to do to win. 'If you do this, this and this, you're going to win.' And that's how it would happen."[440]

Because Belichick realizes players become confused when coaches throw too much information at them, his staff works hard to identify the essential knowledge each player must have each week. Belichick would rather have players feel comfortable with 80% of what their opponent will throw at them than overwhelmed trying to learn many things their opponent is unlikely to throw at them:

> "You have to be careful about defending a lot of ghosts, trying to prepare for 7,000 plays. [Opponents] are only going to be able to run 60 or 70 [plays] out there, so they can't do everything. I think you better take care of the things that you feel sure that they are going to do, cover the things that could be a problem–that there is maybe some good reason to think that they would do–and then you are probably better off taking your chances on everything else or you would be spending a lot of time on things that they might do but will never happen, and it is just a waste of time. And it is confusing to the players. They spend all week worrying about stuff that they might do and then they don't do any of it, but they are thinking about that and the team is never even showing it. So, I think you have to be careful about being–and I don't want to say 'over-prepared'–but I think overemphasizing something that isn't going to come up or doesn't come up, you are just spinning your wheels in the sand."[441]

Teach the basics and add complexity

"I got a little warm up to the basic [defensive play] calls and then once I had to go over [to defense] and play [in real games] I had to learn all the other calls to go along with [the basic ones]. And all the signals they use in the secondary. When I have help [from another defender], when I don't have help, all that stuff."

– Patriots veteran wide receiver Troy Brown, on learning to play nickelback

"You look at Bill Belichick as being rigid, but he gives [Brady] more rope than anyone else he's had, and it shows. And Tom doesn't abuse it. And that means he gets even more rope."[442]

– Former New Orleans Saints GM Randy Mueller

Talented teachers make difficult material easy to learn by explaining simple concepts clearly before building to more complex ideas. We don't start teaching children to multiply 12×19 or even 8×7. We start with 1×1 and 1×2 and 1×3 and 2×2. Even 0×1 is hard to understand initially.

The Patriots' playbook is thick. Rookie offensive lineman Nick Kaczur says his college playbook was about one inch thick compared with six inches for his Patriots playbook.[443] But Patriots coaches are great teachers, and Scott Pioli admits only great students to the Patriots' classrooms. Nose tackle Vince Wilfork picked up the defense fast enough to not only start on opening day of his rookie season but even make some big plays, especially his game-changing fumble recovery: "From the block they gave me, I knew exactly what they were trying to run."[444]

It's easy to frustrate learners because, as a psychologist explains, "people feel anxious when they perceive the challenges in a situation as far exceeding their skills."[445] It's smarter to first teach the fundamentals and then gradually add complexity. The first day of spring mini-camp, Belichick says, "We're… starting from scratch and tak[ing] this weekend to try to indoctrinate these kids into our system. It's about as basic as you could possibly get. We're not out there climbing any mountains. We're just trying to get one foot in front of the other without falling down." May passing camp is building-block stuff: "going through technique, going through bags, hitting big bags, going through steps, going through reads, going through philosophies and blocking schemes."[446]

The Patriots' full playbook is intricate and complicated, but coaches train new players in the basics before adding complexity in a logical, digestible manner at a pace players can absorb. Explains Carl Banks, who played linebacker for Belichick's Giants and Browns:

"Everything he does has a base that you learn from the first day of mini-camp. If he chooses to employ a two-deep zone coverage, then everything is rooted in that defense and all the other plays are like branches off a tree. It's like building a house. First you lay the foundation and then you add the rooms. He may have five coverages in mini-camp, and then he'll start to add to those coverages. Maybe he'll have two zone coverages and three man coverages. If it's a complex man coverage, then he'll do the basics of that first and then he'll add the pieces. Maybe he'll add a blitz and then another blitz off that blitz, and then come back with a third look. But everything is rooted in the basic defense."[447]

As another example, the Patriots use a set of base formations, numbered 0 through 8. They supplement these core formations with additional named formations. I presume that during spring mini-camp they teach only the core formations and supplement these with named formations during fall training camp. This—and other steps to reduce complexity in the spring—could explain why many players have played well soon after joining the Patriots but later faltered. Receiver David Terrell is the latest example. Only great news came out about Terrell during his early weeks with the team, but his performance seemed to slip in later months and he failed to make the final roster. Deion Branch told reporters that coaches were feeding Terrell the playbook in sections, suggesting Terrell had difficulties absorbing it: "He's taking his time in getting everything… He's doing a great job of trying to consume all he can, and the coach is doing a great job of working with him and not pushing a whole load on him."[448]

In training camp, Belichick begins with situational plays in isolation before stringing plays together and worrying about substitutions: "We're [now] working on game situations, tying the game together. We'll get into some more situational substitution… We're still working on fundamental stuff but trying to bring it more into a game-type scenario and how it would work in real-game scenario."[449]

Belichick realizes football teams competing in September are less cohesive and less capable of handling complexity than football teams playing in December or January. So Patriots coaches add complexity as the season progresses. In 2001, offensive coordinator Charlie Weis started second-year quarterback and first-year starter Tom Brady off easy and then ratcheted up the difficulty as Brady absorbed the additional complexity: "We really didn't change the offense. What we really did was started off easy and then worked into the magnitude we would normally have. I often hear that we changed the offense, but we really never changed. It's a matter of being comfortable."[450]

This process did not end in 2001, 2002, or even 2003. In 2004, Charlie Weis asked Brady to score each play in the upcoming game plan on a scale from 1 to 10 and didn't call plays Brady rated low.[451] In 2004, Weis also trusted Brady with more freedom to change plays at the last moment. He gave Brady more control to audible (*i.e.*, announce a different play moments before the ball is snapped than the play called in the huddle) and installed more "check with me" plays that require players to check for Brady's pre-snap instructions. (On a "check with me" play, the quarterback calls multiple plays in the huddle and then surveys the defense and shouts to players which play they will use.) Although Brady changing the play moments before the snap increases complexity, Brady's receivers were excited: "Giving Tom the opportunity to control the offense, that's a good thing for us. We know we can count on him and he can count on us picking up all the calls.[452]"

Also, the coaching staff has treated Brady more and more like a coach: "Brady now plays a key role in game-planning sessions with Belichick and Weis."[453] Here's Brady description of the evolution of his role:

> "My first year, [it was] '[Coaches] call the play and you run it.' And then my second year it was 'OK, we'll do some "check with me" and stuff, we'll go to the line with two plays.' And then my third year, it was 'OK, you got a couple plays and if you want to audible you can do that.' Now it is like 'Let's see what the best play is we can do and let's figure out how to get to it.'"[454]

Patriots center Dan Koppen believes Brady's increasing control makes him even more dangerous:

> "Tom is a smart guy out on the field, and he can really read what the defense is doing and put us in the best situation to make the correct play... He can switch us really into anything he wants done. He's just that good at reading defenses. It's the mental part of the game that he's phenomenal at."[455]

In the Patriots' fourth game of 2004, Koppen says, a Brady audible led to a 36-yard Corey Dillon run: "The look [the Dolphins defense] gave us wasn't a good look for [the play we had called]. Tommy called a play to the other side where we had a better look, where scheme-wise it was a better situation. Tom made the switch, a great audible."[456]

Belichick conceptualizes learning as building "inventory" (i.e., his team's stock of knowledge) throughout the season:

> "There is a lot of inventory that gets built up on a week-by-week basis through September, October, November and December, and even in those couple of weeks in January. Now, you are not anywhere close to that inventory. You might look at the film and say 'Well, yeah. That is something we did [last season] or that is something they did then.' Whether your team could actually go out there and do that now, or whether their team could actually go out there and do that now, after only a few weeks of practice... Maybe you can, maybe you can't, I don't know, but it is not the same as playing it in January. And I think that is a big factor [for] both teams... If you have been playing football for six months, you can do a lot more as a team after six months than you can after six weeks."[457]

The same principle–that learning is an accretive process–applies to individual training. Coaches focus each player on one or two training objectives at a time because people who try to simultaneously do multiple tasks seldom succeed:

> "Multitasking can easily turn into multislacking. It also increases errors, short-circuits attention spans, induces air-traffic-controller-like stress, and elongates the time it takes to accomplish the most basic tasks by… 50% or more, according to University of Michigan psychology professor David Meyer."[458]

A study of CEOs' time-management techniques observed this finding in action: "Successful CEOs do not multitask. They concentrate intensely on one thing at a time."[459] The best way to learn anything is to focus on it. The more you push potential distractions aside, the more successful you will be at learning what you wish to learn. Smart coaches give a player one or two challenges at a time and sequence those challenges by priority.

Teach and re-teach

> "There are several players, even at the [pro] level, [for whom] each week is like starting over. You teach them and then all of a sudden you put in [plays for] the next week and it's like they are talking a foreign language that they have never heard before."[460]
> – *Patriots offensive coordinator Charlie Weis*

> "With the [1980] Giants, our teaching and installation schedule would sometimes be three weeks. Now, it's more like one week. The difference is that now we covered a lot of those things in spring camps… Now, it's more of a review than the first time they're hearing it."[461]
> – *Bill Belichick*

Understanding a play intellectually is not the same as being able to execute it well. The Patriots repeatedly practice every play before using it to ensure each player *feels* the play. In the first minute of his first practice as Notre Dame head coach, Charlie Weis infected his players with his obsessive need to execute each play with precision and to get the basics right before moving to advanced lessons. Though his offense was practicing without a defense, Weis barked, "Get your ass back here. We aren't starting like that. You guys look like crap. We'll keep running the same play. I've got nowhere to go."[462] Wouldn't that time be better used running through more plays? No, because "If you let those little things go by right from the beginning without trying to correct them, you are sending the wrong message."[463]

> "I just wanted the guys to get in a habit of coming in and out of the huddle and have a play called in the huddle with the new language and those types of things. It took the first group three or four times to run the first play

because on the first one, one guy went the wrong way and on the next one I just didn't think the effort was good enough."[464]

If Notre Dame players were surprised by Weis' quality-over-quantity mentality, they weren't surprised in their second practice: "That's the type of attitude where things aren't good enough and you do it over and over again until you get it to where he wants it. That's exactly what this team needs. He obviously knows how to get as close to perfection as you can get."[465] Another player said, "He's real intense. I love the way he coaches—just making sure you're doing things right, and perfecting everything. He's a perfectionist, and that's the way you gotta play football."[466]

College students who "pull all-nighters cramming" for a test may regurgitate enough to pass their test but quickly forget whatever they have "learned." To really understand something, you must learn it several times before it sinks in. During training camp, Patriots players learn everything. Each week of the season, coaches choose a small subset of the playbook for that week's game. Players then re-learn what they learned in training camp by repeatedly practicing that week's plays. Safety Rodney Harrison says, "We have so many adjustments week in and week out to deal with. You have to be able to adjust on the go. Sometimes we might cover something in training camp and we might not get back to it for a month."[467] Troy Brown agrees: "It's not an easy defensive [game] plan. We change the calls from week to week and change our calls during the course of the game. ...The defensive playbook just changes so much from day to day."[468]

Linebacker Willie McGinest says players benefit from learning during training camp and re-learning before games: "The whole package comes in in the offseason, in camp. So we get the foundation [then]. Depending on who we play, you got a week to prepare for what you're going to do. But it's not like you've never done it before."[469] And it's not just sitting in a classroom and saying, "Remember when we did this?" As Tom Brady says, "We always try to run every play a few times."[470] Coaches also encourage players to solidify their knowledge by doing "mental reps." Brady says, "as a quarterback, you see the plays play [out in] your mind a lot."[471]

Patriots coaches' insistence on practice and more practice is so well understood by reporters that Belichick joked—after a reporter asked whether he was surprised when offensive coordinator Charlie Weis called a triple reverse—"Believe it or not, we have practiced the play. We didn't just go out there and say, 'Why don't you give it to Givens, and then you give it to Patten, Givens, and then you flip to Patten.' No, we actually worked on that play and we planned on using it in a game."[472] The Patriots will never be confused with a sandlot team that innovates new plays on the fly by diagramming them in the dirt.

Encourage questions

I mentioned earlier that many teachers move through material so quickly that students cannot keep pace. The material is so obvious to teachers that they fail to realize their students are lost. After becoming a professor, a good friend of mine taught a course and was convinced he taught brilliantly. It turned out students were so confused they couldn't even ask questions. Many students had assumed they were dumb because no one else was expressing confusion. When my friend received his student evaluation results, he thought he was in line for an award after scoring in the top 10% of teachers at his university. But he had misinterpreted his score. He was actually in the bottom 10%. The experience taught him a painful lesson… though not as painful as the experience he had inadvertently inflicted upon his students.

Belichick expects his players to proactively ask questions when they're unclear about something and is glad when they do. Less motivated players won't ask because they don't want to look dumb:

> "This group [of players] is very flexible and adaptable, as far as the ones I've coached. I think that these players are smart, they are conscientious, they work hard, they try to do what you tell them, and if they don't understand it, then they ask questions to try to get it right. It gives you confidence as a coach to put the best configurations on the field."[473]

Adjust teaching to each student

> "The key thing I've learned from [Bill Belichick and Nick Saban] is that everything is not the same for every player. You can't go in there with one coaching philosophy and just say 'Do it this way.' Maybe one guy is more athletic and another is more about using his strength. Maybe it's the other way around. Don't ask players to do things they can't do."[474]
> – Dean Pees, Patriots linebackers coach

As Patriots offensive coordinator, Charlie Weis made creative use of the English language to spur players toward their goals. Because New England has no use for players with fragile egos, Weis never hesitated to embellish or embarrass. After taking over Notre Dame's famed football program, Weis admits to toning down his zingers from 'R' to 'NC-17' because he's dealing with college students, not professional athletes: "I'm choosing my words a little bit more tactfully than I might have done in the past. Not all the time, but most of the time."[475]

Patriots coaches appreciate that coaching is not one-size-fits-all. Belichick says a rookie new to professional football confronts very different challenges than a veteran with who signs as a free agent: "One thing that can be a problem is breaking old habits. If you've been doing something for a long time and you're used to doing it that way, but that's not what's required in the new system, it sometimes requires a little undoing before you start something new."[476]

Patriots cornerback Tyrone Poole admires defensive coordinator Romeo Crennel's sensitivity to players' different needs and his ability to be both tough and approachable:

> "He knows when to press down on players and get the fire started within them, and he also knows when to pat you on the back. There are not too many coaches in this league who can do that. You've got some of those coaches with a military style–hard-nosed. And then you've got some coaches who are too lovable and they don't win. Romeo, he brings a mixture of both. And he brings wins."[477]

Provide tailored training

The Patriots tailor training to individual needs. For example, coaches meet with rookies after practices because rookies require rapid feedback and need to ask extra questions. Patriots defensive coordinator Romeo Crennel explains:

> "You give more attention to the young guys because they don't have the experience, so you are on their every little move, whereas you might not be on Ty [Law]'s every little move. You can tell Ty something, 'Ty, remember this,' and he would know what you are talking about because he has experienced it. Whereas, when you are working with a young player, he hasn't experienced things, so you have to tell him and then you have to reemphasize it to him and point it out on the tape and then you have to show him a clip of somebody else in the game doing it so that he can get the idea."[478]

In his first season as a Patriot, linebacker Chad Brown joins the rookies on post-practice remedial sessions because his three Pro Bowl appearances do not equip him to play in the Patriots' system. After working hard for months to pick up the complex defense, "I told [defensive coordinator Eric Mangini] I was kind of struggling with this, and he said, 'Chad, look back at the first mini-camp films and you'd be shocked at how much better you are now than you were then.'"[479] For smart, hard-working players like Brown, timely encouragement can be as important as constructive criticism.

At the other end of the spectrum is veteran linebacker Willie McGinest. McGinest does not participate in drills early in training camp. Questioned by reporters, he says "I'm ready to go... When it's time for me to be out there, I'll be out there."[480] Belichick hints that, due to McGinest's experience, he does not need practice as much as the new crop of Patriots linebackers:

> "We've been on a schedule with Willie for the last couple of years in terms of training camp and his preparation for the season... It has worked well for him, and it has worked well for the team... We feel like it's mutually beneficial for the player, the team and the unit that he's on."[481]

Also, McGinest's age makes practicing riskier. So, the Patriots let him sit out the drills because they had little to gain and much to lose. Coaches gave Super Bowl MVP Deion Branch star treatment, telling him to sit out all four 2005 preseason games. Belichick explains the differing approaches:

> "When the player's new coming in, that's a little bit different than a player who's been here and been in the system for a year or more… We take it on a case-by-case basis and we do what's best for the player himself physically, the player from a preparation standpoint and then the overall team needs. And that could be different from player to player."[482]

Chad Brown is as old and experienced an NFL linebacker as Willie McGinest, but Brown got few breathers on the sideline–let alone days off–because, as he confessed, he was struggling to learn the Patriots defense: "They recognize it's my 13th year, and they want me to be healthy at the end of the season, but it's one thing to be healthy, it's another to know what the heck you're doing. That comes first."[483]

Late in his 2003 rookie season, Patriots Dan Klecko really appreciated the extra coaching help he was receiving:

> "They do such a good job around here of teaching the rookies. We have earlier meetings. Earlier in the season, me and Tully [Banta-Cain] had to come in and learn extra linebacker stuff with Coach [Rob] Ryan. They do such a good job just bringing you along and trying to teach you everything, to where it's not really by fire. They really have you prepared."[484]

Tailoring training is such a priority that it was Eric Mangini's top assignment after ascending to the defensive coordinator job: "I might need to be a little bit more patient with players learning the material. Everyone learns at different paces, but I expect it to be learned quickly and thoroughly. I need to understand that different guys are going to learn at different paces."[485]

Tailoring training also matters because what works for one player may not for another. Says Belichick:

> "Every player has their own playing style, and eventually players learn how to play into their strengths and kind of play away from their weaknesses. I think that every player goes through that as it applies to each different system. What works for a player in one system may be a little bit different as he goes into another scheme or a slightly different responsibility."[486]

Also, players may need to prove themselves in different ways. In Spring 2005, the Patriots had several promising young running backs, each of whom trained differently. Cedric Cobbs stayed in Foxboro while Kory Chapman played in NFL Europe. Why? They had different training priorities.

4th-round selection Cedric Cobbs' biggest challenge is learning the Patriots' system, which is more complex and demands more pass blocking and pass catching from running backs than the simple scheme his Arkansas Razorbacks used: "Every play, I have a responsibility, and it can change according to the defenses. At Arkansas I never had to worry about that."[487] Belichick elaborates on the simplicity of what the Razorbacks asked Cobbs to do:

> "He either carried the ball or they faked it to him. It was usually a slide protection where the whole line blocked away from the fake and he maybe had [responsibility to block] the end man on the line [on pass plays]. It was pretty simple. Here, it's anything but. There are 20-25 protections in any given game. [NFL defenses] give you a lot of different looks. He hadn't been exposed to what we do or what any pro team does."[488]

The undrafted Chapman has an even bigger challenge: practicing against more NFL-like defenses than his Division I-AA Jacksonville State faced in the Ohio Valley Conference and demonstrating he can run against stronger defenses.[489]

In Spring 2005, Cobbs soaked up the Patriots system while Chapman ran roughshod over NFL Europe defenses: 718 rushing yards on 126 carries (5.7 yards/carry), 5 TDs, 154 receiving yards and 230 kickoff return yards (21 yards/return). Each emerged from the offseason a better player, having grappled with his most pressing challenge.

Train collectively

"It's rarely perfect in football because there are so many moving parts."[490]
– *Tom Brady*

"On the offensive line, [performance] is not about one guy, it's about five guys working together and how those guys fit together and how they perform together as one unit that [defines] the strength of your offensive line."[491]
– *Bill Belichick*

"For a team to be successful, every player has to do what they do within the framework of your organization."[492]
– *Bill Russell, whose Boston Celtics won 11 championships in his 13 seasons*

"You can put together an All-Star team [but] if they can't play together, you aren't going to have much success… We want to go out there and play together and play our roles. We want to be accountable for our roles."[493]
– *Patriots receiver Troy Brown*

"We try to keep our boy [Tom Brady] nice and clean… Everyone plays hard for each other."[494]
– *Patriots offensive lineman Joe Andruzzi*

"You aren't even going to make it in the door if you aren't a team player."[495]
  – Patriots receiver Deion Branch

"We know that without each other we wouldn't be here... Football is a team sport."[496]
  – Patriots receiver David Givens

"If a player jumps offsides, [he feels responsible to] the whole team. And then nothing else needs to be said because the rest of the players are doing it for you. [Building a collective culture] definitely cut down on my profanity."[497]
  – Bill Belichick

When offensive coordinator Charlie Weis shouts to star running back Corey Dillon during a practice or a game, he doesn't yell "Come on, Corey!" or "Come on, Dillon!" or "Come on, Big D!" Weis yells "Come on, two eight!" To Weis, Dillon's name is his jersey number, 28. Calling players by numbers, not names, seems demeaning, but Weis does so to constantly–though subtly–remind each player that he is a cog in the Patriots machine. And each cog must adapt to what other cogs is doing because or the machine will grind to a halt. Optimal performance is possible only when all eleven teammates on the field behave as if controlled by a single brain. As Belichick says, "if you change a tight end's blocking rule or technique... it affects the guard on the other side of the ball."[498]

The Patriots train collectively because they take collective responsibility. Patriots linebacker Willie McGinest says of Terrell Owens and Randy Moss, "I don't think one guy can control everybody else."[499] Before the 2004 AFC Championship Game, Bill Belichick said, "No one guy can stop the Steeler defense." He preaches incessantly about the need for players to coordinate their actions, to respond with collective intelligence to whatever the opponent throws at them:

> "If everyone plays the play as it's designed, the defense fits properly and the line of scrimmage is secure... Everyone is reading keys and all reacting properly to the way they see the play unfold... Playing defensive football, you have to know what you're doing and be smart football players. When you're trying to stop a good offensive football team, one with a lot of misdirection, counter plays and variables, defensive players have to be in the right spot at the right time and recognize [their opponent's trickery]. It's definitely challenging. It's team defense, not about one guy being freed up to make every tackle. It's about the team being in good position."[500]

For example, after joining the Patriots in 2005, veteran linebackers Chad Brown and Monty Beisel struggled to fill the giant shoes of Ted Johnson and Tedy Bruschi until they unlearned their old habit of aggressively pursuing the ball-carrier: "Chad and I both, we were over-running everything. We wanted to get outside, get downhill and make the play. And the [coaches] just kept telling us to slow down. So I think over the last couple of weeks we've kind of slowed it down. And after that it's sort of smoothed out."[501] By pursuing as aggressively as they had elsewhere, they gouged a gap in the defense, allowing opposing runners to cut back into the vacated hole.

The Patriots also believe no one player loses a game. Asked about Troy Brown surrendering the game-winning touchdown pass against Miami, Deion Branch replied, "You can't put anything on one man, and he knows that. He took the blame for it, but we don't do that on our team. It isn't one man's fault."[502]

After his successful rookie season, Patriots nose tackle Vince Wilfork didn't rest on his laurels. He got busy re-learning the playbook from the perspective of all the other defensive positions:

> "My defensive coordinator can ask me about what the linebackers are doing or ask me what the safety's doing on a certain play... I'm learning the defense, and not just the nose [tackle position]. Nose is in my back pocket... I'm done [learning] that. My thing now is to... understand what's going on around me."[503]

Why would Wilfork devote so much time to learning positions he doesn't play? Knowing where his teammates are supposed to be and what they are each trying to accomplish enables Wilfork to adapt his play based on where his teammates actually are as the play unfolds and what opponents are doing. During film study, Belichick constantly preaches that players must adapt their play based on holistic awareness of what is happening around them. He demonstrates this, for example, by crediting Giants defensive lineman Michael Strahan for a teammate's sack. When the play begins, Strahan occupies two Redskins blockers, Jansen and Cartwright. As Strahan's teammate Ralph Brown rushes the quarterback on a delayed blitz, Cartwright tries to slide over and block Brown. Strahan–knowing Brown is blitzing from behind his right shoulder–grabs Cartwright, allowing Brown to make the sack. Belichick similarly credits the Colts' wide receivers for blocking smartly to create a hole for a big running play: "[What's] interesting about this play is how effective the receivers are coming down here and blocking the Houston defensive backs."[504] If Belichick shows us fans several examples of teammates helping teammates, he must show his players a million. He must regularly say, as he did of Strahan helping Brown, "This is the kind of unselfish play that goes unnoticed but... helps his teammates."[505]

The Patriots playbook leaves little room for players to freelance. On every play, each player has a specific role to perform. The roles of all eleven players fit together into a cohesive defensive (or offensive) strategy. If one player deviates from his role, his team suffers because the other ten players will assume he is doing one thing when he is actually doing something different. Out-of-position defenders create holes for runners to run through and zones where receivers can run uncovered. Out-of-position offensive players enable defenders to tackle running backs for a loss, sack quarterbacks and knock down or intercept passes.

For example, when playing a "Cover 0" or "Cover 1" defense, a cornerback has man-to-man coverage responsibility for a wide receiver—wherever he runs. In a standard "Cover 2," the cornerback is responsible for short routes while the safety is responsible for picking up the receiver on deep routes. But in a "Cover 3," the cornerback has deep responsibility while the strong safety or an outside linebacker may have short responsibility. The potential for confusion is obvious. If the corner thinks it's "Cover 1" or "Cover 2" while the strong safety thinks it's "Cover 3," a receiver running a deep route will be wide open for an automatic touchdown.

It's even more confusing because a cornerback with short zone responsibility probably must cover the receiver deep if he runs an outside route while a tight end and/or slot receiver on the same side of the field releases downfield. In that situation, the safety—responsible for deep zone coverage of half the field—cannot handle multiple deep routes because he cannot be in two places at the same time. So one (or more) of the defenders with short zone responsibility must make a "pattern read" and basically switch to man-to-man.[506] Of course, if everyone with short zone responsibility on one side of the field goes deep, the flat is undefended and the quarterback can dump the ball to a running back for a big gain.

In short, covering eleven offensive players with eleven defensive players doesn't leave room for mistakes or seat-of-your-pants decision-making. Every player must know what is expected of him in every possible situation. Poor coordination is lethal. Even in "Cover 3," where cornerbacks usually cover deep zones and the strong safety handles the short zone ("strong-side flat"), their roles are reversed in some variants of "Cover 3." If both cover the deep zone or both cover the flat, some receiver will be running free.

Whenever even one player blows his responsibility—whether because he forgot it or misread the offense—a receiver will likely waltz into the endzone for an easy touchdown. Cornerbacks hate it when safeties blow their responsibility because it makes them look bad and hurts their team. That happened once to Tim Green:

> "When I returned home, my wife's face was glum. She felt bad about my being burned in pass coverage on TV. I told her not only had I not blown my coverage, but that I'd saved a touchdown. We were both incensed at the error the announcer had made in criticizing me."[507]

That is why new Patriots cornerback Duane Starks was excited by Patriots coaches' emphasis on knowing your responsibilities: "[Safety help] makes my job a lot easier, depending on what responsibility I have. The stress that the coaches put on everyone to know what everyone else has to do, that's a big thing for me."[508]

A second reason players study their teammates' playbooks is that if every player on the defense (or offense) knows what everyone else is supposed to be doing, then when something goes wrong, they don't waste time pointing fingers or analyzing the problem... they just fix it immediately:

"If I don't make it [to where the playbook tells me to go], I know who's supposed to [cover for me]. So if it goes wrong, we're not going to the sideline looking at each other—we already know [what went wrong]. It makes it easier for the coaches. Once you understand what's going on around you, you shouldn't have any problems. If you do have a problem, it's fixable just like that."[509]

Cornerback Duane Starks, who helped the Ravens win Super Bowl XXXV and played in Arizona, is impressed: "Every guy knows each other's position and each other's responsibilities, and I think that plays a major part in winning and being on point. The other teams I've been on hadn't stressed it that much."[510] Tedy Bruschi claims he even knows Bill Belichick's position: "I know what Bill's going to call before he calls it."[511] I hope Belichick is not really so predictable!

Players also train together to better predict their teammates' behavior. Charlie Weis–as Notre Dame's new head coach–quickly separated his players into "1s" and "1As" (a euphemism for "backups"). He scrimmages starters against backups because "You [must] maintain as much continuity as you can when you're putting in a new system and everything is new for these guys. The worst thing you can do is take the [starters] all through practice [in separate groups] and bring them into a game situation [together]. You almost defeat the purpose of why you practice."[512] After starters become familiar with one another, Weis will swap players around, but he believes players must practice with the teammates they will play with.

Finally, training together motivates. Running back Kory Chapman credits his teammates for spurring him on every day:

> "The whole running back group [pushes me to improve]. Guys like Patrick Pass, Kevin Faulk. Then there's guys like Rodney Harrison, Willie McGinest. They're picking on me each and every day, asking me 'Are you getting better?' Guys like Mike Vrabel, they push you each day in practice."[513]

Training should simulate games

"If you can't execute a two-minute drill in practice, what makes you think you can execute in a game? If you execute ten out of ten in practice, then your confidence level is pretty good when you're going in the game that you're going to get it done."[514]
– *Tom Brady*

"What [players] need to do is... train for football: explosive strength, explosive speed, change of direction, working on their quickness and things like that. Jogging around the track and doing sit-ups and all is great, but it doesn't really get them ready to play football. ...If the guy wants to play football, the best thing he can do is train for football."[515]
– *Bill Belichick*

"Everything starts at practice."[516]
    – *Patriots receiver Deion Branch*

"If you don't practice special teams full speed, then you will never get any good at them. You need to see if a cover guy running down the field can make somebody miss or whether they are going to run in the lane or whether they are going to have discipline. You need to see how the guy is going to do under pressure. You need to see returners fielding kicks. You don't make any determination until you get to watch all of those things."[517]
    – *Charlie Weis, former Patriots offensive coordinator, after his entire Notre Dame team spent an hour practicing special teams at full speed*

Tom Brady complained that his team's pre-Super Bowl XXXIX practice field was wet and slippery. Is Brady a wimp, afraid of slipping and muddying his uniform? Hardly. Brady simply didn't want to practice on a wet field when the Super Bowl field would be dry: "I don't think it is going to be like the game surface, and that's really what you want. You want the practice fields to be exactly like the game fields."[518]

Patriots players actually love playing in crappy weather. Safety Rodney Harrison–himself a masochist–swears his teammates are insanely masochistic: "We practice when it's freezing, snowing, when its raining. These guys seem to embrace it. Tedy Bruschi and Mike Vrabel are out there with no sleeves on. Guys are out there with shorts on. These guys are crazy."[519] So is Harrison. Here is his description of an October 12, 2003 game in Buffalo: "The weather was awful. It was cold, it was wet, it was damp, it was rainy. Perfect for football."[520]

But there is a method underlying such madness. Football is played outdoors in any weather except hurricanes and severe lightning storms. Therefore, Patriots know they must prepare for all conditions: "The weather affects the playing conditions, and it's our job to go out there and adjust to them."[521] The only way to prepare for crappy weather is to practice in it. That's why "perfect" weather early in 2005 training camp caused Belichick to grumble: "Hopefully, someone will turn up the heat soon."[522]

Against Baltimore in 2005, Patriots punter Josh Miller says, "I threw up on the ball for 10 punts."[523] In fairness to Miller, the top several inches of the field being mud contributed to his wretched performance. Mud splattered in every direction on every play. Punting was treacherous. Try kicking a football in mud if you don't believe me. Though Miller made no excuses, the opposing punter, Matt Stover, complained about the "soupy" field… that the Patriots had watered down by leaving their field uncovered when several inches of snow fell and making no apparent effort to improve the field after their previous game. An angry Stover claimed "Belichick has done that to me before. The NFL shouldn't let that happen… That's ridiculous."[524] So much rain fell during the game that the field would have been a mess anyhow, but it's reasonable to infer that Belichick wanted the field slippery to make it hard for opposing offenses to exploit his depleted secondary, stripped of its top three cornerbacks (Law, Poole, and Samuel) by injuries. Belichick embraces an opportunity to practice on a muddy field because he wants his players prepared for mud games. How can Josh Miller improve his mud punting except by practicing on mud? After Game 11, Belichick probably watered down a patch of ground and scheduled a special punting practice. Miller also learned from that game to stop obsessing about statistics: "I used to be a numbers guy but [now I realize] the weather gets bad so you have to do what you can to help the team. I could care less what I do statistically. I just want to be effective."[525] In treacherous conditions, Miller will undoubtedly kick with less power and more control, now that he has learned to adapt his punting to weather conditions.

Asked about game-time weather conditions, Belichick always says "It is what it is" or "It's the same for both teams." But he knows teams' preparation for weather conditions is never identical. His team usually has the edge. Noting that dome teams are 11-32 in outdoor playoff games, Gary Shelton advises the Colts, Falcons and Vikings to "Go topless," *i.e.*, to uncover their domed stadiums. When dome teams like the Colts come to Foxboro for a playoff game, Shelton says, it's "like watching a polar bear fight a flamingo."[526] To win in the playoffs, you must be prepared for the cold, so he advises that dome teams "spend every minute of your offseason in a meat locker, training the way Rocky trained for Apollo Creed."[527]

Nothing simulates a game better than a game. That's why Bill Belichick took advantage of "garbage time" against the 2-14 49ers the final week of the 2004 regular season. Belichick insisted he inserted backup players (like Don Davis, Earthwind Moreland and Troy Brown in the secondary) as a learning opportunity. He was not pulling starters to protect them from injuries: "The only thing we looked at in this game was getting people in the game. I never thought about taking anybody out. I thought about putting people in who might have to take on a role later in the season."[528] Believe him or not about protecting starters, Belichick undoubtedly valued the opportunity to give his backups real game time.

GUIDANCE COUNSELING

Guidance counseling is one way Patriots coaches help players maximize their potential. After evaluating each player, Patriots coaches try to position him for success. He may be asked to change position, gain or lose weight or concentrate on special teams. Tedy Bruschi was an outstanding defensive end in college, but he had even greater NFL potential at linebacker. Mike Vrabel might have played only special teams in Pittsburgh, but he has become a superb linebacker and even tight end in New England! Logan Mankins played tackle in college but became the Patriots' starting left guard in his first season. Patriots coaches evaluate not only how well a player *is* doing but also what that player is realistically *capable of* doing, given proper training.

Encourage your people to grow

"Leaders don't create followers. They create more leaders."
— Management guru Tom Peters

Patriots coaches provide personalized, one-on-one coaching and want players to succeed: "Coach [Dante] Scarnecchia takes a lot of interest in his players. He takes a lot of time with the players. He makes sure they get the right techniques down and get the assignments, and it really seems that he wants all his players to succeed."[529]

Belichick encourages his assistants to seek promotions and provides them strong references, even when promotions involve leaving the Patriots. And Belichick wants his former assistants to succeed, except when playing his Patriots. After a grateful staffer left for a position with another team Belichick had recommended him for, Belichick refused a thank-you gift, saying: "Don't send me flowers. Don't send me a box of candy. Your thanks to me for the recommendation is to go do a good job. I definitely don't want dinner for two at Joe's Restaurant."[530]

As Belichick protégés take over college and pro football, Belichick's Patriots look increasingly like General Electric, which other top firms have long valued as a bottomless reservoir of management talent.

Provide a vision

"I have a clear-cut, defined role."[531]
— Patriots linebacker Ted Johnson

"Bill has made it very evident to everybody that we are not even close to his expectations for us. From a conditioning standpoint, as a team, I don't think we are where he wants us to be from an effort standpoint, and he has made that very clear... Right from Day 1, he lets us know where we stand, and he lets us know what needs to be done."[532]
— Patriots quarterback Drew Bledsoe, July 2000

"There may be some physical changes that we want to try to get [new draftees] to start making. You know: 'You need to lose ten pounds,' 'You need to put on some weight,' 'You need to work on your lateral quickness,' 'Start catching some balls,' whatever it is, and try to get them ready as much as possible."[533]
— Bill Belichick, after meeting his new crop of college draftees

The Patriots never sign a free agent without a clear vision of his role. Chad Morton's agent says Morton joined the Patriots–rather than the Giants, Raiders or Vikings–because "He had an incredibly positive visit there and enjoyed the vision they outlined for how he might fit."[534] (Morton failed to make the team because a lingering injury kept him off the practice field.) Linebacker Monty Beisel says "I visited a couple of different teams and had the chance to come here and speak with coach Belichick and understand what kind of guy they're looking for. It felt like the right fit... one of those deals where you couldn't say 'no.'"[535] Patriots coaches tell players what they expect from them today, in three months, in six months, in a year, *etc.* New Patriots cornerback Duane Starks says the Patriots act decisively in acquiring players they want and explain clearly to each player why he was brought in:

> "They don't do anything without a plan for you. There's no wasted effort, no wasted energy... They know what they want from you. They know what they're willing to pay to have you come in and do it. And it seems like, if you don't want to do it, they'll find someone else who will."[536]

Safety Rodney Harrison concurs: "There wasn't any hesitation on the Patriots' part. They told me what they liked about me and what they wanted me to do and got it done."[537]

Patriots coaches monitor each player's progress, constantly adjusting expectations–both theirs and the player's. If goals are too easy, that player will not push himself hard enough. If goals are too hard, the player will become frustrated. Finding the "sweet spot" is an art. Also, players must trick themselves: giving their all to achieve and surpass their goals but not getting depressed if they fail to achieve challenging targets. As Robert Kraft advised graduating Foxboro high school students: "Dream big. Pursue things that you are most passionate about. Don't be afraid to fail."[538]

Set stretch goals

"We challenge ourselves to do things that people say we can't do."[539]
– *Patriots linebacker Roman Phifer*

"[My first season] was mind-boggling. They put a lot of pressure on the rookies right away to be right up to speed with everyone else... I wasn't [ready]. It was a new system. It's a lot to learn."[540]
– *Patriots running back Cedric Cobbs*

"[People doubting me] gets me fired up... When people tell you, 'Hey, you can't do this, you can't do this' and you keep overcoming that, you build this confidence in yourself and this belief in yourself that–even when nobody else believes in you–that I'm still going to do it because I don't give a shit what you say. I know what I can do, and I've done it."[541]
– *Tom Brady*

"You can look at all the statistics you want... [but] it's on that person. Don't look at a person's age, look at his heart."[542]
*– Patriots running back Corey Dillon, on the diminishing
performance of running backs as they age*

"Stretch goals" should challenge while being realistic enough to be achievable through intense effort. Patriots offensive coordinator Charlie Weis is a brilliant educator, skilled at setting stretch goals for his trainees. During a day at the beach with his wife and their developmentally-challenged 9-year-old daughter Hannah, Weis displayed his knack for nudging a learner just beyond her comfort zone to a place where she could experience personal growth. Charlie and Maura Weis kept their distance as Hannah played near the shore but remained close enough to avert a serious accident: "She can swim, but it's a little different when you're in a pool... Now you're at the ocean. It's a different deal."[543] Weis knew what his daughter was capable of and monitored her closely: "She'd run out and come back in and sit down in the low water because her butt wasn't going to get taken out there. She wasn't going to let that happen."[544] The Weis' day at the beach also illustrates the joy Charlie Weis experiences watching his students grow: "To us, that was a major deal."[545]

Whether we're learning to handle the ocean's dangerous waves or learning to beat press coverage, stretch goals are not merely a teaching tool but also a formula for satisfaction, perhaps even enjoyment. We all enjoy challenges that utilize our skills and compel us to move slightly beyond our comfort zone, though not all the way into the panic zone where we cannot succeed even with great effort.

Charlie Weis understands this dynamic and never gives players any excuse for complacency. He grades each player and each unit he coaches on a separate curve. No matter how superbly you perform, you will never earn a perfect score from Charlie Weis. Asked how his first Notre Dame intra-squad "game" (the Blue-Gold Game) went, Weis said he was "very pleased with the play of our offense as far as mentally picking up what we've thrown at them"[546] but explained, "I never give an A. How about a C-plus?"[547] Don't expect lavish praise from Charlie Weis, even if your name is "Tom Brady." The better you perform, the harsher his grading standards become. If a player turns in 'A' work, Charlie chides himself for giving too easy an assignment. Weis would love to dangle a carrot on a string just beyond each player's reach so that–no matter how hard a player worked–the carrot would remain just out of reach.

Weis' attitude apparently rubbed off on cornerback Randall Gay, who said of his rookie season–in which he started twelve games and helped the Patriots win a Super Bowl after making the team as an undrafted rookie and not starting for his college team the previous season–"I'm so tough on myself, I would give myself a C-minus. I want As. I will never give myself As, but that's what I'm shooting for."[548]

Players who throw themselves into training as a personal crusade to grow and improve–rather than go through the motions because they "have to"–enjoy the experience much more. Rodney Harrison says, "I came in the league as a fifth-rounder and I had to work my way up… Whatever I have to do. I'm used to coming from the bottom. I'm like a bottom-feeder. Eventually I will get better… Anything worth having is worth working for."[549] One of the world's leading experts on happiness, University of Pennsylvania professor Martin Seligman, would applaud Patriots players' continual striving:

> "The sum total of our momentary feelings turns out to be a very flawed measure of how good or how bad we [later] judge an [event] to be. …It is not just positive feelings we want, we want to be *entitled* to our positive feelings. …The belief that we can rely on shortcuts to happiness… leads to legions of people who in the middle of great wealth are starving spiritually. Positive emotion alienated from the exercise of character leads to inauthenticity [and] depression… The positive feeling that arises from the exercise of strengths and virtues… is authentic. …The highest success in living and the deepest emotional satisfaction comes from building and using your signature strengths. …The good life is using your signature strengths every day to produce authentic happiness and abundant gratification."[550]

In the Patriots locker room, training reflects character and powers performance. Therefore, success derived from training entitles players to feel overjoyed when they succeed on the football field, as Troy Brown explains:

> "I don't think anything could ever beat that first one we won because it was so unexpected of us. The hype was all about the Rams and nobody even gave us a chance. To go out there and do something nobody said you could do was just a great feeling."[551]

Set realistic expectations

As motivating as stretch goals can be, pie-in-the-sky goals eventually lead to disappointment. Few NFL players ever travel to Canton, Ohio for Hall of Fame enshrinement. Most never play in a single Pro Bowl. Unrealistic expectations crush many, so coaches must help each player set attainable goals.

A star and every-down starter in his early seasons with the Patriots, linebacker Ted Johnson later struggled to accept that he–like most of his teammates– is now a role player on Belichick's Patriots: "My ego has taken some shots. It's been a ton of things–your identity and where you fit in, where's your place on this team. You're a starter most of your career, and then you're not."[552] Johnson went through an identity crisis when Tedy Bruschi became the starter, but he learned to enjoy football for its sake rather than for the acclaim and glory:

> "The New England Patriots are going to thrive long after I'm gone. Everyone probably likes to think they couldn't live without you. Sometimes it's easy to

be narrow-minded like that, but that can hurt you. You have to understand it's just a job, not your career. We're all young, some with a lot going for us. There's a lot more to do after football. This is really kind of the beginning."[553]

After soul-searching, Johnson felt relieved of the burden of worrying about his place in history, his reputation around the league, *etc.* Johnson learned to worry only about being the best role player he can be, mentoring young players, doing everything he can to help the Patriots win, and enjoying life:

> "I used to joke I'm not going to make it to the Hall of Fame... You have the success you have and then you think you aspire to be in a Pro Bowl someday so people will consider you one of the best at what you do. I've slowed way down on that. I have a family now. I'm at a totally different place in my life now, and I like where I'm at. It's a comfortable place for me. At this point, I couldn't be happier."[554]

The Patriots encourage each player to strive for excellence and take pride in daily improvement. They stress the satisfaction of contributing to a winning team—in any capacity—and expanding your contribution over time. Every Patriot has performance goals for each practice, each game and each season. Invitations to the Pro Bowl or Hall of Fame can never supplant immediate goals. Patriots focus on doing what they can to help their team win. Doing that well year after year is the only way to play in a Pro Bowl or get a bust in Canton. As Patriots linebacker Mike Vrabel says of defensive lineman Richard Seymour, "He was a professional the day he got drafted, and that's what Hall of Fame-type players do. They do that for 10 or 12 years."[555]

This Goldilocks principle—setting realistic stretch goals—also applies to returning from injuries. Patriots tight end Benjamin Watson appreciates that "The trainers—Jim [Whalen] and Joe [Van Allen]—do a good job holding you back so you don't hurt yourself any more. All the guys that are injured are probably [able to do more] than they allow us to in practice because they want to make sure we're comfortable playing football. In football, you use so many different motions, you have to get yourself acclimated to it... I'm anxious to get there, but I can't rush it, and I won't."[556]

Provide role models

> "There are certain techniques that the [St. Louis Rams'] skill players use that you make a highlight tape of. You take it to a player and say, 'Here, watch the way this guy runs his route or how this guy releases or the way he stems the route,' and work off that. If it's something that's part of our system [and] we can incorporate [it], we will."[557]
> – *Bill Belichick*

Every offseason, defensive lineman Richard Seymour studies film of great defensive linemen. After two Pro Bowl berths and two Super Bowl rings in his first three seasons, Seymour began using the offseason to watch film of himself with a specific objective: detecting when opposing teams were preparing to double-team him. Patriots coaches can't sit with each player throughout the off-season, but they can and do jump-start players' self-study with suggestions like, "Why don't you watch film of the great lineman and discover some of their secrets?" or "Why don't you study how opposing offenses are scheming to stop you?"

After drafting defensive lineman Vince Wilfork in 2004, the Patriots asked him to switch from a penetrate-the-offensive-line-and-tackle-the-ball-carrier style to a hold-the-line-and-don't-let-anyone-run-by-you style. To help Wilfork understand what they wanted, coaches handed him tons of film on two players who play the way they wanted him to play: former Patriots nose tackle Ted Washington and Pittsburgh Steelers nose tackle Casey Hampton. Wilfork says Hampton "made the Pro Bowl last year, and I saw why. He played hard every game. He's a great nose tackle. So I look at both of them and see what I can learn."[558] Having players to admire, observe, and aspire to helps stimulates improvement.

After wide receiver David Terrell–drafted #8 overall in 2001 but released by the Chicago Bears after four disappointing seasons–landed in New England, he worked intensively with Patriots strength coach Mike Woicik to strengthen his lower body. Woicik saw in Terrell a young Michael Irvin–brash and underachieving with a powerful physique–and put Terrell in touch with Irvin, whom Woicik trained in Dallas from 1990 through 1996. Terrell quickly came to see Irvin as an inspiring role model and mentor: "He had an aggressive style on the field. He was feared by defensive backs. He controlled ballgames, and that's what I want to do: be in position to control ballgames with your quarterback and running back. I feel like I can be that type of guy."[559] Months later, Terrell says he has learned a lot from studying Irvin: "I definitely look at his game and try to take as much knowledge from him as I can and put it to my game. Any receiver should be able to do that, whether they're watching Jerry (Rice) or someone else. I do watch Michael and try to take little bits and pieces from his game."[560]

Players should emulate more than one or two role models. One player may have outstanding technique in run defense but poor technique in pass defense, for example. A great role model on the field may be a lousy one off the field. This is why former GE CEO Jack Welch shouts "*Never* get a mentor! Everyone... is a potential mentor. What happens if your mentor gets shot?"[561] Welch's point: always strive to absorb the best ideas from everyone you meet. Always assume each person you meet has ideas of potential value to you. If you listen carefully, everyone can be your mentor. Patriots players most definitely possess this mindset. Welch would be thrilled to hear defensive lineman Richard Seymour say, "I try to stay in touch with [many] guys. I even try to learn from new guys that come into the league. If they have something to teach me, I want to learn. You have to put your pride aside and learn."[562] Asked who helps him improve, Deion Branch replied, "So many guys. Troy and David Patten on offense. On the defensive side of the ball probably Ty Law and Tyrone Poole. Those guys on offense showing me how to watch film and–when we get on the football field–showing me how to go against defensive backs."[563] Patriots players and coaches are constantly sharing ideas with one another. And Patriots learn just from watching one another. Second year safety Guss Scott–who missed his rookie season with an injury but is wowing his teammates in 2005 training camp–says, "You'll be surprised how much you can learn just by watching other people play. You learn techniques and a bunch of other things. A guy like Rodney Harrison, you can learn a lot from him. It's frustrating if you can't contribute to the team, but I got to watch a lot of great people play."[564]

Role models are not just for players. Charlie Weis says he was always humbled by the knowledge of those he worked with:

> "When I first started coaching high school, I thought I knew everything about football, and I was humbled by how much Chironna knew. Then I went to South Carolina. I had been coaching high school for a while, thought I knew a lot and was humbled by what Morrison knew. Then when I went to the Giants, I was doubly humbled by Parcells. You keep on getting humbled. So, even though you're growing, you realize the guys you're working for know a lot more about the game than you do."[565]

As Notre Dame's head coach, Weis continues to emulate his teachers, Bill Parcells and Bill Belichick. One of the NFL's most innovative offensive coordinators, Weis modestly claims, "I'm a copycat, plagiarism guy. I don't believe in reinventing the wheel. I learned under those two guys, and I'm sorry folks, that's all I know."[566]

After five years of improving by studying others, Patriots players have themselves become role models. When Romeo Crennel took over in Cleveland, he ordered his Browns to study film on two teams: the Browns themselves and the Patriots because, says Browns linebacker Ben Taylor, "They're the standard for what we're trying to achieve."[567]

Provide incentives

> "I just want to go out and play hard so that one-year contract can maybe turn into a six-year contract."[568]
>
> – *Receiver David Terrell, after signing with the Patriots after four disappointing seasons in Chicago*

> "Every year I felt like I had to make the team, and that's what motivated me."[569]
>
> – *Former Patriots wide receiver David Patten*

People learn better when they believe the new knowledge will benefit them. The same is true of any kind of training, physical or mental. The more relevant and useful something seems, the more The Patriots keep players motivated to train and perform partly through competition. Competition in training camp is to earn a spot on the team, but players–including the team's stars–naturally engage in good-natured competition year-round because competitive juices are fun and help everyone improve. Patriots safety Guss Scott explains, "Competition makes you better. You don't want to be with an organization that's not doing that. You want to be around the best players and continue to win. Nobody likes to lose. It's something that keeps you on your toes and makes you work to get better every day. Every day at practice, for everybody, is serious."[570]

Channel disappointment into motivation

Ten games into the 2004 season, Patriots punter Josh Miller ranked 3rd in the AFC in net yards/punt (and 7th in gross yards/punt). His eleventh game (the mud game discussed earlier) was so miserable he plummeted to 12th place. Miller says he understood fans booing him: "They pay good money to come in there. If I was a face painter [rabid fan] I'd be booing [myself]. I was livid. It was just an awful, awful night."[571] Miller acknowledges his anger, seeing it as a good thing: "I'm glad I'm still [mad]. If I [were happy], I'd [tell my wife], 'Honey, I think I'm losing it.'"[572] Miller channels his anger into motivation:

> "I want to get better, and [my anger tells me] I still want to play the game. If you take it personally, then you come to the locker room and you're mean to [teammates] for no reason. Then you go home and have a 3- and a 1-year-old and you're not a good dad because you take it home. It's a bad day, you acknowledge it, you learn from it, and move on. If I heard two years of [booing], medication would probably come into the picture. But right now you have to ignore it, blow it off and move to next week."[573]

The Patriots took the same approach after the last eight of their ten 2001 draft picks didn't work out: "Not that we didn't [study] the bottom of the draft in 2001, but obviously we didn't do it well enough. We just didn't appropriate the right amount of time to it. We won't do that again… We allocated a few more resources to college scouting and less on pro free agents."[574] After doing so, they found a future star, David Givens, near the end of 2002's seventh and final round. In 2005, the team reportedly rebuffed queries about trading Givens for a second-round pick.

If someone shows potential, find a position that lets them grow

"We start them out [at whatever position] we feel they are going to play for us or have the opportunity. I respect what they did in college, but I really

don't care what they did in college. [We train them] where we think they have the best chance to compete."[575]
    – *Bill Belichick*

"As long as you're working hard and getting better, they'll find a [roster] spot. But it's stiff competition."[576]
    – *Patriots tight end Andy Stokes, the 2005 Draft's "Mr. Irrelevant" as the final player selected*

"We have a saying within the organization, and it doesn't just apply to players: 'The more you can do, the more you can do.' If a player can do more, if a coach can do more, it's an organizational plus."[577]
    – *Scott Pioli, Patriots VP of Player Personnel*

"[New Patriots defensive coordinator Eric Mangini] came to Cleveland in 1994 as a ballboy. He started out at the bottom and just kept working his butt off… [Belichick asked me], 'What are you going to do with that Eric kid?' …I told him his internship was ending. And then he told me to tell Eric to stop by his office. Next thing I knew, Eric was an offensive assistant with the coaching staff."[578]
    – *Kevin Byrne, former Cleveland Browns VP*

Many Patriots fans remember Tedy Bruschi was a rookie in 1996 when Parcells' Patriots lost the Super Bowl to the Green Bay Packers. Few remember Bruschi played defensive end, his college position, in that Super Bowl. Bruschi could have remained a good defensive lineman. Instead, became a great linebacker:

> "I was playing defensive line. I sacked Brett Favre a couple times, and now here I am in my fourth Super Bowl. Now I am playing… stand-up linebacker. That has been the transition of my career. It has been a learning process since the beginning. I've been fortunate to have good coaches, and– believe me–it was the hardest thing I had to do, transitioning from a defensive lineman to a stand-up middle linebacker. It took a little while, but now I am to the point where I feel comfortable in it and I really feel that I am a linebacker now. …I like to think that I sort of started the thing that maybe if you see an undersized defensive lineman college, maybe you can look at him as a project and turn him into a player."[579]

Patriots receiver David Givens was a late 7th-round draft pick from Notre Dame, a school not famed for its pass-happy "chuck-and-duck" or "run-and-gun" offense. Givens says the Patriots "drafted me mainly as a special teams guy, and even my agent told me I was a longshot to make the team. I took that as a challenge, but there's no doubt I wasn't as polished as the other receivers here. It was almost like I was switching positions again, because it might as well have all been new. I had to change literally everything I'd learned in college."[580] Givens was too raw to play wide receiver in the NFL, but he had talent and motivation. He impressed the coaches by catching every pass the Pats threw at him and carved out a role on special teams while continually striving to become an NFL receiver, eventually blossoming into a Patriots starter. In 2003, Givens caught a game-winning 18-yard touchdown to beat the Denver Broncos with 30 seconds left in the game. Says Belichick:

> "David is a good example of a player who was OK at his position, although not really good enough to get on the field. But he was valuable to us in the kicking game. That's how he earned his roster spot and his playing time. And because he was going to the game as a special team player, we started incorporating him in some of the receiver sets."[581]

Dan Klecko is another guy the Patriots love so much they're trying him at half the positions in all three phases of the game—offense, defense, and special teams: "I've been a nickel rusher (in passing situations). I've played a little linebacker. I've been at fullback. Whatever I have to do to get on the field, that's what I'll do."[582] Belichick compliments Klecko's hustle and drive: "Great motor. You want him on the field somewhere. We just haven't figured out where."[583] Klecko played nose tackle in college and briefly with the Patriots in obvious passing situations but is undersized for an NFL nose tackle: "I was the lightest defensive tackle [in the NFL Draft], but I had good workout numbers. My size was the biggest issue."[584] The Patriots played him at defensive end (again, in passing situations) and fullback. In 2004, the Patriots began using Klecko at fullback to block and catch passes as Brady's outlet receiver until he caught an 8-yarder and Jets defender John Abraham crushed his knee, ending his season in late October.

Belichick takes the same patient approach in developing retired players with potential into coaches. During his playing days, Pepper Johnson analyzed football and studied every position on the field. After taking the reins in New England, Belichick knew Johnson had the persona, playing experience, and football knowledge needed to coach, but Johnson was pure potential. He had no actual coaching experience and had not yet demonstrated his coaching passion. Belichick carved out an opportunity for Johnson to prove himself:

> "[Belichick asked me] to come to New England and help him communicate his system to the other coaches and players… At first he was asking me to come in just for the summer, but I think all along he knew that if I was around it long enough I was going to stay. …I had no title that first year, the 2000 season… I wasn't even on the payroll. I funded my being there."[585]

Over time, Johnson's responsibilities expanded, and he quickly became the official inside linebackers coach. In 2004, he switched to defensive line coach. Shifting to another position gives Johnson broader perspective and keeps him fresh.

Before the 2003 season, Belichick extended an open invitation to former NFL tight end Mark Bavaro to hang out with the team in an unofficial, unpaid capacity… though, Bavaro points out, "I'm getting a lot of free meals in Foxboro."[586]

Bavaro brings an extra pair of trained eyes that can potentially improve the Patriots' tight ends' performance: "Bill is giving me an opportunity to be around the team. I give advice when and if it's wanted. ...I have (job) flexibility, and I like to fill that time with football. It's very therapeutic."[587] Belichick knows that free advice from a former Pro Bowl player can only help. And former stars who hang around Foxboro may, like Pepper Johnson, grow into future coaches, though Bavaro acknowledges he lacks the requisite passion to be a full-time coach:

> "Coaching is very hard. It's long hours and tough on your family. I don't long to be a coach, but I enjoy being around football immensely. Not around it in the sense of being a fan, but just being on the other side of the rope, inside the locker room, being part of the group. I can never recapture the level of gratification you have has a player, but this is as close as you can get."[588]

While serving as the Giants' defensive coordinator in 1985, Belichick even invited a football-loving junior at Central Connecticut State University to stay in the apartment Belichick shared with fellow Giants assistant coach Al Groh! Belichick was impressed by that junior's dedication in spending 2½ hours a day driving back-and-forth from campus just to watch the Giants' practices, saying to him, "What, are you crazy? We've got a spare room. Why don't you just come and stay with us? We'll get you a field pass and you can come onto the field."[589] That kid was amazed by Belichick's generosity:

> "He had nothing to gain by being nice to me and letting me see what he does. Here he was, a defensive coordinator of a Super Bowl championship team. ...He knew I loved football. I wanted to be a better player. And I wanted to be a coach some day. For whatever reason, we hit it off."[590]

> "Here I am a 20-year-old at Central, not going to be a pro player, talking to the defensive coordinator of a team that had just won the Super Bowl. We got talking football and this guy decides to cultivate a relationship with me. He has no agenda. He has nothing to gain from the relationship. To me, that tells you something about the man. At one point he said, 'Why not stay a couple of nights, stay in my room, come to my meetings?' We always kept in touch."[591]

That wide-eyed "kid" is now Bill Belichick's alter ego in the executive suite and back-to-back NFL Executive of the Year, Patriots VP of player personnel Scott Pioli! Belichick and Pioli bonded due to their similar personalities and love of football. Pioli's college position coach says Pioli's "as tough a player as I ever coached, but he's extremely bright. He's an absolute joy."[592] As Cleveland Browns head coach, Belichick hired Pioli as a pro personnel assistant in 1992. As New York Jets interim head coach in early 1997, Belichick hired Pioli away from the Baltimore Ravens as director of player personnel. Later, Pioli married the daughter of his then-boss, Bill Parcells: "People in the office warned me about [dating her]," so "Bill

[Parcells] didn't know we were dating for a long time"[593] even though Parcells had introduced them moments after Pioli asked Parcells' secretary "Hey, who's the blonde?"[594] who had just entered Parcells' office. (Ironically, Parcells' daughter is named "Dallas," and Bill now coaches the Cowboys.)

New Patriots defensive coordinator Eric Mangini began as a Cleveland Browns ballboy and then interned in public relations where "I used to have to cut out every article about the Browns and photocopy them…I tell our PR guys now they have it made because they just have to print the stories off the Internet."[595] One of his duties was picking sweaty uniforms off the locker room floor, a task he recalls with fondness: "The only thing I was running was the laundry."[596] But Mangini had already discovered his knack for coaching before Cleveland. He had coached an Australian football team to a 22-3-1 record. His brother Kyle recalls, "We were always better prepared and in better shape than our opponents. He did a tremendous job of organizing a real defined practice regimen. And, even early on, he did a terrific job of pulling guys together… Guys were out there [practicing late at night, even in cold and rain] for the common goal, winning."[597] After a decade under Belichick's tutelage, Mangini has picked up where Romeo Crennel left off, without skipping a proverbial beat. New Patriots linebacker Monty Beisel says:

> "He's done an outstanding job. He seems to have good poise with the players. He's definitely a personable coach. I've really enjoyed him so far. He's done a lot of coaching and a lot of things I've been learning from, so it's been fun thus far."[598]

Veteran defensive end Jarvis Green agrees: "He's doing the same thing [Romeo Crennel did]. They're pretty much like copy-cats, as far as them coaching. Really, for us, it feels like nothing's changed."[599]

Why is Bill Belichick so willing to take on unproven but enthusiastic guys and give them an opportunity to earn their way into more responsible positions? One reason is that it's a great way to develop talent that has worked extremely well for him. Another is that Belichick himself earned his way up through the ranks, starting when friends (especially his father) convinced the Baltimore Colts to "hire" 24-year-old Belichick for no pay.

Charlie Weis didn't get his start under Belichick, but his career exemplifies the power of passion and dedication Belichick admires and seeks to cultivate. Weis improbably rose from the lowest rung on the coaching ladder. In high school, Charlie Weis was addicted to *Notre Dame Highlights*, a TV show breaking down the team's previous game. Though Weis attended Notre Dame for its football program, his interest was watching and broadcasting, not playing: "I was just a student, sitting in the 59th row, freezing my butt off, second-guessing every call the coach was making. I was just like you, and it got worse as I got older."[600] From the stands in the late '70s, Weis watched some Irish quarterback named "Joe Montana." (Actually, they knew each other reasonably well. When Weis' Giants played the 49ers in 1990, "I went up to him during warm-ups and he looked at me and said, 'What are you doing here?' He didn't even know I was a coach, let alone in the NFL."[601]) Weis attended just about every sporting event at Notre Dame, not just football. And he didn't just watch games. He analyzed them and sometimes did play-by-play. Roommate and fellow sports junkie Jim Benenati says he fought with Weis because Charlie insisted on arriving early enough to watch players warm up, something Benenati felt a waste of time. When Belichick finds a potential coach who enjoys dissecting how players warm up, he pounces because attention to such details signals real coaching potential. Through passion, intelligence and teaching excellence, Weis worked his way up the coaching ranks from high school to college to the pros, surprising his college friends and even himself: "I really didn't think that this was going to lead to the NFL... No one knew I was in coaching, and now everyone is like, 'My buddy Charlie,' especially when it comes to football tickets."[602]

REPORT CARDS

"We're not on the feel-good-for-the-players program."[603]
– *Bill Belichick*

GE's famous approach to human resource management is hardly the only successful model. Southwest Airlines has thrived without ever laying off a single employee. By providing job security, Southwest earns its employees' respect and gratitude. Employees at both GE and Southwest love their company's culture, but those cultures are radically different: GE is competitive where Southwest is collegial.

Though the Patriots locker room is collegial, the team's personnel policy is ruthlessly competitive and meritocratic. This apparent contradiction arises because each Patriot: 1) Perceives himself as competing to attain his full personal potential– not to "beat" his teammates or even other teams; 2) Values competition because it improves him and his team; and, 3) Knows that improving as a football player raises "employability," even if competition knocks him off the final Patriots roster. For such players, "report cards" are more a diagnostic tool than a coercive device. Criticism creates opportunities for improvement.

In its personnel policy, the Patriots are GE, not Southwest. Like GE–which embraces a forced ranking policy informally dubbed "rank and yank"–the Patriots devote substantial time and effort to evaluating employees and giving them detailed and brutally candid performance evaluations.

Avoid snap judgments

"No one is making the team in mini-camp."[604]
– *Bill Belichick*

"You never can tell what a player is until you actually get to be around him for a period of time. Bill, he gives everybody a chance. But if you're not showing your willingness to fit in with the team, you've got to go. We do things a certain way around here, and that's why we win. If you can't fall in line with it, then you've got to go."[605]

– Troy Brown

You can't make a second first impression. Psychologists tell us we seldom change our minds about people after forming a snap judgment seconds after meeting them or hearing them begin a speech.

But first impressions are often wrong, so it is valuable to consciously refrain from allowing first impressions to forever color our perceptions. Bill Belichick understands this. Pressed by reporters for his initial impressions of rookies during rookie training camp, Belichick warns reporters not to form early impressions:

"I learned a long time ago to just kind of take it day-by-day. Guys can have good days, and they can have bad days. Some guys, once they get comfortable doing something, can do it a lot better than the first time they have been asked to do it. ... [The NFL] is an all new ball game [for rookies, so we] just take it day-by-day and evaluate these guys over time once they have had a chance to settle into the situation and develop some degree of comfort with what they are doing and some kind of confidence in doing it... That will happen a little in training camp and in the preseason games. That is really where the big evaluation will come. [Rookie camp is] much more of a teaching/introductory/trying-to-get-them-on-the-right-page type of weekend as opposed to a big evaluation weekend."[606]

Delaying judgment is especially important because NFL rookies are playing against much tougher opponents than in college. Rookies are suddenly competing not against their physical inferiors but against men with similar raw talent and better technique, better training and greater experience. Rookies need to study and practice to raise their game to the NFL level because they have never before experienced anything like it:

"To come to this level where all of a sudden you drop from being one of the top ones ... [to] comparable in ability to all of the other players, that is a whole other ball game and to be that inexperienced and to have relatively little knowledge in terms of what [the Patriots] do, our system and the overall way the NFL game is played relative to college. It is just a different game."[607]

Some rookies progress rapidly while others never do. Coaches must patiently refrain from prematurely judging whether a rookie can grow into an NFL player or was simply outstanding playing against less talented college players. Explains Belichick:

"Most of the defensive lineman taken high in the draft are going to be bigger, stronger, faster and more athletic than all the guys they play against (in college). … Now you come into the NFL and it is probably never that way. The guy across from him is every bit as tough, fast, athletic and more experienced than he is. To be able to take that raw (skill) and transfer that into technique where now you have to do things with hands and your body placement, assignments and all that …to gain an edge over another good football player, that takes some time. It is not just taking him and tossing him and going to get the runner like it is in college a lot of times just because it is a big mismatch."[608]

Poor performance in a player's first weeks in the NFL means almost nothing. Players aren't wearing shoulder pads, familiar with the playbook, hitting each other or used to NFL-caliber competition. Belichick waits until rookies have had a fair opportunity to learn the system, adjust to the stronger competition, and demonstrate their potential: "I don't have any time frame with how long anything is going to take. You give people the information, you give them the opportunity, you evaluate how they are doing and you assess how it is coming along."[609] Teams that judge prematurely shortchange themselves. As Belichick says, "The second and third years are where the rubber meets the road."[610]

College success in no way guarantees NFL success. As Patriots rookie guard Logan Mankins puts it, "College to the NFL is way more plays. Way bigger guys. Way faster guys. Way smarter guys."[611] That's why Heisman Trophy-winning quarterback Jason White and NCAA all-time yardage-gaining quarterback Timmy Chang went undrafted in 2005. Conversely, an underwhelming college career does not mean a player can't play in the NFL. The Patriots passed on White and Chang because they saw greater NFL potential in their Round 7 quarterback selection: Matt Cassel, a career backup quarterback at USC of whom one NFL general manager confessed "I never even heard of the quarterback they took in the seventh round."[612]

Belichick smartly calms new players' nerves by explicitly saying "This is not an evaluation camp. There's no emphasis on timing and execution. [It's] mostly on teaching. We have a long way to go before we have to play."[613] Mini-camp is about teaching players the system and giving them guidance about what to work on between mini-camp and training camp:

"What I really hope we [accomplish] is that we get everything taught that we want to get taught, that the players understand it, that they know what they need to do in different situations and that–generally speaking–they know how they need to train and what things they need to be ready and prepared to play and do this year and they can get ready physically to do that when they come to training camp."[614]

Another focus is identifying and fixing mistakes: "Whether they're doing the techniques right and if they are doing things as they are supposed to be done. If they're not, then you correct them."[615] Knowing that their every move is not being scrutinized allows rookies to focus on learning rather than looking good. Belichick even takes this approach with veterans because performance depends on player interactions: "We have a number of veteran [free agents] who've been through it, but how they'll adapt to our system and fit in with our players remains to be seen. You have quarterbacks working with new receivers, linemen with new players, [and] there's a process in getting comfortable."[616]

Many inventors and writers split the creative process into sequential phases: 1) open-minded, uncritical, non-evaluative brainstorming; and, 2) judgmental, critical evaluation to winnow a long list of ideas to only the best and then refine and polish them. In a similar way, Belichick refrains from judging players' potential during each season's teaching phase. He wants players during training camps to learn, learn, learn. Only as the regular season approaches does he start accumulating evidence to make roster and playing-time decisions.

Scott Pioli says not even the most successful rookies can be evaluated after one season. Asked to evaluate the Patriots' incredible 2003 draft class after those players helped the Patriots win the 2003 season Super Bowl, Pioli replied:

> "We're not grading this rookie class or evaluating this rookie class based on this one season. You evaluate a draft and you evaluate a player's performance over their career and whether or not they have any longevity and any endurance. Tom Brady, if you evaluated him after one year, there's not a whole lot to evaluate."[617]

Keep criticism constructive

> "[Players] like to feel comfortable with the relationships of the people who are going to be coaching them. Just like any other relationship, it's based on trust."[618]
> *– Patriots offensive coordinator Charlie Weis*

To improve future performance, criticism must be constructive. Constructive criticism is forward-looking and uplifting, not backward-looking and harsh. Constructive criticism is offered at an appropriate time and place by an appropriate person in an appropriate manner. Pointing to a past mistake is forward-looking if doing so is intended to inspire learning and future mistake-avoidance rather than allocate blame.

Charlie Weis strikes just the right tone: demanding and challenging but never mean or harsh. Players admire his tough love, with equal parts toughness and love. Former Patriots quarterback Damon Huard says:

"You always wanted to be up to the challenge and ready for a question [he would throw at you], but I never felt that pressure. He never makes you feel stupid if you don't know an answer. You're always comfortable asking questions and working together. At the same time, he took an interest in your personal life. That was something that I really respected about Charlie—he really did care about us as people, in addition to players. He was a coach and also a friend."[619]

Tom Brady offers teammates constructive criticism frequently during practices but seldom during games: "I can get pretty mad, but probably more in practice than in games."[620] The purpose of practices is to improve. The purpose of games is to execute and win. A game is an inappropriate place to offer even constructive criticism. Brady also knows that players attacked for screwing up are seldom receptive to criticism, so he tries to remain calm when criticizing teammates:

"Quarterbacks [must] communicat[e] with their receivers and their linemen if things don't go right. I think the important thing is to be composed because you are a reflection of the entire system. You are a reflection of the coaches. If the players see you lose your poise and composure [during a game], the guys will think 'Wow, something really bad must be going on here.' I don't think you ever want that to happen. There are definitely times [during a game] where I get frustrated with a receiver or something and ask him, 'What were you doing there?' But that doesn't happen very often."[621]

Measure what you want to improve

"One has to measure effectiveness [and] value."[622]
    – Jeff Clarke, Dell's Sr. VP of products and head of R&D

"We rigged a server so that every time somebody downloaded the browser you'd hear a cannon go off."[623]
    – John Giannandrea, on Netscape's early history

"My goal this year is just to get better every week. I go back to Week One and I see a situation where it's a play-action pass and I could've reacted a little faster to it. Then you look down the road three weeks, four weeks, five weeks, and I'm reacting faster to that same play."[624]
    – Patriots defensive lineman Ty Warren

"Last year [2004], I had about three drops in nine games. My second year [2003], I had six. I still got to get better though. You always preach, 'Better.' You have to always think that one drop could be critical."[625]
    – Patriots receiver Deion Branch

Three months after outstanding pass-catcher Deion Branch declared "I still got to get better" at catching passes, *Providence Journal* reporter Tom Curran proclaimed mission accomplished: "Either we've got early-onset memory loss or Deion Branch hasn't dropped a ball in—we give up. Can't remember."[626] Committing to achieve specific goals drives success. In fact, Branch's aspiration is hard to fathom, given that he is the only receiver in the NFL credited by STATS, Inc. with zero dropped passes throughout 2004.[627]

However, Branch explains, "We count everything that touches [a receiver's] hands as a drop, including bad throws."[628] The Patriots are tough graders! If Branch runs full speed and launches horizontally into the air—flying like Superman—and manages to just barely nick the ball with his outstretched middle finger, he dropped that pass.

The team's "No excuses!" approach pays dividends. The second-best receiver in the NFL in percentage of passes dropped, with just one drop in 106 passes thrown his way: teammate David Givens.[629] If your team penalizes you even for bad throws, you're motivated to work with your quarterback to ensure that he throws passes where you want them and that you run your routes as your quarterback expects. Success requires coordination, which is why Tom Brady says, "I'm always trying to encourage guys to do their best. When they play their best, it helps me play better."[630] New England's overall dropped pass percentage ranked second behind the Colts among the 32 teams.

Before they can participate in training camp, each Patriot must pass a grueling endurance shuttle run. The intensity of that run varies based on a player's position. More is expected of wide receivers than offensive linemen. The Patriots also measure each player's bench press, 20-yard shuttle time and 40-yard dash time in early summer and re-measure these in the fall.[631] The fact that the Patriots measure these spurs players to work out in the offseason. Even three-time Pro Bowler Corey Dillon pushed himself to improve in valuable areas:

> "His strength levels, his conditioning level, overall all his testing [improved].
> …If you measure a guy year to year and when you see the testing improve, it does give you somewhat of an indication that, physically, he's made some progress. Corey has worked very hard, and… the results… validate that."[632]

The Patriots don't take such measurements for amusement. They take them seriously. After Belichick arrived in 2000, he found his team had many lazy and out-of-shape players who thought training camp was for getting back into shape and learning the playbook rather than practicing teamwork and situational tactics. Belichick warned players in March that they would have to pass his conditioning test and know the system because training camp would be a *training* camp, not summer school or a Jenny Craig weight loss program. On Day 1 in July, Belichick sent a loud message by cutting offensive tackle Ed Ellis for failing his physical and fining and barring from practice four other players—Derek Fletcher, John Friesz, Tony George and Martinez Williams–for failing the conditioning test. That message thrilled Patriots like safety Lawyer Milloy, who wasn't happy that some of his teammates weren't taking their jobs professionally: "We needed a chewing out. I respect a coach who can walk up to you and say, 'You're not cutting it.'"[633] Belichick had zero sympathy for those he punished: "We're not waiting for anybody. We don't have time. We've got a challenging schedule. Whoever can keep up will keep up. If they can't, we'll find someone else."[634] In 2005, soon after nose tackle Ethan Kelley reportedly failed his conditioning run, he too was cut.

In 2001, Belichick literally dropped a ship's anchor in the middle of the locker room because "We were approximately 700 pounds overweight. The anchor symbolized trying to play with an anchor tied around you. We weren't in the type of condition [we needed to be in]. We were constantly overweight on the weigh-ins, and that was one of the messages for the 2001 season... 'Let's drop the anchor!'"[635] Weighing players helped motivate them to lose weight–especially fat–that slows them down and costs them victories.

The Patriots constantly measure players' knowledge to motivate them to know their assignments and study each upcoming opponent, as three-time Pro Bowl linebacker Chad Brown discovered soon after joining the Patriots: "The defensive coordinator starts every meeting with about 20 minutes of questions–not asking him questions, him asking us questions."[636] The questions aren't easy. In fact, Brown– who has recorded more sacks than any current NFL linebacker–felt like the unlucky kid whose family moved to a new town in the middle of the school year: "I understood the terminology would be different, but I thought some stuff would carry over. There's no carryover at all. It's a whole new language."[637] Another Patriots free agent acquisition, Monty Beisel, felt the same way: "It's been a mental challenge every day,"[638] so "we both asked for the secret learning pill for the Patriots defense."[639] Brown was lucky to be sitting next to class brainiac Tedy Bruschi because "Tedy's been able to whisper in my ear and help me answer some of those questions." Chad Brown, one of the NFL's smartest players, is cheating on tests!

The Patriots are careful to measure important things. They don't measure players' long-jumping because they never ask a player to long-jump during a game. They probably don't measure offensive linemen's vertical jumps because they never ask offensive linemen to jump in the air during games. However, defensive linemen and linebackers probably do train to improve their vertical jumping because the team asks them to leap with arms extended as the quarterback throws the ball–in hopes of deflecting or catching the ball or forcing the quarterback to redirect his pass. As Belichick says, "You can run around the track 1,000 times. You can do pushups. You can do leg lifts and all that... Working out at the gym and doing situps is great, but there's no substitute for playing football."[640]

The Patriots create their own statistics to focus training on desired behaviors. The NFL records "turnovers." The Patriots distinguish between "ball disruptions" (turnover opportunities) and "turnovers" (ball recoveries) because "create turnovers" isn't actionable: "I wish we could scheme for [turnovers]. I wish we [could] say, 'Well, here is our turnover defense. We're going to call this and get a turnover when we need it.'"[641] The Patriots record a "ball disruption" each time "the ball is altered from the course it is designed [by the offense] to be on."[642] Each disruption creates a potential turnover, so Patriots coaches urge players to be alert for ball disruption opportunities. Ball disruption and ball recovery often occur separately. Knocking the ball out of a quarterback's hand or a running back's arm is a valued ball disruption, even if the offense pounces on the fumble. Touching and redirecting a ball as it crosses the line of scrimmage creates an opportunity. Forcing a quarterback to throw around or over a defender disrupts the ball's intended path, creating an opportunity. And touching a pass before the intended receiver is an interception opportunity. Patriots linebacker Eric Alexander (cut after 2004 and 2005 training camps) says, "It's just one of the basic fundamentals that we talk about here all the time on defense: when you have a free path to the quarterback, get your hands up and try to hopefully bat down a ball."[643]

One of the most famous plays in Patriots history was a ball disruption before it was an interception. When Mike Vrabel—with arms stretched into the air—closed in on Kurt Warner during Super Bowl XXXVI, Warner threw sooner and higher than he wanted to. That's ball disruption. The extra second Warner's pass hung in the air allowed Ty Law to step in front of the receiver, snatch the ball and run it back for a touchdown. Vrabel disrupted the pass before Law intercepted it. The Patriots' second touchdown drive in that game also began with ball disruption when Antwan Harris submarined Rams receiver Ricky Proehl, knocking the ball loose with his helmet. Terrell Buckley scooped up the loose ball, setting up a Brady touchdown pass. Counting disruptions is smart because each disruption is a potential big play and counting them focuses players on causing ball disruptions, not just turnovers.

Patriots coaches scrutinize film of upcoming opponents for ball disruption opportunities. Before playing the Giants in 2003, the Patriots knew Tiki Barber coughed the ball up a lot, so Tyrone Poole aimed his left shoulder pad directly at the ball and popped it loose. Matt Chatham transformed Poole's ball disruption into a turnover and touchdown by scooping and scoring. The key to the play was Poole attacking the ball with his shoulder pad at the most effective height and angle. The same is true of Rodney Harrison's strip of Marvin Harrison in the 2003 AFC Championship Game. After Marvin—seeing Rodney bearing down on him—began crouching to brace for the blow, Rodney aimed his left shoulder pad at the ball. He didn't even bother trying to tackle Marvin, instead submarining him and whacking the ball loose with shoulder pad on ball.

Monitor outputs, not inputs

"Making work productive has to start out with the end product, the output of work. It cannot start with the input... Skills, information, knowledge, are tools... The end product determines what work is needed." [644]
 – *Peter Drucker*

"[The Super Bowl trophy] doesn't say what's the best team, which has the most talented players, which team has the biggest payroll, smallest payroll. It stands for the team that played the best in that season."[645]
 – *Bill Belichick*

"The best players will play the most, and the ones that don't play as well will play less."[646]
 – *Bill Belichick*

"They don't really care where you came from. They'll still give you a chance if you can prove it on the field."[647]
 – *Patriots free agent offensive tackle/guard Victor Leyva*

Patriots coaches are too busy breaking down film, drawing up game plans, and coaching players in techniques to watch over players like Big Brother to ensure players are lifting weights, running, eating well, getting enough sleep, refraining from dangerous hobbies, studying their playbooks and watching film. Rather than monitor players' preparation efforts, Patriots coaches advise players on what to do but closely monitor only results, i.e., how players perform in practices and games. They film every game and every practice and watch those films intently, even grading each player's performance on a play-by-play and drill-by-drill basis. They don't care *how* a player becomes great; they care only *that* a player becomes great.

Some managers judge subordinates by how much "face time" they put in. Unless your business requires constant interaction among employees such that one employee's absence harms other employees, monitoring "face time" is sheer idiocy. You shouldn't care how hard someone appears to work when you happen to observe them. You should care about how productive they are. By being organized, taking work home, working passionately and intelligently, *etc.*, some people achieve more with less apparent effort. A manager's only concern should be productivity (output), not time spent in the office (input).

As a corollary, if you can help your people achieve more in less time, that benefits them and you. When the Patriots upgraded their film system to reduce the time and effort required to unearth and watch particular plays, they raised the productivity of their personnel. This not only enables Patriots players and coaches to watch relevant plays with less wasted time but also potentially leaves them a little spare time that they can spend at home with their wife and kids or on the golf course. (Bill Belichick is an impressive 16-handicap golfer;[648] the focused and competitive

Belichick would be a superb golfer if he weren't so busy with his day job.) Since employees are not robots, they value time away from the job and return refreshed after taking some personal time.

Provide detailed, credible, actionable performance feedback

"I was always worried about [Belichick] and [offensive coordinator] Charlie [Weis]. What did he and Charlie think? Because they are the ones that are making the evaluations."[649]
– *Tom Brady*

"I didn't just focus on route running or catching [generally] but the small things in running good routes and catching the ball."[650]
– *Patriots receiver David Givens*

"He cuts through all the [garbage] and gets right to the point. When he looks you in the eye, whatever is coming out of his mouth at the time, you can take it to the bank. You feel like you can… believe in the man."[651]
– *Cleveland Browns cornerback Gary Baxter, on former Patriots defensive coordinator Romeo Crennel*

Performance evaluations should be detailed, credible, and actionable. The Patriots achieve this by disaggregating each player's responsibilities into their constituent elements, teaching how they want each element executed, and giving each player frequent, specific feedback about his performance of each element. Patriots safety Rodney Harrison says:

"[Belichick] gets along with guys. He tells you what he expects out of you, and all you can do is respect a guy like that. He tells you the truth. If you are screwing up, he'll tell you. If you are doing a great job, he'll tell you. …The key that separates him from a lot of coaches is preparation. There is not one detail that he overlooks. He's always on it."[652]

David Givens says Patriots receivers don't think generically about "beating a cornerback." They prepare to beat a cornerback playing specific techniques: "We work on the jam coverage; we work on the press coverage and the off coverage… There are a lot of different techniques a corner can play, so we just try to get prepared for all of them."[653]

Rookie cornerback Ellis Hobbs drills one skill at a time, such as backpedaling, calling it his "point of emphasis *du jour*."[654] "I try to focus on one thing a day… then move to the next thing. You have to keep the little things in check. If you lose sight of the little things, they become big things."[655]

Tom Brady obsesses over every quarterback skill, not merely throwing well. Though one of the NFL's slowest players (whose speed—his dad claims—was once measured with a sundial), Brady works so hard on his footwork that sacking him is like tackling a greased pig. Opponents are awed by his ability to evade tacklers by detecting where pressure is strongest and moving away with just a few small, smooth steps... all the while staring downfield at his receivers:

> "You can't go for the hard hit [because] he has little subtle movements that can make you miss. ...You have to [approach him] under... control and just get him down [because] he just makes you miss... I've seen him shuffle. I've seen him just step to the side a little bit. He might shuffle to the side a little bit, and then on some blitzes he kind of runs away from [defenders] so he can get the ball off."[656]

Former Patriots offensive lineman Damien Woody says, "his awareness in the pocket is second to none. He can feel pressure from anywhere, and he knows how to sidestep. That separates Tom from a lot of pocket passers."[657] After studying film of Brady "in the pocket," former NFL quarterback and current analyst Ron Jaworski insisted Brady is "the NFL's most mobile quarterback." Attention to detail transformed the NFL's slowest player into its most mobile quarterback!

Brady also works hard on handing the ball off and pretending to hand the ball off: "Corey [Dillon] does a great job of carrying out the play-fake, as if he is really getting the football. [And] Brady sells it."[658] Defenders who can't see whether a handoff is real or fake must guess. If defensive backs or linebackers guess wrong or—even worse—hesitate and get trapped in no-man's-land, the Patriots benefit.

Brady has even improved his throwing mechanics: "I was really long and loose my first year. Now, I think I try to be more compact."[659] He also credits weightlifting for his stronger arms and legs that help him "throw a tight spiral or put more zip on [my] passes."[660]

Receiver David Terrell says that—as soon as he joined the Patriots—coaches worked him out in new ways that paid immediate benefits:

> "It's been getting my lower body strength up and the other areas I need to be stronger to be successful. It's drills that tie into playing receiver, whether it's getting in and out of breaks [making sharp cuts while running] or going up to get the ball. It's been a totally different transition here. It's fun because you can see yourself getting better... Explosion, quicker feet. We do a lot of quick feet. Anything that makes you more efficient when you're thinking about the transition from workouts to games."[661]

The Patriots sweat such details because details separate winners from losers. For example, left tackle Matt Light swears the key to stopping great pass rushers is not size or speed but technique: "Whoever has [to block Jevon Kearse has] to... have the right footwork. It comes down to technique. It always does."[662]

Developing great technique requires nuanced feedback from meticulous coaches, precisely the kind of coach Bill Belichick hires and trains. Patriots players trust and act on the feedback they receive because Patriots coaches: 1) are experienced; 2) explain why they're asking for certain behaviors; and, 3) tape and watch everything... and film seldom lies. After playing in the NFL more than a decade, safety Rodney Harrison is still astonished by Belichick's knowledge:

> "I can't believe a coach could know so much about so many different areas of football. Certain things you do, he'll come back and tell you and you probably don't even realize he's looking at you. ...He'll be watching the offense, but he sees things on defense and special teams."[663]

Most people have a very distorted view of themselves. Football players are no exception. Patriots three-time Pro Bowl defensive lineman Richard Seymour credits film sessions with tremendous improvements in his game by showing him what he *actually* did, not what he *believed* he did:

> "I critique myself pretty hard. I'm pretty hard on myself as far as watching film. The first day I came out here, I thought I did pretty good, then I went in to watch film and I was like, 'That's not me.' So I think the more I watch film and the more I continue to come out here, the better off I'm going to be."[664]

Patriots players crave feedback. They want to know how they're doing because they want to improve. They don't want pats on the back. They want honest information. Patriots punter and field goal holder Josh Miller is impressed by longsnapper Lonie Paxton's desire for feedback about his longsnaps: "The thing that I like most about Lonie is he really gets upset when it's not perfect. He really takes it personally. He wants to know what every snap did, he wants feedback. It's not only a job, but it's personal."[665]

Former GE CEO Jack Welch says weak managers fail to provide negative feedback. They believe they're being kind by not telling employees negative things, but "phoney appraisals" instead deny employees the chance to learn and grow or develop a "Plan B" in case they are fired. Welch says managers have "an obligation to let people know where they stand"[666] because the cruelest thing is firing someone without warning. Forthright feedback–even when harsh–is the only kind way to treat employees.

You can't turn a lump of coal into a diamond without pressure. Bill Belichick expects greatness and knows it grows in the soil of competition. Players understand too. Cornerback Asante Samuel played superbly in 2004, yet the Patriots brought in many new cornerbacks after the season:

> "I look at it as 'They're coming in here, so it's time to compete.' That's the only way you can look at it. I don't look at it as a sign that I didn't do my job because I know I did my job and I played very well. I just look at it as 'This is

the NFL, and every year there's going to be people coming in at your position'—that makes competition. Plus, you need depth."[667]

What Richard Nixon said at the 1987 funeral of Ohio State great Woody Hayes is equally applicable to Belichick:

> "He was a Renaissance man, a man with a great sense of history and with a profound understanding of the great forces that move the world... Instead of being just that tyrant that you sometimes see on the football field... he was actually a softy, a warm-hearted man."[668]

Asked whether it was a fact or fiction that "Bill Belichick actually smiles from time to time," Tedy Bruschi joked, "Fiction! Never seen the guy smile ever smile... He's just a very serious guy that just wants to win football games."[669] Belichick's gruffness is not his personality, it is a job requirement. *NFL Film*'s Steve Sabol told Belichick another coach who had always been gruff and tough with his players wished—six months before he died—he could gather all his players together and tell them how much they meant to him. Belichick replied: "Absolutely [I share that sentiment]. And also to be able to say, 'When I criticized you, when I got on you, when I rode you, it was to make you a better player to make the team better. It wasn't personal.'"[670] His insistence on perfection is another job requirement. To quote Woody Hayes:

> "We all have a tendency to ease off at times. That's why you need good teachers and good coaches: To push you a little bit. We *all* have to be pushed... I'm cheating myself and I'm cheating my players if I don't get the best out of them."[671]

For the same reason, each Patriot gives himself feedback by observing himself on film, as nose tackle Vince Wilfork explains: "As long as I have something to work on and film to look at and see myself last year, I know the things I need to work on and what I'm strong at."[672] Patriots always look reality square in the eye. If they don't like what they see, they change it.

Shorten the performance-assessment-feedback cycle

"If there's a problem, I want to hear about it in an hour."[673]
– *Toyota CEO Fujio Cho*

"At Michigan, [Tom Brady] would come up to us... more one-on-one, 'Dave, you want to get in and stick the guy this way. Or you want to get up field at least three more steps and then break.' But now he has the freedom to show you and express it to you on the field, so it's more hands-on."[674]
– *New Patriots receiver David Terrell*

"Work implies… accountability, a deadline, and finally the measurement of results, that is, feedback. …Unless we build expectations into the planning decision in such a way that we can realize early whether they are actually fulfilled or not–including a fair understanding of what are significant deviations [from expectations] both in time and in scale–we cannot plan. We have no feedback, no way of self-control from events back to the planning process."[675]
   – Peter Drucker

Bill Belichick's coaches and players apply Six Sigma to football. They strive to eliminate every error, defect and mistake. When they detect a problem, they halt the entire assembly line until they fix the problem. Patriots nose tackle Keith Traylor cites perfectionism as the key similarity between his Super Bowl-winning 2004 Patriots and his two Super Bowl-winning Broncos teams in the late 1990s: "There's no toleration of mistakes. We pride ourselves on trying to be perfect, with no mental errors. The coaching staffs are similar. They prepare you well."[676] New Miami Dolphins head coach–and long-time Belichick buddy–Nick Saban believes attention to detail is the Patriots' secret sauce:

> "Their trademark as a team is their ability to fundamentally execute against the team they play. They are one of the best tackling teams I see. They are one of the best teams controlling the line of scrimmage I see–both sides of the ball. They get the best fundamental execution out of the quarterback."[677]

Patriots coaches quickly detect and correct weaknesses. After beating the Buffalo Bills for their 18th-straight victory, Patriots coaches weren't ecstatic. They were deeply disappointed in their special teams. They released a player (Shawn Mayer) who missed a tackle on a 98-yard touchdown return, re-signed a former special teamer (Je'Rod Cherry), scratched a player (Bethel Johnson) from the active roster, and tortured special teams players with endless film sessions: "I don't know how many special-teams plays we watched last week. I'm sure the players were sick of hearing about it. It was redundant. It was beaten into them, and I think they responded well."[678] Belichick was as grouchy as a coach on an 18-game winning streak can be. After winning their 19th straight, Patriots safety Rodney Harrison said, "We're happy because he was a very unhappy camper this week, and you really don't want to be around him when he's unhappy. We're happy we got the victory for that reason alone."[679]

Patriots coaches film everything, watch every film, and grade every single player on every single play. They provide players rapid feedback and tailor their coaching to quickly fix problems. Players are kept constantly informed about their performance, areas they must improve, adjustments they must make, etc. By minimizing delays between performance and assessment and between assessment and feedback, coaches maximize players' ability to learn from and fix their mistakes:

"You know where you stand. [Belichick]'s very clear. There's no mixing up what he said. If there's a mix-up, it's not him messing it up, it's you."[680]

An example of shortening the performance-assessment-feedback cycle is the personal coaching Eric Mangini gave Troy Brown in 2004. Because Brown also played on offense and special teams, he missed many defensive meetings, so "He didn't know the [defensive play] calls, and Eric coached him up on every call. Every call was made and Eric was there telling him, 'OK, you need to do this on this one.' …He had to be really coached on the line."[681] Brown says Mangini was totally supportive from Day 1: "I joked with Eric a couple of years ago that I could play defensive back. He agreed and went to Bill and sold him on it. One day, I'm at my locker, and Eric comes up to me and says, 'You got some reps at DB today.' He said, 'Don't worry, I'll be right beside you every step of the way.'"[682]

Computerized animated movies from Pixar and DreamWorks have a much higher success rate than live-action films because animators can iteratively try something, view the results, tweak things, and then re-animate until they love what they see. A traditional director shoots many reels of film and then prays she can splice together a good movie from those reels. If she realizes in the editing room that a scene would work better if filmed or acted differently, it's too late. By giving players rapid feedback, the Patriots coaching staff enables players to optimize their performance in the same way animators at Pixar and DreamWorks fine-tune movies. This is also the concept behind startup Fortify Software. Rather than patch software after it's broken, Fortify aims to analyze code as it is written to immediately identify potential problems. The same is true when learning to swing a golf club or tennis racquet. Novices who learn proper technique from a golf or tennis pro learn much faster than those who teach themselves bad habits they must unlearn before learning proper techniques. Tiger Woods was the world's dominant golfer before changing his swing; he lost ten straight majors over 2½ years before regaining his former dominance.

Coaches themselves are accountable to Belichick. Coaches are expected to identify problems and potential improvements, communicate suggestions to players and improve players' performance. Explains Pepper Johnson, "[my players] have to improve or Coach Belichick will get on me. …The coach has a penetrating look, and everyone knows what it means."[683]

To shorten delays between performance and evaluation, the Patriots in 2004 changed their traditional daily training camp routine (practice-lunch-practice-meeting) to add a meeting after each practice. One day, they'll practice twice (8:45-10:45 in the morning and 5:30-7:30 in the evening); the next day, they'll practice just once (2:30-4:30):

> "This morning we practiced, we'll meet this afternoon. In that afternoon meeting, we'll watch the film from the morning and we'll talk about the things we are going to put in the afternoon. That way after each practice we

can go to the film and show the players the corrections and the techniques and what was good and what wasn't good, before we move into the next phase."[684]

Belichick says the team broke from its two-a-day tradition to sandwich a film session between every two practices so issues arising in one practice are addressed before the next:

"[Alternating one-a-days and two-a-days] facilitate[s] having a good solid meeting before every practice [so] that a) we can cover the film from the previous practice and [film] doesn't back up like it does when you have two practices and one night meeting; and b) to have enough time to install what is going in for the next meeting. That was always a problem... You get to the night meeting after two practices and you have a lot of film that you want to show with a lot of good teaching there and then you have things that you need to install to be able to go out and practice them the next day."[685]

Because Patriots coaches pay such meticulous attention to practice and game film, they can base personnel decisions on current player performance. A player's reputation is irrelevant. When a new season starts, the coaches basically throw out last year's performances as obsolete. Asked whether competition for 2004 Patriots roster spots would be fiercer than in 2003, Belichick said he had no idea:

"We are not going to know until they get out there and start playing. We know how people played last year, but nobody cares about that anymore. It is on a moving forward basis, and that is what the evaluation is going to made on. Some guys may come in here and play better than they did last year, and that could change their status or their opportunity on the team. Others might not play as well, and that could change. I really don't have any idea how that is going to turn out."[686]

The Patriots sign coachable players who love football, help them focus on football, show them what to do to maximize their potential, stress that success derives from goal-driven teamwork, evaluate them accurately and make personnel decisions meritocratically to identify the set of players most capable of winning football games. Without quality employee training, the Patriots would own no Super Bowl trophies.

PLANNING

"Page Scott Pioli over the loudspeaker. Then steal his notes."[687]
– *Ethan Skolnick's "Keys to successful draft"*

"Everyone's basically got the same number of practices [and] preseason games... to get their team at maximum efficiency heading into the regular season and build it from there. So every meeting, every practice, every play is an opportunity to build on that, get better and improve."[688]
– *Bill Belichick*

"As much as the Patriots should be admired for their efficiency, isn't rooting for them like rooting for a smartly run mutual fund?"[689]
– *Buck Harvey, San Antonio Express-News*

Patriots coaches and executives think analytically and plan methodically. As Patriots punter Josh Miller says Belichick "sees a vision [and] knows [how] to make it happen."[690] This chapter describes long-term planning. A separate chapter in Volume 3 ("Strategizing") will analyze game planning.

Planning determines the acquisition and utilization of scarce resources. Effective planners aim for appropriate targets and use efficient methods to hit those targets. Touchdowns and victories are fruits of an unending, unsexy planning process. The Patriots' planning excellence enables Tom Brady to say "We developed something special. It's mental toughness, a sense of complete preparation. And we feel we can overcome any obstacle."[691]

Crisis management is more exciting than planning, but foresightful planning avoids crises. Understanding this, Patriots planners wade neck deep into mundane details. Nothing is overlooked. For example, Belichick's staff decided many months in advance not to play any of the team's 22 starting players in their final 2004 preseason game. That decision was made soon after the NFL released the Patriots' schedule, which gave the team only seven days–not the normal eleven–between its final preseason game and its regular season opener:

> "We looked at the whole situation and the whole preseason schedule. You don't get into training camp and the preseason saying, 'Okay, let's wait until August 20 [to decide] 'What are we going to do today? What do you guys want to do here?' ...Since the opening game is September 9 on a Thursday– and I don't think there are any plans to change that–then you kind of work backwards from there because that is what you are working towards."[692]

Knowing their final preseason game was a throwaway, coaches accelerated the training and evaluation process.

After knocking down the nude streaker who delayed the start of the second half of Super Bowl XXXVIII, Patriots linebacker Matt Chatham joked about his team's obsessive-compulsive planning: "This is a Bill Belichick-coached program. There aren't any surprises. We watched film on that guy during the week."[693]

PLANNING: BORING BUT ESSENTIAL

"You pay the price for not thinking strategically long-term."[694]
– Patriots owner Bob Kraft

If planning sounds dull, consider its value. American Airlines lost $162 million in the first quarter of 2005. Had American locked up oil at $26/barrel–as Southwest Airlines smartly did–it would have earned a $184 million profit![695] Failing to protect against higher future oil prices cost American $346 million in just three months.

Bad planning can be lethal. As this book goes to press, too many have died in New Orleans and Mississippi after Hurricane Katrina because equipment and National Guard troops were in Iraq, funding for FEMA and for the Army Corps of Engineers' work on New Orleans' levees had been diverted elsewhere[696] and the top three officials at FEMA were, according to *The New York Daily News*, "political cronies with no apparent experience coping with catastrophes."[697] Unlike the Patriots, who stress hiring the right people, our government placed post-9/11 emergency preparedness in the hands of two public relations executives and a man "ousted"[698] from a job as judges and stewards commissioner of the International Arabian Horses Association.[699] I have been unable to focus on editing because I have been so upset by our government's fatally slow response. Writing a book about football–a game–seemed trivial while hundreds of thousands of our fellow citizens suffered or died as the nation watched.

I was able to resume editing only after realizing how many lives could have been saved had those responsible for America's (disastrous) disaster response followed the Patriots' planning principles. Here's just one horrible example:

> "He said, 'Yeah, mama, somebody's coming to get ya' on Tuesday, 'Somebody's coming to get ya' on Wednesday, 'Somebody's coming to get ya' on Thursday, 'Somebody's coming to get you' on Friday. And she drowned Friday night."[700]

Though football is fun, the lessons of this book are not at all frivolous.

Michael Chertoff, Secretary of Homeland Security–which oversees FEMA–claims the impact of a hurricane strike on New Orleans "exceeded the foresight of the planners and maybe anybody's foresight" and was "breathtaking in its surprise."[701] President Bush agreed: "I don't think anyone anticipated the breach of the levees."[702] Perhaps that belief explains why Bush flew to California–not Louisiana or Mississippi–after the Category 4 hurricane struck? But FEMA director Michael Brown had already said Katrina "caused the same kind of damage that we anticipated. So we planned for it two years ago. Last year, we exercised it."[703] Indeed. In July 2004, a five-day government disaster preparedness training exercise about hypothetical "Hurricane Pam" striking New Orleans assumed 20 feet of water would flood the city and burst levees. Virtually identical scenarios have been described in *Scientific American*, NPR's *"All Things Considered," National Geographic* and New Orleans' paper, *The Times-Picayune*. An early 2001 FEMA study concluded America's three greatest potential catastrophes were an earthquake in San Francisco, a terrorist attack in New York and a hurricane strike on New Orleans.[704]

So, what plans were in place? In July 2005, government officials and the regional Red Cross executive director jointly warned New Orleans residents– including the estimated 134,000 who lacked cars–that they would be on their own if a hurricane struck: "You're responsible for your safety… We don't have the transportation."[705] Three days before Katrina's landfall, the *National Hurricane Center* predicted a Category 4 hurricane would strike New Orleans,[706] but buses were not brought in to evacuate the poor, ill, aged or carless who lacked means to flee. Despite this, Secretary Chertoff later said, "The critical thing was to get people out of there before the disaster. Some people chose not to obey that order. That was a mistake on their part."[707] Also, despite three-day advance warning, food, water and medicines were never pre-positioned in downtown New Orleans–as is standard procedure before a predicted crisis–or air-dropped for days afterwards. After relief finally arrived, *NBC News* anchor Brian Williams–who was on the scene–wrote, "There was water, there was food, and there were choppers to drop them both. Why no one was able to combine them in an air drop is a cruel and criminal mystery."[708]

Days into the crisis, television crews were on the scene but our government somehow couldn't get water or food in. Louisiana's governor said the federal government–rather than being part of the solution–"has caused us a lot of stress. We would have wanted massive numbers of helicopters on Day One."[709] Hospital ships and water-pumping ships that FEMA in the 1990s planned to bring to New Orleans were nowhere. The Red Cross was not allowed to provide relief:

> "Access to New Orleans is controlled by the National Guard and local authorities… We simply cannot enter New Orleans against their orders. The Homeland Security Department had requested–and continues to request– that the American Red Cross not come back into New Orleans following the hurricane. Our presence would keep people from evacuating and encourage others to come into the city."[710]

Chicago's mayor said "I was shocked" after his offer of police, firefighters and vehicles was rebuffed.[711] On Wednesday morning, Louisiana citizens–organized by state senator Nick Gautreaux–brought between 100 and 500 boats (estimates vary) to conduct search-and-rescue but were turned back.[712]

According to the *Chicago Tribune*, the massive USS Bataan, with a crew of 1,200, "has helicopters, doctors, hospital beds, food and water. It also can make its own water, up to 100,000 gallons a day."[713] It followed right behind the hurricane and was ready to help immediately but did nothing. Its massive hovercraft–loaded with supplies–was zipping to New Orleans when the Bataan was ordered to divert to Biloxi. U.S. Northern Command spokesman Lt. Commander Sean Kelly said "Because we have exercised our response to hurricanes and actually assisted with several smaller hurricanes last year, we had a pretty good sense of the kinds of help that would be needed, and we essentially pre-positioned it in the region in advance so that we could react quicker when FEMA called."[714] He also said on *BBC World News*:

> "We had the USS Bataan sailing almost behind the hurricane so that after [it] made landfall its search and rescue helicopters would be available almost immediately. So we had things ready. The only caveat is, we have to wait until the President authorizes us to do so. The laws of the United States say that the military can't just act in this fashion. We have to wait for the President to give us permission."[715]

More than 72 hours after Katrina struck, New Orleans' head of emergency operations declared, "This is a national disgrace… We're not getting any supplies. This is not a FEMA operation. I haven't seen a single FEMA guy."[716] The president of Jefferson Parish told *Meet the Press* that FEMA turned away three trailer trucks of water Wal-Mart sent, barred local officials from accepting 1,000 gallons of diesel fuel offered by the Coast Guard and shut down all the parish's emergency communication lines, concluding "bureaucracy has committed murder here."[717] The expert who ran the "Hurricane Pam" exercise said, less hyperbolically but equally grimly, "What bothers me the most is all the people who've died unnecessarily. Those FEMA officials wouldn't listen to me. Those Corps of Engineers people giggled in the back of the room when we tried to present information."[718] Thursday night, FEMA's director told *CNN* "the federal government did not even know about the convention center people until today."[719] Friday night, 4½ days into the crisis, *Fox News* reporters Shepard Smith and Geraldo Rivera were tearful, livid and screaming about the continuing tragedy and the fact that troops were blocking people from leaving the city.

The planning disaster began earlier. The city might never have flooded had work continued on strengthening the levees, according to *The Chicago Tribune*:

> "The Bush administration and Congress in recent years have repeatedly cut funding for hurricane preparation and flood control. The cuts have delayed construction of levees around the city and stymied an ambitious project to improve drainage in New Orleans' neighborhoods. For instance, the U.S. Army Corps of Engineers requested $27 million for this fiscal year to pay for hurricane protection projects around Lake Pontchartrain. The Bush

administration countered with $3.9 million, and Congress eventually provided $5.7 million… Because of the budget cuts, which were caused in part by the rising costs of the war in Iraq, the Corps delayed seven contracts that included enlarging the levees."[720]

When–a year earlier–the Army Corps of Engineers had stopped working on the levees for the first time in 37 years, Jefferson Parish's disappointed emergency management chief explained, "The money has been moved in the President's budget to handle homeland security and the war in Iraq, and I suppose that's the price we pay."[721] Even earlier, in 2002, Mike Parker was forced to resign as head of the Army Corps of Engineers after pleading for more funds with Director Mitch Daniels of the president's Office of Management and Budget:

> "I took two pieces of steel into Mitch Daniels' office. They were exactly the same pieces of steel, except one had been under water in a Mississippi lock for 30 years and the other was new. The first piece was completely corroded and falling apart because of a lack of funding. I said, 'Mitch, it doesn't matter if a terrorist blows the lock up or if it falls down because it disintegrates–either way, it's the same effect, and if we let it fall down, we have only ourselves to blame.' It made no impact on him whatsoever."[722]

By contrast, thanks to House Transportation chairman Don Young, Alaska received funds to build the Gravina Island Bridge to connect Ketchikan (population 8,000) to Gravina Island (population 50) at a cost of $315 million and the Knik Arm Bridge to connect Anchorage to undeveloped wetlands at a cost of $600 million.[723]

The New York Times called the response to Katrina "The Man-Made Disaster,"[724] and *Newsday* called it "the single most catastrophic collapse of American government in our times."[725] Any private firm that planned so poorly would be bankrupt. Because no organization can succeed with poor planning, this chapter shows you proper planning, Patriots-style.

FOCUS ON RESULTS

> "The mentality of this team is 'win or die.'"[726]
> – *Patriots running back Corey Dillon*

> "Any book of management that does not begin with the tasks to be [accomplished] misconceives management. Such a book sees management as something in itself, rather than as a means to an end. It fails to understand that management exists only in contemplation of performance."[727]
> – *Peter Drucker*

Smart organizations "manage by objective." They envision their desired results and then work backwards to determine a tactical path that leads to their objectives. The Patriots are relentlessly focused on winning football games. Everything derives from that objective. The Patriots would hire a three-eyed midget with a wooden leg, six fingers and glow-in-the-dark hair if he played well and was a good teammate:

> "Whether [a cornerback]'s 6´2˝ and covers [a receiver] or 5´9˝ and covers him... if they're covered, the quarterback's not going to throw to him. If they're not covered, it doesn't make any difference how tall, short, fast [he is or] how many pushups he does."[728]
> – *Bill Belichick*

> "If he's 290 [pounds] and runs fast and can open his hips and drop [into pass coverage], hey he could be a *good* linebacker!"
> – *Romeo Crennel, asked "Is there a size where you won't even attempt to convert a [college defensive end to linebacker]? 290?"*

> "The scheme is [for our inside linebackers] to go up, take on guards, shed them and make tackles. Whatever niche you have–TJ [Ted Johnson] had that hard-nosed mentality–you have to get that job done. There's many different ways. You can beat guys to a spot, give guys a flipper, head-butt a guy, hands a guy. It all depends on what your strength is."[729]
> – *Patriots special teamer and reserve linebacker/safety Don Davis*

> "Whether [a receiver gets open] because he's strong and he pushes off [the defender] and he creates separation or whether he does it with quickness, whether he does it with technique or whatever it is, if the quarterback sees an open receiver, he's going to be happy and he'll throw him the ball."[730]
> – *Bill Belichick*

Bill Belichick makes every decision based on what he believes gives his team the best chance to win football games:

> "I have to make decisions in the best interest of the football team. I can't answer to any one particular constituency, like the linebackers or the cornerbacks. I have to make a decision. Whether the players understand that or respect that, I don't know. I hope they do. I think they do."[731]

It is human nature to allow sentiment to sway decisions. Many coaches would have paid Joe Andruzzi, David Patten and Ty Law–integral members of three Super Bowl-winning teams–to stay on for a fourth Super Bowl run. Many coaches would never have cut fan favorite Troy Brown and risked losing him to the Saints. But Bill Belichick is not your ordinary coach. Belichick suppresses his humanity and makes personnel decisions as a robot might. As he says, "I just want to improve our team and make it as good as it can possibly be. That's what I try to do this year and every year."[732] If your singular focus is winning, you must release aging, overpaid players, no matter how unpopular doing so is. As much as David Patten contributed to three Super Bowl-winning teams, he is not quite the player he once was, and he was not worth to the Patriots the $13 million–including $3.5 mil. signing bonus–the Redskins are paying him over the next five years. Early in Super Bowl XXXIX, Patten appeared shell-shocked. Tom Brady threw a pass that Patten might have caught by diving low instead of remaining upright and staring at the Eagle defender about to smash him. Had Patten gone low–instead of attempt a standing basket catch–he might have caught the ball and avoided the wallop he actually received. His mistake thrilled Eagles players, who shouted excitedly to one another on the sideline. Defensive tackle Paul Grasmanis screamed: "They don't want to come across the middle no more!" Linebacker Jeremiah Trotter was thrilled: "He's scared. He's scared!" In KC Joyner's analysis of all NFL wide receivers, Patten ranked "85th, or 3rd worst among qualifying receivers," though Joyner said Brady underthrew Patten many times.[733] The Patriots expect their receivers to catch passes, so Belichick decided Patten was not worth the money he expected as a free agent and Redskins coach Joe Gibbs was on the phone with Patten a moment after the midnight start of free agency.

Set goals and move toward them

"[Belichick] keeps putting goals up there for you. You never want to stay the same. You want to keep going up… Even after a victory like today [locking up the AFC East championship], the goal now is to maintain the No. 1 seed and beat a Jacksonville squad that's on the rise."[734]
– *Former Patriots offensive lineman Damien Woody*

"The team has goals. Just as much as any individual player goal, there is also a team goal of trying to win Super Bowls, which is most important. Anyone that chooses to play on the Patriots realizes that goal supersedes any other individual player goal."[735]
– *Tom Brady*

Bill Belichick's Patriots are masters at setting goals: individual goals, unit goals, and team goals. Short-term goals, medium-term goals and long-term goals. Coaches and players seize every possible "hook" to motivate themselves to push harder. Every Patriots coach and player maintains in his mind a continually updated copy of the table below and uses it for motivation. The following are all actual goals:

	Individual	Unit	Team
Short term	"Gain at least four yards on this (and every) run" (Corey Dillon)	"Block this field goal attempt" (special teams)	"Score first in this game" (Belichick challenge before every game)
Medium term	"In 2004, break Ray Clayborn's record of 36 interceptions as a Patriot" (Ty Law)	"Don't surrender any sacks" (offensive line)	"Play as well after Thanksgiving as the 2001 Patriots" (2003 Patriots)

Long term	"Study the great players at my position and become the NFL's best player at my position" (Richard Seymour)	"Return two punts for touchdowns this season" (special teams)	"Repeat as Super Bowl champion" (2004 Patriots)

Patriots coaches have their own goals. Eric Mangini is working to tailor his coaching to particular players' needs and learning styles. And in the summer of 2004, offensive coordinator Charlie Weis sat down with Bill Belichick to devise a plan for becoming a college head coach: "It was time to lay out a plan. I had no idea what jobs might open up, but the example we used when talking about this was Notre Dame."[736] That's smart planning!

Short-term goals

"I don't think of repeating. It's such a long road. I think of trying to get this team to play well in Week 1."[737]
– *Bill Belichick, 2002*

"Take it one play at a time… I just look forward to that one play and then the next play and the next play."[738]
– *Patriots backup linebacker Tully Banta-Cain*

"You can't look too far ahead or look in the past. Just live for the moment, man. Right now. Enjoy what each day brings."[739]
– *Patriots receiver Troy Brown*

Short-term goals are fundamental because only short-term goals are actionable. "Win the game" and "Win the Super Bowl" fail to tell players what to do. They are useful only insofar as they motivate players to accomplish substantive short-term goals. So, every long-term goal must be disaggregated into a sequence of short-term goals. Tom Brady says, "The [goal] is to make an improvement on a daily basis."[740] Left tackle Matt Light equates practice with improvement: "That's my plan: go out there and get better."[741] Former Patriots offensive coordinator Charlie Weis says each player sets a bar for himself at each practice. The next practice, "There's two ways you can go."[742] As Notre Dame's new head coach, Weis huddles up his players and has them each reach a hand into the middle and shout "1-2-3-Get better!" to emphasize that each player should strive to elevate his play each practice. That's a clear objective with a short time horizon and rapid feedback. Weis uses incremental goals to motivate himself for the tedious task of recruiting high schoolers to Notre Dame, something he traveled school to school doing from April 28th through May 27th, never once returning home:

> "I have a passion for recruiting, as much as I like to coach… because I look
> at recruiting like a game with wins and losses and setbacks and small steps.

When you go after a guy and you don't get him, sometimes it's a setback, and sometimes it feels like you just got punched in the mouth."[743]

Weis' comment raises another point: short-term goals create challenges and provide rapid feedback. A steady stream of short-term feedback motivates far more effectively than a distant goal. Belichick advises against worrying about the future because, as he told Bryant University students, "No matter where you think you'll be in the future… it's going to change. So my advice is to look at the short term and explore something you can put all your passion into."[744] Special teams captain Larry Izzo broke into the NFL because his first special teams coach (Mike Westhoff) gave him daily goals:

> "Throughout camp he was always very supportive and motivated me as far as what I needed to do… to show [up] every day on film and do something every day that sets [me] apart from the rest of the guys. Having him there telling me that every day really kept me going, and throughout camp [head coach] Jimmy [Johnson] took notice. I had some good practices consistently and made plays. From the early part of camp, I moved up the depth chart."[745]

The father of management science, Peter Drucker, says success is impossible without short-term goals: "Achievement is never possible except against specific, limited, clearly defined targets… Only if targets are defined can resources be allocated to their attainment, priorities and deadlines set, and somebody be held accountable for results."[746] Setting goals focuses players' preparation on essential tasks and creates a sense of urgency that spurs players to constantly improve, prepare, and perform. New Patriots–like free agent defensive lineman Keith Traylor in 2004–immediately sense their new team's goal-focused intensity:

> "The feeling I get here is the urgency to [win the Super Bowl] again. We don't want to do it like the year they won it and [the next season] went 9-7 and didn't make the playoffs. Now it's the urgency of, 'Let's do it again.'"[747]

The kind of "overachieving" player the Patriots seek tends to constantly challenge himself with short-term goals without prodding from coaches. 2005 Patriots draftee Ellis Hobbs, for example, was working toward a goal in his first mini-camp, just one week after being drafted: "I'm not going to learn everything right away, but I want to move ahead at a faster pace than they expect. You wouldn't get picked at this level if you didn't have talent. The thing I stress the most is knowledge of the game, because that's what puts you ahead of everyone else."[748]

Patriot running back Corey Dillon has long set a goal for himself of gaining at least four yards on each carry. Anything extra is great, but four yards is his minimum standard. Dillon set this reasonable stretch goal before joining the Patriots, and his achievement focus helped him become a Patriot.

Belichick believes players must be continually challenged with short- and medium-term goals because "Win the Super Bowl" is too remote, hypothetical and intangible to prevent the deadly *mañana* syndrome. Belichick believes his 2002 Patriots were so overconfident that they were unchastened even by defeats:

> "When you [become] overconfident, another team will usually come along and put everything in perspective in a hurry. But whenever players or coaches start to take the attitude of, 'We'll be there when it counts, don't worry about things, there's no urgency,' it usually doesn't get straightened out, and when you try to, it doesn't happen."[749]

You must make the playoffs to win the Super Bowl. And you must win many games to make the playoffs. And you must have a good team at the end of training camp to win games. And you must have well-conditioned athletes at the start of training camp to have a productive training camp. Therefore, a coach must chop long-term objectives into a long chain of short- and medium-term objectives and motivate his players and assistants to achieve those shorter-term goals without which the ultimate long-term goal is unattainable. As Charlie Weis said after his new Notre Dame team's first spring practice, "right now our intention is to go out tomorrow and get an improvement over where we were today."[750]

While many teams preach "one game at a time," Belichick preaches "one game at a time, one week at a time, one practice at a time, and one play at a time."[751] To help players stay focused every minute of every game, Belichick divides each game into mini-games. To focus players' minds on performing well early in games rather than worrying just about the final score, Belichick emphasizes scoring first. Every week, Belichick presents his team a list of keys to winning that week's game. Almost every week, his list includes "score first."[752] Tom Brady says, "Playing from a lead is critical when you're playing a good team."[753]

Belichick's emphasis on scoring first is smart because playing well early is as important as playing well late. 70% of NFL games in 2003 were won by whichever team scored first, and teams that scored twice before their opponent scored won 84% of the time.[754] Elias Sports Bureau says that over the past five seasons, teams with a 3-0 lead won 59% of games, teams with a 7-0 lead won 71% of the time, teams with a 10-0 lead won 82% of games and teams with a 14-0 lead won 87% of the time.[755]

Conversely, falling behind in a game affects players' attitudes and coaches' play-calling strategies. More often than not, a team that digs itself into an early hole digs itself in deeper as the game progresses. In 2003, 70% of NFL interceptions were thrown by teams that were losing at the time.[756]

The Patriots' NFL-record 21-game winning streak is well known. Less well known is that the 2003-2004 Patriots shattered the NFL record for consecutive games scoring first. The previous record, 15 straight, was held by the 1978 Dolphins. The 2003-2004 Patriots scored first in an astonishing 23 straight games! The NFL does not count the Patriots' three playoff wins, so the NFL record book says the Patriots scored first in 20 straight games, five more than the previous record.

The odds of scoring first in 23 straight games by chance is 0.00001192%. The contrast from before their streak is stark: "Before that streak, there weren't many times we scored first… We hadn't scored (first) in eight weeks. The coach was dogging us saying that we couldn't score on the opening drive. Maybe he dogged us enough and we finally figured it out."[757] Another eye-opening stat is that the Patriots have not surrendered an opening-drive touchdown in 37 games![758]

Patriots games since the start of the 21-game winning streak

Opponent	First score in game	Patriots' first scoring drive	Did Patriots score first?
Titans	Titans FG	2nd drive TD (missed 34-yard FG on opening drive)	No
Giants	Giants FG	7th drive TD (missed 42-yard FG on opening drive)	No
Miami	Patriots FG	3rd drive FG	Yes
Browns	Patriots FG	1st drive FG	Yes
Broncos	Broncos TD	3rd drive TD	No
Cowboys	Patriots FG	2nd drive FG	Yes
Texans	Houston FG	2nd drive TD	No
Colts	Patriots FG	1st drive FG	Yes
Dolphins	Patriots FG	2nd drive FG	Yes
Jaguars	Patriots TD	1st drive TD	Yes
Jets	Patriots TD	1st drive TD	Yes
Bills	Patriots TD	1st drive TD	Yes
Titans	Patriots TD	1st drive TD	Yes
Colts	Patriots TD	1st drive TD	Yes
Panthers (Super Bowl XXXVIII)	Patriots TD	6th drive TD (missed 31-yard FG on 1st drive and 36-yard FG blocked on 5th drive)	Yes
Colts	Patriots FG	1st drive FG	Yes
Cardinals	Patriots TD	2nd drive TD	Yes
Bills	Patriots TD	1st drive TD	Yes
Dolphins	Patriots TD	3rd drive TD	Yes
Seahawks	Patriots TD	1st drive TD	Yes
Jets	Patriots FG	1st drive FG	Yes

Opponent	First score in game	Patriots' first scoring drive	Did Patriots score first?
Steelers	Patriots FG	1ˢᵗ drive FG	Yes
Rams	Patriots FG	1ˢᵗ drive FG	Yes
Bills	Patriots FG	1ˢᵗ drive FG	Yes
Chiefs	Patriots TD	1ˢᵗ drive TD	Yes
Ravens	Patriots FG	3ʳᵈ drive FG	Yes
Browns	Patriots TD	Kickoff return TD	Yes
Bengals	Patriots TD	1ˢᵗ drive TD	Yes
Dolphins	Patriots TD	1ˢᵗ drive TD	Yes
Jets	Patriots FG	3ʳᵈ drive FG	Yes
49ers	49ers TD	4ᵗʰ drive TD	No
Colts	Patriots FG	3ʳᵈ drive FG	Yes
Steelers	Patriots FG	1ˢᵗ drive FG	Yes
Eagles (Super Bowl XXXIX)	Eagles TD	6ᵗʰ drive TD	No

The Patriots don't score first by accident. They script each game's opening so they're as comfortable as a chess grandmaster playing his opening moves:

> "We tell the team sometimes on Friday and at the latest on Saturday and again on Sunday morning, 'This is the way we'll start the game. This is the sequence. Some of [the play calls] are situational–the first third-and-long is this; the first third-and-short will be that–but we make sure they're prepared so they know what to expect on those plays. [They know], 'If we get this look, this is what happens; if we get that look, this is what happens.' You want to make sure you start the game in a positive way and with the best execution you can have."[759]

Grabbing an early lead helps avoid desperate situations that force players to gamble. Two nights before the Patriots' first Super Bowl victory, for example: "Belichick showed his players video clips of games in which turnovers had led to early Rams leads. (Included was the Patriots' last loss, a 24-17 setback against St. Louis in Foxboro, Mass., on Nov. 18.) 'If you can get through those first few minutes,' he told the team, 'you've got a fighting chance.'"[760]

Scoring first in the second half is another short-term goal. With the game tied at halftime 17-17 against the Buffalo Bills in 2004, the Patriots knew how important the early minutes of the second half would be: "As we went in at halftime, [our attitude] was, 'Hey, it's 0-0. We've got to win a half. We've got to start by winning the third quarter and we've got to start by winning the first play of the 3rd quarter."[761]

Intermediate-term goals

"You go through training camp and try to prove you're the better player out there. You try to show these coaches and scouts that you belong on that 45-man [game day] roster. That's what I want them to think on that opening kickoff Thursday night–that I deserve to be one of those players out there... There are a lot of guys trying to take my job from me. I want to hold onto it... When they're in that meeting room deciding who to keep, I want to make it tough. I want them saying, 'Troy did this well. Troy did that well.' These young guys are fighting hard, too, and I don't want to make it easy on them, either."[762]

– Patriots receiver/returner/nickelback Troy Brown

Intermediate goals often imply obvious short-term goals. Patriots center Dan Koppen provides an example: "We try and go out there to get better each week. We try to give Corey and Kevin lanes to run in and try to keep Tom [Brady] clean."[763] Striving each week to create more holes for running backs and protect Brady better obviously implies doing this on every play too.

After Thanksgiving 2003, Belichick challenged his players with a medium-term goal: "comparisons were being made [between] the '03 team [and] the '01 team that won [the Super Bowl] and the big difference was that [2001] team won nine games in a row after Thanksgiving, so that was a big challenge for us."[764] The implied message: "You may think you've accomplished something, but you haven't. What made the '01 team great was what they accomplished from this point in the season onward."

After the NFL scheduled a potentially distracting pre-game extravaganza (with stars like Elton John celebrating the 2003 Patriots' Super Bowl victory) before the 2004 Patriots' season opener, Foxboro became a construction zone the week before the game. Players were not distracted. In fact, Tom Brady set as his week's goal "to upstage any of the performers with the game."[765] According to linebacker Tedy Bruschi, after the Patriots won Super Bowl XXXVIII, players motivated themselves during the off-season with a medium-term goal of breaking the all-time NFL consecutive victories record of eighteen games. Bruschi quickly emphasized that this medium-term goal is really three short-term goals: "Can we win our first three in a row? That is something we'll keep in the background. We want to win three in a row, but we do that by trying to win one in a row."[766] Patriots players know that every medium- and long-term goal can–and must–be decomposed into short-term goals.

Long-term goals

Long-term goals supplement short- and medium-term goals by helping motivate effort day-to-day. "Win the Super Bowl" is like "build a great house." What actually creates the house is not the dream or even the detailed blueprint but the laborious process of laying a brick, adding mortar, then laying another brick and adding more mortar. Patriots players worry about bricks, not dream houses. They pridefully strive to become the NFL's most precise and efficient bricklayers and lay each brick perfectly, always motivated by their ultimate goal of a dream house. Being bricklayers, not dreamers, they concentrate not on "winning" but on performing their best. Troy Brown explains: "We're coming into [Super Bowl XXXIX] with the mentality that if we go out there and play well we've got a chance to win the game. We never came in [to any game] with the top dog mentality... just... the expectation to go out there and play well, knowing that if we played well we could win."[767]

Long-term goals give meaning to short- and medium-term goals. For example, Charlie Weis has a clear vision for his tenure as Notre Dame head coach: "I would really like to be here at least 10 years... I'm hoping that by the time I leave, the Notre Dame fans, the alumni [and] anyone who has a positive light on Notre Dame will be able to look at me and say, 'We're glad we hired that guy.'"[768]

Before bricklayers can begin, an architect must translate the long-term goal (a dream house) into blueprints (short- and medium-term goals). The design process illuminates tradeoffs, sets priorities and assigns responsibilities. Working intensely at the wrong tasks is as productive as driving 100 miles an hour in the wrong direction. Coaches' and players' medium- and short-term goals must add up to their collective long-term goal. Patriots defensive lineman Ty Warren says exactly this: "Everybody's short-term goal is going to lead up to everybody's long-term goal."[769] Each team member must appropriately allocate his scarce time across his various short-term goals to achieve his medium-term goals. This is why effective managers always budget their time. Charlie Weis, for example, has his secretary give him a "two-minute warning"[770] when he needs to wrap up an interview with a journalist. Weis knows that meeting the media matters, but he cannot allow an interview to crowd out other important tasks.

Winning the Super Bowl comes into focus as an actionable goal only after winning the AFC Championship Game. According to Tom Brady:

"The goal is really just to continue playing. Late in the year when you realize you qualify for the playoffs, you try to get a great seed. Then you play your first playoff game, which we did in the second week of the playoffs. We won that one and then we go to Pittsburgh. And then before you know it, we win one game, and we're flying down here. [Looking ahead] just takes away from how much fun it is and how much I think we enjoy going out there and preparing each week and how much fun it is to go out there and play each week."[771]

Personal goals: "Do your job"

Team goals always trump personal goals. As Super Bowl MVP Deion Branch explains, "Every year I want to get better. I want my numbers to be better. But–at the same time–if we are winning and my numbers are low, I am happy. I am good."[772] Patriots set their personal goals in support of unit and team goals. Individual achievements are meaningful only when they contribute to unit and team objectives. "Ability" doesn't win football games. Actions that help one's team score or prevent one's opponent from scoring win football games. "Ability" is simply the raw potential to perform actions that benefit one's team. "Ability" is not "talent" unless it is expressed on a football field in concert with ten teammates to help one's team outscore one's opponent. Troy Brown says his teammates apply their talents to winning games, not looking good:

> "Here, there are no egos. Everybody gets along. Nobody gets mad because somebody is catching more balls then somebody else or somebody is playing 'X' amount plays, or… 'He gets to blitz; I don't get to blitz.' Nobody gets mad about that. Everybody falls in and plays their role. That's how you've got to win football games. Everybody's got to be a role player, and everybody is not going to be that star player. …Do your job… well and you'll be successful, and that's why we are. That's why you see a lot of teams that people say has more talent then we have that just fall off because they can't get along, they can't learn to play in that system like that. When… everybody wants to be the star, most of the time it's going to be a failure."[773]

Safety Rodney Harrison agrees: "We always stress the importance of doing your job and not try to do someone else's job."[774] Linebacker Mike Vrabel surprised a reporter who asked if Patriots linebackers tried to control the game: "I don't think we take it upon ourselves. I think we try to play within the framework of the defense."[775] Over-emphasizing and over-rewarding non-contextualized individual behavior–such as the number of sacks or touchdowns a player records–undermines selfless, team-benefiting behaviors. Grading and rewarding a player in a team sport according to individual statistics encourages him to pad his stats at the expense of his team and teammates.

The Patriots ensure that every player is always striving to achieve specific personal goals. After tying Ray Clayborn's record of 36 interceptions as a Patriot, cornerback Ty Law said, "That was one of my personal goals this year. That was real important to me. I'm glad I own a piece of it."[776] Offensive lineman Stephen Neal says, "I try not to lose any time I'm out on the football field. But you do get beat [by a defender] here and there, and so that's what I'm striving for–to have a perfect game, which a lot of people say you can't have, but that's my goal."[777] I wouldn't bet against Neal, who won back-to-back NCAA Division 1 wrestling championships without losing a match. Patriots coaches help each player set goals consistent with team needs, even during the "offseason." For example, coaches experimented in 2003 using defensive linemen Ty Warren and Jarvis Green at nose tackle. After determining Warren and Green were better suited to defensive end, coaches encouraged both to become quicker by losing weight during the offseason: "Warren played last season at 308 pounds, but is now down to 298 and looks to have more muscle definition. ...Ditto for Green, who played at 290 last season but is down in the 280 neighborhood."[778] Warren, who actually lost 18 pounds, explains "One of my goals was to get lighter. The fact is, you get more agile when you're lighter."[779] Dan Klecko, who played defensive line in college and his first season (2003) with the Patriots, dropped twenty pounds in the offseason after Patriots coaches told him they would try him at linebacker in 2004.

After the coaching staff highlighted safety Rodney Harrison's penchant for penalties–because, as Harrison puts it, "every once in a while I think, 'Maybe unnecessary roughness may be necessary'"–Harrison improved dramatically:

> "Coach Belichick brings us into a meeting and I'm leading the team in penalties. So he's getting on my back. I think I might have had eight penalties in the first eight games of the season. The last eight games of the season, I had zero penalties. So I improved."[780]

An example of individual incentives diverging from team incentives is intercepting passes on 4th down. If a 4th down pass falls incomplete, it's the equivalent of a fumble recovery at the original line of scrimmage. If a defensive player intercepts the pass, his team instead gets the ball wherever he is tackled, so the defensive team is usually better off knocking down a 4th down pass than intercepting it. But defenders love making interceptions because INTs is a major defensive statistic. Patriots defenders want to win, so they always knock down 4th down passes–unless they're confident they can run beyond the original line of scrimmage.

Even the Patriots punter, Josh Miller, has goals and strives to improve. You might think a punt is a punt, but Miller says punting is as situational as every other dimension of the game, based on the location of the snap (high, low, right, left), field position, the importance of kicking long versus kicking high to give the punt coverage team time to get downfield, etc. Miller also reshaped his body for the 2005 season: "I lost about 19 pounds. I was working with a trainer... a lot of diet, a lot of running, a lot of fast stuff."[781] Why bother? Miller had clear goals:

"I felt slow and felt my get-offs from catch to kick looked slow. I used to be strong and 235, then I had a couple of shoulder surgeries and I felt weak and 235. I said, 'I don't need this crap anymore. I'm getting older.' The most important thing is your back, stomach, and flexibility, so I got rid of [excess weight] and it helped out a lot. I got a little faster, quicker, and I feel like my hang time got a lot better for coverage."[782]

Players should be judged by whether their behavior helps their team win football games. Belichick praises Tom Brady for caring only about the team performing its collective best and for setting his teammates up to succeed:

"His preparation... is exceptional. He studies the game plan very hard. He studies his opponents well and has a good command of not only what he's doing, but what our offense is doing as a unit and some things to expect... He works well with his teammates–the other receivers, the offensive linemen–on things that will make their jobs easier, whether it's things related to the snap count, the cadence, receiver splits, the different techniques on routes and those kinds of things. He works very hard with those people, and it helps us with our overall execution."[783]

When Belichick says "Nobody works any harder or does any more to prepare for a game than Tom,"[784] he is praising Brady's preparation of his teammates as much as his self-preparation. Brady works hard to prepare his offensive teammates because his success is intertwined with theirs.

Patriots players' all-for-one-and-one-for-all mindset is real and deeply embedded. Their unity derives from their intensely-held shared goal of performing their collective best. Economists traditionally view all behavior through the lens of "methodological individualism," *i.e.*, the assumption that anyone who helps someone else has an ulterior motive, most likely expecting reciprocity or wanting to feel good about him/herself for helping another. Patriots players certainly expect reciprocity, but their selflessness can only be accurately described in terms of "interdependent preferences," *i.e.*, each player truly cares about the interests of his teammates. Each *wants* his teammates to succeed. Interdependent preferences violate economists' standard assumptions. Fixation on methodological individualism is a major reason why economists long ignored bottom-up movements, such as peace rallies and the rise of open source software like Linux. Thousands of programmers work on Linux because they believe in the mission of building something that benefits millions. They receive recognition from their fellow programmers, but many receive no money. Even rival corporations–including Hewlett-Packard, IBM, and Intel–are now contributing cash and programmers' time to the movement. The decentralized Linux community collaborates effectively because, according to one of the movement's leaders, "Cooperating gets you farther along than screwing your neighbor."[785] Patriots players and coaches feel this in their bones.

Focus on excellence, not winning

"Guys here take pride in working hard, paying attention to details, and doing things right."[786]
— *Patriots linebacker Rosevelt Colvin*

"The more prepared you are, the better your chances are of being successful."[787]
— *Patriots safety Rodney Harrison*

"I just go to practice and try and improve what I do. I can't worry about [who's starting]. Just worry about yourself... It never changes around here. Everybody is playing for a spot—at every position. It hasn't changed for me at all since I came here as a rookie."[788]
— *Patriots right tackle Tom Ashworth*

Because no player can—by himself—win a football game, the Patriots' objective is performing their collective best. Each Patriot worries about performing his role to the best of his ability, not "winning," which is beyond his control. Even playing time is beyond a player's control, something Belichick stresses in preseason:

"I've told [players] to be ready to go for 60 minutes, just like it's a regular-season game. They can't control any of the decisions on playing time, so don't even try to. Just get ready to go for 60 minutes and whoever we put in, we'll put in."[789]

Making the roster is also beyond any player's direct control. Belichick spells out the implications for players each offseason:

"I try to impart to them: 'Rather than worrying about how many linemen we're going to keep or how many linebackers we're going to keep—which is a coach's decision and a personnel decision the player can stay up all night worrying about but there's nothing he can do about that—let's concentrate on what you can do better and how to create a role on the team.'"[790]

Players certainly want to make the roster, get into games and help their team win, but all are by-products of professionalism. Veteran receiver Troy Brown knows there are no guarantees: "I don't pick the team. I don't scout the players. They bring in a new guy, I can't worry about that. It's all competition. New guys come in. Somebody leaves. You get friendly with guys, then someone has got to go. It's the same as nature. The strong survive."[791] Each player should strive to perform his role to the best of his ability. If he does, he should feel proud—even if he stands on the sideline and watches his team lose—because he did everything his team asked of him. Similarly, a team that prepares and plays well deserves praise, even if it loses a tight battle against a great opponent. Conversely, a team that wins a tight game against a weak opponent after preparing and playing poorly deserves criticism. Win or lose, each player should judge himself according to his preparation and performance relative to his potential and what his team asked of him.

If Patriots linebacker Willie McGinest wanted more than anything to win Super Bowl XXXIX, he would have been saddened by news that the Eagles' star receiver, Terrell Owens–who had missed many games following a fibula fracture and serious ankle injury forced doctors to drill a large syndesmotic screw through his fibula and tibia to stabilize the joint–would return for the Super Bowl. Instead, McGinest was happy to hear his opponent would have its star back:

> "That's great. We hope he does play. As a professional, this is our work. This is our job. We hate to see anybody with injuries. This is how we eat. This is how we provide. We hope he plays. We hope he's feeling fine. He's worked so hard in his career to get to this point."[792]

Safety Rodney Harrison answered "the T.O. question" similarly: "We want to see their best. You never want to go out there and see someone missing, regardless if it's on us or on them. We don't want any excuses. We're not going to give any excuses, and we don't want anyone else to make excuses. We expect Terrell Owens to be 100 percent."[793] Asked whether Eagles receiver Freddie Mitchell–who had disparaged Harrison a week earlier–would be "carried off in a stretcher," Harrison again displayed his emphasis on playing great, not on winning: "I hope not. I don't wish that on anyone… You never want anyone to get hurt."[794] Harrison proved that in a 2005 preseason game. After smacking his shoulder into Green Bay receiver Antonio Chatman so hard Chatman felt "tingling" in his arms and had to be carried off the field, Harrison–as Chatman lay on the ground–prayed for him. After visiting the Packers locker room and feeling relief seeing Chatman walking around, Harrison told reporters, "You never want to see anyone down. And I just felt really bad… The guys kind of cheered me up, saying, 'You're just playing football, Rod. Just keep playing.' It made me feel a little better, but the fact remained he got carried off on a cart, and you never want to see that."[795]

The greater the opponent, the greater the thrill of victory. When Tedy Bruschi sees his 2004 championship ring, he relishes the agony he experienced while striving to defeat the world's best football teams: "This symbolizes fighting to stay awake in meetings, pushing yourself in the weight room, sucking it up for those three-hour practices and going out and giving it everything you have on game day. I see all of that. I experience all of that. I hear the fans when I look at this. I smell the grass. All of that. It's all encapsulated into this ring."[796] Rodney Harrison emphasizes that it is a symbol of and reward for players' intense struggle to win: "It… signifies all the hard work and dedication that the guys put in as well as the coaches. To get something like this as a reward is very fulfilling."[797] "Guys know exactly what's behind this: blood, sweat, guts, sacrifice with your family, your kids. So many hours of hard work. So many years of sacrificing."[798] Players are rich enough to pay jewelers to design them gorgeous rings, but no player will ever see a ring as beautiful as one he earned. Linebacker Ted Johnson: "The rings are symbols of the effort that was put in and what we were able to accomplish. Having three of those puts you in pretty small company... The symbolism in the ring is what I enjoy the most."[799]

Players value their rings in proportion to the sweat they lost to earn them. After receiving his first Super Bowl ring, Rosevelt Colvin felt hollow because his fractured hip had prevented him from contributing much during his first season in New England, 2003. Tight end Benjamin Watson feels that same emptiness now after missing almost his entire 2004 rookie year with a knee injury: "We [injured players] will still get the hardware–the ring–but it'll mean something a little bit different to me, because I was hurt."[800]

Patriots love facing challenges and striving to overcome them. Linebacker Mike Vrabel says "we go out there... to win and to play up to our ability and our potential."[801] Tom Brady says "It's a tough battle, and it continues to be. That's one of the fun parts of success, that you can look back on all the tough experiences."[802] The process is fun only when the challenges are great. The Patriots don't enjoy beating up weak opponents. And they never relax because "it always is [competitive] in the NFL, and that's what we expect. In this league, if you are not ready to play your best football, any Sunday, any week, then you're probably not going to be happy with the result."[803]

Patriots love reaching down deep into their souls to rouse the courage and determination and spirit that enable them to achieve greatness. Linebacker Rosevelt Colvin says his fractured hip early in the 2003 season "was heartbreaking to me,"[804] but he stayed positive. Getting healthy became Colvin's new job, and he embraced it. Belichick advises players–whether they've just won a Super Bowl or fractured their hip–to strive to get better every day: "[Rosey] always had a positive attitude and worked very hard... He was in there every day working on his rehab... He had a smile on his face [and said], 'I'm going to work hard. I'm going to be back... You're having a great season, coach. The team is having a great year and I'm excited for them, but I'll be there next year.'"[805] Colvin continued rehabbing throughout the 2004 season, grimacing through pain and physical limitations. In 2005, he explained:

> "I don't have to push to get out of bed in the morning anymore. I don't have
> to get in the ice tub after every practice. I'm not limping in between every
> rep or trying to push through every rep. I can focus on football... Now, you
> don't have a guy that's out there not full-speed. The toughest part last year
> was getting to the point where I wasn't always sore pushing off the leg. It was
> so painful–so much discomfort–that I didn't want to do that. Certain moves I
> couldn't do. Certain stances, I couldn't line up in."[806]

After watching his teammates win Super Bowl XXXVIII, Colvin derived special satisfaction from torturing his body in 2004 and starting in Super Bowl XXXIX:

"I'm tickled... Everything that I had to go through to get myself back in the position of where I'm at today: the hard work I had to endure, the long hours, the ice tubs, the stiffness, not being able to play with my kids for two or three months. You have to thank the training staff, everything they've done and their knowledge of the situation. It shows you what hard work can do. You can come back from anything if you put your mind to it... It's a dream come true. I couldn't stop smiling after we beat Pittsburgh. On the bus and on the plane, when I thought about everything that happened last year and I thought back to where I came from and where we are."[807]

The only meaningful statistic is wins and losses

"We [won] by a single point, but that was just as good as winning by fifty."[808]
   – Patriots assistant coach Pepper Johnson on the 2001 Patriots' 17-16 triumph over the Jets

"Our goals are to be No. 1 at the end. That's really all that matters."[809]
   – Tom Brady

"I'm not even excited about [gaining 1,000 receiving yards in a season for the first time in my career]. I'm more excited about our [record]. We're 8-5, and that's the biggest issue that I'm dealing with right now."[810]
   – Troy Brown in 2001

"I've been starting since my rookie year here, for 10 years. ...I've done everything I can do and been every place I can be, the Super Bowl, the Pro Bowl, all that. All those years, the only thing that matters at the end of the day is winning the game."[811]
   – Patriots linebacker Willie McGinest

"Losing ain't fun. Every week we get to go out there and play hard and every week we've come out on top. That's very fun."[812]
   – Patriots running back Corey Dillon

"There's winning and then there's complete misery. I don't think there's any gray area."[813]
   – Patriots tight end Christian Fauria

"The most underrated stat in football is points scored. That's what it's all about, keeping the other team off the scoreboard. So any time they get in the red zone, we tighten down, they're not getting in. That's something that we take very seriously."[814]
   – Patriots defensive lineman Richard Seymour

"It was an uncharacteristically poor performance on special teams. We were basically responsible for [surrendering] 14 points, and that's the worst feeling in the world. Actually, it's the second worst feeling in the world. The worst would have been giving up those points and losing."[815]
– Patriots special teams captain Larry Izzo

"Just win, baby!" is the Oakland Raiders' motto. The Raiders even sell a shirt with that phrase translated into Mandarin to promote themselves in China, but Belichick's Patriots should own the trademark because all they do is find ways to win most every game. Belichick says football is simple: "This game comes down to points. There are a million stats out there, but the big one is points."[816] He actually walks around reminding players that "The team that scores more points will win."[817] Players understand. Cornerback Ty Law says "[Winning by] 3 points, 14 points, 2 points… it doesn't matter to us."[818]

In every situation—on and off the field—the Patriots do whatever gives them the best chance to win football games. Everything else is a distraction. Interceptions. Yardage. Margin of victory. Time of possession. Sacks. Journalists consider these important statistics, but Patriots know that only one statistic *really* matters: wins and losses. Cornerback Ty Law asks, "What do stats mean when you're sitting at home [not competing in the playoffs]?"[819] Linebacker Mike Vrabel agrees: "It doesn't matter who gets the sack or who gets the interception. That's the way we are around here. We have people that put personal gain aside to win. What matters most to everyone here is winning."[820] Asked what his 2004 team was doing well, Belichick answered: "Score more points than the… teams that we played. That is the bottom line. We have made a few more plays than our opponents have, and that is what the games are all about."[821] Patriots kicker Adam Vinatieri, a holdover from Bill Parcells' mid-90s Patriots, remembers "Parcells said 'Statistics are for losers.'"[822]

Winning games is the only real stat because, as tight end Christian Fauria says, "your team is going to be ultimately judged on how many Super Bowls you win."[823] Every Patriot has swallowed Belichick's Kool-Aid and been brainwashed into his "Just win, baby!" cult.

Patriots don't care about style points

"We don't have a bunch of glamor guys around here. All we do is win ballgames. We don't care about being pretty. We care about winning championships."[824]
– Patriots linebacker Tedy Bruschi

"What other team has been 24th on defense, 19th on offense, and #1 at the end?"[825]
– Denver Broncos head coach Mike Shanahan, on the 2001 Patriots

Football is about scoring more points than your opponent. Period. How you outscore your opponent is irrelevant. In a 12-0 victory over the Miami Dolphins on December 7, 2003, the Patriots defense outscored the Patriots offense 9-3. (Tedy Bruschi returned an interception for a touchdown, and Jarvis Green scored a safety by sacking the Dolphins' quarterback in his endzone.) Tom Brady wasn't embarrassed. He explained the offense's conservatism as follows: "There weren't many mistakes, and I think a lot of times we play to the score, and we were winning."[826] While the Dolphins were busy turning the ball over three times, the Patriots offense was squeezing the ball tight and punting a team record-tying eleven times.

Flashy but sloppy teams, like the 2001 St. Louis Rams, dominate time of possession and yardage but sometimes stumble by fumbling or throwing interceptions. The Rams are a thrilling team to watch, but a "boring" team like the Patriots can beat the Rams despite surrendering 427 yards while gaining only 267–as the Patriots did in Super Bowl XXXVI–if they put more points up on the scoreboard– as the Patriots did. The Rams marched up and down the field on the Patriots, but the Patriots won the February 2002 Super Bowl by not turning the ball over while causing three Rams turnovers–two interceptions and a forced fumble–and converting them into 17 of their 20 points.

Entering that game, the world knew that "The Rams Achilles' heel is turnovers."[827] The Rams' 44 turnovers "led" the league. As Rams running back Marshall Faulk said after the defeat, "I've said before that the only team that can beat the Rams is ourselves. You can't win a game turning the ball over three times and not forcing any yourself."[828] Instead of committing to reduce their fumbles and interceptions, the Rams seemed almost proud to win despite so many turnovers, as if to say, "We're so damn great, we'll keep handing you the ball and still kick your butt." Joe Theismann accurately pointed to hubris as the Rams' fatal flaw: "The offense is so cocky and arrogant that they feel like they don't have to adhere to the rules of football. Maybe during the regular season it isn't necessary, but it is in the playoffs."[829]

The Patriots are the anti-Rams. Winning is everything. They don't care about style points or margin of victory. In the 2001 regular season, the Patriots defense surrendered more yards (5,352) than the offense gained (4,882)... but the team scored 99 more points (371) than it surrendered (272). Most importantly, it won every game it needed to win, including the Super Bowl. Asked two seasons later what type of Super Bowl he expected against the Carolina Panthers, Patriots defensive lineman Richard Seymour said he didn't care as long as the Patriots won:

"It really doesn't matter. What matters is how we go out and play on Sunday. Once we get another ring on our finger, that's the only thing that matters. What type of game it's going to be or whether it's going to be a defensive struggle isn't that important. I really don't care if it's 3-0. As long as we get another ring on our finger is all that matters."[830]

Tennessee Titans defensive coordinator Jim Schwartz–who broke into the NFL as "Schwartzie," a number-crunching assistant and scout on Belichick's Cleveland Browns–inherited Belichick's philosophy:

> "One of the things I learned from Bill was he couldn't give a [expletive] about how many yards he allowed. Every year, look at where he's going to rank, and he's not usually going to be near the top. But he's always going to be near the top in points allowed. Always at the top in key areas. I took some of his philosophies and proved them mathematically."[831]

In young Jim Schwartz, Belichick found an eager disciple. Schwartz reminisces, "I remember listening to a Colts-Lions game on the radio, the Colts were up three points very late in game. They tried to punt against an 11-man rush and got the punt blocked for a touchdown. I was about 10 years old but still wondered, 'Why didn't they just take a safety?'"[832]

Belichick says "I don't think it's any secret that teams that turn the ball over a lot more than they take it away aren't going to win too many games."[833] So he will gladly sacrifice yards for turnovers. He'll run a more conservative offense to avoid turnovers. He'll run a more aggressive, risk-taking defense to create turnovers.

In 2003, for example, Belichick's Patriots were 2nd-best in the NFL in takeaways (with 41) and 7th-best in giveaways (with only 24). Overall, their +17 net turnovers ranked second behind the Kansas City Chiefs' +19. In 2004, they tied for 3rd-best in takeaways (with 36) but were 14th in giveaways (with 27) for an 8th-ranked +9 net turnovers. Over the Patriots' four-year period of dominance, they forced 38 more regular season turnovers than they surrendered, one behind the Jets. 38 net turnovers over 64 regular season games means the Patriots averaged .594 more turnovers per game than their opponents:

Team (2001-2004)	Net turnovers recovered	Team (2001-2004)	Net turnovers recovered
New York Jets	+39	Carolina	+1
New England	+38	Oakland	-7
Philadelphia	+32	Washington	-7
Tampa Bay	+27	Denver	-8
Kansas City	+21	Houston	-8
San Francisco	+17	Chicago	-11
Atlanta	+16	New York Giants	-15
Green Bay	+15	Cleveland	-16

Team (2001-2004)	Net turnovers recovered	Team (2001-2004)	Net turnovers recovered
Pittsburgh	+15	Cincinnati	-18
Seattle	+15	Detroit	-19
Tennessee	+12	Arizona	-25
Indianapolis	+11	Miami	-25
Jacksonville	+10	Minnesota	-27
New Orleans	+9	Buffalo	-32
San Diego	+9	Dallas	-33
Baltimore	+5	St. Louis	-46

Source: www.infoplease.com/ipsa/A0901317.html (2001); www.nfl.com/stats (2002-2004).

The Patriots gained an additional +18 net turnovers in the nine games of their three Super Bowl runs: +6 in 2001, +3 in 2003 and +10 in 2004. That's two more turnovers per playoff game than their opponents! The Patriots have +56 net turnovers from 2001-2004.

You might expect all teams to focus on winning, but individualism is a cancer in many locker rooms. The NFL's best all-time pass-catching running back, 14-year veteran fullback Larry Centers, says the Patriots win because they have their priorities straight:

> "I've been other places where winning isn't the No. 1 priority. It's not that way here. Winning is No. 1. You don't hear guys grumbling about contracts. You don't hear guys grumbling about schedules. The players on this team are committed to going out and doing whatever it takes to win football games. And that's the way it ought to be. I knew coming here would give me the best chance to win a championship and the Patriots organization didn't disappoint me one bit. Scott Pioli, Bill Belichick, Charlie Weis, they all have the same goal. It's a like-minded organization from top to bottom and that's why this organization's successful."[834]

As time is running out late in a game (or the first half), a defense protecting a lead often benefits by letting its opponent gain additional yards if doing so allows them to tackle the ball-carrier in-bounds–keeping the clock running–rather than let him escape to the sidelines–automatically stopping the clock. Conversely, teams losing late in a game are often better off getting out of bounds to stop the clock rather than gaining additional yards and risking getting tackled in-bounds. In such details, the Patriots play to win, not to look good.

Patriots don't care about reputations

"[Popularity]'s never been a huge priority. I don't think it affects the final score."[835]
– Bill Belichick

"Every Monday morning, we pick up the paper in the NFL and some games go a lot differently than how they were projected to go."[836]
– Bill Belichick

"We don't really care about what [respect] people give us... We have the attitude that we're going to go out there and take it. The only time you get respect is if you take it. That's all that matters is what the group of guys in our locker-room does and thinks."[837]
– Patriots linebacker Willie McGinest, asked whether the Pats were finally getting some respect

"Whatever we get out there [in Super Bowl XXXIX], we're gonna have to earn it."[838]
– Patriots running back Corey Dillon

Tom Brady personifies the Patriots' focus on winning and blindness to "reputation." Every year, three to six quarterbacks are drafted in Round 1 of the NFL draft, usually several near the top of Round 1. Brady was drafted in Round 6 because many questioned his arm strength, speed, and other "measurables" and because he never nailed down the Michigan starting job. He didn't star at Michigan because he overlapped with two future NFL quarterbacks, first Brian Griese and later Drew Henson:

> "[Scouts and NFL teams] didn't like his speed, said he didn't run fast enough. Second, he didn't look the part of a quarterback. Skinny upper body, not a lot of muscle, almost fragile. But the most damaging thing was that we didn't play him full time, that he was sharing the field with Drew Henson. That really hurt him. Brady was doing a super job for us, but this Henson was an unbelievable talent that the staff didn't want sitting on the bench. ... [Scouts] saw it is a sign that Brady wasn't good enough to win the job outright."[839]

Former Patriots quarterback Drew Bledsoe's initial impression of young Brady: "I just figured on him being a skinny, scrawny kid [with] a great attitude."[840] But the Patriots loved Brady's winning attitude: his heart, head, competitiveness, toughness, and charisma... traits that have helped him become this generation's Joe Montana. The Patriots knew that it's much easier to strengthen one's arm than one's character. After lifting weights religiously since the Patriots drafted him, Brady now has, according to Colts quarterback Peyton Manning, "a sneaky strong arm."[841]

Coaches also knew they could correct Brady's footwork that was so lousy in college that it scared off Seattle Seahawks coach Mike Holmgren.[842]

NFL personnel expert Gil Brandt says Brady's strengths were on display at Michigan but scouts overlooked them because they were obsessed with arm strength and stats:

> "What the pros didn't see was his confidence, his mental toughness. Football smarts. Those are difficult things to quantify. You don't pull out a scale or a measuring tape for that stuff. But his teammates at Michigan knew what he had. They responded to him on the field."[843]

Brady is not flashy, self-absorbed, or self-promoting, but reputations don't win football games... except in video games. Brady's all about winning and team. Running back J.R. Redmond found Brady inspirational: "Some guys just say the play. He makes you think we're about to do something big."[844] After Brady marched his offense downfield in 81 seconds to set up its first Super Bowl-winning field goal, wide receiver David Patten was astonished by Brady's knack for winning:

> "You can't say enough about that kid. He has a tremendous amount of confidence; he has led this team. Maybe he doesn't have the most impressive statistics, but it doesn't matter. The kid knows how to win; he knows how to motivate other players. My hat is off to the guy."[845]

It was *déjà vu* all over again after Brady marched the offense downfield in 68 seconds to win the February 2004 Super Bowl. As wide receiver Troy Brown said so eloquently:

> "There are still some critics who say, 'Well, he can't do this very well, and he's not too good at that.' Well, he's pretty good at winning Super Bowls, isn't he? And there are a lot of guys with the big arms and the mobility, and all that stuff, who don't have even one ring."[846]

Brady's teammates at Michigan had more respect and appreciation for Brady than outside observers and had already witnessed his trademark calmness under pressure. Michigan guard Steve Hutchinson said:

> "Tom is always–no matter if things are going good or bad–he's always the same. He makes sure everybody in the huddle is on the same page, and everybody respects him for that. Like when we were down at Penn State, when we had to score two touchdowns to win, his composure, he never lost it. It was: 'All right, guys. Here's what we have to do.'"[847]

Ty Law agrees: "I want to go out there with Tom Brady. With all due respect to [league co-MVPs for 2003] Steve [McNair] and Peyton [Manning], winning is the card that trumps everything."[848] Brady wins not with a barrage of 50-yard *Sports Center* highlight reel passes but by avoiding mental mistakes and throwing errors. Former Patriots assistant coach Steve Szabo says, "He really understands the game and what he's doing. He just doesn't throw a lot of errant balls, and it's balls with velocity and balls with a soft touch, but they are all where they need to be."[849]

Substance over style

"[Corey Dillon] runs hard, and I think guys respect that more than anything. You can't tell anything about a guy from the way [someone] walks or talks, but you can when they play, and this man plays hard."[850]
  – *Patriots tight end Christian Fauria*

"I don't really care [whether 'people realize how good we are']... We're just doing what we have been doing all year, and that is playing good football. It just so happens that we are in the Super Bowl now, and now all we have to do is play one more football game. ...What people think... we're really not into that."[851]
  – *Patriots linebacker Tedy Bruschi*

New York Giants head coach Tom Coughlin dominated the balloting of 354 current and former NFL players in the category of "worst coach."[852] Many Giants players despise Coughlin's arbitrary rules. For example, Giants players in 2004 had to tuck their helmets under their left arms during the National Anthem and were prohibited from wearing hats during meetings. Coughlin also ordered players to wear collared shirts, slacks, and dress socks at all times in hotels, even if briefly visiting a vending machine. An unnamed Giants player complained: "I'd rather worry about the playbook than how I look."[853] He should join the Patriots. Bill Belichick insists on what is important and disregards what is unimportant. Coughlin treats players like children: requiring them to arrive five minutes before a meeting. Giants who arrive "late"–which Coughlin defines as "less than five minutes early"–are fined. Patriots safety Eugene Wilson's college coaches–like Coughlin–held Wilson's extreme punctuality ("I was never late, but I am [quite] aware of the time"[854]) against him. Their lowered assessment of Wilson possibly caused him to slide into Round 2. *Boston Herald* reporter Michael Felger wrote:

"If [the Patriots] want their players in their seats at 8:55, that's when they schedule the meeting. Simple. They don't like lateness, naturally, which is why they made sure to schedule several pre-draft meetings with Wilson. He was on time to every one."[855]

Wilson is glad he's not a Giant: "I guess I'm in the right program here, because... you can actually be 30 seconds late."[856] In short, the Patriots treat players like adults and overlook occasional minor mistakes in areas that don't impact performance.

Bill Belichick is indisputably the worst-dressed coach in the NFL. On the sidelines some weeks, wearing just a gray hooded sweatshirt, Belichick looks like a homeless person or "The Emperor" from *Return of the Jedi*. Scott Pioli explains that his friend simply doesn't care about appearances: "As you can see by the way he dresses, he's not concerned about being polished. He doesn't spend a lot of time and energy playing to things that aren't important. He's just who he is."[857] Belichick pleads guilty: "There are only two things that anyone has: name and reputation. It's not style. I mean, look at me." When controversy raged after the NFL denied 49ers head coach Mike Nolan's request to wear a suit and tie–as his father had when he coached the 49ers–rather than NFL-sanctioned Reebok gear, the Patriots signaled Belichick's satisfaction with his gear: "Hey, when the president of the United States talks about [Belichick's] gray sweatshirt, you know it's a fashion trend."[858] One Super Bowl sweatshirt even now resides in The Pro Football Hall of Fame in Canton, OH. Bill's dad–Steve Belichick–believes Bill learned while growing up at the Naval Academy surrounded by Naval cadets that "You don't waste 10 minutes trying to figure out what kind of tie to wear."[859] Belichick reportedly now earns $4.2 million per season,[860] so what flashy sports car does he drive? A blue Volvo station wagon.[861] Phil Simms says, "[Belichick] just plods along. He's so not cool, he's hip."[862] Simms gives an example from Belichick's days as Giants defensive coordinator:

> "I can't explain how hard he worked. He was legendary. I mean, he'd pull out his exercise machine in front of the projector, and he'd be there exercising as he watched films. We kind of made fun of him. But that's Bill Belichick."[863]

Belichick's lack of style is a symptom of his wasting no time worrying about what people think of him:

> "You can be 16-0 and there will be people who hate you, just as you can be 0-16 and there will be some people who will defend you. That's always the way it's going to be. Knowing that, it's easier just to do your job and hope people like what they see. I don't think I can be 100 percent of what everyone wants me to be."[864]

Belichick even makes fun of himself. A year after winning Super Bowl XXXVI, he addressed a *New York Times* editorial to the winning coach of that day's Super Bowl. He advised: "800 million people will be watching you. Try to remember to fix your hair."[865] Asked about the transformation of his reputation from the 1990s to the 2000s, Belichick answered, "[Winning our upcoming game] is really what I am concerned about, not what somebody is calling me. I have heard plenty of those good and bad things. I can't really worry about that."[866]

Many Patriots fans, myself included, find Belichick's disregard for superficiality endearing. But Cleveland Browns fans and journalists found Belichick obnoxiously prickly and protective: "One Browns official said that Belichick's imperious manner and general aloofness antagonized season ticket-holders as much as the decision to move the team to Baltimore."[867] Belichick no longer spurns the media and fans, as he did his first year or two in Cleveland. He now sends Christmas cards to some reporters and calls on reporters by name at press conferences. He has matured over the past decade to be less defensive about sharing information about his team and himself because he appreciates that he is the public face of his team and that appearances are not completely irrelevant to the team's performance. He realizes that controversy and animosity over his unapproachability in Cleveland harmed his Browns.

Patriots executive Scott Pioli is a much flashier dresser than his friend Bill Belichick, but he shares Belichick's low regard for formality, prestige, glamor, and recognition: "It's about the team winning championships. If you're in this for the trappings of the game, you're in this for the wrong reasons. And that higher-profile garbage is part of the trappings."[868]

Patriots owner Robert Kraft was repeatedly warned against hiring Belichick in 2000 because of Belichick's poor communication skills while in Cleveland: "I had some people I respected a lot telling me what a mistake I was making. They sent me tapes of Bill doing press conferences in Cleveland. They spoke about his interpersonal skills."[869] Fortunately for New England, Kraft, like Belichick, is "not into lipstick and powder. I'm into substance, and substance is winning football games."[870] Kraft hired Belichick because Kraft trusted the man who coached the Browns to victory over his Patriots in the 1994 playoffs and coached his 1996 Patriots to the Super Bowl. Kraft judged Belichick on the quality coach he had become, not the reputation he acquired as a rookie head coach in 1991. Kraft didn't care what fans or reporters thought. He cares only about building a winning franchise, as Ted Johnson attests: "If you were paired with [Bob Kraft] in a golf tournament, you'd see how competitive he is. He is a winner. Everything he does is to win, whether it is business or not."[871]

BALANCE SHORT-RUN AND LONG-RUN OBJECTIVES

"Management always has to consider both the present and the future; both the short run and the long run. A management problem is not solved if immediate profits are purchased by endangering the long-range health, perhaps even the survival, of the company. ...[Management] has to make the enterprise capable of performance, growth, and change in the future."[872]
– *Management expert Peter Drucker*

"When you get good people who have a long term commitment and share your vision on how you want to do things, then good things can happen... When there isn't stability–whenever there is change–it's very disruptive to an organization. ...You really have to have a long view, and when you sign people, you have to fit it in a total system."[873]
– *Patriots owner Robert Kraft*

Impatience was a likely factor in the Buffalo Bills' relenting to the Patriots' demand for a 1st-round draft pick for quarterback Drew Bledsoe. Jerry Magee–a *San Diego Union-Tribune* football columnist since 1961–believes "New England gaining what it did for Bledsoe… could be classified with the team's 20-17 conquest of the St. Louis Rams in Super Bowl XXXVI."[874] Magee pointed out that 83-year-old Bills owner Ralph Wilson "wants a winner and he might not have too many more years to get one."[875] The Kraft-Belichick Patriots never act impulsively or impatiently: "We built this thing… so that year in and year out we have a good shot at making the playoffs."[876] With their long view, the Patriots take frequent advantage of other teams' impulsiveness and impatience.

Managers confront two time tradeoffs: 1) Change is disruptive, so you often must get worse to get better; and, 2) Investing in the future detracts from current performance. Bob Kraft realized this from the moment he purchased the Patriots. His goal–seemingly absurd when he stated it in August 1994–was to become the San Francisco 49ers: "Why not think big? …We don't just want to win a championship. We want to win lots of championships. And nobody exemplifies that better than the 49ers organization."[877] In the decade since, not only have the Patriots become the 49ers but the 49ers have become the Patriots. Dynasty to dust. Dust to dynasty. The exclamation point was added at Foxboro in the final game of the 2004 regular season, from which the victorious Patriots emerged 14-2 and the embarrassed 49ers skulked away 2-14. The Niners are now so bad that Vegas' Plaza hotel predicts they will win just 3½ games in 2005 in a weak NFC West.[878]

Don't panic if needed changes erode short-term performance

"You just jump in the water and start swimming… You are dealing with cap situations, roster formations as well as developing an attitude and a mentality of doing things the way you feel they need to be done [and] installing a system for evaluating players."[879]
– *Bill Belichick, on the challenges of taking over a new team*

After Belichick's Patriots went 5-11 in 2000 under their new head coach, many fans and journalists attacked Belichick as a hopeless loser of a head coach because he appeared to be repeating his lack of success–four losing seasons in five years–as the Cleveland Browns' head coach. The boos grew louder in early 2001 when the Patriots were 3½ minutes from starting 1-4. After the Miami Dolphins embarrassed the Patriots 30-10, the San Diego Chargers came to Foxboro and led by ten points until the Patriots scored twice in the final 3:31 and again in overtime. With the team lucky to be 2-3, no one was thinking Super Bowl. But Patriots owner Bob Kraft knew Belichick had implemented many personnel and managerial changes that would eventually strengthen the team and translate into victories, so he did not panic after Belichick's Patriots lost 14 of their first 20 games. Kraft had also stayed in the background four years earlier when new coach Pete Carroll's defending AFC champions lost five of seven games following a strong start:

> "It was suggested to me that I fire the coach or trade the quarterback... There's a tendency for people to make quick, short-term decisions. My job is to sit back and stay cool. This is a highly emotional business. It's extremely fulfilling when things are going well, and very draining when they aren't. As the person ultimately responsible for the franchise, I can't get caught up in that. Instead of making a passing comment in the heat of the moment, I wanted to stay cool and make the right evaluation at the end of the year. I wanted to eliminate off-field distractions—including me—and let the product speak for itself."[880]

The 2001 team's gutsy come-from-behind win over the Chargers demonstrated their new intensity and willpower. Afterwards, Tom Brady said of his third game as starting quarterback: "That shows a Patriot team that is fighting, fighting and fighting."[881] That victory showcased a new Patriots quarterback soaking up the Patriots' outstanding coaching and applying it on the field. Offensive coordinator Charlie Weis realized following that game, "Whoa, [Brady] has a chance of doing something special!" because:

> "We had practiced all week long against a specific blitz that San Diego had been running against multiple wide receiver sets. We had told him that if this look comes up, we want him to check [to a different play] and have Patton run an 'out go.' The first play that we had the ball in overtime there is the look. [He]'s a kid, it's his first year playing, the team is [below] .500, he just played a few games, and there is the look. And sure enough he checks off to the 'out go' to Patton, throws about 50 yards down the field. They tackle Patton for a pass interference, we kick a field goal three plays later and end up winning the game and going on to win the Super Bowl."[882]

Bob Kraft appreciated that first-year coaches face daunting challenges and must be supported—not criticized or dumped—if they have a plan for winning but their early tenure goes poorly due to forces beyond their control. Change is disruptive and costly. Because performance often slips while changes are being implemented, a long-term performance boost usually requires a short-term performance dip. Kraft was wise (and gutsy) to be so patient.

Belichick's 2000 Patriots surrendered more points than they scored. There were many reasons for their poor performance:

- Transitioning to a new playbook, new coaches, and a new culture. The culture certainly needed changing: "In the late 1990s, former Patriots cornerback Jimmy Hitchcock said that there was a hierarchy within the team where stars and high-salaried players hung out with others of the same ilk. There were cliques."[883]

- Lousy drafts in 1997, 1998, and 1999, and a mediocre draft in 2000 (aside from diamond-in-the-rough Tom Brady who rode the bench in 2000 but led the team to a Super Bowl victory in 2001) left the team with only a handful of quality NFL players. *The Eagle-Tribune* called them "the kind of drafts that keep sports radio in business."[884]

- Dramatic personnel change. Many players were unfamiliar with one another and needed to learn to play together.

- Belichick was forced to cut many good players, like wide receiver Shawn Jefferson, because the Patriots had overspent in the late 1990s—handing out giant signing bonuses whose salary cap impact was spread over the length of each contract—and needed to underspend during Belichick's early seasons to escape "Salary Cap Jail."

- Replacing high-priced veterans with a mix of inexpensive veterans and younger players with less experience but greater potential initially hurts performance. Like many teams in "rebuilding years," the 2000 Patriots sacrificed wins to "invest" playing time in the future performance of new players. Belichick generally runs a meritocracy but makes one exception… he favors promising younger players because playing them—rather than veterans—lets them accumulate experience that improves team performance tomorrow. In 2004, Belichick explained his philosophy:

  > "We have kept the players that performed the best. …[But] You always reach a point with a younger player who is ascending and an older player whose play may be declining a little bit and where those paths/intersections cross, or if they cross, or maybe you think that they will cross and you have to make a determination on that, that is a little bit of a different story."[885]

In short, the Patriots were "under renovation" and "under new management" in 2000. Rather than allow the team's complacent star-driven culture to continue, Belichick overhauled the team, bringing in team-oriented and hard-working but unsung veterans, developing younger players and shrinking the payroll to pay down accumulated debt and lay a foundation for success.

First, clean up the mess

"When we started to [reshape the Browns], we knew the kind of player we wanted: Winners. Quality people. Leaders. ...With the guys we brought in, we're hoping some of what they've got rubs off on people, mixes in well and then, boom, you've got something."[886]

— New Cleveland head coach (and former Patriots defensive coordinator) Romeo Crennel, who has been busily overhauling personnel

When Belichick and Pioli took over in early 2000, they discovered their predecessors (coach Pete Carroll and VP of player personnel Bobby Grier) had gone on a wild spending spree and stuck them with the bill. Even worse, they had squandered the money and draft picks. Only fourteen players wearing Patriots uniforms in 1999 contributed at all to the 2001 Super Bowl season.[887] Of those fourteen, three (Brown, Bruschi, and Milloy) became free agents in early 2000 before Belichick and Pioli re-signed them and two (Bledsoe and Glenn) contributed only minimally in 2001. The new regime scrounged up well over 40 NFL-caliber players in 2000 and 2001. And only eight players from the 1999 Patriots contributed to the 2003 Super Bowl season.[888]

Eliminating players who were popular with fans and teammates and insisting that other players take pay cuts–as Belichick did–was obviously painful and upsetting... not an obvious formula for building team chemistry. But getting under the NFL salary cap required substantial slashing because the Patriots had led the league in payroll from 1997 through 1999[889] and were stuck with a bloated salary cap. The Patriots' late-1990s payroll far exceeded the cap because the team was handing out lavish signing bonuses. The Patriots had been able to spend more cash than the official salary cap figure because salary cap accounting treats a signing bonus as if that cash were paid in equal annual installments over the contract's lifetime. But every dollar a team hands out in signing bonuses is a dollar it must underspend in future years. For example: if a player signs a five-year contract, only one-fifth of his signing bonus counts against the team's current-year cap figure, but another fifth counts in each of the following four years.

Signing bonuses restrict a team's future payroll as surely as buying a car on an installment plan or a house with a mortgage restricts a family's disposable income. Late 1990s signing bonuses larded the Patriots' salary cap in the early Belichick years with many millions of dollars of "dead money," i.e., salary cap space unavailable to pay current players because it was spent during the Carroll/Grier years and allocated to the Belichick/Pioli years. Cutting players who received those large signing bonuses offered no panacea because those players' not-yet-amortized signing bonuses accelerate, for salary cap purposes, to the season they are cut. The "ghost of signing bonuses past" forced Belichick's Patriots to drop their payroll substantially below the salary cap.

When Belichick took over, just 36 Patriots' salaries (of their 53-player roster) exceeded the salary cap by $10.5 million, yet "the roster showed scant signs of promising young talent."[890] By June 2000, Belichick was able to joke, "We're about twenty bucks under the ($57-million cap) limit."[891] Getting there was painful. One Patriots coach euphemistically termed the bloodletting "a large graduation class."[892] The Patriots slashed payroll to 29th in the NFL in both 2000 and 2001 and 26th in 2002.[893]

The Patriots used 2000 to escape "Salary Cap Jail" and carve out training and playing time for young players who would help win a Super Bowl in 2001: Tom Brady, Matt Chatham, Kevin Faulk, Antwan Harris, Tebucky Jones, Patrick Pass, Lonie Paxton, J.R. Redmond, Greg Robinson-Randall, Grey Ruegamer, Jermaine Wiggins, and Damien Woody. They also signed some low-cost veteran free agents who would contribute to the 2001 championship season: Grant Williams (March); Bobby Hamilton (July); Otis Smith (August); and Joe Andruzzi (September). They worked hard to bring in high-character veterans who knew Belichick's system and could build a professional team culture:

> "Having a veteran presence, particularly with players who understood our system and understood how we do business and how all of the football operation runs—guys like Brian Cox, Anthony Pleasant, Rick Lyle—those were some critical guys who were in place to get things started."[894]

Before the 2001 season, the Patriots continued cleaning house and brought in 23 low-cost free agents, 17 of whom contributed to the Patriots' Cinderella season.[895] Fourteen contributed substantially, despite being virtually anonymous signings at the time and receiving an average annual compensation of just $865,232, far below the 2001 average NFL player's compensation of $1,100,500, the average starter's compensation of $1,799,047, and the average 2001 unrestricted free agent compensation of $1,389,300.[896] The Patriots basically signed fourteen starters and paid them backup money:

Player	Position	Month signed	Avg. annual compensation
Larry Izzo	Special teams	March	$525,750

Mike Vrabel	LB	March	$1,766,667
Anthony Pleasant	DL	March	$1,575,000
Terrance Shaw	CB	March	$1,750,000
Marc Edwards	FB	March	$567,500
David Patten	WR	April	$580,000
Damon Huard	QB	April	$700,000
Mike Compton	OL	April	$1,433,333
Antowain Smith	RB	June	$500,000
Terrell Buckley	WR	July	$500,000
Je'Rod Cherry	Special teams	July	$477,000
Bryan Cox	LB	July	$800,000
Roman Phifer	LB	August	$520,000
Ken Walter	P	October	$418,000

Avg. annual compensation calculated from chart in: John Clayton, "Patriots shopping spree pays off," ESPN, 20 December 2001, http://espn.go.com/nfl/columns/clayton_john/1298726.html.

This was a motley collection of unwanted "street" free agents, most of whom signed for close to the NFL minimum. When the Seattle Seahawks signed Patriots defensive tackle Chad Eaton, Eaton received a $3.5 million signing bonus. The Patriots paid a total of $2.123 million in signing bonuses to *all* their 2001 free agents.[897] The largest bonus ($625,000) went to guard Mike Compton, whose former team–the Detroit Lions–was about to go 2-14 in 2001 but didn't even make him an offer.[898] The second-largest bonus–Damon Huard's–was only $375,000. Personnel experts around the league actually wondered whether Belichick and Pioli had lost their sanity: "Pioli allowed that, during the offseason, some of his friends in the personnel community called him to ask if he and Belichick knew what they were doing with some of their acquisitions."[899]

But the Patriots' apparent madness was brilliance. They did not confuse salary with value and believed character was an underpriced commodity in the free agent market. In Cleveland, Pioli and Belichick had watched in agony as players' bad attitudes defeated their efforts to build the Browns into a winner. Belichick said in August 2001, "We really looked for [high-character] kinds of guys. It can make a difference. We brought in some solid people."[900] Quarterback Drew Bledsoe quickly noticed the winning attitude brought by the new crop of Patriots: "The guys we signed seem to bring not only some talent, but some attitude, some leadership qualities."[901] After that season culminated in an improbable Super Bowl victory, Belichick explained their thinking:

> "We just didn't have the flexibility or the cap space and resources to be able to go out and sign the (big-ticket) players. I think the players that we did sign are good players; they're guys that have worked hard, have some experience, are team players, are unselfish and they've molded well with the young players that we've drafted and some of the experienced Patriots players."[902]

With hindsight, *Providence Journal* reporter Tom Curran believes "The Pats' 2001 free-agent class of castoffs and underutilized players like David Patten, Antowain Smith, Mike Vrabel and Roman Phifer was quite likely the best crop since free agency came into being."[903] Even before his team lost the Super Bowl, St. Louis Rams general manager Charley Armey declared, "Unbelievable. For some reason, the chemistry of all these guys melded with what they already had."[904] *Boston Globe* sportswriter Ron Borges was similarly dazzled:

> "The first problem Belichick had to overcome was the mess he inherited...
> The Patriots' salary cap situation was atrocious and so was the roster.
> Somehow he and personnel director Scott Pioli lessened the cap problem
> while reconstructing the roster through adept drafting and careful shopping
> in the free agent market."[905]

One series against the New York Jets in early 2002 epitomizes the Patriots' ability to extract performance from other team's unwanteds: "[Jets quarterback] Testaverde was sacked on consecutive plays by the former Jets Bobby Hamilton, Rick Lyle and Anthony Pleasant. And on the next possession... [former Jet Victor] Green had his interception [that he ran back for a touchdown]."[906]

Shrewd personnel decisions–especially the focus on character–helped the Patriots win the 2001 Super Bowl with a minimal payroll. By 2003, the Patriots had busted out of "Salary Cap Jail," and their payroll ballooned to $74.7 million, 10th in the league.[907]

The culture transplant Belichick and his assistants performed was a huge and underappreciated factor in the team's long-term success. A reporter dubbed 2001's training camp and preseason "Camp Doom and Gloom" following the death of quarterbacks coach Dick Rehbein, wide receiver Terry Glenn and linebacker Andy Katzenmoyer both going AWOL, and the surprise retirement of newly-signed guard Joe Panos, a projected starter. But players kept plugging away, both because Belichick had assembled a team of mentally tough players and because they bought into his philosophy of self-reliance, staying positive, ignoring distractions and focusing on only what they could control, *etc.* By early August, Belichick had already instilled much of the mental toughness his 2001 team would show the world in winning that season's Super Bowl. Receiver Charles Johnson said:

> "As long as I've been playing in the league, I can't ever remember being with
> a team that went through such a tough stretch. It's just been one thing after
> another. But I know these two things: In this league, no one feels sorry for
> you, so there's no sense feeling sorry for yourself. And, second, no matter
> what happens, you've got to find a way to keep moving on."[908]

Don't sacrifice tomorrow for today

"We try to put something in place that is there for the long term. There are no 'quickies.'"[909]
   – Patriots owner Robert Kraft

"Free agency is a little like having a credit card. You can only run up the bill so high. At some point, you have to pay those bills. You can keep borrowing, but we've seen teams in this league who have those bills come in and it's a big hit, a crash."[910]
   – Bill Belichick

"On Wall Street, they're in the business of making money between now and next Thursday. ...We want to build a company that will still be here 50 and 60 years from now."[911]
   – Costco CEO Jim Sinegal, responding to criticism that Costco is too generous to customers and employees

"[Miami] fans should expect a dominant organization and team, long-term, that will be a consistent winner. That doesn't address what next year's team will be like. If we compromise the future of the franchise, relating to the salary cap and draft picks, we might be able to win a game or two more next year. But we might not be able to be a consistent, winning team long-term."[912]
   – Belichick confidante Nick Saban, former LSU head coach and new Miami Dolphins head coach

A critical decision the 2004 Patriots made was not placing receiver Deion Branch on injured reserve. They could have freed up a roster spot that might have helped them over the 7½ games Branch missed. Instead, Branch returned, sparked the Patriots' playoff offense and ended the season with Super Bowl MVP honors. Though Belichick never wants his players looking beyond their upcoming game, as head coach, Belichick must balance immediate and longer-term concerns.

The only thing harder than winning a Super Bowl is winning multiple Super Bowls. As Intel's Andy Grove points out: "If it is hard to make a success out of something, it is an order of magnitude harder to sustain the success."[913]

Belichick and Pioli quickly decided against the "easy" way to "save" salary cap money. Many NFL teams restructure contracts by turning salary–which counts against the salary cap in the year it's paid–into signing bonuses–which are prorated over the term of the player's contract in cap calculations. The Patriots didn't want to boost short-term performance by saddling the team with "dead money" long into the future:

"We could have restructured deals and made [existing contracts] more workable under the cap. All that does, though, is push your money problems out to future years, rob Peter to pay Paul. But we decided from the start, we weren't walking in here for the short term, trying to turn things around in a matter of minutes and, in so doing, perpetuate those financial problems."[914]

Instead, the Patriots simply cut, or did not re-sign, many of the team's high-paid players in 2000 or 2001,[915] some for performance or attitude reasons and others for financial reasons:

"We would have loved to keep Shawn Jefferson, but the numbers just didn't work for us. ...We loved Chad Eaton as a player, as a person. We wanted him on our football team, but he had an opportunity [to sign a four-year, $10.7 million contract with the Seahawks] that was something we felt we couldn't do because we felt it would have an impact on the entire football team."[916]

After winning a Super Bowl, the Patriots resisted using Enron-Worldcom accounting to pump up spending to keep their team intact for another run at a Super Bowl. Some teams load up for one or two strong years and then starve themselves. Instead of 'yo-yo' or 'binge-and-purge' dieting, the Patriots stuck with their goal of fielding a championship-caliber team each season. Belichick says his Patriots "try to be consistent, not to... have this one big year and the next year we know we're going to pay the price."[917]

Bob Kraft is also in business for the long term. He's a strong advocate of bringing football back to L.A. because "we're losing an entire generation of fans."[918] More tellingly, as owner of the NFL's only dynasty, Bob Kraft could make far more money by scrapping the NFL's revenue sharing arrangement because, as he notes, "No other business punishes you for success the way the National Football League does."[919] Nevertheless, when revenue sharing renewal came before NFL owners in 2004, Kraft led the charge to extend it. He argued that revenue sharing's continuation is in the long-term interest of all teams, even though it reduces the short-term profit of some teams, including the Patriots:

"If we didn't continue [revenue sharing], we, the New England Patriots, would be in good shape, because we are a larger market team. But I think the strength of this league is the revenue sharing. Selfishly, if we didn't keep this going it would have been good for us financially in the short run. But I think it would be bad for the league, and therefore it would be bad for the Patriots long-term. So I'm happy we kept that in place."[920]

In fact, according to NFL commissioner Paul Tagliabue, Kraft decided to become an NFL owner in part because he knew revenue sharing created a solid foundation for a strong league: "Robert... has said many times that it is one of the major reasons he bought the team. He knows that for the league to thrive all franchises must be strong and have the ability to compete. It's the philosophy that has been the foundation of the NFL's success."[921]

Another example: the Patriots masterfully stockpile picks for future drafts. They have repeatedly traded current-year draft picks to a team desperate to improve their team immediately for better draft picks the following year. For example, the Patriots traded their 2003 3rd-rounder for Miami's 2004 2nd-rounder. By patiently deferring gratification a year, the Patriots get a substantially better player. They occasionally get two picks for one, as they did by trading their 2003 1st-round pick for the Baltimore Raven's 2003 2nd-round pick and 2004 1st-round pick. The 2003 2nd-rounder became starting safety Eugene Wilson. With the Ravens' 2004 pick, the 21st in that draft, the Patriots landed a superior player–defensive lineman Vince Wilfork–whom many draftniks expected to be grabbed in the Top 10 and one of four players Belichick considered trading up for. Wilfork is a huge addition, both figuratively and physically, whom the Patriots could never have selected with their own pick: 32nd and last in Round 1, due to their Super Bowl victory. Though a rookie, Wilfork played many snaps in 2004 and was a key contributor to the team's third Super Bowl victory.

A major reason the Patriots have been willing to defer gratification–and benefit from other teams' desperation–is the organization's stable leadership. NFL coaches and general managers live under microscopes, scrutinized by owners and fans. In some cities, pressure to win is so intense that coaching your team into the playoffs each season isn't enough. You're expected to win the Super Bowl. Inflated expectations leave coaches and GMs desperate to strengthen their teams immediately. Like CEOs, many NFL coaches and general managers whose jobs are in jeopardy often recklessly sacrifice their team's future in hopes of saving their endangered jobs. Former Packers GM Ron Wolf complains about the Wall Street-like pressure for instant results:

> "You can't blame coaches. This is a two-year league now. Never thought I would say that, but that's how sad it is. Do it quickly or you are fired and someone else is brought in. There is no thought to development of teams. It is quick fix, do it right away. So now you have people playing not to lose. John Paul Jones once said, 'He who will not risk cannot win.' It's not that way anymore with the NFL."[922]

The Patriots' stability and patience make them one of the few teams able to give away something today to get more back tomorrow.

Yet another example of how the Patriots prepare for the long term is their conscious effort to stock their roster with a mix of youngsters, prime-age players, and veterans:

> "You want... older players... in the prime of their careers, in that three to eight-year range. And then you want some younger players. There is going to

be some type of a circulation of those guys. The younger ones are going to step up, and they are going to get into the prime of their careers. And guys that are in their prime are going to move to closer to the end. And then there are guys that eventually their careers are going to end. And, I think that is a healthy flow for your team."[923]

Age balance yields three benefits: 1) Players of different ages complement one another. Older players mentor younger players and improve their performance, while younger players generally possess superior physical talent and energy and are less susceptible to injury. 2) Involving younger players sets your team up for sustained success and builds "institutional memory." Relying heavily on veterans risks a rash of injuries or retirements that devastate team talent and destroy team chemistry and culture. And, 3) Age balance helps players perceive a career trajectory and think long-term about their careers, which should encourage them to take better care of their bodies.

A perfect example of the value of age balance is how quickly Eugene Wilson– a rookie in 2003 who had never previously played safety, even in preseason–became a superb safety. The Patriots threw Wilson into the fire after releasing Lawyer Milloy just days before the start of the 2003 season. Belichick and Crennel moved Wilson to safety in desperation in Week 2 after the Patriots lost 31-0 in Week 1. Opposing teams often exploit a rookie, especially a rookie playing a position he has never before played. But the Patriots are 34-3 with Wilson as their starting safety. Wilson's development benefited from veteran Rodney Harrison manning the other safety position and veterans Ty Law and Tyrone Poole playing cornerback: "Guys like Rodney Harrison and Ty Law are still teaching me things when they see something I might be doing wrong."[924] Another example is the help veteran tight end Christian Fauria has given young tight end Daniel Graham.

Belichick also wants a balanced staff of assistant coaches. He expects his assistants to learn and improve and be promoted within his system whenever possible and outside his system whenever necessary. It is not possible for his coordinators to become the Patriots' head coach, so Belichick recommends them for coaching openings elsewhere. Belichick won't selfishly constrain an assistant's career, and he can recover from the loss of any assistant because he constantly grooms talent at all levels so talented assistants are prepared to fill coaching vacancies, just as backup players step up when starters are injured. The prospect of promotions helps engage everyone.

PREPARE FOR DECISIONS

"The ability to make good decisions comes from being prepared."[925]
– *Bill Belichick*

"Bill and Scott go into the draft and there's not a lot left to uncertainty and chance. They go over it in great detail. They're very businesslike, not haphazard. It's not... 'Let's spin the wheel [and take a] chance.'"[926]
  – Jonathan Kraft

"Each individual–all of us on the football team, coaches and players–are responsible and accountable for what we do. There is some guidance at times. [But] you can't legislate or monitor every single second of every person's day. So we all have to make decisions and judgments. Sometimes we make good ones, sometimes we make not so good ones. But we try to make the best ones we can for ourselves, our team, and our organization."[927]
  – Bill Belichick

Time is a coach's scarcest commodity. Countless problems fall into the head coach's lap, and many issues get addressed only if he ensures that someone addresses them. And coaches are teachers as well as decision-makers. A head coach must allocate his time and the time of his assistants and players. Which issues are worth worrying about? Which issues can be ignored today? When do we need to stop analyzing and make a decision? Coaches must worry about the most important issues, ask the essential questions, and do the highest-productivity activities.

A head coach can't possibly decide everything, so he must equip his assistant coaches and players to make smart decisions. Many games are won or lost by players' decisions during games. Smart coaches worry constantly about preparing those around them to make intelligent decisions because, as linebacker Mike Vrabel explains, what looks great as Xs and Os on chalkboards breaks down as a football play unfolds: "People think that Bill Belichick is over there with a joystick putting guys in the right spot. We have guys that can go out there and instinctively make football plays."[928] Defensive line coach Pepper Johnson agrees:

> "People figure, 'Oh, Tedy is getting that interception and running it back for a touchdown because Coach Belichick put him in a position to do that.' It's not that easy. We could sit up there and spend hours trying to teach the guys one thing [but] if he doesn't see it on the field, react, and make it happen personally, that's what separates the elites and the average guys."[929]

Here's an example. In the 2004 AFC Championship Game at Pittsburgh, Patriots nose tackle Vince Wilfork decided he could beat the combo block double-team he was receiving from Steelers center Jeff Hastings and a guard–who were twisting him sideways–by attacking Hastings aggressively rather than waiting for them to attack him, as the Patriots usually expect Wilfork to: "I saw [Hastings] was vulnerable to power. I thought, 'Just let me go and get to his chest and see what happens.' So I got into his chest."[930] Wilfork's innovation worked so successfully–a smiling Wilfork explained–that Hastings got upset: "He finally said to me, 'If you're going to bull [rush] me every time, our running backs will [illegally] cut [block] you.' I said, 'Let them cut me then.'"[931] The better trained a player is in various tactics and techniques, the more likely he is to improvise successfully during a game.

Because much of Belichick's time is spent training players to make smart decisions, he loves guys like linebacker Tedy Bruschi who make him look good:

> "[Tedy] is a smart player who just instinctively seems to do everything right in the right situation… You can't go over every single thing that happens, so [I love that]–when something comes up–he almost always does the right thing. He just knows how to play. He knows when to play with power. He knows when to try to slip people in the pass rush. He knows when to try to tackle a guy low, when to go for the big hit, when to make the play against the Colts when he stripped the guy on the screen pass."[932]

Know your options

"Right after the season–after a little time passes–we get together collectively as a coaching staff and myself and we spend time evaluating players, what was good, what wasn't good and what we need to improve on."[933]
– Scott Pioli, Patriots VP of player personnel

In the 2004 NFL Draft, the Patriots surprised most Patriot-watchers by using all eight draft choices and trading none of them. Most years, Belichick and Pioli "invest" several mid- or low-round picks by trading them to teams desperate enough to offer picks a round higher the following year, usually average-to-poor teams whose draft position will be substantially higher than the Patriots'. In 2004, the Patriots didn't bother because they knew the 2004 draft was strong and the 2005 draft would be weak. By April 2005, it was abundantly clear how weak the draft class was: "One NFL source said Friday night that if [Vince] Wilfork [whom the Patriots took at #21 in 2004] was in the 2005 draft, he would have been a top-five selection."[934] In both 2003 and 2005, the Patriots postponed gratification because they had scouted college players and knew the next draft would contain more attractive players. So they traded picks in weak drafts for higher selections in stronger drafts. They now own three extra picks, in the 3rd, 4th and 5th rounds of the 2006 NFL Draft:

· The Ravens' 3rd rounder, acquired along with the Ravens' 2005 3rd rounder (Ellis Hobbs) and the Ravens' 2005 6th rounder (which the Patriots later traded) in exchange for the Patriots' 2005 2nd round pick

· The Lion's 4th rounder (which should be high), acquired for the Patriots' 5th and 6th round picks in 2005

· The Raiders' 5th rounder, acquired along with a 2005 7th rounder (which became Matt Cassel) in exchange for the Patriots' 2005 6th round pick

Also, before the weak 2005 draft, the Patriots traded a 3rd-round pick for cornerback Duane Starks–the 10th player chosen in the 1998 draft and a starter on the Baltimore Ravens' Super Bowl XXXV championship team–whom, Scott Pioli later said, was better than anyone still available in Round 3 when they would have selected.

The quality of the current draft class and next year's draft class are crucial variables the Patriots consider. Knowing their options enables them to use each draft pick optimally, whether that means drafting a player, trading the pick for future picks or trading the pick for a veteran player. In financial terms, the Patriots are informed enough to "arbitrage" their draft picks, trading them for whatever maximizes the value of those picks.

Gather information systematically

"Our grading system… evaluate[s] certain characteristics in every football player: their physical ability, their competitiveness, and so forth. Then, we do it specifically [by position], say for a defensive lineman, his ability to play the run, to rush the passer, to pursue, his ability to play on his feet and stay off the ground, his tackling. So, when you add all that up, you have an athlete… Then you look at his playing. Maybe… this guy is not that great of a physical athlete but he's a really good player or vice versa."[935]
– *Bill Belichick*

The Patriots begin spring draft preparations a year in advance. After one NFL draft concludes, scouts draw up a list of 4,000 potential draftees in the next draft.

The Patriots overlook no one. They drafted tight end Andy Stokes from William Penn… not UPenn or Penn State but the Oskaloosa, Iowa school that compiled a 3-8 record playing against religious colleges in the Mid-States Football Association. Heading into the 2004 season, the news was grim for Stokes' team: "The 2004 William Penn football schedule is a killer… Early predictions indicate five Penn opponents this season will be ranked."[936] Wow! Michigan? USC? Oklahoma? Miami? Not exactly. The teams are "ranked" by the Olathe, Kansas-based NAIA, whose 2004 champion and 2005 preseason #1 is Helena, Montana's Carroll College Saints. The fearsome "ranked" teams threatening William Penn were St. Xavier, Trinity International, Olivet Nazarene, McKendree and St. Ambrose.[937] Pow! "Add to that… Drake University on Sept. 11 and the clincher…a road trip to Southern Illinois… That is a tough schedule!"[938] William Penn lost to all those "ranked" teams and to perennial powerhouses SIU-Carbondale, Drake and Quincy. When your scariest competitor sounds like a snack cake manufacturer and you still manage just a 3-8 record, it's truly a miracle the Patriots know you exist, which is why a Cleveland Browns coach once told Stokes, "You have about a one-in-one-million chance of getting drafted from here."[939]

Stokes couldn't make the Patriots' roster. Looking good against Olivet Nazarene is easier than playing well against the Colts and Steelers. But Belichick speaks with indisputable credibility when he says, "We go to every school. There aren't very many schools that we don't scout."

After preparing their list, they research each player to assign him–by June 1–a provisional grade: "A" for a Round 1 to 3 selection; "B" for a Round 4 to 7 selection; and "C" for potentially useful players unlikely to be drafted. These provisional grades are used to allocate scouts' time, especially national scouts'. Using three overlapping sets of geographically-focused scouts–area, regional and national– plus position scouts and position coaches ensures that each prospect worthy of further consideration is evaluated by many eyes: "If a[n area] scout gives a player a good grade, that could push them to a regional scout or somebody who's responsible for that position. Players then go from being scouted by somebody in an area to being cross-checked by somebody with broader responsibility. Ultimately, if the player has a grade that's high enough, they may be seen by the Director [of Scouting] or one of the people more responsible for seeing the top-rated players."[940] Scouts are on the road more than half the year, writing up player reports that the organization reads not just before the draft but also later, if a player becomes a free agent.

The system standardizes evaluation criteria and reporting terms so Belichick and Pioli can grasp each scout's opinions and rationale and compare the opinions of all scouts. Scouts sign their reports and are held accountable for evaluations of players who become Patriots. Because scouts are asked to evaluate only a player's suitability to New England's system–not the player's generic "talent" level–they are not punished if a player they rated poorly becomes a star elsewhere or if a player they loved flops elsewhere.

For the same reasons the Patriots hire professional, passionate players, they seek the same traits in their scouts. The Patriots' player evaluations are so good, says Director of College Scouting Tom Dimitroff, Jr., because "There's an unspoken energy and rule about the commitment and approach here. People know that to work here, in New England, you can't glide through this. We have such diligent, hard-working scouts. Our scouts get after it. Everyone is passionate about the game."[941] Patriots scouts dig for facts, assigning numerical grades to every aspect of a player's physical makeup, mental makeup, and on-field performance. Their fact-rich reports must include strong opinions, never vague, hedging speculation or unsubstantiated opinions. Belichick wants as many facts as possible because:

> "When you bring a player into a team, you bring all that comes with him. You bring his attitude, his speed, strength, mental toughness, quickness. Our evaluation is comprehensive. Scott Pioli and the scouting department do a great job of getting a lot of details by going into the history of a player, his mental and physical makeup as well as attitude and character. He eventually receives one grade and that establishes his overall value to the team."[942]

Anticipate and prepare for every possible scenario

"Coach prepares us for every little thing. We never go into a game not expecting a situation. We go over every situation, every little thing in practice."[943]
– Patriots defensive lineman Dan Klecko

"I've got total confidence in [Belichick] and the rest of the coaching staff. I wouldn't want to play for anyone else… Every week we go into a game we are as prepared as anybody, and we always feel we have somewhat of an edge."[944]
– Patriots special teams captain Larry Izzo

Bill Belichick says, "I know a team is prepared when everyone knows what every player should do in a certain situation."[945] Well, he must have known his 2003 squad was prepared because *Boston Globe* reporter Dan Shaughnessy wrote, "At times, it looked as if they had 11 coaches on the field."[946] Though I wasn't playing, I was a nervous wreck during the Patriots' game-winning drive of Super Bowl XXXVI. So was Tom Brady's dad: "My cardiologist loves this stuff. He says, 'I hope this kid keeps throwing, because the Brady family is putting my kids through college.'"[947] Surely the players on the field were stressed out? Not at all. They felt comfortably prepared. Tom Brady, just 24½ years old, said afterwards, "You're feeling like you're at practice because this is how we practice it."[948] Tight end Jermaine Wiggins said of his final six-yard reception that set up Adam Vinatieri's field goal, "It wasn't something I had to think about."[949] Offensive coordinator Charlie Weis explained "There was no lack of composure by the offense because everyone knew exactly what to do."[950] Two years later, Brady said of his second last-minute Super Bowl-winning drive, "This is something we work on all the time in practice."[951] "We're good at [the two-minute drill] in practice, and we don't do it any differently in the game. We know the coverages we'll face, and we know the plays. I don't worry about being down with two minutes left. I just feel like it's a great opportunity."[952] Three days after receiver Dedric Ward joined the Patriots in November 2003, "We were down seven points in Houston with a minute-and-some left, and he comes in the huddle laughing and telling us we're going to score a touchdown and take this to overtime."[953] They won in OT. Brady's preparation allows him to perform superbly in more than just two-minute drills. His calm in every situation drives Pittsburgh Steelers coach Bill Cowher nuts: "Tom Brady is a very, very special quarterback. Very smart. He can use the whole field to throw the ball. And he knows the weakness of every coverage that is thrown at him. He's not flashy maybe, but this guy, if you make a mistake, he'll make you pay."[954]

Patriots coaches train players to understand the game's nuances. I screamed at the television set when Kevin Faulk called "fair catch" on a punt at the 6-yard line against the St. Louis Rams in 2004. Everyone "knows" you shouldn't field a punt about to land close to your own goal line because such punts almost always bounce backwards (upfield) in your favor or bounce forward into the endzone for a touchback that–by rule–brings the ball out to the 20-yard line. You're better off letting it bounce in any direction than catching it at the 6. But, after the game, Belichick wasn't upset because special circumstances–that I had not even considered–made Faulk's decision reasonable. This particular punt was so high that the Rams punt coverage team got downfield to give themselves a good chance to down the punt on the 1- or 2-yard line. Letting such a high punt bounce might have pinned the Patriots near their goal line. Calling for a "fair catch" guaranteed the team would not lose five precious yards:

> "It's a judgment the returner has to make. There's a point where you'd rather have the ball on the 6- or 7-yard line than it either be on the 1 or the 20. If it's on the 1, you're so limited offensively, it's a tough place to play from. Being on the 20 is certainly better, but there's not a lot of difference between the 6 or the 10 or the 20. You can [run your offense]… Kevin felt like it was up there for a long time, he was concerned someone would circle it from behind, which they were closing in on. I'm not going to second-guess him."[955]

In spring 2004, defensive backs coach Eric Mangini recommended to Belichick that they train receiver Troy Brown to play nickelback and special teamer Don Davis to play safety as insurance against personnel emergencies. The Patriots had nearly lost Super Bowl XXXVIII after the Panthers exploited injuries that knocked both starting safeties–Rodney Harrison and Eugene Wilson–from that game. Mangini's creative insurance policy paid off in Week 9 after injuries knocked out the Patriots' top three cornerbacks–Ty Law, Tyrone Poole and Asante Samuel. With both Troy Brown and Don Davis playing defense, the Patriots managed to defeat the pass-happy St. Louis Rams. Belichick praised his coaching staff: "That's the kind of thing this staff does, looking ahead, not just seeing what the next day will bring but trying to anticipate your needs through the course of the season."[956] Don Davis as safety and Troy Brown as nickelback were gifts that kept on giving. Brown's presence in the injury-ravaged defensive secondary was essential to the Patriots' 2004-05 Super Bowl run, so essential fans started waving "What can Brown do for you?" signs. Asked before the Super Bowl whether he would rather be playing offense than defense, he said simply, "I'd rather be playing football period, no matter what that is. Special teams are a part of the game. Everything is a part of the game. …Whatever [winning] calls for me to do, I'm going to do."[957]

Spread your knowledge

> "We are always having situational practices. Coach drills it into us to think the way he is thinking."[958]

Great leaders inspire employees to emulate their behavior, adopt their bedrock beliefs and embrace their core philosophies. Even in death, Sam Walton, Bill Hewlett and David Packard continue shaping the companies they founded because the power of their vision infected so many hearts and minds. Vince Lombardi still inspires coaches. General George Patton–"Old Blood and Guts... His guts and our blood"–still inspires. Netscape founder Jim Barksdale says of FedEx founder and CEO Fred Smith, "When you work for Fred, you either become like him or you leave."[959] Patriots linebacker Ted Johnson says the same is true of Bill Belichick:

> "We take our cues from him. Talk about a guy who's demanding and has a vision and won't deviate from his plan! He won't be influenced by any external factors... He won't change for anybody. So, if you've been around him long enough, you buy into that and you become that. That's what our team has become: a mirror image of Coach Belichick."[960]

Belichick has built a professional organization by inspiring players to follow his professional example. He also has the world's smartest, best-prepared football players because Patriots players receive a Ph.D. in footballology from their coaches. Patriots coaches have coached for decades and understand the nuances of every position and the dynamics of eleven guys choreographing their play to defeat eleven other guys, and they are skilled at communicating that knowledge to players. Belichick equates preparation with savings:

> "It's like putting money in the bank. It's an investment. There are so many things you can draw from–situational work, conditioning, and execution of certain plays. When those situations come up again during the season you feel you're prepared because you've gone over them before during camp."[961]

After Patriots quarterback coach Dick Rehbein suddenly passed away in 2001, Belichick took over some of Rehbein's positional coaching duties and astonished Tom Brady:

> "If I ever show you some of those sheets that [Belichick] brings in, it's just– *God*, I mean, it's incredible. Sometimes I think he knows what their defense is doing, more so than their defensive players know what they're doing. And to have him come in each day and break down the film with us, to understand why teams are playing certain coverages, certain schemes each week, you go into a game realizing that, hey, there's nothing this defense can do to surprise us because we've seen it all."[962]

Belichick's objective is to transfer all his knowledge into the mind of each of his players. As Patriots safety Lawyer Milloy once explained: "[Belichick] wants to give you, as a player, all the knowledge he has. He wants you to be prepared for everything, because he's always prepared for everything."[963] It seems to be working.

Patriots outside linebackers coach Rob Ryan (now the Raiders' defensive coordinator) says, "Having Brady is like having Belichick on the field–only Brady has a better arm."[964] (Belichick admits he has no future as an NFL quarterback. Asked whether completing 70% of one's passes is "more mental or physical," Belichick joked "Both. I can read defenses, but I doubt I could hit 70%."[965])

Practice as you want to perform

"They expect perfection in practice. It doesn't always happen, but they expect it. You never know how close to perfection you can get."[966]
    – *Patriots offensive lineman Stephen Neal*

"I don't have an 'On' and 'Off' switch like that. I can't say, 'It's preseason. I'm only going to go 60 percent.'"[967]
    – *Patriots safety Rodney Harrison*

"If you're confident in your two-minute offense and you execute it on the practice field, then you have the confidence to push the envelope in the game."[968]
    – *Bill Belichick*

"You can't go out and practice average on Wednesday, average on Thursday, okay on Friday and then expect to play well on Sunday. ...We're going to start practicing great every day."[969]
    – *Tom Brady to teammates after the 2001 Patriots fell to 1-3*

"I practiced the way I wanted to play ...There were certain moves I worked on in practice that I [used] today [in the game]."[970]
    – *Patriots rookie defensive tackle Vince Wilfork*

"Our practices are more intense than some games."[971]
    – *Patriots defensive end Marquise Hill*

"[Wide receiver David Patten] just keeps going. He won't slow down. He only knows one speed. He only runs routes one speed out there in practice. It doesn't matter whether it is Friday, Saturday walkthrough, whatever he does, he just goes 100 percent."[972]
    – *Bill Belichick*

Belichick makes practices at least as hard as games. Backup quarterback Rohan Davey says Belichick's "big on preparation" because "the harder you prepare, the easier the games are."[973] For example, Belichick drills his punt returners by having them catch punts with one arm while holding another ball in their other arm: "If you can go back there and catch two balls, I think you can feel pretty confident having to catch just one. It's like swinging two bats and then stepping into the batter's box with (one)."[974] Belichick refused to tell third-string quarterback Kliff Kingsbury when he was likely to play during 2004 preseason games because "a third quarterback has to be able to go at any time, [so] you better be ready to go at any time. I don't know when I'm going to put you in, and you don't know either, and that's the way it would be in the season."[975] Belichick also ensures that some practices are as physically intense as real games because players cannot practice hitting and tackling unless everyone's going full speed: "We could sit around here and talk about [football] and we wouldn't get anybody hurt, but we wouldn't be any good."[976]

Tom Brady says he loves practice because practicing well is the only way to ensure you play well on game day. Practicing well gives you confidence–justifiable confidence–that you are prepared to execute well:

> "As sick as it sounds, I think I probably enjoy the practices sometimes as much as the games. I enjoy the preparation part of it, and I take practices very seriously. I believe you practice how you play [so] if you don't practice well usually there is not a lot of confidence going into those games that you're going to go out and play very well… [So] it's very important for our team to go out and practice well and execute very well."[977]

> "I still try to approach practice that way–as a competition. You compete against yourself every day. You compete against the defense you [scrimmage] against. If you don't do that, then you get out there and it's like you're flipping a coin to see how well you do on the weekend. I think if you can be very good throughout the week, the chances are you'll be pretty good when you go out and play on the weekend."[978]

Understanding this, Brady says, Patriots coaches push the scout team to simulate each upcoming opponent and make practice maximally challenging on the starting players. Before Super Bowl XXXIX,

> "Coach was trying to instigate all of the defensive scout team players to go out there and try to ruin our practice. He had them all riled up, each time they make a play or bat down a pass, they go crazy. [Defensive line coach] Pepper Johnson has nicknames for them all, and they were hooting and hollering, and it was making the offensive guys really mad. The practice wasn't going well, and you know what the meetings will be like later when you're going to get cussed out by your coach for not doing the right thing."[979]

Players get as excited about touchdowns and interceptions during scrimmages as they do during games because they love beating their teammates. After safety Don Davis intercepted a pass during 2005 training camp, only quarterback Doug Flutie stood between him and a touchdown. Flutie–like all Patriots quarterbacks–was wearing a red scrimmage jersey that screams "No contact allowed!" but Davis pushed him down anyhow and then held the ball aloft as he crossed the goal line, jumped skyward and spiked the ball between his legs. The entire defensive unit went bonkers. Linebacker Rosevelt Colvin "rushed from the sideline and gave Wesley Mallard a flying chest bump," later telling reporters, "We had a good time today. I don't know about the offense, but we had a good time."[980]

By ratcheting up the competitiveness of practices, coaches ensure that players engross themselves in them and prepare mentally and physically. Brady says some practices are too effective, forcing him to obsess over his plans for the upcoming game: "Sometimes things don't go right [in practice], but that's part of being a quarterback is. Sometimes things don't go right and you lose sleep during the week because things don't go well. That happens too often for me."[981] With each team and individual success, Belichick just ratchets up expectations and competition, a trick Ohio State's legendary coach Woody Hayes had to explain to a *BBC* reporter stunned after Hayes verbally savaged his players following a 10-0 opening day victory:

> BBC reporter: "[Your players] must be pretty dispirited now and low in morale after the ticking off and harassing you gave them."

> Woody Hayes: "Oh no. I don't think you quite understand because kids are buoyant. They snap back. I didn't tear them down that much. But now we'll get pretty dog gone serious about this thing. Cause, you see, worse [would be] if I'd have said, 'Oh well, fellas. Don't worry about that. We played a pretty good game.' We'd never get better. That'd be it. But this way, we'll get better."[982]

Patriots players don't shrink from contact during "meaningless" preseason games. When Tom Brady took a shot from Philadelphia Eagles defensive end N.D. Kalu early in their first 2004 preseason game, Brady didn't curl into the fetal position to protect his multi-million dollar body. He drew on his countless hours pumping iron in the gym to out-muscle Kalu and then throw a sweet 19-yard completion to David Patten while Kalu struggled to pull Brady down. Watching live at Gillette Stadium, I couldn't believe Brady had not only avoided the sack but even managed a big completion. Kalu later said he too was impressed: "I just underestimated [Brady's] strength. Usually, a quarterback just goes down in that situation. But he kind of has a fighter's attitude."[983] Was Bill Belichick shell-shocked after witnessing his star quarterback in a potentially season-ending injury situation during an irrelevant game one month before the start of the real season? No, because preseason games aren't meaningless to Belichick:

> "It was an excellent play. I've never told him [to protect himself]. We try to play the game, every situation, the best way we can play it... I can't really envision doing it any other way. You play to that standard, and that's how you get better. You just can't sit around and talk about [executing well] all year. At some point you have to go out there and experience it."[984]

Belichick has convinced his players to give their all, even in preseason because–as Brady puts it, "The better you can do it now, the better you can do it when it counts."[985] Brady wants to look his best on Week 1 of the regular season, not just on Super Bowl Sunday: "You want to knock the rust off early in training camp so you can hit the first game like you're in midseason form."[986]

Belichick finds players who love practicing intensely and physically because this is the best way to prepare. Safety Rodney Harrison—who made an explosive statement by initiating several violent collisions on his first day as a Patriot in 2003 training camp—exemplifies the spirit Belichick admires: "When we're out here [scrimmaging in training camp], if you're not wearing the same blue [defensive] jersey I am, you're my teammate but you're my enemy in the same breath."[987] Constantly simulating pressure situations in practices helps players relax and focus— rather than tighten up—during games. Running back Corey Dillon says, "It's so different here. Here, when it's a tight situation, we're just so relaxed. We just stay calm and go out and execute."[988]

Preparation breeds confidence. Safety Eugene Wilson says Patriots feel no pressure to repeat as champions because they focus on doing their jobs well and know they are prepared:

> "I wouldn't say there was any pressure at all. No. We just went out there every game and played our game. We prepared the same way we prepared the year before and we didn't put any of the media hype on us or anything. We went out there and just played ball, had fun, and we got it done."[989]

Situational practice

> "There's probably not a situation over the course of last season or this season that we haven't been in or practiced. Our preparation is good and we're confident in our preparation and in each other."[990]
> – Patriots linebacker Roman Phifer

> "You just never know what set of plays [will determine the winner] this week and what situations are going to be the key situations in this game or any other game in the future. You just try to cover all your bases on that stuff and react to [situations] as they come along."[991]
> – Bill Belichick

Most Patriots practice sessions focus on specific situations that might arise in actual games. A team can have the greatest athletes in the world and the most brilliant game plan ever devised and still get trounced if its players don't execute on game day. A team can dominate most of a game and lose after committing several costly errors. Belichick tells players this motivational metaphor: "Wile E. Coyote has a great game plan. He's got the (dynamite) and the trap door, but he doesn't execute. The (dynamite) goes off in his hands and the Roadrunner gets away."[992]

To minimize risk of bad game day execution, Belichick makes each moment of practice simulate a game situation. Patriots cornerback Ty Law says, "He's unique in… how he conducts practices. Seventy percent of our practices are situational. I think that helps us."[993] Over the course of many practices, every possible situation is covered. This attention to detail reminds me of the German national soccer team. The Germans play like they know a thing or two about soccer. One reason is that they break the entire sport down into specific skills and then monotonously drill each of those skills. They then monotonously drill skill combinations. Tedious but effective. The NFL's Paul Brown coaching tree embraces this deconstructivist approach. Before Bill Belichick, the most famous offshoot of the Paul Brown-rooted coaching tree was a fellow named Bill Walsh who coached a San Francisco-based team called "the 49ers." Walsh said the following:

> "I would… practice being behind by two touchdowns, in practice and in training camp. I would work and plan on being ahead by two touchdowns, with just minutes to go, to use the clock, not fumble, go out of bounds, have a penalty, get sacked, or throw interceptions. We would isolate each contingency that we felt important and practice it."[994]

But even three-time Super Bowl champion and Hall of Fame coach Bill Walsh is amazed that "Belichick's teams are so well drilled."[995]

The Patriots are a technically sound and situationally smart football team because players are drilled in proper technique. Former Buffalo head coach Marv Levy–who led the Bills to four consecutive Super Bowls–also sees telltale signs of dedicated coaching:

> "What I've seen is a tremendously focused team… You can see it just the way they go after tipped balls. That's not luck, believe me. That's taught in drills. He has his people alert to it. You can get very exotic with X's and O's, but they don't mean anything if you don't have the players out there aware, and executing. Wasn't it another New Englander–Ralph Waldo Emerson–who said that a brilliant idea is a job half done? I think that was Emerson. Well, they've got the game plan, and they're taking care of the other half."[996]

For example, the Patriots don't merely practice recovering loose balls. They practice recovering loose balls in different loose ball situations:

- *If the ball is loose near the Patriots' own goal line*, players are taught not to recover the ball but to instead hit it out their own end zone to surrender a 2-point safety rather than risk the other team recovering and scoring a 7-point touchdown. They actually practice knocking the ball through their end zone.

- *If the ball is loose near their opponent's end zone*, Patriot players' primary focus is falling on it. Trying to pick up the ball and score while surrounded by opponents is a sin because 1st-and-goal from the 5 is great while failing to gain control is a major setback. Coaches teach players that this situation dictates caution and drill players in falling on loose balls.

- *If the ball is loose after the Patriots have blocked their opponent's field goal attempt or punt*, players try to scoop it up and run for a touchdown ("scoop and score") because their opponent's kicking team is a motley collection of slow, stout blockers, a slow, skinny holder, and a slow, skinny kicker. Since the kicking team's players can't run fast or tackle well and since the Patriots will gain possession even if the kicking team recovers the ball (because teams kick on 4th down), Patriots players are taught to try for a quick touchdown. Aggressively gambling to score is a smart risk, since the sizable potential gain (a touchdown) far outweighs the negligible consequences of failure.

Meticulous situational preparedness paid off with a Patriots special teams touchdown in the 2001 AFC Championship Game against the Steelers. After the Patriots blocked a field goal, Troy Brown recovered and started running upfield. Rather than get tackled, Brown tossed the ball to Antwan Harris who ran it the rest of the way for a touchdown.

Neither brilliance nor luck is responsible for Patriots players' many "smart plays." The team scripts practices carefully to simulate the full variety of game situations. Few "heads-up" plays are improvisations. The coaching staff anticipated the situation and taught players what to do. Players then recognized and responded to that situation by doing what they were taught. For example, as Buffalo Bills linebacker London Fletcher was streaking toward a touchdown with a fumble he had scooped up, Patriots offensive lineman Stephen Neal remembered Coach Belichick instructing players to punch the ball hard enough to knock it loose with enough force to propel it out the back of the end zone. Knocking the ball out of bounds to a sideline is useless because whichever team last had possession–the Bills, in this case–retains possession. So, with Fletcher just two yards from a touchdown, Neal smacked the ball in the right direction with enough force to bounce it through the end zone. Instead of a Bills touchdown, the "touchback" gave the Patriots the ball back with a 1st-and-10 from the 20. (Actually, the Bills successfully challenged the "fumble" ruling–that ironically had enabled them to gain possession–and the play was ruled an incomplete pass. Nevertheless, Neal's outstanding play prevented the Bills from tying the game because the Patriots had exhausted their officiating challenges and could not have challenged the "fumble" ruling if the Bills had scored a game-tying touchdown.)

Because offenses aren't skilled at defense, Patriots defenders aren't satisfied with an interception. Linebacker Tedy Bruschi said after a superb interception return, "When you get it, score with it. That's what I was trying to do" and joked he was a running back: "I'm not going to go down. I've got a feel for how to run the ball and how to read blocks."[997] Bruschi's not completely joking; the Patriots defense practices running back interceptions. Similarly, the Patriots offense practices preventing turnovers from becoming scores.

The Patriots also commit fewer "stupid plays" than most NFL teams. For example, defensive players who intercept passes or pick up fumbles aren't used to running with the ball, so they are prone to hand the ball right back to the offense. Many defensive players are so eager to score touchdowns that they recklessly flip the ball to a teammate or hold it with one hand as they swing their arms to run faster. Realizing this, Patriots offensive players practice knocking balls loose and have accomplished this during games. And Patriots defensive players practice securing the ball while running. After Patriots linebacker Willie McGinest intercepted a pass and ran 27 yards before getting tackled from behind in a 2004 game against Seattle, McGinest suggested he might have been able to score a touchdown by running full speed gripping the ball with one hand and swinging his arms but focused on retaining possession by securing the ball like a running back: "Of course, I wanted to score a touchdown, but I just don't want somebody to try to knock the ball out. Anytime you get an interception or a turnover, the worst thing that can happen is somebody to come up and knock the ball out and they get it back."[998]

Tom Brady says the Patriots offense understands "The difference, at the end of the game, between having 22 seconds on the clock and 16 seconds on the clock."[999] Those six seconds presumably determine, for example, whether a receiver runs upfield or out of bounds to stop the clock. I can only speculate, but Patriot players know how to play with 22 seconds left and with 16 seconds left. And they practice each situation.

Patriots practices are as demanding mentally as physically. Players must be in shape on Day 1 because camp is about learning to play smart and play cohesively. Belichick places players in simulated situations requiring them to adjust their routes or their throws or their blocking or their coverage according to what their opponent is showing before the snap and doing after the snap. Each Patriot must also know his teammates' responsibilities in any situation their opponent creates; otherwise, receivers may run into one another when one runs the wrong pattern or two linebackers may cover the same receiver, leaving the other wide open:

> "There's no way for a player to learn how to execute his plays and for a team to learn how to execute them together—and all the variations that can occur when something happens on the other side of the ball—without going out there and doing it, going through the process, seeing things and collectively three or four guys seeing things together and reacting together. There's no way you can cut the corner on that."[1000]

Patriots players play especially well in obscure, arcane situations because they practice every situation. The Patriots don't practice plain vanilla field goals. They practice rushing onto the field without a huddle to kick a field goal with seconds remaining and no timeouts. They practice punting from their endzone. They practice onside kicks and free kicks. Everything. While putting his Notre Dame team through end-of-game simulated practice, Charlie Weis told his quarterback to intentionally throw an incomplete pass just to see whether the defense would waste a timeout. According to Tom Brady, situational preparation pays off:

> "They make it as tough as they possibly can. It's not like we sit there and say, 'They're not going to blitz much this week.' We run every blitz known to man in practice. I'm like, 'How are they going to run that?' But that's the stuff you have to [know] about. [Receivers] getting open in man coverage. [Receivers] getting open in zone coverage, and the zone blitzes. We work on pretty much everything."[1001]

Preparation helps the Patriots win many close games. After the Patriots won their 2003 regular season matchup with the Colts by stopping Peyton Manning's offense on four straight plays from within two yards of a game-winning touchdown, Patriots linebacker Mike Vrabel suspected Belichick was psychic: "It's kinda funny. The first thing Bill did this week was point out the Cleveland game where the Colts made two goal-line stands to win their opener. He [also] brought up a goal-line situation at the end of the Jacksonville game."[1002]

Preparation also enables the Patriots to salvage wins in games that appear beyond hope. Most NFL fans and commentators were initially shocked and then impressed after the Patriots took an intentional safety while already trailing Denver 24-23 with just 2:51 left to play. Teams with large leads occasionally surrender a meaningless intentional safety (two points) rather than give their opponent the ball back in excellent field position to score a touchdown (seven points). But no one ever recalls a team taking an intentional safety while losing! By putting themselves behind 26-23, the Patriots appeared to have dug themselves a deeper grave. Wrote long-time NFL observer Peter King,

> "This was the kind of play that, when it happens, you yell at the TV: 'Idiot! The Pats are screwed now!' Then you think about it and you say: 'Hey, that was pretty smart.' Then it works and you say: 'Belichick's a friggin' genius.'"[1003]

Watching live, I thought it was a bad snap. But this was no mistake or spur-of-the-moment improvisation. Patriots director of football research Ernie Adams—yes, the team has someone whose job is researching football strategy—had systematically analyzed every possible game scenario, in terms of point differential, field position and time remaining. Adams' analysis had determined that on 4th-and-long late in a game close to their own goal line down a point, they have a better chance to win by surrendering two points and free-kicking the ball deep downfield to the other team—

in hopes of getting the ball back in better field position–than by punting the ball from their own end zone or going for it on 4th down.

Bill Belichick rattles off from memory the list of situations in which he might surrender an intentional safety:

> "Most of the time you'd think of doing this if you're ahead. You're up by six, or 10 or 11. There've been very few times, if ever, where you take a safety when you're actually behind. But think about it. There's not a lot of great options in that situation. I just figured, if you're down one or three, what's the big difference? You've still got to get at least a field goal."[1004]

Surrendering an intentional safety while losing by a point late in a game was a situation the Patriots had not only *planned* for but had even *practiced*. They had literally practiced intentionally snapping the ball out of their end zone! That anticipation proved masterful, as the Patriots won in Denver just minutes after the game appeared hopeless. Coaches' preparation gave the team a chance to snatch victory from the jaws of defeat, and players seized the opportunity. After Ken Walter free-kicked the ball away, the Patriots' special teams stopped the Broncos' punt returner at Denver's 15. The Patriots defense stood tall, forcing the Broncos to punt back to the Patriots four plays later. Brady took over at the Patriots' 42-yard line with 2:15 left. In the exchange of possessions, the Patriots moved the ball 41 yards–from their own 1-yard line to their 42-yard line–while giving up two points and losing just 36 seconds. (The Patriots were able to stop the clock during the Broncos' possession with their timeouts.) Brady then drove his offense 58 yards for a game-winning touchdown pass to David Givens.

Throughout 2001, the Patriots practiced *ad nauseam* faking a field goal and instead punting the ball and trying to down it near their opponent's end zone. In December, with the Patriots leading the Browns 20-16, Adam Vinatieri faked a 53-yarder and instead punted. Tight end Jermaine Wiggins successfully killed the ball at the 2-yard line, trapping the Browns 98 yards from the Patriots' end zone:

> "We've been working on that play since the beginning of training camp. Sixteen, 17 weeks. It's the last thing we do on Fridays and we worked on it again Saturday. After the first five or six weeks of doing it, the players are rolling their eyes. But we were ready."[1005]

Bob George wrote that it "may go down as the key moment in the game."[1006]

It's fortunate Tom Brady practiced punting before surprising the Dolphins in 2003 by pretending to go for it and instead punting. In the actual game, David Givens downed Brady's 36-yard punt at the 1-yard line. In Brady's first practice, however, "the first one I kicked hit [offensive lineman] Joe [Andruzzi] in the butt. It went about 8 yards, and that was not a very good audition right there. The next time, I kicked it about 20 yards."[1007] Brady's 36-yard net surpassed the Patriots' punter in that game, Brooks Barnard, whose punts netted 32.5 yards.

In Super Bowl XXXVIII, the Patriots pulled from their bag of tricks a two-point conversion play they had never used but had practiced every Friday all season.[1008] The center snapped the ball directly to running back Kevin Faulk–rather than the quarterback–resulting in an easy two-point conversion that put the Patriots up by a touchdown, 29-22. They hadn't attempted a single two-point conversion all season because their analysis indicated that few situations warranted a risky two-point conversion attempt rather than a nearly-automatic extra point.

When a reporter asked Brady to explain why Belichick says Brady seldom makes two consecutive poor plays, Brady credited situational practices:

> "We do a good job here of putting ourselves in pressurized situations in practices and in mini-camps, so when it does get to game day we are so prepared. And when you are prepared there is no hesitation. You just let loose. You just be the player that you are. Because of that, those bad plays don't happen repetitively. You don't give in to the mental aspects of the game because you believe in yourself and you have too much confidence in your teammates."[1009]

Heading out to snap the ball that won Super Bowl XXXVI, Patriots long snapper Lonie Paxton felt little anxiety because he trusted himself and his teammates: "Because I know I'm automatic, [holder Ken Walter] is automatic, Adam's automatic. I knew the field goal was going to be made."[1010] In fact, Paxton didn't even bother watching the ball: "Once I threw a strike, I knew the game was won, so I just took off toward the end zone"[1011] where he celebrated by lying down and making a snow angel by waving his arms as he had following the "Snow Bowl" playoff victory over the Raiders... except there was no snow in the temperature-controlled, domed Louisiana Superdome.

The Patriots' "hands team" covers kickoffs in likely onside kick situations. Watching a replay of the hands team seemingly effortlessly smothering the Eagles' onside kick in the final minutes of Super Bowl XXXIX, Patriots left tackle Matt Light was astonished the kick went "again, the way we practiced it. You go grab the practice film and you'll see that exact [play]."[1012] Everyone but Christian Fauria blocked onrushing Eagles players, creating a protective pocket for Fauria to calmly catch the ball and fall down. The Patriots execute with such precision because they practice relentlessly. Light recalled another play the team practiced and practiced before kicker Adam Vinatieri threw a touchdown to a wide open Troy Brown: "This year, we did the Troy Brown fake field goal. Remember? We practiced that forever. [Groan in the background.] I mean, how many years have we been practicing that?"[1013] With more moaning in the background, Ted Johnson answered, "All the time, and we never ran it."[1014] When they did, it worked brilliantly. Had Troy Brown run completely off the field, he would not have been allowed to sneak back on right before the play. He instead–as planned and practiced–walked just close enough to the sideline that the Rams ignored him. When the Minnesota Vikings tried to copy the

Patriots, they screwed up. Randy Moss—playing the role of Troy Brown—noticed the Vikings had twelve players on the field (because lineman Cory Withrow went onto the field as he normally does on field goals). Moss saved his team a penalty by stepping out of bounds, but Gus Frerotte—who was supposed to pass Moss the ball—had no one to throw to, so the Vikings squandered a scoring opportunity.

Clock management

The Patriots' superior preparation is especially apparent in their clock management. In a tight game, clock management can decide who wins and who loses. Patriots linebackers coach Dean Pees—who joined in 2004—says his Kent State team won its 2003 opener thanks to a strategy for using timeouts Belichick devised: "We… were down 14 points with 2:30 left to go and we won by three. And it was all because we used our timeouts a certain way. It's a formula, and I learned it from Nick [Saban], who learned it from Bill."[1015]

The Patriots seldom have the wrong personnel in the game, fail to call a play quickly enough, get penalized for too many men on the field or waste a timeout because they have too many or too few players. Players and coaches always know their responsibilities. One playbook page even tells players where to huddle (eight yards behind the ball), where to stand (each playing position has an assigned location in the circular huddle… center closest to ball; guards flanking the center; tackles outside the guards; quarterback closest to sideline; *etc.*), how to stand (hands on hips; no leaning), what to say (nothing unless you're the quarterback, in which case you should speak parallel to the ground, not into the air or down at the ground), how to exit the huddle ("ready," pause, clap, then "Jog away from the huddle! Never loaf!").[1016] It even tells offensive linemen which direction to turn (toward the ball) when exiting the huddle. Through diligent practice, the Patriots operate smoothly and conserve timeouts, no matter the situation. They coordinate the flow of players into and out of the game and choose and transmit play calls in a timely manner. And Tom Brady never fails to snap the ball (or call a timeout) in time: "Brady has never—I still can't even believe this one—had a delay of game penalty called when he was behind center."[1017] In 2004, he finally was penalized for delay of game once. I know because I remember feeling stunned.

After a questionable ruling by officials results in a big Patriots gain that the defense might challenge, the Patriots offense skips its huddle, sets up quickly and snaps the ball immediately. Players sometimes reposition themselves and hike the ball a second before the opposing team throws its challenge flag. Once the ball is snapped, the opponent can no longer challenge the prior play.

As you might guess by the Patriots' two Super Bowl victories won on last-second field goals, the Patriots go to great lengths to make the clock their friend. Their last-second heroics are no flukes. Patriots director of football research Ernie Adams sits in the press box during games worrying about quality control issues: clock management, which referee decisions to challenge, *etc*. (A successful challenge benefits the team, but an unsuccessful challenge costs the team a timeout.) The Patriots spend oodles of time during training camp and practices preparing to save precious seconds in end-of-half and end-of-game situations. Coaches motivate players to pay attention by showing game film of teams losing games by mismanaging the clock.

As important as clock management seems when the Patriots' intense focus on it is pointed out and when the Patriots' three Super Bowl victories required it, many coaches wing it. Even the head coach of the excellent New York Jets, Herman Edwards, admits to being sloppy with time:

> "We had some things that came up [in 2003] and [2002]. So many things happen so fast. You say, 'I kind of let that get away. We could have saved five seconds on the clock.' It didn't hurt us, but how would I have done it different? Sometimes, I'm into the game too much instead of watching the clock and saying, 'We need to do this at this point.'"[1018]

For example, on December 1, 2003, the Jets had a 1st down and a lead against the Tennessee Titans with 1:51 left in the game. The Titans had no remaining timeouts, so the Jets could have won risklessly by having their quarterback kneel down four times, burning thirty seconds per play. Instead, they ran two plays that needlessly risked a bad quarterback-to-running-back handoff or a running back fumble. As another example, "Due largely to indecision, shoddy communication and, ultimately, confusion, the Jets [during 2003] burned five timeouts in the first and third quarters and five in the first seven minutes of the fourth quarter."[1019] In 2004, the Jets finally assigned Dick Curl to the full-time task of clock management.

Against the Patriots in 2004, the Arizona Cardinals wasted timeouts—one in the 1st quarter and another with 8:49 left in the 2nd quarter—forcing themselves to attempt (and miss) a 58-yard field goal on 2nd down after running out of time.

For years, the Patriots have had Ernie Adams optimize time management, says Patriots linebacker Mike Vrabel: "One of his things [Adams] says is you don't want to call a timeout with less than 2:17 left in the half. Don't ask me why, but that's what he's come up with."[1020] (The Patriots likely determined that a timeout can save more than 16 seconds after the automatic timeout at the two-minute warning.)

With a 1st down fourteen yards from tying Super Bowl XXXVIII, the Carolina Panthers called time out with 103 seconds left. The Panthers scored the game-tying touchdown but left too much time on the clock. The Panthers gifted the Patriots half a minute without which Tom Brady could not have moved his offense downfield for Adam Vinatieri's game-winning field goal with four seconds left. The Panthers left Brady 68 seconds but could have left 30 seconds or less.

Had the Patriots been in the Panthers' position, they would have let the clock run, saving their timeout to stop time if and only if they trailed with the game nearly over. We know this because offensive coordinator Charlie Weis complained Brady spiked the ball to kill the clock too quickly after leading the Patriots downfield for the Patriots' first Super Bowl victory–against the Rams–in February 2002: "We actually clocked it too early."[1021] Weis wanted Brady to squeeze another second or two off the clock before spiking the ball because, if Vinatieri's field goal had not consumed the remaining seven seconds, the Patriots would have been forced to kick to the Rams with several ticks left on the clock, needlessly giving the Rams an extra chance to score on a kickoff return. To Weis, leaving even a second or two was a sin. The Panthers left the Patriots *68 seconds* and compounded that blunder when kicker John Kasay miss-hit the kickoff out of bounds, giving the Patriots the ball at the 40 without any time elapsing. After the game, Brady said, "[Moving] thirty yards [for a field goal attempt] in 1:08 with timeouts is way more than enough time."[1022] In fact, even after a ticky-tack penalty pushed the Patriots backwards thirty yards during that drive, Brady again chastised himself for leading a Super Bowl-winning drive that left too much time on the clock: "I kind of lost track of time and I called the timeout too quickly with nine seconds left instead of letting it run to five."[1023]

The Patriots further appreciate that clock management involves time-aware play calling as well as time-aware execution by players. Says Belichick:

"A lot of clock management is done by play-calling. You can say we want to run plays that stop the clock, but if you're running inside routes, it's going to be hard to stop the clock. You're going to have to have plays built into your system that are appropriate to what you're trying to do from a clock management standpoint."[1024]

So Patriots coaches prepare special lists of plays for end-of-game situations:

"There's times when we're going fast and we just don't have time to go through the communication. But a lot of that is preprogrammed too. You know here are the plays we're looking at. If the ball's on the left hashmark, we want to be in this [formation]. If the ball's on the right hashmark, we want to do that. That kind of thing. So even though it's going quick, I don't think Tom is sitting there thinking, 'What am I going to call here?' It's probably one of one, two or three things that, based on the situation or where the ball is, here's what we're going to do."[1025]

All great teams possess great situational awareness. I recently re-watched Game 7 of the 1987 Eastern Conference Championship between the Celtics and Bucks. Late in a tight game, Robert Parrish blocked a shot. Dennis Johnson recklessly hurtled over fans to redirect the ball an instant before it touched out of bounds, sending it straight at a Buck player off of whom it then bounced out of bounds. A minute later, Parrish got a rebound and had a decent chance to score a quick bucket but instead passed the ball so a teammate could kill the clock.

Contrast the poise of those Celtic greats with the impulsiveness of current Celtic Paul Pierce who—with just 13 seconds remaining and a one point lead in Game 6 against the Pacers—was intentionally fouled by Jamaal Tinsley. Instead of shooting his free throws, Pierce took a swing at Tinsley, getting himself ejected and gifting the Pacers a technical foul shot that Reggie Miller hit to tie the game. Pierce's ejection also allowed the Pacers to choose the Celtics' worst foul shooter to take the two shots for Tinsley's foul. Celtic Kendrick Perkins hadn't warmed up and missed both. Pierce's elbow cost his team three points and got him tossed from a tight playoff game.

Prepare for your actual opponent, not a faceless opponent

"Remember Sunday when Miami tried to run a quick play on third-and-1 and false-started? We were ready for that. We had seen they tried to quick-snap on third-and-short so we lined up quick, eight in the box, and they wound up false-starting."[1026]
    – Patriots linebacker Ted Johnson

"A big, tall, athletic guy like [Randy Moss], I expected the fade [pattern to the corner of the endzone]. I played for the fade, and I went up for the ball and he slung me down."[1027]
    – Patriots cornerback Asante Samuel, after getting such perfect position that Moss grabbed and pulled him to the ground

"[Belichick] does a great job of preparing us for different opponents, letting us see things we need to see and do the things we need to execute to... win that particular game."[1028]
    – Patriots linebacker Roman Phifer

"You have to have a lot of football knowledge and understand what an offense is trying to do and create mismatches. The NFL... is very situational, so we... come up with schemes and plays that play to our strengths and can hopefully shut down their strengths."[1029]
    – Patriots linebacker Ted Johnson

"If you don't work hard in practice on what you're going to play against, you're not going to have a chance... We keep going over [the game plan] and over it again. We watch a lot of film. We study hard... The preparation [enables us] to go into the game and execute it."[1030]
    – Patriots linebacker Willie McGinest

Players on the Patriots' scout team are primarily backups and non-roster practice squad players but take pride in preparing the starters to play their best by simulating each upcoming opponent's players, plays, techniques and tactics, a role Belichick says is underappreciated:

> "All of our players try to simulate the other team's individual players and also their schemes. Some guys have certain individual strengths: the way [Marvin] Harrison runs routes or the way [Dwight] Freeney [plays his] pass-rush techniques and that kind of thing. You try to talk to the players and get them to replicate that and also scheme-wise to try to get everybody to run the play the way that your opponent runs it so that your team can see it close to the way it's going to look when they run it [during the game]. And that's part of working together, practicing together, helping each other out... it probably never gets enough credit and is always understated, but... a big part of the preparation is how your scout teams can prepare your regular team for being ready to play on game day."[1031]

Every Patriot must study the opponent's plays and players and then pass written tests and answer oral questions in front of their peers. Any unprepared player will be embarrassed in front of his teammates. Questions aren't always about the player's position: "[New defensive coordinator Eric Mangini] makes sure everybody knows [everything]. He'll ask questions to a linebacker that's a safety question, or to a safety that's a D-line question. So he wants everybody to know what everyone else is doing."[1032] Prepared players receive greater respect from teammates, says Brady: "You put the work in like everybody else, you try hard to prepare and be held accountable. You gain respect by working hard and not asking anything more of [others] than you would ask of yourself."[1033] Patriots non-starters then simulate that week's opponent as realistically and competitively as possible. Cornerback Ty Law: "We don't get nervous or tight as players because we make practice so realistic."[1034] For example? Before playing the speedy St. Louis Rams in Super Bowl XXXVI, scout team receivers and defensive ends lined up beyond the line of scrimmage to give themselves a headstart and force Patriots starters to prepare for the Rams' sprinters.[1035]

On many teams, serving on the scout team is considered a thankless chore. On the Patriots, starters sometimes participate on "The Dirty Team." And all members–whether starters, backups or practice squad players–take pride in their mission-critical task that–they believe–determines whether the Patriots win or lose: "If we're not roughing up the offense, pushing them, they'll get not only a false look but false confidence."[1036] If they can harass Tom Brady while simulating the upcoming opponent, they have prepared Brady for the actual game:

> "They have a dirty job and someone has to do it. Their job is to bother Tom Brady. They have to be as distracting as they can to him. Anything an opponent's defense can do, we're going to throw it at him. We're not a 'look' team. We're not out there to give the offense a good look. That's our period to get better. Guys like Larry Izzo are not out there just to stay in shape. He's

out there to make plays and show Coach Belichick that they can make plays when given the opportunity. If Brady has a bad game, that means 'The Dirty Show' didn't get the job done during the week. I would say twice this season we didn't take care of our responsibility."[1037]

Belichick acknowledges scout team contributors, underscoring their value:

"In the locker room after the Patriots beat the Indianapolis Colts in the AFC Championship Game, coach Bill Belichick credited [backup quarterback Damon] Huard for having as big of a role as anyone in the victory, even though Huard didn't take a snap. The reason? Huard did an outstanding job of mimicking [Colts quarterback] Peyton Manning in practice to prepare the Patriots' defense."[1038]

Two days before playing the New York Jets in 2004, the Patriots offense ran a two-minute drill against "the Jets defense" as simulated by the scout team. That practice led coaches to change the plays they called two days later, helping the Patriots drive 62 yards for a touchdown in 1:49 against the real New York Jets defense:

"We didn't like exactly where we were. The way the drill turned out, was that we didn't really finish it very well. Part of [the problem] was just what we had in the game plan. We took a look at it Friday and revised it a little bit, went back over it on Saturday, and ironically it came up exactly the way that we had planned it. It was a good thing that we went in and talked about it. It probably resulted in more points than we would have otherwise. It was a nice job by Charlie to have the mental telepathy to practice that exact situation."[1039]

Belichick says his players simulate opponents so well that "Every time we do the two-minute drill in practice we learn something as coaches and players. It seems like there's always a teaching point that comes out of there."[1040]

Willie McGinest says Tom Brady studies opposing defenses so meticulously that he understands them as well as they understand themselves:

"He's a student of the game. [Quarterbacks] have to study [and] break down defenses. You have to understand it yourself. You can't just get a game plan from a coach and go out and try to do it. You've got to actually go in and understand every intricacy of that defense. If you hear [Brady] talk about [some] pass, he knew where he was going with the ball a lot of times in different games just on a look [the defense] gave him or just what happens."[1041]

Offensive coordinator Charlie Weis offers as an example a Chargers game in 2001: "The first play [in overtime], they show a blitz that we practiced all week. We were [planning] to audible to a specific play if this [situation] presented itself. He picked it up and got us into field goal range. We won, and that game spearheaded us into our [first] championship run."[1042]

Even when an opponent does something the Patriots have not prepared for, they understand the opponent well enough to adjust quickly and painlessly: "Sometimes you get surprised in a game with something that a team does, and it is something fairly easy for you to handle. Maybe you haven't worked on it but (you say), 'OK, here is what we want to do about it.' And you adjust to it."[1043]

Prepare for plan failure

"Everyone has a plan until they get hit."
– *Heavyweight boxing champion Mike Tyson*

"There are two ways to run an NFL franchise. One is to believe everything will go wrong and plan accordingly. The second is to assume everything will go right and plan for a victory parade. The New England Patriots are firm believers in Plan A, which has pretty much proven to be a winner."[1044]
– *Jonathan Comey, Standard-Times*

"[The salary cap]'s like a household budget; you could always have an emergency... Somebody could get hurt–will get hurt–and you have to get somebody. You have to budget a cushion, and I believe we're OK on that."[1045]
– *Bill Belichick*

Another reason the Patriots always appear prepared is that they know their plan won't always work. The Patriots plan for failure of their plan. They always want a "Plan B" and a "Plan C." Hope for the best, but expect the worst. Midway through 2004, they were forced to dust off "Plan C" after injuries to three of their four starting defensive backs (only Rodney Harrison remaining healthy). Special teamer and backup linebacker Don Davis–who became an emergency safety–said:

"I'm very amazed. We went from Ty Law [and] Tyrone Poole to [street] free agents and linebackers and a wide receiver, so it was kind of a joke around here, but it's fun. Guys are doing good. It's indicative of the good coaching that's going on around here, and it's also good players."[1046]

Wishful thinking has no home in Foxboro. Tom Brady's realism extends even to dealing with his fame:

"[Joe Montana] told me a story of being at an airport, huddled [so no one would recognize him] in the side of a bar with his two buddies drinking a beer, and I said, 'That's me.' You just want to be with your buddies. I said, if he's still feeling that way... I don't think I'm ever going to get over that. You always think you'll be more comfortable with things [in the future], but I don't think I ever will. Rather than say, 'It's going to get better,' just [admit], 'It's not going to get better. I'm just going to have to deal with it better.'"[1047]

Before Super Bowl XXXIX, Patriots cornerback Asante Samuel tuned out speculation that star Eagles receiver Terrell Owens would not be healthy: "He's on the 53-man roster. He's not on injured reserve, so I expect to see him play... We're preparing for him like we do for anybody else... I'm going out there like he's 100 percent. You don't ever underestimate anybody when you're going on the battlefield. He's explosive. He's fast. He's strong. He's big."[1048] That is Belichick's philosophy: "We expect all [our opponents'] players to be at their best... [Terrell Owens]'s not going to be out there on crutches... He's going to be able to run and play. Whether we can cover him or not, that remains to be seen. But they're not going to put the guy out there in a wheelchair."[1049] If Belichick managed FEMA, every hurricane would be assumed to be Category 5, until proven otherwise.

The Patriots protect against future-blindness through "positional flexibility," a major Belichick focus. The Patriots signed linebacker Chad Brown because, Belichick said, "He's a versatile player who can do a lot of different things on the defensive side of the ball, and you can never have too many of those."[1050] Versatile players enable Patriots coaches to plug someone in whenever a starter is injured:

> "Any time a player creates a role for himself it doesn't mean necessarily that the player who's doing that is better than everybody else at doing it, but when you can only take 45 active players to the game, and if one guy can do five things second best on the team than five different guys, you just run out of people. So, that can have a lot of value in itself–to be versatile. Versatility and durability are two of the most important things in the National Football League. ...If you can only be good at one thing, you'd better be really, really, really good at it, and it better make a difference in the game"[1051]

The Patriots not only acquire versatile players but also teach players to play multiple positions. After cornerback Chad Scott–who played left cornerback during his entire tenure with the Steelers–signed with the Patriots, he found himself playing almost exclusively at right cornerback throughout the 2005 preseason because, Belichick explained, "We wanted to give him more work on the right so that if he had to go back to the left, it would be an area more familiar to him, rather than vice versa... We're starting to build our overall versatility and depth within that position."[1052] Eugene Wilson played cornerback in college and during his first training camp but was thrown into the fire at safety after the Patriots released Lawyer Milloy days before the start of the 2003 season. In training camp 2004, Wilson split time between safety and cornerback. Belichick says, "He still has some corner responsibilities even when he plays safety, and we know that if we have to play him at corner that he's trained to do that and has the skill and confidence to do it. I think his versatility back there has been a really big plus."[1053] Wide receiver David Givens played some running back in high school and college and was prepared to run in the

Patriots' 2004 season opener if Corey Dillon and Patrick Pass had been injured.[1054] In early 2005, Belichick said, "There are a lot of multiple crossover trainings going on [so we can] cover multiple spots with only a few players."[1055]

Flexible players simplify injury adjustments. The NFL allows a team to activate only 45 players for a game, so a team can't have a dedicated backup for every position. Belichick: "If you only go to the game with seven [offensive] linemen–which is what we normally go with–you have 10 spots, really, that you have to fill, the starter and the backup at each of those spots. Somebody has to double up and... if you ever lose two players in the same position, you are in trouble."[1056] A team truly needs multiple backups at each position because–during a season–some positions suffer multiple injuries (or one injury plus a player being shifted as a substitute to another position). Belichick says, "It's much easier [to call plays] when you don't care what players are in there and you're able to do whatever you want. Basically we have six [linebackers] that allow us do that. It's very comforting."[1057]

The Patriots fill their roster with adaptable players who collectively maximize the team's expected winning percentage, given the inevitability of injuries throughout the season:

> "You have to make up your team so you can cover all the situations and all the aspects of the game. ...What you do at linebacker has something to do with what you do at tight end and what you do at running back. What you do at receiver is going to have something to do with what you do at tight end and what you do at defensive backs, especially when you cross over into special teams."[1058]

The Patriots released veteran fullback Fred McCrary before the 2004 season, though many reported he had a strong training camp. McCrary was likely released because he lacked positional flexibility. The Patriots kept three tight ends who can also play fullback. They kept two defensive players (Klecko and Seymour) who have also learned to play goal-line fullback. They also kept Patrick Pass, who can return kickoffs and punts and play three offensive positions: "I knows the offense well. I can line up at fullback. I can line up tailback. And I can line up as a receiver and still be productive."[1059] The Patriots similarly released mountainous former Pro Bowl right tackle James "Big Cat" Williams, in part because he plays only right tackle. Were Williams more adaptable, like other Patriots offensive linemen, he would have been more valuable. Linebacker Mike Vrabel has become a touchdown-catching machine as a tight end.

Patriots executives and coaches also prepare for inevitable personnel challenges by maintaining an "emergency list" of players at each position they might sign if an injury fells one of their players:

> "If you have an injury during the season, who would you go to next? That's just procedural. It's policy. We do it every year, with every position... So, if

we needed somebody at a certain position, at least there would be some kind of priority or group of players that we would want to look at before another group."[1060]

That list helped fill a gaping hole punched in the Patriots roster when a knee injury ended starting tight end Benjamin Watson's 2004 season in Week 1. The moment a surgeon told Watson he needed season-ending surgery, the Patriots were on the phone with tight end Jed Weaver.[1061] Belichick felt fortunate to snag Weaver, who had been a surprise cut of the Denver Broncos:

> "I'm glad we were able to sign him. We go through [available personnel] every week. At this time of year there's a handful of guys who you say, 'I'm really surprised that guy's not on a team. You look at the rosters and know he's better than some of the guys who are on teams. Those players don't figure to be available much longer. It depletes quickly which is what you'd expect. It's not long before the good ones get picked off."[1062]

As Notre Dame's new head coach, Charlie Weis' depth chart covers players and coaches: "I have a contingency plan if I lose anybody."[1063] Belichick's undoubtedly does too.

The Patriots also prepare intelligently for the annual roster culling NFL teams engage in each fall to get down to the 53-man limit. Instead of trying to study every player on every team to decide whom the Patriots might want to acquire, the Patriots figure out who might get cut and focus on evaluating that subset of players:

> "People in the personnel department look at each team's roster, and they see how many offensive linemen they have. They see how many receivers they have. Here are the guys they are pretty sure are going to make the team. Here are the guys they are pretty sure are not going to make the team. Here are some guys that, maybe it could go either way on, depending on what their evaluations are with that team. Those are the ones you kind of look at the most, those guys you think may be available."[1064]

The college draft is another area where the Patriots display their Boy Scout-like "be prepared" mentality. Says Belichick: "We always feel like we need to know the whole draft. You never know what can happen on draft day. You might move up or down. You can start the draft at (pick No.) 20, but you'd [better] be ready to draft sixth."[1065] Speaking to students at Boston College, Belichick compared the Patriots' preparations for the draft to students' preparation for a final exam:

> "You study all semester for your final exam. You cram for it the week before. We don't know what questions will be on the test. We don't know who is going to be available, but we try to do all our preparation and react to the situation as it comes to us."[1066]

Patriots executive Jonathan Kraft says the Krafts were blown away by Belichick and Pioli's pre-draft preparations:

> "Bill and Scott led mock drafts the night before and the morning of the draft. It was amazing how much planning went into it. We were ready for every scenario. It wasn't like in past drafts where we'd just wait. These guys had every scenario mapped out and then how we would react."[1067]

After intensively studying potential draftees, the Patriots do a "vertical stack" (ranking/scoring of players at each position), then a "horizontal stack" (merging position-by-position grades into a single scoring system so players playing different positions can be compared with one another), and then a final vertical stack (relative ranking of players within each cluster of players with identical scores).

As costly and time-consuming as player evaluation and ranking is, the team must also strategize based on what it expects other teams to do. So, after assessing how well each potential draftee would perform in a Patriots uniform, the Patriots assess other teams' needs: "After every pick we make, we talk about what the needs of teams five, six, seven spots ahead of [our next selection] are so we have idea of what they're looking at." [1068] Throughout the draft, director of football research Ernie Adams guesses what other teams might do. Adams' scenarios define the team's options and buy extra time to consider each selection. Understanding other teams' needs occasionally enables the Patriots to get two players they want by strategically selecting the one they want less first because they feel he is more likely to be grabbed by another team: "You may have graded the player [ranked] 55 higher because of your system and you know you're higher on him than other teams. So we're going to take the player [ranked] 63 and hope for the 55 on the next pick."[1069]

Avoid worst-case scenarios

> "We are very clear when we call a certain play... 'This is what can't happen. This can't go wrong.' There are certain things we can't do. And sometimes understanding what you can't do is as important as understanding what to do."[1070]
>
> – Bill Belichick

"Avoid worst-case scenarios" may sound like worthless advice. But there are "bad" situations and "really, really bad" situations. Smart coaches list the "really, really bad" situations that might arise and figure out how to avoid them.

For example, many football commentators note how "lucky" the Patriots have been to keep Tom Brady on the field and out of the hospital. Many argue the Patriots would be an average team without Brady. More than "luck" is involved in protecting Brady. Patriots coaches stress over protecting Brady like chess grandmasters scheming to protect their king. Since Brady joined the Patriots, coaches have urged him to strengthen his body. More muscle makes Brady more durable. Coaches designed the offense so the quarterback usually takes a 3-step drop and releases the ball quickly rather than take 5-step or 7-stop drops and throw deep. The coaches also design superb pass protections. Incredibly, Brady was not sacked once during the entire 2003 playoffs, despite facing three powerful defensive lines (Tennessee, Indianapolis, and Carolina).

Belichick also emphasizes strength training, stretching, eating right, and anything else that aids durability. After signing Tim Dwight, Patriots coaches asked him to regain–as protection against injury–the ten pounds he lost from early in his career.[1071] Keeping players healthy maximizes the team's chances to utilize their entire playbook and win games. Durability is so important that the Patriots' training room has a big sign proclaiming "Durability is more important than ability."[1072]

Regularly review your assumptions

"[The quality of linebackers available in the NFL Draft] hasn't been good for several years, and I don't think it's good this year [2005] either. We've gone back and asked ourselves if our standards are unrealistic, if we've set the bar too high. And I don't think so. We've looked at some of the guys who've been drafted high the last several years around the league, and the conclusion you come up with is that maybe they've been a little over-drafted."[1073]
– *Bill Belichick*

Patriots coaches periodically re-examine their assumptions about which situations might arise during a game. Developing a plan for every known situation is important, but you must also update your list of possible situations to avoid getting caught by surprise. Explains Belichick:

"We go through every [in-game] situation we can think of that we want to be prepared for. Let's say there's 70 of them. Then in the offseason we go through all our games and see if there's anything that came up unusually that would not fit cleanly into one of those situations. An example of that would be the Denver game when we were down by one and we took the safety. It was a relatively easy decision. But let's just say the score was tied or we were ahead by one. Now let's take a look at that decision and see what we'd want to do. Maybe it would change it. Maybe it wouldn't. But those are some new situations based on the experience we've had… Those will be discussed."[1074]

The Patriots staff doesn't wait till season's end to refine its tactics:

"Game management is something that you probably learn a little bit about in every single game. You prepare certain situational strategies and plays at the beginning of the season to use in those situations and sometimes modify them a little bit as you got through the year as maybe new situations occur or your personnel changes."[1075]

Avoid avoidable mistakes

"You can't win [games] if you're losing them."[1076]
    – *Bill Belichick*

"We are going to go in there and make the least amount of mistakes as possible."[1077]
    – *Patriots defensive end Ty Warren*

"Playing New England is very much like playing chess. When two very good people play chess, the one that makes a mistake loses, and that's [how they beat us] today."[1078]
    – *Curtis Martin, star running back of the New York Jets and skilled chess player*

"There are so many situations in football, and they happen so quickly. When you've played 58 minutes and it's still a tie game–like so many of our games are–it's going to come down to three or four select plays. If a player fails at that point, chances are you're going to lose."[1079]
    – *Bill Belichick*

"15 times in a row people haven't found a way to beat them. You see them in a close game and someone gets a field goal blocked. Someone snaps the ball over the punter's head. Someone throws an interception in the end zone. Someone fumbles the ball or blows a coverage, and it's usually not them."[1080]
    – *Colts head coach Tony Dungy, after Colts mistakes helped the Patriots end Indianapolis' 2003 season with a playoff loss and before Colts mistakes helped the Patriots start Indianapolis' 2004 season with an opening day loss*

In 2003, the Miami Dolphins lost to the Patriots in overtime after repeatedly blowing opportunities to seal a victory. Patriots receiver Troy Brown, who caught the game-winning 82-yard TD pass, said "It was almost like they were trying to give it to us."[1081] Patriots linebacker Ted Johnson says the Patriots win because "We don't make many mistakes. That's the key."[1082] Each of the 2004 Patriots' first six opponents walked off the field beating themselves up for committing more errors than the Patriots. After Indianapolis head coach Tony Dungy spent the entire off-season preaching incessantly to his Colts about the need to avoid mistakes against the Patriots on opening day 2004, the Colts lost another winnable game to the Patriots by again making several more mistakes than the Patriots. Colts GM Bill Polian went insane: "We shot ourselves in the foot, in the head, in the left ear lobe, in the right eye. We killed ourselves. ...This is the worst football game we've played in three years."[1083] The Colts blew that game even after referees kept them in it with dubious penalties against Patriots defensive backs–encroachment, illegal use of the hands, illegal contact, pass interference and defensive holding–likely called because the Colts and other teams had pushed through an offseason "point of emphasis" (aimed squarely at the Patriots) ordering referees to crack down on aggressive pass defense:

> "Two of the six penalties came on a key 4th quarter drive, resulted in automatic first downs, and led directly to an Indianapolis touchdown... Replays on at least two calls shows that there was virtually no contact between the New England defender and the Indy receiver."[1084]

Asked the keys to beating the Patriots, Bills head coach Mike Mularky replied, "One is don't beat yourself. Two... I don't know if there is a number two. I know if you do number one, you really have no chance."[1085] After losing to the Patriots, Bills quarterback Drew Bledsoe said, "We're making mistakes at the wrong time and–especially against the defending world champs–you can't make mistakes like that."[1086] Miami Dolphins coach Dave Wannstedt said, after his team outgained the Patriots 295 yards to 204 yards but lost 24-10, "We are just making too many negative plays. We get a first down and somebody jumps offside. Turnovers, we're giving them the short field."[1087] Seattle Seahawks quarterback Matt Hasselbeck said, "We're not a good enough team to do that stuff and beat the New England Patriots."[1088] Every New York Jet walked off the field muttering exactly what they all said before the game: Justin McCareins said, "You can't afford to make many mistakes against a team like that."[1089] Jets head coach Herm Edwards said, "Errors like that kill you."[1090] Guard Pete Kendall: "That team's so good you can't give them any extra chances. You can't make it any harder than they already make it."[1091]

Mistakes killed the St. Louis Rams in Super Bowl XXXVI. Three crucial plays were: 1) Patriots cornerback Otis Smith picking off a pass and running it back 30 yards; 2) Patriots defensive back Antwan Harris stripping the ball from wide receiver Ricky Proehl and Terrell Buckley recovering it for the Patriots; and, 3) Ty Law intercepting a pass and running it back for a touchdown. All three turnovers killed Rams drives and led to Patriots scores: a field goal and two touchdowns, respectively. Turnovers proved the Rams' undoing, as coach Mike Martz admitted: "We seemed to move the ball well enough. We just had too many errors that they were able to take advantage of."[1092] Ironically, the Rams said all season that the only team that could beat them was themselves. They "led" the NFL in giveaways (with 44 on the season) and had turned the ball over an incredible fourteen times in their only two pre-Super Bowl losses.

Every team wants to cut down on mistakes. But talking in generalities about what *not* to do accomplishes nothing. You reduce mistakes by practicing intensely and not tolerating mistakes, even during practices. A less famous key play in Super Bowl XXXVI occurred when Patriots running back "Kevin Faulk made a good decision not to throw on a designed halfback pass."[1093] By drilling that trick play, Faulk learned when to throw the ball and when to tuck it and run. Avoiding high-risk, low-reward gambles can tip games in a team's favor. Tom Brady knows this, so he continues to emphasize avoiding mistakes. In 2003, Brady didn't throw a single interception in any of the Patriots' regular season games in Foxboro. That's an astounding eight interception-free games and 241 pass attempts.[1094]

The same conservatism is apparent on defense. The Patriots allow short catches but tackle—or smash—receivers before they turn a short catch into a long catch-and-run. In 2003, "Only 2.7% of completed passes allowed by the Patriots went for 30 yards or more; only Chicago allowed fewer."[1095] Most "long passes" are actually short-to-medium passes with long runs after the catch. The Patriots defense's motto is "run and hit."[1096] Running-and-hitting prevents opponents from turning short gains into long gains. Patriots safety Rodney Harrison's personal motto, "seek and destroy,"[1097] says the same thing with more punch.

Running-and-hitting also produces powerful, high-speed collisions that smack balls loose. Harrison says the Patriots defense wins by smashing offensive players:

> "This League is geared for offense. They don't want the receivers touched; they want them to prance up and down the field. That's why when you get a shot to knock one of their heads off, you try to take it. …These guys getting in the end zone. They celebrate and they want to make you look bad, so whenever we get a chance, we're going to try play physical… We're going to try and take your head off."[1098]

Colts tight end Marcus Pollard says, "They beat us up, cold. They literally were so physical that we never got our offense going when we played them."[1099]

But Patriots defenders don't hit ferociously each play. They calibrate the aggressiveness of each hit, balancing the risk of missing a tackle against the value of a helmet-rattling collision. Before the 1996 season's Patriots-Packers Super Bowl, Packers offensive coordinator Sherm Lewis said of the Belichick-coordinated Patriots defense: "You don't see [offensive players] running loose and wide open."[1100] Belichick and Crennel train defenders to conservatively tackle opponents in one-on-one situations and to aggressively seek interceptions and fumbles whenever teammates are nearby to back them up. Facing elimination while losing to the Oakland Raiders 13-3 in "the Snow Bowl" playoff game, the Patriots defense sorely wanted to force a turnover but remained disciplined, waiting for a low-risk gang-tackling opportunity to try to step in front of a receiver or strip or smash the ball away from a ball carrier rather than risk gifting the Raiders an easy touchdown:

"We wanted [our defenders] to begin going after the ball a little more, but... we didn't want a one-on-one situation where the defender goes for the ball, misses, and gives up the long gain. We needed a situation where two or three guys are covering and then one of them can go for the ball."[1101]

The defense couldn't force another turnover, but its avoidance of sink-or-swim desperation defense prevented the Raiders from scoring again. Their patience was rewarded when the Patriots triumphed, 16-13.

The power of disciplined running-and-hitting was showcased in Super Bowl XXXVI. As Rams receiver Az-Zahir Hakim tries to catch a ball, he is surrounded by Roman Phifer, Otis Smith, and Lawyer Milloy. He drops the pass as defenders rudely pound him into the ground. Patriots defenders could body-slam Hakim–despite his speed–because they had a three-on-one advantage. Even if Hakim had eluded or bounced away from the first hit, he would not have waltzed in for an easy touchdown because two other players would have dragged him down.

Do you win a Super Bowl or avoid losing?

"For the quarterback on this team, it is real important not to make a mistake, an interception or fumble. Our defense is tough, and if [I] don't give [our opponent] a short field... they make it tough."[1102]
– *Tom Brady*

"They limit their mistakes... I [watched] their last two Super Bowls, and they really capitalize off the other team's turnovers... Kind of like tennis and unforced errors. They just let [their opponents] make mistakes. Unforced errors: you can win all day off those."[1103]
– *Philadelphia Eagles receiver Freddie Mitchell, before the Patriots did the same to his team in Super Bowl XXXIX*

"They won [Super Bowl XXXIX] methodically, smartly... Bill Belichick's men don't knock your socks off in any one area. Their true greatness lies in their completeness... It's not their strengths so much as their utter lack of weaknesses that make them so invincible."[1104]
– *Steve Sabol, NFL Films*

The first thing Belichick drills into his quarterbacks' heads–and was unable to convince Drew Bledsoe of–is the crucial importance of avoiding interceptions. As Belichick packed Rohan Davey off to NFL Europe to accumulate playing time, Davey knew his coaches wanted him to avoid risky throws:

"We sat down and talked about what I should be getting out of this experience. One of the things was about being smart and... not trying to make something happen when it's not there. That's a big thing I've been taught by coach Belichick and (offensive coordinator) Charlie (Weis). You never lose a game by punting the football."[1105]

Belichick knows NFL championships are not won by quarterbacks who carry their teams on their shoulders. Dan Marino was one of the most talented and accomplished quarterbacks of all time, but he reached just one Super Bowl, which his team lost. Rams quarterback and league MVP Kurt Warner blamed himself for losing Super Bowl XXXVI: "The offense basically gave up the first 17 points on turnovers. Our defense played well enough to be world champions. And that's what hurts most: that I let some of the guys down."[1106]

The clearest example is Denver's John Elway. As Broncos quarterback, Elway won more regular season games than any quarterback in NFL history, but he lost three Super Bowls (in January 1987, 1988, and 1990) while chucking the ball all over the field. After calming down and becoming a cog in the machine, he ended his career with consecutive Super Bowl victories (in January 1998 and 1999). According to Elway's former offensive coordinator, Jim Fassel:

> "If John ever got in trouble... it was because everything was always written that the Broncos will go as John Elway goes. I don't care who you are or how great a player you are, if you carry that burden into the game, sometimes you are going to take unnecessary risks that might blow up. As long as he just plays within the framework and allows other players to do their jobs, he can raise the whole team's level of play. And that's what they have done, because they have a good overall team and he's just a part of it."[1107]

Early in his career, Elway played like Bledsoe, putting up gaudy statistics and single-handedly winning games while also making mistakes that cost his team games. Later in his career, Elway played like Brady. From 1983 through 1992, Elway threw as many interceptions (157) as touchdowns (158). From 1993 through 1998, he threw twice as many touchdowns (142) as interceptions (69). His yards-per-attempt was 4.87% higher later in his career, but his touchdowns-per-attempt rose 34% (from 3.64 to 4.88 touchdowns-per-100-attempts) and his interceptions-per-attempt plunged 34.5% (from 3.62 to 2.37 interceptions-per-100-attempts). Smarter, more conservative decision-making helped three-time Super Bowl-losing quarterback John Elway close his career as a back-to-back champion.

As if to prove Belichick's point that a quarterback's first priority is to avoid losing, in his first Super Bowl victory, Elway completed only twelve of twenty-two pass attempts for 123 yards, tossed no touchdowns and one interception, and ran for a touchdown. On most plays, Elway was handing off to Terrell Davis, who ran for 157 yards. Elway knew he was on a great team and could rely on the Broncos' defense and powerful running attack. Late in his career, Elway discovered the power of the Patriots' philosophy–as expressed by Mike Vrabel–that "if we wind up with 45 sacks and we've got ten guys with 4.5 sacks, that's fine. It works for us."[1108] This mindset works in part because no player feels winning requires that he freelance outside the framework of the playbook. In his younger days, Elway gambled too often, trying to make something out of broken plays, rather than throw the ball away and punt.

After Tom Brady's first Super Bowl season, many observers felt Brady was merely an adequate quarterback whose primary strength was avoiding interceptions and sacks: "The only thing spectacular about Tom Brady is his success."[1109] Brady threw for only 145 yards in his first Super Bowl. Many even complained that Drew Bledsoe deserved "his" starting job back. But casual fans don't appreciate how crucial avoiding costly mistakes is. Young Brady was not a flashy down-the-field passer, though he has developed a good long-ball. But he has always avoided mistakes and completed quick, short passes with accuracy. Brady doesn't always post gaudy yardage numbers, but he racks up wins. Former Patriots running back Antowain Smith says "he's not selfish. I mean, every quarterback dreams of the deep ball, that is what they are bred for, but if he doesn't throw any in a game, he doesn't care. He realizes he doesn't want to hurt the team by making mistakes."[1110] Even football scholar Gary Shelton confesses to failing this test:

> "Bill Belichick is smarter than I am. …When the Patriots played the high-powered Rams, I was convinced–absolutely convinced–they had one shot at an upset and his name was Drew Bledsoe. Like a lot of people, I noticed Bledsoe was bigger, more experienced and had a better arm than the Pats' other quarterback."[1111]

Fans enjoy high-scoring shootouts featuring strong offenses. But the offense-happy Kansas City Chiefs must buy tickets to attend a Super Bowl. And the offense-happy 2002 Oakland Raiders got spanked by the defense-first Buccaneers in Super Bowl XXXVII. The Patriots' stout defense and no-turnover offense has proven a winning combination. In Super Bowl XXXVI, Kurt Warner threw two interceptions (one run back 47 yards for a touchdown by Ty Law), while Tom Brady threw none. Without those two plays in the 60-minute game, the Patriots lose and the Rams are world champions. Avoiding mistakes is not luck. Tom Brady would never have thrown the high-risk, low-reward wobbler of a sideline pass that Warner threw with linebacker Mike Vrabel in his face and Ty Law returned for an easy touchdown. Minimizing risk isn't sexy, but it is extremely effective.

You can also lose by being unprepared for the weather. In Super Bowl XXXIX, Jacksonville was much warmer than recent Eagles and Patriots games, and heat affected the game. Patriots linebacker Rosevelt Colvin explained that, at halftime, "Guys were just trying to hydrate as much as they could. I think [Eagles receiver Todd] Pinkston goes out [of the game] with cramps later on."[1112] He indeed did, probably from dehydration, insufficient stretching or potassium/sodium/calcium deficiency. (Cramping can also result from use of the performance-enhancing substance creatine–which improves leaping ability, something I wondered about watching Pinkston make some great leaping catches in the Super Bowl–though the aforementioned causes are more likely.) The Patriots appeared better prepared for the heat, likely because, as linebacker Roman Phifer says, "We pride ourselves on conditioning around here, whether it's hydrating, lifting weights or eating the proper food."[1113] Various Eagles reported that–late in the game–Eagles quarterback Donovan McNabb was exhausted and/or vomiting and/or unable to talk, perhaps due to the heat or extreme nerves or perhaps because he ate a pre-game meal of "pot roast savory beef."[1114]

Weather conditions also affected pre-Super Bowl practices. According to Belichick, rain and cold transformed his team's practice field at Bartram Trail High School into "an ice rink" where "We're not even going full speed and guys are falling all over the place." Belichick smartly held star defensive lineman Richard Seymour (and some other players) out of the scrimmage because he was still recovering from an injury: "After I saw the field, there was no way I was going to put him out there... when everyone was slipping and sliding." Instead, Seymour drilled safely on the sideline against a single offensive lineman. Had the Patriots not handled weather conditions so adroitly, they might have lost players to the "ice rink" or heat stroke. Super Bowl XXXIX was not the Patriots' most dominant game, but they didn't make deadly mistakes, and the Eagles did. And the Patriots believed that "the team that comes out and makes the least amount of mistakes and the most good plays is going to win... I'm confident that our team will do their job because we take... a business approach."[1115]

Patriots focus not on making spectacularly great plays but on avoiding spectacularly bad mistakes. Safety Rodney Harrison says the key is "Don't give up the cheap, easy play."[1116] They strive to play smart football, not jaw-dropping football. Linebacker Mike Vrabel says, "we have football players that... pride [our]selves on not making mistakes."[1117] Fellow linebacker Ted Johnson concurs, "We have to limit the mistakes. We have to play mistake-free football."[1118]

Fool me once…

"[My main offseason priority] is making sure that my body is as close to 100% as it can possibly be so I'm able to go all out from the first day. Last year I hurt my hamstring right off the top. [I misjudged] the speed and the pace of this level. Now I understand."[1119]
– *Patriots running back Cedric Cobbs*

"I got a big head because I was doing so well in high school. I started hanging with my friends and stopped going to class and my grades fell. [Losing my University of Florida scholarship and having to attend junior

college] was a learning experience that I can go and talk to some of the younger guys [about]. It happened to me, and I learned from it."[1120]
     – Super Bowl XXXIX MVP Deion Branch

George Santayana famously said "Those who do not remember the past are doomed to repeat it." If Santayana is correct, logic theory assures us that his proverb's converse–"Those who never repeat the past remember it"–is also true, though less famously so. Because Bill Belichick makes few mistakes, we should suspect he is a historian. He indeed is. Belichick has lived a football life and studied football history and management science, learning vicariously from others' mistakes and successes. And he has distilled his knowledge into a detailed plan for winning that he has embedded within his team's playbook, its offseason procedures manual, its scouting manual, its training camp procedures manual, its daily schedule and its culture.

The most easily avoided mistakes are those you have previously made. Whenever the Patriots screw up, they study their mistake, figure out why they made it and devise a strategy for never repeating it. Bill Belichick tolerates "rookie mistakes" but loses patience with repeat mistakes.

Media requests and exciting invitations lured Tom Brady away from football too much following his first Super Bowl win. After he suffered a down season in 2002, he learned to say "no" and hired sister Nancy part time to manage his schedule: "I wasn't handling anything well. I think the one thing I have learned in the last couple of years is that you have to find time to keep your sanity. You have to find time for yourself."[1121]

Consider the evolution of the Patriots' offensive line hires. Pass blocking has been solid, though not as strong as statistics suggest because Brady releases the ball so quickly and throws the ball away to avoid sacks. Patriots coaches were apparently especially unhappy with the offensive line's run blocking, which thrives on a knock-'em-on-their-butts, bash-their-heads-in, kick-'em-the-groin mentality. The Patriots are now signing only offensive linemen who are: 1) nasty on the field; and, 2) frat boys off the field, tight with their offensive linemates. No matter how technically sound or physically imposing you are, you will not play along the Patriots offensive line if you don't fit this profile. Those who don't match these two criteria are being thrown overboard. In 2005, the Patriots made only a token effort to re-sign left guard Joe Andruzzi, one of the kindest men you will ever meet. In came 2005 offensive guard/tackle draftees Logan Mankins (Round 1) and Nick Kaczur (Round 3). Both are vicious competitors who delight in hitting opponents. Mankins says, "I am always trying to push guys until they fall down." Mankins' sadistic joy at physically dominating his opponents is obvious on film–even to a non-expert like me–in just seconds. If Mankins' pancaked opponent foolishly tries to stand up, Mankins knocks him down again… and again until he learns to take the fetal position until well after the play is blown dead. He'll love playing next to left tackle Matt Light, whom Richard

Seymour calls "Extra Light"[1122] because Light enjoys squeezing in an extra hit the moment the referee blows the play dead.

Boston Herald reporter Michael Felger noted that two earlier Patriots offensive line draftees who, he argued, flopped in New England—Adrian Klemm and Greg Robinson-Randall—relied on finesse more than violence. They pass-block adequately but lack passion for punching defensive linemen in the mouth and shoving them aside to clear a lane for Patriots running backs. To bolster their running attack, the Patriots have developed a taste for nasty. Also, "Off the field, [Kenyatta Jones, Adrian Klemm and Greg Robinson-Randall] never seemed to fit with the fun-loving, good-guy core of linemen like Damien Woody, Matt Light, Joe Andruzzi and Dan Koppen. That might seem like a side issue, but the Pats believe [chemistry is] important because offensive line play is not a function of individuality."[1123] (I disagree that Klemm's failure reflected his style. I blame his many injuries, including two broken feet, major knee surgery, a torn calf muscle and an ankle injury that caused him to miss 54 of 80 regular season games as a Patriot. The Patriots offered Klemm a new contract soon after he broke his foot, but Klemm wanted a fresh start elsewhere.) Mankins and Kaczur will excel as enthusiastic hitters and enthusiastic participants in the Patriots' locker room fun and games (dominoes, backgammon, practical jokes, good-natured insults, *etc.*). Mankins' only obvious flaw is his selective hearing loss: "I have had personal fouls for late hits when I didn't hear the whistle." Will he become the Rodney Harrison of the Patriots' offensive line? Belichick is counting on it. He doesn't want any more nice offensive linemen.

Study your industry

"Bill was the [New York Giants] special teams coach, and I was a punter [in 1978]. We were both the same age. …He was so thorough that I felt he knew as much about my punting as I did."[1124]
– Dave Jennings

"The [St. Louis Rams'] execution in the passing game—in terms of route running techniques—is as good as anybody in football. They are a team that every year in the offseason, I watch them. I study them. I try to learn more about the passing game from them so that I can implement certain aspects of it into our team. Our assistant coaches, Brian [Daboll], Josh [McDaniels] and Charlie [Weis], we spend time in the offseason watching them throw the ball because—in all honesty—nobody throws it better."[1125]
– Bill Belichick

"I'm a big believer in Sam [Walton]'s philosophy that when it comes to good ideas, you should steal shamelessly."[1126]
– Joe Hatfield, Wal-Mart's Asia CEO

"Our success in some areas could be from something else that we've seen other teams do and copied from them."[1127]
– *Bill Belichick*

Bill Belichick *knows* football. He understands every position on the field at a deep technical level. Belichick's interview of Kirk Ferentz–then a 17-year football veteran and, a decade later, college football's 2002 Coach of the Year–for the offensive line coach opening on his Cleveland Browns scared the heck out of Ferentz: "That interview was a lesson in detail. The whole process was a workout in itself. I went home frazzled, tail between my legs."[1128] Scott Pioli, who drove Ferentz to the airport after his interview, knew a Belichick grilling indicated serious interest: "Scott told me, 'I'm sure you did better than you think. It will work out.'"[1129]

Patriots executives also know their industry: "[In 2003], the Pats were $3 million under the cap for much of the year... Belichick and Pioli [executed] an obscure salary cap maneuver that pushed those savings into 2004."[1130] Similarly, the Patriots extensively use the "qualifying contracts" loophole in the salary cap that enables them to pay players more than their salary cap figure:

> "The qualifying contract says that the veteran players minimum, depending on his years of service, could be $600,000, $650,000, $750,000, whatever it is. Under certain conditions, the club would only count $450,000 of that toward the cap. ...And there's no limit to the number of contracts that you can do. So in essence, every qualifying contract is that much cash over the cap. If we're not leading the league in those contracts, we're right at the top."[1131]

Patriots special teams ace Don Davis, for example, earned $660,000 in 2004 but counted only $455,000 against the cap.[1132] The numbers were identical for Je'Rod Cherry, another special teams standout, except Cherry's numbers were pro-rated because he was not a Patriot for the first three games.

The Patriots study other leading teams each offseason. Belichick says:

> "The Eagles franchise–starting at the top Jeff Lurie, Joe Banner, and Andy Reid, down to the coordinators, the players, the way they have managed the cap, the team by integrating young players into their system–I think they have done a fantastic job. It is a team we look at very closely in the offseason and when we have to evaluate how they manage their team, I think they are one of the model franchises."[1133]

The Patriots even go beyond studying their industry to studying top organizations in other professional sports. Scott Pioli collaborates closely with Cleveland Indians GM Mark Shapiro and San Antonio Spurs general manager R.C. Buford and director of player personnel Sam Presti. They all constantly swap ideas and insights.

The Patriots' analytical approach to determining the optimal strategy in every possible situation seems nerdy but helps them win. Consider this analysis from *FootballOutsiders.com*:

> "Teams [seem to] get pass-wacky on third-and-short instead of just pounding the ball for the first down. ...I consulted the comprehensive *Football Outsiders* database of every single play from the 2003 season. The results are pretty clear. In almost every single short yardage situation, running the ball is more likely to lead to a first down or touchdown than passing the ball. ... Which team was most likely to run in power situations? Would you believe that it was a team with a terrible running game–and the best record in football? Yes, the New England Patriots ran on 40 'power' plays, and passed on only 12 'power' plays."[1134]

Due to their poor running attack in 2003, the Patriots didn't derive as much advantage from their wise decision to run, rather than pass, in short yardage situations as other teams could have: "Despite [using the correct strategy], the Patriots actually weren't much better running (63% conversions) than passing (58% conversions)."[1135] But they were the *only* team in the NFL using the proper strategy!

Though the Patriots derived little advantage from running in short-yardage situations, they may have won the two biggest games of their amazing 2003 season– the AFC Championship Game against the Indianapolis Colts and the Super Bowl against the Carolina Panthers–by out-researching their opponents.

How the Panthers lost Super Bowl XXXVIII

The New York Times published the following seemingly arcane statistical tidbit the very day the Patriots beat the Panthers in Super Bowl XXXVIII:

> "After Harold Sackrowitz, a Rutgers statistician, was quoted in the *New York Times*... saying that teams try for a two-point conversion too often after scoring a touchdown, he received a call from Ernie Adams, the Patriots' football research director [who] sent Professor Sackrowitz a copy of the team's chart telling coaches when to go for two points, and the statistician critiqued it. 'Nobody had any real interest other than the Patriots,' said Professor Sackrowitz... New England did not try a single two-point conversion this year."[1136]

Ironically, two-point conversion strategy may have cost the Panthers a world championship.

If your team is losing by two points with one second left in a game, it's obvious you should go for two. But going for two rather than one early in a game is foolish because extra points are nearly automatic (98.7%[1137]) whereas two-point conversion attempts succeed less than half the time (43% in 1997; 39% in 1998;[1138] 44% since 2000[1139]). In other words: if you kick 100 extra points, you should expect to score 98.7 points, but if you attempt 100 two-point conversions, you should expect to score somewhere between 78 and 88 points. Extra points are more reliable and, on average, gain you more points. You don't need a statistics professor to tell you to kick extra points. Phil Simms wrote a September 2003 column explaining why "Unless it's late in the game, just kick the extra point."[1140]

In Super Bowl XXXVIII, the Carolina Panthers twice went for two points (with 12:39 left in the game and again with 6:53 left) and twice came away empty-handed. As the following chart shows, attempting two extra points yields 2 points 97.42% of the time and 1 point 2.57% of the time. While it is virtually impossible to miss two extra points, it is quite possible (31.36%) to come away from two two-point conversion attempts with zero points:

If a team...	Points scored (% of the time)
Attempts two extra points (assuming 98.7% success rate)	2 (97.42%) 1 (2.57%) 0 (0.0%)
Attempts two two-point conversions (assuming 44% success rate)	4 (19.36%) 2 (49.28%) 0 (31.36%)

The smart strategy is kicking extra points, except very late in a game when one point is of little value (e.g., because you trail by two points or lead by five points). By attempting two two-point conversions instead of two extra points, the Panthers basically accepted a 31.36% chance of scoring zero points for a 19.36% chance at two extra points (4 instead of 2).[1141]

Sackrowitz' paper demonstrates that going for two makes sense only when you don't expect much more scoring. If you expect more scoring, you're wiser to take your (nearly) automatic one point, regardless of the score differential.

How did two-point conversion strategy win the Patriots the Super Bowl? After the Carolina Panthers' two failed two-point conversions, the Panthers led 22-21 instead of 24-21, as they almost certainly would have had they just kicked extra points. The Patriots then scored a touchdown, putting them up by five points with just 2:51 left in the game. Because it was safe to assume there wouldn't be tons of scoring in the final 2:51, the Patriots successfully attempted a two-point conversion to go up by a full touchdown, 29-22. (Also noteworthy: Where the Panthers tried low-probability passes on each of their attempts, the Patriots used a higher-probability run on their successful attempt.) Had the score been 24-21 before the Patriots' touchdown, the Patriots would not have tried a two-point conversion and would instead have led 28-24. The Panthers' touchdown that tied the game at 29-29 would, instead, have put the Panthers up by a field goal, 31-28. The Patriots' game-winning field goal would instead have been a game-tying field goal, and the Super Bowl would have gone into overtime. The following chart summarizes what happened and what "should" have happened:

What actually happened	Time left	Actual score	What likely would have happened	Could have been...
Panthers TD + missed two-point conversion	12:39	21-16, Patriots	Panthers TD + extra point	21-17, Patriots
Panthers TD + missed two-point conversion	6:53	22-21, Panthers	Panthers TD + extra point	24-21, Panthers
Patriots TD + two-point conversion	2:51	29-22, Patriots	Patriots TD + extra point	28-24, Patriots
Panthers TD + extra point	1:08	29-29	Panthers TD + extra point	31-28, Panthers
Patriots kick game-winning field goal as time nearly expires	0:04	32-29, Patriots win	Patriots kick game-tying field goal as time nearly expires	31-31, go to overtime

Carolina coach John Fox's decision to go for two with 12:39 remaining was a mistake but not idiotic. It's wise to go for two when losing by five if you expect little additional scoring. Sackrowitz' paper even suggests going for two may be optimal for the average team in Fox's situation. But this situation was far from average. Fox should have expected more scoring, and he should have had little confidence in his team's ability to convert a two-point attempt against the Patriots.

Fox should have expected more scoring because: 1) The Patriots and Panthers combined to score 24 points in the final 3:05 of the first half; 2) Both defenses were exhausted and having trouble stopping anyone; 3) The Panthers offense had just driven 81 yards for a touchdown; 4) Two years earlier, the same Patriots had marched the length of the field in the final minute to win Super Bowl XXXVI on a last-second field goal; 5) Belichick's Patriots are superb clock managers and can milk the clock to squeeze in many additional plays; and, 6) The Patriots still had all three timeouts.

But perhaps Fox's biggest blunder was assuming that a two-point conversion attempt against the Patriots had a decent chance of success. The Panthers were 0-for-3 on two-point conversions during the regular season. And the Patriots had a stout goal-line defense that had famously stuffed the Indianapolis Colts on four consecutive goal line plays earlier in the season. Belichick's players constantly practice their goal-line offense and defense. The Patriots defense surrenders yards but toughens near the goal line. It's difficult to punch the ball into the end zone against Belichick's boys.

Most teams rely on a pre-printed card indicating score differentials where it is purportedly wise to go for two. Even if the conventional wisdom embodied in those cards is correct, many teams–including the Panthers in Super Bowl XXXVIII–attempt two-point conversions too early. *ESPN* analyst John Clayton's intuition is correct that "head coaches [should] hide the card until late in the fourth quarter"[1142] because two-point conversion attempts fail more often than they succeed and–as the Panthers demonstrated–teams shoot themselves in the foot with two-point conversions more often than not. The Panthers transformed a likely tie into defeat. And the Panthers would have had the upper hand in overtime because both Patriots starting safeties–Eugene Wilson and Rodney Harrison–had been knocked out of the game with injuries.

Many coaches still haven't learned. Dennis Green's Cardinals went for two late in the 3rd quarter of their 2004 Week 2 game against the Patriots and got nothing.

How the Colts lost the 2003 AFC Championship

How did strategic smarts help the Patriots win the AFC Championship Game against the Colts? The Patriots won by ten points (24-14) after scoring ten points–a touchdown and a field goal–on 1st quarter drives kept alive by 4th down conversions:

- On the game's first series, the Patriots faced 4th-and-1 from their own 44 yard line, an "obvious" punting situation. Instead, they ran a quarterback sneak. One reporter called that play, just 90 seconds into the game, "a huge gamble."[1143] That "huge gamble" made possible a 65-yard touchdown drive.

- Leading 10-0, the Patriots drove to a 4th-and-8 at the Colts' 29 nearly twenty minutes into the game. Brady threw to Troy Brown for 16 yards. After gaining six more yards, the drive stalled. But those 22 yards let Vinatieri kick an easy 25-yarder–rather than attempt a 47-yarder–to take a 13-0 lead.

Few coaches gamble on 4th down unless they're losing and time is running out. And only desperate coaches "go for broke" from their own half of the field. The Patriots were neither desperate nor reckless. The Patriots employed the counterintuitive statistical conclusions of UC-Berkeley economist David Romer. Professor Romer drafted what he assumed was an obscure, unpublished, highly-technical academic paper with the alluring title *It's Fourth Down and What Does the Bellman Equation Say? A Dynamic-Programming Analysis of Football Strategy*.[1144] Romer analyzed the optimal strategy for an NFL team facing 4th down at various locations on the field: should it punt, attempt a field goal, or attempt to gain a 1st down? Romer's empirical analysis, based on real NFL data, claimed to demonstrate that NFL teams kick punts and field goals far too frequently on 4th down and could increase their odds of winning games by "going for it" more often. For example, the paper says, "A team facing fourth-and-goal is better off on average trying for a touchdown as long as it is within 5 yards of the end zone." Instead, teams facing 4th-and-goal from the 5-yard line almost always kick field goals. Romer's analysis says teams are ignoring the value of pinning opponents deep in their own territory. Going for it close to an opponent's endzone is like a "heads I win; tails you lose" gamble. Teams that fail to score a touchdown on 4th down often either quickly score a safety–gaining two points and getting the ball back–or get the ball back with excellent field position via a punt from the opponent's end zone.

Even more startlingly, Romer's analysis also indicates it is often wise to go for it on 4th-down at midfield or even in one's own territory: "At midfield, being within 5 yards of a first down makes going for it on average desirable. Even on its 10-yard line–90 yards from a score–a team within 3 yards of a first down is better off on average going for it."[1145] This is as close to heresy as it gets in NFL circles. It contradicts decades of coaching wisdom and practice. No coach has ever "recklessly" gone for it on 4th down with the gusto Romer's study suggests is optimal behavior.

Bill Belichick was asked about Romer's unpublished paper in September 2002 and astonished everyone when he answered, "I read it. I don't know much of the math involved, but I think I understand the conclusions, and he has some valid points."[1146] The *Boston Herald*'s Michael Gee was incredulous:

"How in the world did Belichick even find out about Romer's work... let alone find time to read it? There's no stone Belichick will leave unturned in the pursuit of victory. The last thing the Pats coach must do before going to bed at night is run a Google search typing in the words 'pro football.'" [1147]

In fact, Belichick had not only read it... he even raised an intelligent, valid criticism–suggesting the results might apply only to football-playing robots: "There are motivational and momentum issues involved that I don't know how you calculate."[1148] Romer's paper had not factored in the possibility that human emotions might swing as a result of the 4th down play and affect teams' relative performance the rest of the game. Going for it on 4th-and-short and turning the ball over is an emotional blow to one's team and gives an morale boost to one's opponent, compared with punting or kicking a field goal. So, failure on 4th down might lower a team's performance and boost its opponent's. Belichick had not only analyzed the academic paper and absorbed its arguments but even transcended it by raising a real world issue ignored by the academic paper.

Like reporters attending Belichick's news conference, Professor Romer was stunned that an NFL coach had read his paper: "Upon hearing that, Professor Romer's jaw dropped, he said. His paper was available only on his Berkeley Internet site, emlab.berkeley.edu/users/dromer and the site of a group called the National Bureau of Economic Research."[1149]

Professor Romer was also impressed by Belichick's critique that his model failed to consider emotion. Romer created a new model to test Belichick's hunch that results might change after accounting for momentum shifts after a gusty 4th down play. The result? Belichick's hunch was wrong: Team performance doesn't drop after failing to make a 4th-down play. The only logical conclusion seemed to be that coaches are overly cautious and overly eager to kick, perhaps due to imitation or perhaps because failing conventionally is less hazardous to one's coaching career than failing unconventionally.

Belichick apparently accepted Romer's analysis and decided to put it to work. Belichick's aggressiveness early in the 2003 AFC Championship Game against the Colts suggests Belichick really grasped Romer's paper because the paper restricts its analysis to the early portion of football games. Romer intentionally avoided analyzing situations near the end of the first half because time constraints distort the optimal strategy. For example, with one second left, you should kick a field goal because there's no value in pinning your opponent on their 1-yard line before the half ends because time will expire before you can get a safety or get the ball back. Romer also avoided analyzing the second half because the value of points varies according to the current score differential... something not relevant early in a game when teams can be considered approximately "risk neutral" *vis-à-vis* points.

Bill Belichick's open-minded attitude toward Romer's paper contrasts with the scorn and ridicule of many other coaches. Then-New York Giants head coach Jim Fassel mocked Romer: "What does the professor coach? Maybe he needs a few more classes to teach. Too much free time?"[1150] Pittsburgh Steelers coach Bill Cowher joined in the Romer-bashing: "Asked what would happen if more coaches follow the economist's suggestions, Cowher smiled and said, 'There will be a lot more unemployed coaches looking for professors' jobs.'"[1151] Realizing that Bill Belichick's job is in no jeopardy, a Steelers fan wrote "Tale of Two Coaches," contrasting Belichick and Cowher:

> "Belichick not only took the time to read the Professor's thesis, but he also took something from it. So while Cowher was busy denouncing the Professor, Belichick was shrewdly using it to his advantage. This folks is another in a litany of reasons why Belichick is a champion and Cowher will always be an also-ran. Belichick is always striving to learn and grow and does not clutch to the past and play favorites. And Cowher is pretty much the anti-Belichick, in that he is extremely stubborn, does clutch to the past and refuses to acknowledge the idiocy in keeping players like Gildon and Bettis way past their prime."[1152]

Though Belichick revised his thinking based on Romer's paper, he is also smart enough not to delegate his decision-making to "optimal" strategies calculated using league-wide data:

> "The more 3rd-and-ones you make, the more likely you are to go for it on 4th-and-1. You also factor in the defensive side of the ball. How good of a short-yardage or goal-line team is your opponent? When you add those two up and you're real good and you don't think the other team is that proficient at it, that's one thing. If it's vice versa, then maybe that skews you."[1153]

Consciously or unconsciously, Belichick probably realizes another weakness of Romer's analysis: football teams go for it so infrequently on 4th down that Romer used 3rd down data as a proxy for 4th down performance. If defenses stack defenders along the line of scrimmage more aggressively on 4th down than 3rd down, Romer is assuming a higher 4th-down success rate than an actual coach would experience. NFL teams have converted only 44% of two-point conversions from the 2½-yard line since 2000[1154] and between 43% and 51% of 4th-down attempts.[1155] But Romer's 3rd-down data implies a roughly 64% chance of succeeding on 4th-and-1 from outside the opponent's 17-yard line, which seems too high. The optimal strategy would be more conservative if actual 4th down data were used.

A year later, Colts coach Tony Dungy was still playing conservatively. Losing 6-3 in a 2004 playoff game against the Patriots, the Colts punted on 4th-and-1 from the Patriots' 49-yard line with 24:54 left to play in the game. The Patriots won 20-3.

Study industry trends

"It's interesting to see the evolution of Bill's defense. He's always staying ahead of the curve. That's why the defense evolves and changes."[1156]
– *New defensive coordinator Eric Mangini*

"It's a game that's always changing. There are always new trends, new ways to attack each other. You have to keep moving those 11 men around, and that's a constant challenge on both sides of the ball. It'll never get stale, because of the number of men involved and the unlimited possibilities of what you can do with them."[1157]
– *Bill Belichick*

The Patriots never stand pat with either their personnel or their tactics. The Patriots are always eager to improve because their competitors are not standing still but innovating new strategies. Ever vigilant Patriots coaches study industry trends and adjust and adapt quickly.

For decades, Bill Belichick has studied other teams in search of new wrinkles and new ideas. When Belichick spots a new trend, he starts devising counter-strategies. And, if the new ideas would help his team, Belichick appropriates them. After someone invents the wheel, why stick with square tires?

In 1975, for example, Belichick studied game film of the L.A. Rams using two tight ends to beat the Redskins. In 2004, every NFL team uses two tight end sets. In 1975, this was odd. But Belichick noticed how effective this strategy was and brought the concept with him when he became the Detroit Lions' tight ends coach in 1976. The Lions went 6-8 that season while the Patriots went 11-3. Nevertheless, Belichick's Lions embarrassed the Patriots 30-10 by unleashing two tight ends.[1158]

After playing the St. Louis Rams in 2001 and again in the February 2002 Super Bowl, Belichick appreciated how hard it was to stop the powerful the Rams' spread-'em-out offense, so he copied it. He drafted receiver Deion Branch in Round 2 of the NFL Draft and signed free agent receiver Donald Hayes and tight end

Christian Fauria. After Tom Brady's new toys helped blow out the Steelers in Week 1 of 2002, a game in which Brady threw 25 straight passes without a single running play, Belichick explained, "We spread 'em out and found a way to make plays" and joked that he had passed so much "to establish the run."[1159] Christian Fauria confirmed the strategy: "The key for us is to spread the wealth... There are a lot of weapons on this team."[1160]

2002 ended unhappily, with a 9-7 record, partly because opposing offenses ran very successfully against the Patriots' defense. Out of that wreckage Belichick would pull an innovative strategy that would produce the outstanding Patriots defenses of 2003 and 2004. The 2002 Patriots defense surrendered 4.7 yards/rush (28th worst of 32 teams) and 137.4 yards/game (31st worst of 32 teams). Before 2003, the Patriots shored up their run defense by adjusting defensive tactics to better stop opposing runners, trading for mammoth and talented run-stopper Ted Washington and signing hard-hitting safety Rodney Harrison. In 2003, the Patriots' defense was superb against the run, giving up just 3.6 yards/rush (6th-best of 32 teams) and 89.6 yards/game (4th-best of 32 teams). The Patriots surrendered fifteen runs of 20+ yards in 2002 but just two in 2003.[1161]

Most notable is that the Patriots' dramatic improvement against the run did not come at the expense of a weaker pass defense. The defense remained superb against the pass in 2003, surrendering the fewest touchdown passes (11) in the NFL, intercepting the most passes (29), and yielding the fewest yards per pass attempt (5.64).[1162]

Belichick strengthened his run defense without hurting his pass defense by detecting and adapting to an industry trend. After 2002, Belichick perceived a league-wide trend toward "spread offense," wherein an offense lines up with no running back and many pass-catching wide receivers and tight ends. Belichick also knew offensive coordinators were becoming increasingly creative at using sophisticated computer analysis to identify and exploit weaknesses and mismatches. So he knew he could not easily "fix" his defense by substituting run-stoppers for pass-protectors. His base defense needed to be prepared for anything opposing offenses might throw at it: multiple running backs or empty backfields. If his defense had a weakness, opposing offenses would find and exploit it. So Belichick went out and acquired flexible players.

The 2003 and 2004 Patriots' ability to simultaneously play strong against the run and the pass revolves around the remarkable flexibility of Patriots defenders. Both of the 2003 Patriots' newly-arrived safeties are smart, love to hit and defend well against the pass and the run. Eugene Wilson was a cornerback in college, played safety for the Patriots in his 2003 rookie season, and often plays man-on-man like a third cornerback when offenses attempt to saturate the Patriots' pass defense. Wilson always seems to arrive at the right place at the right time. Belichick raves that his other starting safety, Rodney Harrison, can pretty much do it all:

"I just think Rodney Harrison is a good football player from 'A' to 'Z.' He's a pro–on the field, off the field. He has the ability to play in all situations–run, pass, blitz, tackle, special teams when he's been asked to do that. I think he is a complete player. He has had a good year for us, and he's had it in a lot of different areas. It's not all in the run. It's not all in the pass. It's not all on blitzes. It's on everything."[1163]

With flexible players who possess the intelligence to adapt to whatever tactic an offense throws at them, the Patriots defense adapts well to any offense without resorting to "sub packages"–players entering and leaving the game based on the situation or opponent's personnel. In the 2003 playoffs, Tennessee Titans offensive coordinator Mike Heimerdinger believed he could beat the Patriots by stretching their pass defense beyond its breaking point. The Titans played empty backfield, five-receiver sets to place maximal stress on the Patriots' pass defense and–by forcing the Patriots to move men away from the line of scrimmage–neutralize the Patriots' unpredictable blitzes that confuse offensive linemen and quarterbacks. The Titans did better passing (6.9 yards/attempt) than the Patriots' regular season opponents (5.64 yards/attempt), but the Patriots withstood the attempt to overwhelm their pass defense and prevailed, 17-14.[1164] The Patriots' subsequent 2003 playoff opponents copied the Titans, de-emphasizing running and attempting to flood the Patriots' pass defense with extra receivers. All three opponents removed running backs from their backfields and replaced them with extra wide receivers and tight ends. This "spread offense" forced the Patriots to move defenders out of "the box" near the line of scrimmage, where they have maximal flexibility to tackle runners, rush the quarterback, or drop into pass coverage:

"If [an offense] can't run, boom, let's spread [players] out and look for matchups that we can take advantage of. Now offenses are beginning to take that a step further. Rather than moving one guy away from the formation, they're moving [more] guys away, and having more empty formations."[1165]

The spread offense is giving defensive coordinators around the league nightmares, especially coordinators who lack enough fast, agile guys to cover opponents' third, fourth and fifth receivers: "Someone has to move out to cover those [additional receivers]. If you have a fast wide receiver and a slower defender, then offensively they feel they have the ability to match up."[1166] According to Tennessee Titans head coach Jeff Fisher, NFL passing attacks have evolved so quickly that "we look at that position [nickelback] as another starter. It has become that important of an issue."[1167] By noting this trend early, Belichick crafted a personnel strategy that immunized his team from getting victimized.

The Patriots continued preparing for the barrage of spread offenses they expected in 2004 by: 1) Spending two mid-round draft picks on productive college safeties–Guss Scott from Florida in Round 3 and Dexter Reid from UNC in Round 4; 2) Signing undrafted free agent cornerback Randall Gay; 3) Signing a slew of veteran defensive backs (Terrell Buckley, Otis Smith, Earthwind Moreland, Jeff Burris and Je'Rod Cherry); and, 4) Teaching Don Davis to play safety and Troy Brown to play nickelback. At one point, the Patriots had "no less than seven former starting cornerbacks on its roster."[1168] Burris decided not to report to training camp. Scott suffered a season-ending injury in preseason. Moreland played poorly. And Cherry, Buckley, and Smith failed to make the final roster. But Reid, Gay, Davis and Brown (and, later, Hank Poteat) provided better depth than the Patriots had in 2003.

In 2005, Belichick tried to corner the cornerback talent market. In adding cornerbacks, he adapted to another trend–the tighter enforcement of physical pass coverage–by de-emphasizing physicality and stressing coverage ability. He allowed muscular "press" cornerback Ty Law to depart and spent two 3rd round draft picks–trading for Duane Starks and drafting Ellis Hobbs–on small, quick, agile cornerbacks who can cover speedy NFL receivers stride-for-stride and time their leaps to bat down or intercept passes. The Patriots also signed former Steelers starter Chad Scott and kept ten defensive backs on their final 2005 roster, including four recent Super Bowl starters: Starks, Samuel, Gay and Poole. Another Super Bowl starter, Eugene Wilson, could move back from safety to his traditional cornerback spot whenever necessary.

After the NFL's Competition Committee instructed officials to enforce defensive pass interference more tightly in 2004 and they did so, the Patriots wisely grabbed cornerbacks who are quick enough to play on the line of scrimmage (where they can legally hit receivers) without getting burned and fast enough to cover receivers step-for-step. Tighter enforcement of pass interference is encouraging defenses to play more man-to-man and less zone coverage, placing a premium on cornerbacks who can blanket a receiver without "muscling" him. After quickly noticing the spread offense and officials' lower tolerance for clutching-and-grabbing pass defense, Belichick smartly rebalanced his portfolio by adding fast, quick, agile defensive backs far cheaper than Ty Law, whose physicality is now less of an asset.

Sweat the small stuff

"I thought I looked at football in too much detail until I met you."[1169]
– Patriots inside linebackers coach Pepper Johnson thanking Coach Belichick in his book on the 2001 season

"When [former Eagles tight end John] Spagnola would [spread his fingers] like this, it would be a pass play. When he would keep his hand clenched like this, it would be a run."[1170]
– Bill Belichick

"It's an intricate game. With every team in the NFL working full time to study their opponents and prepare their teams to compete, the margins are small, and it is often the details and the subtleties that can give one team an edge."[1171]

– Ernie Adams, Patriots director of football research

"It's the little things that have always made us what we are, and we have to make sure we don't lose sight of that."[1172]

– Willie McGinest

"He doesn't leave a rock unturned. Detail is what it's all about. When we'd break down film… we had to diagram the front, the cover, the numbers, the yards where they lined up. You'd go through all the cards and if anybody had a tendency when No. 88 was on the right, the slot, the inside left, he wanted to know about it. …It would take me four hours to [chart] one game. I used to think, 'Golly, what are we doing?' but then you see how important it is. Nothing is taken for granted."[1173]

– Fresno State head coach Pat Hill, describing his four years as
tight ends coach on Belichick's Cleveland Browns

Tom Brady is right-handed but shakes strangers' hands with his left.[1174] Why risk an injury to his throwing hand? Little things like protecting your throwing hand can make a difference in a season. So can distracting a kicker…

As Cardinals kicker Neil Rackers lined up to attempt his third field goal of the day, Patriots linebacker Mike Vrabel knew his team had no timeouts remaining but made a dramatic show out of madly waving for a timeout. Doing this technically violates the rules, but there was no penalty other than officials ignoring you. Officials called their own timeout to explain to Rackers why they would ignore Vrabel if he did it again. Vrabel then repeated his spectacle just as the Cardinals snapped the ball, hoping to again distract the kicker. After kicking successfully from 51 and 53 yards away, Rackers finally missed: "It's just something to get into the kicker's head. Whether it distracted him at all, I don't know. I hope it did. …Every little bit helps."[1175] Kickers are notoriously unflappable, but Rackers complained to an official after his miss, so perhaps Vrabel did get inside his head. Regardless, Vrabel says the Patriots enjoy using every potential edge:

"If you know the rules, you can use them to your advantage. We have tried to do that at different times, and the refs haven't called it before. This time, they did call it. I know the Emmys are [Sunday], so I figured I might work that."[1176]

Vrabel had previously used the same ploy twice on critical end-of-game field goals: the Dolphins' Olindo Mare's game-winning attempt in Miami in 2003; and the Colts' Mike Vanderjagt's game-tying attempt on opening day of 2004. On both of those attempts the opposing kicker also missed and the Patriots went on to victory! In fact, Vanderjagt's miss was his first miss since 2002. Vrabel even practices his distracting behavior during scrimmages, which helps Adam Vinatieri practice tuning out such theatrics.

After the Cardinals game, Vrabel stopped practicing his "move." Why? The NFL immediately closed the rules loophole Vrabel had been exploiting by assessing a 15-yard unsportsmanlike conduct penalty for intentionally calling a timeout in such a situation.

Belichick's 1994 Cleveland Browns defeated Bill Parcells' Patriots in a playoff game. Before that game, Belichick determined that a key to victory was shutting down Drew Bledsoe's favorite target and security blanket, All Pro tight end Ben Coates. Belichick blanketed Coates with Pro Bowl linebacker Carl Banks. But Belichick had devised a scheme that enabled Banks to hold Coates all game long. Before the game, Belichick sent Banks to talk with an official and to stick his hands against the official's chest to "demonstrate" what he planned to do to Coates. Banks told the official: "Look, I'm going to get pretty physical with this tight end, so let me show you what I'm doing... This is OK, right?"[1177] The official said "yes" and then paid no heed to Banks during the game, even as "I held the sh-- out of Ben Coates."[1178] To Banks, that incident was just one example of "the stuff we used to do with Belichick. It's the nuances. That's what makes him so special" and why "He's the most thorough coach out there."[1179]

Belichick says, "I don't think there's any real magic to it."[1180] But if there is just one secret to Belichick's NFL success, it is his fascination with football's technical details. He teaches his players to be smart and observant and to react appropriately to whatever their opponent is doing. Belichick showed a reporter film of a pre-Belichick Patriots defense getting fooled by an offense pretending to go right and instead "bootlegging" to the left (meaning the quarterback kept the ball and ran left even as the rest of his team went right). To Belichick, the offense's lack of intensity screamed "we're not really going right," but the Patriots missed the "obvious" clue: "Look at this. It's such a phoney play. Look at this lineman. He's not even blocking anybody. He's just running. [Patriot defender Chris Carter] bought it."[1181] Belichick's foreword to *Football Physics* contains this analysis of punts:

> "If a right-footed punter is kicking, the ball will most likely have a counter-clockwise rotation on it as it approaches. If the punt turns over and descends with the nose down, the ball will break to the left and the returner will have to move quickly in that direction in order to be in position to catch the ball. If the ball is coming down with the nose up, it will break right. A wobbling or end-over-end punt will be short."[1182]

Such attention to detail pays off. With the score tied at 14 and the Tennessee Titans driving downfield in a tough 2003 playoff battle, Patriots linebacker Willie McGinest sniffed out a Titans trick play. McGinest felt strange as he rushed toward Titans quarterback Steve McNair, so he diverted toward Frank Wycheck just as McNair started tossing the ball to Wycheck. McGinest tackled Wycheck for a ten-yard loss before Wycheck could throw the ball downfield. Belichick was thrilled:

"You could see trouble coming… on the double pass that [tight end Frank] Wycheck was going to throw. Willie made a great read on the play. Normally, he would be rushing the passer. But he read it on his first step and then flattened out, and by the time Wycheck got the ball, he was right on top of him. …It made me look like a good coach."[1183]

Patriots linebacker Mike Vrabel said the team actually knew what was coming: "We were 90 percent sure we were going to get the bubble screen-pass off that set [configuration of players]. We got it the first game. They ran the same [pre-snap] motion they ran before. They ran the pass off it and Willie made a great play on it."[1184]

With the Buffalo Bills going for it on 4th down late in a game, Patriots linebacker Tedy Bruschi broke into the Bills' backfield and could tackle either the running back or the quarterback. Bruschi had noticed multiple clues suggesting quarterback Drew Bledsoe was only faking a handoff to running back Travis Henry. So Bruschi ignored the running back and chased the quarterback. One-on-one with Bledsoe, Bruschi knocked the ball loose. Teammate Richard Seymour scooped it up and ran it back for a touchdown. Bruschi explained, "The way the guard and the center were set up, it just felt like a pass. I didn't think Travis could pull off the fake quick enough to come back and block me":[1185]

"I'd seen [the fake handoff] a couple of times. I wasn't going to bite on it. …The whole picture told me [the running back] wasn't getting the ball. The center-guard alignment. The situation. Drew has a certain little hop he does when he's trying to sell play-action. A few quarterbacks do that, trying to oversell the play-action. It all just told me it wasn't a run."[1186]

Bills quarterback Drew Bledsoe hadn't expected Bruschi to be so observant: "Hopefully Bruschi would have tackled Travis on the play fake and [I could have run for the first down]."[1187]

Aeneas Williams says inattention to details cost his St. Louis Rams Super Bowl XXXVI:

"The Patriots did a tremendous job of taking what we gave 'em. They took advantage of little dump passes and guys missing tackles. And what came to my mind was Coach Lovie, our defensive coordinator. He used to always talk about mistakes. He said, 'We're doing pretty good and we're feeling pretty good about [ourselves], but there are some guys [repeating] the same mistakes and I'm telling you right now, we're looking to replace you.' [On] that [final] series, we had people who were not where they were supposed to be. Those little things that were talked about all the time came back to bite us at the most significant time."[1188]

Belichick and his protégés–including Nick Saban who coached the LSU Tigers to the NCAA Division 1 national championship in 2003–sweat the details because little things add up and tip close games. Explains Patriots rookie Marquise Hill, who played on Saban's 2003 championship team:

> "(Saban) runs a tight ship, on every little thing. He pays attention to all of the details. He's real specific in everything we do–Belichick (as well). Little things like how you carry yourself off the field, how you respect the team–it's the same thing coach Saban prides our (LSU) team on. That's what you've got to do to be a winning program."[1189]

Tom Brady says Belichick insists his Patriots be as detail-focused as he is: "[Belichick]'s very well prepared. I don't think anybody works as hard as he does. He makes us understand that these are the things that it's going to take to win and these are the type things that are going to beat you. I think everyone buys into that."[1190] Patriots receiver David Givens agrees: "It starts with Belichick and goes down. We thrive on doing the right thing. We try to do the little things right, and the big things will come. It's why we win."[1191]

After losing by two touchdowns to the Patriots, Buffalo running back Travis Henry said, "Little things are killing us, man. We played great. I guess when it comes to the little things, I guess that's why they've won two of the last three Super Bowls."[1192] For example, the Bills botched the critical 4th down play mentioned earlier. The offensive line failed to touch Patriot linebacker Tedy Bruschi, and quarterback Drew Bledsoe and running back Travis Henry failed to coordinate their fake handoff. Henry apparently wasn't even sure what play had been called: "I think it was a running play. I don't know what happened and why [Bruschi] came up the middle like that. It was miscommunication somewhere."[1193] Bills receiver Eric Moulds succinctly said, "That's the difference between a 3-0 team and an 0-3 team. They make their own breaks. We shoot ourselves in the foot."[1194]

Sometimes, sweating the details is the only thing. With talk swirling that the 2005 NFL Draft was of low quality, Scott Pioli was oblivious: "This is the pool of players we all have to pick from, all 32 teams, and we have to find a way to make the best of it. ...I always look at it from the standpoint, 'We have a need. This is the pool of players. This is what we've got to do.' That's just one of those things where I don't waste a lot of time and energy looking at the whole big picture."[1195]

The Colts' "one yard from the Super Bowl" myth

The Patriots visited the Indianapolis Colts on November 30, 2003 in a fight for playoff positioning. The winner would have a huge advantage in the battle for home field advantage in the playoffs and a coveted first-round bye. (The top two teams in each conference relax and heal their wounds during the first week of the playoffs while the four lower-seeded teams fight for the right to take on the top two teams.) The Patriots shot out to a 24-10 halftime lead. After Coach Belichick smartly warned his players at halftime to play as if the game were tied, the Patriots increased their lead to 31-10, but Peyton Manning's offense caught fire and the Colts came storming back, transforming a Patriots rout into a nail-biter. The Patriots held a 38-34 lead when they punted from their own 30-yard line with 3:07 left. After an awful 18-yard Ken Walter punt, the Colts had the ball on the Patriots' 48-yard line. The Colts drove downfield and had a 1st-and-goal from the Patriots' 2-yard line with 40 seconds left. The Colts had four plays to seal the victory by moving the ball two measly yards. In golf, this is a tap in. In basketball, a slam dunk. In poker, it's getting dealt a full house. In the NFL, it's nearly "checkmate."

But the Patriots defense stiffened and simply refused to yield those two yards. Sweating the small stuff decided this game. After stopping the Colts three times, the game came down to, as Patriots linebacker Willie McGinest said, "No time left on the clock … fourth-and-one… that is what championship teams are made of."[1196] On that final play, McGinest feigned dropping into pass coverage before blitzing just as the ball was snapped. With no Colt to block him, McGinest corralled Colts running back Edgerrin James in his backfield to save the game. McGinest actually *knew* what play was coming when he saw Peyton Manning pat his hip just before the snap. In fact, McGinest may have faked Manning into calling a run. The Patriots had studied the Colts' signals, and the Colts did a poor job of disguising their plans:

> "I walked up to the slot receiver and tried to make it look like I was in coverage. I saw Peyton turn and tap his backside. That's usually a check for them to switch to a run. I was never in coverage. I was only baiting them. I stayed there for a little while and I crept and I crept and I crept. The big guys were going to clog the middle. I came off the edge like a bat out of hell. It was either going to be a great play-action play or I was going to get Edgerrin."[1197]

Back in 2001, the Patriots were already exploiting ways that Manning "tips some of the things he's going to do"![1198] Manning may be the unnamed quarterback of whom Belichick said, "He would come up to the line of scrimmage, he'd look one way, then he'd look the other way, and his head would come forward when he snapped the ball. Whichever way he looked first was the way the play was going to go."[1199]

The Patriots' goal-line stuffing of the Colts was huge. *ESPN*'s John Clayton called it "the stop heard 'round the NFL."[1200] At the time, the Kansas City Chiefs were 11-1, so everyone assumed the Colts-Patriots winner would probably earn the second seed in the AFC playoffs, a first-round playoff bye and home field advantage over all teams except the top seed.

Had the Colts earned the bye, the Patriots would have played an extra playoff game while the Colts rested, and the Patriots would have traveled to Indianapolis for the AFC Championship Game. During the playoffs, *The Boston Globe* reported that the Patriots' November triumph had decided that the AFC Championship Game would be played in Foxboro rather than Indianapolis and that the Colts, not the Patriots, had to play an extra playoff game.[1201] Television coverage of the playoffs repeated this "fact" endlessly. In October 2004, *The Boston Globe* again asserted that "Had James scored, the Colts would have had home-field advantage for the AFC title game and there might never have been a Super Bowl trip for New England."[1202] *The Buffalo News* still says, "Bill Polian's Indianapolis Colts lost to the New England Patriots in the waning seconds of regular-season games in each of the past two seasons. Both times, the losses cost the Colts home-field advantage over the Patriots in the playoffs."[1203] Even Colts head coach Tony Dungy says so. After the 2004 season, he told Peter King: "We've played them twice during the regular season in the last two years with a chance to win at the end, and if we won, we'd have played them at home in the playoffs."[1204] And in 2005, *USA Today* declared, "Had the Colts won those games, the ensuing playoff meetings would have been held indoors at the RCA Dome rather than wintry Gillette Stadium."[1205]

Though Willie McGinest's big play demonstrates the importance of details, the oft-stated "fact" that the Colts would have hosted the AFC Championship Game had they beaten the Patriots November 30th is simply untrue. It is a myth sustained by repetition. Winning that game actually gave the Patriots nothing except a psychological edge. The myth persists—especially in Indianapolis—that the Colts were inches away from a Super Bowl because a fresh Colts team playing in their home dome might have defeated a weary Patriots team. Instead, the fresh Patriots hosted the tired Colts on a cold January day, and the Patriots won another Super Bowl.

NFL tie-breaking rules are nearly inscrutable. "NFL tiebreaking procedures" posted on NFL.com (www.nfl.com/news/981202ties.html) don't even define two tiebreakers, "strength of victory" and "strength of schedule." Many fans incorrectly believe "strength of victory" is about point differential or number of blowouts. After figuring everything out, I discovered the Patriots still would have won first seed in the AFC—on the fourth tie-breaker—if they had lost to Indianapolis on November 30, 2003. The Colts, Patriots, and Chiefs each would have finished with a 13-3 record, a 10-2 AFC record, and a 4-1 record against their common opponents: Buffalo, Cleveland, Denver, and Houston. (Each played five games against the four teams because New England played Buffalo twice, Kansas City played Denver twice, and Indianapolis played Houston twice.) The first tie-breaker (head-to-head sweep) would have been ignored because Kansas City played neither New England nor Indianapolis and the tie-breaker applies "only if one club has defeated each of the others or if one club has lost to each of the others." The teams would have tied on the second tie-breaker (AFC record) and third (common opponents). It would have come down to the fourth tie-breaker, "strength of victory," which is the collective winning percentage of all teams that team defeated. The Patriots beat many playoff teams and had a stronger "strength of victory" (.5044) than the Colts (.4479) or Chiefs (.3846). Even if the Patriots had lost to Indianapolis, they still would have had a higher "strength of victory" (.4856) than the Colts (.4760).

	What actually happened...	*If Colts had beaten Patriots...*
Patriots' record	14-2	13-3
Colts' record	12-4	13-3
Chiefs' record	13-3	13-3
Patriots' common opponents	One loss (Buffalo)	One loss (Buffalo)
Colts' common opponents	One loss (Denver)	One loss (Denver)
Chiefs' common opponents	One loss (Denver)	One loss (Denver)
Patriots' strength of victory	.5044	.4856
Colts' strength of victory	.4479	.4760
Chiefs' strength of victory	.3846	.3846

My calculation. "Strength of Victory" stats in my "What actually happened" column match www.nfl.com/standings/conference, so I am confident I am using the correct formula.

In 2004, the Patriots had a better record (14-2) than the Colts (12-4), beat the Colts head-to-head, and had the edge in common opponents (since the Patriots beat the Chiefs while the Colts lost to them). Nevertheless, it is true the Colts would have nosed past the Patriots if they had beaten them in Week 1 and everything else had played out the same. They would have had identical 13-3 records, and the Colts would have won head-to-head... though I suspect the Patriots would have avoided losing to Miami 29-28 (a game in which they blew an 11 point lead in the final three minutes) and finished 14-2 to edge the Colts. Regardless, home field advantage didn't help mighty Pittsburgh, and it's doubtful the Colts—who lost their playoff game to the Patriots 20-3 at Foxboro—would have won in Indianapolis.

Expand your options

"We have, like, 35 linebackers in [training] camp. Is that even legal?"[1206]
– Patriots linebacker Ted Johnson

Apparently 35 linebackers wasn't enough for the Patriots because Ted Johnson joked at another time that, "We've got like 50 linebackers in camp."[1207]

Joking aside, widening your options is an excellent way to improve the quality of your decisions. For example, before the 2004 NFL Draft, the Patriots made several player transactions that filled roster holes. This set them up to use each draft choice on the "best player available" rather than the "best player available at a position of need":

- Realizing they would probably not re-sign aging starting defensive end Bobby Hamilton (because they wanted to get younger on defense), the Patriots signed Steelers defensive end Rodney Bailey. Because Bailey was a restricted free agent originally drafted in Round 6, the Patriots surrendered their 6th-round draft pick to Pittsburgh when the Steelers chose not to match the Patriots' offer. The Patriots are excited about Bailey (and the Steelers nearly chose to match), believing him superior to anyone available in Round 6. Unfortunately, Bailey missed the 2004 season after a training camp injury.

- The Patriots took out another pre-draft insurance policy on another hole in their lineup—nose tackle—by signing 34-year-old veteran Keith Traylor. Traylor is no Ted Washington (the Patriots' 2003 nose tackle), but Traylor possesses the size and defensive line experience to clog the middle. His signing eliminated another glaring need.

- Even before trading a 2nd-round draft pick for disgruntled Cincinnati Bengals star running back Corey Dillon, Belichick was able to say, nine days before the 2004 draft, "I think we can play with what we've got. We've got guys that have won quite a few games the last few years."[1208] But he could have added an exclamation point days later after filling the only remaining hole: running back. Dillon had run for more than 1,000 yards in six of his seven NFL seasons. Like Bailey, Dillon—a *bona fide* star running back—was more valuable to the Patriots than any college player available with the draft choice they traded to acquire him: "Looking at the relative options that were available around No. 56, the New England Patriots were happy to have Corey Dillon."[1209] In 2004, Dillon (1,635 yards) outgained all three Round 2 running backs combined: Tatum Bell (396), Julius Jones (819) and Greg Jones (162). And he easily outpaced every Round 1 running back: Kevin Jones (1,133), Steven Jackson (673) and Chris Perry (1).

The Patriots' pre-draft maneuvering brilliantly positioned them to draft the best talent available in the draft, regardless of position, rather than be held hostage by a weak position of need. With no "needs," they were able to draft for value. Had they not acquired Traylor, they might have felt an urgent need to trade draft picks to move up and select Miami Hurricanes defensive tackle Vince Wilfork. Had they not signed Dillon, they might have felt compelled to draft a running back when Wilfork, whom many expected to be a top 10 selection, unexpectedly fell to the 21st pick. With no needs, the Patriots grabbed this "massive" talent, a true steal at #21. One unnamed NFC general manager told a reporter after the draft, "We had him in our top 10."[1210] An unnamed AFC general manager said Wilfork was perfect for the Patriots' system: "Wilfork is younger and quicker and in better health [than Ted Washington]. In the system New England plays—with the two-gap assignments that put the premium on controlling the line and attracting blockers—Wilfork is absolutely the right guy."[1211] (According to defensive end Ty Warren, "We two-gapped on every play, except on passing downs."[1212])

Thanks to pre-draft maneuvering, the Patriots could also afford to grab tight end Benjamin Watson at the end of the Round 1 and defensive end Marquise Hill at the end of Round 2, though they had no particular need for another tight end or defensive end.

As the draft neared completion, the Patriots continued expanding their options by hoarding undrafted football players. During the draft's final round, they were on the phone with Florida State longsnapper Brian Sawyer, whom they quickly signed to a free agent contract along with other promising undrafted players, like LSU cornerback Randall Gay. The Patriots released Sawyer just before the season after the Patriots' veteran longsnapper recovered from his injury, but Gay became a starting cornerback on a Super Bowl champion! The Patriots always expand their options by signing many more quality football players than can make the team to create depth and competition. Not all signings work out. They said "good bye" to the ageless Otis Smith before training camp, and Jeff Burris decided at the last minute not to report, but the team still had more cornerbacks than could make the roster. Randall Gay excited the coaches enough to cut Terrell Buckley, a veteran of the 2001 Patriots Super Bowl season. (Though fans were shocked Gay made the team, Gay himself said, "Coming in, I thought I had a real good shot to make the team."[1213] He had played in an LSU defense virtually identical to the Patriots' and could play safety and cornerback.)

Corey Dillon

In the spring of 2004, several teams–including the Patriots, Dallas Cowboys, Miami Dolphins and Oakland Raiders–needed a running back and considered trading for Corey Dillon, but no team was offering the Bengals more than a 3rd-round pick. Many experts believed the Patriots wouldn't touch Dillon because of his bad reputation: "Belichick would probably prefer an athlete's foot epidemic in his locker-room to a questionable guy like Dillon."[1214] But Patriots safety Rodney Harrison pushed the team to consider Dillon:

> "I knew Corey was one of the hardest-working guys I was around. I used to watch Corey in warmups and watch him play, and he just worked so hard and ran the ball so hard. How could a guy like that not help you? I kind of put myself in his shoes, like maybe this could be a Rodney Harrison kind of story."[1215]

Belichick and Pioli refused to disqualify Dillon based on his reputation. They collected facts. Between ages 12 and 19 (1987 through 1994), Dillon was constantly in trouble with the law. In the late 1980s and early 1990s, "Dillon was arrested and charged with assault, malicious mischief, obstruction, possessing stolen property, reckless endangerment, and theft. ... [In 1989] Dillon and two other boys were arrested and later convicted of attempting to sell cocaine to undercover Seattle police."[1216] Dillon has always denied selling cocaine, calling himself "a victim of certain circumstances" and "guilty by association," though he partially chose those circumstances and associations. In March 1998, "he was arrested and charged in Seattle with driving under the influence, negligent driving, and driving with a suspended license."[1217] In January 2002, *Maxim* magazine "inducted" Dillon into its "Sports Felon Hall of Fame":

> *"Arrested for: DUI, theft (twice), intent to sell cocaine, obstructing a police officer (thrice), resisting arrest (twice), assault (five times), criminal trespass, malicious mischief (twice), reckless endangerment (twice)* Corey Dillon has committed so many crimes (with such variety!), we inducted him early. He had 11 arrests before age 17. Since going pro Corey's been busted for DUI, driving with a suspended license, and assaulting his wife… We still expect a lot of jail time from this promising youngster."[1218]

But the Patriots explore options rather than assume they know the best option before investigating carefully. Scott Pioli says, "There are certain guys who are perceived as bad character guys that, until we really knew who they were, I don't think we would make a judgment."[1219] Dillon fit this category:

> "We went into the whole situation with an open mind. We didn't have a preconceived belief of who Corey Dillon was or supposed to be, and that's the approach we take with any player. All of us have reputations that precede us that are either good or bad and so you sit with a person, man or woman, and find out what and who they are for yourself. We try to avoid judging people before we spend time with them."[1220]

> "I'm not sure that our personal feelings about Corey Dillon were what seemed to be the general public's perception or how he was portrayed… In the time we spent with Corey, we didn't go in with preconceived notions… It's important to us to meet face-to-face [and] see their eyes, hear them."[1221]

Many were shocked when the Patriots, who sign only "character guys," traded a 2nd-round draft pick for Dillon, who landed himself in trouble galore since his early teen years and became visibly and audibly disgruntled in Cincinnati. But, after researching Dillon exhaustively and meeting with him personally, the Patriots determined he had put his troubles behind him and would likely shine in New England. Dillon described the process as follows:

> "They just wanted to be reassured that I am a good guy. They did a two-month investigation—that's what I call it—and they spoke with a lot of people, and everybody told them I am a good guy and that he's a hard worker. They [then] just wanted to bring me in [for a long face-to-face meeting] and reassure what they are thinking."[1222]

The Patriots got inside Dillon's head. They may have understood Dillon as well as he understood himself. In their face-to-face meeting, the Patriots asked about every incident since Dillon's childhood:

"We went over all the incidents, and if I was wrong, I told them I was wrong. And there were times I was wrong. I can admit it. But I think some of the things I did were magnified because for a long time in Cincinnati I was the only guy everyone looked at."[1223]

Dillon didn't feel uncomfortable under the Patriots' microscope because he felt the Patriots questioned him respectfully and appreciated that no longer applicable environmental factors had contributed to many of his serious problems years earlier:

"If Bill didn't think I was a good guy, there wouldn't have been a meeting. Obviously, he thought I was a good guy, and it was more of me and him sitting down and getting familiar with one another. It was a great meeting. We talked about football. I don't think it was an interrogation of what I had been doing 20 years prior. We talked about me coming there and contributing and helping the team win."[1224]

Patriots decision-makers believed they understood why Dillon acted as he did when he did and why he was unlikely to repeat such behaviors: "the Pats determined Dillon was a Bryan Cox-type, a player with a bad reputation on the outside, but a good football personality on the inside."[1225] They decided his recent whining was also forgivable, a natural reaction of a competitor to seven straight losing seasons with the Bengals.

Dillon's troubles with the Bengals reflected not Dillon being a jerk but a player who desperately, passionately wants to win. As Dillon puts it, "nobody thought they'd [trade for me] because, 'Everybody knows Corey Dillon ain't a New England type.' I was kind of baffled. If you look at it, I'm a hard worker, I'm a team player, and I give 110 percent. That's a New England guy."[1226] Having rushed for over 1,000 yards in each of his first six seasons and been a Pro Bowl running back three times, Dillon's talent was beyond dispute. When questioned about his complaining even during the best Bengals season this decade (2003), Dillon replied, "I have been there a long, long time. It got a little better, but it didn't get that much better. If 8-8 is a good season to you, I don't know what to think. I have a high standard, and that just did not sit right with me."[1227] He has also said, "in seven years [with the Bengals], I won a total of [34] games. Who would be satisfied with that? I'm a competitor. And if I feel like I'm not given an opportunity to compete, yeah, I'm going to be upset, and there's a lot of times I've been upset down there. It's not that I'm a bad guy. A lot of people in my position would be angry, too."[1228] Dillon wanted to play for a winner, and his Bengals never once made the playoffs. Even before meeting with Dillon, Belichick says, the deal "was pretty much all done."[1229]

Patriots players adopted a similar mindset in judging their new teammate. Tight end Christian Fauria said, "I'd always kind of heard the rumors but decided to make my own impression of him. It's been nothing but good."[1230]

Maxim was wrong. Dillon has been a model citizen since August 26, 2000, when he was charged with fourth-degree domestic assault on his wife, Desiree.[1231]

Real options

The Patriots taught receivers David Givens and Troy Brown to play as defensive backs in a pinch. When secondary coach Eric Mangini initially convinced Belichick to try Brown on defense during 2004 training camp, no one knew how the experiment would turn out. Did Brown have NFL nickelback potential? Could the Patriots train him quickly enough? And, if Brown learned the position, would he be needed?

Mangini was effectively proposing a development project. But the risk was low because the project could be abandoned at any time if it appeared headed for failure. Mangini sought only an initial trial. As long as Brown showed sufficient potential and learned fast enough, his training would continue.

Brown's training is an example of a "real option," something of potential but uncertain value. At every step along his development process, coaches decided he had shown enough potential to continue. Eventually, Brown helped his team win a Super Bowl. That would have been impossible if the Patriots had not initiated the project during training camp.

Belichick and Mangini continually weighed the experiment's cost (the time and energy Mangini and Brown devoted to it) against its potential value ("How well could Brown play nickelback?" and "How likely are we to need Brown at nickelback?"). Every investment of time and energy raised Brown's ability closer to his potential and reduced uncertainty about his potential. Simultaneously, the Patriots' need for Brown was rising. When Tyrone Poole was injured in Week 3 against Buffalo, the probability that the team would need Brown rose. When Ty Law broke his foot early in the Halloween game in Pittsburgh, the probability rose further. When an injury knocked Asante Samuel from the St. Louis game on the defense's second play, Troy Brown was on the field. Brown was an active defender from early November through early February.

Teams require multiple personnel trained for each role. Belichick wisely uses the preseason to teach experienced players new positions because:

> "It is a little late to wait until the tenth week and say, 'Oh, geez, we have got a couple corners hurt, who are we going to move over?' It is a lot easier to try to build [player flexibility and positional depth] now... If we are going to do it, I would rather look at it now than right in the middle of the season where everybody has got a lot of other things to worry about."[1232]

Another tenet of real options is not foreclosing options prematurely. "Fungible" assets with multiple potential uses are more valuable than assets dedicated to a single use. That's one reason I built a video recorder on a computer rather than buy a Tivo. I also use that computer as a jukebox and for accounting. Businesses must frequently choose between purchasing specialized equipment that performs a few tasks superbly and multi-purpose equipment capable of performing more tasks but none especially well. Doing your taxes in a spreadsheet is not as easy as using specialized tax software, but having your financial data in a spreadsheet opens up other options–such as analyzing your spending patterns–that specialized tax software lacks.

Bill Belichick may not formally understand "real options" theory–though I would not be surprised if he does–but he certainly understands it intuitively because he keeps his options open. Consider the importance he places on personnel flexibility, which lets his team change its plans moments before–and even after–the ball is snapped. Rather than pay top dollar for the NFL's greatest run-stuffing linebacker and pay top dollar again for the NFL's greatest pass-covering linebacker, the Patriots have many linebackers who cover both the run and the pass well: "We sort of look for those guys, the players that don't just do one thing. We really don't look for the player that is really just one-dimensional because I think to be able to play on this team you have to be multi-dimensional."[1233]

Other examples of the Patriots keeping their options open include:

- Stockpiling extra players but not evaluating them until late in training camp.

- Belichick's willingness to tear up his game plan early in a game if it isn't working. Many coaches stubbornly stick with their game plan. Belichick knows following the game plan is just an option.

- The Patriots' defensive and offensive schemes, personnel, and coaching are designed to enable them to run different plays from identical "pre-snap looks." The Patriots carefully disguise which play they're actually running. Even players don't always know because the play can change based on what players see the other team doing. Charlie Weis says players must understand: "here is where the play is called and how it is designed to go but–based on the pre-snap look–this is probably where it is going to go."[1234]

- As Tom Brady's football instincts have improved, Belichick and Weis have expanded his freedom to change plays at the last moment based on what he's seeing from the opposing defense.

THINK CREATIVELY

"It's not that I'm so smart. It's that I stay with problems longer."
   – Einstein

Bill Belichick is always searching for better ideas. He encourages subordinates to bring him new ideas. He seeks out the opinions of former colleagues. And his subconscious dwells on problems and surprises him with new insights he uses to refine his strategies. Belichick is never afraid to change his mind in light of new facts and new ideas:

> "[Situations] are not always quite the way you draw them up. There's always some little wrinkle–field position, field conditions, the weather, time, time outs, score, etc.–so I think you are always learning on that. It is something as a coach, a quarterback, and coordinator and play caller, you've always got to stay on top of it and keep thinking about it. The more you think about it, the quicker I think you can react when those things do occur during the game. It's a lot easier when you can plan ahead."[1235]

Zero-based budgeting

> "There's no shortcut to [building a team each season]. You build the foundation brick by brick."[1236]
> – *Bill Belichick*

> "Every day is a new day. You have to come out here and re-establish yourself every day."[1237]
> – *Former Patriot running back J.R. Redmond*

> *Andy Grove*: "If we got kicked out and the board brought in a new CEO, what do you think he would do?"
> *Gordon Moore*: "He would get us out of [computer] memory."
> *Andy Grove*: "Why shouldn't you and I walk out the door, come back, and do it ourselves?"
> – *Intel's president and CEO deciding to exit computer memory and produce microprocessors*

> "You can come up with any [defensive play]. If it will help us win, we will do it. We'll do anything."[1238]
> – *Patriots linebacker Mike Vrabel*

Belichick takes a "zero-based budgeting" approach to football. In zero-based budgeting, last year's funding decisions have no impact on this year's funding decisions. Each project or program must justify itself anew each year, and the budget is determined without reference to last year's budget. Belichick's take-nothing-for-granted mindset is smart, according to management guru Peter Drucker:

> "The key to doing something different tomorrow is getting rid of the no-longer-productive, the obsolescent, the obsolete. The first step in planning is to ask of any activity, any product, any process or market, 'If we were not committed to this today, would we go into it?' If the answer is no, one says,

'How can we get out–fast?' Systematic sloughing off of yesterday… will force thinking and action. It will make available men and money for new things. It will create willingness to act."[1239]

We observe this principle throughout the Patriots organization:

1) *Upgrading the roster*: Belichick and Pioli's attitude seems to be "If it ain't broke, fix it anyhow." Pioli says they will upgrade any position at any time: "If there's a player out there that can upgrade our football team and make us better– regardless of the position on the field and regardless of the depth on the football team–we're going to do that."[1240] Patriots scout Larry Cook explains: "You've got to be cruel at times. …What you really have to guard against is becoming complacent with the personnel you have… Our job is to have people in place, ready to be future Patriots."[1241] After overhauling a chunk of his roster following back-to-back Super Bowl wins, Belichick explained, "There's always a to-do list for the offseason, and it's always long and comprehensive. I've never gone into an offseason saying, 'Well, we've got everything set here. See you in July. We're done.'"[1242] After winning several Super Bowls, the Patriots identified 23 personnel needs.[1243]

Although Antowain Smith helped carry the ball–and the Patriots–to two Super Bowl victories, the Patriots decided to upgrade. After looking critically and objectively at the Patriots' weak running game, Belichick and Pioli determined Smith was a weakness. Belichick's Patriots have never had a powerful running attack, and the 2003 Patriots had a lousy "red zone" offense; fifty visits to within twenty yards of their opponent's end zone resulted in just 22 touchdowns, the next-to-worst conversion rate in the AFC. The Patriots addressed both problems by trading for three-time Pro Bowl running back Corey Dillon:

> "[Red zone productivity] is part of Corey's resume and part of what he's done. He is a power runner, and having a power runner at that area of the field could be beneficial because there are smaller spaces. There are going to be bodies in the way, and you are going to have to deal with them and create spaces. I think he is a good interior runner and he is good on the goal line, so hopefully he will help our production down there."[1244]

Belichick and Pioli never let sentimentality or familiarity or a "good enough" mindset prevent them from improving their roster.

2) *Salaries*: Zero-based budgeting implies making contract offers and roster decisions based on projected future performance, not past performance. As Troy Brown can attest, the Patriots do not overpay for past performance:

> "Looking at [a player's past play] is usually somewhat of an indicator, but what is more important is where you think it is going to be [in the future]. Some guys have years that aren't as good and then their [subsequent] years are a lot better. Other guys have good years and the next years aren't as good. What you want to do is decide when you want to buy."[1245]

After Ty Law had a great season in 2003—most notably snaring three interceptions of Peyton Manning in the AFC Championship Game—he mouthed off about deserving more money, though he had long been the NFL's best-paid cornerback. The Patriots refused, arguing Law's an aging player and that cornerback performance invariably declines after age 30. Law and the Patriots eventually left Law's contract as it was and focused on working together toward another Super Bowl. The Patriots' refusal to renegotiate Law's contract exemplifies the Patriots' focus on paying for projected performance, not past performance.

3) *Evaluating players' personal histories*: The Patriots acquired Corey Dillon after determining his troubles would not likely recur when surrounded by a winning locker room. After making that determination, the Patriots never looked back to Dillon's past. As with all their players, they let Dillon's on-field and off-field performance as a Patriot decide his fate:

> "We look into all of the players that we draft and obviously if we draft them we are ready to bring them onto the Patriots team and we are really going to evaluate them on a moving forward basis. ...We look at all of the players as they come on our team and evaluate their performance and their actions on the Patriots. ...I don't want to try to judge everybody on what happened in other environments."[1246]

To the Patriots, Dillon's past was relevant only to the extent it predicted his future as a Patriot, something they felt confident about. The Patriots probably felt Dillon was even better than his statistics because he had gained over 1,100 yards in six straight seasons as the Bengals' best player and their opponents' #1 focus. If they thought he would post even better stats as just another weapon in the Patriots offense, they were right. His average of 4.7 yards/carry in his first Patriots season is better than all but his rookie season in Cincinnati, when he gained 4.8 yards/carry. They probably also realized joining the Patriots would energize Dillon, which it did: "I rededicated myself to what I want to do and what I want to become... It just gave me extra incentive to come in here and be the best I could be. And it makes it a lot easier when you're playing with guys like this."[1247]

4) *Preseason preparations*: Belichick has convinced his players that each season's team is an entirely new team that must re-learn football basics: "You've got to walk before you can run. Right now, we're crawling."[1248]

> "There is no shortcut to it. You can't take two days and say, 'OK, we're all set.' The only way to have all your bases covered is to go out and cover them. That's something I've explained to the team and individually. Those elements are not going to be skimmed over. At times it's going to be drudgery, especially for the players that have been through it a number of times. But it's a process we have to go through."[1249]

Belichick's players spout his brick-laying metaphor. Kicker Adam Vinatieri explains, "It's one brick at a time. We've got a long ways to go before the house is built."[1250]

After the Cincinnati Bengals beat the Patriots 31-3 in a 2004 preseason game, Tom Brady was asked whether he took solace in the Patriots' proven ability to overcome adversity. Brady's response illustrates zero-based budgeting: "Not this team. This team hasn't responded to anything. 'Poor' would be the way to summarize us right now."[1251] After winning 17 straight games, safety Rodney Harrison was asked about the streak: "I don't know about streaks or any of that other crap. It's just one game."[1252] Players read from the same script as their coach, who insisted in early 2004 that his Patriots had no winning streak or championship because those were accomplishments of a completely different team–the 2003 Patriots: "There's no championship team. There's been one game played this year, and that's it. And so nobody's won anything, nobody's done anything."[1253]

Charlie Weis brought zero-based budgeting to Notre Dame. Though virtually every 2004 starting offensive player returned for 2005, the staff watched barely any film from 2004 because they cared only how players would perform in their new system.

Patriots outside linebackers coach Rob Ryan carried this philosophy to Oakland after the Raiders hired him–following the 2003 season–as their defensive coordinator. Ryan signed two of the NFL's most prolific and accomplished linemen– Ted Washington (a Patriot in 2003) and Warren Sapp–but didn't assume they were using the right techniques. Ryan personally tutored these stars in defensive line fundamentals: "We'll teach fundamentals first, then the scheme. That's one thing I learned from the Patriots and [defensive coordinator] Romeo Crennel."[1254]

5) *The irrelevance of past team performance*: Zero-based budgeting is such an emphasis within the Patriots locker room that even the freshest rookies "get it" within days of arriving in Foxboro. Special teamer and backup linebacker/safety Don Davis reports, "It's what have you done for me lately. We're in the production business. What you did before is irrelevant. Everyone knows that."[1255] How proud was Patriots rookie Marquise Hill that his team, the LSU Tigers, became co-national champions just months before he was drafted?

> "It means nothing. There's nothing to talk about now. Time to move on. Once you've done it, it's done. That's one of the things I learned playing under coach Saban. This business is about 'what have you done for me lately,' not dealing with the past."[1256]

Linebacker Mike Vrabel says his teammates know a Super Bowl trophy doesn't help win football games: "One of the things we've done a great job with [in 2004] is not defending anything. We've gone out and fought for games. We haven't pretended that we own this title and that we carry this with us. [After winning] a Super Bowl... you have to come back and start all over."[1257]

Belichick lives zero-based budgeting. Philadelphia Eagles head coach Andy Reid says, "I wear [my 1996 Super Bowl ring] year round."[1258] Belichick could wear his five Super Bowl championship rings (two from the Giants; three from the Patriots), but that would be living in the past: "I don't have any jewelry. I don't wear a watch or a ring. When you're on the football field, it's not about where you came from. It's not what you have. It's all about performance. That's all that matters."[1259] Belichick's behavior illustrates Patriots coaches practicing what they preach. Belichick's players respect their coach because he doesn't hold himself to a lesser standard. Patriots offensive lineman Russ "Frodo" Hochstein even (jokingly) complains about lugging his giant Super Bowl rings around: "I might take the first one back [to my hometown] to show it off... It sucks going through the airport with them things because a lot of people notice them. It gets you nervous."[1260] Linebacker Ted Johnson is also burdened by his rings: "It's so funny to me. People ask me about my ring—'Where's your ring?'—as I'm lifting at the gym."[1261]

"Streaks" are another backward-looking topic Belichick refuses to discuss. As the Patriots kept extending their NFL-record winning streak, Belichick denied its relevance. He refused to let "streak" talk distract his team from doing everything in its power to prepare for their next game: "Whether we won 15 in a row or didn't win 15 in a row, nobody cares about that now, certainly not Indianapolis."[1262] But opposing players *did* care. The Buffalo Bills swore the Patriots would not extend their streak to 18 games at their expense. Afterwards, Bills linebacker Takeo Spikes was awed: "You're talking about 18 straight wins, man. *Eighteen straight*! That's a big, big number, OK? The way this league is, you have to be playing great to win three or four games in a row."[1263] The Patriots eventually achieved 21 straight by preparing for each upcoming game, not by daydreaming about their streak.

Asked whether the Patriots felt advantaged going into Super Bowl XXXIX because they had won two recent Super Bowls, Troy Brown explained "There is no comfort level at all. The two teams in this Super Bowl are very good teams... We've got to go out and play well. The team that plays the best is going to win."[1264]

6) *Player assessment*: Belichick doesn't care how a player performed last year or three years ago or what round of the draft he was drafted in: "Coach Belichick told me, 'We don't care where you come from or what you did in college. You're a Patriot now. We'll judge you from this day forward. It's performance-based.'"[1265] When players arrive in Foxboro, no matter how they got there, Belichick's only concern is how well they're likely to play in future games:

"Everybody is in the same boat. At this point, I don't think it really matters how anybody got here... The only thing they are being judged on is what they do going forward. I don't think anybody cares how many touchdown passes some guy caught last year or how many tackles he made or missed or whatever. All it is about is what he can do for our team, what he can do for himself in terms of finding a role on the team and that all will be based on his performance, not based on some game he had in college."[1266]

Belichick says that whether the team paid a signing bonus or traded a draft pick to acquire a player has "zero" relevance: "It doesn't matter whether the guy played Division I or Division VI, was in 12 Pro Bowls or was a rookie free agent... A player's performance, to me, is based on what he does in your system on the football field."[1267] Asked about the Patriots' rare all-1st-round defensive line, nose tackle Vince Wilfork sniffed that "That doesn't mean anything. Everyone in this league is good, so I don't care if it's three 1st-rounders, three free agents or three 3rd-rounders. Whoever can get the job done will play."[1268] Pressed to know what players must do to make the team, Belichick said players are measured with a "what-have-you-done-for-me-lately" yardstick:

> "Play better than the competition. The same things that David Givens did in the seventh round, the same thing that Tom Ashworth has done, you can go right down the line, [Tom] Brady, those guys didn't come in here with some of the hype that somebody else comes in with. They came in and they played well enough to establish themselves and earn a role and be able to contribute to the team. Everybody will get the same opportunity. What each guy does with it will be up to him."[1269]

Investment companies warn that "past performance is not necessarily indicative of future results." Certain teams pay outsized contracts to free agents who have had one or two statistically strong seasons. (The Washington Redskins are the NFL's poster boy for overpaying free agents.) Such players frequently disappoint their new teams. This is partly due to players being suited to one system but not another. It also partly results from "regression toward the mean," meaning that players who have been lucky in the recent past are likely to have average luck in coming seasons. The Patriots try to extrapolate how a free agent would perform within the Patriots' system. They often find players–like Joe Andruzzi, Monty Beisel and Mike Vrabel–who can't get into games for their current teams but project to be valuable Patriots:

> "When you are comparing players, you are definitely taking a look at where they are now and where you think they're going to be... doing the things you want them to do. And maybe the things that he did in another system either were very favorable and accentuated his strengths or maybe they really didn't and you think he may be able to blossom or be more productive in your system or in the things you're going to ask him to do."[1270]

As the team's fourth-string quarterback in 2000, Tom Brady was unknown even to Patriots fans. Through superior play, Brady-the-Nobody leapt over Michael Bishop and Damon Huard on the depth chart to become Bledsoe's backup and lead the team after Bledsoe's injury. Brady has done OK since then, despite his humble beginnings.

Knowing they must continually earn their roster spots, Patriots players are motivated to improve. After playing left guard on the victorious Super Bowl XXXVIII team, Russ Hochstein knew he could easily have failed to earn a roster spot in 2004: "I approach it as, 'I have to start all over again. I have no job. I signed a contract, but it means nothing. I have to go out and perform better than I did a year ago.' I'm looking at it like there's no one penciled in [as the starting left guard], and that's the way it is."[1271]

Zero-based budgeting is a philosophy and a mindset. Veteran players don't show up at the beginning of training camp with "blank slate" minds. Belichick simply assumes they do. Belichick runs through every play until the team proves it is ready to execute that play under game conditions. Of course, Patriot players study their playbooks during the off-season and arrive at training camp remarkably prepared. Tom Brady was immediately impressed on the first day of 2004 training camp: "We ran a bunch of plays that we didn't even really install. We just ran them, and everyone did them perfect. That just shows you we can be ahead of schedule if we continue working at it."[1272] But successful coaches assume nothing and believe only what they see with their eyes. Belichick says roster decisions are "based on what a player's performance is out on the field, and [I] have to stand up there in front of the team and say, 'These are the players that we've selected [for] the team based on performance,' not based on other things [they] don't even care about. They're just... seeing performance. I think that's what the coaching staff is looking for too."[1273]

Don't mindlessly copy others; Seek unfair advantage

"The thing that separated [Belichick] from all the other guys was that he was very interested in the technical aspects of the game. ...Bill didn't stop all those offenses just by doing what everybody else did. He's always used a lot of data in problem solving."[1274]
– *Belichick's college football coach, John Biddiscombe*

"As recently as 2001, Pittsburgh was the only team that used the 3-4 as its base defense, and New England was the only other team that made some use of it. In 2004, the Steelers, Texans and Ravens are being joined by the Chargers as entrenched 3-4 teams, and the Patriots, Raiders, 49ers, Jets, Cowboys and Giants plan to mix it in with the 4-3."[1275]
– *Phil Barber, The Sporting News*

Bill Belichick's teams are like snowflakes: they never play the same game twice. They throw new and unexpected twists at each opponent. Former Patriots safety Victor Green says this freshness excites and challenges Belichick's smart players:

"You're always surprised when it comes to Belichick. He's such a master of the game plan. It's always fun coming in. You know you're going to get four or five plays that you've never gotten before. ...You can't be a dummy in the system, or you're not going to last long."[1276]

The Patriots' defense is designed to maximize the confusion offenses face. The Patriots continually switch defensive fronts and pass coverages throughout a game, often switching a moment before the ball is snapped to confound the offensive line's blocking scheme and receivers' decisions about which routes will beat the Patriots' coverage. In their first Super Bowl victory, "the Patriots made the Rams guess which player was acting as the middle linebacker. There were times when they took funky blocking angles, making it appear that there was no nose tackle."[1277] The Patriots once deployed an "11 Guys Milling Around Defense" against the Buffalo Bills; not a single Patriot defender dropped down into a standard defensive lineman stance with a hand touching the ground. The havoc and confusion such unorthodox tactics create in opposing players' minds give the Patriots an unfair advantage.

Other teams are rushing to copy the Pats. After Patriots secondary coach Eric Mangini rebuffed Oakland's attempt to hire him as their defensive coordinator, the Raiders hired Patriots outside linebackers coach Rob Ryan–son of famous defensive genius Buddy Ryan. Ryan brought not only the "3-4" to Oakland (which he is scrapping after a disappointing 2004, though more teams are switching to a "3-4") but also Patriots defensive lineman Bobby Hamilton and the 2003 Patriots' anchor player, mountainous Ted Washington, the nose tackle who clogged the middle of the defensive line, preventing opponents from running through the 2003 Patriots. The Patriots wanted to retain Washington–of whom Patriots linebacker Willie McGinest said, "That's two people right there when you talk about Washington, so we had a little bit of an advantage"[1278]–but the Raiders signed him to a long-term deal the Patriots were unwilling to match for an aging player who had broken a leg in each of the past two seasons. (I have heard a rumor the Patriots feel they screwed up by letting Washington get away.)

Teams have also copied the Patriots' offensive innovations. *ESPN*'s John Clayton writes:

"I still can't forget calling defensive coordinators before the 2002 season asking about how to defense [Charlie] Weis' offense. Some pointed out Tom Brady's shaky numbers down the stretch run of 2001 and said that New England's short-passing attack was nothing to worry about. Guess what, other teams copied some of the Patriots ideas and the impact was huge."[1279]

Former Patriots defensive back Terrell Buckley–cut by the Patriots during 2004 training camp–says his current team, the New York Jets, patterns itself on the Patriots: "A lot of what we're doing is very similar to what they're doing in New England. You know, it's a copy-cat league, anyway."[1280] After a horrible 2003 season, the San Diego Chargers copied the Steelers and Patriots and switched from a 4-3 defense to a 3-4. Doing so helped the Chargers also switch from a 4-12 team to a 12-4 playoff team.

But copying Patriots tactics is of little use because their greatest innovation is not particular tactics but ingenuity, flexibility and relentless creativity. Every week, Patriots coaches give their players an edge by dissecting their upcoming opponent and innovating new tactics that leverage their players' capabilities while exploiting their opponents' weaknesses. For example, football broadcaster and Super Bowl-winning quarterback Phil Simms admired the way the Patriots neutralized the quickness of the Indianapolis Colts' star pass rushing defensive end, Dwight Freeney, in the 2003 AFC Championship Game by slamming a wide receiver into him at the start of each play. Simms said, "It ruined Freeney."[1281] If another team had tried this a week later, they might not have had the personnel to make it work or the Colts might have learned to defend it. The Patriots' unfair advantage derives from springing creative tactics on unsuspecting opponents, as Steelers receiver Hines Ward appreciates: "We know coach Belichick. He's going to have something up for us that we are going to have to adjust to on the run."[1282] Knowing that it will be surprised doesn't help a team prepare. Ingenuity is hard to copy because it is an approach/process, not a tactic.

Also, successfully copying the Patriots' innovations requires smart players. Some teams confuse themselves more than opponents by trying to switch plays just before the ball is snapped. Jacksonville Jaguars defensive coordinator Mike Smith, for example, says his defenders lack the mental agility to adjust to Indianapolis Colts quarterback Peyton Manning:

> "When we made the adjustments, [Manning] just changes again. You want to be clear-cut with your plan in terms of disguising (coverages). But if you overdo that, your guys have a tendency to not play fast. They start thinking about it. You just want to find something, (get set) and go."[1283]

Patriots players know exactly what they are doing, even when they are playing man-to-man on one side of the field and zone on the other but pretending to do something totally different before the snap. Even after backing up two Heisman Trophy-winning quarterbacks at USC, Patriots rookie quarterback Matt Cassel is still astonished by Tom Brady's creativity:

> "What makes him really special is his ability to think outside the box. The questions he poses in meetings–whether it relates to a defense or a possible route combination which he thinks might work… It's pretty amazing stuff a lot of people, including myself, would never even think about. He's put his game to that level where he's asking questions that are thinking way beyond the level a lot of experienced quarterbacks are probably even thinking."[1284]

Tom Brady's creativity is not hit-or-miss trial-and-error. Like his coach, Brady innovates in productive directions because he understands "the box" so well that he knows what he's doing when he "thinks outside" it. Brady–like Belichick–understands what offenses and defenses are trying to accomplish, so he can mentally simulate a "what if" to test its value in his brain before trying it in a game, just as companies use their knowledge of their markets and their customers to raise the "success rate" of their products and marketing campaigns.

In business books, "creativity" is synonymous with "thinking outside the box," but creativity also requires expertise. As Louis Pasteur–who discovered that germs cause disease and invented pasteurization–said, "Chance favors the prepared mind." How did venture capitalist John Doerr know to invest in Netscape? He had listened to Sun Microsystems founder Bill Joy: "Bill Joy had said to me, 'John, this Internet thing is going to be enormous. It is moving very, very rapidly. When you see an opportunity, just dive in.' …So I was prepared when I saw the Mosaic browser in '94."[1285]

Seek advantage in unsexy areas

"The easiest way to improve the fastest is on special teams, because not enough people spend enough time on special teams."[1286]
– Charlie Weis, former Patriots offensive coordinator

"I have an important role, whether I'm catching balls or not. If it's a running play, I have to make the blocks for our running backs."[1287]
– Patriots tight end Daniel Graham

Why did the Patriots prevail in their 2003 playoff match against the Tennessee Titans? Titans defensive coordinator Jim Schwartz points to a play by Tom Brady. No, not a touchdown pass. Not even a long run. Schwartz points to a block Brady made as that game's difference-maker:

"The one that sticks in my brain is the 3rd-and-13 we had them in in the 1st quarter when [Patriots wide receiver] Bethel Johnson reversed direction–and got sprung by a nice block by Tom Brady–and turned it into a long gain [14 yards] for a first down. Just one tackle and we had them. It's one of those plays where I'm sure Bill [Belichick] and Charlie [Weis] are on the sideline yelling, 'No! No!' when he's reversing his field, and then at the end of the play they're saying, 'Good decision.'"[1288]

In a league with such even talent across teams, little things like Tom Brady's block can determine a game's outcome.

Special teams

"When you see a guy like Rodney Harrison playing on special teams, someone else can't say that they don't want to do it."[1289]
 – Patriots offensive lineman Stephen Neal

"As soon as you start talking about one guy too much, another guy can burn you because [the Patriots] have a bunch of really good special teams players that are veteran players who've been around."[1290]
 – Philadelphia Eagles special teams coordinator John Harbaugh

"I've always looked at [special teams] as a third of the game. When I came into the league, I basically came in as a special teams coach. I was involved in the kicking game in my first five, six years directly as either the head or assistant special teams coach on four different teams and so it's always been a very important part of the game for me. I've never taken that for granted or considered it less than instrumental in the outcome of a game. ...Points are the name of the game. Field position is a critical factor, and a lot of that is determined in the kicking game, and any time that you have big plays or big swings with a blocked kick or a turnover or something like that, that could be a huge impact."[1291]
 – Bill Belichick

In football, "Offense sells tickets, but defense wins championships." The Patriots sell tickets and win championships, but where they often distinguish themselves is in the game's neglected third phase: special teams. Receiver Troy Brown wrote, "We really believed that our special teams could make a difference in winning and losing."[1292] Since Belichick took over, the Patriots have gone out of their way to hire "star" special teamers—an oxymoron on many teams. Philadelphia Eagles special teams coordinator John Harbaugh says Patriots special teams captain Larry Izzo is practically unstoppable: In one game, "We actually set up our kickoff return schemes around [Izzo], and he still made every tackle."[1293] Harbaugh says the Patriots use many veterans on special teams who "have been around the league for a long time [so they] know what they are doing."[1294] Izzo agrees, "I've been around a while, so I recognize things quickly."[1295] Therefore,

"You aren't going to trick them. They are going to make all the right moves. And, when you set up a kickoff return, by the time they get to the 50-yard-line, they already know the return. So they read and react to it... How many returns has Rabih [Abdullah] covered over his career? Hundreds."[1296]

Most teams let their inexperienced, expendable players cut their teeth on special teams. Linebacker Mike Vrabel says, "It's assumed here... that you're going to make contributions in the kicking game. That's just protocol here. We complain about it and we joke about it, but we're out there busting our humps trying to cover kicks and trying to help out in the return game."[1297] Few fans realized Vrabel played on special teams until he injured his ankle during the first preseason game, after which Belichick had to explain to reporters:

> "We look at a special teams play just like any other play in the game. It's important. It's important to winning and losing. I don't think anyone wants to go out there and play hard for 60 and 65 plays on the offensive and defensive side of the ball and then see the game slip away on a play in the kicking game."[1298]

The Patriots know special teams is the most chaotic and unscriptable phase of the game. Mistakes lead to 80- or 100-yard touchdowns, so the Patriots employ smart, experienced players who have seen most everything and react instinctively to most anything:

> "When Izzo gets double-teamed, he knows it. When he gets trapped, he doesn't get caught by surprise. ...He's covered hundreds and hundreds of kickoffs in his career, [so] he pretty much knows where all the blocks are coming from. He knows where the traps are at. He can anticipate what's going to happen well before it happens."[1299]

Belichick knows football intelligence is essential on special teams because:

> "Once that ball's kicked, everything breaks loose; everything's set in a certain framework, but then once the ball hits the kicker's or a punter's foot, then it's chaos, it's kind of an organized chaos. Everybody has a responsibility and an area that they are working in, but because the types of kicks vary—the length, the direction, the hang time and so forth—every play is a little bit different. It takes on a life of its own and that's where decision-making becomes such a critical part of special teams. Having players who are good decision makers and really understand the situation and what's going on in the play are ones who are the best players and the most productive."[1300]

The Patriots win games with special teams. Special teams preparation led to an 85-yard Troy Brown punt return against the Cleveland Browns in 2001: "That was something we thought we matched up pretty well with them. We worked on the punt returns in pads Thursday and we thought we could make a play in the game. Not everybody was real excited about doing that."[1301]

The Patriots emphasize special teams in several ways. First, some Patriots starters—like linebacker Roman Phifer (the Patriots' leading tackler from 2001 through 2003), Tedy Bruschi, and Mike Vrabel—proudly play on special teams. Bruschi played on 86% of the team's 2004 defensive plays and 40% of that season's special teams plays.[1302] Punter Josh Miller joined the Patriots in part because he admires their dedication to special teams: "They play a lot of their starters on special teams and that's rare in this league."[1303] Defensive coordinator Romeo Crennel is proud of his starting linebacker's special teams performance:

> "Roman is truly a professional. ...The thing that's a little surprising about Roman is that last year, and even two years ago, not only did he play just about every play on defense, he played every play on special teams. We tried to cut back on that a little bit this year. But he's the kind of guy that we look for—guys that are football players, guys who will make contributions wherever they're needed and then go out there and do it at a high level."[1304]

After returning a punt 55 yards for a touchdown in the 2001 AFC Championship Game against the Pittsburgh Steelers, the Patriots' #1 wide receiver Troy Brown said, "I always said that special teams is crucial. If you're good at what you do and your team needs you on special teams, that's what you go out and do."[1305] The Patriots won that game (and a berth in Super Bowl XXXVI) with two special teams touchdowns. Troy Brown was also a key player in the other, a 60-yard touchdown return after Patriots defensive lineman Brandon Mitchell blocked a Steelers field goal attempt. Brown scooped up the ball while running full speed (as the Patriots train to do in that situation), ran eleven yards upfield, and then tossed the ball to Antwan Harris who ran 49 yards more for the touchdown. Though the Patriots had regularly practiced "scoop and score"—their plan for scoring after blocking a field goal—many Pittsburgh players and fans still insist the 2001 Patriots "got lucky" or that the Steelers *really* won the AFC Championship because the Patriots' margin of victory was achieved through outstanding special teams, as if that phase of the game doesn't count.

Second, the Patriots acquire game-changing, difference-making special teams players. Many said the Patriots blundered in drafting wide receiver Bethel Johnson in Round 2 of the 2003 NFL Draft because his college performance didn't justify it and because he had missed many games with injuries. But the Patriots were in awe of Johnson's speed and knew they could use it on special teams, even if Johnson contributed nothing as a receiver. In 2003, Johnson had the best kickoff return average in the entire AFC. Against the Colts in the wild 38-34 Pats victory that concluded when the Patriots stuffed the Colts on four consecutive 4th-and-goal plays, Johnson's 92-yard kickoff return for a touchdown to end the first half and a later 67-yard return were arguably game-changing. Unfortunately, Johnson appears to be one of the least mature Patriots, something pre-draft reports noted: "*ESPN* had some scathing things to say about Johnson, calling him 'dumb,' 'immature,' 'inconsistent,' 'sloppy' and 'underachiever.'"[1306]

Another example is veteran backup linebacker Don Davis who played almost exclusively on special teams until a rash of injuries in the secondary forced him to play safety in 2004: "A lot of teams don't want to pay a veteran [to play special teams]. But here, they realize special teams is a very important part of the game."[1307]

Longsnapper is the least glorified position on a football team. Few longsnappers have ever been drafted. Nevertheless, the Patriots evaluated 125 longsnappers to find the right one because it's hard to kick field goals without a reliable longsnapper. They were on the phone with Florida State's Brian Sawyer during the 2003 draft's final round, telling him how much they liked him and promising a signing bonus equal to the player they drafted with their final pick. Sawyer had impressed NFL scouts by "consistently fir[ing] footballs back to a kicker in less than .70 seconds."[1308] But, once Sawyer arrived in New England, "Brad Seely, the special teams coach, told me when I got here that they knew I could throw it back there plenty fast. He said they'd rather me take something off it and hit my mark than just try to wing it back there. Once you get here, it's all about consistency." [1309]

And special teams captain Larry Izzo has played in three Pro Bowls as the AFC's best special teamer. In 2003, Izzo racked up a team-leading 31 special teams tackles (27 in 2004), helped Bethel Johnson lead the league in kickoff return average and helped the Patriots' punt coverage team hold opposing punt returners to a measly 6.3 yards per return, second lowest in the AFC. Izzo is tough as nails and beloved by his teammates for his gung-ho attitude. Says fellow linebacker Ted Johnson,

> "I always have fun when we're in there together… He's been a joy to play with. He's got a great personality. He's a guy's guy. He thoroughly enjoys what he does. He's just the kind of guy you want on your football team. His attitude is just so positive–it permeates throughout the whole team. I consider him a very good friend too, so I'm a little biased."[1310]

How badly did Bill Belichick want Izzo on his team? According to assistant coach Pepper Johnson, "When Larry came on his recruiting visit, Coach Belichick told me that if I let Larry leave New England without verbally committing to a contract I might not have a contract myself."[1311] Fortunately for Johnson, he got extra arm-twisting time. Belichick recalls "when [Izzo] became a free agent, we got in on that, and pretty quickly, too. He was signed right away. He came up, we had the snowstorm up here. Fortunately he couldn't get out."[1312]

Third, Patriots coaches understand special teams. Special teams coach Brad Seely is a true expert. According to Patriots punter Josh Miller:

> "[Seely's] not a linebackers coach that got stuck coaching special teams. [He's a] special teams professional… To draw an analogy to college, that's [his] major. …He really knows kicking and punting. A lot of coaches leave it up to the punter and the kicker and hope he makes it. Brad knows what I do wrong, and he's showed me a lot of good drills to get ready."[1313]

Belichick–who earned his early NFL reputation coaching special teams–is actually as much a special teams expert as a defensive expert. Belichick rattles off the names of special teamers who have impressed him over the decades, players anonymous even to their teams' fans while they played: "The Tony Bertucas with the Colts, and the Leonard Thompsons at Detroit, and Joe McLaughlin, and Mike Whittington, and Nate Thompson with the Giants, Randy Baldwin and all those guys. They weren't all great football players in their offensive and defensive position, but they were highly productive in the kicking game."[1314]

Unsurprisingly, the Patriots' special teams performance is usually among the league's best. According to NFL expert Rick Gosselin in early 2004, "The [Philadelphia] Eagles are one of only two teams to rank in the Top 10 in special teams all four seasons of the 2000 decade. The two-time Super Bowl champion New England Patriots are the other."[1315] Gosselin's analysis indicates that "Both Super Bowl teams, Carolina and New England, ranked in the Top 5 in special teams [in 2003]. Six of the eight division champions ranked in the Top 10. Counting the Patriots, six of the last seven NFL champions ranked in the Top 10 in special teams on their way to a Lombardi Trophy. ...New England... excelled in coverage." [1316]

Rick Gosselin's Rating of 2003 NFL Special Teams Performances
(based on data in 21 kicking-game categories) by Team[1317]

Rank. Team	Points
1. Philadelphia Eagles	260
2. Carolina Panthers	279.5
3. Pittsburgh Steelers	281.5
4. Baltimore Ravens	282.5
5. **New England Patriots**	**285.5**
6. Oakland Raiders	296.5
7. Chicago Bears	298.5
8. Green Bay Packers	310.5
9. Buffalo Bills	312.5
10. Detroit Lions	314.5
11. Kansas City Chiefs	314.5
12. Houston Texans	317.5
13. Indianapolis Colts	319.5
14. Seattle Seahawks	321.5
15. New York Jets	326
16. New Orleans Saints	332
17. Tennessee Titans	335.5
18. Cleveland Browns	346
19. Washington Redskins	347
20. Miami Dolphins	360
21. Dallas Cowboys	366
22. Atlanta Falcons	367
23. New York Giants	369
24. St. Louis Rams	377.5

25. Cincinnati Bengals	380
26. Denver Broncos	393.5
27. San Francisco 49ers	397
28. Arizona Cardinals	425
29. San Diego Chargers	429.5
30. Minnesota Vikings	437
31. Tampa Bay Buccaneers	442
32. Jacksonville Jaguars	463.5

"We're the baddest mothers out there"

"We've lost other games before, but this is the first time anybody's beaten us up physically."[1318]
   – *Buffalo Bills safety Lawyer Milloy, after losing to the Patriots 29-6 in 2004*

"The coaches keep talking to us about making sure we wrap the guy up and make the tackle, but the way me and the other safeties see it, we're not wrapping you up, we're knocking you out."[1319]
   – *Safety Tebucky Jones while he played for the Patriots in 2001*

As a college senior, tight end Kellen Winslow Jr. was pummeled by the press for saying, "It's war. They're out there to kill you, so I'm out there to kill them. We don't care about anybody but this U[niversity]. They're going after my legs. I'm going to come right back at them. I'm a f*&#$@' soldier." Winslow's unfortunate metaphor and unnecessarily graphic language notwithstanding, he's got a point. In just his second NFL game, Winslow himself was one of *six* Cleveland Browns injured against the Dallas Cowboys in 2004. The Cowboys broke Winslow's fibula–requiring a metal plate and screws to repair–and wrenched ligaments in his ankle so severely that they required surgery; Winslow missed the rest of his rookie season. The 2004 Patriots lost two starters–Deion Branch and Benjamin Watson–to knee injuries in their opening game against the Colts. Watson missed the season after damage to his ACL required surgery.

NFL football combines the strategic complexity of chess and Rubik's Cube with the violence of demolition derby, boxing and Battlebots. Some teams, like the Patriots under coach Pete Carroll, hope to win through finesse. Belichick's Patriots proudly out-hit their opponents to intimidate them, tire them, de-motivate them and force them into mistakes (dropped passes, poor throws, fumbles, interceptions, *etc.*). Pounding opponents is painful but necessary, so the Patriots excel at it. According to former NFL great tight end Mark Bavaro, the Patriots are "one of the hardest hitting teams you'll see. The opponent can count on walking away with some bumps and bruises after facing these guys."[1320] Belichick has long emphasized hitting hard because he believes it's essential to slowing down opposing offenses:

"Hard hitting safeties are an important element of your defense. One thing you want to do defensively is control the middle of the field. You want receivers, tight ends, when they come across for passes thinking what will happen when they go there. (A big hit) is a good tempo to set."[1321]

Many hard-hitting defensive players followed Belichick from the Jets to the Patriots because they love Belichick's swarming, attacking, aggressive, violent defensive style. After making eleven spine-compressing tackles in an early 2001 game, linebacker Bryan Cox said in clear, no-nonsense Belichickian style, "I get paid to do that. I'm a football player."[1322] Another Jet-to-Patriot linebacker, Roman Phifer, said, "It's the only way to play the game. That's what (Belichick) looks for. We wanted to set a standard of how we play the game. Aggressive and physical."[1323] A third former Jet defender turned Patriot, Bobby Hamilton said, "When we step on the field, we think we're the baddest mothers out there." [1324]

Patriots players embrace their sport's physicality and believe toughness livens up practices, sharpens focus and intensity and, eventually, leads to victories. After winning Super Bowl XXXVI, linebacker Ted Johnson looked back to a fight at the beginning of preseason that, to him, augured success: "I remember the first day of mini-camp, and two guys on the offensive line had this big fight. It was great. It sort of set a tone, especially with all of the new guys that were brought in. We were going to be tough."[1325]

That toughness paid off in the Super Bowl when the Patriots, according to linebacker Roman Phifer, "hit everyone as much as possible."[1326] Rams receivers started running tentative routes, fearing they would get smashed by Patriots defenders. One powerful hit by Patriots safety Antwan Harris popped the ball loose from Rams wide receiver Ricky Proehl. The Patriots recovered that fumble. And Marshall Faulk sacrificed yards to save his body: "We [hit] Marshall Faulk early, too. You hit him hard a few times and he puts his hat on. He may get his yards, but did you notice him running out of bounds a few times rather than get the extra yards? We did."[1327] At least one fan noticed:

> "Marshall Faulk ran out of bounds more Sunday night than any player I can remember. ...He kept missing blocks, not reaching out for the extra yard, first down, goal line or anything that required him to take a hit. I don't know if he was hurt, but watching him play, it seemed like we were watching Barry Sanders without the toughness."[1328]

Faulk confessed noticing the Patriots' hitting. "They took some shots at me that I thought were unnecessary shots, but within the game of football."[1329]

Bill Belichick loves hard-hitting safeties, so he aggressively pursued safety Rodney Harrison after San Diego foolishly released him. What did Harrison bring to the 2003 Patriots? Linebacker Roman Phifer says Harrison brought an infectious attitude that inspires teammates to hit even harder:

"When there's a guy like Rodney, he really fires you up. When he comes in and makes a big hit on the runner or a receiver across the middle, it really ignites you, ignites the defense and sparks everyone, you know, 'Hey, I want a piece of that.' We pride ourselves on being a physical defense. I really think Rodney fits that mold and I think it's really contagious. I mean, look at [rookie safety] Eugene (Wilson). You can't be a soft guy playing back there playing with Rodney and I think (Wilson) has stepped up too, and it's affected everyone."[1330]

The offense also enjoys pounding opponents. The Patriots opened the 2002 season against their 2001 AFC Championship Game opponent, the Pittsburgh Steelers. Patriots rookie receiver Deion Branch caught six passes for 83 yards and a touchdown, a tremendous first-game performance. Which catch was Branch most proud of that day? Fellow receiver Donald Hayes' catch! Branch hit Steelers safety Lee Flowers and knocked him out of the way so Hayes could turn a short pass reception into a 40-yard touchdown: "The block made it feel like I scored the touchdown."[1331]

Toughness and athleticism are expected even of Patriots kickers. Linebacker Roman Phifer jokes with kicker Adam Vinatieri that "he's got the best job in football. When we're still in meetings, he's hanging out in the hot tub, or having lunch."[1332] And Patriots punter Josh Miller confessed before Super Bowl XXXIX that "My playbook is very thin [and] I'm not podium worthy." Jokes aside, Patriots kickers are tough, as training camp longsnapper Brian Sawyer explains:

"The long-snappers, the kickers, the punters, we all [train hard]. Everybody here is seen as a professional football player. In the workouts and running, we're no different than any linebacker or tight end. During the conditioning drills, I'm actually running routes with the tight ends."[1333]

Belichick and Bill Parcells both love Adam Vinatieri. Back in 1996, Vinatieri somehow outran the great running back Herschel Walker—who was sprinting for a touchdown—and tackled him from behind: "I don't know how I got 10 seconds of speed, but that one day I was fast."[1334] Troy Brown said, "The guy ran down Herschel Walker, so you have to classify him as a football player."[1335] Even before Vinatieri drilled some of the most famous field goals in NFL history in the 2001 playoffs, Belichick admired his physical and mental toughness: "I look at Adam and I don't see a kicker. I see a football player. He so steady and consistent. He's a tough guy and a good tackler. He saved us earlier in the year when our coverage wasn't so good."[1336] Special teams captain Larry Izzo vouches for Vinatieri's toughness:

"He's a great athlete, a tremendous competitor. He's able—if needed—to make a good open field tackle on a great athlete who would be a returner. So he's a guy that's obviously got some athletic ability and he's shown that."[1337]

Belichick's belief that physical teams win football games is no hunch. It's a fact: "If you look at all of the successful teams over the years, one thing you notice is the physical nature of those teams. Even the teams that can score, they usually set the tone on defense."[1338]

Take calculated risks

"Nothing's dangerous if you know what you're doing."[1339]
  – Johnny Unitas, after throwing an apparently dangerous pass on the 86-yard game-winning drive of the 1958 championship game

"You need to be bold when it's time to be bold."[1340]
  – Patriots owner Robert Kraft

"I don't just want a sack in that situation. I want the ball. I want the big play. I want it all. If the situation presents itself, you've got to go for it."[1341]
  – Patriots linebacker Tedy Bruschi, after stripping Bills quarterback Drew Bledsoe of the ball that Richard Seymour then returned for a Patriots touchdown

"There is always a little bit of risk and reward. You don't want to risk a lot to gain two yards. If you have a shot [for a long completion] down the field and you take it there is some pretty good reward there also."[1342]
  – Tom Brady

The Patriots won their first world championship on a last-minute drive many considered reckless, even dumb. With Super Bowl XXXVI tied 17-17, 1:21 left in regulation and the ball at their own 17-yard line, the Patriots decided to try to score. A Patriots fumble or interception at their 17-yard line would gift the Rams an automatic game-winning field goal. Moving the ball 83 yards in just over a minute is unlikely. And the Patriots' quarterback was only one season removed from being a 4th-string quarterback. But Patriots coaches and players knew Tom Brady would throw only low-risk passes to whichever receiver the Rams left open on each play.

After the Patriots marched downfield and won the game with a field goal, Belichick said going for it was much less risky than most believed. Why? Tom Brady. "With a quarterback like Brady, going for the win is not that dangerous because he's not going to make a mistake."[1343] Offensive coordinator Charlie Weis shared Belichick's faith in Brady's preparation: "There was no doubt in my mind Tom could handle this drive. That thought never even crossed my mind. I had total confidence he'd handle the situation."[1344]

Belichick and Weis had trained Brady to avoid "big plays" and focus instead on making "positive plays." Weis believes the formula for winning is as simple as avoiding negative, game-losing plays and instead stringing together positive plays: "There is one significant statistic in offensive football. It's the total of rushing attempts and pass completions. When those numbers combine to total 48 or more, teams win 80% of their games."[1345] This basically boils down to avoiding interceptions and incompletions because runs seldom lose yards. Avoiding interceptions–the ultimate "negative play"–is of extreme importance. In NFL games since 1970, teams that returned an interception for a touchdown won 77.1% of the time.[1346]

Had the 2001 Patriots been losing Super Bowl XXXVI, Brady would have taken risks. With the game tied, however, Brady knew he didn't have to take risks and wind up either the hero or the goat. Brady simply hoped to string together enough safe passes to win. Brady later explained that, coming out for that drive, "I was thinking, 'Let's get a positive play.' First play of the drive, most important thing is to gain some yards."[1347] If Brady couldn't stitch together a field goal drive using safe plays, the team would take its chances in overtime. So he did not force anything. He took whatever the defense gave him. For example, on the drive's first play–according to Charlie Weis–the Patriots intended to throw a bomb to David Patten if the Rams covered him with just one defender but dump off to Troy Brown or J.R. Redmond if the Rams double-covered Patten:

> "If [defenders] played man[-to-man], we wanted to score on that first play to David Patten down the left sideline. If they zoned, we wanted to look to Troy Brown. If he wasn't available, then J.R. All we wanted to do was make positive yardage. What we weren't going to do was make a mistake. Tom dumped the ball to J.R., and that's what he was supposed to do."[1348]

Coaches had taught Brady that no defense can cover everyone and he should find the open receiver. Patriots running back J.R. Redmond explained, "On all the plays [of that drive], I was an outlet, meaning that if no one else was open downfield, that meant nine times out of ten I'd be open because they were double-covering someone."[1349]

Brady took other steps to avoid "negative plays" that risked losing the game. On that first play, Brady avoided fumbling: "I felt edge pressure stepping up in the pocket [from Rams end Leonard Little], and I know those guys wrap around, so I tried to get both hands on the ball instinctively realizing I should."[1350] On the fifth play, Brady smartly threw the ball away rather than risk getting sacked or intercepted or completing a short pass that would chew up precious seconds:

> "They were bringing the weak-safety blitz. Normally I'd throw a sight adjustment to the weak side, but I figured why throw an 8-yard slant and lose 25 seconds on the clock, so I just faded away from the rush and threw it out of bounds."[1351]

On that play Brady was also savvy enough, Weis comments, to avoid an intentional grounding penalty: "They brought the blitz from the left and Tom rolled right and threw the ball away. We didn't have the blitz picked up and he realized it. He did a nice job avoiding the grounding by getting outside [the tackles]."[1352]

KC Joyner, who has systematically analyzed film of every play of every NFL game in 2004 (and every Patriots game in 2003 too), also sees what I see:

> "When the Pats pass short, they are going to be certain they don't make mistakes on it. They are more willing to make mistakes on vertical [deep] passes... The Patriots seem to have a risk/reward ratio in mind when they pass the ball... They are much more willing to take chances on deeper passes because the reward is higher... You'd be amazed how many teams don't have this philosophical clarity."[1353]

Another example of a calculated risk is throwing a "smart interception." There are times when it's acceptable–even desirable–to throw an interception. Patriots backup quarterback Rohan Davey explains:

> "[My] second interception came on a long pass where we were just taking a shot down the field. It was third down and you just take a shot. If you hit it that's good and if you don't then it's just like a punt because they caught it on like the two-yard line. It was one of those things where you just take one [statistically] for the team."[1354]

The Patriots defense takes similarly smart risks. Patriots coaches instruct defensive backs, "If you can't get two hands on the ball, you try to knock the ball down with one hand and secure the tackle with the other hand."[1355] So, after rookie cornerback Ellis Hobbs surrendered a touchdown after trying to step in front of a pass during his second preseason game and failing to knock it down or tackle the receiver, Coach Belichick explained his displeasure in risk-reward terms:

> "You can't go out there and miss an interception and give up a touchdown. You can't play like that. It's not worth it. There's nobody behind you. If the safety or the corner misjudges the ball and the guy goes in for a touchdown, you think the nose tackle is going to catch him? It's all over. [Cornerbacks] can't play like that. If there's any doubt in your mind, then you have to make the secure play."[1356]

Hobbs got the message that his gamble was especially dumb because the Patriots had an 11-point lead (and wound up losing the game): "You have to... [know] the mindset you have to be in, to pick and choose your gambles, pick and choose your fights. Sometimes, you want to go for a risk like that; sometimes you don't."[1357] Another situational factor affecting whether Patriots defensive backs should take chances is whether a teammate is in position to make the tackle. After joining the Patriots in 2005, cornerback Duane Starks grew excited reading the Patriots' playbook because "it gives me the opportunity to jump routes."[1358] Starks' former team, the Arizona Cardinals, required him to play cautious man-on-man defense on almost every play. When a cornerback plays "on an island," his top priority is tackling the receiver and his secondary priority is knocking down the ball. Only when he is certain the receiver cannot possibly catch the ball can he step in front of the receiver and try to intercept it. The Patriots' system does not always place its cornerbacks in isolated coverage. Starks was excited to receive help from safeties on some plays. Whenever he does, he can defend more aggressively and take greater risks to intercept passes or knock down passes rather than ensure he makes the tackle. To take only smart risks, Starks must know when he has help and when he is "on an island," which is why he said, "everyone is learning their position and trying to get things done the right way. They put a little more emphasis on learning everyone else's position, which is a good thing because once you know what they're doing, that helps you out doing your job."[1359] Because they emphasize avoiding big plays, the Patriots–along with the Buffalo Bills and New York Jets–surrendered only five touchdowns on drives of four or fewer plays in 2003 and 2004 combined, lowest in the NFL.[1360]

MAKE DECISIONS

Avoiding decisions has consequences

"We need to encourage people to take initiatives, look at the problems very quickly, and make sure they make the decision. You can't stay on problems because you have to move quickly."[1361]
– *Carlos Ghosn, CEO of Nissan and Renault*

"You have to make decisions that aren't popular. If it's 4th-and-1, half the people in the stands want you to go for it, the other half don't want you to go for it. Whichever way you decide, you're going to make people angry. At that point, I get paid to make the decision. I'll make them."[1362]
– *Bill Belichick*

Decisions must be made. Postponing or avoiding unpleasant decisions can be psychologically comforting. But avoiding decisions doesn't solve problems, as Bill Belichick understood in 2001 when he gave talented-but-troubled receiver Terry Glenn no more chances:

"The player was notified when he left camp that it was unexcused. [I made the suspension decision approximately 11 days later.] The situation needed definition. For a player not to be where he's supposed to be for that amount of time, unexcused–at some point, if you don't do something, what's that say to everybody else?"[1363]

Patriots safety Lawyer Milloy was glad Belichick canceled the soap opera: "It's just a cancer to us right now. As a whole, that situation probably needed to die as soon as possible."[1364] But the courts intervened to prolong the sideshow throughout 2001, undoing Belichick's attempt to resolve the Terry Glenn saga. The subsequent distractions proved both the wisdom of Belichick's decision and the troublesome nature of festering problems.

Terry Glenn has every physical gift a wide receiver could possibly lust after. From the neck down, Glenn was a lock for the Hall of Fame. But his head repeatedly landed him in trouble, and he was never able to consistently translate his immense physical gifts into on-field performance. *ESPN's* Len Pasquarelli dubbed Glenn a "fruitcake."[1365] Bob McGinn called him "a poster child for messed up professional football players."[1366]

Glenn's first season is still his best. With mother hen Bill Parcells and receivers coach Charlie Weis prodding and challenging him, Glenn broke the NFL rookie record with 90 receptions in 1996. An apocryphal story was reported in 2003[1367] that Parcells goaded Glenn in 1996 by saying, "I recovered from open heart surgery faster" than Glenn was recovering from a hamstring injury. Parcells uttered those words but aimed them at receiver Vincent Brisby, not Terry Glenn. Though apocryphal, the story has the ring of truth, given Glenn's history and the fact that Glenn also had a hamstring injury at the time "that sidelined him for the entire preseason and the first regular-season game."[1368] Also, Parcells once famously insulted Glenn, referring to him as "she" while talking with reporters.

Many players, fans and journalists felt Glenn's laziness, inconsistency and unreliability hurt his team: "Glenn was an infrequent participant during the strength and conditioning program and, as a result, there were all kinds of rumors floating around. Terry Glenn's lazy. He's unmotivated. He's checked himself into the Betty Ford Clinic."[1369] His poor attitude, injuries, constant complaining and off-field troubles (including a substance abuse suspension by the NFL) also hurt. In 1998, the *Standard-Times'* Dan Pires summed up Glenn with this superb analogy:

> "I think of Terry Glenn as being like a fine automobile. A Jaguar XKE to be specific. When it's running, it's a great vehicle and a real head-turner. The crummy part is that it's always broken down and is always in need of repairs. At some point you're going to get completely frustrated and trade the Jag in for a Honda Accord. In a nutshell, that's Terry Glenn."[1370]

Glenn strengthened his cry-baby reputation after a series of seemingly minor injuries kept him out of countless practices and games. From 1997 through 1999, Glenn didn't start in 17 of 48 Patriots games due to injuries.[1371]

In 1999, Glenn publicly dissed then-head coach Pete Carroll after Carroll said all the receivers had to work harder at breaking loose from bump-and-run coverage: "I don't know what Pete's talking about. You can ask any other receiver (about) that, too. That's his opinion. As a receiver, it's not mine."[1372] By contrast, the mature and classy Shawn Jefferson accepted his coach's critique: "If Pete says we've got to work harder, we've got to work harder. He's the boss." [1373] One of Carroll's final acts in late 1999–before he was fired–was suspending Glenn after "Glenn refused to come in to have his flu checked out and did not come in for treatment either Monday or Tuesday. He showed up Wednesday and was told to go see Pete Carroll. He responded with an epithet against Carroll."[1374] After a strong 2000 season under Belichick and Weis (hauling in 79 passes for 963 yards), Glenn skipped the mandatory spring training camp in 2001[1375] and was arrested on May 16, 2001 on an alleged domestic abuse charge against the mother of his son, Terry Jr.: "He was charged with assault, battery and intimidating a witness."[1376] In June, the Patriots temporarily withheld $1 million of his signing bonus because he skipped mini-camp and because–the team claimed–his assault charge violated a "character clause" in his contract. Glenn later missed an NFL drug test and was suspended by the league for the first four games of 2001 for again violating its drug policy. Since failing a marijuana test three years earlier, Glenn had been required to pass a drug test three times a week. After learning of his suspension and apparently also learning that the Patriots decided to seek recovery of at least $8 million of his $11.5 million signing bonus for his alleged violations of good-behavior clauses in his contract, Glenn disappeared from training camp August 3rd and refused to return. The Patriots sent Glenn a formal letter demanding his return within five days and threatening a season-long suspension without pay if he failed to comply. Against his attorney's advice, Glenn remained AWOL. After Glenn remained AWOL a full eleven days, Belichick suspended him for the 2001 season: "This is about being in training camp and playing football. I'm going to spend my time and my energy with the players that are here."[1377] But Glenn's lawyer fought the suspension in the courts and had it overturned. After Glenn served his league-mandated four-game suspension, he gained 110 yards on seven receptions in Week 5 after practicing just one week, again proving his incredible physical ability. But Glenn then missed the next six games with what he termed a hamstring injury though "team doctors deem[ed] his hamstring to be healthy."[1378] In Week 12, Belichick suspended him again. Belichick suspended him yet again in January "for allegedly missing numerous team functions."[1379] Belichick knew Glenn would never fit in his system, so he tried to find a win-win solution by trading him to a Green Bay Packers team with a history of productively channeling players' talents and keeping them out of trouble: "The situation just didn't work out here, and I think, mutually, Terry and I both felt it would be better for him to go somewhere else. Green Bay was a place he wanted to go, so we made the trade."[1380]

In 2003, Glenn's embarrassing, childish, sour grapes statement before returning to Foxboro to play the Patriots underscored Belichick's wisdom in no longer tolerating Glenn's immaturity: "I just hate everything about everything over there. I can't wait to get up there. I hate everything about New England."[1381]

Don't fall for fads

"The best guys in this business–the successful ones–set their own trends. My job, and the job of everyone here, from ownership to the personnel staff to the coaches and the players, is to know what trends are best for our team, not what others have."[1382]
– *Scott Pioli, Patriots VP of player personnel*

After the Patriots shocked the football world by winning the February 2002 Super Bowl, NFL executives and coaches searching for secrets to the Patriots' success put the Patriots under a microscope. One widespread conclusion: the Patriots had disproved the conventional wisdom that the way to win a Super Bowl is by signing high-priced free agents to put the team "over the top." Many, including the current GM of the New York Giants, decided that success comes from signing "bargain" free agents. Many inferred the Patriots won by re-signing their own players rather than chasing big-name free agents. Scott Pioli insists teams are naïve to seek a simple formula underlying the Patriots' success:

"Initially, we all believed that when free agency comes around, you've got to sign other players. Lately that's changed to, 'the teams that are successful are the ones that sign their own players.' The reality is that the best way to succeed in free agency is to sign the right players."[1383]

The Patriots never re-signed all their free agents or spurned other team's free agents. In 2000, they wanted to retain Shawn Jefferson and Chad Eaton but could not afford to. And the Patriots let their best offensive lineman, Damien Woody, walk after the Detroit Lions basically loaded up a Brinks truck with money. And the Patriots have won two Super Bowls since signing big-name free agents Rodney Harrison, Tyrone Poole, and Rosevelt Colvin.

Pioli's alter ego, Belichick, agrees success is not about easy formulas like "sign cheap free agents" or "re-sign your players." It's about finding players who provide maximal performance-per-dollar within your system: "The only factor that goes into our decisions is what's best for our football team. There are no set rules or regulations on that. There are a lot of players in this league that have high contracts and earn every penny."[1384]

Nevertheless, in 2002, a conventional wisdom quickly spread throughout the NFL and the media that the Patriots had won by: 1) "clearing the deck" of high-priced veterans; 2) shunning high-priced free agents; and, 3) acquiring low-priced free agents. Some teams adopted these tactics. As other teams started following the Patriots' purported blueprint, the Patriots began violating "their" principles. The Patriots had signed a slew of "street" free agents in 2000 and 2001 because that was all their bloated salary cap could afford. By 2003, they had cleared some space and signed linebacker Rosevelt Colvin (for $30 million) and safety Rodney Harrison (for

$14 million) to large contracts in the spring of 2003. Owner Bob Kraft joked with Belichick and Pioli: "Thanks a lot. After spending all this money, my wife can't go shopping now."[1385]

Another overly simplistic analysis we often hear is that the Patriots build through the draft, not free agency. Also untrue. Before the 2003 season, they traded a 4th-round draft pick to the Bears for the rights to veteran nose tackle Ted Washington. Result: another Super Bowl victory in February 2004. Before the 2004 season, they traded a 2nd-round draft pick to the Bengals for Corey Dillon. Result: another Super Bowl. And before the 2005 season, they traded a 3rd-round pick to the Cardinals for cornerback Duane Starks. The common thread: the Patriots perceived greater value in those particular proven players than in the draft picks they surrendered. Whether a player or a draft pick is more valuable depends on circumstances.

The media and other NFL teams looked primarily at patterns in *what* the Patriots did while neglecting to uncover *why*. The Patriots care about: 1) finding players who match their profile and fit their system; and, 2) acquiring those players at a price low enough to justify their value to overall team performance. Outsiders were hung up on the fact that the Patriots had dumped high-priced veterans when the real issue was that those veterans who were dumped were either overpaid or unaffordable, given the team's salary cap bind. Some, but not all, of the overpaid players had slacked off and not performed at a level commensurate with their high price tags. The Patriots retained other veterans (like Willie McGinest, Troy Brown, Ty Law, and Ted Johnson) who would contribute to three Super Bowl seasons.

Outsiders were similarly mesmerized by the way the Patriots signed many veterans to inexpensive contracts. The Patriots had nothing against paying high-value players high pay, but they had been forced to avoid signing high-priced free agents because they were burdened by a legacy of overspending and burdened by the bloated salary structure they inherited. After freeing cap space, the Patriots signed some high-value players to big contracts. Scott Pioli does not care how he acquires players so long as he acquires the right players for the right price:

> "Sometimes finding the right players is through the draft, sometimes through free agency, sometimes trades. Whatever vehicle is available for you to improve the talent on your team, that's what you use. ...The philosophy of saying 'the draft only' or 'free agency only' or 'trading,' you have to use all the vehicles afforded to you in building your team. What doesn't change is the type of players you're looking for and how you're trying to build a team. Don't get how you're trying to build a team confused with which vehicle you use to get players. You're looking for a certain type of player to fit the system."[1386]

Indianapolis Colts general manager Bill Polian has revealed the real secret to the Patriots' personnel success: "That's the real secret to free agency. Find the right role players and have Bill Belichick as your coach."[1387]

Research a decision intensively, then don't second-guess it

The time to worry about a decision is *before* you make it, not afterwards. Careful analysis before a decision usually results in a wiser choice. Fretting about decisions you have already made is generally counterproductive and a waste of time… unless new information arises that suggests you made the wrong decision.

Bill Belichick appreciates that irresolute decisions are the bane of management: "If [decisions are] wishy-washy and if I'm not definitive, it's worse than anything, because nobody will have any direction."[1388]

Steve Belichick says his son learned decisiveness growing up with the Naval Academy football team, where "Billy" became a *de facto* assistant coach at age 8:

> "If you are around military men, you learn to make a tough decision and stand by it… You look at life this way: You formulate a plan, and you follow it. You take the heat. You stay the course. You don't worry about what other people think. You don't worry about entertaining reporters."[1389]

You must trust your decisions. But never confuse confidence with blind faith. You must always remain receptive to new facts and ideas. A decision that was smart yesterday may later appear dumb. For thirteen years, Autodesk CEO Carol Bartz has led her firm to great success. She says, "I've turned this company around three times. It's like a sailboat. The weather changed, and I had to change. The economy changed [or] the technology changed, [so I shifted direction]."[1390] Rams head coach Mike Martz should have studied sailing and the need to adapt when your plan is failing. Patriots players claim they overheard Rams players during Super Bowl XXXVI begging Martz–who was calling pass after pass–to mix in more runs, to which Martz supposedly replied, "F--- it! I'm going to win it my way."[1391]

COLLABORATING

"We talk every day in our meeting room. We talk about what we need to do to get better. I bounce ideas off of [backup quarterback Doug Flutie], and he bounces things off of me."[1392]
   – *Tom Brady*

"[Charles Schwab CEO David] Pottruck had a personality so overbearing that… after a second failed marriage, he'd sought counseling for what he thought was a 'wife selection problem' only to be told he had a 'husband behavior problem' and needed to learn how to compromise."[1393]
   – *Betsy Morris, Fortune magazine*

"If you give [Belichick] an idea and it is sound and he thinks it is a good idea, he will go for it. If he doesn't think it is a good idea, he is not going to go for it. He is open-minded. He is flexible."[1394]
   – *Patriots defensive coordinator Romeo Crennel*

"[Belichick] listens to the advice of his assistants, and he's not one of those guys who will take ill heed of anyone's advice. If he thinks it gives him a better chance to win, he'll do it."[1395]
   – *Patriots offensive coordinator Charlie Weis*

Bill Belichick is arguably the universe's foremost football authority. Romeo Crennel says he's "a very thorough football-oriented guy. He knows football. He knows offense. He knows defense. He knows special teams because he has coached all of those positions. He is willing to put in the time to work, the study, and the effort that it has to have."[1396] But no coach has time to devise every creative idea, teach every player, study every game of each upcoming opponent, analyze thousands of prospective draftees and make every decision. So, Belichick relies on Charlie Weis to oversee his offense, Romeo Crennel to oversee his defense, Brad Seely to oversee his special teams and Scott Pioli to oversee personnel.

Belichick's effective collaboration with these men and their subordinates is another component of the team's success. Patriots director of football research Ernie Adams says Patriots collaborate so well because players and coaches "are not out to satisfy their own egos. They are committed to getting along and being on the same page. Everyone knows there is plenty of glory to go around if we win."[1397] Jealous Chicago Bears head coach Dick Jauron says this is the perfect formula:

"They have what everybody is looking for: quality ownership at the top. They have a guy in Bill Belichick in charge who is making all the decisions and making the right ones. And they all seem to be on the same page as an organization. They look at issues and seem to agree."[1398]

DELEGATE DECISIONS

"I run the Patriots like all of my other businesses. I figure out what I can't do and find good people that I can trust [to do them]."[1399]
– *Robert Kraft*

Patriots owner Robert Kraft delegates complete authority over football operations to Bill Belichick because Belichick possesses far greater football knowledge. Belichick does not delegate such unfettered authority to his assistants because–after a lifetime in football–he knows at least as much about his assistants' jobs as they do. Belichick delegates to his assistants conditional authority. He expects them to make decisions as he himself would in their position. If a decision seems unsound to Belichick and the assistant cannot persuade him of its wisdom, Belichick will likely overrule it:

> "I am responsible for all the things that happen out there on the field. I have the final say on them. If I want to change them, I can change them. And if I don't, then they're out there with my approval. If they don't go right, I still feel accountable for it. I'm not trying to put it on anybody else, but that's the way it's been, and that's the way it's going to be. Whatever we've run out there, regardless of who called it–me, Charlie, someone else suggested it– ultimately, it's my decision, and that's not going to change. It will be the same way on defense."[1400]

The buck in New England stops with Bill Belichick. Coach Belichick retains authority over every Patriots decision and accepts responsibility for everything that goes wrong.

This arrangement is not as dictatorial or adversarial as it sounds because Belichick hires assistants who share his mindset and possess deep football knowledge, so Belichick and his assistants usually agree. And most disagreements are resolved amicably, following an intense but respectful exchange of ideas and facts that convinces everyone of the final decision's appropriateness and leads to greater understanding. Debates are civil because Belichick and his assistants care only about *what*'s right, never *who*'s right. No one ever "wins" or "loses" an argument. The team makes either a smart decision or a dumb one. Belichick respects his assistants and overrules them only when he's confident his logic is more valid than theirs, never arbitrarily. Belichick never seeks to impose his will. Instead, he consciously strives to judge all ideas–his and others'–on their merits, not their origin. "Not invented here" does not afflict the Patriots, and Belichick always does whatever he perceives is best for the team. Peter Drucker says this is a proper use of authority:

> "What people mean by bureaucracy, and rightly condemn, is management that has come to misconstrue itself as an end and the institution as a means. This is the degenerative disease to which managements are prone... Business management must always, in every decision and action, put economic performance first. It can justify its existence and its authority only by the economic results it produces."[1401]

A corollary is that coaches should pride themselves on offering input (suggestions, ideas, critiques, facts, evidence, *etc.*) that helps the team make the best possible decision, not on whether the final decision is "theirs." They should pride themselves on contributing to something great, not on how much "power" they have. For example, new defensive coordinator Eric Mangini is not at all interested in rewriting half the defensive playbook just because others developed it: "There are a lot of names on this defense, and there'll probably be a lot of names in the future on this defense. Everybody kind of adds to it, and it evolves... I'm hoping that 'Mangini' will be another name on a defense that's done a lot of good things."[1402] Mangini's goal is not to prove how smart he is but to tweak and adapt the existing playbook–itself the product of collective effort–into something even greater.

Though Belichick runs nothing by himself and does not micromanage his assistants, he is aware of and involved in everything, as defensive coordinator Romeo Crennel explains:

> "Bill lets me coach the defense. You can talk to the players. I put in the game plan. I make the calls on the sideline. Just like any other manager or CEO, if he has something that he wants, I try to give it to him because otherwise he will get somebody else that will try to give it to him. That is kind of the way we operate. He looks at an opponent and he has some ideas and we might talk early in the week about the ideas, 'Who do we need to stop? How do you perceive this game?' If there is something different than I see that he is seeing, he will say, 'Look, I would like to do this,' or, 'Get it done for me this way.' Then, boom, we get it done the way he wants to do it. Most of the time, like I said, because we have been together for so long and we have grown up in the same system, we are kind of on the same page."[1403]

Belichick relies heavily on his staff but can overrule anything. He views his coaching and personnel assistants as extensions of himself. He enjoys digging into details and will overrule a decision after robust debate yields no consensus:

> "A lot of times I've delegated [tasks] and will continue to do that. But at the same time, if there is something I don't feel comfortable with, or I don't like the call, or if (there is) something I want to do, then we'll do it."[1404]

This arrangement violates the principle that managers should delegate authority and responsibility to subordinates and trust them to make the proper decisions. But Bill Belichick is so aware of details and so knowledgeable about football that he is fully capable of overruling decisions for smart reasons and explaining his reasons to those whose decisions he is overruling. He never overrules anything arbitrarily, and his subordinates learn from his decisions. Belichick does not hog his assistants' glory and accepts personal responsibility whenever he fails to overrule a poor decision. Employees resent bosses who claim credit and point fingers. Belichick does the opposite, so assistants do not resent his meddling and looking over their shoulders as they otherwise might.

Belichick never publicly blames subordinates for making bad decisions because Belichick considers it his responsibility to overrule their bad decisions. Since the buck always stops with Belichick, subordinates' mistakes are ultimately his mistakes: "It's [my] responsibility to take the information and go with it."[1405] Pressed in late 2001, for example, to say who else within the Patriots organization was involved in the controversial decision that Tom Brady would continue as starting quarterback after Drew Bledsoe returned from his injury, Belichick refused to name names because who advised him was irrelevant: "I made the decision. It falls on me."[1406]

Delegate all non-essentials

"It is a law of governance that it restrict itself to the *necessary* decisions. Any governing body will be the more effective, and more powerful, the more it eschews decisions that it does not have to make."[1407]
– *Management expert Peter Drucker*

"I've tried to budget my time probably a little more efficiently, and delegate things to people that maybe I wasn't as quick to delegate [while] in Cleveland."[1408]
– *Bill Belichick*

Bill Belichick learned from unnecessary distractions during his disappointing tenure as Cleveland Browns head coach from 1991 to 1995 to avoid involving himself in unproductive activities: "I've tried to take some of the non-football things out of my domain, all the things that come across my desk that don't have to do with performance directly."[1409] To focus on football and avoid distractions, for example, Belichick uses a personal assistant, Berj Najarian–previously a public relations assistant with the Jets. Najarian filters the news to ensure that Belichick knows the major issues the media is covering, much as the CIA prepares a "PDB" or *Presidential Daily Briefing*. This allows Belichick to anticipate and prepare answers to likely press conference questions without spending hours every day reading papers and listening to talk radio.

For two years in Cleveland, Belichick served as both head coach and offensive coordinator, two full-time jobs. After joining New England in 2000, Belichick immediately hired Charlie Weis as offensive coordinator and handed him the keys to the offense: "I have complete confidence in Charlie. We've worked together before, both here [in 1996] and with the Jets [1997-1999]. He knows what I want and expect. It's his responsibility to see that our players get it."[1410]

The following season, Belichick relinquished control of the Patriots' defense to Romeo Crennel. During the 2000 season, when the Patriots finished a disappointing 5-11, Belichick ran both the team and the defense. He didn't trust anyone else with the defense, so he trained defenders and called defensive plays himself. In early 2001, Belichick wisely leapt at the opportunity to hire Crennel, whom he had known for two decades and with whom he had shared defensive coaching responsibilities for fourteen years. Belichick knew that delegating the defense to Crennel meant "We got better today."[1411] Belichick trusted Crennel, and the two shared a defensive philosophy: "I feel real comfortable with Romeo. Nobody has worked more closely with me since (I've been in the NFL) than Romeo."[1412] Crennel's signing freed Belichick from defensive coordinator responsibilities to worry only about head coaching duties:

> "What the assistant coaches or coordinators do really isn't what a head coach does. The coordinator calls plays, puts in game plans and works with one side of the ball. It's tremendously important. But as a head coach, you're in a lot of different administrative areas—salary cap, the weight program, special teams, the media, on and on and on."[1413]

Following Crennel's hiring, offensive coordinator Charlie Weis witnessed a huge boost in Belichick's effectiveness as head coach:

> "When he first came here, I ran the offense, he ran the defense, and the one thing he wasn't allowed to do was really manage the team. Then, when he brought in Romeo this year and turned over the defense to Romeo and other guys, that allowed him to become a head coach, and I think he's really flourished. His personality has come out as he's gotten more familiar with guys on both sides of the ball."[1414]

Belichick gets angry when the media tosses him rose petals for the Patriots' defensive dominance. Belichick goes out of his way to say Romeo calls the defensive plays.

Let the best-informed person decide

> "Controlling the work process means control of the work, and not control of the worker. Control is a tool of the worker and must never be his master... The purpose of control is to make the process go smoothly, properly, and according to high standards."[1415]
> – Peter Drucker

A decision should be made by whoever possesses the most information about possible choices and their likely consequences. The Patriots follow that rule. Here are three simple examples:

First, before Super Bowl XXXIX, reporters asked Patriots defensive lineman Richard Seymour whether coaches or trainers had given him the green light to play. Seymour replied, "I'm the official word."[1416] Leaving the decision to the injured player makes sense because no one else knows better how he feels and how productive he could be. Of course, players are tempted to make emotional, not rational, decisions because, as Patriots defensive end Ty Warren explains, "When you want to be out there… It's like your little brother's out there in the yard in a fistfight and you want to go out and help him."[1417] But Seymour knew he needed to decide based on his health, not his desire to play in the Super Bowl: "I didn't want the magnitude of the game to dictate whether I would play… It was important that I make a smart decision for myself and also for the football team… If I wasn't healthy enough to go out there and play, I wouldn't be on the football field. Even though it's tough, you still have to be smart about the situation and not let your emotions take over and get the best of you."[1418] Patriots coaches trusted Seymour to make that decision based on the team's best interest, not his own. Had they feared Seymour might make a self-serving decision, coaches likely would have overruled him.

Second, Troy Brown–training on offense, defense and special teams–was never unsure which meeting to attend: "I just go where Bill tells me to go."[1419] Belichick allocated Brown's practice time based on sound coaching logic:

> "He gets bounced back and forth a lot. When we are working on things defensively that he would have a role in, we try to get him there, feeling that the catch-up on offense is a little easier than the catch-up on defense. But, there are times when offensively we are doing things that have application to him and we don't need him as much on defense, like goal-line and some of our first down calls where he is not as involved. We just have to split him up. I think at this point if it comes down to offense or defense, it is going to go to defense just because he has so much more of a background on the offensive side of the ball."[1420]

Third, who decides whether the Patriots challenge an official's ruling? Ernie Adams is the primary decision-maker, not Bill Belichick. Why? Because Belichick knows only what he witnessed and what his players have told him whereas Adams– sitting in the press box–sees all the video angles the officials will see if the team challenges their ruling. The rules dictate that the referee can overrule the initial ruling only based on indisputable video evidence. It doesn't matter what players witnessed or what actually happened. Only what is captured on video matters. Adams is best informed to choose which rulings to challenge because he sees–on the press box monitor–whether the video provides indisputable evidence.

Decisions are ideally made by whoever possesses the most relevant information, but decision-making power must be withheld from those who make self-serving decisions.

Trust, empower and hold accountable

"In [my] other businesses, I would always hire, give authority to the people I hired, hold them accountable and give them support. I should have done that earlier here, and I'm clear on it now. But it is so much fun to be involved that maybe you do some things until you realize you'll just get knocked around. ...Since we've owned the team, I probably got into the most trouble when I strayed from the core values in how I run my life and run my businesses."[1421]

    – Patriots owner Robert Kraft

"Your balls weren't on the line [before Belichick and Pioli took over]... [Now] if you say a player isn't going to be a problem off the field [and] he is, then it's your fault."[1422]

    – Former Patriots scout Jason Licht (Philadelphia Eagles assistant director of player personnel since 2003)

Leaders must find managers they trust, grant them authority and responsibility, train, monitor and assist them and hold them accountable.

Like effective corporate board members who operate "nose in, fingers out,"[1423] Patriots owner Bob Kraft understands his team's business and communicates frequently and productively with his team's "CEO" (Belichick) but never grabs the steering wheel and always lets his executives and coaches do their jobs: "I try to hire the best managers I can and then I try to ask them very tough questions and hold them accountable."[1424] Belichick has the authority and responsibility to make all football decisions but keeps Kraft informed: "We talk all the time. We have open lines of communication. ...I feel that's my obligation. He doesn't want to read in the paper what we've done."[1425]

Kraft also encourages his managers to take smart risks, telling them: "Don't be afraid to take a chance, but you'd better be right."[1426] An excellent example of the trust Patriots management has earned in Kraft's mind and of Kraft's willingness to delegate responsibility is the Patriots' early 2004 decision to trade their 2nd-round draft pick to the Cincinnati Bengals for talented-but-troubled Corey Dillon. The Krafts have famously refused to allow low character individuals to become Patriots. Many observers were therefore surprised–even shocked–after the Patriots acquired Dillon. It appeared completely out of character and against Kraft family policy.

But Kraft didn't graduate from Columbia University and Harvard Business School and become a successful businessman without being open-minded. Kraft accepted his coaches' and executives' judgment that Dillon had truly changed and was Patriot-worthy, despite a nasty reputation "earned" over a long period.

Kraft wisely trusted his managers to investigate and make the correct determination:

> "In the discussions I've had–predicting the future–our people feel pretty good about [the trade]. They feel [Dillon] is a good person to have here... I think he wants to win–that's whats been represented to me. He wants to come here and be part of a winning program and not be someone who is the 'The Man.' He understands we're about 'team.' Our managers believe we have a better football team with him here [and that he possesses] all the things that are important to our family. I think everybody understands it, and they feel this is someone who can help us... It's felt that he's going to fit in and make a great contribution."[1427]

To the shock of many NFL executives who were convinced Dillon was not a Patriots-type player, Dillon not only excelled on the field (1,635 yards rushing for 4.7 yards/carry in 2004) but also instantly earned his new teammates' admiration. Dillon's agent said he's "by far, the happiest I've ever seen him."[1428] The Patriots had even spoken with Dillon's high school coach who now says, "I always figured that if he got on a good team, he could hold his ego in check. I knew he could blend in. Winning was always so important to Corey. Winning takes care of all that pain... He can be part of a cog in the wheel and not the whole dang car."[1429]

Many professional sports teams are hamstrung by meddlesome owners. Owners interfere with executives' and coaches' decision-making because they are habituated to exercising authority, enjoy running a football team or deceive themselves into believing they know more than the professionals they hired to run their team. Patriots owner Bob Kraft interfered during the 1990s when the Patriots had four "top" guys: Kraft, VP of player personnel Bobby Grier, the head coach (first Bill Parcells and later Pete Carroll), and quarterback Drew Bledsoe. Kraft eventually figured that out that a team with four "top" guys doesn't have a top guy. If Kraft didn't figure it out on his own, Carroll certainly told him: "There were no clear lines on how it was all supposed to be done. It was, 'Work it out,' and it was very difficult. And Robert knows this. It's the conversation we had on the day I walked out."[1430] Carroll believes "it totally would have been different" if he had controlled human resources:

> "Any organization that's run with a divided leadership, how can you expect to have a clear message? That was obvious to me early, and I couldn't do anything about it... We won the division in 1997, then we gave [star running back] Curtis [Martin] away to the Jets, and they won the division. It couldn't be any more obvious... The best player on the team was given away, to our opponent."[1431]

Kraft knew the top guy could not be the quarterback or owner. After years of problems arising from Kraft's effort to separate personnel decisions from coaching decisions, Kraft was convinced of the value of unifying power. With that power, Bill Belichick smartly delegated personnel responsibilities–though not final authority–to Scott Pioli, who operates as an extension of Belichick.

Since hiring Belichick in 2000, Kraft has extended him nearly complete authority to run his football program. Kraft occasionally interfered–by giving Drew Bledsoe a $103 mil. contract in 2001, for example–but a Super Bowl championship cemented Kraft's trust in Belichick. By not interfering and screwing things up for his executives and coaches, Bob Kraft helps the Patriots succeed on the field, perhaps as much as Tom Brady helps the team succeed by avoiding sacks and interceptions. Mistakes at any level of the organization erode on-field performance. Bob Kraft may not catch touchdowns or return punts or sack quarterbacks, but he has the power to quickly destroy the organization he has so smartly built into the NFL's best.

Owners who feel compelled to overrule their professional managers have hired the wrong professionals. By choosing the right professionals and standing aside as they do their jobs superbly, Kraft demonstrates the value of finding the right people and delegating to them both authority and responsibility.

As Kraft delegates to Belichick, Belichick in turn trusts Scott Pioli to run the Patriots' scouting system with little interference: "Bill has given me so much autonomy. He respects me and trusts me."[1432] Kraft confirms that "Ego doesn't get involved with those two" and that they're "on the same page."[1433] In Pioli, Belichick has an assistant who both completely shares his vision and works tirelessly toward team success. Pioli not only works Belichickian hours but also has the brains to work productively: "People tell stories of his ability to remember obscure offensive tackles from other franchises' scout squads. During an hour-long Super Bowl media session, Pioli greeted reporter after reporter by first name. He answered their questions with great detail."[1434] (I would pay to watch Belichick, Pioli, and Ernie Adams play *Trivial Pursuit*. Each has unnatural memory and might give Ken Jennings a run for his money on *Jeopardy!* On second thought, they're all too obsessed with football to know much about pop culture or literature.)

While earning his economics degree, Belichick studied the theory of comparative advantage that says people should not build their own homes and cars, grow their own food, fix their own roofs, repair their plumbing, *etc.* but should instead specialize in whatever they do relatively well. In Cleveland, Belichick fully absorbed the lesson that efficiency requires "delegating things to other people in the organization. I am a detail-oriented person, and sometimes that is not good, it's better to let somebody else worry about the things they can do and let me worry about the things that only a head coach can do."[1435] Belichick might be able to do Scott Pioli's job better than Pioli (in economics-speak, possess an "absolute advantage"), but he could never be as effective as a part-timer as Pioli is as a full-timer. A wise manager delegates to subordinates because he lacks the time to do everyone's jobs. No matter how bright a manager is, he cannot succeed by hoarding power and making every decision. As Belichick puts it, "I can't do Scott's job and he can't do mine. We work perfectly together."[1436]

Delegating is also necessary because smart people shun positions of responsibility that lack commensurate authority. If you lack control over outcomes but will be held accountable for results, you are placing your fate in the hands of others. The same Cleveland experience that taught Belichick the necessity of delegating responsibility to his coordinators also taught him to flee the New York Jets head coaching job in 2000 because Bill Parcells would have pulled all the strings, especially on player acquisition, and Belichick had no relationship with the soon-to-be owner as he had had with the recently-deceased Leon Hess:

> "The uncertainty surrounding the ownership of the team, and a number of other things, had an effect on my decision. I know the commitment that needs to be made, and I don't feel in the current situation I can lead the Jets with 100 percent conviction... I've been in a situation and, more importantly, my family has been in a situation where I was the head coach of a team in transition, of a team that went through a lot of changes, and frankly it wasn't a real good experience for me or them."[1437]

Recently asked why he quit the Jets to join the Patriots, Belichick explained his decisions were sequential: "It wasn't a decision to go any where. It was a decision to leave that organization because I just didn't feel like I could fully commit to it based on all the circumstances that were in place. I didn't know where I was going. I didn't know what I was doing. I knew what I wasn't doing. I didn't know the Patriot opportunity was going to present itself."[1438] He said the same thing the day he resigned: "I haven't thought about the future. I've thought about the situation that I'm in. 'Long term' for me is 'I've got to pick up my kids at four o'clock.'"[1439] Belichick knows quality assistants demand and deserve significant autonomy.

William Davidson's championship trifecta

> "Just like our other businesses, I hire good people I can trust. No Lone Rangers. If you keep the turkeys out of your life, then good things can happen."[1440]
> *– Patriots owner Bob Kraft*

Like Bob Kraft, 82-year-old billionaire businessman William Davidson ("Mr. D" to most of his employees) exemplifies the value of hands-off ownership. In 2004, Richardson became the only owner ever to win NBA and NHL championships in the same season. Davidson's M.O.? "He invests in troubled businesses or teams, hires the best people he can find to fix them, then waits. He gives his managers latitude to make big decisions."[1441] Davidson says finding the right people is his greatest challenge: "The main thing is to find the right people and empower them. The word 'right' is easy to say but hard to do. ...In a lot of instances, we found what we thought were the right people, empowered them and, basically, they weren't the right people."[1442]

Davidson's Detroit Pistons defied all the experts' predictions and beat the Lakers four games to one in the 2004 NBA Finals. How? Richardson hired a smart, hard-working, no-nonsense former basketball star, Joe Dumars, as general manager and empowered him to trust his instincts, which were downright Belichickian. Dumars traded away famous stars and signed lesser-known but hungry, talented, team-oriented players: "The Pistons' 'Goin' to Work' marketing campaign, devised several years ago to juice lagging attendance, reflected Dumars' persona and philosophy–hard work, no knucklehead behavior."[1443] The 2003-2004 Pistons had great chemistry and maturity. Many have compared the 2003-2004 Pistons to Belichick's Patriots, for obvious reasons. For instance, the Pistons play superb team defense, a signature of Belichick's Patriots. (The Pistons returned to the Finals in 2005 but lost in seven games to a San Antonio Spurs team whose executives practically worship at the altar of Belichick and Pioli.)

Davidson's formula also yielded success in the NHL. In 1999, Davidson paid $100 million for the Tampa Bay Lightning, which *Sports Illustrated* in 1997 called the worst franchise in all of professional sports. On June 7, 2004, the Lightning shocked the hockey world by winning the Stanley Cup. Not only had the Lightning recently missed the playoffs six straight seasons, but they also had only the 21st-highest salary in the NHL, a league where wins and salary are highly correlated.

Davidson's hands-off approach and willingness to let his professionals make occasional mistakes built league champions in 2004 out of teams few thought could win it all. Davidson's formula sounds eerily like something Scott Pioli or Bill Belichick would say:

> "I try to have an organization that has integrity, that has some proper knowledge of the sport, whether it's hockey or basketball, and hopefully makes the right decisions in regard to the players, the players' contracts and getting value in those contracts. You need to know the concept of the team you need to have. ...They may not be the best players at their position, but they fit with one another."[1444]

Davidson's Pistons won the 1989 and 1990 NBA championships under coach Chuck Daly, who appreciated Davidson's non-meddlesome style:

> "He's the kind of guy that hires you and basically leaves you alone... which is all you can ask when you are in the professional sports business. You can succeed or fail. I didn't have any real meetings with him the whole time. He would come through at halftime, but he would never say much."[1445]

Even Davidson's WNBA team, the Detroit Shock, won its league's 2003 championship. The common thread among the Pistons, Lightning, and Shock? Lunch pail, blue-collar players, just like the Patriots:

> "The teams were crafted by different men—Dumars with the Pistons, Bill Laimbeer with the Shock and Jay Feaster with the Lightning—but they all have the same workingman's attitude. Dumars, Laimbeer and Feaster each looked for toughness first. These days, most sports executives look for talent first, figuring that toughness will come."[1446]

Davidson even shares the self-assurance that led Bob Kraft to purchase the Patriots against his financial advisors' advice and to later completely self-finance construction of Gillette Stadium, now the best stadium in the NFL and a money-maker even in the off-season:

> "When Davidson first proposed building Auburn Hills ["The Palace" where the Pistons play] for $92 million in 1986, without public support, friends and colleagues called Wilson and asked him to talk his boss out of it. Davidson went ahead and built a revolutionary arena with luxury suites placed close to the floor so the Pistons could charge more for their rent. The arena has always been profitable and has been copied throughout the sports world."[1447]

Surround yourself with the smartest, most talented assistants

> "Bill is the best listener I've ever known, and he wouldn't have had those [great assistants in Cleveland who have done great things since then] around unless he was learning from them too. The give-and-take is a major reason he's grown and evolved."[1448]
> – *Scott Pioli*

> "I have a board of directors to try to balance me, and I need it… There's always got to be an entrepreneurial streak, but… having really good, sort of conservative people… is important. We try to surround ourselves with great people."[1449]
> – *Richard Branson, Virgin CEO*

> "What we have here is a real group effort. It's not just Bill. It's [defensive coordinator] Romeo Crennel and [defensive backs coach] Eric Mangini and [outside linebackers coach] Rob Ryan. Bill has done a good job putting quality minds around him."[1450]
> – *Patriots linebacker Tedy Bruschi*

Many "smart" people enjoy feeling like the smartest person in the room. Truly smart people want to be the dumbest. As Rick Pitino says, "I don't hire assistant coaches; I hire future head coaches."[1451] Charlie Weis takes this a step further, hiring three former head coaches for his new Notre Dame staff. A smart coach surrounds himself with greatness because he measures himself by his team's success, not by how fastidiously he micro-manages his team or how thoroughly he dominates his assistants. Bill Belichick loves smart people, and it shows. Phil Simms reports, "I've had a couple of head coaches in the NFL tell me that they think the New England Patriots have the best coaching staff in the league."[1452] With hindsight, the same has been said of Belichick's Cleveland Browns coaching staff.

Another problem "smart" people often create for themselves is believing they know everything. There's simply too much knowledge in the world for anyone to possess it all, so we are each ignorant in our own unique way. Truly smart people: 1) Know what they don't know; 2) Know that they don't actually know some of what they believe they know; and, 3) Know that they don't even know about some of the stuff that they don't know. (That is a brain-teaser of a sentence! If you re-read it, it should make sense.) "Know-it-alls" are deceiving themselves. Belichick knows more about football than anyone else, but he knows he's no know-it-all. During a Bryant University Q&A session in which one student referred to the quintuple Super Bowl-winning coach as "Your Greatness,"[1453] Belichick self-effacingly—and humorously—reminded students that he himself was fired in 1995: "Don't be afraid to fail. Has anyone here been fired?"[1454] Belichick was telling students: you may think I'm a genius, but not that long ago people thought I was a failure, so don't let temporary setbacks crush your passion for pursing your dreams. Belichick was simultaneously reminding himself that he is thoroughly capable of losing in the NFL. The Cleveland Browns fired Belichick even after he surrounded himself with one of the greatest coaching staffs in NFL history. Success is much harder to achieve than Bill Belichick now makes it appear. Just ask the 31 other NFL head coaches… not to mention the many fired each season. Recognizing his need for quality ideas, even Bill Belichick seeks the best assistants he can find and relies on their advice.

By hiring assistants he trusts and respects, Belichick maximizes the likelihood he will receive and heed good ideas. Romeo Crennel says, "I have worked with Bill so long, it is just like second nature to me because we were assistants together. We have kind of grown up together."[1455]

Belichick is smart enough to listen to his assistants, and his assistants are smart enough to offer up useful ideas. Rob Ryan—Patriots outside linebackers coach until he accepted the Oakland Raiders' offer to coordinate their defense—said the Patriots coaching staff is a team, not a hierarchy:

> "Our defense is a hell of a lot more multiple [varied] than it used to be, and I like to think that I've bounced a few ideas off people that have worked. With me and [secondary coach] Eric Mangini, we're pretty consistent. We're going to bring something up and it's either going to get thrown out, or it's going to hit. We have an open line of communication. We're not there to be

yes-men. We're there to do our job and if we believe in something, put it up there."[1456]

Belichick agrees:

"The assistants generate a lot of the ideas... (They'll offer) 'We really need to think about this,' or 'This was something that worked in the past.' There's a good flow on that. We have a lot of experience together. I get a lot of input from them, and I use it."[1457]

And the assistants Belichick hires are also excellent listeners. If a player has a good idea, it will receive serious consideration. Patriots safety Rodney Harrison says of new defensive coordinator Eric Mangini: "We like Eric. He's open-minded. He's a smart, innovative guy, and we have a lot of respect for him... Just being open to us and listening... a lot of coaches think they know it all and are very close-minded. I respect the fact Eric is open-minded."[1458]

Because Belichick hires talented assistants, trains them well and enables them to grow, the "Belichick coaching tree" is expanding rapidly in today's NFL.

Belichick's New England Patriots assistants

One indication of the quality of Belichick's staff is its experience, over 300 years of collective football coaching:

Name	Position	NFL coaching years	Football coaching years
Bill Belichick	Head coach	30	30
Dante Scarnecchia	Assistant head coach & offensive line coach	23	35
Romeo Crennel	Defensive coordinator	24	35
Charlie Weis	Offensive coordinator	15	26
Brian Daboll	Wide receivers coach	5	8
Jeff Davidson	Tight ends coach & asst. offensive line coach	10	10
Ivan Fears	Running backs coach	14	28
Pepper Johnson	Defensive line coach	5	5
Eric Mangini	Defensive backs coach and defensive coordinator (2005)	10	10
Joel Collier	Assistant defensive backs coach (2005)	14	16
Josh McDaniels	Quarterbacks coach	4	6
Dean Pees	Linebackers coach	1	31
Brad Seely	Special teams coordinator	16	27
Mike Woicik	Strength & conditioning coach	15	27

| Markus Paul | Strength & conditioning assistant coach (through 2004) | 7 | 7 |

Source: *New England Patriots 2004 Media Guide and Patriots.com.*

Consider just one of these men, Dante Scarnecchia. His deep knowledge of the game is evidenced by his advice to a rookie Tedy Bruschi that he develop "positional flexibility," something Belichick craves in his players. Amazingly, 2005 will be Scarnecchia's 36th season as a football coach and 22nd with the Patriots. He survived the regimes of Ron Meyer, Raymond Berry, Dick McPherson, Bill Parcells, Pete Carroll, and Bill Belichick. He served under three owners. It's no coincidence Scarnecchia was the only assistant retained when Bill Parcells took over in the 1990s or that Scarnecchia is one of four assistants remaining from the pre-Belichick Patriots. (Belichick also retained running backs coach Ivan Fears, special teams coach Brad Seely, and tight ends coach Jeff Davidson–who called the offensive plays while Charlie Weis was hospitalized in 2002. With modesty characteristic of Belichick assistants, Davidson claims he was retained because "it didn't cost him much to keep me on the staff."[1459] Davidson followed Romeo Crennel to Cleveland in 2005.) Belichick fell in love with Scarnecchia when they spoke after Belichick joined the Patriots and the two discovered they shared similar football philosophies. Belichick made Scarnecchia his assistant head coach because "He's the best. Dante is as good a coach as I've been around. He does a great job from top to bottom, from rookie to 13-year veteran, from tackle to center to backup guys and guys that are on the practice squad and don't play that eventually develop into solid players. He is outstanding."[1460] Patriots guard Joe Andruzzi agrees: "He knows this game. He knows his players. He gets everybody ready, no matter who it is."[1461]

Experience is not the only measure of quality. Belichick is grooming the younger coaches in whom he perceives great potential. Asked in 2002 whether Josh McDaniels–himself the son of a football coach–reminded him of himself at that age, Belichick replied, "He's a lot better than I was."[1462] McDaniels is now the quarterbacks coach and appears to be calling offensive plays in the 2005 preseason.

Ernie Adams

The most cerebral Belichick assistant is not even listed above. Belichick's best friend from Phillips Andover, Ernie Adams, is the Patriots' director of football research. Bill and Ernie stuck together during stints with the New York Giants, Cleveland Browns and New England Patriots. Adams discusses strategy and tactics with Belichick, most famously leading to the realization that they could disrupt the entire St. Louis Rams' offense in Super Bowl XXXVI by attacking Marshall Faulk. Adams' insight derives from his analytical skill: "Adams is in charge of computer analysis and statistical evaluation [and] has a hand in nearly all of the major personnel and game-planning decisions… Adams also plays a huge role in coordinating the film study that is at the core of the Pats' evaluation process."[1463]

Tennessee Titans defensive coordinator Jim Schwartz, who broke into NFL coaching with Belichick's Cleveland Browns in the early 1990s, says he learned his analytical, data-driven approach to coaching by watching Belichick and Adams: "Ernie Adams was doing a lot of research for Bill. They were doing stuff on turnovers, and they do a lot of stats on things like, 'If you block a punt [what are] your chances of winning?'"[1464] Schwartz says Belichick "used to assign me [statistical] projects"[1465] and "I got a PhD in footballology [in Cleveland]."[1466] Schwartz has used that knowledge to mine football data for factors that correlate with scoring and winning, seeking opportunities to improve. For example, "If red-zone efficiency means so much, we need to practice our ass off in the red zone. If third-down efficiency means so much, then we want to practice that stuff more."[1467] In Cleveland in 1994, Schwartz's analysis found that fumbles "were damn near random. Bill had a hard time buying that one. He'd say, 'No, no, good teams don't fumble.' I researched 10 years of data and the good teams fumble every bit as much as the bad teams."[1468]

Ernie always remains behind the scenes but serves as Belichick's second brain. And what a brain Ernie has! A rare article on Ernie titled "Is Adams a genius' genius?" says, "Adams, those few who know him say, has a photographic memory whereby he can instantly recall plays from games 15 years ago and the offenses or defenses used in them."[1469] A Pittsburgh Steelers video coordinator was blown away by Adams' uncanny ability to recall past football games and predict what was about to unfold in a game:

> "I remember sitting on the roof of old Cleveland Stadium and watching this guy know exactly what play was coming. He could tell you what play Terry Bradshaw ran against a certain defense, how many times he ran it; just an incredible guy. If you asked him what play the Pittsburgh Steelers ran against the Cleveland Browns, he'd give you the terminology, the defense, who blocked what and who ran what. They talk about how smart Bill Belichick is … he's a good coach, but here's one of the guys he's had around for a long time."[1470]

San Francisco 49ers director of player personnel Bill Rees confirms that "His ability to recall particular instances is the best I've ever seen. He could tell you a play from when he was at Northwestern in 1974 that someone ran against him, the down and distance, the yardage and how they blocked it."[1471]

Adams' memory helped him earn–according to Belichick–"tons of money"[1472] in finance. Adams left the New York Giants in 1985 to work on Wall Street but returned to the NFL after Belichick became Browns head coach in 1991. He returned to Wall Street after Belichick's firing but re-reunited with Belichick when he took over the Patriots in 2000. Patriots linebacker Mike Vrabel says Adams is a walking, talking Google: "I use Ernie for trivia. You know, like who held the longest field goal record before Tom Dempsey? Bert Rechichar of the Colts (56 yards in 1953)."[1473] Belichick is the same way, says Patriots punter Josh Miller: "He'll relive a play that happened in the third quarter in 1974, and know all the guys who played for his team and the other team, and who [officiated] the game."[1474]

Adams keeps a low profile. Patriots secondary coach Eric Mangini calls Adams "the man of mystery."[1475] Special teams coach Brad Seely says, "I know he helps Bill a lot with the philosophy of the game. But beyond that, I have no idea."[1476] Running backs coach Ivan Fears says, "I'm not sure what he does. ...He's important to Bill, I know that."[1477]

Adams says his job is to "think of things to help us win."[1478] He scouts each opponent and helps with game planning. He watches countless hours of film on potential Patriots draft choices. He absolutely has Belichick's ear on any issue. He construes his job as being an extra pair of eyes and ears for Belichick: "I stick my finger in as many pies as possible. It's important that I don't have everyone in the organization thinking I'm in their way. If I come to a conclusion on something, I go to Bill and give it to him."[1479] Belichick entrusts challenging special assignments to Adams. Adams is basically an in-house management consultant who always has the CEO's attention: "My responsibility is to do whatever I can think of to help us win. Part of it, I make up as I go along. Bill and I work together. If I think I can help us win, my job is to do it."[1480] The Patriots are most fortunate to have Adams. Baltimore Ravens' senior VP Kevin Byrne, who knew Adams when they were both with the Cleveland Browns, calls Adams "a genius." [1481] Wearing large glasses, surrounding himself with books, wearing out-of-fashion clothes, and burying himself in statistical analysis, Adams is certainly a nerd's nerd... which suits Belichick perfectly.

Adams' grasp of football minutiae and statistics gives the Patriots a definite advantage, even if the man and his process are shrouded in mystery. According to Tennessee Titans defensive coordinator Jim Schwartz, "Mike Martz, Mike Sherman, Bill Belichick, Brian Billick, Dick Vermeil, and Jim Haslett are the head coaches who I know pay attention to statistical analysis."[1482] The complete list is likely longer and growing rapidly, but Belichick and Adams were statistical pioneers, and empirical analysis is a continuing Patriots strength.

Belichick's Cleveland Browns staff (1991-95)

"Being on that staff was an amazing experience."[1483]
– *Phil Savage, current Cleveland Browns GM*

"We all worked together and had a good group of people to learn from."[1484]
– *Nick Saban, Bill Belichick's defensive coordinator, 1991-94*

Belichick surrounded himself with smart, experienced, analytical, open-minded assistant coaches in Cleveland too. Rick Gosselin–who won a long and distinguished reporting award from the Pro Football Hall of Fame–called Belichick's Cleveland coaching staff "one of the greatest football think tanks ever assembled."[1485]

Belichick says the coaches he brought to Cleveland had all drawn similar conclusions from their experiences: "There are some common denominators, in terms of work ethic, overall philosophy, toughness and consistency."[1486] Their interaction generated great ideas that all have benefited from ever since. Former Browns offensive line coach Kirk Ferentz says, "I would imagine that we all went to Cleveland with ideas about how things ought to be done, and there's no question that they got reshaped a little bit. We all learned quite a lot."[1487] Virtually every coach and executive in that Cleveland organization went on to achieve greatness somewhere:

Former Browns staffer	*Position with Browns*	*Post-Browns accomplishments*
Kirk Ferentz	Offensive line coach	· As head coach at the University of Iowa, transformed a 1-10 team into a perennial national powerhouse · College football's Coach of the Year in 2002 when Iowa (11-1 regular season) won the Big Ten and played in the Orange Bowl · Led Iowa (10-3) to 8th place ranking in final 2003 AP poll and an Outback Bowl victory over Florida · Led Iowa (10-2) to 8th place ranking in final 2004 AP poll after a Capital One Bowl victory over 9-2 LSU · Interviewed by Jacksonville Jaguars for head coach opening
Nick Saban	Defensive coordinator (1991-1994)	· Head coach at LSU where he inherited a back-to-back losing team and went 8-4 with a Peach Bowl victory in his first season (2000). 10-3 in 2001, 8-5 in 2002, 13-1 and co-national champ in 2003, 9-3 in 2004 (one play from 10-2 before surrendering a last-second 56-yard touchdown to the Iowa Hawkeyes in their bowl game) · NCAA Coach of the Year in 2003 · LSU Tigers: 2003 college football co-champions · Turned down opportunity to be head coach of the Chicago Bears[1488]; "spurned at least five N.F.L. offers"[1489] · Became Miami Dolphins head coach in 2005
Pat Hill	Tight ends coach	· Head coach at Fresno State · Coached Fresno State to six consecutive bowl games (1999-2004) · Fresno State ranked #22 in nation in final 2004 AP poll

Scott Pioli	Personnel assistant	· Patriots VP of player personnel · NFL Executive of the Year in 2003 and 2004 · Helped Patriots win three Super Bowls · Spurned $15 million offer to become Seattle Seahawks general manager
Mike Lombardi	General manager and player personnel director	· Oakland Raiders personnel director · Helped Raiders earn spot in Super Bowl XXXVII
Chuck Bresnahan	Linebackers coach	· Former Oakland Raiders defensive coordinator · Helped Raiders earn spot in Super Bowl XXXVII · Named Cincinnati Bengals defensive coordinator in 2005
Scott O'Brien	Special teams coach (NFL special teams coach of the year in 1994)	· Special teams coach and assistant head coach of the Carolina Panthers · Helped Panthers nearly win Super Bowl XXXVIII · "Is considered the best special teams coach in the NFL."[1490] · Named Miami Dolphins Coordinator of Football Operations in Jan 2005
Rick Venturi	Defensive backs coach (1994-1995)	· Became New Orleans Saints defensive coordinator in January 2002 · Helped improve Saints defense. The Saints defense gave up 25.6 points/game in 2001, 24.3 in 2002, and only 20.4 in 2003[1491] (but 25.3 in 2004)
Ozzie Newsome	Coaching intern; later pro personnel director	· Baltimore Ravens general manager and executive VP · Former Ravens senior VP of football operations · Helped draft Peter Boulware, Todd Heap, Jermaine Lewis, Ray Lewis, Jonathan Ogden and Ed Reed · Helped Baltimore Ravens win Super Bowl XXXV
Phil Savage	Assistant to Nick Saban and personnel scout	· Baltimore Ravens director of player personnel · Baltimore Ravens director of college scouting since 1996. Helped draft Peter Boulware, Todd Heap, Jermaine Lewis, Ray Lewis and Jonathan Ogden and Ed Reed · Helped Baltimore Ravens win Super Bowl XXXV · Named Cleveland Browns general manager in January 2005
Jim Schwartz	Personnel assistant	· Defensive coordinator of the Tennessee Titans · Titans were NFL's sixth stingiest defense in 2003 in points/game, surrendering 17.6 · Titans were NFL's sixth stingiest defense in 2004 in points/game, surrendering 16.8

Ernie Adams	Special assistant to the head coach	· Patriots director of football research · Helped Patriots win three Super Bowls
Jim Bates	Linebackers coach ('91); Defensive ends coach ('92 & '93); ? ('95)	· Named Miami Dolphins interim head coach in mid-November 2004 · Became Green Bay Packers' defensive coordinator in 2005
George Kokinis	Scouting assistant	· Baltimore Ravens director of pro personnel · Previously Ravens assistant director of pro personnel · Helped Baltimore Ravens win Super Bowl XXXV
Terry McDonough (son of the late Will McDonough)	Southeast area scout (hired by Belichick)	· Former Baltimore Ravens eastern college scouting supervisor and "one of the best young talent evaluators in the league"[1492] · Helped Baltimore Ravens win Super Bowl XXXV · Jacksonville Jaguars' executive scout since 2003
Eric Mangini	Ball boy, then intern, then coaching assistant	· New England Patriots' secondary coach · Helped Patriots win three Super Bowls · Turned down offer to become Oakland Raiders' defensive coordinator · Just 33, Mangini succeeded Romeo Crennel as Patriots defensive coordinator after turning down defensive coordinator offers from the Miami Dolphins and Cleveland Browns
Kevin Spencer	Assistant	· Four years as special teams coach of the Indianapolis Colts · In three years as special teams coach of the Pittsburgh Steelers, has lifted them from embarrassing to a top-10 team in most categories · 2003 NFL Special Teams Coach of the Year
Mike Tannenbaum	Personnel assistant	· New York Jets Sr. VP of football operations and assistant GM

Nick Saban says of the staff Belichick assembled and nurtured: "It's pretty amazing. Obviously, we all learned a lot about how to do things the right way when we were in Cleveland. It also says a lot about Bill's ability to acquire and develop good people."[1493] Saban says the talented coaches learned from one another in Cleveland. Belichick agrees: "[Nick] taught me a lot about defense. I learned more from him than he learned from me when we were together in Cleveland."[1494]

New Orleans Saints defensive coordinator Rick Venturi, who compares notes with Belichick frequently during the regular season regarding common opponents, is another member of the mutual admiration society that developed in Cleveland: "Bill and Nick are two of my closest friends in this business. I talk a lot to both of those guys. I've maintained not only a coaching friendship, but also a personal friendship… Both guys are tremendous coaches, period. They're terrific at what they do, and they have a lot in common… They're brilliant."[1495]

ADVICE: HEEDING AND IGNORING

Kenny Rogers says we "gotta know when to hold 'em and know when to fold 'em." Decision-makers must know whom to trust and when to trust them. They must solicit advice but cannot follow it blindly. In other words, they must know when to continue believing in themselves even when everyone else thinks they're insane.

In 1965, "C" student Fred Smith wrote an undergraduate paper proposing a radical business idea. Though his professor thought little of his idea, "I knew the idea was profound. There wasn't any doubt in my mind about that. The fundamental forces that were driving it were inexorable."[1496] As obvious as the idea was to Fred, he had trouble raising capital in 1969. Fortunately, he had inherited millions and was willing to invest it. He eventually raised the rest of what he needed. The day "Federal Express" opened for business in 1973, it handled just seven packages. Virtually without revenue, FedEx was nearly bankrupt. But Smith refused to surrender. He flew to Las Vegas. The $27,000 he won playing blackjack kept the doors open. Smart move. FedEx is now worth over $25 billion.

Robert Kraft and Bill Belichick are tough like Fred Smith, so confident in their intuition that they will bet their fortune and reputation on gambles no one else would consider.

If you're an expert, trust your gut

"When you believe in something, you have to just follow it and do it, even when so-called gurus tell you it's wrong."[1497]
– *Patriots owner Robert Kraft*

Robert Kraft earned fellowships to Columbia (where he earned his B.A.) and Harvard Business School before founding The Kraft Group and building it into a successful company. Kraft and his four sons became Patriots season ticket holders–to the chagrin of wife Myra–in 1971. Kraft decided in the early 1970s to someday buy his favorite team. He owns it today only because he repeatedly ignored the advice of his bankers.

Kraft buys Patriots against his bankers' advice

"In pursuing the team, I probably broke every one of my personal financial rules."[1498]
– *Patriots owner Bob Kraft*

"My wife was scared I'd lost my marbles."[1499]
– *Patriots owner Bob Kraft*

In 1985, Bob Kraft purchased a $1 million/year lease and a ten-year option to buy–for $18 million–300 acres surrounding Foxboro Stadium. Kraft's banker disapproved, thinking it a bad investment. On November 23, 1988, Kraft paid a bankruptcy court $25 million to lease the stadium through 2001. Kraft's banker again disapproved, thinking it unwise to pay $25 million to lease a crappy, decrepit stadium built for just $6.7 million in 1971. Even the Patriots' then-owner Victor Kiam bid only $16 million (or $19 million... I have seen both figures). But Kraft had witnessed Boston University rake in concession stand and parking revenue from the Boston Lobsters tennis team he owned, so he knew he could generate good revenue without owning the team. And he knew leasing the stadium might give him an opportunity to buy the Patriots because the team was locked into a rock-solid stadium lease and had to play in Foxboro: "Some franchises never go up for sale, so I realized I needed a competitive advantage."[1500]

In 1994, Kraft finally got the chance he craved to purchase his beloved team when the team's owner decided to move the team to St. Louis. James Busch Orthwein ("Busch" as in beer) offered Kraft $75 million to escape the stadium lease. Mrs. Myra Kraft was ecstatic: "That's great. You're going to take it. You still have the stadium. You'll find another team."[1501] But Kraft wanted the Patriots–even though the team had the lowest revenue and attendance in the entire NFL and 19 wins and 61 losses over the past five seasons–because "If you look at teams like the Giants, the Bears, the Steelers, they've never changed hands in over 70 years... I always said I had a greater chance of being a starting quarterback in the NFL–of which there are 32–than owning a team in my hometown where it might not ever happen again in my lifetime."[1502] Twenty-three years earlier, Kraft had endured his wife's wrath after buying season tickets for the family, something son Jonathan remembers vividly: "It was the only time I ever heard her yell at him."[1503] Kraft would not be dissuaded from saving his beloved team from being uprooted *and* owning it. Kraft's investment bankers estimated $115 million to be a fair price. But instead of taking Orthwein's $75 million, Kraft wound up paying Orthwein $172 million for the team on February 25, 1994 and immediately launched an exhausting three-month campaign to excite New England about the Patriots.

In 1994, $172 million was "the highest price ever paid for a sports franchise" and "Many people thought I'd made a foolhardy move" [1504] in overpaying for a horrible team. On paper, Kraft got robbed. The Patriots were 5-11 in 1989, 1-15 in 1990, 6-10 in 1991, 2-14 in 1992, and 5-11 in 1993! The team was so horrible that the NFL seriously considered buying it to eliminate a perpetual embarrassment.[1505] Most everyone thought Kraft was either insane or a hopeless Patriots romantic who wildly overpaid for a hopeless team.

But Kraft was also a wise businessman who saw a hidden gem and had a plan to polish off its grime and make it shine again: "The thing on the balance sheet that nobody noticed was the potential fan base. If you understood the passion of the people."[1506] Kraft knew the team had drafted quarterback Drew Bledsoe #1 overall in the NFL Draft on April 25, 1993 and legendary head coach Bill Parcells had the team moving in the right direction. The team had won only one of its first twelve games under Parcells but ended 1993 on a four-game winning streak. Jonathan Kraft recalls his dad turning to him–like a shark smelling blood in the water–as the Patriots' last victory drove the crowd into a mad frenzy: "The crowd was just going nuts. They were just dying to have stability and commitment to a championship. Robert turned to me and said, 'There's no way I'm not buying this franchise.'"[1507] Kraft was also convinced he could use his business skills to help build a winner: "That was the dream, to get a system in place where we could be competitive from year to year."[1508]

A decade later, $172 million looks like a steal. Even before the Patriots won their third Super Bowl, *Forbes* estimated they were the fourth most valuable NFL team, worth $861 million.[1509] A year later, *Forbes* estimated its value at an astonishing $1.04 billion, the world's fourth most valuable sports team, trailing only the Dallas Cowboys, Washington Redskins and British soccer team Manchester United.[1510] The Patriots generate $236 million in revenue and $50 million in gross profit annually.[1511] Kraft has operated like a savvy homebuyer who buys and fixes up a structurally solid but unsexy house undervalued because it requires superficial repairs: landscaping, a fresh coat of paint or a new roof. Kraft didn't overpay for an inherently dreadful team in a lousy location. He bought an under-performing, poorly managed asset with substantial appreciation potential and has managed it effectively, after early missteps. After reviving the team, he created–for example–80 luxury suites, each bringing in $165,000 a year.

Bill Parcells' no-nonsense mindset whipped players into a nearly miraculous 10-6 season in 1994, but the team lost to the Belichick-coached Cleveland Browns in their playoff game. The Patriots suffered a setback in 1995–falling to 6-10–but Parcells hired Belichick as defensive coordinator in 1996 and the Patriots went 11-5 in the regular season and swept through the playoffs to the Super Bowl before Kraft and Parcells parted ways.

Kraft hires Belichick

"People were calling us from the league office and saying we were crazy. They said that he was a difficult guy and definitely not a head coach candidate."[1512]
– *Patriots president Jonathan Kraft*

"Harvard Business School doesn't teach you how to feel something in your gut. [Belichick] had a system and he also understood the economics of football."[1513]
– *Patriots owner Bob Kraft*

With hindsight, Bob Kraft's hiring of Bill Belichick appears an obvious decision. At the time, however, it was wildly unpopular. As revered as Bill Belichick is today, Belichick was equally reviled by Cleveland fans and reporters after serving as the Browns' head coach from 1991 through 1995. One of Belichick's closest friends, Scott Pioli, noted that Belichick circa 2001 was succeeding on many levels where he had been perceived as failing in Cleveland, but few outsiders appreciated Belichick's success because his Cleveland reputation cast a long shadow: "All the perceptions of Bill based on history–his inability to communicate and handle and deal with people– what he has done here [in New England] is the antithesis of the perception that's out there."[1514]

Many believe, incorrectly, that Belichick's experience in Cleveland was an unmitigated disaster aside from a 1994 playoff appearance. I refuted this myth in Volume 1. Many inferred from Belichick's Cleveland "disaster" that his earlier achievements–two Super Bowl victories while defensive coordinator of the New York Giants and a Super Bowl appearance as defensive coordinator of the Patriots–were tainted… more a reflection on head coach Bill Parcells' genius than on Bill Belichick. Sure, Belichick was defensive coordinator of some great defenses, but was he just in the right place at the right time? How else to explain Belichick's "failure" in Cleveland? Using this logic, many believed Bob Kraft had hired the wrong coach, a lifeless retread whose resume highlights deserve giant asterisks due to his umbilical cord to Parcells. After Belichick severed his lifeline, his Browns floundered, and he scampered back to his "mentor" with his tail between his legs.

Kraft's decision was even worse, in the minds–and words–of many, because the Patriots were forced to surrender a 1st-round draft pick to the New York Jets for stealing Belichick, then under contract to the Jets. "Even members of Kraft's family questioned the wisdom of parting with a first-round draft pick to acquire a coach who had failed miserably in his first head coaching job."[1515] Even if Belichick proved a good coach, could he possibly be worth a #1 draft pick? Kraft had no doubt: "For a No. 1 draft choice, we can bring in a man that I feel certain can do something, rather than the uncertainty of a draft choice. And [the decision] wasn't even close when I thought about it that way."[1516]

Many in the media assumed Kraft hired Belichick because they had become buddies during the Parcells era. But Bob Kraft was not hiring a drinking buddy or a weak-willed puppet. Kraft knew Belichick well and believed in him, his unparalleled football knowledge, his deep passion for the game, his desire to win, his ability to coach better after absorbing lessons from his Cleveland experience, *etc*. Kraft knew far better than any sportswriter or fan what Bill Belichick was all about. And, to his great credit, Kraft knew what he knew, trusted his gut, and hired the guy he believed in–at a steep price–though few agreed with his decision.

Kraft knew Belichick's value to Bill Parcells. On January 3rd, Kraft fired Pete Carroll and faxed Parcells seeking permission to pursue Belichick. (That same day,

Parcells resigned as Jets head coach, allowing the Jets to retain Belichick, whose contract stated that he automatically became head coach upon Parcells' resignation. Belichick himself then resigned the next morning.) Kraft saw through speculation that Belichick had merely ridden Parcells' coattails to begin his Super Bowl ring collection. If you visit the Pro Football Hall of Fame in Canton, OH, you can view Belichick's defensive game plan the Giants used to shut down the Buffalo Bills' #1 offense–that had scored a league-high 428 regular season points in 1990–in Super Bowl XXV. *Sports Illustrated's* Peter King makes clear the magnitude of Belichick's accomplishment: "That Buffalo team beat its first two playoff foes by about a million to 3. I thought there was no way on God's green earth the Giants would win [the Super Bowl] after Buffalo stomped the Raiders 51-3 in the AFC Championship Game."[1517] But Belichick had cracked the code on the Bills offense: "[Bills quarterback Jim] Kelly, for instance, would say 'Black 33, Monday, Monday.' That meant the ball would be snapped on 1. Or he would say 'Red 85, Wednesday.' He called low numbers for runs and high numbers for passes. When he said 'Wednesday,' the snap was on 3."[1518]

Tales from the Parcells/Belichick years with the Giants make clear Belichick fully deserved his reputation as a defensive genius and even knew a thing or two about Parcells' strength, psychology. Patriots assistant coach Pepper Johnson has written of his years as a Giants defensive player:

> "Our front seven [defenders] had so much pride in being able to get the job done that when the coaches would design plays to bring the strong safety down to help stop a runner like Bo Jackson, we would really get mad. ...No way you're going to bring the damned safety down... Belichick tells me now they used to do it just to make us mad."[1519]

Belichick whipped up his defense to knock the back-to-back world champion Montana-led 49ers out of the playoffs in the NFC Championship Game:

> "We were two-touchdown underdogs. I remember Bill making a big deal about that. He told the defensive players, 'Two touchdowns! They didn't even score two touchdowns against us [in our regular season meeting], so how can we be a two-touchdown underdog?' Bill convinced all of the corners that they were going to jam the heck out of those wide receivers and they weren't going to get off the line of scrimmage, and they didn't. It totally disrupted the timing of Montana's passes. Bill had the players sold that it was going to happen, and it happened."[1520]

Belichick later issued the following backhanded compliment to Parcells that implies Parcells had little to do with the Giants' defensive success: "The thing that I really appreciated the most was the latitude that [Parcells] gave me as a defensive coordinator to set up the defensive game plans and make personnel decisions and call the defenses within the framework that he wanted it done."[1521] The dramatic turnaround of Parcells' Patriots defense after Belichick and Romeo Crennel arrived in 1996 confirmed this. The 1995 Patriots were generous to opposing offenses: surrendering twice as many passing touchdowns (29) as they grabbed interceptions (15). The 1996 Patriots were stingy grinches: surrendering just 17 passing touchdowns while grabbing 23 interceptions.[1522]

Successful coaches must be great teachers and great innovators, and Belichick had demonstrated both skills even before becoming Cleveland's head coach. Bob Glauber, a *Newsday* sportswriter who has known Belichick since 1985, has written about what a great teacher and innovator Belichick was in his Giants days:

> "He taught me more about football than any single coach. He'd diagram plays, explain zone defenses, different coverages and everything that was happening on the field. For the first time, I realized that Bill Parcells didn't handle every coaching assignment on the Giants. Belichick ran the defense. Parcells, no doubt, was a brilliant head coach and motivator. But it was Belichick who was the guy getting it done."[1523]

Evidence of Belichick's potential greatness was abundant. Belichick simply had the wrong players in Cleveland and had to overcome a steep head coaching learning curve. Kraft knew Belichick was absolutely ready for a second chance and would likely hit a home run. Most importantly, Kraft trusted his brain and his gut and ignored shrill cries from reporters whose views on Bill Belichick were stuck in 1992.

Belichick's QB controversies

> "Some said 'We will regret it,' some said 'Good riddance, Drew'
> And the bloody controversy reared its ugly head anew
> Now Halloween's approaching and the Bledsoe Bowl is 'nigh
> This QB controversy is like 'The Thing That Wouldn't Die'"[1524]
> – *"Drew Has Left the Building" by PatriotsPlanet.net's Jack Thornton*

Bill Belichick is a decisive decision-maker. He attempts to anticipate decisions so he can research them thoroughly and know in advance what he wants to do in any given situation. Patriots special teams captain and Pro Bowler Larry Izzo appreciates Belichick's informed and clear decisions:

> "The guy is so sure of himself. There is no 'maybe' with him. It's one way or the other. It's a good trait for a leader to have. The guy is prepared, and he makes tough decisions look easy. I don't question him. I just do what I'm told and good things happen. Have you noticed the last fourteen games [all wins]?"[1525]

Belichick and his assistants share a clear vision of what they're trying to accomplish and how they intend to accomplish it, and they know they are experienced and knowledgeable, so they refuse to deviate, even when their vision differs from other "experts." Scott Pioli says:

> "We don't concern ourselves with the model for the league [that emphasizes building around a small core of star players]. Our model is the right thing for us because we believe you have to build an organization that fits the attitudes and personalities and philosophies of the people in the leadership group. Our leadership group believes there's no one person bigger than the team."[1526]

Bernie Kosar

Belichick does whatever he believes is right, even when it's unpopular or contrary to conventional wisdom. Reflecting on his hate-inspiring decision—while coaching the Cleveland Browns—to cut popular quarterback Bernie Kosar and replace him with the backup to injured backup Vinny Testaverde, Belichick says: "You have to put the team first. And I think I did. You're going to be criticized whatever you do… You have to make decisions that aren't popular… I get paid to make the [tough] decision[s]. I'll make them."[1527] Today, many Browns fans and reporters—once livid—confess that Belichick's assessment of Kosar was accurate:

> "His timing on Bernie Kosar's release was awkward and detrimental to the Browns' season. But the 'diminished skills' line we used to hammer him with was, in retrospect, one of the most accurate things he might have said at that point in Kosar's career."[1528]

"Diminished skills" was only the official explanation for Kosar's release. Belichick was also reportedly angry at Kosar for repeatedly and insubordinately calling his own plays instead of the coaches' plays and for complaining about what he perceived as the team's predictable play-calling. (Even before Belichick took over, Kosar had overruled Browns coach Bud Carson. In 1989, Kosar tossed Webster Slaughter a 97-yard touchdown pass. Before the play, on the sideline, Kosar had told Slaughter to run a "fly" pattern, no matter what Kosar said on the field. When the Browns lined up, Kosar pretended to audible to a slant before connecting with Slaughter as he streaked down the sideline.[1529]) When Belichick took over, he inherited a clique of Browns players, many of whom saw Kosar as their true leader. For years, Belichick and Kosar battled for control. After Kosar's release, Browns receiver Michael Jackson said, "The whole thing's a power play between Bernie and Belichick… Every day we expect it."[1530] Like talented, confident quarterbacks before him—including Colts legend Johnny Unitas—Kosar preferred calling his own passing plays to handing the ball off on running plays sent in from the sideline he felt would fail. The day before Belichick cut him, Kosar "drew [a play] up in the dirt" and threw for a 38-yard touchdown to Michael Jackson.[1531] It was Kosar's last pass as a Brown. Belichick basically said, "I knew Johnny Unitas, and you, sir, are no Johnny Unitas." Because Belichick doesn't tolerate players overruling coaches, he must have been itching to send a message that coaches coach and players play. Otherwise, Belichick could have allowed Kosar to play out the season and leave quietly rather than cut him during the season with the Browns in the thick of the playoff hunt. Former Browns receiver Reggie Langhorne said in 2002:

> "Nobody… hated Belichick more than Bernie Kosar and me. But as I've gotten older, I understood some of the moves that he's made. He realized some of the mistakes he made, and I'm sure he's handled things a little differently. You have to remember that we players, as a group, had been together for six or seven years, and he changed the way we had been doing things. We all bumped heads. But right now, I respect what he's done, and if I were to ever coach, I'd do some of the same."[1532]

Had Belichick thought Kosar was Johnny Unitas, he might have opened the barn door and let him run free. During Super Bowl XXV, Belichick told Lawrence Taylor on the sideline, "Run whatever you need to run to get [to the quarterback] because they ain't gonna beat us running the ball."[1533] And Belichick has steadily expanded Tom Brady's authority to modify play-calls–such as ratcheting up his authority to audible at the line of scrimmage–over their years together.

Recently, Belichick said "Brady and Kosar could absorb as much, manage as much, and have as expansive an offense as you wanted to. They could pretty much handle whatever you throw at them."[1534] Had Belichick inherited a young Bernie Kosar–rather than a strong-willed veteran with "diminished skills"–they might have thrived together.

Drew Bledsoe

> "We keep a special place for some, and never can forget
> The ones whose exit you rejoice or those that you regret
> The ones who made a difference and the ones who left their mark
> Or coaxed a raging bonfire from a tiny fading spark…
>
> While he's here I hope he takes some time to look around
> At last year's flag and good King Kraft's new stately castle grounds
> While Drew may have his regrets - you just know he'll never quit.
> He need not hang his head because he's part of all of it."[1535]
> – *"Return of a Favored Son" by PatriotsPlanet.net's Jack Thornton*

With his Patriots embroiled in a quarterback controversy after former starter Drew Bledsoe returned from an injury late in 2001, Belichick made a similarly resolute decision. Belichick announced that former backup and previously unknown Tom Brady would continue as the Patriots' starting quarterback. He didn't even give Bledsoe a chance to compete for "his" job. As in the Kosar situation, Belichick based his decision on solid facts and reasoning but did not lay out his his analysis for the media. *Boston Globe* reporter Nick Cafardo wrote, quite possibly accurately,

"[Belichick] may not last the length of his five-year deal if the decision to sit Bledsoe turns out badly."[1536]

Lacking Belichick's facts and experience, reporters and fans misperceived the decision to continue playing a no-name, inexperienced, 6th-round quarterback over a proven commodity and former #1 draft pick as a riverboat gamble. Before the 2001 season began, *Pro Football Weekly's* Glen Farley confidently declared, "For all the changes, there is this constant: This team will go, in large part, as far as Bledsoe and his right arm can carry it."[1537] Many New Englanders couldn't imagine anyone other than Drew Bledsoe as the team's #1 quarterback.

Many who lacked Belichick's intimate knowledge of the two quarterbacks questioned his judgment and implied he was playing craps with his team's playoff chances. The most outspoken was *Boston Globe* sportswriter Ron Borges, who warned that Belichick was making a career-threatening decision: "Bill Belichick walked the plank this week. Now Tom Brady will decide if he goes off the end of it or not. …If Bill Belichick is wrong and Brady… is not a quarterback he can rely on to win for him and win immediately, he will pay the ultimate price, just as he did in Cleveland. He will get himself fired. The difference is this time he will not be given another head coaching job in the National Football League."[1538]

Borges stated without reservation that Belichick lied to Bledsoe "that when [Bledsoe] was declared fit to play, he would get enough snaps at practice to compete with Brady."[1539] No one else was present when Belichick spoke with Bledsoe, so Borges' claim rests completely on Bledsoe's recollection. Every expert on human memory knows that our brains are notoriously faulty and susceptible to believing what they want to believe. Eyewitnesses often tell strikingly different stories about the same event, sometimes with all witnesses believing their conflicting memories with absolute certitude. And when we have a stake in the matter, our brains filter facts through our pre-existing beliefs and desires. I'm sure Bledsoe *believes* he heard Belichick say that, but that does not mean Belichick did. Nevertheless, Borges wrote:

> "The facts are simply these. He lied to Drew Bledsoe about what the competitive situation would be when the quarterback regained his health. There was no miscommunication. There was no misunderstanding. There was no hedging of the bet. He fibbed."[1540]

Belichick disagrees: "I don't feel like I misled him. I really don't. You know, that really kind of bothered me."[1541] Belichick believes he was clear that he planned to give Bledsoe practice time with starting receivers to prepare in case he had to come off the bench but promised nothing more.

It's possible Belichick lied. It's more plausible that he stated his intent–rather than promise–to let Bledsoe compete for the job but later realized that would be unwise; if so, he changed his mind rather than maliciously deceived Bledsoe. Another plausible scenario–given that Belichick plays whichever players he believes give his team the best chance to win—is that Belichick tried to assure Bledsoe he would not be rudely shoved aside and communicated his message in a way he hoped would soften the emotional blow but that Bledsoe heard as confirming what he wanted to hear.

I suspect Belichick preferred Brady but could not politically move him ahead of a healthy Bledsoe, given Bledsoe's emotional hold on fans and the owner and his newly-inked $103 million contract. If so, then Belichick had even less incentive to promise Bledsoe a chance to win his job back, and this whole mess sounds more like a failure to communicate.

Whatever Belichick said to Bledsoe, Borges condemned Belichick's decision, ironically saying Belichick had caused so much damage in denying Bledsoe "his" job that it could be undone only by multiple Super Bowl victories and that "this Patriot team [obviously] isn't going to win two Super Bowls any time soon." Borges could have taken the advice of a frustrated Jim Mora—former NFL Coach of the Year—who once admonished reporters with these words: "You just never know. You think you know, but you don't. And you never will." Instead, Borges blasted Belichick:

> "The minute Belichick looked Bledsoe in the eye in his office and told him one thing and did another, he severed, probably irreparably, his relationship with the team's franchise player. Jimmy Johnson did the same thing with Troy Aikman in his rookie season, and it took him four years and several Super Bowls to repair the damage. Belichick will not be so lucky. He doesn't have Johnson's personality, which can be as jovial and charming as a snake oil salesman's."[1542]

Borges also predicted, with sardonic humor, that Bledsoe would come back to haunt the Patriots:

> "Maybe Bledsoe fails miserably and fades into the night, although I doubt it. He's much more likely to fade the way Curtis Martin faded when he went to the Jets and Roger Clemens did when he left Boston in 'the twilight of his career.' ... [If he lands in Tampa or Baltimore], the bet here is he would light the football world on fire again for another half-dozen years or so."[1543]

Belichick never blinked: "My job is to make the decisions for the football team, and that's what I'm going to do. I'm going to make the best decisions I can for the football team. That's what Mr. Kraft's paying me to do, and that's what I'm going to do. I'm going to make the decisions that I think are the best for the football team, T-E-A-M."[1544] He dared the world to blame him later if time proved him wrong: "There is no sense in being wishy-washy. That's not what I'm paid to do. ... I'm accountable for all the decisions I make. That's the way it was when I took the job. That's the way it should be. That's the way I want it to be."[1545] He later explained that "Any time you make a decision, it's gonna maybe be good for somebody and not be good for somebody else, but in the long run it's good for the team, and that's why you make it."[1546]

Belichick was hardly the only insider who felt Brady gave the Patriots the best chance to win. Offensive coordinator Charlie Weis said before the Super Bowl: "Brady was a big part of the chemistry that developed after Drew's injury. You can't deny that. How do you take a guy, if he's healthy, out of that? You don't."[1547] And nearly a year earlier, former 3rd-string quarterback Michael Bishop had said of 4th-string Tom Brady, "You guys are going to find out that Tom Brady is the best quarterback here."[1548]

Belichick smartly refused to engage the press in a debate over his decision. When one reporter trotted out statistics suggesting Bledsoe was the better quarterback, Belichick said tersely, "That's just not the way it is."[1549] Pressed further, during the playoffs, Belichick said simply, "Drew hadn't been playing for two months. Tom had been playing. Tom kept playing."[1550] Several insiders–including Belichick and Pepper Johnson[1551]–believed Bledsoe had not physically recovered from his injury. Bledsoe was twenty pounds lighter[1552] and had not regained full health. Also, Belichick felt it important for the starting quarterback to get most of the "snaps" during practices. He believed that opening up a competition and giving each half the snaps would have created a media circus and weakened the performance of whichever quarterback started. Besides, Brady was making the smart decisions and safe throws Belichick and Weis asked him to make. They didn't have the same confidence in Bledsoe to take what the defense gave him. Finally, the Patriots hadn't played well under Bledsoe and were winning under Brady. Other than violating the unwritten rule that starting quarterbacks should not lose their jobs due to injuries, there was little reason to hand the starting job back to Bledsoe. Brady had the Pats on a roll, and Bledsoe's health was dubious.

Despite this, Bledsoe was unhappy, telling reporters "I look forward to the chance to compete for *my* job,"[1553] emphasizing "my" as if he owned it. Behind the scenes–Belichick said four years later–Bledsoe told Belichick "the team needed an experienced quarterback for the playoffs, that they could not win in the playoffs with a rookie quarterback."[1554] Just before the Super Bowl, "Bob Kraft said the club would be receptive to off-season trade offers for either quarterback."[1555] Perhaps even Kraft distrusted Belichick's choice?

Twenty-six months later, two Super Bowl MVP trophies were collecting dust in that no-name quarterback's apartment. That quarterback now has both a name and a face recognized around the world. An impressed Patriots defensive lineman Richard Seymour later noted, "[Belichick] makes the tough decisions. Drew Bledsoe. Lawyer Milloy. All the changes he's made. If those moves backfire, he's taking bullets."[1556] Hindsight is 20-20. But Belichick and Weis knew exactly what they were doing because they were intimately familiar with the two quarterbacks and what they were capable of. Brady was a much better quarterback than media "experts" believed, and Drew Bledsoe was overrated. In a Belichick-Weis offense—emphasizing error-free football—a quarterback's primary job is not winning games… it's not losing games due to mental mistakes or poorly-thrown passes. Bledsoe's dangerous penchant for feast-or-famine risky passes was legendary. Bledsoe's arm was so powerful Bledsoe thought it could win every game. Sometimes the arm won; other times it threw away games the Patriots should have won. Bill Burt of the *Eagle Tribune* noted that Bledsoe's 32 minutes in the AFC Championship Game victory over the Steelers—which Bledsoe-backers held up as Exhibit A for why Drew should be the Super Bowl starter—was a "microcosm of his career":

> "Bledsoe also made two of the dumbest passes a 3-time Pro Bowl quarterback could make. His hook shot, while falling down, was lucky to fall to the ground untouched. And his pass that hit Steelers linebacker [Joey Porter] in the numbers probably should have been returned for a game-winning touchdown, but instead fell incomplete."[1557]

Despite dodging those bullets, Bledsoe's stats in that game were still marginally worse than Brady's. Brady completed 12 of 18 pass attempts for 115 yards, while Bledsoe completed just 10 of 21 for 102 yards.[1558] Bledsoe did throw one touchdown, but he threw two passes that could easily have been intercepted. After the game, Patriots coaches graded Bledsoe with four poor passes, one mental mistake, and four bad decisions.[1559]

What terrified Patriots coaches was that Bledsoe always looked for the big play downfield, not the quick, easy, short pass to the open receiver. Patriots coaches want their quarterbacks to throw to whoever's open. In 2004, Belichick was asked, "After Bethel [Johnson]'s big catch last week, might he get the ball more often?" Belichick's reply: "If he's open."[1560] Brady was only too happy to buy into the get-rid-of-the-ball-quickly-to-whoever's-open philosophy because "If you are standing around too long with that ball in your hand, you are going to have helmet marks right in the middle of your back."[1561] Bledsoe's dropping back seven steps and holding the ball till receivers ran deep downfield resulted in countless sacks that many fans unfairly blamed completely on the offensive line. Bledsoe's big play mindset deserved some "credit."

It's hard to teach an old dog new tricks. After Bledsoe played poorly in Buffalo in 2003 because he held the ball too long, Bills coaches held an alarm clock behind Drew's helmet during 2004 training camp to alert him when four seconds passed. Bledsoe was already an 11-year NFL veteran. After landing in Dallas in 2005, Bledsoe's new coach—same as the old coach—Bill Parcells said, "I'm trying to get him to throw it out on time as much as I can. I'm on him pretty hard about that."[1562]

The Patriots' less-than-overpowering offensive line forced offensive coordinator Charlie Weis to design the Patriots offense around a mix of runs and short, quick, safe passes: "[A quick pass to the sideline] gives me Troy Brown in the open field with one guy [the cornerback] to beat. I like those odds. He makes lots of yards on those plays. It is like a sweep for us."[1563] Weis says Brady–who drops back only three or five steps before releasing the ball–is perfect for his system and implies Bledsoe was not:

> "Having a trigger man like Tommy makes it work. When you throw a lot of those short passes, you better complete 80 percent of them. Tommy does. He knows right away where the ball should go and he gets it there fast. Some people are suited to different offenses. Number 12 is suited to this one."[1564]

Asked about the offensive line's apparently outstanding pass protection in 2003, Belichick was less than gushing, hinting Brady's quick passing papered over some less-than-stellar offensive line performances:

> "[The offensive line's performance] was all right. I think a big part of it in the passing game was our efficiency in getting the ball out quickly. I thought the line and the backs did a pretty good job on picking up blitzes. There is a lot of room for improvement but it was adequate."[1565]

Playing behind a porous offensive line, the statuesque Bledsoe would have gotten himself killed. In fact, he did in Buffalo: 54 sacks in 2002 (Brady: 31), and 49 in 2003 (Brady: 32). In 2003, Bledsoe was sacked on more than 10% of his pass attempts (49 times in 471 attempts). After alarm clock training in 2004, 37 more sacks (Brady: 26). Thanks to Belichick, Bledsoe has taken his licks in Buffalo, not New England.

Finally, Tom Brady considers himself just one football player on a team of 53 where Drew Bledsoe considered himself *the quarterback*. This difference was apparent in their press conferences. Where Bledsoe spoke from a podium at his personal press conference in the middle of every week, Brady spoke to reporters only in the locker room surrounded by his teammates, a symbolic move that inspired them. In April 2002, then-Patriots safety Lawyer Milloy said, "I'm a big fan of Drew's, but it was obvious that the team needed something different, and Tom brought that youthful energy. What we have in him is a personable quarterback. Guys on the team don't feel he's untouchable."[1566]

I like Drew Bledsoe the person and thank Drew Bledsoe the quarterback for helping revive Patriots football. I also think it's classy that he said in 2005: "I'm very, very happy for my friends who are on that team and have had so much success. At the same time, I'm jealous at what happened after I left."[1567] That's why I'm sad he was never able to adapt his game to a short passing attack. The Patriots lost Belichick's first four games as Patriots head coach in 2000. All were winnable, with margins of defeat of 5, 1, 8, and 7 points. In Game 1, against Tampa Bay, Bledsoe took needless risks early in the game and failed to take a necessary gamble on the final play; he was sacked six times and threw the ball out-of-bounds on the last play rather than try to make something happen.[1568] In a 20-19 Week 2 loss to the Jets, the Patriots had great field position all game–due to two big Troy Brown punt returns and an Antonio

Langham interception return—but settled for one touchdown plus five short field goal attempts: Vinatieri hit from 30, 32, 33, and 35 yards and missed another attempt from the Jets' 11.[1569] Three of the Patriots' field goal "drives" covered 2, 19, and 30 yards. Before Game 3, rumors were already flying over Boston airwaves that the Patriots might trade Bledsoe to Seattle.[1570] After Game 3, a pattern had emerged: "The Patriots (0-3) lost their third straight close game. In each one, they had the ball in the last two minutes with a chance to win or tie, but Bledsoe fell short. On Sunday, he had the ball at the Minnesota 14 but was sacked on fourth down by Bryce Paup with 54 seconds left."[1571] In Game 4, the pattern continued. Down 10-3 with a first down at the Dolphins' 14-yard line, the Patriots offense couldn't score. On the final play, Bledsoe's intended receiver (tight end Eric Bjornson) stretched for but couldn't reach Bledsoe's off-target throw.[1572]

By contrast, everything Brady touches turns to gold. He quickly offloads the hot potato to an open receiver because he prepares thoroughly for each opponent and has an unnatural ability—like his coach—to glance at a football field and know exactly what the other 21 players are doing. When Brady recalls past plays, he describes in vivid detail what he saw and why he did what he did. His answers explain what the defense was doing, what the offensive players were doing, and why his decision was optimal, given what the defense and offense were doing. For example:

> "We called 80-hot-rock-opec with Deion and Troy running the rock portion of the route, which is a return route by the outside guy where he comes inside and pulls back out, and a flag route by Deion. The [Panthers] were in …cover-5, which is a two-deep zone with man coverage underneath with a four-man rush. When they play it, all their help is to the inside so any out-breaking route by the receivers is the best route to run against it. Deion made a nice move on Terry Cousins, got open and I threw it."[1573]

Belichick treasures this quality in his star quarterback: "He sees the game and can explain very quickly and succinctly what happened on the field. I think that separates him from a lot of guys. He's mentally sharp."[1574] Brady developed this ability by emulating Belichick who, Brady says, can step into a film session and immediately describe what the opposing team is about to do: "He'll say, 'This is probably what they will do, but if they don't do this, they are going to do this,' And you can bank on that."[1575]

Compared with Bledsoe, the star who single-handedly wins or loses games, Tom Brady is steady and unspectacular but a more consistent winner: "Tom Brady is a winner. He is the best field manager I've ever seen. He plays within the scheme. He does not try to be bigger than the team."[1576] This from a player who knows quarterbacks, Larry Centers, the running back who has caught more passes than any running back in NFL history and more passes than all but six wide receivers.

After Bledsoe's Bills bageled the Patriots 31-0 in Week 1 of the 2003 season (immediately following the sudden departure of Lawyer Milloy to those same Bills), the Bledsoe-is-better crowd was emboldened. One Patriots fan later blogged:

"Week 1 this year looked for all the world like Bledsoe and the Bills were going to the Super Bowl. Nothing was going to stop them—shit, all the pundits had their Super Bowl tickets printed, had [Bills coach] Gregg Williams anointed as the next big genius, and depicted Bill Belichick as being a grumpy, misanthropic yutz possessing slightly more football sense than my cocker spaniels."[1577]

By season's end, the Patriots had turned the tables on the Bills, bageling them 31-0, Gregg Williams was fired, and the Patriots earned their second Super Bowl victory. Bledsoe was and is a good guy with a great arm, but he proved unwilling to discipline himself to play within a system emphasizing avoiding mistakes and taking what the defense is giving. Because Tom Brady throws to every receiver and finds whoever is open, he is the more effective quarterback. Also, Brady is young and maturing while Bledsoe is old and declining. Trading Bledsoe to the Bills for a 1st-round draft pick was another widely criticized move (especially after Bledsoe returned to the Pro Bowl after the 2002 season) that looks brilliant several years later.

Belichick made these moves not because he's a riverboat gambler—which he most certainly is not: "I wouldn't be the one to go drop a couple of paychecks on the lottery. That isn't really my style."[1578]—but because he counts cards, knows when the odds are in his favor, and is willing to place big bets when he thinks he has an edge. He believed Tom Brady was a safe bet: "Look. I don't think I'm going to be up here after every game answering questions about all the things that Tom Brady did wrong. I just don't."[1579] If he weren't so obsessed with football, Belichick could make a good living playing blackjack. With his ability to conceal emotions, he might even star in the World Series of Poker. Belichick admires intelligent risk-taking by others who—armed with facts and experience-based intuition—trust themselves to make unpopular decisions:

"Another thing I really respect about [Tennessee Titans general manager] Floyd [Reese] is that he's not afraid to pull the trigger, not afraid to take chances. A lot of people thought he made a huge mistake when he took (Steve) McNair (in the 1995 first round), because he was so far away [experience-wise]; he had a lot of talent, but the level of competition, the experience wasn't there. But Floyd wasn't afraid to stick his neck out there and it turned out to be a great decision for him. When he has a conviction, he's not afraid to act on it."[1580]

Belichick's decision to release star safety Lawyer Milloy after Milloy refused to shave his pay was another highly criticized decision that many thought might destroy the Patriots' 2003 season. Though the team did suffer a meltdown in its first game, a 31-0 drubbing at the hands of Milloy's new team, the Buffalo Bills, the team pulled itself together and lost only one more game all season *en route* to winning its second Super Bowl. Belichick's friend Charles Barkley stood by his friend and admired his fact-based analytical approach and resoluteness: "[Bill] was taking a lot of heat [for releasing Milloy]. What makes him a great coach, though, is that he knew what he was doing was right. He had faith in the players he'd kept and assembled."[1581] One reason Belichick decided to cut Milloy is that Milloy was not the essential leader outsiders perceived him to be ("Milloy [had] many sulking days on the practice field"[1582]), so he knew the team would overcome Milloy's departure.

If you're an expert, ignore non-experts

"It's a fair question if you're worrying about what people are thinking. I'm not."[1583]
– Former Patriots offensive coordinator Charlie Weis

Fullback Marc Edwards–who played for Belichick's Browns and Patriots–says Belichick "definitely sticks to his guns. He doesn't let outside influences mar his decision-making."[1584] The Patriots boldly and decisively make unpopular decisions–such as trading Drew Bledsoe, waiving Lawyer Milloy and drafting Benjamin Watson and Logan Mankins in Round 1, even though no mock draft rated either as Round 1 material–because they know the facts better than any fan or sportswriter.

Here's another example, based on the Patriots giving the Chicago Bears a 6th-round pick to move up from 14th to 13th in Round 1 of the 2003 draft:

"The [Patriots] were accused of 'wasting' a draft pick to be sure they got Ty Warren. But what if they had been 'stuck' with Michael Haynes? The former Penn State star, a smallish defensive end (280 pounds), was taken by Chicago one pick after Warren and has been something less than an impact player (four starts in two seasons, 52 total tackles, 4 sacks)... Belichick has three Super Bowl rings and a dirty sweatshirt. Mel Kiper has a hairdo."[1585]

And Belichick explicitly said he didn't care what sportswriters thought about Corey Dillon, instead relying completely on conversations with people who really knew him before trading for the "troubled" running back:

"Nobody [we spoke with] ever said that he was anything other than a guy that they wanted to have the ball [with the game on the line] and that they wanted on their team. I didn't talk to a couple of the sportswriters out there in Cincinnati. Maybe they might have said something different. From a teammate standpoint, a coaching standpoint and assistant coaches, none of them expressed any real problems with him."[1586]

Belichick ignored rumors and sought opinions from those who had coached or played with Dillon:

"The people I talked to were coaches and players who had been with Corey at Cincinnati, and nobody had one negative thing to say about him. They talked about his toughness, his consistency, and how in key situations they would want him to have the ball... Everybody wanted [him] on their team... That's really what carried a lot of weight with me... Other things people have referred to, I never got that from people who were with him on a day-to-day basis. Those must have come from somewhere else."[1587]

Fans and reporters aren't football professionals

Some coaches and executives distort their decisions to please fans and journalists. Not Bill Belichick. Belichick knows players play, coaches coach and reporters report. If reporters coached, they would be called "coaches."

Insecure coaches and executives appease fans, sportswriters and owners by distorting decisions:

· Some teams bring in a big-name, big-money star who excites fans but helps his team less than two or three solid but unsensational players would. Example: most free agents signed by the Washington Redskins.

· Some teams play popular, aging stars rather than replace them with lower-cost younger players with more energy and upside potential. Example: After the Cowboys released their once-great running back Emmitt Smith, the Cardinals paid more than any other team for two seasons Smith should have watched from the comfort of his living room recliner. Smith–with a career yards-per-carry above 4.2–struggled to gain 2.8 in 2003 and 3.5 in 2004.

· Some teams rely too heavily on conventional wisdom on draft day, just as business people avoid risk because "no one ever lost their job for buying IBM." Teams that defy conventional wisdom are punished by reporters telling their fans what a lousy draft their team just had.

· Many fans and owners–impatiently seeking a "quick fix" to their team's ills–want their team to draft high-profile players at sexy "skill" positions: wide receiver, running back and quarterback. If the passing (running) game is lousy, people blame the quarterback and receivers (running backs) and overlook poor blocking by the offensive line. Because television coverage tracks the ball-carrier so closely, fans can be forgiven for underappreciating the importance of players who seldom touch the ball.

New England makes none of these mistakes. Let's focus on the last one. The Patriots have not spent half their high draft picks on "skill positions," as the Redskins have. If the Patriots love any position, it's defensive line. The chart below demonstrates that perennial non-playoff teams spend many high draft picks on so-called "skill" positions (ball-touching positions) whereas perennial playoff teams, including the Patriots, spend fewer high draft picks on "skill" positions:

Perennial playoff team	% of Round 1 & 2 draftees at offensive skill positions ('00-'05)	Perennial non-playoff team	% of Round 1 & 2 draftees at offensive skill positions ('00-'05)
Colts	13.64%	Redskins	50.00%
Patriots	25.00%	Browns	45.83%
Eagles	25.00%	Bears	41.67%
Steelers	29.17%	Cardinals	36.20%
		Lions	35.71%
NFL average	29.47%	Bengals	30.77%

Source: Author's calculations based on www.nfl.com/draft/history/drafts. Skill positions: QBs, WRs, RBs. TEs counted as 50% skill players because they block and catch passes.

Because Belichick is secure in his professional knowledge, he couldn't care less about arrogant reporters or "draft gurus" who insist they understand football better than he does, especially those who present their opinions as unassailable truths.

Boston Globe columnist Ron Borges was appalled by the Patriots' first two selections in the 2001 NFL Draft, grading their draft a "D-":

> "You hate to fail anybody who shows up for class but what are they doing? If you didn't know better, you'd think the Jets sent Bill Belichick north to destroy the Patriots from within. On a day when they could have had impact players David Terrell or Koren Robinson or the second-best tackle in the draft in Kenyatta Walker, they took Georgia defensive tackle Richard Seymour, who had 1½ sacks last season in the pass-happy SEC and is too tall to play tackle at 6-6 and too slow to play defensive end. This genius move was followed by trading out of a spot where they could have gotten the last decent receiver in Robert Ferguson and settled for tackle Matt Light, who will not help any time soon."[1588]

Borges was not alone. An NFL fan website agreed so precisely with Borges that you almost wonder whether one plagiarized the other:

> "What do you get when you combine the worst coach in the NFL, a stupid owner who gave up a first round pick to get him, and the year long suspension of the teams [sic] best player in a needless confrontation created by said coach and owner? The worst team in the league, which is what the Patriots are... This team has no offense, no defense, and hopelessly screwed up its draft, passing on future stars Kenyatta Walker, Koren Robinson and David Terrell to take DT Richard Seymour, who is third on the depth chart.

This is a team in total disarray… They could easily be 0-13 when they host Cleveland… Couldn't happen to a nicer bunch of idiots."[1589]

Such scathing critiques gave Belichick and Pioli a week of insomnia followed by a week of cold sweats and nightmares… not! "Luckily" for Belichick and Pioli, their "blundered" 2001 draft picks proved less-than-complete disasters. Seymour and Light helped the "team in total disarray" win three Super Bowls (so far).

Conversely, Terrell, Walker and Robinson have all been disappointments. After "impact player" and "future star" David Terrell busted in Chicago, the Bears dumped him and irony-loving Belichick scooped him up for free in 2005. (Terrell was unable to survive the final round of cuts.) The Seattle Seahawks dumped "impact player" and "future star" Koren Robinson after his arrest for DUI, speeding, unsafe lane travel and reckless driving. That arrest came a week after Robinson–who had reportedly just rehabbed for substance abuse problems and been involved in "13 other traffic-related cases"[1590]–swore to reporters he was no longer drinking. His release also followed incidents like a four-game league suspension for failing an ecstasy test[1591] and two benchings by his coach. *Seahawks.net*'s Doug Farrar summarized Robinson's Seahawks career as "four frustrating, infuriating, potential-filled, but mostly unrewarding years."[1592] The third "future star"–Kenyatta Walker– has been arrested only once since the Bucs drafted him but "has not caught fire at [right tackle], despite several opportunities, although in the 2nd half of 2004 he was clearly better than Todd Steussie."[1593] If teams could re-draft the 2001 NFL Draft, Seymour would be chosen no later than #3. In a simulated re-draft on *KFFL.com*, Seymour was the overwhelming #3, receiving 36 of 72 votes; his closest competition was Kris Jenkins with 11 votes.[1594]

Being wrong does not make these predictions idiotic. I too might have questioned the selection of Seymour and Light. But I don't understand why any outsider would feel so certain of his beliefs as to question the competence and sanity of football experts paid to run professional teams. Belichick already owned two Super Bowl rings (from the Giants); his 1994 Browns had won a playoff game over Parcells' Patriots; and his year coordinating New England's defense in 1996 culminated in a Super Bowl appearance. Belichick's 2000 season had been disappointing, but he had basically dynamited the old Patriots and begun building from scratch. How could any sportswriter judge Belichick using the 6th pick in the draft on Mel Kiper's 14th-ranked player as tantamount to "destroy[ing] the Patriots"? Even before the 2001 draft, *Salon.com* warned fans:

"NFL teams spend far more time studying the draft than Kiper does, pouring millions into scouting every Kutztown offensive lineman and Bethune-Cookman nose tackle… Last year, his mock draft proved worthless on Draft Day. His frequent on-air explosions–once a sure sign that a team had flubbed its pick–now show how poorly he anticipates the selection process.

He has practically surrendered his guru status to Rick Gosselin... who consistently upstages him."[1595]

Rick Gosselin–who creates his pre-draft ranking after polling NFL scouts, coaches and executives–had Seymour ranked 10th.[1596] And a player like Seymour could be more valuable in the Patriots' system than in a different system.

Some reporters have agendas other than reporting the truth. Some believe it's easier to sell newspapers and attract listeners to their radio shows by shouting extremist, controversial opinions rather than providing accurate but nuanced opinions. Others apparently resented Belichick for: 1) Repeatedly making decisions they called "dumb" but later turned out great; 2) Restricting their access to players, coaches, executives and owners; 3) Not being their buddy, as Parcells was to some reporters; and 4) Not feeding them juicy quotations. Under Parcells and Carroll, some reporters had tight relationships with loose-lipped Patriots players and executives:

> "Bledsoe was also very close to the Kraft family and was 'in the loop' about many things going on 'behind the scenes' with regard to the operations of the Patriots. He shared some of this information with some of the media members he was closest to. As a result, the media people always covered Bledsoe positively in their articles, even when he struggled, blaming it instead on his lack of weapons, or having had so many offensive coordinators over the years, or not having enough protection from his offensive line."[1597]

Those sources dried up after Belichick arrived and convinced the entire organization to drink his Kool-Aid... and shipped Bledsoe to Buffalo. Several reporters apparently wanted to undermine Belichick simply because they didn't like him. No one's private life is a Disney film, and Belichick's is no exception, something I know colors at least one reporter's view of him. And some reporters resented Belichick's decision that Brady would continue at quarterback after Bledsoe returned from his life-threatening injury in late 2001. Bruce Allen–who runs *BostonSportsMedia.com*–writes that "from that day until now, Borges has been on a seeming crusade to discredit everything the coach has done... Borges made numerous attacks of the coach and [Tom Brady] for the remainder of the season. The Patriots made it all the way to the Super Bowl and as a show of his displeasure with the team, Borges... said that the Rams would win 73-0."[1598]

Releasing Lawyer Milloy

"Bill Belichick is pond scum again. Arrogant, megalomaniacal, duplicitous pond scum."[1599]
  – Kevin Mannix of the Boston Herald, after Milloy's release

When the Patriots signed former Chargers safety Rodney Harrison and later released safety Lawyer Milloy (who earned *much* more than the Patriots paid Harrison), *Pro Football Weekly*'s Andy Hanacek believed he knew better than Belichick:

> "[Milloy]'s a fantastic player who makes your defense that much better... In four consecutive seasons (1998-2001), Milloy led the team in tackles... The previous strangest thing I've seen the Patriots do was to add former Chargers S Rodney Harrison this offseason via free agency. That baffled me, since Harrison is nearly identical in his skills package and is older than Milloy by a year, but played as though he were five years older than Milloy in 2002... Harrison might develop into another defensive leader, but he cannot step up and be a leader like Milloy was right away because he needs to inherit his teammates' respect first."[1600]

Hanacek could not have been more wrong: 1) He ignored that Harrison was playing for much less than Milloy and that Milloy was cut only after refusing to accept a pay cut; 2) Harrison's slowness the previous season was due to a groin problem so severe that he returned to the Chargers six weeks before doctors recommended, proving what a tough S.O.B. Harrison is; 3) Milloy's productivity had dropped, a fact Hanacek downplayed; 4) Harrison made such an impression on his new teammates that they almost immediately elected him a team captain, and Harrison soon proved instrumental in rallying the team after Milloy's emotional departure; 5) Harrison was as good against the run as Milloy but better against the pass; and, 6) Harrison played so well on the 2003 and 2004 championship teams that many believe he deserved to play in the Pro Bowl and was robbed of free trips to Honolulu by players who voted against him not based on performance–which was Pro Bowl-worthy–but on his reputation for overly aggressive play that sometimes crossed the boundary into cheap shots, a reputation that does not fit his behavior as a Patriot. (15% of 354 current and former NFL players polled voted Harrison the NFL's "dirtiest player," earning him top "honors."[1601] Harrison hits so hard and has such a bad reputation that officials inexplicably called "roughing the passer" after Harrison completely legally pounded Drew Bledsoe's thigh, causing Harrison to say, "If you hit him high [in the head] you get a penalty. If you hit him low [below the knees] you get a penalty. Can't even touch the quarterback now?"[1602]) Harrison says he's not bothered because the Pro Bowl is a popularity contest: "Pro Bowl balloting is a bunch of crap. How long did it take Tedy Bruschi to get voted [in]? ...I don't validate how well I play by the Pro Bowl balloting."[1603] But perhaps the most ironic statement Hanacek made is the one that best demonstrates how little we outsiders know:

> "Milloy will be an instant boost to another team's defense right away... If Milloy signs with Buffalo, the Patriots will have given their up-and-coming, hard-charging division rival yet another gift of a player who could give the

Bills enough power on defense and enough desire to make it to the Super Bowl."[1604]

Pro Football Weekly was hardly alone in condemning Milloy's release. Countless reporters and fans did too. *The Boston Globe*'s Nick Cafardo was swamped with letters from enraged fans: "I've never seen such a backlash. If this forum is any indication, and I think it is, people are fuming over this."[1605] He added: "I don't think Bill explained the reasons for the release to the satisfaction of the fans. On the one hand he's acknowledging the impact of the player and how hard it is to replace him, but some of the answers such as it was done 'for the good of the team' or 'the good of the organization.' Who buys that except some of his fan and media supporters?"[1606]

Belichick could have justified his release of Milloy but only by insulting Milloy publicly, something the media would have (rightly) attacked him for. For example, Tom E. Curran of the *Providence Journal* later wrote that Milloy "was every bit the mercurial diva."[1607] But smart organizations don't embarrass employees after firing them, and doing so can trigger character defamation lawsuits.

More generally, Belichick doesn't justify his decisions to the media. Providing details would often make Belichick look smart and avoid embarrassment and controversy, but why reveal team secrets and Belichick's "special sauce" just to satisfy fans' curiosity? Consider, for example, Belichick's incredible restraint when the 2002 Patriots, having lost their previous four games, headed to Buffalo to face Drew Bledsoe's Bills, who had won three straight. Belichick was asked why he traded Bledsoe instead of Brady. The *Eagle Tribune*'s Hector Longo noted that the prickly Bill Parcells might have exploded at the stupidity of that question:

> "Parcells answer might have been something like this, 'Hmm, other than the $6 million salary cap difference, the five-year difference in age, the fact that Brady is healthier and has taken about 500 less NFL hits might have had something to do with our decision. THAT AND THE FACT HE WON THE @#$%^#@ SUPER BOWL FOR US!' Instead Belichick noted calmly that he made the 'decisions I felt were in the best interests of this football team.'"[1608]

Patriots fans should be ecstatic Belichick doesn't care what fans think or reporters write or talk radio shouts. Though the Bills—with Milloy and Bledsoe—began 2003 by crushing the Patriots, they finished 6-10 while the Patriots finished 17-2 and earned another Vince Lombardi Trophy for their rapidly expanding trophy case.

Drafting Richard Seymour

Because Belichick knows more about football than perhaps anyone else, he is smart to trust his gut. Above, I addressed criticism of Belichick and Pioli for drafting Richard Seymour on the grounds that he was unworthy of their high 1st-round draft pick (#6 overall). Let's now examine another criticism: that the team "needed" a receiver or running back, not a defensive lineman:

"Most Patriots fans… begged for excitement… They wanted touchdowns… They wanted University of Michigan wide receiver David Terrell… From the media headquarters, we could see the Patriots practice bubble, which hosted yesterday's draft day festivities for the fans, deflate like the falling Hindenburg seconds after the pick was announced… [Seymour] garnered only 1.5 sacks his last season."[1609]

Massachusetts Congressman Marty Meehan–a Patriots fan to whom the team had given the ceremonial responsibility of delivering their selection to the NFL commissioner–was so disappointed when he saw Seymour's name that "I thought, 'I could write the name David Terrell and I'd bet a lot of people in New England would be happy with me.'"[1610] But the team's decision wasn't even close: "We went into the draft with a game plan. And Richard Seymour and Gerard Warren were the guys we were keying on. It wasn't a surprise we picked Seymour. That was the plan."[1611] The Patriots were drooling to draft Seymour, according to Patriots executive Jonathan Kraft:

"[College scouting director] Larry Cook looked at every play the kid played in college. And he said he couldn't find one play that he took off. Talk about a motor… I couldn't believe how ripped he was. Other than the WWF, I've never seen a 300-pounder look so muscular. He definitely looks like he can put on another 20 to 30 pounds and you wouldn't even be able to tell."[1612]

It's fortunate for Rep. Meehan–and all of New England–that he didn't overrule Belichick's informed judgment. Four years later, that unsexy, unpopular decision is recognized as brilliant:

"The construction of a powerful defense began four drafts ago, when Belichick and Pioli took defensive lineman Richard Seymour on the first round instead of succumbing to the rants of sports talk show hosts and callers who felt wide receiver David Terrell was a can't-miss star. Seymour is now the anchor of the defensive line as well as a team leader; Terrell has been little more than a journeyman with the Chicago Bears."[1613]

In fact, a May 2004 poll of 22 NFL personnel directors rated Richard Seymour the very best defensive tackle in the entire NFL.[1614]

Seymour's great value can be inferred by comparing the Patriots' 3-4 record while Seymour missed most of the first seven games of the 2001 season (due to hamstring problems in both legs[1615]) with the team's 11-1 record after his return. Many attribute the Patriots' improvement during the 2001 campaign to Tom Brady's emergence, but the defense also played remarkably better following Seymour's healthy return. Over its first seven games, the Pats surrendered an average of 21½ points per game. In the twelve games following Seymour's return, the Pats gave up an average of just 14 points, more than a touchdown per game improvement! Some of this is attributable to the team's many free agents becoming more comfortable with the playbook and their new teammates, but they played superior competition over their final twelve games, including three playoff games against the Raiders, Steelers and Rams and a regular season game against the Rams. Seymour has been honored with Pro Bowl starts in 2002, 2003 and 2004 and is one of the most valuable Patriots.

Fans continue to lust after a dominant receiver. Three years after the Patriots chose Seymour over Terrell, *Providence Journal* reporter Tom Curran echoed the sentiment of many when he wrote, "This [2004] draft class is just too stocked at wide receiver for the Patriots not take a guy to complement Givens and Branch over the next three to five seasons."[1616] The Patriots ignored the 2004 and 2005 drafts' wide receivers, drafting only P.K. Sam at the bottom of 2004's 5th round. They instead brought to training camp Chicago Bears bust David Terrell and undrafted unknowns like "Bam" Childress, Jason Anderson, Cedric James and Eugene Baker and traded a 5th round pick for Andre Davis. Belichick's Patriots were not built around dominating wide receivers. The offensive philosophy is to spread the ball around, and Brady does: "No wideout caught 60 passes this year, posted a 100-yard receiving game or caught more than eight passes in a single contest."[1617] (An exception is Deion Branch, who films *Receivers Gone Wild* videos at Super Bowls. He caught ten passes in XXXVIII and eleven in XXXIX.) An amazing sixteen Patriots caught Tom Brady passes in 2003. With their egalitarian passing attack, the Patriots have done fine with their two 2nd-round receivers (Branch and Johnson) and a bunch of cast-offs and overachieving late-round receivers (Brown, Givens, Patten, *etc.*). When a reporter pointed out how well tight end Daniel Graham was catching passes in early 2004, Belichick saw this almost as a negative: "We need to try to balance it out: our receivers, our running backs and our tight ends."[1618]

Listen when someone you trust knows more than you

"Pat has obviously spent the majority of his career coaching offensive linemen, and his players are always fundamentally sound. Suffice to say, Pat recommended [Patriots 2005 1st-round draft choice] Logan [Mankins]."
– Bill Belichick, after drafting an offensive lineman coached by Fresno State head coach Pat Hill, former offensive line coach of Belichick's Cleveland Browns

After the Patriots won their first championship, Bill Belichick researched why repeating as champion is so hard. He picked the brains of former L.A. Lakers head coach Pat Riley, NFL legend Jim Brown, and Celtic great Bill Russell. He even re-read Peter King's *The Season After*, which argued dynasties are a thing of the past and used the Parcells/Belichick Giants as a case study. Belichick also sought lessons from his Giants experience: "In '87, seven guys wrote books. Everyone thought we could just slap the team back together and win, and it was a disaster."[1619]

Belichick seeks advice and new ideas from his network of trusted football advisors, not just from Patriots assistants. Three top college football programs operate very similarly to the Patriots program because their head coaches were Belichick's Cleveland Browns assistants in the early 1990s:

· Pat Hill's Fresno State Bulldogs (#22 in final 2004 AP poll)

· Kirk Ferentz' University of Iowa Hawkeyes (#8 in final 2004 AP poll)

· Nick Saban's LSU Tigers (#16 in final 2004 AP poll), until Saban became Miami Dolphins head coach in 2005

Because Belichick's former assistants know what he wants in a player, he listens carefully when one of them recommends a player, as when Hill recommended Logan Mankins: "I worked for Bill for a long time and we had talked a lot. Logan had the types of things they were looking for: intelligence, toughness, position flexibility. [The Patriots] are very demanding. They want to get guys who know what hard work is all about. Logan definitely fits that bill. He's as hard a worker as I've ever coached."[1620] Current Patriots Dan Klecko and Tully Banta-Cain were also personally recommended to Belichick by Pat Hill who—after coaching Fresno State to a successful season—coached Klecko and Banta-Cain in the East-West Shrine Game.[1621]

Belichick similarly heeded a personal recommendation from UNLV head coach John Robinson about linebacker Ryan Claridge, selecting him in 2005's 5th round. Why listen to Robinson? Robinson possesses nearly a half century of coaching experience and served as head coach of both the USC Trojans and Los Angeles Rams. As USC head coach, Robinson once developed a kid named "Willie McGinest" into the #4 pick in the entire 1994 NFL Draft. (For Robinson's recent retirement, the always appreciative McGinest pitched in to buy his former coach a Mercedes!) McGinest has helped Belichick win three of the last four Super Bowls, so Belichick listened carefully when Robinson said of Claridge, "He's got size and quickness. He's 'sudden.' He's perfect for that kind of defense, an edge linebacker who can rush."[1622] Belichick spoke after the draft of the similarities between McGinest and Claridge.

Iowa coach Kirk Ferentz handed Belichick another potential diamond-in-the-rough. After Iowa longsnapper/linebacker Grant Steen went undrafted in 2004, the Patriots brought him in for a look as a free agent, presumably because Ferentz touted Steen as a worthy prospect. Steen played linebacker in NFL Europe in 2005 and will try again to make the Patriots roster and is also the Patriots' insurance policy against an injury to regular longsnapper Lonie Paxton.

Nick Saban

Until the moment LSU Tigers head coach Nick Saban took control of the Miami Dolphins, the Patriots profited from Bill Belichick's close and mutually beneficial relationship with Saban, 2003 NCAA Coach of the Year and NCAA Division 1 champion. The two met in the early 1980s when Saban worked with Bill's dad Steve on Navy's football staff. Belichick admired Saban and his football philosophy even before 1991, when Belichick appointed Saban defensive coordinator of his Cleveland Browns:

> "I really respected him and his knowledge. He's very bright and every time we talked about football I learned things from him that were a little different than how I viewed it. As I gained more respect for that knowledge, philosophically there were a lot of similarities in the type and style of football we would play."[1623]

Belichick raves about how much Saban has taught him: "A lot of the ideas, the things we're doing now are concepts or adjustments that I really got initially from him when we came together in Cleveland."[1624] Michael Holley reports that "Belichick will shake his head and say [to Saban], 'That makes a lot of sense. Why didn't I think of that?'"[1625]

The friends captain their football programs so similarly that former LSU and current Patriot defensive lineman Jarvis Green says Belichick and Saban are two peas in a pod: "The biggest difference is coach Saban screams a lot more. Their philosophy is the same, their mannerisms are the same, and their mindset is the same. But coach Saban yells a lot more. ...Other than that, they're the same exact guys."[1626] Green's description of Saban sounds like a swashbuckling Belichick:

> "I had blonde hair. He said, 'You want to play in the NFL one day?' I said, 'Yeah.' He said, 'Number one, get that stuff out your hair. This isn't Hollywood.' Then he told me I played slow. My first two years I had 16 sacks and 39 (tackles for losses). It felt like an insult. ...It took me a year to realize what he meant by playing slow. He meant I didn't see reads. I didn't see where the tackles went, I didn't see pass-run reads. (Saban) taught me to do all that."[1627]

Dean Pees, who worked for Saban at Toledo and Michigan State and is now New England's linebackers coach, agrees with the peas analogy: "Those guys just don't leave a stone unturned. They think everything out. And then they go out and get smart players. Everything is just very thorough."[1628]

Saban—known in Cleveland as "Grumpy,"[1629] which is quite a feat, given his competition from Cleveland's dour head coach—accentuates Belichick's "personality" as Joe Lieberman brought out Al Gore's "dynamism." The two coaches even talk similarly. Saban said the following, but I could have told you Belichick said it and you wouldn't have blinked:

> "I haven't invented anything in this game, so everything I have, I've learned from [others]... You have to work hard. There's no easy way to do it. You have to pay attention to detail so you're not surprised by things that can bite

you in a game. And if you can't talk to people and help them be successful, it's going to be rough."[1630]

Saban's Tigers and Belichick's Patriots use similar philosophies, similar terms, and similar playbooks. This makes it easier for the Patriots to evaluate LSU players because it's easier to project performance when you'll be asking someone to do things similar to what they have done in the past. As more LSU grads headed to New England, the LSU locker room began calling the Patriots "LSU North." Explained Belichick:

> "Marquise Hill is a guy that played defensive end in a system similar to the one that we use and everybody knows... Based on the fact that he has been at LSU and has been in their program and been in that system, we can evaluate and see him do a lot of things similar to what we are doing."[1631]

Saban adds: "We have similar philosophy. There are certain things you really want in a guy, and the definition of what Bill is looking for in a defensive end or defensive tackle or offensive lineman is very similar to ours."[1632]

The Patriots' enthusiasm for LSU players goes beyond their ability to evaluate talent. The coaches' friendship guaranteed that Belichick received Saban's unvarnished advice about players (something that obviously changed when Saban took control of a division rival). Who knows LSU players better than LSU's head coach? Rohan Davey, a Patriots backup quarterback who terrorized NFL Europe defenses in 2004, is a 2002 LSU product. So too is defensive lineman Jarvis Green, who threw Peyton Manning to the turf three times during the 2003 AFC Championship Game. Randall Gay didn't even start for LSU his senior season, but he started for New England throughout much of 2004 and helped win another Lombardi Trophy. The Patriots also brought in LSU linebacker Eric Alexander for tryouts in 2004 and 2005.

After undrafted cornerback Randall Gay made the final 2004 Patriots roster, Belichick said, "Nick recommended him. We looked at him, and we thought he would be a good fit in our system. We were probably lucky to get him."[1633] They certainly were! Gay started many games, including the Super Bowl. Following injuries, Gay–who took over for Ty Law–was the surprise of the season. Gay credits the similarity between Saban and Belichick for helping him succeed in New England: "You can tell they worked together at the same time. I could tell that the first day here they were so much alike, right down to the words they use."[1634] Another recent Patriots acquisition from LSU is 21-year-old Marquise Hill, a raw defensive lineman with 305 lean pounds on his 6'6" frame who left college after his junior year with great potential but uncertain NFL prospects. Some believe he would have been a top-15 pick in the 2005 NFL Draft but fell to the Patriots at the end of 2004's Round 2 because he needed more experience and because teams had difficulty evaluating whether he would be an NFL star or a bust. He also had some maturity issues. But Belichick trusted Saban's judgment and grabbed the potential star because Saban's endorsement greatly reduced the uncertainty–in Belichick's mind–about Hill's NFL prospects: "DE Marquise Hill was involved in a firearms incident that frightened some teams. But LSU coach Nick Saban cleared Hill and that was good enough for Bill Belichick."[1635] Saban must now regret stocking his main AFC East rival with so much talent.

Two heads (sharing a philosophy and objective) better than one

"We all collectively agree on what we will do [offensively and defensively] going into a game, and then sometimes you modify that based on the game."[1636]
– *Bill Belichick*

"We want the same eyes to see the same players. First we scout regionally, then we have our scouts who scout nationally come in and look at those players. [The national scouts] will see all the players on offense, defense, east of the Mississippi, west of the Mississippi. Then by the end of November we break it up and do it positionally. By the time the combine comes [in March], a regional scout, the national scout, a position scout, a position coach and, ultimately, Scott and I will look at them. We get six or seven looks at a guy."[1637]
– *Bill Belichick, describing the college scouting process*

"I lean on [Patriots owner Bob Kraft] quite a bit in terms of the big-picture decisions and input on things like financial management and the direction of the team. He is the owner and he is the boss, but he is also a friend."[1638]
– *Bill Belichick*

Belichick delegates responsibility wherever appropriate. But delegating to those you trust and know well does not preclude collaboration. Romeo Crennel says Patriots coaches brainstorm together every day:

"We kind of know how each other thinks. If [Bill] has an idea and he wants to look at something or [says] 'Do this' or 'Implement this,' then boom, we do it and get it done. If I have an idea, I bounce it off of him and see what he thinks, and then we go from there. It's a good interaction."[1639]

"If [Bill] has something that is really important that [I] didn't think of or we haven't done, then he will say, 'I will like to see how this works,' or 'Get this done for me.' So it's up to us to get it done. If the way we get it done, he doesn't like, he'll say 'Hey I don't like that.' Or if we come up with something, [we say] 'We have a good idea.' We [explain] why we want to do [it]. He'll say 'That's good. Go on ahead.' If he doesn't like it, he will say 'I will put that on the back burner.' So that's the give and take we have week in and week out."[1640]

Another Belichick "force multiplier" is his special assistant, football research director and prep school best friend Ernie Adams, who handles key projects and brings Belichick insights about every aspect of the football program. Having been friends for a third of a century, the two trust each other implicitly and understand each other completely.

Belichick strives to make major decisions only after collective consideration and debate, ideally after reaching consensus. But when consensus cannot be achieved, Belichick will not delay a necessary decision:

> "Our decisions are really made collectively. I don't think there's a lot of independence where one guy does something and everybody else finds out about it, whether it's a game plan or a personnel decision or whatever. We try to plan things out and work them out and get everybody's input. Everybody may not agree with the final decision, I'm not saying that, and there's a time and a place for people to voice their opinions and then at some point somebody has to make a decision or collectively we make a decision. Then everybody goes forward with it, whatever that decision is... There is a time and a place to discuss them, but at some point you have to pull the trigger and do whatever it is you're doing and move forward."[1641]

Belichick involves others in decision-making because he is smart enough to know what he doesn't know... and what he thinks he knows but isn't sure he knows:

> "[I have always] tried to get as much input from people who are in the know, who see things that I don't see. Or, who may see it from a different perspective. Sometimes I'll seek input from people I respect, though sometimes it's not appropriate to bring someone into it that shouldn't be involved. I'm mindful of that, too."[1642]

Scott Pioli

Bill Belichick and VP of player personnel Scott Pioli are such fast friends and close colleagues that some suspect they are actually the mythological dual-bodied creature called "Belipioli" in some fables and "Piolichick" in others.

Belichick values Pioli's counsel because Scott shares his philosophy (about what a great football team looks like) and objective (winning) and has earned his respect: "I have a lot of respect for how hard he works, how well prepared he is and [I] know that his opinions are well thought out."[1643] Several sportswriters have suggested that Bill Belichick and Scott Pioli are linked in a "Vulcan mind-meld" regarding the Patriots system and what types of players fit best in that system because, as Belichick admits, "There just aren't many things we disagree about. We tend to look at players through the same set of eyes, I guess, and see the same things."[1644]

This is partly because "We've spent so much time together that we both have a good understanding of what we need collectively as a team."[1645]

When they do disagree, Belichick says, it's never personal: "Scott and I both recognize that business is business and friendship is friendship."[1646] Pioli says their disagreements are always rooted in inadequate research and asymmetric knowledge, not in differing philosophies, and are always resolved through further fact-finding, information sharing and truth-seeking, never by yelling and screaming:

> "It's never 'Are you kidding me?' It means I'll go back and do some work on it and he'll do the same. ...It's not a matter of him caving in to me or me caving in to him. It's what we know. It's not about me proving myself right and Bill wrong. It's about coming to the right decision."[1647]

Belichick and Pioli debate decisions in a cooperative, results-focused manner. Pioli recalls them strongly disagreeing "less than three [times]" because they share a common objective and are not trying to "win" the debate but to come to the wisest decision:

> "If there is [a player] Bill is adamantly opposed to, I know that there is probably a sound reason. If there is [a player] I'm adamantly opposed to, he knows there is a sound reason. That's part of the beauty of our leadership. It's never about trying to prove yourself right, it's doing what's best for the football team. When egos get involved in contract negotiations, when you're negotiating with an agent and you're worrying about your own personal feelings and how you are going to win this deal with an agent, it's the wrong way to do business. When you start to get into ego things and worry about who's right or not instead of what's best for the team, go do something else."[1648]

Their unity of mind and mutual trust and respect enables them to complement one another. Belichick can offload most scouting chores to the scouting department and feel confident they will be done as he would do them himself. Pioli explains they're both focused on Super Bowl victories, not personal glory: "Neither of us has separate agendas because we're only interested in winning [Super Bowl] rings."[1649] Earlier in his career, Belichick had trouble delegating responsibility and authority to others. As he matured, he learned to trust particular people and realized that he could not accomplish everything by himself. Belichick understands that "There's no way I can coach a team and go out there and scout players or keep up with pro personnel. There's no way a person in charge of keeping up with personnel—college, pro and etc.—is going to be able to coach the team. So you have two people doing it."[1650] Scott Pioli is an extension of Bill Belichick in terms of scouting and signing talent. Their relationship has deepened over time. Belichick calls Pioli "one of my best friends."[1651] Pioli can even tease Belichick about his painful years as head coach of the Browns: "Pioli... has repeatedly accused

Belichick of 'turning soft' …'I only kid him about it because it's one of those things that bothers him.'"[1652]

Belichick and Pioli's shared clarity of vision and mutual respect enable them to evaluate players more carefully and screen out riskier potential hires. Explains Belichick:

> "Usually, if we disagree, then we're better off moving on from that guy and finding somebody else because there are so many players we do agree on, that every once in a while, when we don't, we feel like rather than force it down the other guy's throat, we just move on to somebody we both feel the same way about."[1653]

Pioli agrees that when they occasionally disagree on a player, they err on the side of caution rather than fight it out:

> "We just know each other so well, that we know there's a flaw somewhere if we're not seeing things the same way. Neither one of us has a problem telling the other when we think they are wrong. If there's a difference, we'll both just put more work into it to solve things."[1654]

The agent of Patriots cornerback Tyrone Poole correctly said, "I don't think one would be nearly as effective without the other."[1655] Pioli and the Patriots' scouts sift through 4,000 potential draftees each year, rejecting 3,900 before Belichick gets involved.[1656] By evaluating only the 100 most suitable draftable players, Belichick maximizes the value of his limited time. Belichick and his assistants can watch extensive film on their top prospects. If Belichick were not completely confident in Pioli's judgment, he might feel compelled to study several hundred college players rather than just one hundred. Also, Pioli and his scouts accumulate better information on potential draftees by zooming in early on those players Pioli knows Belichick might conceivably select. By February, for example, the team has already created a preliminary draft board (*i.e.*, player ranking) that it uses to focus its limited time observing and interviewing players at the annual NFL Combine.

Force debate on hidden disagreements

Two heads are better than one only when they avoid "groupthink": the tendency of humans to uncritically adopt the beliefs of those around them or to suppress expression of their independent thoughts.

The Patriots' internal decision-making process operates so smoothly and so successfully (and is so effectively hidden from outsiders) that it potentially blinds us to a critical challenge faced by every organization: identifying and debating contentious issues. Belichick and Pioli have a rare bond and ability to separate professional beliefs from personal friendship. Belichick stresses this dichotomy to all his coaches, executives and scouts and also preaches the need to engage in provocative debate. He demands that everyone state their opinions loudly and with conviction backed by facts.

People with valuable ideas or valid concerns that threaten vested interests or powerful leaders often "go along to get along." There's a reason we so often hear the phrase "shoot the messenger": no one enjoys bad news. And whistleblowers–like Daniel Ellsberg (Vietnam War), Jeffrey Wigand (tobacco and cancer), Cynthia Cooper (Worldcom), Sherron Watkins (Enron), Colleen Rowley (FBI & 9/11) and Dr. David Kelly (Iraq's supposed WMDs)–are more likely to suffer retribution than receive a medal or a promotion. Uncomfortable truths are uncomfortable, and myopic self-interest often outweighs long-term concern for the organization or society. Ignoring painful realities feels good ("out of sight, out of mind") but destroys organizations over time. The bigger the problem or danger, the more hesitant people are to raise it and the more eager others are to suppress it. If you believe your company's core strategy is wrong, you're jeopardizing your career to speak up. Belichick expects to hear bad news quickly because denial is never an effective strategy. Ignoring signs of tooth decay or heart disease or cancer only allows problems to grow more severe.

Hesitance to raise unpleasant realities is compounded when business partners are also friends. Friends naturally seek friendship. In business or government, desire for tranquility–especially when our colleagues are also our golf buddies–can lead to problems being left unstated and unaddressed.

In a speech to Harvard students, former Secretary of Defense Robert McNamara begged students in their future leadership roles to encourage conflict and force unspoken anxieties into open debate. McNamara is haunted by the fact that neither he nor any of his fellow leaders in either the Kennedy or Johnson administrations ever debated two fundamental questions: 1) Was the "justification" for the Vietnam War–the so-called "domino effect"–real? And, 2) Even if real, could such a domino effect be prevented by external force?[1657] With hindsight, McNamara believes the answer to both questions was "no" because the U.S. was fighting an unwinnable war against national self-determination. But, McNamara says, the real shame is not that they got the answers wrong but that they failed to even ask the questions. Whatever the answers, these critical questions were never debated by the men (and they were men) who brought America to war and continued the war in the face of mounting Vietnamese and American deaths. Failing to ask tough questions leads to colossal leadership failures.

The Patriots understand this leadership challenge so thoroughly and fear it so profoundly that they have institutionalized a culture that: 1) Demands that everyone express their concerns; 2) Tolerates dissent; 3) Focuses debate on ideas, not on who originated those ideas; and, 4) Rewards those who challenge the status quo in intelligent and productive ways. Many firms instead foolishly reward "yes men." The importance of exposing questions for debate cannot be overstated.

MOTIVATING

"I try to show [players] that I have confidence in them. ...Motivational speeches have a place, but the first priority is to do the tangible things you need to do to [improve]. If you couple self-motivation with the proper coaching and guidance, there's a pretty good chance they will be successful."[1658]

– *Bill Belichick*

"It [is] the job of management to make the individual's values and aspirations redound to organizational energy and performance. It will simply not be good enough to be satisfied... with the absence of discontent... Adapting the individual to the demands of the organization [is less important than] adapt[ing] the organization to the needs, aspirations, and potential of the individual."[1659]

– *Peter Drucker*

The New York Giants won Super Bowls XXI and XXV with "Big Bill" (head coach Bill Parcells) and "Little Bill" (defensive coordinator Bill Belichick). Patriots linebacker Ted Johnson admires both: "I had Coach Bill Parcells–who I thought was a hell of a coach–that I got to work with for two years too. There's more than one way to skin a cat. You can certainly find different ways to win."[1660] But it has become fashionable to reassess their relative contributions to the Giants in light of Belichick's victories in Super Bowls XXXVI, XXXVIII and XXXIX and Parcells' lack of success without Belichick. Parcells' only other Super Bowl visit–with the 1996 Patriots–also came with Belichick as his defensive coordinator.

Most football commentators give Belichick the overall edge, but virtually everyone considers Parcells the superior "motivator." This chapter explains why Belichick is an outstanding motivator, even better than Parcells:

1) Belichick's approach–challenging players to achieve excellence–is more effective than Parcells' slave-driving. Parcells rules through threats, yelling, finger-pointing, psychological manipulation and fear. A reporter wrote that "The percentage of football fans who like Parcells is low, but the percentage of media members who like him is even lower."[1661] Imagine how players must feel. Belichick accomplishes more by motivating with professional standards, challenges, commitment to teammates and other high principles.

2) Coaches/bosses who rule through fear encourage individualistic, self-serving behavior. Coaches/bosses who create collective challenges encourage cooperative, mutually-beneficial teamwork. Players on such true teams motivate one another.

3) Those who praise Parcells equate motivation with pre-game pep talks. Motivating 365 days a year, season after season–at which Belichick excels–is far more important because winning requires superior preparation. Adrenaline bursts last–at most–through a game, so they cannot motivate players to give their all 24/7/52. Players on adrenaline highs during the week are burned out by game day.

4) Belichick worries about preparing players, instilling confidence and calming nerves, not hyping players up. Belichick understands that football players perform better under the influence of "flow" (an excited, hyper-aware mental state that arises when deeply, passionately engrossed in a challenging activity one has trained for) than hopped up on adrenaline (artificial hyperactivity). As Belichick says, "What makes the difference [in the final minute of a close game] is the players being able to perform and execute under pressure."[1662]

Those who criticize Bill Belichick as a less effective motivator than Bill Parcells fail to understand that Belichick does a brilliant job motivating his style of player to play his brand of football, which requires intelligence and coordination, not racing around the football field like madmen.

The Patriots locker room has tremendous positive energy. New players immediately feel their new teammates' excitement, enthusiasm and intensity. Relative to other teams, the Patriots are: 1) more intense and energized during off-season training and weekly preparation; and, 2) more calm, focused and deliberative during games. That's precisely what Belichick wants.

Parcells is a master at using psychology to squeeze greater production out of less mature players, like Terry Glenn. Belichick's approach does not work with players like Glenn, which is why Belichick benched and later traded him. But Belichick succeeds in getting his players to prepare productively all week and to optimize their game-day performance by avoiding excessive emotions that might result in stupid decisions on the field. Belichick finds players who need little external motivation and feeds them facts that provide whatever motivational spur they require. He ensures players have an optimal blend of emotion and intellect during games. That is superb motivating.

As Parcells himself said before his 1986 Giants won Super Bowl XXI, "I don't have to motivate this team for this game. Are you kidding? This is the Super Bowl. If you can't get ready to play this game, you ought to take a hike."[1663] Belichick and Pioli believe that if a Patriot can't get himself ready to play each and every Sunday, he ought to take a hike. Motivational effectiveness should be judged by players' mindsets and performance, not by how furiously a coach pumps his fist in the air or how loudly he screams at his players.

CHALLENGE; DON'T THREATEN

"Men want to be treated like men."[1664]
— *Romeo Crennel, former Patriots defensive coordinator*

"The way you manage innovative companies is you get people excited about the cause… Passion motivates more than money."[1665]
— *Eric Schmidt, Google CEO*

"I would probably retire before I'd accept another coach or go to another staff that doesn't put in as much work. The way [Belichick] demands us to play the game, what he asks of us, his approach to the game is so demanding… Why would you want it any other way? It's proven."[1666]
— *Patriots linebacker Willie McGinest*

"It's pride. It has to come from within each individual. Exterior motivation isn't going to work. They have to want it, and want it badly. And apparently, they [the Patriots] do."[1667]
— *Chuck Noll, Hall of Fame coach of the Pittsburgh Steelers*

"[Bill]'s very analytical. He'll pull out his notebook and he'll say: 'We know we have to stop the run. We know that they like to blitz on second down…' He'll go through this list of things, the same things he has hammered into your head all week. Then, he'll end up by saying something like: 'Now, damn it, let's go kill 'em.'"[1668]
— *Center Mike Baab, who played on Belichick's Cleveland Browns*

The best leaders tap into employees' natural passions. They don't instill fear. Intrinsic motivation–striving to satisfy internal, personal desires–is a strong and inexhaustible force. Extrinsic motivation–striving to avoid punishment or win external rewards–is a weak and exhaustible force. Leaders seeking sustained success must tap into employees' intrinsic motivators. Only short-term success is possible relying on carrots and sticks.

Bill Parcells permanently poisoned his successful relationship with Bill Belichick when he reportedly screamed into a live microphone during a Giants game in the late '90s after Belichick called a successful blitz: "Yeah, you're a genius… a goddamn genius, but that's why you failed a head coach [and] that's why you'll never be a head coach."[1669]

Inspire with challenges and high principles

"You earn your reputation, and that's all you've got."[1670]
— *Bill Belichick*

"I love the [Notre Dame] culture. I think there's an aura here. And as I've told [recruits], if you can't feel this place–if you can't *feel* it–then it probably isn't right for you."[1671]
– *New Notre Dame head coach Charlie Weis, while playing the Notre Dame fight song on his cell phone*

"If you come [to practice] and be lackadaisical, you not only disrespect yourself and your teammates, but you disrespect the guys who laid down the groundwork of this game for us."[1672]
– *Patriots receiver Deion Branch*

"I wouldn't trade my two [Super Bowl] rings for Gonzalez-like or Sharpe-like stats ever. No one bitched about their personal numbers on [our Giants] teams. The only stat that mattered was the Super Bowl, much like Belichick's Pats today. I could have caught more balls, but Bill [Parcells'] plan didn't call for it. I caught as many as he wanted me to. But to me, that's what being a part of a team was all about."[1673]
– *Former New York Giants tight end Mark Bavaro*

Riddle: How can someone run a marathon faster while pushing someone in a wheelchair than running unencumbered? Answer: After Dick Hoyt's son Rick was born, doctors urged him to institutionalize Rick who–doctors said–would never do or say anything after his umbilical cord severed his brain's oxygen supply, leaving him a non-speaking spastic quadriplegic with cerebral palsy. Thirteen years later, in 1975, Rick tapped a message with the side of his head into a computerized device Tufts University engineers specially designed for him to communicate. Rick told his dad he wanted to participate in a race to benefit a local athlete who had become paralyzed, to show him there was life after paralysis. Over the 25 years since, Dick and Rick Hoyt (TeamHoyt.com) have run 64 marathons, with an astonishing best time of two hours and 40 minutes, just half an hour slower than the world record! Dick even learned to swim and trained to ride a bike with an 80-pound bag in the front so Team Hoyt could participate in triathlons. They have completed 206 triathlons, including six Ironmans. Rick–a happy, humorous man who tricked his parents with his first words, "Go Bruins"–is living a fulfilling life and graduated from Boston University. But I tell their story because Dick swears he could never run as fast unencumbered as he does pushing Rick since "He inspires me. He motivates me."[1674] Dick became a world-class athlete because he runs and swims and bikes with passion and purpose.

People want to be part of something greater than themselves. People want to inspire and help others. People want to embody the principles they hold dear. The Patriots tap into such wellsprings of inspiration. Preparing to win football games is not fundamentally about winning. Preparing to win football games is about enduring pain to improve oneself, sacrificing to help your teammates, proving that you can accomplish what people say you cannot and becoming a role model for teammates, family and fans. Belichick said of his 2001 champions, "The bottom line was how those guys held together and supported each other. Guys had to give up things they wanted for the good of the group."[1675] That attitude attracts players like receiver/punt returner Tim Dwight to the Patriots: "It's good to be part of something that's bigger than you... This organization believes in that, and the players believe in that."[1676]

Patriots receiver/returner/nickelback Troy Brown's 2004 performance exemplifies the many reasons why Patriots pursue excellence with such intensity:

> "I get home sometimes, 7 or 8 o'clock each night. That is the sacrifice you have to make sometimes. I did it because I wanted to win. I did it because they needed me to do something I hadn't done and I was willing to step up and do it. Most of all, be an example to a lot of the players on this team. This is what Patriots football is all about. You've got to do things you don't want to do sometimes, but you go out there and do it, and you try to do it well, try to do it to the best of your ability and the rest will take care of itself. That's what we're about here in New England."[1677]

Throughout the nineteen-week 2004 season, Brown gave his all to the point that he said, before Super Bowl XXXIX, "I'm just exhausted,"[1678] "The way I feel right now, I wouldn't put it on anybody"[1679] and "I spend a lot of time in meetings, and there's been a lot of late nights."[1680] The stress was severe:

> "It has been real nerve-wracking for me knowing that I have to play a defensive game in the Super Bowl. I kind of feel like a rookie all over again. Just getting ready and bouncing back and forth [between] different meetings is unusual for me in a Super Bowl atmosphere. Instead of ten million people watching, it is going to be three hundred million people watching... I am nervous."[1681]

Though nervous, Brown was no quitter: "Hopefully I can go out there and help our team win... I am going to step up to the challenge that has been offered. There are only two things you can do. Fight or run. I pretty much have to be a fighter."[1682] Brown fought, and the Patriots emerged champions. But the 2004 season so drained Brown that he reportedly said–following the Super Bowl–that he wanted off the defense in 2005, further proof of how hard he pushed himself. After recovering from exhaustion and re-signing with the Patriots in May, Brown sounded like his old self again: "Wherever they put me at, that is what I'm going to do... On offense, defense, special teams or whatever, you just want to be on the field being a part of the game. It would be a little tough for me to sit back and watch from the sidelines."[1683]

When the most veteran Patriot, who joined the team even before Robert Kraft bought it, willingly switches from offense to defense following a coaching request, his selflessness sets a tone that inspires teammates to ratchet up their effort and even inspires fans, something Brown feels justifiably proud about:

"You try and set good examples for [others]. ... [Belichick] asked me to do something that I hadn't done [since high school], and I was willing to go out there and step out there and do it. He was talking about that type of attitude: 'You've got a guy that is an offensive player going out there to play defense because I asked him to, not because he wanted to or because he was good at. I asked him to go out there and do something because we needed help.' What better way to send a message to your football team about how we play around here than have one of your better players, one of your long-tenured players switch over to... play defense for you?"[1684]

Brown inspired safety Rodney Harrison: "He's a consummate professional, and that's something you don't see a lot of nowadays. Just to see a guy maintain such professionalism and not complain one time, always working hard, always doing the right thing. Troy is what the NFL should represent."[1685]

Bill Belichick always finds new ways to challenge his players. How do you motivate a team that has won three of four Super Bowls? A day after joining the team, linebacker Monty Beisel grasped that Belichick's newest challenge to players is "sustaining success": "There's an obligation there, if you do get a chance as a player, to come in there and help them win. It's a winning program, and you want to help keep it that way."[1686]

Because the Patriots win with "old fashioned" values of teamwork, high standards and collective responsibility, football coaches at all levels–NFL, college, high school and pee wee–hold the Patriots up as their model. Buffalo Bills head coach Mike Mularkey explains:

> "It's easy for me to get up in front of [my] team because what I preach, [the Patriots] do. I can use them as an example that if you play smart football and you don't beat yourself on Sundays, if you have players that push each other, you don't have coaches pushing the players, you have guys that are playing for each other and making sacrifices for each other and a team that's physical, you've got chances to win every week."[1687]

Spell out the challenge

"[Sustaining success] is about getting our people to understand that we're in a real dogfight now and not to let success get to their heads. We're always giving updates, so they understand how constantly under siege we are. They get it."[1688]
– David Neeleman, JetBlue CEO

"It only took a practice for him to knock the swagger out of us."[1689]
– Patriots safety Lawyer Milloy in 2002, after the Patriots won their first Super Bowl

"This week's game should be an easy win."
– *Words you will NEVER hear from Bill Belichick*

Bill Belichick tells graduating students that the only way to know whether they can succeed in their chosen field is by pursuing it with everything they've got: "The best you can do is put everything you have into the position that you're in. If you don't put everything into it, I don't know if you'll ever be able to evaluate what you're trying to accomplish."[1690]

Belichick's style isn't "Win one for the Gipper!" sentimentality. It's not whipping players into emotional frenzies. It's not scaring players senseless. It's impressing on players the seriousness of their upcoming challenge and making clear the steps required to overcome that challenge. Patriots players perform professionally–even without pep talks–because, as linebacker Tedy Bruschi explains, "We respect who we play. Anybody who puts on that helmet has enough guts to go out there on the field, and that garners my respect because this is a tough game to play."[1691] Asked about defending the incredible Randy Moss in their 2005 season opener, safety Rodney Harrison said the same thing: "It doesn't matter if it's Randy Moss [or] Chris Chambers. It doesn't matter. Any guy out there that's starting in the National Football League is capable of beating you."[1692]

Belichick wants his players feeling like underdogs every week. He wants them feeling they must prove something... to disrespectful opponents, Vegas oddsmakers, skeptical reporters, opposing fans, it doesn't matter who. After *Colts.com* foolishly put "AFC Conference Champions" t-shirts on sale before the Colts played the Patriots in January 2005, Belichick extracted full motivational value. If Belichick could have snatched a shirt before the Colts quickly fixed their mistake, he would have waved it in the locker room before the game like a matador taunting a bull. Belichick loves planting slights in his players' brains much like a pearl grafter placing irritants inside oysters to grow giant pearls.

Belichick manipulates facts to paint a picture of the Patriots as little shepherd boy David with a slingshot and stones and their opponent as sword-wielding giant Goliath, decked out in full body armor and taunting poor little David. If any opposing player ever said anything remotely disrespectful–or even something that can be twisted into sounding disrespectful–Belichick makes certain his players froth at the mouth like rabid dogs over those "fighting words." Belichick also scrounges whatever evidence he can conjure up to convince players their next opponent is the greatest team in the history of the NFL. As one reporter wrote, "You would think [the Seattle Seahawks] were God's gift to the NFL after hearing Belichick... If I were Bobby Taylor, I'd be outraged–Belichick slighted him by calling the Seahawks' cornerback 'pretty good.'"[1693]

Finding motivational facts is tougher some weeks than others, but Belichick always spurs players to prepare and perform well by presenting "evidence" of their upcoming opponent's: 1) talent, which scares Patriots players–willing dupes eager to be convinced—into believing they could lose; and, 2) disrespect for the Patriots, which energizes players. For example, before playing the Tennessee Titans in the 2003 game that launched the Patriots' NFL-record 21-game winning streak, Patriots players were ticked off because their coaches kept reminding them of their 2002 loss to the Titans and telling them how much tougher the Titans were. After victory, Patriots guard Damien Woody relished avenging their earlier humiliation: "They beat the [expletive] out of us last year. The only way to put that away was to go out and return the favor."[1694] Though vengeance did not motivate safety Rodney Harrison—who wore a Chargers uniform in 2002—he felt ecstatic after a week of coaches taunting him about the Titans' toughness: "All week, that's all we heard was how physical they were. It was up to us to go out there and match their intensity ...just knuckling up with those guys."[1695] When the Patriots and Titans met again in the playoffs, Belichick ignored the Patriots' regular season win and again focused players' minds on the 20-11 Patriots defeat in 2002 in which "They beat us every which way."[1696]

In 2003, as the Patriots prepared to play the 0-2 Jets, a team that had scored just 23 points in its first two games, Belichick pulled out film of the Jets beating the Patriots 30-17 in 2002 and pointed out: 1) how soundly the Jets had beaten them; and, 2) how the Jets' victory had propelled the Jets—rather than the Patriots—into the playoffs:

> "We'll take out last year's game where they came up here and beat us. In the end, that is really the game, from our standpoint, that made them the division champions. Just look at the game. Just look at the score. Just look at what happened. I think that is all we need to see. I don't care what they did against anybody else. I don't care what anybody else did against them. I know what they did against us. They beat us, and they deserved to win that night. That's why they ended up ahead of us."[1697]

Belichick used the same tactic in early 2004 before playing the mediocre Buffalo Bills, 6-10 in 2003 and 0-2 to that point in 2004. In their previous matchup (at Foxboro), the Patriots crushed the Bills 31-0, but Patriots players developed collective amnesia. The locker room fixated on 2003 opening day, more than a year earlier. Belichick: "The last time we went to Buffalo, we got beat, 31-0... I would like to go out there this year and not get beat, 31-0."[1698] Before facing the 4-6 Houston Texans (who would finish 5-11 in 2003), Belichick "reminded us that Houston is a tough team. They went up there to Buffalo and did something we didn't do, and that's beat those guys."[1699] The Patriots were supposed to fear Houston—a 4-6 team—because it beat the 4-7 Buffalo Bills (who would finish 6-10 in 2003) by two points, 12-10? Belichick always finds something, however tenuous. And his players, eager to grasp at motivational straws, latch onto it.

In 2004, Belichick lavished such praise on the 5-0 Jets that a clever reporter humorously asked, "Bill, is there any way you can beat the Jets?"[1700] Belichick didn't surprise anyone by conveniently ignoring that his Patriots were 20-0 over their last twenty games, instead saying: "We'd be the first ones to do it, if we do."[1701]

Each week, Belichick builds his team a giant sand castle to knock down. Tom Curran of *The Providence Journal* terms this weekly cycle of creation and destruction "Beli-hype. Build 'em up on Wednesday, Thursday and Friday, tear 'em down on Sunday."[1702] Though few teams ever live up to "Beli-hype," Belichick wants his players aiming to beat their upcoming opponent's best performance, not hoping their opponent shows up with its "B game": "We expect every [Philadelphia Eagle] to be at their very best for [Super Bowl XXXIX]. That's the only way we ever think about it. We never expect anything less from our opponents. That's what we try to get ready for."[1703]

When even Belichick can find no motivating facts, he argues the past is irrelevant. Before the Indianapolis Colts invaded Foxboro to open the 2004 season, the media asked Belichick about his team's success against the Colts (5-1 since Belichick took over the Patriots). Since he couldn't point to a recent game the Patriots had lost, he said:

> "None of that makes any difference. All that matters is [this game]. That's all that matters. You guys were all saying the same thing last year before Buffalo since we beat them twice the year before. That doesn't mean anything. We can talk about what happened in 1997; what difference does it make? ...It's going to be how those teams play on that day. It's as simple as that."[1704]

Even without Belichick's prodding, Tom Brady and his teammates exaggerate upcoming opponents and seize any flimsy "rationale" for fear:

> "A few years ago we were 0-2–like [the Bills] are–and we had the Colts coming in to our stadium and they were 2-0, and we beat them [44-13]. 2-0 doesn't mean anything. 0-2 doesn't mean anything, especially for a team that barely lost the last two games. Two plays and they could be 2-0."[1705]

Confronted with a challenge, Patriots work tirelessly to prepare to meet it. Preparation is the key because, as Tom Brady says, "Once you kind of figure out you're prepared and you're confident, you want to get out there and play."[1706] Because they prepare so thoroughly, Patriots players always deny feeling "pressure," instead perceiving a "challenge" or an "opportunity" or a "test." Defensive end Jarvis Green was asked about pressure to become the first back-to-back-to-back Super Bowl champion:

> "As far as pressure, I really don't look at it that way. Everybody has to do what they have been doing the last two years and come together. It's going to be a good year for us. It's going to be another test to see how we [respond to] losing some guys and being the Super Bowl champs... It's just a challenge and a test for us to see how we come together to play."[1707]

Set high standards

"Again and again, [Belichick] got back to one basic theme: the individual player knowing what to do and making the right decisions instantly in ever changing situations, decisions that hinged on their understanding of their distinctive role in a collective effort."[1708]

– Ken Hartnett, on a two-hour teaching session Belichick held for reporters

When Bill Belichick gets angry, you know someone screwed up and Belichick is about to explain—probably using colorful language and sardonic humor—who did what wrong and how to fix it. Belichick makes clear his expectations and may shout profanities when players fall short of his lofty expectations. Second year nose tackle Vince Wilfork says, "The coaches expect a lot out of you. There are no excuses now. You're not a rookie anymore. You have no business out there making dumb mistakes, rookie mistakes."[1709] But Belichick also praises players—though seldom profusely—for executing well. Patriots offensive lineman Russ Hochstein says Belichick "treats us well, and he rewards us when we do well. We try to keep him happy."[1710] Belichick's goal is correcting mistakes, so he tells you, after every practice and every game, everything you did well and everything you did poorly. Win or lose, there is always a long list of good and another long list of bad. After rookie quarterback and Round 7 draft pick Matt Cassel detected an all-out blitz and threw a 20-yard touchdown pass to undrafted rookie Jason Anderson in their first game as Patriots, Belichick didn't toss confetti: "We still screwed it up... Without getting too technical, we got away with a few things on the play that ordinarily we might not have gotten away with."[1711]

When Bill Parcells blows up, on the other hand, someone may or may not have screwed up. It's possible Parcells is just putting on a show to keep players on edge. He may yell at a player to "Pay attention!" or "Stop relaxing!" without the faintest clue whether that player actually did anything wrong. Parcells will yell and scream even when players are playing well. NFL commissioner Paul Tagliabue was once chatting with Parcells fifty yards from the practice when Parcells wheeled around 180° and screamed at one player, "You'd better start doing things right... I don't want to see any more mistakes out here!"[1712] A stunned Tagliabue asked whether Parcells had eyes in the back of his head. Parcells answered, "I didn't see what he was doing. I just wanted to yell at him. I knew I was going to yell at him at some point in practice, and I just picked my spot."[1713] Also, throughout the season, Parcells tries to moderate players' emotional highs and lows by cheering them up after losses and knocking them down after victories.

Belichick yells at you only when you're screwing up, and he always explains precisely how you're screwing up. Once you stop screwing up, he stops yelling. That's what Russ Hochstein means when he says players "try to keep [Coach] happy."

Belichick never attacks a player arbitrarily, just to scare him. As Patriots center Dan Koppen puts it, "He just tells us the truth, and—as players—that's all we can ask of him. We should take what he says to heart and learn from it."[1714] Offensive coordinator Charlie Weis yells at players constantly—but always with a valid reason and clear purpose: "The number one thing is that the players know you're not being condescending and demeaning. I think it's important that when you're getting on them, you're getting on them to raise their expectations. Because [their performance] just isn't good enough."[1715]

Belichick's error correction approach is superior to Parcells' psychological manipulation—especially over time—because players don't enjoy getting screamed at for no reason but will try to improve after coaches point out their mistakes. Success with Parcells' approach also requires rare ability to read and manipulate players. *ESPN*'s Len Pasquarelli says Cleveland coach Butch Davis failed with this approach, "leading" his Browns to a 4-12 season: "[Davis] developed a reputation for lacking accuracy. Davis became, in these parts, the pro of con. But he also became so transparent in his dealings with players, he lost their trust, he lost face, and ultimately, he lost his job."[1716]

If Belichick's players were not so mature and responsible, Bill would likely yell more. But his primary disciplining device is bringing in players of character, in part because this allows his coaching staff to concentrate on teaching, not discipline and mind games. Former secondary coach Eric Mangini chose the defensive coordinator opening in New England, over offers from Cleveland and Miami, in part because:

> "I believe in the people that are here. It's fun to work with the people that we have here because you're focused on winning. It's a universal focus and that's what's important across the board. You don't have to fight a lot of the things you may have to fight at other places just to get to the game."[1717]

In a locker room dedicated to winning, every player focuses on maximizing collective performance. That's why an angry Rodney Harrison declared to reporters following a 37-27 preseason defeat to the New Orleans Saints (in which Harrison caught an interception and made five tackles in one half), "What difference does it make how I played? We lost. All I care about is that we lost."[1718]

Cultivate happy, hard-working employees

Happy, enthusiastic employees work harder because, although our rational brain (frontal cortex) makes long-term planning decisions, our emotional "reptilian" brain (limbic system) dominates short-term decision-making. Consequently, an employee works harder at any given moment if he feels good about what he's doing than if he merely perceives that working hard will benefit his career. The emotional nature of short-term "thinking" is on display at shopping malls and auto dealers every day in the form of "impulse buying."

Every company tells workers *what* to accomplish, but some give workers great control over *how* they accomplish their objectives. Every job lies somewhere along a spectrum between pure command-and-control ("rules") and pure worker empowerment ("discretion"). In my dissertation, I showed statistically that a job's use of rules or discretion is correlated with many other workplace and job features and the quantity and quality of employee effort. In a "high performance work organization" (HPWO):

· *Workers* are smarter and better educated

· *Jobs* involve more discretion, creativity, task variety, flexibility and learning

· *Workplace culture* is more collaborative and collegial

· *Managers* are more supportive, pleasant and appreciative and reward employees for doing well

· *The physical work environment* is more pleasant

· *Job performance* is more apparent to workers

· *Workers* are more satisfied with their bosses and colleagues, take greater pride in their work and derive greater satisfaction and meaning from their work; and,

· *Work* is done with greater passion, effort and creativity

If you want to see empirical proof that HPWOs exist or understand HPWOs in greater detail, please see the Appendix (p. 391) where I have placed a table of results from my dissertation. I have not placed the table here because it simply demonstrates the list above.

HPWOs are thriving in many industries: Adobe (graphics software), Alston & Bird (law), CDW (computer retailing), The Container Store (storage supplies), Edward Jones (investment brokerage), SAS (statistical software), S.C. Johnson (maker of Windex, Ziploc, *etc.*), Southwest (airlines), TDIndustries (plumbing and air conditioning) and Wegmans (groceries). These firms all have happy employees and healthy profits.

Workers who are told what to do–such as line workers at McDonalds–tend to be unhappy, take little initiative or pride in their work and do only what they're specifically told to do. Workers–such as Patriots players–who are treated with respect and given responsibility tend to be happier, more collaborative, harder working, more prideful, and more productive.

Even incremental efforts to improve a work environment pay dividends. Cardinal Health, which routinely gauges employees' engagement with a 12-question survey, finds that up to 10% of company profit depends on how engaged its employees feel.[1719] After manufacturer Hunter Douglas discovered that only 30% of new employees in its divisions with the highest defect rates stayed beyond six months, further investigation revealed that new employees "didn't feel respected... didn't have input in decisions [and] felt a lack of connection," so Hunter Douglas created a mentoring program that led to 84% of new employees remaining six months and improved attendance, productivity and product quality.[1720]

Belichick's Patriots are an outstanding example of a "high performance work organization." Any manager who wants happy, productive employees can benefit from studying the Patriots. The Patriots teach lessons of value beyond the NFL or even professional sports.

Professionalism is its own reward

"I can only control what Troy is doing today."[1721]
  – *Patriots receiver/nickelback/returner Troy Brown*

"You've just got to be the master of your craft. I've got to be the best middle linebacker I can be, and it doesn't matter who [else]'s there."[1722]
  – *Patriots special teamer and backup linebacker Matt Chatham*

"When we hire people, the most important thing is loyalty, integrity and character. And #2 with us is work ethic, and #3 is brains. But if you don't have 1 and 2, 3 doesn't matter."[1723]
  – *Patriots owner Robert Kraft*

"[This team] *is* boring... Boring works for us, though. It's a professional attitude... Being a professional... is making the hard look easy... It's not fun, and it's not flashy for you [media] guys, but it works for us, and we enjoy it."[1724]
  – *Patriots linebacker Mike Vrabel*

"[Belichick] keeps everybody level-headed. It isn't a team of superstars. He has a real solid team atmosphere, and he keeps their feet on the ground because he has his feet on the ground... That's how he coaches. That's why he's got it going so well."[1725]
  – *St. Louis Rams head coach Mike Martz*

Before the 2003 AFC Championship Game, Colts tight end Marcus Pollard suggested "If we keep playing like this, then you can just go ahead and hand us the [Super Bowl] rings."[1726] After the Patriots shamelessly stole poor Marcus Pollard's ring, Belichick told his players: "We talked about it last night: Nobody gives those rings to anybody. You've got to earn them."[1727] The Patriots don't want anyone's charity. They don't want handouts or freebies. They enjoy the painstaking process by which they earn respect, earn victories and even earn Super Bowl rings. As defensive lineman Richard Seymour says, "If you want to be the best, you've got to come out and work... I'm a product of hard work, and no one's going to give me anything. If I want something, I'm going to have to continue to work at it."[1728]

For Belichick's Patriots, professionalism–proper technique, close coordination and maximal effort–is its own reward. Patriot players pride themselves on performance quality, not quantity. Backup linebacker Matt Chatham is a pretty solid linebacker, but he derives satisfaction from special teams rather than sulking over being a backup linebacker:

> "In the Super Bowl, for example, there's a guy like [Eagles linebacker] Dhani Jones–a guy probably making more [money] and doing more on his roster, but I get to face him on the punt team and throw him on his head. I get a little personal satisfaction out of that. You get your little bits and pieces from each game... In my mind, I've been preparing to just be the best I can be."[1729]

Practicing and playing professionally matters even more than winning because wins and losses are under the direct control of no single player. But every player can strive to perform his best at whatever tasks his team assigns him. Former Patriots starting linebacker Ted Johnson came to peace with a backup role after realizing that becoming the best player he can be is its own reward. Johnson plays many snaps, but even if Coach Belichick never calls for him to step onto the field, Johnson is always ready to be called on, and he helps his teammates improve. These are real contributions:

> "Personally, it's very satisfying to know that I can still play at a high level if I want to. There are so many things that are out of your hands: injuries and personnel decisions. There are a lot of things that you can't control, but you just hope that [setbacks] make you a tougher person."[1730]

Johnson learned to prevent his mood from moving in lockstep with his playing time:

> "Football is still, predominantly, the most important thing in my life. I want to be the best football player I can be. But now that I have a family... I'm a little more relaxed about my performance, my esteem isn't so caught up in performance. Everyone can suffer from performance-based esteem because everyone likes praise, everybody likes to hear they're doing a great job."[1731]

Another example is Troy Brown, the longest-serving Patriot and–for many years–the team's star wide receiver and punt returner. Brown has also accepted his diminished role with class. In fact, he found a silver lining–career extension: "We've got a lot of good receivers at New England that take some of the pressure off me. It might put a couple more years on me."[1732]

Cornerback Asante Samuel says, "You prepare for the worst and–if you're a fourth-stringer–you never know if you're going to play or not but you still prepare as if you're the starter. When your number is called, you have to go out and do your job."[1733] Kicker Adam Vinatieri has also memorized the team propaganda: "You always prepare and assume that you will have an opportunity on the field. You never know if you're going to be a cheerleader at the end of the game or your number is going to get called."[1734]

The Patriots expect players to prepare to play their best and to trust coaches to make coaching decisions. Belichick tells players that not everyone can march in the parade; someone must watch and cheer. Patriots rotate between marching in the parade and cheering as it passes.

Professionalism requires knowing and handling your responsibilities. Belichick has been stressing mental alertness for decades. During the 1986 New York Giants' run to victory in Super Bowl XXI, then-defensive coordinator Belichick huddled his Giants defenders during their 17-0 NFC Championship Game shutout of the Washington Redskins and exhorted them to "Keep the intensity and stay alert. Know what the hell down it is. Know what the situation is. Get in the huddle, get the call and play hard."[1735] That mentality worked pretty well for the '86 Giants. A week earlier, Belichick's defense had held Joe Montana's 49ers to a puny three points in a 49-3 rout (28-3 when the Giants knocked Montana out of the divisional championship game). It would soon hold John Elway's Broncos to just 20 points in Super Bowl XXI. Belichick gave his Patriots team pretty much the same speech the morning of Super Bowl XXXIX:

> "Do... your... job. Don't try to take care of somebody else's responsibility. Just take care of your assignment. Know what it is. Execute it. And get it taken care of. Don't let anything today get in the way of your focus and your concentration and your ability to... execute the plays the way they're supposed to be executed. Follow the game plan. Do your assignment. Have confidence that the other ten guys ...are going to do theirs. ...And you'll be champions tonight."[1736]

This is a brilliant speech because it takes players' minds off of "Will we win?" Belichick focuses each player on the question, "What do I need to do to perform my best?" No player should feel they need to play the game of their life for their team to win, a burden that weighed on running back Corey Dillon in Cincinnati:

> "The pressure [isn't] on me to strap a franchise on my back and take them to a Super Bowl... Without me, they won two out of the last three... I'm only one person. It takes a team to get to a situation like this [Super Bowl XXXIX], and I'm just glad that I'm part of this team. All I have to do is just go out there and do my part. There are 52 other guys who will go out there and do theirs. It's much more relaxing. It's a different atmosphere [than in Cincinnati]."[1737]

A great team enables each individual to concentrate on individual responsibilities. On a poorly-run team, individuals worry about teammates' responsibilities. Trying to carry your team on your shoulders leads to breakdowns. So Patriots players know they *must* trust their teammates. Explains Tom Brady:

> "You [must] do your job. I play quarterback. I've got to trust that those receivers are going to do their job. I can't sit there [during a game] and... worry that a certain guy won't run the right route... I have to worry about doing the best job I can... If I don't do that, we're all going to [stink]."[1738]

This mentality is helping the 2005 Patriots cope with the sudden loss of Tedy Bruschi and Ted Johnson and the holdout of Richard Seymour. Brady told reporters "I can't control it, so I'm just going to go out there and worry about playing quarterback,"[1739] adding: "I don't have to play left tackle. I don't have to play running back. I just have to play quarterback. And I think that's all we ask of any player—just play your position. You've got to trust in the other guys that they'll do their job."[1740]

Belichick wants players to focus on process (preparation and execution), not outcome (winning or losing). As *St. Petersburg Times* columnist Gary Shelton writes, "The Patriots do not think of their place in history; they think of their place in the end zone... [The team] cares about victory. It doesn't seem to care about the spoils."[1741] This action focus is productive for two reasons: 1) Contemplating one's future actions—as opposed to future rewards—improves performance; and, 2) Thinking proactively about performing well—as opposed to winning—inoculates players against counterproductive stress and worry over a game's outcome and even their individual performance.

To accomplish this, Belichick encourages players before games to visualize scenarios and decide how to react to each scenario: "If we do this, what if they do that? What if this happens? What if that happens?"[1742] Troy Brown visualizes on pre-game rest days: "I just try to sit back, relax and go through all of the plays in my head."[1743] Linebacker Willie McGinest—who began using visualization in college—used it to prepare for Super Bowl XXXIX:

> "I just sit and think of plays that I can make. Sometimes it happens. We would do this at USC. They brought in a guy to help us with visualization tricks. He would have you close your eyes and think about the things you were going to do and relax your mind. We would go through the game before we played it... [While] watching film on Philadelphia and seeing some of the stuff they do, [you imagine] putting yourself on the field and try to visualize what you are going to do."[1744]

What does McGinest see? "Mostly sacks. I always dream about getting sacks."[1745] Tom Brady also visualizes extensively. Before Super Bowl XXXIX, he explained:

> "We have to counter [the Eagles' excellence] with being prepared. We have to make sure we know what we're doing and what our adjustments are. We

have to know all the looks that we will get from them, and I think any time you can carry that into the game, you will do well. I'm going to be sitting there the night before the game and going through my game plan and going the through the plays and saying, 'If they go to this coverage, this is who I'm throwing to,' or 'if they blitz, I'm going to do this.' ...I feel most confident [going] into the game prepared... You feel like you have the answers to the test and you're prepared, and you are just anxious to go out there and play."[1746]

During games, Belichick wants his players to "react to the game," by which he means, "Do your function, which is all you can do. If you are a quarterback, a coach, a linebacker, whatever it is, only you can do that job. You zero in on it and do the best you can."[1747] The Patriots playbook requires players to analyze their opponent and adjust their behavior accordingly, something that requires preparation and concentration. Tom Brady gives this example:

"It's about making the quickest decision and the best decision. [Let's say] you have a play where it's 'Z' read. You know on 'Z' read with Cover 2 [defense] you throw one place, Cover 4 throw another, Cover 1 you throw another. If you get a certain defensive front, then you check to another play."[1748]

Belichick offers receiver Deion Branch as an example. Because Branch "knows where the other receivers are and he understands where he needs to be," Branch can focus on reacting to the action on the field:

"When there are traffic problems, he almost always does the right thing to clear that traffic up—going over guys, going under guys, stopping, throttling down, keeping moving, speeding up, pulling out of routes, sitting down in holes. If you run one play ten times, it could happen differently every time, and he would almost always do the right thing."[1749]

Eagles special teams coordinator John Harbaugh observes this reactive intelligence even on special teams, the most chaotic, unpredictable phase of football: "They are kind of a reaction-type team. It's like a two-gap defense. They read and react to what they see."[1750] Patriots players must always know what their opponent is doing and adapt appropriately, as defensive lineman Ty Warren explains: "Your primary goal on every play is to... do whatever your job calls for on that play. Whatever move [the offensive lineman] gives me... I just try to counter that."[1751] Even a blitz can suddenly become a non-blitz, if the offense does something unexpected, something new Patriots linebacker Chad Brown has had trouble adjusting to: "This defense definitely has layers to it. Even when they call a blitz, you might still have to alter things."[1752]

Patriots running back Corey Dillon says the first thing Belichick taught him is "discipline and playing calm in tough and difficult situations. Those are the things that were emphasized. I picked that up the first day I got here. He stressed it."[1753]

Belichick even tells players the "P-A-T" in "Patriots" stands for preparation, attitude, and teamwork.

The Patriots' preparation to play the Rams in Super Bowl XXXVI was so palpable that team owner Bob Kraft smelled victory. Though few felt the Patriots could win, Kraft says, "I knew we were going to win the game. I could just feel it in the locker room. Bill was calm. The players were calm. They had that look."[1754] Players developed such confidence during months of pushing themselves and their teammates to physical and mental extremes, as then-rookie defensive lineman Richard Seymour said of training camp 2001: "I remember being tired and [veteran linebacker] Bryan Cox saying, 'C'mon big fella, we need to step it up another notch today.' He would tell me that the days you don't want to be out there—which is a lot— are the times when you get better, and they are the times you'll look back to and appreciate when you're winning."[1755]

Opponents marvel at the Patriots' mistake-avoidance. The Patriots avoid mental errors through intensive preparation. Game-day passion causes mistakes. Only productive practice prepares players to play mistake-free football. This requires constant, sustained passion and intensive, dedicated training, not short spurts of passion. For example, in praising Tedy Bruschi, Belichick links Bruschi's outstanding instincts to his preparedness: "He's a very smart and instinctive player. He has a very good feel for the game, both in running and passing. As a blitzer, he knows where the ball is. He knows where to hit on plays. We ask him to do a lot, and he is prepared."[1756]

On game days, Belichick Ball is as much about brain as heart. Belichick praised Mike Vrabel's 2001 season by saying Vrabel "didn't have one mental error the entire year."[1757] Vrabel is so well prepared in part because he takes "copious notes on opposing offenses, schemes and players."[1758] It's a mutual admiration society because Vrabel says of Belichick, "I've never been around a guy who is so prepared. He's uncanny … His attention to detail is amazing. I've never been around someone like him."[1759]

Belichick himself is quiet and understated. Writes inside linebackers coach Pepper Johnson, "I've known him for seventeen years, and sometimes we just walk past each other without saying a word."[1760] Linebacker Mike Vrabel says it's just because Belichick is focused on optimal preparation, which sometimes necessitates talking and sometimes necessitates contemplation: "If he's passing somebody in the hall and thinks of something he needs to say, yeah, he'll… stop and talk to guys… Sometimes he'll be thinking about who-knows-what and he'll walk right by you, but you understand that's just him."[1761]

Though Belichick is low key and contemplative, he's passionately focused on winning, and his players and assistant coaches admire his dedication and trust his decisions. They know he is always busy devising winning strategies. Even after a disappointing 5-11 first season in 2000 and a lousy early 2001, defensive lineman

Bobby Hamilton–who followed Belichick from the Jets to the Patriots–knew Belichick had a practical plan for making the Patriots winners: "If you get to know the guy well, you know he just wants to win so badly. You see him here [all the time] with the guys. Winning is what he's about. He has a great system. All we have to do is believe in it, and in him."[1762]

Use gimmicks thoughtfully

"Let me just read you a little something… about the Philadelphia parade after the [Super Bowl]. It's 11:00, in case any of you want to attend that… It's gonna go from Broad St up to Washington Avenue past City Hall then down to Benjamin Franklin Parkway and will end up at the Hart Museum. This is the reverse of the route that they took for the '80 Phillies and the '70 Flyers parades. But, since this one's a lot bigger, it seems to be organized a little bit differently… The Eagles will be in double-decker buses. And the Royal Grove Naval Air Station is gonna fly over with their jets, in case you're interested in that."[1763]
– *Bill Belichick to his players before Super Bowl XXXIX*

Belichick uses gimmicks sparingly but effectively to solve specific problems. Over-reliance on gimmicks as a primary motivator is foolish. Belichick's gimmicks are tasteful desserts following a steady diet of professional preparation. He uses them because "You can say the same things only so often. No matter how important they are, at some point the message isn't going to get through unless you vary it a little."[1764] Here are some of the gimmicks that helped the 2001 Patriots become world champions:

- After a 5-11 2000 season, the Patriots in 2001 training camp passed out t-shirts with "Wanted: Winners" in large font and the definition of a "winner" in small print underneath.

- Belichick herded his players onto buses and drove to an IMAX theater to watch "Shackleton's Antarctic Adventure," a movie depicting a crew stranded a thousand miles from civilization after their boat was crushed by ice. All 28 men survived the 22-month ordeal through incredible teamwork, trust and ingenuity. Tom Brady later said the movie drove home to players that "There are always going to be obstacles in the way. You have to keep your faith, keep believing in each other, keep working together, even if you think you're never going to make it."[1765] The movie made such a powerful impact that it motivated players throughout the season.

- After a 30-10 defeat to Miami dropped the 2001 Patriots to 1-3, Belichick held a ball-burying ceremony to signal to players that they should put that game behind them and focus on their upcoming opponent. The Patriots won 13 of their remaining 15 games, including the Super Bowl.

- Belichick handed out a sheet stating that "if 99.9 percent was good enough," each day the post office would lose 400,000 letters, eighteen planes would crash, 3,700 prescriptions would be filled incorrectly, and ten newborns would be dropped during delivery.[1766]

- After his 2001 team improved from 1-3 to 6-5, Belichick feared complacency, so he showed players footage of racehorse Tiznow's victory in that October's $4 million Breeders' Cup Classic in which–according to Tiznow's owner–"he came [from behind] and gutted it out right down the line"[1767] to become the only horse ever to repeat as Breeders' Cup champion. 12 of the 14 horses reached the back stretch bunched together. Belichick emphasized his point by pausing the video with six horses neck-and-neck after the turn onto the home stretch.[1768] He asked players to predict the winner, drilling home the lesson that the Patriots' 2001 season could end in glory or ignominy, depending on how they performed down the home stretch: "I stopped the tape because we were at about that point in our season as well. I said, 'OK, who's going to win?' The answer? You don't know. And it doesn't matter who's ahead until they get to the finish line. I wanted to show the players that we hadn't accomplished anything because we still had five games to go."[1769]

- The week before a December 2001 game against the Cleveland Browns, Patriots players found themselves walking past posters of the Browns beating them the previous season. Coaches had posted them to generate urgency and fear. After the Patriots won 27-16, Belichick gave Lawyer Milloy the poster showing him getting burned for a touchdown by Browns tight end Aaron Shea. Milloy enthusiastically shredded it.

- Throughout 2001, Belichick motivated players by reminding them of the 2000 season's numerous humiliations. Following each victory, players sounded like mafia members who had defended their family's honor by avenging wrongs done to their wives and daughters the previous (5-11) season. Said Tedy Bruschi, "That was my motivation all week. [Belichick] told us in a meeting that we had to settle some family business. We settled things with the Jets, and this week we had to right the wrong from the Cleveland game. Last year, a lot of guys got the better of us. You remember things like that. That was the worst feeling I ever had on a football field, in Cleveland last year."[1770]

After their Super Bowl victory, Belichick knew repeating as champion would be an extreme challenge. So he brought the entire team to watch a documentary on NBA legend Bill Russell, who led the Boston Celtics to eleven championships in his thirteen seasons. Russell epitomizes "team first." After the movie, Russell appeared and spoke to a hushed room of Patriots awed by his accomplishments.

As new Notre Dame head coach, Charlie Weis wasted no time in using Belichick's cinema gimmick. To restore Irish pride, he showed his football players the movie *Rudy* and then–as Rudy Ruettiger explains–"Charlie comes up afterward and says, 'We could talk about the movie all you want. But let's have Rudy come up and tell you about the movie.' They were, like, side-swiped. Their eyes were big. They cheered."[1771]

Fear fails to inspire

"Parcells was all about scaring the crap out of you."[1772]
  – Patriots kicker Adam Vinatieri

Coaches can be too domineering. Fear is a lousy long-term motivator. Sports should be fun. I've never heard of an athlete make it to the pros after his parents forced him to play a sport he or she hated. Look at Iraq. After Uday Hussein took control of the Iraqi Olympic committee and soccer federation in 1984, he began torturing Iraq's athletes with fists, razors, electric cables, electric prods... even an iron maiden (a sarcophagus with spikes). He tortured some athletes to death. Performance plummeted across the board:

> "Iraqi sports are worse today than ever. Our teams used to win. There was much pride in playing for your country. But Uday never understood pride, only fear. He was never an athlete. He thought he could use his father's sadistic approach to improve performance. He has failed."[1773]

Immediately after the regime was removed, Iraqi soccer flourished. The team surprised everyone by qualifying for its first Olympics. It startled everyone again by beating powerhouse Portugal 4-2, winning its group, qualifying for the semi-finals and narrowly missing a bronze medal after arguably outplaying Italy but losing 1-0.

Bill Parcells rules through fear. Consider his reason for deciding to draft former Ohio State running back Maurice Clarett with Dallas' high 4th-round pick in the 2005 NFL Draft (a plan foiled when the Broncos selected Clarett with the last pick in Round 3). Parcells was excited that Clarett was, in his words, "cornered,"[1774] meaning that Clarett had burned so many bridges that he had to play well for whichever team drafted him or he would be out of the NFL and searching for his next job in his local paper's want ads. Parcells' players' motivation is avoiding his wrath. Actually, it's *minimizing* his wrath because avoidance is impossible, even if you play perfectly. Just days after poor Dallas Cowboys tight end Dan Campbell had an emergency appendectomy, Parcells started calling him "Milk Truck" "because he says I am milking my injury."[1775] Here are more examples from Mike Freeman's book *Bloody Sundays*:

- "Kratch! Stop worrying about your lungs!" - To Bob Kratch, after a staph infection and pneumonia hospitalized him nine days, during which he lost 25 pounds

- "You will never play for me again" - To guard Lonnie Palelei, after he surrendered a sack while playing tackle after the starting tackle was injured

- "Parcells exploded at [rookie Dedric] Ward in front of the entire team, cursing him out and questioning his intelligence."[1776]

As similar as Belichick and his close friend Nick Saban are, Saban is a mix of Belichick (getting annoyed only when someone screws up) and Parcells (unrestrained intimidation and screaming to "motivate" players): "What makes Nick really angry is when you bust a play or you're not doing something the way he wants you do to it. You can tell when he's about to get really mad, and when he does, keep your mouth shut. That's one thing people will learn. When he's mad, don't say nothing."[1777] On the first day of his first training camp as Dolphins head coach, Saban reportedly "took off his hat and pointed to his head while yelling at"[1778] a rookie till he burst into tears:

> "Manuel Wright… was in tears Tuesday. The 6-foot-6, 290-pound defensive tackle… broke down during an on-field workout session. Dolphins coach Nick Saban appeared to be shouting, or at least talking very sternly, to Wright, who was later seen walking off the field, escorted by a member of the team's staff, and lifting the front of his shirt to wipe away tears."[1779]

Saban said afterward that he was upset with Wright's poor conditioning and muscle soreness, but I don't understand how hollering at him could solve either problem. Belichick might have cut Wright on the spot or made him run laps or ride a bike for hours to get into shape. Wright had also reportedly shown up without shoulder pads, but yelling at and humiliating him does not instill the passion needed to become a champion. Punitive punishment is not a sustainable motivation source, so conveying the same message with less anger would have been more productive. By screaming, Saban scared all his players, who realized immediately that "You don't want to make him mad. You've just got to go about your business. He's not one for jokes or antics, so you just go with the flow. You've got to have your guard up at all times, just doing the right things."[1780] But what will happen when players eventually tire of Saban's screams and start ignoring them?

Compared with his disciplinarian former colleagues Parcells and Saban, Belichick focuses more on conveying information and less on cussing players out at high volume. Belichick expects players to listen to coaches and to perform professionally. He replaces the few who repeatedly disappoint him. But he no longer relies on artificial fear as a motivator. And Belichick would never resort to psychological manipulation or terror to get a player to take his job seriously.

Belichick today is neither a gruff, fear-inspiring disciplinarian (like Parcells or Bobby Knight) nor a cheery, chummy, pat-his-players-on-the-back type (like former Patriots coach Pete Carroll). Belichick keeps emotional distance from his players to maintain his objectivity because you can't run a meritocracy if you're playing favorites. Early in his coaching career, Belichick was warned repeatedly by more seasoned coaches to avoid getting too buddy-buddy with players.[1781] Belichick felt this especially strongly because he was younger than some of the players. After becoming the Giants' special teams coordinator at a tender age, he solidified his authority immediately: "Shut the fuck up, all right? If you don't want to sit here, then just get the fuck out of here. But this is important. Everybody else is listening."[1782] Belichick learned this lesson too well; some of his troubles in Cleveland stemmed from excessive toughness and emotional distance from his players.

Belichick's current approach–showing competitive, self-disciplined players how to win–is not the only successful approach. Vince Lombardi shared many characteristics with Belichick, especially dedication to precise execution and teamwork. But Lombardi was a domineering father figure who won by imposing his will on his players and having his players impose their will on opponents through brute force. Belichick does not believe in hierarchical command-and-control or bossing others around. He believes in roles, teamwork and self-discipline. Having carefully defined his playbook and each role on his team, he strives to find and train players with the traits and skills to best fulfill each role. He wins by training and inspiring his players to out-maneuver opponents through alertness, attention to detail, and tactical brilliance. Each player is responsible for his success. The dominance of teams like the Patriots and San Antonio Spurs and Detroit Pistons suggests that setting high expectations and building an achievement culture without continual monitoring works as well in sports as it does in business. But this approach requires self-motivated personnel. You will never see a Randy Moss on Belichick's Patriots or an Allen Iverson on Gregg Popovich's Spurs because such teams value passionate professionalism above sheer "talent."

Criticize to spur self-improvement

"The only way a player can improve is to understand what he did wrong, accept it–not try to make excuses and rationalize it and all that–and then try to improve on it. When that gets better, then you work on something else."[1783]

– Bill Belichick

Patriots players trust the accuracy and importance of their coaches' criticism and advice. Competitive players eager to improve love tough criticism, especially when offered in a helpful, future-focused–not a punitive or accusatory–way. As Patriots rookie cornerback Ellis Hobbs explains, "If somebody is telling you your brakes don't work, you don't go get your oil changed. You have to get your brakes fixed first. You have to concentrate on your weaknesses. Because that's what they're going to attack."[1784]

Fear is a lousy motivator because few humans respond positively to heavy-handed criticism and abuse. People become defensive when criticism is presented with a "You stink" undertone rather than an encouraging "Let's eliminate this mistake" or "I know you can do better" vibe. Ideally, criticism is offered in a supportive, light-hearted, humorous way.

Patriots offensive coordinator Charlie Weis rides his players hard, but players know he's trying to help them improve, and Weis criticizes players with a sense of humor they enjoy. Says Patriots backup quarterback Damon Huard:

> "It's that good, intelligent, sarcastic, Seinfeldian sense of humor and wit that you love. He cannot pronounce my name. He says, 'U-erd.' And I'm like, 'How can the H be silent?' He's a lot of fun to be around. Keeps you on your toes. At the same time, he'll bring you down to earth if you think you are good."[1785]

Listening to Weis, you realize why players don't mind him ridiculing them. He skewers people without being mean-spirited. And his humor takes the sting out of awkward situations. Asked whether he was bothered that he and his former boss–Bill Parcells–no longer talk (due to a falling out), Weis replied, "I don't even get to talk to my wife I'm so busy."[1786] (Belichick's defensive coordinator, Romeo Crennel, shares with Scott Pioli the rare distinction of remaining friends with both Bill Belichick and Bill Parcells: "I'm neutral."[1787]) Another illustrative Weis wisecrack relates to the Super Bowl touchdown pass Brady threw to linebacker Mike Vrabel. Vrabel, normally a defensive player, relentlessly teased his teammates by saying he was inserted into the goal-line ("red zone") offense to take advantage of his superior athleticism. That play is designed for Brady to first look for Richard Seymour and then look for Christian Fauria. The Carolina Panthers had Seymour and Fauria covered, so Brady threw the touchdown to his third option, Vrabel. Weis explained Vrabel is only the third read on the play because "We don't like throwing to him because we have to listen to his mouth."[1788]

Weis' wisecracks spur players to train harder. Here's a line Weis must enjoy throwing at young receivers: "I love speed, but speed can be overrated. If he's not a football player, what difference does it make how fast he is?"[1789] And, instead of telling a quarterback, "You must throw accurately," he asks rhetorically, "What good does it do you if you can throw the ball 80 yards down the field and can't complete it?"[1790] Weis doesn't even spare his 9-year-old daughter Hannah, who suffers from global development delay: "We like to say she's a globally developmentally delayed spoiled brat. She has no problem communicating to the people at home what she wants."[1791] Weis doesn't coddle anyone. He is an equal opportunity sarcasm-hurler on a life-long mission to stamp out all traces of complacency and arrogance in everyone everywhere. He took his comedy routine on the road recruiting for Notre Dame. At the Angelo Coaching Clinic in Texas, Weis indignantly denied his presence had anything to do with recruiting because it would be "wrong for [me] to go into a recruiting pitch to lure Texas' NCAA Division I football players to South Bend, the Mecca of the universe."[1792]

Charlie Weis has a my-way-or-the-highway approach to coaching, but he markets it in a brilliantly self-deprecating way. He says the willingness of his new Notre Dame players to absorb his coaching "gives me hope that my lack of versatility in calling a game won't slow us up. I mean, I only know how to call a game one way."[1793] Before smothering his Notre Dame players with tough love, he gave them fair warning: "I let the players know in no uncertain terms: don't expect me to be in my best disposition for quite some time because I think we have a lot of ground to catch up."[1794] Smart leaders are both firm and humble. They punch with velvet gloves. Presidential scholar Richard Neustadt famously wrote that "The power of the presidency is the power to persuade." All great leaders understand this eternal truth.

Weis has a magic hat full of persuasive techniques: charm, cajoling, insults, inspiration, taunts, disparagement, praise, condescension, humility… whatever works. Weis is a genius at understanding a player's character and choosing the most effective motivational tactics.

Belichick has a similarly sardonic sense of humor. He told players, for example, he was mad they were "giving the ball away like we don't give a shit about it. Just turn it over to 'em. Leave the ball lying on the field there for five seconds while [the other team's players] come from 30 yards away."[1795] He told reporters after a practice:

> "We ought to be able to get the snap from center, to hand the ball to the back standing behind the quarterback running straight up the middle. We ought to be able to stop him before he gets 20 yards. We ought to be able to catch a pass that hits us right in the numbers. We're doing the two-minute drill, we're trying to get into field goal range and we don't catch the ball. We're not talking about some big scheme or skill that we've never practiced. We've been out here practicing. We're a professional football team. We ought to be able to do that."[1796]

Messages delivered inside humorous, sarcastic wrappers evade the human brain's censors that attempt to block out unpleasant news. Humor acts like the outer surface of a virus that tricks the body's immune system into letting it pass.

Don't criticize publicly

> "Have you seen that movie, 'The Green Mile?' That's the way we approach things. It's going to be taken care of internally. If we have to pull a guy aside or joke with a guy, [we do]."[1797]
> *– Patriots linebacker Tedy Bruschi*

In 2001, Patriots cornerback Terrell Buckley rotated in and out of games with fellow cornerback Otis Smith. Buckley had always been a starting cornerback on his previous teams, so he wasn't thrilled about sharing the job. When coaches held Buckley out of a series against the Indianapolis Colts when it was his turn to go in, he got angry and refused when coaches later asked him to go in. Belichick suspended

Buckley for the next game against the Denver Broncos but did so privately and unofficially to protect Buckley's pride. By handling the delicate situation secretly, Belichick defused a potentially explosive situation that might have spiraled out of control had Buckley's punishment landed in the newspapers, further bruising his ego and hardening his heart. What could have been a disaster instead became a learning experience for Buckley and the entire team:

> "Terrell asked [defensive coordinator Romeo Crennel] if he could address his teammates. He stood up and admitted he was wrong, that his actions had been selfish, and he apologized for them. Then he said he had been so emotional and got caught up in the game, as we all do, and was thinking of himself rather than his teammates."[1798]

A very public player-coach dispute arose after each of the Patriots' first two Super Bowl victories. Belichick defused both disputes by avoiding inflammatory rhetoric and rash decisions. In 2002, linebacker Ted Johnson basically walked off the job in anger at his diminishing role in the Patriots defense. Despite Johnson's insubordination, Belichick listened carefully to Johnson and treated him respectfully:

> "I have a lot of respect for Ted as a person and as a player. I've known him, been with him for a long time and have a lot of respect for him personally and professionally. That being said, nevertheless there are procedures that I've followed on the team when we've had situations similar to this in the past, and we've had a number of them, and I'll be consistent on those procedures."[1799]

Johnson cooled down, cleared his head, returned to the team and helped win two more Super Bowls.

Almost immediately after Super Bowl XXXVIII, star cornerback Ty Law started mouthing off, insisting the Patriots trade him ("let the trading begin") or allow him to buy out the balance of his contract. Law called the Patriots' initial offer of $26 million for four years ($15.6 million guaranteed) "an insult"[1800] and "a slap in the face."[1801] Law even said Coach Belichick "gets paid to lie," called Belichick a "professional liar"[1802] and "a liar who lies to feed his family,"[1803] and insisted nothing would change his mind about his former team: "That bridge is burned. I no longer want to be a Patriot. I can't even see myself putting on that uniform again, that's how bad I feel about playing here."[1804] After the Patriots rejected Law's agent's request for a 7-year, $63 million deal (including a $20 million signing bonus), most fans were angered by Law's greed and his un-Patriotic mouth. More than a few reporters pointedly recommended that the "shutdown corner" shut up.

Unfortunately for the greedy Law, he remained under contract to the Patriots, and the Patriots knew they held all the cards. They knew Law wouldn't walk away from more than $7 million to play in 2004 and couldn't afford to prepare or play half-heartedly because his 2004 performance would impact his next contract.

The Patriots also wisely understood they had nothing to gain by attacking their star in public. So, neither the Patriots as an organization nor Belichick as an individual said anything derogatory toward Law. Every time Belichick was asked about the Law situation, he refused to answer: "I'm not going to talk about him."[1805] After speaking to students at Brown University, Belichick fielded questions and recoiled from a question about Law as if it were radioactive: "Are you a correspondent for *The Globe*? What, are you kidding me? I'm not going to talk about that."[1806] Simultaneously, owner Kraft was playing the role of good cop, proclaiming Law one of his favorite players and trumpeting Law's many contributions:

> "He's one of my favorite players. I think he's a great favorite of the fans. He's made great contributions that have helped us go to three Super Bowls. He's someone I like a lot, and I hope he'll be playing next year for the New England Patriots. I'm sure all our fans feel that way as well."[1807]

Law insisted his complaints were less about money than respect. He argued he's the league's best cornerback and deserved to be paid accordingly. Law said he felt insulted by the Patriots' opening contract offer. But Law, whose old contract averaged $7.3 million a year, was the league's best-paid cornerback for years, until Champ Bailey signed an even fatter 7-year, $63 million contract with the Denver Broncos. As Peter King wrote: "Law... has been the highest paid defensive back in football over the past five years... [so] to say in any way that he hasn't been treated with respect is one of the silliest misuses of the English language I have ever heard."[1808]

Law appears obsessed with money. In an interview that aired on Fox before the 2004 Patriots-Seahawks game, Terry Bradshaw asked Law whether he preferred PlayStation or Nintendo. Law answered that he didn't like either because he doesn't enjoy video games but immediately backtracked and asked to re-tape his answer to choose whichever had more lucrative endorsement potential.[1809] Like many people, Ty Law seems to believe money can purchase material comforts that will make him happier. Facts suggest the wealth-happiness link is far stronger in our imaginations than in reality. The best scientific analyses of what makes people happy conclude that money raises happiness only when: 1) It raises us out of poverty; 2) It buys us superior health care; 3) It allows us to feel superior to others; or, 4) We give it away to the needy. For all his wealth, Bill Gates isn't a whole lot happier than you or me, and whatever extra happiness his money buys him comes not from spending it but from the high social status it gives him and from the pride he feels when giving it away to important causes like malaria research and vaccinating developing-world children. The surprisingly weak relationship between wealth and happiness holds cross-nationally: "While Americans are the richest people in the world, the Dutch, Irish, Canadians, Danes, and Swiss are happier. Mexicans and Indonesians are about as happy."[1810] As American wealth has risen, overall happiness has not. Only wealth relative to our peers affects happiness, and even this effect is small. A study of 20,000 people over thirty years found that "An individual who earns $20,000 more than the peer group average is 10% more likely to be 'very happy' than someone who earns $20,000 less than the average. The absolute size of an individual's income had only a small effect on happiness."[1811]

Bottom line: Ty Law is chasing a mirage if he believes $10 mil./year will make him happier than $7 mil./year... unless he is obsessed with feeling superior to his NFL peers. Perhaps he is. Ty Law and Richard Seymour measure their salaries against the NFL's best-paid players. Tedy Bruschi and Tom Brady measure their incomes against the national average and speak of how fortunate they are to be paid so richly to play a game they love. Bruschi says he lives in a modest house in a modest neighborhood and has no need for more money. Bruschi and Brady agree with Belichick when he says the reputation you earn is worth so much more:

> "It's not style. I mean, look at me. It's not what car you drive or what watch you wear. Think about our team. You think about Adam Vinatieri, you think 'clutch.' Tom Brady, 'poised.' Willie McGinest, 'tough.' Mike Vrabel, 'versatile.' Corey Dillon, 'dependable.' Troy Brown, 'team player.' Tedy Bruschi, 'energetic.' All of those players earned that. You can't buy that."[1812]

In May, Law added that he was mad because Belichick's silence concerning his injuries early in the 2003 season made him appear lazy:

> "You [the media] were writing that I failed the conditioning run, right? Hell. I had had groin surgery. Surgery. And [Belichick] didn't back me once. He just let it hang out there without saying a word. I was dying to say something. So I had the groin thing. Then after the season started I had the (high) ankle (sprain). Then I tore an abdominal muscle. Some guys don't play hurt, never mind injured. I play injured. And then they throw that stuff at me (in the contract talks)? That's when I was like, 'Let me out of here.'" [1813]

Regardless of Law's motives, the Patriots were smart to refrain from criticizing their star and, instead, praise him. Doing so calmed Law down. By May, Belichick's "high road" non-response response was paying off. Said Law, "[My relationship with Belichick will be] like it always is. 'Hey, what's up Bill, how you doing? ... [I'll] shake his hand and acknowledge him as a head coach trying to defend his championship."[1814] Did Law expect to be welcomed back into the fold by Belichick after publicly calling him a liar? "Why not? I mean, if you're a professional, why not? I mean, we're here now, no sense in arguing on the field. We're trying to defend a championship."[1815] Bob Kraft kept up his charm offensive. Another article was a Kraft love letter to Law:

> "'Ty Law is one of my favorite players. We've been to three Super Bowls and he's been a big part of each.' In his office there's a photo of Kraft boogeying (well, trying to) with Law after the Super Bowl win over the Rams. Ty Law

wrote on the photo: 'Who said white men can't dance?' Kraft smiles every time he looks at it."[1816]

Belichick maintained his non-provocative silence. Asked whether he expected Law to show up for summer mini-camp, Belichick replied simply "We'll run it whether he's here or not."[1817]

Law skipped the team's "voluntary" practices but showed up on June 10th, the first day of mandatory mini-camp, and Law and Belichick met face-to-face. Following that meeting, Law told the media: "This is home for me. It's the only place I've ever known, and I'm glad to be a part of the tradition here and the history, and, hopefully, I can continue to be."[1818] "I would love to play here and retire as a Patriot."[1819] He said, "It's just time to move on, the past is the past. Things happen. This is a business. I'm a Patriot, and I'm glad to be."[1820] He added, "When we're out there as a team, we're all trying to accomplish the same thing and that's to bring home another championship."[1821] Law implied that he hadn't been serious about his greedy contract demands: "I never had a problem with the contract I have. As long as I'm playing under that contract, I'm more than happy."[1822] He even tried to pass the entire incident off as a media misunderstanding: "You know how people twist your words. You guys (in the media) do it all the time. Things happen, man."[1823] Law was probably referring to his "we've all gotta eat" comment that had especially offended fans, few of whom earn millions of dollars a year. But Law had made many inflammatory remarks, not just that one.

Whatever ideas were bouncing around Ty Law's head, the Patriots responded intelligently to his tirades and smoothed over a volatile situation. And Belichick held true to his "it's all business" belief that teammates must respect one another but need not like one another. After Law and Belichick met and shook hands, Belichick's Belichickian comment was "I'm a coach. He's a player. We've got a team. We're going to go out there and try to win"[1824] and "It is my job to coach the team and get the team ready for the opener and the regular season. It is his job to prepare to play. I expect both of us will do that."[1825] More notably, Law emerged from the meeting echoing Belichick: "He's going to coach. I'm going to play and try to bring home a championship"[1826] and "Now we're out there accomplishing the same mission... We have to be out here together fighting for a championship, fighting for the guys out here."[1827]

There is one time when public criticism is wise: when it helps a player come back down to Earth. Ken Hartnett, who covered legendary Packers coach Vince Lombardi, gives this example:

> "The Packers had a rookie kick returner, a shy, unpolished kid named Travis Williams who for a brief spell was unstoppable. He was becoming a media moment. After one of Williams' big games, Lombardi began to talk about why the kid was doing so well... He drew up... 'the wedge.' All Williams had to do was run as fast as he could in a straight line and keep

going. The blockers would do the rest. It was the only time in three seasons I can remember Lombardi stopping to explain. I realize now he wasn't doing it for me; he was doing it for Travis Williams."[1828]

Leaders need respect, not love or fear

"What I'd like is for the players to have respect for me. That's what really counts."[1829]
   – *Bill Belichick*

"We play for a coach we have great respect for."[1830]
   – *Tom Brady*

"[Our coaches] have put us through every situation that could possibly come up. We buy into the system. We realize that the guys know what they're talking about. If we can get out and do what they ask of us, we should have a pretty good day at the office."[1831]
   – *Patriots nose tackle Keith Traylor*

"A man can work very well with somebody …for whom he feels neither friendship nor warmth nor liking. He can even function well in a work relationship with somebody whom he cordially dislikes–if only he respects the other man's workmanship… The work relationship has an objective, outside focus, the work itself."[1832]
   – *Peter Drucker*

"I don't think you can argue with all the things he's done. He can get rid of me. I don't care. He's still the best coach of [2003]."[1833]
   – *Patriots cornerback Ty Law*

"If that man tells me to throw the ball into Row 17… you know where the ball is going? Right between Row 16 and Row 18, that's where. I'm not about to question him. I mean, the guy has five Super Bowl rings. *Five* of them. That's good enough for me."[1834]
   – *Cleveland Browns quarterback Trent Dilfer, on coach Romeo Crennel*

In sports, there are disciplinarians and "players' coaches." Belichick is neither. In 1991, 38-year-old first-time head coach Bill Belichick tried being a disciplinarian. In 1994, former Cleveland Browns center Mike Baab recalled:

"I'll never forget Bill's first team meeting. He stood in front of us and said: 'I've worked too long and too hard for this chance to let you guys (bleep) it up for me.' I mean, he came down hard. He'll get very profane, and he'll get right in your face. He'll put together words that usually don't go together. He'll do it to anyone from the starting quarterback to the last man on the special teams. If he thinks you're a dumb so-and-so, he'll tell you in very blunt terms."[1835]

Belichick mellowed some during his five years with the Browns after discovering in Cleveland that constantly cracking the whip is counterproductive. He figured out that piling on insults does little good. A player who fails to discipline himself is more trouble than he's worth because coaches are too busy strategizing, teaching, and evaluating to be tyrannical dictators. You'll never witness 21st Century Bill Belichick pulling Bobby Knight-like stunts like hurling a chair in disgust. Belichick will cuss a player out for not doing his job, but only to wake him up, not gratuitously:

> David Letterman: "Do you ever raise your voice?"
> Belichick (smiling): "Oh, occasionally."
> David Letterman: "Do you ever call them names?"
> Belichick (still smiling): "Sometimes."
> David Letterman: "What kind of names might you call a player?"
> Belichick (laughing): "Family TV here."[1836]

Bill Belichick no longer gets in a guy's face and tells him how ugly his mother is. The new Belichick would release or trade any player who repeatedly screwed up long before he would start hurling personal insults. One reporter joked, "Beneath that cautious exterior beats the heart of an accountant," adding "His own players will tell you he's too careful as a speaker, too controlling as a taskmaster and too intense to take his own pulse, let alone that of his team."[1837] Belichick's not wholly undeserved reputation notwithstanding, he now knows that he coaches human beings, not robots. Nevertheless, he believes it wise to coach with more intellect and less emotion–whether "rah-rah" cheerleader emotion or "you suck!" emotion–than the average coach. Most great coaches agree. Hall of Fame coach Don Shula was volatile early in his NFL coaching career and blew up at players. Shula says he learned over time that restraining his anger made him more effective.

Belichick has not become a "softie." New Patriot receiver David Terrell says, "I'm still scared of the head coach when he looks at me."[1838] And every Patriot knows, as offensive lineman Russ Hochstein says, "if you're not performing, you're not playing."[1839] Though Belichick realizes it's important to listen to and show respect toward his players, he's running neither a popularity contest nor a commune where he is first among equals. He is the New England Patriots' ultimate decision-maker. As leader, he is in charge, but he's no tyrant. He has *earned* the admiration and respect of his players. As cornerback Ty Law said, "I can't say that everyone here loves Bill. Some don't really know him that well. But he has the respect and the ear of every player."[1840] Belichick's former Giants players, who nicknamed him "Doom,"[1841] no doubt agreed. (There are two theories of the meaning of the "Doom" label: 1) Belichick's charisma, personality, demeanor, and fashion sense match those of the Grim Reaper; and, 2) The fate to which Belichick's players must resign themselves under the burden of his grueling training sessions and lofty expectations.) Because

Belichick's players know how hard he works and how intensely he has studied the game of football for longer than many of them have been alive, they trust his decisions. Says defensive lineman Bobby Hamilton:

> "When Coach Belichick makes a decision, we know he's worked hard at coming up with that decision. I respect it. I know he's doing it for a reason, and whatever that reason is, I agree with it because I know that he spends a lot of time on those things."[1842]

Belichick hires as assistants teachers, not psychological manipulators. Special teamer and backup linebacker/safety Don Davis says of Romeo Crennel and Eric Mangini, the Patriots' former and new defensive coordinators, "They both are very mellow. They're not screamers."[1843]

A talented coach whose players admire him can accomplish great things, so I expect great things from Charlie Weis' Notre Dame program. Weis' flashy Super Bowl rings blind players with his achievements. His players listen to him: "Coach Weis is a coach who doesn't have to repeat himself. When he says something once, it resonates and stays with you."[1844] If that's not enough, famous NFL players are singing Weis' praises. Weis has motivated his Notre Dame players by bringing in famous alumni, like Super Bowl XVII-winning quarterback Joe Theismann and legendary quarterback Joe Montana. Current Notre Dame quarterback Brady Quinn is tickled to receive advice and encouragement from Montana: "I called some of my buddies who play at other schools and I told them, 'I just got off the phone with Joe.' They said 'Joe who?' And I go 'Montana, you know.'"[1845] These greats–because they understand the magnitude of Weis' accomplishments–spontaneously raise players' respect for their new coach. Heisman-winning Oakland Raiders receiver Tim Brown advised players:

> "This guy [Weis] has all the tools. He's obviously won at the highest level of football several times, unfortunately for me, a couple of times. He's a guy who knows how to get it done. ...You have to pay attention to this guy. You have to believe in what he says because he can take you to where you want to go. It may not be this year, it may not happen next year. But certainly in the future you can see him getting this program to the very, very top, where everyone wants to be."[1846]

Behind closed doors, the Patriots are messier than the polished facade they expose to reporters and fans. I have no access to private meetings, and the Patriots do an outstanding job of concealing disagreements from public scrutiny. But it's clear from *Patriot Reign*–whose author, Michael Holley, was granted unprecedented access–that Patriots coaches can disagree heatedly and profanely. And *Boston Globe* reporter Ron Borges reportedly told WWZN listeners that "Belichick fired Charlie Weis [before the 2004 season] but the Krafts made Belichick take Weis back" and that "Romeo Crennel 'hates' Belichick but is too classy to say anything."[1847] If personal relations between Belichick and his top aides were strained in 2004–and my sources do not discredit these claims–it is further proof that professional collaboration does not require friendship.

Belichick's reported firing of Weis was presumably triggered by Weis' agent's campaign to win Weis a pay raise and contract extension, something I have been told Weis had been seeking since the team's first Super Bowl victory. Earning $500,000/season, Weis–who had helped win multiple Super Bowls–was earning less than half of what top offensive coordinators were receiving.[1848] The Patriots gave Romeo Crennel a raise but shot down Weis' 2004 request, at which point Weis' agent declared Weis would flee New England after the 2004 season: "We tried to reach an agreement and corporately the Patriots decided against it. So for Charlie, all he can do is work as hard as he can, devote himself, and know he will not be back next year."[1849] Belichick probably did not enjoy reading that "Charlie Weis' agent continues to make the rounds, as Tom Curran is the next to report on the Pats offensive coordinator's inability to reach an agreement on a new contract. The agent says this is Weis' last year with the Patriots."[1850] Ron Borges later wrote that "Weis publicly claimed that statement was only his agent's opinion following a private dressing down from Belichick. But the rift between him and his boss... was well known among Patriots insiders."[1851] Belichick's refusal to award Weis a raise was likely based on Weis' dream of becoming a head coach, either in college or the NFL. Bill Belichick wants everyone throughout his organization passionately devoted to the Patriots, not dreaming of a future beyond New England.

As Belichick often says, professional respect is more important to collaboration than friendship. Even if Weis and Belichick were mad at one another throughout the 2004 season and even if Crennel dislikes Belichick, the three men managed to win another championship together, proving that respect is necessary while friendship is desirable.

Seek success, not popularity

"You have to be able to deliver your message and get your point across the way you want to and not care about how guys perceive you. He's going to come across sometimes as bitter, and that's understandable."[1852]
– *Patriots nose tackle Keith Traylor*

"Everybody has feelings, and I'm sure [Belichick] does too."[1853]
– *Troy Brown*

The star of a popular British comedy series, *The Office*, is a manager with a fatal flaw: "He's not a bad bloke [fellow]. He's just confused popularity with respect. And they're not related. He wants everyone to say, 'You are the best boss and my best mate [friend].'"[1854] Patriots kicker Adam Vinatieri describes former Patriots coach Pete Carroll in similar terms:

"Pete tended to always look on the bright side and see the best in people. So somebody would do something wrong and he'd give them another chance. Someone would screw up and it would be like, 'Oh, well. Whatever.' Sometimes you have to hold people accountable."[1855]

How did Carroll's players respond? An unnamed "veteran" says,

"Guys totally took advantage [and] started being late for meetings. Even Pete wouldn't show up on time. Guys were falling asleep in the film room. The sight of Chris Canty with his sunglasses on and his feet up on the desk was all you needed to know. I can't remember how many times Pete would have to stop meetings and say, 'Guys, shush, quiet down!' When Bill [Parcells] was here, everyone was 15 minutes early and you could hear a pin drop. Everyone was on eggshells."[1856]

Being right does not necessarily make one popular. And being popular does not necessarily make one right. Smart coaches worry about being right, not being popular.

Belichick and his assistants scrupulously avoid being too nice or becoming too friendly with players. Belichick explains: "I'm looking for a player-coach relationship. I want to respect them and them to respect me. I don't think the players would be happy if we had some type of a social relationship but we didn't win as many games."[1857] During his playing days with the New York Giants, Patriots assistant coach Pepper Johnson spurned Bill Parcells' attempt to become his friend, not just his head coach, because Johnson thought players and coaches should not mix business and friendship.[1858] Coaches cannot become so friendly with players that they lose their willingness to make objective personnel and disciplinary decisions. Coaches who "let the inmates run the prison" make some players happy in the short term, but team performance degrades and, in the long run, leaves many players unhappy when they find themselves stuck on a lazy, losing team with a defeatist attitude. Troy Brown acknowledges this: "People may say [Belichick]'s not attached to players but I think somewhere deep down inside him he is... He is a great teacher of the game, and that is all you can ask for in a coach in this business. You can't ask him to be your best friend."[1859]

Recent Oakland Raiders and Dallas Cowboys teams have demonstrated how weak, indecisive coaches can produce losing seasons. Both teams had meddlesome owners who dealt directly with players, undermining their coaches' control. The coaches were never secure in their jobs, so they tried to win players' hearts but opportunistic players took advantage. NFL teams with entrenched, demanding–though not necessarily mean–coaches generally perform better. For example, every time Bill Parcells takes the reins (at the Giants, Patriots, Jets, and Cowboys), players' effort and performance skyrocket, at least for a year or two. But the effectiveness of Parcells' iron-willed tough guy routine–which motivates through fear, cajoling and scaring up superior performance–weakens over time, whereas Belichick's competition-and-professionalism-based approach is "sustainable."

Belichick stays close enough to his players to inspire them but aloof and dispassionate enough to make tough decisions. Reporter Bill Burt admires this: "Unlike coaches like Jon Gruden, who regularly blurt out 'I love these guys,' Belichick never crosses that line."[1860]

Belichick's praise for Nick Saban's LSU program demonstrates Belichick's emphasis on respect and lack of concern for popularity:

> "Anybody that's been associated with Nick in any capacity in football– whether it be playing for him, coaching with him–they respect him. They respect what he says and they respect what he does, because they know he's put a lot of time and thought into it and he's trying do what's best for the team and what's best for the person. Whether they really like it or not is not the point. The point is they respect it for what it is."[1861]

Former LSU Tiger and current Patriot cornerback Randall Gay agrees that respect outweighs congeniality: "I learned so much from [Saban], and I have so much respect for him. When you're a young player under Coach Saban, you might not like him as much, but he's trying to get the most out of you. As you get older, you start to realize what he's doing."[1862]

In the locker room and the media room, says Patriots linebacker Tedy Bruschi, "[Belichick]'s not a comedian. He's the head football coach, one that takes football seriously."[1863] Some mistake Belichick's standoffish public persona for his personality. Though Belichick is a cerebral, introspective man, he also has a humorous personality. He adopts a more reserved, austere, stern persona because he believes doing so improves his coaching. In social settings, however, Belichick is fun and intellectually stimulating. He was warm and funny on *The David Letterman Show* in February 2004. And when Belichick was defensive coordinator of the New York Jets, *NFL Today* host Jim Nantz had a memorable dinner with Belichick the night before Belichick's Jets played in the AFC Championship Game: "Contrary to his reputation in the press, Belichick was… open, honest, engaging and the owner of a great sense of humor. It was a thoroughly enjoyable social evening."[1864]

Competitive players and coaches need not love their teammates. It is sufficient that they respect their job performance. And Patriots coaches have certainly earned their players' respect. Cornerback Ty Law speaks glowingly, for example, of quiet defensive coordinator Romeo Crennel: "He is a man of class and he is a distinguished person. He would be a distinguished head coach."[1865] You cannot lead without such respect.

Being loved is often incompatible with the challenges and responsibilities of running a large organization. Wal-Mart founder Sam Walton managed to earn his employees' love. So did Bill Hewlett and David Packard. But leadership often requires making unpopular decisions. HP's famous founders' heirs–Walter Hewlett and David Woodley Packard–found leadership quite unpleasant when they openly opposed HP's decision to merge with Compaq. Though later events proved the wisdom of their opposition and led to the ouster of HP CEO Carly Fiorina, Hewlett and Packard were savaged in the press by those running the company their fathers founded: "Hewlett-Packard on Friday released a letter to shareholders bashing dissident board member Walter Hewlett."[1866]

Just as a general must maintain some emotional detachment from the men he leads into battle and potential death, so too Belichick knows he must maintain "professional distance" from those he leads. Otherwise, his heart might override his mind and place individual needs above team needs. But underneath his quiet, contemplative, unemotional public exterior, Belichick is a fun guy. Belichick even has celebrity friends, though he isn't starry-eyed about celebrity. Says his dad: "People that know him, people that are his friends know he's a nice guy. And his friends are the same way. He doesn't care about that other stuff. I think that's why his friends like him so much."[1867]

"Cruel to be kind, in the right measure"

"He's a laid-back guy till you ain't doing what you're supposed to do."[1868]
– Cleveland Browns defensive lineman Orpheus Roye, on Romeo Crennel

A 1979 song by one-hit-wonder Nick Lowe proclaims, "You've gotta be cruel to be kind, in the right measure." Former Patriots coach Pete Carroll emphasizes "be kind." Bill Parcells believes in "you've gotta be cruel." Belichick smartly stresses "in the right measure."

Most successful coaches are hard on players who aren't achieving to their potential but respectful toward players who are. Bill Belichick is on no power trip. He exercises authority if and when doing so will improve his team's performance. By constantly evaluating and grading players, the Patriots enable their hard workers to fix their mistakes and take responsibility for self-improvement. It's pointless to beat up on a hard-working, disciplined player who's generally performing well when he makes an occasional mistake. A mature player will beat himself up inside when he makes a mistake. Coaches must bring mistakes to players' attention because players are not always aware of the many subtle mistakes they make, but players–not coaches–are responsible for getting mad at themselves and taking corrective action. New defensive coordinator Eric Mangini explains this philosophy:

> "I [enjoy] it when they do it right. That's the goal. If we learn from our mistakes, that's OK. The problem is when we consistently make the same mistakes. As long we make a mistake and correct the mistake and it doesn't

happen again, then that's OK. The problem is more or less when we make the same error multiple times."[1869]

Mangini holds himself to the same standard: "I'm looking to improve from each week and learn from some of the mistakes that I make. Hopefully, just like the players, the mistakes won't repeat and I'll get better as we go."[1870] Belichick also makes mistakes but never repeats them. A week before the Patriots' Super Bowl XXXVI triumph, he admitted to players that he had coached poorly in the Patriots' most recent loss—a regular season game against the same St. Louis Rams they would face in the Super Bowl—and vowed "I'm not going to screw it up again."[1871]

Here's another example. Patriots running back Corey Dillon fumbled five yards shy of a touchdown with just 12 minutes left to play against the Kansas City Chiefs in 2004. A touchdown would have given the Patriots a commanding 31-13 lead. Instead, the Chiefs marched 95 yards for a touchdown to pull within five (after a failed two-point conversion attempt). Patriots players and coaches knew that Dillon didn't want to fumble and seldom does. So, rather than get mad at him, they urged him not to get discouraged:

> "I'm disgusted. I was just trying too hard to make things happen. Immediately after that, the team told me, 'We need you to come through, run the ball hard, and get us down there.' That's what I did. That's what I love about this team. They believe in me. I believe in them. We fight until the end for each other."[1872]

Dillon composed himself and—on the next drive—had runs of 5, 9, 6, 3, 4, and 1 yards that chewed up the clock and set up a field goal that gave the Patriots an 8-point lead with just 1:40 remaining. That proved the final margin.

Conversely, it's foolish and harmful to retain players who screw up repeatedly just because they're nice guys. Belichick's immediate predecessor as Patriots head coach, Pete Carroll, was too lenient. Under Carroll's "country club" environment, team performance suffered. After Carroll's firing, the Patriots' starting quarterback Drew Bledsoe said:

> "Guys took advantage of the freedom and the responsibility that Pete Carroll gave us. I think in some situations, guys just tried to see how much they could get away with. Now, with Belichick, you can't get away with anything. He's going to be right there, he's going to embarrass you in front of the team."[1873]

Linebacker Tedy Bruschi also expressed frustration:

> "(Attitudes) needed to be changed... There were non-professionals who didn't approach their jobs very seriously. Those people were a problem before. That's not the case any more. ...A guy like Belichick, coming from the old school, won't put up with any of that stuff."[1874]

If several players slack off and suffer no consequences, others begin asking "Why should I work so hard?" When coaches tolerate such unprofessionalism, they invite a cascade. More and more players slack off, and overall team performance spirals downward. After Pete Carroll inherited the 11-5 Super Bowl team of 1996, performance eroded steadily: 10-6 in 1997, 9-7 in 1998, and 8-8 in 1999 (finishing 2-6 after starting 6-2). Near the end, reporter Bob Hanna wrote, "this is a ship without a captain, caught in a whirlpool. It is spinning around and around and around before what would seem to be an inescapable plunge to the bottom of the ocean."[1875] Pete Carroll has since coached USC to two national championships. Perhaps his nice guy approach is better suited to the college game, where recruiting is more important (because there is no salary cap) and motivating players less important (because players train far fewer hours than in the NFL and have not yet signed million-dollar NFL contracts).

When Belichick took over, things got tougher immediately. Rookie mini-camp shifted from Carroll's one-a-day workouts to two-a-day workouts.[1876] And coaches no longer ignored "little" disciplinary problems because they knew that festering "little" problems metastasize into big problems. In fact, "little" problems are often merely visible symptoms of larger latent problems. Patriots inside linebackers coach Pepper Johnson detailed several incidents in which players disrespected his coaching or the rules established by Coach Belichick. In both cases, Johnson acted quickly, decisively, and aggressively to make clear that such behavior was completely unacceptable because, otherwise, "other guys would try it, and it would end up snowballing."[1877]

After a rookie talked back to Johnson and apparently mocked the importance of the Johnson-led scout team (which simulates the opposing team's style to prepare players for their upcoming competitor), Johnson didn't attack the rookie or even name him but instead ripped the problem up by its roots. Johnson gave an impassioned speech to all the players. He explained how he, as a rookie, had won his roster spot by performing well on the scout team and on special teams. Rather than attack and embarrass a single player whose inappropriate behavior was merely symptomatic of the real problem, Johnson ensured that everyone realized the importance of the scout team to the team's success and to each player's ability to make the team. "After that, I had guys fighting to get on The Dirty Show,"[1878] Johnson's nickname for the scout team. Johnson uses all kinds of marketing gimmicks to excite players about participating in the scout team, even talking about it like James Bond: "I can't talk about 'The Dirty Show.' If I talk about them, if I tell you any information about them, I'd have to kill you. I don't want to go to jail while I'm down here in Jacksonville. We can talk about them after it's all done. It's a lot of prideful guys who go out there and do their business very dirty."[1879] Giving players positive reasons to want to do something is much smarter than yelling at them for refusing to do it.

COLLECTIVE CHALLENGES ENCOURAGE TEAMWORK

"When you get employees headed in the same direction, they demonstrate power you can't even imagine."[1880]
— *Sharp president Katsuhiko Machida*

"Tom Brady… takes practice as seriously as anybody. That rubs off on the team."[1881]
— *Patriots receiver Deion Branch*

Before the 2003 season's AFC Championship Game, a Colts coach huddled his players and whipped them up with, "Let's go 'Knockout!' 1-2-3-Knockout!"[1882] Three hours later, the Patriots had knocked the Colts out by TKO, a 24-14 win with 17 of the Patriots' points coming on a safety and five field goals. Bill Belichick doesn't want his Patriots players thinking "knockout!" because a player who tries to make a "big play" outside the framework of the playbook leaves his entire team exposed to an opponent's uppercut. The Patriots jab relentlessly. They play defensive rope-a-dope. They don't go for the jugular. They are a pack of hyenas who tire their prey, surround it, gang-tackle it, immobilize it and—only then—go for the kill. By coordinating their attacks, hyenas can kill faster animals—like gazelles and zebras—and larger animals—like rhinoceroses and hippopotamuses.

Like hyenas, Patriots players collaborate intelligently—and communicate effectively—to achieve their collective goals. Patriots defensive end Jarvis Green believes this is the Patriots' greatest weapon:

"I think [our secret is] 'It's not I, it's we'—the team concept, and we are going to live and die with it. When we come together, we play together and we are a very humble team altogether, from top down to bottom. We look at that and know that—all of us—we need each other. When it comes time to play football, we all know we need each other in order to go out there and play at a high level."[1883]

Former Patriots safety Lawyer Milloy criticizes his old team because "You can't feed your families off of Super Bowl rings. The more they focus on, 'We don't have any stars' and all that, the more you get overlooked as far as individual accolades and contracts."[1884] What Milloy fails to grasp is that Super Bowl rings can feed your soul! To players like Tedy Bruschi, winning championships is of far greater value than luxury yachts, precious metals or rare furs. Like the Beatles, Bruschi "don't care too much for money" and wants "those kind of things that money just can't buy" because "money can't buy me love." Bruschi does, however, dispute that he "don't need no diamond ring." So does Bruschi's 2005 replacement, veteran NFL linebacker Chad Brown, who joined the Patriots because "I've played awhile, so I've done OK [financially], but the allure of the ring is strong."[1885]

The other reason many free agents accept lower pay to become or remain Patriots is that upbeat, competitive, football-loving guys love the Patriots' locker room energy. Being around similarly upbeat, competitive, football-loving guys gives them a "high." Together, they push one another to improve and achieve greatness, both individually and collectively. And they hold one another to an exceptionally high standard. Tedy Bruschi explains:

> "There's one way we do things around here, and that's collectively, that's as a team, that's hard work, that's preparation, and we all do the best we can. And if we don't think you're doing enough, we're going to let you know. We may joke about it, but still, we put it out there."[1886]

Asked why the Patriots are so successful, receiver Deion Branch answered, "We're just a bunch of guys who like to play the game. We work hard. We compete every day in practice, like who'll make the most plays every day. We just have fun."[1887]

Motivate one another

> "I'm more focused, and my [new Patriots] teammates help me to be focused... I'm just coming out here having fun. You can feel the energy every day. Even if you're hurt and you're bumped up, you still want to be out here and want to be working."[1888]
> — *New Patriots receiver David Terrell, who underperformed relative to expectations as a Chicago Bear*

> "Our core of veterans sets the example. When we add people to the team, they see those guys working out in the morning and doing things after practice, and they do the same things. It's not something that's talked about. It just happens as new people come, and it snowballs."[1889]
> — *Patriots linebacker Mike Vrabel*

> "[Selfishness] can be a cancer to a team that can gut a team from the inside and cause things to fall apart. We have great character guys, and they're not about to let that happen."[1890]
> — *Patriots linebacker Roman Phifer*

> "I look at Tedy Bruschi and admire him. He practices hard every day. He plays with a lot of energy. Whatever it takes, he gives everything that he has. Even if the coaching staff gives him a day off, he's out there giving it his all. I'm ecstatic that he's in the Pro Bowl."[1891]
> — *Patriots defensive lineman Richard Seymour*

> "[Tom Brady] motivates guys to do more and give more... [Tom] gives everything he has every time he touches the field... There is no letdown in that guy. If we were going to play a game of basketball, he would be the one

out there screaming and yelling, scoring all the points and taking it very seriously."[1892]
– *Patriots left tackle Matt Light*

When tackle Tom Ashworth caught a training camp touchdown, players cheered. When nose tackle Vince Wilfork caught a punt–in an annual Belichick stunt in which a 300+ pounder attempts to catch a punt after his teammates coach him up–players cheered madly "with Wilfork high-stepping to his teammates' cheers."[1893] The Patriots love watching teammates perform well and cheering their accomplishments.

The idea that Knute Rockne–or any other coach–is responsible for motivating players is absurd. Each player and coach must motivate himself. And each player and coach should help motivate everyone else. Everyone in the Patriots organization understands this. Running back Corey Dillon says, "The camaraderie in the locker room is a good thing, man. You can't beat this. I love coming back [to Patriots training camp]."[1894] It's shocking that any player–especially a player with as little to prove as Corey Dillon following the shortest offseason of his career–would be eager for the arrival of training camp. Patriots training camp is "fun" only in the way running a marathon or surviving medical school is fun. Patriots tight end Christian Fauria explains:

> "It's not fun. It's not enjoyable. No ghost stories, no sitting around the campfire. We're not roasting marshmallows. You want your mom. I don't want to say you just try to get through it, but you wake up in the morning and it's like 'Groundhog Day.' The same Sonny and Cher song is playing on the radio. You're wearing the same clothes you wore the day before... At the end of the day, I am so damn tired that I don't want to talk to anyone. Even the easiest conversation with my wife becomes too much effort. I'm short with everyone."[1895]

Persevering together through the agony of training camp is such an essential bonding experience that Tom Brady smartly joined his offensive teammates for their punishment lap when they were punished with a lap around the field during a 2005 training camp session Belichick had ordered Brady to skip. The togetherness forged during training camp motivates everyone throughout the season.

"I am Spartacus!" / "We are Borg"

"When we were in the heat of battle with Microsoft, a venture capitalist forwarded us an e-mail written by a Microsoft executive. All it said was 'Boy waves red cape in front of bull, boy gets gored.' ...Downplay [your rivalry]. Do the 'aw shucks' thing."[1896]
– *Former Netscape employee Mike Homer*

"I'm reading *The Sporting News* two months ago that says something about me being an 'average' player. I just tore it out and put it in my wallet... to remind me."[1897]
– *Tom Brady*

"Sundays are... that day for Rodney [Harrison] when he has that chip on his shoulder. He has a chip on his shoulder every day, really."[1898]
– *Patriots running back Kevin Faulk*

To Patriots players, disrespect is like Brylcreem: "a little dab'll do ya!" Patriots receiver Troy Brown says, "There are all kinds of things you can use to get motivated."[1899] Watching Patriots players latch onto any tiny irritant they can use to pump themselves up is hilarious. And disrespect is contagious in the Patriots locker room. After Eagles receiver Freddie Mitchell brainlessly tossed out the playful boast that "I got something for you, Harrison, when I meet you" in Super Bowl XXXIX, Patriots safety Rodney Harrison knew those words would fire up his teammates: "It's not just me against Freddie Mitchell. It's 53 guys against 53 guys. [So] it's not just me getting motivated. I'm always on a high level of motivation. I always have something to prove. You get so many other guys... motivated when trash talking starts."[1900]

Patriots linebacker Willie McGinest basically stepped forward and declared, "I am Spartacus!" (or, for younger readers, "We are Borg!"):

"We're all one. He called out our offense and our special teams, he called out everybody. What he doesn't get is that Rodney is me. He is Bruschi is Vrabel is Seymour. He's everyone on our team. We're all one, so if you call out one guy, you call out the whole team. He said what he said, and it upset us."[1901]

McGinest continued by insulting Mitchell, the only player I recall the Patriots ever disrespecting before a game: "We are not going to go back and forth wasting time commenting on a guy like that who's been unproductive in his career, who is only [playing] because one of their star players is hurt. So now he gets a little limelight and he starts talking and doing a lot of interviews."[1902]

Freddie Mitchell's remark made headlines because the Patriots and Eagles were on their best behavior during the two pre-Super Bowl weeks, and everyone but Mitchell seemed to understand that Harrison and his teammates start drooling like Pavlov's dog the moment any opponent says anything less-than-fawning about any of them. After the controversy erupted, Eagles quarterback Donovan McNabb correctly explained, "Everybody is going to take it and turn it to the way that they want it to sound. When it gets back to the [Patriots], all of a sudden, he's basically challenged their manhood."[1903]

Willie McGinest said, "Rodney is not one of those guys that you want to rile up... You don't want to get him going. He is already walking around ready to play yesterday. To hear comments like [Freddie's], it just gets him going."[1904] Indeed!

Harrison's passion came pouring out even while interning as an NFL Europe referee in Spring 2005: "I saw one guy get annihilated, and I almost jumped through the sky. I was pumped up. I was yelling and screaming and [then] I was like, 'Man, what are you doing? Are you officiating or are you a fan?'"[1905] Instead of throwing a flag for illegal contact or unnecessary roughness, Harrison was whooping it up like a drunken fan. (Did you expect objectivity from one of the most heavily fined players in NFL history who is, ironically, training to become an NFL ref following his playing career? *Sportsline.com* termed Harrison's career aspirations "Pot, meet kettle.") In Super Bowl XXXIX, Harrison intercepted two passes and held up an Eagle ball-carrier while teammate Randall Gay stripped the ball away. In victory, Harrison's joy was as much for proving his doubters wrong as for winning back-to-back world championships: "It's unbelievable, being that I can't play anymore, that I'm washed up. Everyone has different motivations. With some people it's money. ...Mine is from people doubting me."[1906] If a Patriots opponent kicked dirt into the air, I wouldn't be shocked to watch Rodney Harrison dive to the ground and convince himself his opponent had deliberately kicked dirt in his face. Anything to motivate.

Freddie Mitchell pushed the wrong button on the wrong player at the wrong time, and his teammates paid the price. Harrison is angry when he walks off the field after a *victory*. After beating Tennessee in 2003, Harrison was livid: "Nobody picked us [to win]. Everybody hated us!"[1907] Amazingly, Mitchell—more self-obsessed than Cuba Gooding Jr.'s character in *Jerry McGuire*—never understood the consequences of his loose jaw: "I never feel bad for anything I say. It's interesting though how they [the Patriots] blew it up. It's cool. Whatever happens, happens. ...I'm definitely shocked [by the reaction] but that doesn't bother me at all."[1908] He even added, "It's still funny to me."[1909]

Harrison is hardly the only Patriot who scrounges for scraps of motivational disrespect. Linebacker Willie McGinest explained that the Patriots' fire was raging even before Freddie's remark:

> "We don't need people to throw things out there to get us motivated. This is a highly motivated team as it is. ...We're a highly competitive bunch of guys that push each other, and anytime something comes out, we use it as fuel. It adds fire for us."[1910]

The Patriots are such famous self-deluders that *SportsPickle.com* spoofed them as ticked off being only 3-to-1 preseason favorites to repeat as champions and only seven-point Super Bowl favorites, calling it "total disrespect." In the parody, Willie McGinest took umbrage at *ESPN* for predicting the Patriots would be "almost impossible to dethrone" following their acquisition of Corey Dillon: "What's this 'almost' stuff? It's that type of constant disrespect that motivates this team every week." According to the spoof, Belichick manufactures fake newspaper articles and TV shows to anger his players and bans them from watching sports news—lest they discover that "the media gushes over them incessantly"—and supposedly told his players that everyone expected them to lose the AFC Championship Game in Pittsburgh (despite being favored on the road against a team that destroyed them in the regular season), afterwards thinking to himself, "I didn't see one player roll his eyes or do that cough 'bullsh-t' thing or be like: 'Uh, coach, doesn't everyone think we're going to beat them fairly easily?' It was amazing. After a while you have to wonder if these guys are retarded."[1911] What makes the parody so funny is how close it comes to the truth.

Before the Super Bowl, Freddie Mitchell said his remarks had "been blown way out of proportion."[1912] Afterward, he chastised the Patriots! "[I was] being facetious and kidding around. They blew it way out of proportion. [Their overreaction] reminded me of little girls. They're sensitive. Real, real sensitive." Mitchell totally misunderstands the Patriots' psyche. Mitchell thinks they're the NFL equivalent of the fairy tale princess who complained about a pea underneath her mattress keeping her awake at night. Mitchell doesn't realize that Harrison found Mitchell's pea and deliberately placed it under his mattress in the most uncomfortable spot, so he couldn't sleep. Mitchell should have asked Broncos safety John Lynch about Harrison: "You could walk up to Rodney right now and you could tell him that you think he's the second-greatest safety of all time. Somehow, Rodney would come away convinced you have disrespected him."[1913] Heck, Freddie could have asked either of the Eagles' safeties. Brian Dawkins said, "[Rodney]'s a crazy man. That's my dog. I love the way he plays the game. Almost every play you see him getting into it with somebody, some kind of altercation."[1914] And Michael Lewis told reporters, "I love his game… I try to pattern my game after [Rodney]. He is a high intensity guy. He is going to hit you and let you know that he hit you… He's going to take your head off."[1915]

Harrison bought a bag of peas and handed out peas to teammates to place under their mattresses, so everyone would be disturbed:

> "When you attack me, you are not just attacking me. You are attacking ten other guys on defense as well as any substitutions that come into the game. A lot of guys take that personally because we are such a close-knit group and we are so tight. So it is not like he has to watch out for me. He has to watch out for everyone because everyone is pumped up, and we all take offense to smart comments like that. You are calling out Tedy Bruschi, Willie McGinest, Roman Phifer and all the other guys out there. Remember, you've got a trained assassin in Eugene Wilson back there [at free safety]."[1916]

How dumb was Mitchell? Harrison suspects "Maybe he was drinking before he started talking because when you attack me, you attack the whole defense… Normally, most guys who have played long enough in this league wouldn't attack someone a week before the Super Bowl, especially a guy [like me] who gets riled up because of things like that. Trust me, I don't need any added motivation. I need some things to calm me down."[1917]

After the game, Belichick uncharacteristically joined in the Freddie-bashing, calling him "terrible" and saying the Patriots were happy to see him in the game. Freddie responded with characteristic idiocy: "It takes a big man to talk after the game is over." Mitchell acted like a moron who gleefully pokes a beehive with a stick and then blames the bees for stinging him. If you taunt someone and dare them to fight you, you can't whine after they knock you unconscious, especially if you said "everything gets settled on the football field"[1918] before catching just one lousy pass in the biggest game of your life.

Another outspoken Eagles receiver, Terrell Owens, also handed the Patriots motivational ammunition when he called the Patriots defense "very simplistic."[1919] (Owens is wrong. Chad Brown—one of the NFL's smartest and most experienced linebackers, who has played for nine different defensive coordinators—said after three months learning the Patriots defense, "This is difficult. Yes it is. …It's a huge challenge… There's a lot to it. I don't think it's an insurmountable obstacle, but it's going to take a lot of hard work… The complexity of this defense is a huge challenge."[1920]) Owens also challenged Patriots cornerbacks' virility when he said, "I welcome man-to-man [defense], but Belichick is a smart coach, and I don't think that is a situation that he is going to want to put his guys in."[1921] (Again, wrong. After the game, Rodney Harrison said the Patriots' cornerbacks "did a tremendous job considering they were in man-to-man coverage for most of the game."[1922] On many plays, Owens was single-covered by the undrafted Randall Gay who said, "we were trying to… make it look like we were double-covering him, but we were in the same coverages—man-to-man—every play."[1923])

By April 2005, Mitchell was bashing his Eagles teammates. He caught just one pass in the Super Bowl because "You need that rapport [with your quarterback], and it just wasn't there."[1924] McNabb threw to him only "to get his ass out of a jam."[1925] "I can't throw myself the ball. …I got more tired doing jumping jacks [waving for the ball] than actually playing."[1926] Mitchell's one-catch, 11-yard performance wasn't his fault: "I did all I could do to win. I can't ask any more of myself. I feel great."[1927]

Months later, Mitchell still couldn't comprehend that insulting his opponent had hurt his team: "The media took that like, 'Oh my god! I can't believe you said that.' What's [Harrison] going to do? Hit me less hard if I didn't talk about him?"[1928] In Mitchell's mind, his pathetic teammates had screwed him by not defending him more vigorously after he insanely called out Harrison: "I could have sworn we were playing tennis. They didn't back me up because they were scared."[1929] Mitchell refuses to take responsibility for anything. When he strikes out, he literally believes it's the pitcher's fault: "I've been thrown so many curveballs on 2-0 counts when everyone else is getting damn fastballs down the middle."[1930] He underperformed in Philadelphia because "Other receivers learn one [position] and just have to perfect that. It hindered my performance to have so many plays running through my mind."[1931]

By Draft Day, the Eagles were shopping Freddie, only to find no interest. So, they released their trouble-making former 1st-round draft pick who averaged a shade over 1½ catches per game as an Eagle, though he would have cost the Eagles only $540,000 in 2005. Mitchell said "I'm very happy to be out of there" and lashed out at fans: "Fans should have been glad to have a... player that actually cares enough to tell [media people] that they don't know what they're talking about."[1932] Mitchell is the anti-Patriot, and his role in Super Bowl XXXIX proves the wisdom of everything Bill Belichick preaches.

Eagles quarterback Donovan McNabb also handed the Patriots bulletin board material by violating the Patriots' rule of never speaking ill of an upcoming opponent. Seemingly trying to convince himself, McNabb told reporters, "If they were invincible, they wouldn't have lost two games this year... They were fighting just to have home field advantage... This team is not invincible. This team can be beat."[1933] McNabb's factual and seemingly innocuous words were hardly fighting words... except to the Patriots' always-eager-to-be-disrespected players. Even the slightest slight turns them into frenzied piranhas. As Willie McGinest puts it, "If somebody is disrespecting you... be humble and handle it on the field. Nobody wins games doing interviews, nobody wins game in articles."[1934]

Belichick is an expert at finding facts that irritate players into passionate preparation. Swears Patriots cornerback Ty Law:

> "He's great at it. Just like he's a great coach, he's a great motivator. He knows his X's and O's, but he knows how to push those buttons on, you know, as far as the team and as far as individuals. If he knows that we need Rodney [Harrison] to step up and have a good game, he'll find something about Rodney from another team—whether it be a lineman, whether it be a receiver, a quarterback—he'll find something to strike a nerve in Rodney. He'll do a search on Google: 'whoever and Rodney Harrison' [and then] come in there and read it to everybody."[1935]

Law shared a personal example:

> "[Belichick] found tapes of [a Seattle Seahawks player] ...on TV... that he had to show the whole team about what [that player] said about me, and [Belichick] was like, 'Uh-oh Ty, he's gonna kick your ass.' ...He'll do that in front of everybody. But I mean we take it all in fun. But you know deep down inside it's going to strike a little nerve to make you go out there and play better. And that's just the fun that we have sometimes amongst that team."[1936]

Willie McGinest agrees Belichick "keeps us hungry and ready to go."[1937] Patriots players respond to such facts with mature preparation.

How can the Patriots possibly find anyone to insult them in 2005, after winning three of the past four Super Bowl trophies? Rodney Harrison, unsurprisingly, seems to have found the answer, finding motivation not in insults but in jealousy and hostility: "The whole world is against us, basically, and people want us to lose, people want to see us fall."[1938]

The Patriots are also smart enough not to help motivate their opponents. They are respectful to the utmost. Patriots left tackle Matt Light, for example, emphasized before Super Bowl XXXIX that—as great a player as Jevon Kearse is—"I don't know if I have every played Jevon when he has been 100 percent healthy."[1939] In other words, "This guy's even more incredible than he looks!"

Enjoy helping your teammates win

"Help the team win… Giving it my all for my teammates. That's pretty much what I've been thinking about all [Super Bowl] week."[1940]
   – *Patriots running back Corey Dillon*

"It takes a total team effort. If we can't get pressure on the quarterback or can't stop the run, then we leave our secondary more vulnerable."[1941]
   – *Patriots linebacker Ted Johnson*

"[My Super Bowl MVP trophy]'s been [untouched] in the little case that they send it in for a long time. It's a great honor. I am very thankful, but it's another year and now hopefully we… move on and get somebody else to make that step up."[1942]
   – *Patriots receiver Deion Branch*

"Even though I've won …a couple [Super Bowls], you still want to go out and play your heart out for a guy like [Corey Dillon] who has never been in a playoff game at all."[1943]
   – *Patriots wide receiver / nickel back / punt returner Troy Brown*

Do the Patriots have star players? Players themselves are divided. Some say they need no stars. Others—like Rodney Harrison—believe "Every one of us that lines up on the field is a superstar."[1944] Many Patriots don't care because, as linebacker Mike Vrabel points out, "the media are the people that create stars"[1945] and they crave only their teammates' respect.

When Scott Pioli won his second consecutive NFL Executive of the Year award, he said he's just "trying to win championships. And this [award] is just a byproduct of the team success and what the players do and what the coaches do. This is a collaborative effort. …Our leadership group doesn't believe in egos [and] we've surrounded ourselves with a group of players who are similar to us personality-wise, who are more selfless than selfish. …No one cares about who's getting credit.

Everything that everyone does is geared toward winning games, not things like this [award]."[1946] Tom Brady agrees:

> "[In] football, you're entirely dependent upon the guys you're with. Ultimately, the pride and the enjoyment come from succeeding as a group, which is very different than [individual] sports... It's about how you can try to get everyone else doing the right thing so they can rise to that level too. We've got guys that are really capable of that. When you really push Deion Branch, he responds. When you push Corey [Dillon], he responds. When you push the linemen—because they are so well coached—they respond. I think when you look back at the end of the year like we did last year, you look back and you say, 'Man, that was so much fun because we continued to meet every challenge that we faced.'"[1947]

Being a team player is about doing your best at all times, whether or not you touch the ball. As receiver Deion Branch explains:

> "We aren't greedy. One week it might be Troy's game, the next might be Patten's game and the next week might be David's game. It happens like that and if we are winning, we are happy... I can only contribute when my number is called. If an opportunity happens, I try to take advantage."[1948]

When Branch runs his routes well, he clears space for his fellow receivers to catch balls and pulls defensive backs away from the line of scrimmage so Corey Dillon has more room to run. If Brady throws the ball in Branch's direction, he tries his darnedest to catch it. But he doesn't measure success by counting catches or yardage. He measures success by how much he helps his team win. And his teammates measure their performance the same way. Only Fantasy Football fans should obsess over numbers. But many coaches baby their "stars." Tampa Bay Buccaneers coach Jon Gruden confesses that his game day cheat sheet—which places every play he might call in that game in a column representing a situation, such as 3rd-and-long—"might even have a Keyshawn Johnson column, and [I might] say, 'I've got to get him the *damn* ball.'"[1949] Bill Belichick calls plays only to win games, never to please a particular player.

Belichick himself is a team player who enjoys watching his "teammates" succeed. Though Belichick is "first among equals" or, as Orwell put it, "more equal" than the other Patriots, Belichick himself would never say he was more important than others or act that way. Belichick knows he—on his own—wins no football games. He has an important role and executes it brilliantly, but winning requires nearly a hundred players and coaches, not to mention scouts, owners, and support staff, all working productively together. Harvard Business School professor Nancy Koehn distilled this key insight from her entrepreneurship expertise: "The most successful entrepreneurs think of their companies as a separate entity from themselves... They have a sense that if they have done their work well, the proof will be in their companies outgrowing, outpacing–and even outliving–them."[1950] Bill Parcells, Bobby Knight, and Lee Iacocca saw little distinction between their organizations and themselves. Many innovative small companies fail to grow because the entrepreneurs who run them are too proud to relinquish some control to create an organization greater than themselves. In great organizations, no one monopolizes leadership.

On great teams, players respect their teammates and coaches and crave their appreciation. On the Patriots, players even want the front office to appreciate them. Defensive lineman Marquise Hill worries about disappointing those who drafted him: "You don't want to let the people in the front office down because they drafted you. The main thing is to just go out there and show them, 'You didn't waste your draft pick.' So there is a lot of pressure."[1951]

Patriots players love cheering for their teammates and helping them succeed. Left tackle Matt Light loves blocking for Corey Dillon because "You would be hard pressed to find somebody that works harder than him… He refuses to go out of bounds."[1952] Dillon reciprocates Light's respect. Asked whether his offensive linemen get enough credit, Dillon answers "No, not at all. There's a lot of guys on that offensive line that should be All-Pro or Pro Bowl players but they get overlooked, and that's not right. But I respect what they do, and they're one of the reasons I've been so successful this year. They go out there and do a great job."[1953]

Unlike many NFL players who treat kickers like "the help," Patriots players love their kicker. Defensive lineman Richard Seymour raves about Adam Vinatieri: "The kick in the snow against the Raiders–the one that the Raiders cry about now– that would be the best, because it was clutch, in the snow. He's the ultimate professional. He doesn't get rattled. When you need a game-winning field goal, he's the guy you want."[1954] In fact, Vinatieri works out with Seymour, one of the strongest men in the NFL: "He trains with me in the off-season. He and I did a workout together. We ran and lifted weights. He does all the things to go out there and hit. He wants to go out there and hit. That's the type of mentality he has."[1955] Vinatieri attributes the respect he receives from his teammates to the team's emphasis on "do your job":

> "We're the punch line of some jokes. We don't necessarily get the same respect, but maybe that's because we are on the field for a minute and a half [of] the 60 minutes… Our jerseys are always clean, and we usually don't get a lot of blood on our jerseys. It's OK if that's the situation. I think guys respect us for doing our job. I can't do what Tom [Brady] does, and Tom can't do what Troy [Brown] does. They can't do what I do, and I can't do what they do. Each one of us does our own job and has our own responsibilities."[1956]

Adam's teammates also likely respect him because he is prepared to make tackles, though he seldom needs to:

"We are a bunch of guys that try to do whatever we can to help our team. That [sometimes] means making a tackle–as ugly as it may be–or at least divert[ing] the guy back so someone else can make the tackle. I try to do whatever I can to help the team. Lifting and running and getting as strong as you can be can only help this team."[1957]

Vinatieri says he pushes himself because he enjoys helping his teammates: "You look across the locker room here and go, 'Hey, I don't only want to do it for myself. I want to do it for the other guys in here.'"[1958]

Nose tackle in the Patriots' 3-4 defense is another inglorious position. The nose can play a perfect game and record zero sacks and zero tackles. Vince Wilfork–who played a more glamorous attacking role in a 4-3 scheme at the University of Miami–had to change his mindset:

"The hardest part I had to learn was being frustrated every day. All the big plays I made [in college], I'm not making them anymore. All the sacks I made, I'm not making them any more. The coaches had to sit down with me and tell me this was my job. I had to be a patient player. I wasn't going anywhere fast. Everything I had to do was backside. Until I understood that, I was going home mad every day because I wasn't making plays. Sometimes I'd [finish] with no tackles, and that was real frustrating to me coming from the background I did. Once I learned what I had to do and understood the different [style of] play, it really is OK. I'd go through practice and I would think I'm messing up, and I'd get in the film room and the coaches would tell me I was doing a great job."[1959]

The Patriots' other nose tackle, Keith Traylor, says grunt work is worth it because winning trumps all personal accolades and statistics:

"Everybody has an assignment. I try to do my part and take on a blocker or two and let the guys behind me fly around and make plays. If you can buy into the system, it works. If you come in wanting to be a superstar, you may not be so lucky. I don't care about the dirty work. I'll get in the trenches and do whatever I have to."[1960]

Vince Wilfork says playing nose is more enjoyable in New England because his teammates–especially the linebackers who make many tackles because he keeps the center and guards off them–appreciate him doing the dirty but essential job:

"I just love playing around this group of people. We have Ted Bruschi, Ted Johnson... They let us know every day what a good job we're doing and how much they love us. I just found out that Bruschi got named to the Pro Bowl, so I'm proud of that. He was behind me in my first year as a rookie and I was able to contribute to the team and help him make the Pro Bowl. That says a lot about this defense."[1961]

Lead by example

"Example is not the main thing in influencing others. It is the only thing."
   – *Albert Schweitzer*

"I hope to be a leader on the field by example."[1962]
   – *Wide receiver Deion Branch, days after the Patriots drafted him in 2002*

"You hear of coaches leaving the office at 4 or 5 o'clock to go play golf. [Belichick] and his staff put in a tremendous amount of hours. They put in so much to give us every edge, every possible little thing they can do to make us better and help us have a better chance at winning."[1963]
   – *Patriots linebacker Willie McGinest*

"I don't lead by talk. I lead by example. A lot of guys can talk."[1964]
   – *Rookie cornerback Ellis Hobbs*

"Leadership is about… attitude. Leadership is not about getting up and giving long speeches or [throwing] pizza parties. It's about working hard and putting the team first."[1965]
   – *Bill Belichick*

"Bill Belichick has always been one of the hardest-working coaches in the league… His strong work ethic is imparted to us, simple as that."[1966]
   – *Patriots inside linebackers coach Pepper Johnson*

"100% [effort] every single play, every single day. That's just me. And hopefully guys–especially the young guys–feed off of it and hopefully they learn how to be a professional and bring their 'A' game every day."[1967]
   – *Patriots safety Rodney Harrison*

"[Belichick] knows the game in-and-out. He's always going to strive to do his best, and that's what he relays [to] the players. We're going to strive to do our best and work together as a team and a coaching staff. Nobody is going to do it themselves. He's not going to go out there and call a play and hike it to himself. It runs down from him to the coaching staff down to the players on the field. Everyone's got to go out there and do their best."[1968]
   – *Patriots offensive lineman Joe Andruzzi*

"When [new] guys come in and they see older veterans being unselfish, they see guys coming back from injury working hard, or they see people gel as a unit, it sets a foundation for them. It shows them that this is the way it should be… That's just the way they do it around here. I'm glad to be a part of it."[1969]
   – *Patriots linebacker Rosevelt Colvin*

> "Troy [Brown]'s not going to stand up and give a team speech; he's never one to be extremely vocal, yet he's one of the very best leaders I've been around in my 30 years in the National Football League. Troy works hard; he's very team-oriented, he's dependable, he'll do anything that you ask him to help the team win, and he does it to the very best of his ability. ...He puts himself last and everyone else first."[1970]
> – Bill Belichick

Leaders whose deeds match their words motivate most effectively because employees are inspired by leaders who walk the talk. Bill Belichick's definition of "leadership"–as doing your job to the best of your ability–embodies this principle. And Belichick certainly studies, strategizes and trains players as intensely as any coach anywhere. Defensive coordinator and former secondary coach Eric Mangini says of his mentor:

> "He's the best example or the best role model you can get... He works as hard as anybody I've ever seen, and he never stops learning, and he never stops trying to stay ahead of the curve. Here's a guy who's had success upon success upon success, but that hasn't changed him. He's the same guy today that he was however many years ago."[1971]

Another way Belichick leads by example is by putting himself through rigorous workouts like those he puts his players through. Belichick works out daily at high intensity. Cleveland Browns broadcaster Casey Coleman said in 1994: "I've been with [Belichick] while he has the Stairmaster geared up to the highest level for an hour and 10 minutes. And he'll be watching a film and talking to you the whole time. Most of us couldn't even breathe after that long on a Stairmaster."[1972] Belichick's players certainly notice and admire his toughness. Browns center Mike Baab said, "It's an amazing display of endurance and agony–and he loves it."[1973]

Belichick also leads by example every time he pokes fun at himself, implicitly telling each team member never to get too high on himself. While handing President Bush one of his trademark hooded gray sweatshirts, for example, Belichick self-mockingly told the president, "As the leader of our country and a world leader, we want you to be out front in fashion."[1974]

Patriots defensive coordinator Romeo Crennel demonstrated leadership before Super Bowl XXXIX. Barraged with questions about his future–especially whether he would become Cleveland's head coach–Crennel insisted "My mind is concentrated on the game at hand because [otherwise] you are going to probably end up losing it."[1975] Pressed further about his "expectation for next week," Crennel artfully dodged the question: "My expectation next week is to try to win the game this week. Then we will see what happens next week."[1976] Crennel even explicitly said that he must follow his own advice: "I tell my players never to assume. I don't have the job. I work for the New England Patriots. As long as I am a Patriot, I am a Patriot... If you focus on other things, then you are going to lose the game, and that is what we tell our players."[1977]

Patriots defensive coach Pepper Johnson stresses himself physically to bond with players:

> "When I instruct the guys as a coach, I go through the workouts with them for the most part. It draws me a little closer to them. I remember that from my Giants days [as a player], how good I felt when the team's strength and conditioning coach, Johnny Parker, used to work out with us. ...It motivated me, and I try to do the same thing with the Patriots."[1978]

Leaders who get their hands dirty also relate better to employees and their challenges. When CEOs take time to do an entry-level job for a day or a week, they invariably come away humbled by the demands of the job and gain insights that enable them to make more informed decisions. The co-CEOs of *California Pizza Kitchen* were shocked to learn they were under-qualified to bake pizzas with sufficient speed and quality. Their experience prompted employee-friendly innovations and motivated them to do more in-store stints. After washing duties educated Rick Rosenfield about its perils ("It's the forks that get you"), procedures were changed to sort utensils before throwing them into the sink.[1979]

Conversely, when employees see their bosses arriving late and leaving early, insulating themselves in posh offices and living large on company expense accounts, they feel resentful. I still recall how bitter I felt the two months I rowed crew my freshman year at Harvard as the coach rode his motorboat alongside our boat while yelling through his bullhorn for us to pull harder. I would almost swear he had a cold beer in his other hand.

Patriots linebacker Mike Vrabel will be a superb football coach after he "retires." After earning his second Super Bowl ring, Vrabel returned to Ohio State to complete the biochem course he needed to receive a diploma. He did so because he was already planning to lead his future team by example and be a role model for his children:

> "Ultimately, I want to coach. It's tough to recruit kids to come play for you and talk to their parents and say 'I'm going to make sure your son goes to class, and I'm going to make sure he graduates,' when you don't have a degree yourself. It's tough to tell kids to go to class when they're looking at a coach who hasn't graduated. For my kids also it's important."[1980]

Another example of leading by example is offensive coordinator Charlie Weis preventing a contract situation from becoming a distraction. With one year left on Weis' three-year contract, Weis' agent approached the Patriots, seeking an extension and a raise after Weis helped the Patriots win two Super Bowls because top offensive coordinators were earning more than twice Weis' salary. Weis' agent gave the media the impression Weis was disappointed the Patriots left his contract unchanged. Weis quickly squelched rumors before they inflicted more damage:

> "I've become a bit of a distraction. I'm very uneasy talking about money. It creates uneasy feelings and animosity. I'm not interested in contract negotiations. I signed a contract after 2001. I signed for three years and I thought it was pretty damn good. All I want to do is win. ...What's an agent's job? He's an agent. I'm a coach. All I do is coach. Everyone wants more money. But that's not the point. When you have a contract, until that's up, that's what you're getting paid. Am I unhappy with my contract? No. Do I want to be a distraction? No. Do I want to work to help us win? Yes. ...I'm not unhappy with the Patriots. How can I be unhappy with a team that's won two Super Bowls? All I want to do is coach. All I want to do is win."[1981]

Had the Patriots ripped up Weis' contract and given him more money, players might have wondered why they seldom receive similar treatment (though the Patriots had done so for Bill Belichick and have subsequently done so for quarterback Tom Brady and defensive lineman Richard Seymour). Though Weis' salary was low, the Patriots have a reputation for paying somewhat below-market salaries. They can do this because they emphasize team over individual and dangle the chance of winning a Super Bowl in front of hungry players. Had Weis demanded a contract renegotiation or left the impression he was giving less than 100% effort due to unhappiness over his contract, players would have smelled hypocrisy on the coaching staff. Coaches' salaries are not subject to the salary cap, so the Patriots could have paid Weis more without affecting the team (whereas a dollar paid to Player A is a dollar that can't be paid to Player B). But impressions matter. Coaches should follow the rules they hold players to. A contract obligates the signer to play or coach at a certain salary. Requesting more is legitimate, but demanding more is arrogant and selfish.

After Weis took over Notre Dame's football program, he didn't settle into his fancy new office. He packed his bags and lived on the road for an entire month because "I said all along that recruiting was the lifeblood of our program. If I send seven guys on the road recruiting and the head coach isn't one of them, what kind of message would I be sending?"[1982] After he returned, Weis found a loophole that allows him to stay in touch with recruits, despite the NCAA's one phone call per week limit, telling reporters at the end of one Q&A with "I'm going to go upstairs and [send] a few text [messages]."[1983] Instead of outsourcing the task, Weis has become a text messaging fanatic: "We sit down and we start typing away. It's a different message for each kid... I just want to get them. I just want to get them and follow the rules and do all I can to help get the players we want."[1984]

SUSTAINED MOTIVATION BETTER THAN MOTIVATIONAL BURSTS

"Football is preparation, preparation, preparation, and then you get one chance to play."[1985]
  – Bill Belichick

"Bill [Belichick] has a saying, 'When you get out there in the middle of the ocean, you're either going to drown or swim, so keep swimming.' Dog-paddling and stroking have gotten me where I am today."[1986]
  – Patriots linebacker Rosevelt Colvin, on his recovery from a fractured hip

Professionalism requires 24/7/52 passion, not 60-minute passion. Belichick wrote in 2002:

"The 2001 Patriots… did a tremendous job getting ready to play the games. But that commitment to prepare didn't start the week of Opening Day, and it didn't start in training camp, either. It went back to the off-season program in March, the passing camp in May, the mini-camp in June and all the hours of meetings and work that led up to training camp."[1987]

Games are not won on game day. They can be lost on game day, but they're won in the months and weeks leading up to games. Belichick enjoys Sunzi's ancient Chinese text *The Art of War*, which taught him that "most battles are won before they're fought."[1988] Patriots offensive lineman Joe Andruzzi says players "get it":

"Practice makes perfect. That's what Bill enforces on his coaching staff and on the rest of the players here. We've been working all week as it is, and we're trying to do our best. Trying to get into game plans and trying to improve and get better because no one is perfect. Those guys over there [their Super Bowl opponent, the Eagles] are getting paid too. You want to go out there and have every play be a good play. Bill enforces that, and we're going to go out there and do our best."[1989]

Romeo Crennel says, "You don't want your players thinking too much [during games]. You want them to feel confident when they walk out on the field and then be able to execute and react. If you have to think, you're going to be a step slow, and when you're a step slow, you give up [big] plays."[1990] Belichick would applaude the great Ohio State coach Woody Hayes' description of the state of practiced excellence–"the thinking of no thinking"–he expected from his players:

"The more you work now [to prepare], the more you think over the job you do, [then] in a ballgame the thinking you do [will be] the thinking of no thinking. You don't dare sit there and philosophize… If you've got to stop and think, 'Well, what do I do now?' you're all done. The play's by you…

> [We need] alert football players that are really thinking and learning. You don't just say [something] to them and they wag their head and forget about it."[1991]

Performance suffers when a player thinks too hard, as new Patriots linebacker Chad Brown discovered in a preseason game: "I was still thinking of the call and running it through my head rather than looking at what the offense was running. I just have to get more comfortable with the defense."[1992] Conversely, says Patriots linebacker Rosevelt Colvin, "Knowing my responsibility–as far as what I'm doing on every play, knowing where I'm supposed to be, where I'm supposed to line up–gives [me] the opportunity to relax a little bit. When you feel comfortable knowing you can get your job done, then you have the opportunity to do other things... You're pretty much going all out."[1993] This is why Belichick and his assistants quiz players each week and why players who don't know the answers don't play that week. Patriot linebacker Monty Beisel hadn't experienced this earlier in his NFL career: "I'm sitting in a meeting the first day and they start asking me questions about what I know about the defense, right in front of everyone else."[1994] Patriots quarterback Doug Flutie says:

> "There's an attitude of hard work, of being accountable for what you do every day. When we step into a team meeting, you're accountable for everything that's been given to you information-wise and you have got to answer to it."[1995]

Many motivational speakers entertain brilliantly and leave spellbound audiences feeling wonderful but have little impact on listeners' day-to-day behavior. Showmanship and motivational speeches are often as impactful as New Year's resolutions. They're like candy bars... providing a brief burst of energy that fades quickly, leaving you even hungrier.

This is why Bill Belichick is no Knute Rockne. Charlie Weis says Belichick will never pop an artery whipping his players into a frenzy: "He's never going to be a rah-rah, win-one-for-the-Gipper guy. He's a cerebral coach, but [he dishes out] many [motivating] off-color comments."[1996] Belichick takes a workmanlike, blue-collar approach to football and expects each player to act professionally and intelligently at all times.

Patriots players don't let their coach down. They aren't pleasure-seekers who slack off the moment their coach turns his back. For Patriots players and coaches, work is fun. And hard work is really fun. As Belichick's close friend Nick Saban puts it, "Fun-loving is not something you [should aspire to]. You work. You work hard. And good things happen."[1997] Defensive lineman Richard Seymour motivates himself with the example of Michael Jordan:

> "When he came back [in 1994 from retirement], he was rusty and he had to kick off some of the dirt, and he didn't do that well that season. But the following season, he came back and won a championship. It doesn't matter

how good of a football player you are or how talented you are. You still have to put in the work."[1998]

Strive for consistency

"It's hard for linebackers to play when the defensive linemen in front of them aren't consistent. If they don't consistently do what they're supposed to do, then the linebackers are at the mercy of what goes on in front of them. They don't know whether to be here or there because they don't know where the guy in front of them is going to be. So they're hesitant; they're kind of waiting to see where he's going to go so they can kind of fit off him. And that's no good. You can't play that way."[1999]
– *Bill Belichick*

Two of Belichick's favorite words are "consistent" and "consistency," and he praises most highly not players who make spectacular plays but those who perform "consistently":

"When the game's on the line, you want the ball in his hands, and we have confidence that he'll come through. He's been very consistent for us every day in practice in terms of running the ball, catching it, blitz pickup, knowing his assignments… He's been one of our most consistent players, day in and day out. The great thing about Corey Dillon is that when you walk out on that practice field on Wednesday or into the stadium on Sunday, you know exactly what you're gonna get. He gives it to you every single time. And that's a very secure feeling as a head coach."[2000]

Patriots players talk consistently about consistency. Linebacker Mike Vrabel: "We're all so consistent, which is the key in the NFL. You're not going to get Willie [McGinest] bring some superstar [performance] and then the next week just slacking off. You know exactly what you're getting."[2001] Vrabel says no team can become champion playing brilliantly one week and horribly the next: "It's tough to line up week in and week out and be consistent. I think that's the key to every playoff team… The goal is consistency."[2002] Players hyped up on adrenaline and flying after the ball carrier at full speed with little tactical awareness or group cohesion are easily exploited by misdirection: screen passes, reverses, play-action passes, flea flickers, fake punts, and other gadget plays. Passion and intensity are important, but they must be leavened with tactical savvy, and they must be character traits, not fleeting emotional outbursts dialed up minutes before a game. That's why, as Patriots safety Rodney Harrison says, "We strive for consistency. To be up, to be down, it's not good."[2003] Defensive lineman Richard Seymour says, "the biggest issue is consistency for a football team, because you can have a good day, a bad day, but you can never get too high or too low. You just have to float along and stay consistent."[2004] Belichick emphasizes consistency when he describes his ideal team: "Professional, hard working, playing with physical and mental toughness, and able to stand up to a competitive challenge on a week-in and week-out basis."[2005]

Consistency requires more than emotional control. Consistency also requires knowing your job and doing it properly every time. During training, Belichick tells players, "I can't put you in game if you don't know consistently what to do. Just can't do it! Penalties. First-and-twenties. First-and-fifteens. We can't play that way. All right? Fellas, look. Just relax. You've got to concentrate on what the hell you're doing."[2006] Belichick's players have adopted his execution-based mindset. Patriots offensive lineman Joe Andruzzi loves Tom Brady because:

> "He's calm, cool, and collected. He's not a guy that's going to get all nervous and start screaming and stuff. Take for instance the last two Super Bowl's. The last two minutes of the game you just get in that huddle as an offense and (he'd say) 'Alright guys, it's up to us. Let's go do this thing.' That just reflects [on] everybody else on the offense. We want to go out there, and he calms everybody when we're in a tough position but we know what has to be done. Let's go out and do our jobs. He relaxes the huddle."[2007]

Massachusetts General Hospital president Peter L. Slavin, applauds this approach: "A lot of teams rely on emotional highs to succeed. What [Belichick] has is a sustainable solution."[2008] It's also an approach that fosters consistency and predictability. After taking over Notre Dame's football program, former Patriots offensive coordinator Charlie Weis said, "If there's anything we're working to get rid of, it's …inconsistency."[2009] Belichick absorbed his emphasis on preparation and situational awareness over game-day adrenaline while growing up in Navy's football program and observing his father's friendship with and admiration for legendary Cleveland Browns and Cincinnati Bengals head coach Paul Brown. According to father Steve Belichick, "As great as Paul was, I don't think he ever walked into a room and took it over."[2010]

Involve everyone

> "It's hard to keep guys on the bench. It's hard to tell a guy, 'You aren't going to play this week. We're going to play this guy.' The guys do an excellent job of taking a step back... from 'me, me, me,' and really worrying about 'team, team, team.' …Everybody knows that they are going to have an opportunity to play, regardless of whether it's 10 plays or 50 plays."[2011]
> — *Patriots linebacker Rosevelt Colvin*

> "[Rotating players] keeps everybody involved. It can create some different combinations and matchups for you. …At some point along the line, if you ever have to [deviate from] that rotation, then everybody has a lot more

experience than they would if it was one guy playing and the other guy not playing."[2012]

– Bill Belichick

No athlete enjoys sitting on the bench. On most teams, however, there are "starters" and "backups." On the Patriots, such labels are fluid and not particularly meaningful. The Patriots' depth chart is written with a pencil, not a permanent marker. And coaches try to involve every player in every game. As Patriots linebacker Willie McGinest says,

> "'First string,' 'second string,' whatever. Everybody gets reps. Everybody prepares hard. Everybody understands the game plan, because we've been in situations in the last few years where you have two guys go down [with injuries] and other guys step in and play really well."[2013]

Ty Warren and Richard Seymour are the Patriots' normal starters at defensive end. But Jarvis Green is effectively a "starter" in 3rd-and-long situations, where coaches like to use his pass rushing skills. Conversely, run-stuffing nose tackle Ted Washington was a starter but always stood on the sideline on 3rd-and-long because he is a poor pass rusher. Coaches take advantage of players' different strengths by using them in different situations. Even when one player is arguably "better," few Patriots can sleep through a game on the bench. Ty Warren (a former 1st round draft pick) is arguably a "better" defensive end than Jarvis Green (a former 4th round pick), but Green often replaces Warren on passing downs. Coaches rotate players in and out of games for four reasons:

- To boost motivation

- To keep everyone fresh and avoid burnout

- To survive injuries with minimal impact

- To gain strategic and tactical advantage

After several months as Notre Dame's head coach, Charlie Weis said, "We have a pretty good idea who is No. 1 and who's 1A at each position."[2014] It's just a label, but "1A" sounds much better than "backup" or "#2."

Patriots players understand why coaches keep everyone involved, and they embrace rotations as essential to winning. Says Troy Brown, "You can want [the ball in your hands] every play, but you're not going to get it, and you can't complain about it. You've just got to go out there and play ball within the system and success will come."[2015]

Boosts motivation

"Hopefully, what you end up doing is… put people in place and positions, not just at the player level, but the coaching level, the scouting level, the video people, the equipment people, and… everyone understands they're part of the success."[2016]
 – *Scott Pioli, Patriots VP of player personnel*

The Patriots keep every player excited and motivated in part by by singling out each player for recognition and special treatment:

"It actually became fun. We had a blitz for everyone on the defense– everyone who played, not just the starters. The third and fourth corners, for example, had blitzes designed for them with their names attached to the play call. Other formations were named after defensive linemen. If a player knew his blitz was going to be called during the game, his eyes would light up in the meeting room. …sometimes just calling that play once would spark the player to excel for the rest of the game."[2017]

Rotating players obviously motivates "backups." If a boss keeps handing the tough assignments to the same people, others will get bored, slack off, feel resentful, or worse. Less obviously, but perhaps even more importantly, rotating also motivates "starters" by preventing them from becoming too comfortable. Patriots coaches keep "starters" hungry by occasionally handing "their job" to another player:

"When we faced teams with a good gunner [a player who lines up wide on punts and runs downfield to tackle the returner], Ty Law and Lawyer Milloy would come out with the receiving team to block and hold up the gunner… The guys whose positions they take… will get pissed off and even more fired up. Then you rotate them so you get more out of the normal guys."[2018]

Keeps everyone fresh and avoids burnout

"Your front seven has to be kick-[butt] if you want to be successful… [We] keep guys fresh because–when it comes to the 4th quarter–we don't want to known as a team that laid down for anyone."[2019]
 – *Patriots nose tackle Vince Wilfork*

"When guys go down, you have to have guys that can step in without a drop-off. We've got veterans who know how to play the game. They're prepared, and it's fun to watch Bill rotate a lot of guys like that. Everybody gets to play, and that adds years to [the careers of old] guys like me."[2020]
 – *Patriots nose tackle Keith Traylor*

People perform best when they're mentally and physically engaged. Patriots coaches know uninvolved players lose their mental focus and tighten up physically, so "We really don't like the players to sit around for 20, 30, 40 minutes and then stick him back [into the game]. I don't think that is a really good way to take care of players, especially the older ones."[2021] The opposite is also true: if you push someone too hard for too long, you will exhaust them. That's why a Patriots assistant coach repeatedly screamed "Get your rest!" at defensive players as they came off the field following a defensive touchdown during Super Bowl XXXVI. Players must push themselves, but everyone has a breaking point. Wise coaches and wise managers apply optimal pressure, tension and stress, pushing hard but never all the way to the precipice.

The Patriots keep players involved and fresh by swapping them during each game. In 2003, for example, nose tackle Ted Washington and defensive ends Bobby Hamilton and Richard Seymour were usually "starters" but Jarvis Green, Ty Warren, Rick Lyle and Dan Klecko also saw action. The same was true at many positions:

> "Other teams may rotate defensive linemen, but I don't see them rotating much with linebackers and safeties. We rotated everyone. Even Ty [Law] rotated somewhat during [our 2001 Super Bowl season]. ...Belichick's system really made everyone feel they were part of the team. Creating intense competition paid dividends."[2022]

Minimizes impact of injuries

> "[We're] loaded [at cornerback]. And that's a good problem to have. If one goes down, you have another one and you don't lose a beat."[2023]
> *– Patriots cornerback Duane Starks*

NFL players are at severe risk of injury, and that risk has risen in recent seasons. NFL teams had 243 players on injured reserve at the conclusion of the 2002 season, 258 at the finish of the 2003 season, and 296 at the close of 2004.[2024] This prompted the following humorous exchange:

> *Patriots trainer:* "This guy's got a dislocated elbow... He's probably going to be out about eight weeks."
> *Steve Belichick (Bill's father):* "Are you kidding me?! Eight weeks? I dislocated my elbow in college, and I didn't miss a game. I played the whole season with a dislocated elbow. Couldn't bend it. But I played with it."
> *Bill Belichick:* "Didn't seem like we ever had [high ankle sprains] before [ten years ago]. I guess we must have, but it seemed like everybody had a low ankle sprain. But that caught on like bell-bottom pants."[2025]

For many teams, losing a key player is devastating because: 1) The injured starter is more skilled than his backup; 2) The injured starter has had more practice and game time than his backup, so he has absorbed the playbook more completely and is better able to communicate and coordinate with his teammates; and, 3) Teammates become demoralized after losing an "irreplaceable" star.

According to Patriots linebacker Willie McGinest, the Patriots' linebacker rotation minimized all three factors in 2003: "After Rosie [shattered his hip]... Mike Vrabel broke his hand. Ted Johnson missed time. I missed a couple of games. But what we did was rotate. We were on a rotation anyway, so we all kind of picked each other up."[2026] Rotations enable players to cover for one another, helping the team continue winning following injuries. They also help players heal injuries rather than rush back. The Patriots can afford to be cautious with injuries, as kick returner Chad Morton explained after he felt ready to return following ACL surgery: "They're smart about it. They just want me to be healthy. It's a good approach... What's the point if I get out there too early and I get hurt again?"[2027]

The 2005 Patriots will be sorely tested at linebacker after losing three of their 2004 starting linebackers: Roman Phifer failed his physical and was released in early 2005, and in July Tedy Bruschi decided to sit out the season due to a stroke and Ted Johnson suddenly retired due to concern over the many concussions he suffered during his ten-year career: "I just felt like I was really putting myself at risk by playing again. There could be irreparable damage."[2028] With top defensive lineman Richard Seymour holding out, linebacker Rosevelt Colvin joked, "Drama, man. The Patriots are like a soap opera–it's like 'As The World Turns.'"[2029] The Patriots' rotation gives them a better chance to overcome the loss of three starting linebackers, a loss that would devastate most teams. They still have three "starting" linebackers because they have used a rotation of six linebackers: Bruschi, Colvin, Johnson, McGinest, Phifer and Vrabel. Special teamers have also rotated in at linebacker and, therefore, possess some experience: Tully Banta-Cain played some late in the 2004 season. Dan Klecko got some linebacker work early in 2004 before a knee injury ended his season. And Matt Chatham played significant time at linebacker in 2003, including four starts. Surviving the loss of three starters at the same position is almost unheard of, but no one is betting against these Patriots. Their rotation gives them a fighting chance to overcome even multiple losses at a position.

Creates tactical advantage

Rotating players into and out of each game also makes it hard for opponents to figure out what the Patriots are up to. The Patriots can hit opponents too many ways for any team to prepare for every possible attack:

> "[Belichick] seems to play every player on the roster and has neat little packages for each and every one of them. His tight ends are a great example of how hard it is to get a feel for what he's doing. Christian Fauria, Cameron Cleeland and rookie Daniel Graham can all be in together, or any two of them in, or one of them or none of them. In the Pats' first 20 plays I recorded, [the tight ends] were in six different personnel groupings."[2030]

Tom Brady is successful for many reasons, one being that he doesn't fixate on throwing to any particular receiver or location. He spreads the ball around, denying opponents the opportunity to shut down his offense by blanketing one or two "go to" receivers or protecting a certain area of the field. As Patriots quarterback, Drew Bledsoe always looked to tight end Ben Coates when his primary receiver was covered. Over-reliance on Coates helped opponents stop the Patriots offense. No longer. Belichick says: "Tom does a good job of seeing the field. I think he does a good job of utilizing the different receivers and being able to find where the coverage is the lightest and put the ball in those places. And he's pretty accurate with the ball."[2031] When a quarterback always looks to the same receivers, the defense has a major advantage. Instead of forcing throws to his favorite guys, Brady throws to whoever the defense isn't covering. That makes it harder for opponents, acknowledges Eagles safety Brian Dawkins: "Brady does a good job of spreading the ball around to each of them, so you can't key too much on one guy."[2032] As inside linebackers coach Pepper Johnson wrote after the 2001 season, "It's no secret that Troy Brown is our best receiver, but it's hard for a defense to focus on him when there are seven other guys catching the ball."[2033] That's why the Eagles' Sheldon Brown says, "We view all of their receivers as number one guys."[2034] Eagles linebacker Dhani Jones adds that "Brady does a great job on distribution between the middle and the outside of the field... He just sees his receivers [wherever they're open]."[2035]

The Patriots successfully run plays using four or five receivers because: 1) Brady is willing and able to throw to whoever's open; 2) The Patriots have a stable of five or six quality wide receivers, each of whom gets enough practice and game time to perform well; 3) Patriots receivers are unselfish; 4) Patriots receivers are quick off the line of scrimmage, fast and practiced at eluding press coverage, so they force defenders to defend lots of territory soon after the ball is snapped, thus widening the gaps between defensive backs for one another to run into; and, 5) Patriots receivers are, pound-for-pound, the NFL's toughest blockers. The Patriots' "spread offense" forces defenses to drop more defenders into pass protection, simplifies blocking challenges for Patriots offensive linemen, and buys Brady more time to throw the ball. Explains Brady:

> "I like to see the field. I like to spread people out and see who's covering who, where my mismatches are and where the blitzes are coming from. ... It's hard when you line up in a regular set, a regular pro formation [with a fullback and halfback]. The [defense] can bring any one of nine players (on blitzes). They can bring anyone other than the two corners. In the spread or empty formation, we can figure out who's gonna blitz, and then if they're not blitzing, you can just [look at each potential receiver in order] like you normally would."[2036]

On many teams, top receivers zealously guard their playing time. Patriots players focus on running great routes whenever coaches put them in the game and catching the ball whenever Brady throws it their way. Decisions by coaches and quarterbacks are out of their control, so they don't worry about them. Was former #1 receiver Troy Brown anticipating more action after #1 receiver Deion Branch was injured early in 2004? "Hey, I just show up, man. We just have a lot of good players who can play the position well. The more guys you can have to play at a position, the better it is."[2037]

In a television commercial, Tom Brady plugs *Sirius Satellite Radio* as his "new favorite receiver," but—when not filming commercials—Brady confesses his real favorite receiver is "whoever's open"[2038] because "You might be able to throw the ball great, but if you're never throwing it to the right guy then it doesn't matter."[2039] Also, Patriots receivers are well-conditioned and rotated in and out of the game, which drives defensive backs nuts. Eagles cornerback Sheldon Brown says, "They play hard every play... They try to block when they are running the ball and they get after you for sixty minutes. What is impressive too is that they get down the field fast."[2040] And every Patriots receiver runs a mix of short, medium and long routes whereas many other teams have certain receivers run primarily short while other receivers run primarily deep.[2041]

Another reason Brady is successful is that the Patriots don't expect his arm to win every game. Offensive coordinator Charlie Weis believes it's essential to balance the run and the pass. Though the Patriots lacked a strong running attack before 2004 (when Pro Bowl running back Corey Dillon joined), Weis kept defenses on their toes with a mix of runs and passes. The threat of running improves the effectiveness of play-action passes (i.e., passing plays that start off looking like running plays) by forcing defensive players to stay in position to tackle the runner rather than commit fully to stopping the pass. The Patriots beautifully balanced running and passing in their 2001 Super Bowl season, running 506 times and passing 505 times.[2042] When they got pass happy in the first two months of 2002 (running 159 times and passing 307 times[2043]), they struggled. Trying to involve everyone helps ensure your play-calling is balanced.

Don't burn out

After Tom Brady threw in the first thirteen training camp practices of 2005, Coach Belichick ordered him to skip the next one. Knowing how much Brady hates forced vacations, quarterbacks coach Josh McDaniels delivered the message forcefully: "Belichick doesn't want you to practice today. Don't fight him on it, and don't be a pain in the butt."[2044] Brady confessed, "over the long haul, it's always good [to take an occasional break]. And the coach does a great job of trying to keep guys fresh."[2045] The next day, Belichick gave his whole team 2½ days off in the middle of training camp. Brady threw much less over the next two weeks, explaining:

> "It's a long, long season. There's been a few years where my arm hasn't felt very good, and I think a lot of it is the precaution of making sure it never gets to the point where you have to back off in the regular season because

that is not really what you want to do. You try to take advantage of some of the rest while you can afford it."[2046]

Brady adds that he's hardly the only veteran given time off:

> "A lot of… the older guys get a day off or an afternoon off. Troy [Brown] gets an afternoon off every once in a while. Christian [Fauria] does. Willie [McGinest] does. You just try to make sure you're fresh, because the last thing you want is to start the regular season in Week 1 and miss Wednesday or Thursday practice because something is sore or because you're tired."[2047]

As Cleveland Browns head coach, Bill Belichick made sure his assistants took time off every Wednesday and Thursday to spend with their families.[2048] Belichick expects great effort from his assistants, but his consistent, predictable scheduling of family time helps his assistants and their families maximizes the value of their time together, raising the quality of free time, though not its quantity.

When Notre Dame called Patriots offensive coordinator Charlie Weis during the 2004 season to set up an interview for its head coach vacancy, Weis knew exactly when he would be available: "They asked if they could come visit me in person, and I said, 'Yeah, but it will have to be after 11:30 at night because that's what time I work until.' So they came [then]."[2049] Maura Weis knows when to expect Charlie home, almost never: "We don't see him a lot during the football season. Sometimes in the NFL, we'd only see him six to eight hours a week. That's besides sleep time, which he doesn't get much of at all during football season."[2050] Belichick is not the only Weis abuser. When Bill Parcells offered Weis his first NFL job, Parcells told him he "wanted to hire a guy with basically no life."[2051] But Charlie and Maura have a strong bond and enjoy watching movies, relaxing on the beach and just talking together.

Wise managers avoid overworking employees or themselves. But "burnout" is about enthusiasm and energy, not the number of hours spent working. Some workers are exhausted and depressed by their jobs after just several hours. Others can work all day, every day and still feel a thrill. Belichick loves his job. He works insane hours because he wants to, not because he has to. He also carefully screens potential assistants and players to ensure they love football so much that they will *want* to put in the hours he expects of them. He doesn't want his assistants or players burning out. Finding people who love their jobs is even more important in staving off burnout than the number of hours worked.

Belichick works hours no boss could ever force an employee to work, but he doesn't consider it "work." And Belichick is blessed with a body that can tolerate less sleep than mere mortals: "Even when he was a child, Bill never needed much sleep. We'd send him up to bed, then find him reading or drawing. He can go on five hours' sleep a night for quite a while."[2052] Pepper Johnson claims "in the sixteen years I've known him I've never seen the man yawn—not once."[2053] Former Patriots defensive lineman Chad Eaton agrees "You'll never see him yawn. He's tireless."[2054]

Rodney Harrison: "I don't think he sleeps, and he never looks tired. He's unbelievable."[2055] After his first game as Patriots head coach, "Belichick went home, slept, and returned to the office. At 1:30 a.m."[2056] *60 Minutes* reports Belichick arrives at his office at 5:00 a.m.[2057] Despite his inhuman schedule, Belichick doesn't let football consume his life: "It is a pretty full-time job, I have been down this road, especially to the point of diminishing returns, and I think it is important that I come in every day fresh and ready to go."[2058] For Belichick, several hours is a great night's sleep.

Though Belichick spends less time at home than most parents, he does have a strong bond with his daughter Amanda. He enjoys watching her lacrosse games at Wesleyan when his schedule permits. They have fun boating and fishing on Nantucket every summer. And she hugged him just seconds after he won his first Super Bowl. Belichick is a supportive–not a demanding–father whose only concern is "That she'll be happy... Whatever [she] want[s], as long as she's happy and feels fulfilled."[2059] He says Rod Stewart's song "Forever Young," which includes the words "Whatever road you choose, I'm right behind you, win or lose," sums up his feelings. Sadly, the stress of coaching in the NFL (a.k.a. "No Fun League" and "No Family Life") apparently contributed to Belichick' separation from his wife and high school sweetheart. An unnamed source said, "He's a machine at work. He's there literally around the clock, but he's also a great father. The only time he skips out [of work] is to get to one of the kids' games. But would you want to be his wife?"[2060] Belichick isn't even unusual in this respect; an NFL executive says the divorce rate over two decades is 70%.[2061]

Even those who love their work can burn out. So, after the Patriots won their second Super Bowl, taskmaster Belichick dialed down the training camp torture level from his standard "unbearable" to "barely tolerable." He apparently figured his team was in less need of pounding since: 1) Their offseason was one month shorter than the offseasons of non-playoff teams; and, 2) His players had continued training intensely during the offseason. Belichick didn't want to overwork them.

Tom Brady similarly strives to avoid burnout despite incredible demands on his time following Super Bowl victories:

> "There are a lot of obligations and expectations I'm expected to fulfill, and I try to do as many as I can, but... [after winning my first Super Bowl], I didn't have much free time and that mentally tired me out. I'd go from working out straight to something else, straight to something else and back to working out. Now, I'm scheduling more time to relax my mind."[2062]

Not coincidentally, the only other coach to win a Super Bowl during the Patriots dynasty–Tampa Bay Bucs coach Jon Gruden–shares both Belichick's minimal need for sleep and his childlike love of football. Gruden writes that "I'm up at 3:17 A.M. most days."[2063] This is no hardship because "as a little kid I was always up way before the crack of dawn... I've [always] been able to stay up late and still get up early and still feel pretty fresh."[2064] In college, Gruden was worried enough to try sleeping pills and consult doctors and even a hypnotist before being diagnosed as having "a gift [for] function[ing] perfectly well on minimal sleep."[2065] Gruden does not fill his spare hours with frivolity: "[Football is] really the only interest I have outside of my wife and our three boys."[2066]

If you are lucky enough that your job is also your favorite hobby, count yourself blessed and work like mad. If you feel rested after several hours sleep and your job feels like "fun," not "work," then you too may win your profession's Super Bowl some day. But if your name's not "Gruden" or "Belichick," you will burn out if you do not budget time to sleep well and do things you enjoy.

Stay loose

Patriots players and coaches make sure the team stays loose. "Work hard, and play hard" could be players' motto, but they would define "playing hard" as playing practical jokes on one another and playing dominoes, backgammon, and video games together, not doing tequila shots at wild parties with scantily-clad women. Compared with many other professional athletes, Patriots players are nerdy teacher's pets.

To relieve stress and keep players loose before Super Bowl XXXVIII, Belichick pulled out a "scandalous" tape of assistant coach Pepper Johnson:

> "Many of the Patriots always will associate the song 'Brick House' with their Super Bowl experience. In a midweek meeting, 'coaches tape' took on a different meaning when the team was shown a tape of inside linebackers coach Pepper Johnson awkwardly dancing to the tune at a Super Bowl event during his rookie season 17 years ago. The team was rolling in the aisles."[2067]

Commit to be happy

> "We have a lot of respect and love for [Tedy] Bruschi, but he's gone… There's nothing he can do to help us on the field, physically… You can't keep referring back to Bruschi and [Ted] Johnson. We love them, but they're gone. That's unfortunate for us, but we have to move on."[2068]
> *– Patriots safety Rodney Harrison*

> "Yeah, they're gone, but it's a sport about opportunities. We got a lot of guys that have been presented opportunities, and I'm one of those guys… It's an adjustment, something different."[2069]
> *– Patriots linebacker Mike Vrabel, on moving from outside LB to insider LB because of Bruschi and Johnson's disappearance*

"Change is inevitable, and we deal with it."[2070]
– *Bill Belichick*

Bill Belichick says that when playing on the road "in a hostile environment… We'll have to generate our own energy and enthusiasm for the game. We're not going to get any from the crowd."[2071] Patriots safety Rodney Harrison has an even more positive way of coping with deafening fan noise: "When they're cheering, I just think of them as cheering for me."[2072] Because your brain interprets the world around you, you can–to a substantial degree–control your reactions to external events… or at least moderate their intensity. We're not leaves blowing in the wind. Wise people don't let their environment push them around. In the brilliant movie *Life is Beautiful*, Roberto Benigni's character Guido not only uses humor to keep himself and those around him sane in a Nazi death camp but also hides the terrible truth from his young son by tricking him into believing the concentration camp is actually a reality show where contestants are competing to win a tank.

In English, we say "someone provoked me," but the truth is usually that "someone tried to provoke me, and I responded as they hoped I would." Others can't manipulate your mind unless you follow their script. The more conscious you are of the dichotomy between external events and your reaction to external events, the better equipped you are to react in ways that benefit you, as Harrison does when he interprets cheering as support. Harrison understands the power of his mind so well that he even tricks himself into imagining slights and provocations because he plays better with "something to prove." Choosing a constructive response is equally important when "fate" deals you a blow, as Apple and Pixar CEO Steve Jobs explains:

> "How can you get fired from a company you started? …At 30, I was out. And very publicly out. What had been the focus of my entire adult life was gone, and it was devastating. …It turned out that getting fired from Apple was the best thing that could ever have happened to me… It freed me to enter one of the most creative periods of my life… Sometimes life hits you in the head with a brick. Don't lose faith."[2073]

In 2004, Troy Brown experienced the life of an Arena League player–never stepping off the field–wide receiver, punt returner, defensive back, ballboy, jock strap holder, bus driver, vending machine repairman, whatever. Bill Belichick became mean old boss Bill Lumbergh from the movie *Office Space*: "If you could just go ahead and make sure you play nickelback from now on, that would be greeeaaaat!"

> "Troy, we're gonna need to go ahead and move you downstairs into 'Storage B.' We have some new receivers coming in on offense, and we need all the space we can get. So if you could go ahead and pack up your stuff and move it down to defense, that would be terrific, OK?"

After Brown helped his team win its third Super Bowl by moving to defense and learning a totally new position in his twelfth season–sacrificing potential bonuses of "$200,000 for 50 catches and $400,000 for 60 catches,"[2074] how did his team reward him? How did the Patriots organization thank a player for giving 100% of himself to the team for more seasons than his coach, any teammate or even the team owner? They cut him.

After the New Orleans Saints made Brown an offer and virtually guaranteed him its third receiver slot, the Patriots offered less money–practically the veteran minimum–and, unlike the Saints, promised him nothing: no starting job, no playing time, no roster spot. So, when Troy Brown re-signed with the Patriots, he was bitter, right?

Brown held court at a news conference decked out in Patriots gear and beaming gleefully. He told reporters how thrilled he was to be back. What of the $5 million his original contract called for him to earn in 2005 being slashed to $800,000?

> "My goal was to get [a new deal] worked out. It didn't happen, and free agency started. ...I'm here now. Everything that happened in between there, I didn't want to come in here holding any grudges. I wanted to come in here and be happy and be the player I always have been and be the guy I've always been in the locker room and not bring any extra baggage in with me. That is all cleaned up."[2075]

Will Brown reduce his effort a tad now that he's earning just 16% of what he was scheduled to earn? "Whatever I am asked to do, I am going to give them 110 percent."[2076]

My freshman year at Harvard, the weather was gloomy, cold and rainy all fall, and I repeatedly, audibly and only half-jokingly beat myself up for turning down Stanford. One day, my annoyed roommate said something to the effect of, "Either shut up or transfer." He said it far more politely, but his words hit me hard–as I imagine getting hit by Corey Dillon must feel–and the lesson stuck: Once you make a decision, make the best of it. Looking back with regret or anger helps no one. Patriots sacrifice their finances and free time to be Patriots. Belichick and Pioli make clear to free agents that they expect such sacrifices, and players who sign on the dotted line maturely accept these sacrifices as the cost of belonging to a great team.

At least one Patriots fan learned this lesson from Troy Brown: "Hard work, positive attitude and desire to win. He not only rubbed off on his teammates but many fans as well, myself included. Troy Brown is in my [Hall of Fame] ... He changed my attitude from negative to positive over the last 6 or 7 years."[2077]

Determination to remain upbeat enables Patriots to shrug off bad news and stay focused on doing their jobs. After the Patriots released aging linebacker Roman Phifer and Tedy Bruschi decided to skip the 2005 season due to health concerns following his stroke, fellow linebacker Ted Johnson wasn't panicking or gloomy about the loss of two starters, including the defense's heart and soul: "We just will [survive Tedy's loss]. We have no choice. There's no time for self-pity. Not in this business. [Coach] doesn't allow that."[2078]

Staying positive, however, does not mean stupidly ignoring reality. A week after making the statement above, Ted Johnson himself retired, but not because of Bruschi: "Something didn't feel right with my body, really, this whole off-season." He said doctors had uncovered "enough evidence to have serious concerns for some head trauma" and "The closer I got to camp, the more I started feeling my body was telling me something, and I just couldn't ignore the evidence," so "I can no longer ignore the severe short- and long-term complications of the concussive head injuries I have sustained over the years."

Whichever Patriots take over for Bruschi and Johnson will undoubtedly adopt the "no surrender" mentality Johnson expressed over Bruschi's loss. As one of those new linebackers, Monty Beisel, says, "Unfortunately, we've lost a couple of our core guys that have been around here in the past, so I guess it's time for new leaders to step up."[2079]

Enjoy pleasing your customers

"I was going to my hotel [in Mexico], and these little kids ran up to me [asking for my autograph]. It was surprising, but at the same time it was good to see the effect you can have on others by doing good things. For the little kids to look up to me like that, I was very proud of that."[2080]
– *Patriots receiver Deion Branch*

Patriots players draw energy from their "customers": fans, family, and teammates.

Starting in training camp, players feed off fans' excitement. Before Super Bowl XXXIX, special teams captain Larry Izzo acknowledged the fans:

"We had a nice send off at the stadium before we left on our flight. It was really special to see fans come out to wish us well. It was a large group, and it was cold. As always, the Patriots fans showed how much they love football and their team. The fans have played a big part in our success over the years. …Foxboro is always a tough place for teams to come in and play, and I think [our fans] play a big factor in that."[2081]

Patriots nose tackle Ted Washington called Patriots fans "the greatest in the league" and admitted he got all choked up as the Patriots' team bus departed Gillette Stadium for Super Bowl XXXVIII:

"When we were leaving the stadium to come here on Sunday and all of those people were lined up in freezing cold temperatures to see us off, I got really emotional. It took everything I had to hold back the tears as we were driving off. We kept going, and the fans just kept going right on down the line. It was very emotional to me."[2082]

Offensive guard Joe Andruzzi also was awed by the pre-Super Bowl XXXVIII send-off rally, "I was freezing. To see our fans out there; I think we've got the best fans in the league. It's unbelievable. They've been behind us week-in and week-out, no matter what goes on. Without them, it wouldn't be a game. It's unbelievable, and it's great support for us."[2083]

Patriots also love making their families happy by winning. Troy Brown said of Super Bowl XXXVIII:

> "I had my two boys there with me to go over to the stands, and to be able to grab them and pull them down onto the field with me. To see the look on their faces with all the confetti falling down, it was just wonderful, just great. To see everybody with their kids and enjoying the moment—nothing can beat [that feeling]."[2084]

Offensive coordinator Charlie Weis takes special care of his favorite fans: "Before every game, I look for my wife and my son... I make eye contact with them and point to them just to say hello... I've been doing that for years. That's why a lot of times there are a lot of people in the stands figuring I was waving at them."[2085]

But winning for one another is players' biggest motivator. Troy Brown says, "I'd do anything for these players on this team. Playing defense happened to be one [contribution] this year, and if I have to do it again, I'd do it again."[2086] Special teams captain Larry Izzo agrees: "It's a unique situation running onto to the field celebrating with your teammates that you're Super Bowl champs... That high carries through when you [return home] and have 10,000 people at the stadium that are there to greet you. Then the next day you have a parade and there are 1.5 million people there. You feel like a rock star."[2087]

If you build a great product or organization, your customers will become fans, perhaps even fanatics. And this loyalty will motivate and inspire your personnel. Says Patriots owner Robert Kraft:

> "The fans really made a difference... the way they supported us in the games in the rain and the games in the snow, minus-15 degrees—the coldest day in my life when we played Tennessee. It was unbelievable. We thought our no-shows would be huge. The only difference we did is we gave away coffee and hot chocolate to people coming in and then we spiked it in the stands (joke). ...Nobody left. Did you see the Miami game? The Miami game when [fans] threw the snow up—it was a spontaneous thing. It's just a great tribute to the fans of our region and how they've supported the team."[2088]

EXCESSIVE EMOTION SHORT-CIRCUITS THINKING

"Revenge is a dish best served cold."
– *Sicilian proverb*

"You can play hard. You can play aggressive. You can give 120 percent. But if one guy is out of position, then someone's running through the line of scrimmage and he's going to gain a bunch of yards."[2089]
– *Bill Belichick*

"We just got too excited. We let all the emotion and adrenaline get the best of us, and if we can control that, we'll be OK."[2090]
– *Tennessee Volunteers linebacker Jason Mitchell, after a bad first half against Auburn in 2004*

"There are different mentalities among linebackers and quarterbacks. As a linebacker, you can let the adrenaline flow and sort of let it take over you. You become animalistic. As a quarterback, if you get too excited and too ramped up, it can affect your game."[2091]
– *Patriots linebacker Tedy Bruschi*

After reading numerous disparaging remarks about themselves in the recently-released book *Patriot Reign*, the 2004 Bills were as pumped up as any team could be, and their overzealousness hurt them in a two-touchdown loss. They repeatedly committed avoidable penalties: a 15-yard unnecessary roughness penalty for a late hit (body-slamming Patriots running back Corey Dillon after he dropped a pass) on the very first play of the game; an offsides penalty on the second play of the game; a 15-yard roughing-the-passer penalty ("blow to the head"); an unsportsmanlike conduct penalty on receiver Eric Moulds for saying nasty things to an official; many false starts; *etc.* Afterwards, Patriots tight end Christian Fauria said, "We knew this game was going to come down to us being poised, confident, and executing."[2092] He implied Bills players had pressed too hard while the Patriots had played alert team football: "The more chances we get, the more we think we'll do something good. It's just poise. When people try too hard to make plays, it's like a round peg in a square hole. We just play. We just do our stuff."[2093]

Before Super Bowl XXXVIII, did Belichick whip his players into a frenzy? Were players "excited"? Were they "pumped"? Were they "psyched"? Were they "revved up"? No. Wide receiver David Givens says, "We just came out focused, and we knew we had to execute."[2094] Focus and execution. Reason, not passion, is what Belichick believes wins football games:

"Winning or losing in the NFL is about execution. It's not about banging your head against a wall or a locker on your way out to the field. That's not what this game is about. That's over by the second play. What this game is about is whether or not you can execute under pressure in critical situations."[2095]

Late in the Super Bowl, after the Panthers scored to take the lead, Willie McGinest said to a defensive teammate on the sideline: "Hey, this is the Super Bowl, man. We're going to have some adversity. We just got to stay together. We're gonna work it out."[2096] Simultaneously, Charlie Weis was exhorting his offense: "Let's answer right back now. Let's go. Composure! Let's answer right back."[2097] They responded with a touchdown drive. After Carolina fired back with another touchdown, Panthers kicker John Kasay kicked off with so much emotion that he hooked his kick out of bounds like a ferocious but wayward tee shot that soars into the air before swerving into the trees. The Patriots calmly and methodically marched down for another Super Bowl-winning field goal drive. Clinical. Methodical. Surgical.

Belichick stresses that pre-game emotions can drain players' energy even before kickoff and cause players to play too hard early in games. Anyone who watched the fourth quarter of Super Bowl XXXVIII witnessed two defenses that had burned all the fuel in their tanks and were running on fumes. So, before Super Bowl XXXIX, every Patriot understood—as soon-to-be Super Bowl MVP Deion Branch explained—"You don't want to get too excited early in the week."[2098] As Patriots players conserved energy, Eagles head coach Andy Reid said his players were "wound up every day," "always talking and always going 100 miles per hour" and "wired up and ready to go."[2099] According to Tom Brady:

> "The one thing Coach doesn't want us to do is to get all this emotion and energy going and try to sustain it for two weeks. At some point, it needs to build, and I think that first week of practice is getting your feet wet, and understand[ing] what we're trying to do and understand[ing our opponent]. [During the second week], it's going to be fine tuning and really kind of ratcheting [the emotion] up."[2100]

Even the always excited Tedy Bruschi read his coach's memo: "You don't want to get yourself worked up [early in the week]. You just want to stay calm, and as the week goes on you really start to get serious about physical preparation as well as mental preparation."[2101] Bruschi had the same clock-punching mindset in the 2003 playoffs:

> "You have to look at it just the way you have looked at every other game. You prepare the same. You focus the same. It just so happens to be the AFC championship game, and—if we win this—we will get to the big one. You don't want to magnify it too big where you get too stressed out or too excited or too anxious or anything like that. Just realize we will get it done."[2102]

Another reason Belichick discourages excessive emotion—in himself and his players—is that it interferes with thinking:

> "I have to make a lot of decisions, and I don't have a lot of time to make them. If I'm emotionally caught up in a game, it's hard for me to calculate

the information that I need to make the decisions. I try to remain calm and be analytical and to leave the emotional aspect of the game to the participants."[2103]

"I make better decisions when I try to stay even-keeled and try to think about the next situation—what's coming up—and think about the decisions I have to make rather than jumping up and down about a play that's already over, good or bad. ...[Making decisions] is what people are counting on me for... The worst thing is for [others] to be waiting for me to make a decision and me not making it because I'm out doing cartwheels because we just made a first down."[2104]

So, while many coaches give rousing locker room speeches, Coach Belichick urges players to remain calm, especially during games. Patriots cornerback Tyrone Poole feels a lunch pail pre-game vibe from Belichick: "Normally, with the couple of teams I've been on, the coach walks around and says, 'Good luck,' and things like that. But he's a serious guy, and that's the way he wants his players to be—serious when we go out there. We're out there to do a job, even in a preseason game."[2105] Kicker Adam Vinatieri shares Belichick's view that emotion is his enemy: "You try to just make every kick the same, no matter what the situation. A 40-yard field goal is a 40-yard field goal."[2106]

On the sidelines during Super Bowl XXXIX, Belichick gave players another de-motivational speech: "Let's spend a little more time focusing on our job and less time jawing and pushing them. Just do our job and get on to the next play."[2107] Players who are too pumped up jump offsides, commit late-hit and roughing-the-passer penalties, get fooled by screens and draws and reverses, blow blocking assignments, *etc*.

Though Belichick realizes many players are excessively emotional, he isn't anti-emotion: "When you step out on the field, you're trying to hit them [and] they're trying to hit you. That's the game... When you step out there, you don't want to be just going for a Sunday stroll. You'll get blown up in a hurry."[2108] In fifth gear, race cars are hard to control and prone to overheating. Belichick wants his players playing in fourth gear: fast, but under control.

Balancing emotion and conscious thought has been scientifically proven to produce optimal sports performance, at least in the narrow domain of golf putting. Arizona State professor Debbie Crews won *Golf Magazine*'s "Best Science in Golf" award for proving that many amateur putters over-think each putt, especially when anxious and stressed. By monitoring brain waves as people putted in a lab, she demonstrated that the best putters quell extraneous stress-related activity in their brains' left hemispheres (the hemisphere primarily responsible for logical, sequential and analytical reasoning) before striking the ball. The left hemispheres of amateurs are so energized by these extraneous stress-induced thoughts that their left brain images become bright red.[2109] Successful putters have less left hemisphere "chatter" and somewhat more active right hemispheres (the right hemisphere being primarily responsible for creativity, intuition and integrated, synthetic, holistic analysis). Optimal performance occurs when players know what they're doing so well that they don't need to think about it (left hemisphere) and instead "just do it" instinctively (right hemisphere) with neither excessive emotion nor excessive conscious thought:

> "As people get ready to perform, the left hemisphere tends to quiet and the right hemisphere becomes slightly more active. ...What we end up with is more balance in the brain. It's very important that the left side quiets. That's our verbal, analytic side. When an athlete is performing well, it's automatic, it's effortless."[2110]

Crews' studies confirm earlier psychology research findings that anxiousness erodes the left hemisphere's ability to function properly. This in turn confirms a tenet of Zen Buddhism:

> "Crucial to the philosophy of Zen [Buddhism] is the idea that our normal state of consciousness ruins the quality of the Zen experience. As soon as we consciously think about our performance, we are no longer one with it. Trying harder at a task only compounds this separation. The discipline of the Zen archer can be found in the performer's ability to still the mind, remove mental interference, and allow instinctively honed skills to manifest themselves naturally."[2111]

Crews' results also confirm the finding that athletes "in flow" feel confident and shut off their self-critical minds and don't worry about external critics:

> "When energy is taken up in worrying about yourself, it is taken away from the performance. Worry often manifests itself as distractibility. Attention wanders from the task, and often in moments of pressure, the self-worrying athlete fails because of a lack of focus that stems simply from insufficient confidence... Awareness of the body and its movements is often heightened in flow. It is the awareness of one's ego, or social identity, that recedes into the background. The more attention we invest in the body and its performance, the less is left over to ruminate about saving face or impressing others."[2112]

Sports psychologists say too much excitement is as harmful as too little excitement. Getting too "pumped up" before a football game inhibits performance identically to stress and anxiety. Over-stimulation makes it hard to think and react properly:

> "[When] athletes are over-amped... [they] frequently dread the performance and can't wait for it to end. They're plagued by self-doubts and negative thinking. They may feel sick to their stomach and even throw up

before the start. Or they may have made the performance so important in their head that they press and try too hard."[2113]

The Patriots traded the Cardinals a third-round draft pick for cornerback Duane Starks in part because Starks remained calm in the 2000 playoffs, intercepting two passes in the AFC Championship Game and another in Super Bowl XXXV. Starks says:

> "You can't be overanxious just because you're in the playoffs. You have to stay calm and stay disciplined, because if you've been playing well the whole year and you get to the playoffs, then try to do something different, you're messing your game up… Whatever you've been doing that's been working, you have to do the same thing, because no matter what, you're still facing a receiver, you're still facing the same type of guy that's going to go out there and make plays. Error-free football wins games."[2114]

Anyone lucky enough to have watched legendary Baltimore Colts quarterback Johnny Unitas observed Brady-like calm. Unitas himself said, "Anything I do, I always have a reason for." Unitas' receiver Raymond Berry admired "his uncanny instinct for calling the right play at the right time [and] his icy composure under fire," and running back Buddy Young couldn't believe how "He'd get knocked on his fanny play after play, yet he'd be right up there at the spot where the referee was putting the ball down, and then he'd be checking the clock and knowing how much yardage he needed."[2115] Rationality under fire was Unitas' not-so-secret weapon. And Unitas' confidence was infectious in the huddle. Colts tight end John Mackey famously said it's "like being in the huddle with God." Patriots describe Brady in similar terms.

If Knute Rockne spoke to Patriots players before a game, over-excited heads would start exploding in the locker room. Linebacker Rosevelt Colvin says he once got so excited during a game that he nearly passed out. Before every game, I recoil in horror watching Tom Brady and tight end Daniel Graham bang heads like dueling rams. Receiver Deion Branch agrees this emotional spectacle is insane: "You have to watch out for that… They [bang helmets] three times. I sit and watch them. I think there is something wrong with both of them, but they do that and I guess they get going from that. I don't know."[2116] Belichick realizes that his players love football so passionately and hate losing so intensely that he must guard about excessive emotion, not insufficient emotion. Deion Branch says, "Coach always came to me and told me not to get so emotional about the game."[2117] Branch says Belichick lectures the team to stay calm and avoid committing dumb "emotional" penalties:

> "He talks to the whole team. I know I'm one of the guys he's talking about though. It's just my nature. You've got to get yourself going. You've got to get your team going. I try to let my emotions and my play get the guys going sometimes. I feel like if I'm going, then the team will get going. I haven't

been in a game where I haven't been up, and we've been winning. So that's a good thing."[2118]

Some players naturally possess the construction zone ethic Belichick lusts after. Nose tackle Vince Wilfork, for example, says "I'm not a talker... I wasn't brought up that way. You'll never see me jawing at offensive linemen. You'll never see me dancing and all that stuff in a game."[2119]

While striving together toward collective excellence, each Patriot experiences a steady stream of "flow," a near-magical sensation of being so engrossed in their favorite activity that they lose track of time and feel "in the zone." Pursuing a challenge that engages you and unites you with others who also love pursuing that same challenge produces wonderful "flow" experiences that money cannot buy. A team full of players in love with their "work" will outperform a team whose players are playing for fame or fortune rather than the pure joy of the experience itself. The same is true of any organization. Any company whose employees love coming to work every morning, enjoy collaborating with colleagues to accomplish things, and are too engaged by their work to clock-watch will be extremely successful.

The Patriots are not the first Super Bowl champion to rely on flow. When the Dallas Cowboys won back-to-back Super Bowls in 1992 and 1993, head coach Jimmy Johnson built his teams around the concept of "flow":

> "For many years, I've admired Dr. Csikszentmihalyi's pioneering work and tried to apply his concepts on the football field. Some people have labeled my approach as 'intense,' but the more accurate term might be 'in flow.' Being totally absorbed in the task at hand is essential to becoming a sports champion. *Flow in Sports* tells you how to get into that positive, winning mindset."[2120]

Emotions can be especially counterproductive for players who rely heavily on their brains during games. The Patriots drafted Tom Brady after falling in love with his competitiveness and calmness under pressure. As Michigan's quarterback, Brady threw an interception to Penn State cornerback Bhawoh Joe that dumped his team into a 27-17 hole with just 9:44 left to play. Instead of sulking or getting mad, Brady focused even more intensely before leading Michigan to two touchdowns and a 31-27 victory. Brady wanted to win so badly that "Brady—who is one quarterback that might lose to Bernie Kosar in a foot race—decided to impersonate Antwaan Randle El during the waning moments of the game, scrambling 15 yards for a key first down and rumbling five yards for a touchdown."[2121] Brady "runs" as fast as Jesse Owens... with two broken legs, so Brady running twenty yards on one drive is mind over matter. How slow is Brady? Michigan designed a play in which Brady was supposed to fake a leg injury to get backup quarterback Drew Henson in. While practicing, teammate Aaron Shea told Brady to "Just run normal. People will think you're hurt."[2122] When you build a team full of guys like Brady–who will run to win football games even though he couldn't run to save his life–you have a locker room full of winners who will do anything to prepare to win. But, as competitive as Brady is, he raises his game not by pumping himself up but by calming himself down.

Brady's inhuman calm and focus during the closing minutes of Super Bowls–when even most fans are nervous wrecks–is one of his greatest assets. Patriots offensive tackle Matt Light says "Tom never lets his emotions get in the way of the game."[2123] Patriots cornerback Ty Law is awed: "'Cool as the other side of the pillow.' That's how he is. That's his biggest attribute–he never gets rattled. He's probably as calm as any quarterback that's ever played the game. To me, to be so young and do that is incredible."[2124] Most incredibly, Brady even fell asleep before starting in his first Super Bowl: "I was relaxed ... calm and confident. The locker room was quiet, so I just put my head back and had a little snooze."[2125]

> "I was laying in the locker room before the game, and I fell asleep. I woke up and said to myself, 'I didn't think I'd feel this good.' I don't know how to explain it. You just convince yourself that it's just a game. It's just another game–even though everything leading up to it tells you how big it is."[2126]

Though Belichick's speeches are fact-laden and low-key, they do inspire players. Belichick's logic and understated delivery can be as motivational and inspirational as any fiery speech. Consider his pre-game talk before his team avenged a 31-0 loss to the Bills with a 31-0 victory: "Need a big push this week. Those guys got us pretty good [last time]. You don't always get a chance to settle the score during the season, but we got this one. We're going to need to take advantage of it this week." Here's the end of his pep talk before Super Bowl XXXVIII as he unveils the 2001 team's Vince Lombardi Trophy for players to admire:

> "You earn a championship. It's yours. No one can take it away from you. You keep it. This [trophy] isn't about the past. It stands for team, not statistics. It's the team that's toughest, smartest, and most confident. It's all about execution, as it has been all season."[2127]

Belichick's delivery lacks fire-and-brimstone, but his impact is equally powerful. Five months after that speech, players were still buzzing:

> "I was just kidding with Deion (Branch) and Troy (Brown), going over the speech Bill gave before the Super Bowl. Troy said he was ready to run through a brick wall. It was just that feeling. We want that again. Once you get that taste in your mouth, anything less is unacceptable."[2128]

Almost immediately after arriving at Patriots training camp, Grant Steen sensed Belichick's no-nonsense attitude and noted the similarity to his college coach, Kirk Ferentz–college football's Coach of the Year in 2002 after rebuilding University of Iowa football–who served as the Cleveland Browns' offensive line coach in the 1990s while Belichick was the Browns' head coach:

"Coach Ferentz is real even-keeled. After games, he's not jumping up and down high-fiving everybody. He doesn't get really rah-rah. And, again, just in the short time with Coach Belichick it's that same business attitude. He's coaching everyone to get better. Coach Ferentz demands respect from everybody and that's one of the first things coach Belichick mentioned in our meetings–just respect everybody."[2129]

REWARD SUCCESS

"What matters is whether resources are being allocated to produce results and on the basis of results."[2130]
 – Peter Drucker

"Coach Belichick gives six preferred parking spots to the hardest working players in the offseason, and Tom [Brady] was right at the top again this offseason."[2131]
 – Patriots owner Bob Kraft

"I'd drive [Belichick] to the airport, and on the way out of the car, he would throw me a Ben Franklin [$100 bill] and tell me to fill up the tank. Hey, he'd lived those jobs himself, so he understood. At the end of the season in Cleveland, he would turn around and write me a personal check–and I'm not talking $100 here. He'd write this check, money that made a difference, and if you objected he would say, 'Look, you did a good job. Shut up and take it.'"[2132]
 – Scott Pioli, reflecting back on his $14,000-a-year job with Belichick's Cleveland Browns

Communist societies eventually collapse because people lacking incentives eventually become lazy. As a Russian joke says, "They pretend to pay us, and we pretend to work." But suffering is great in excessively capitalistic societies because few corporations have morals other than maximizing profit and because minimalist government provides no safety net or regulatory oversight to protect individuals against crippling medical costs, lousy schools, unemployment, pollution, monopolistic exploitation, counterfeit products, scams, accounting fraud, market manipulation, etc.

Just as a great society requires both a vibrant private economy and a government that curbs the worst business behaviors, so too–I believe–a great employee compensation scheme provides rewards significant enough to acknowledge good performance but not so substantial that reward-seeking warps behavior, encourages individualism or promotes ass-kissing. One firm I worked for gave me a framed piece of paper acknowledging my contributions. Had executives really wanted to thank me, they could have given me a gift of some value, perhaps a $200 gift certificate. Belichick gives such rewards: post-season "thank you" checks to young Scott Pioli, prime parking spots for the most diligent players, etc. "He tossed a Reebok catalogue to a few of the 20-somethings on his office staff and told them to pick what they wanted."[2133]

In 2002, the Patriots acknowledged defensive end Bobby Hamilton's contribution to their Super Bowl championship by giving him "an unsolicited raise worth around $200,000."[2134] In 2004, the Patriots rewarded two selfless and loyal wide receivers: In March, they gave a $250,000 bonus to David Patten, whom many believed wouldn't survive the intensive competition for wide receiver spots on the 2004 roster. (He did but became a free agent after 2004.) And in May 2004 they guaranteed Troy Brown's $2.25 million 2004 salary, high for an aging player whose production had been declining.

The Patriots attempt to reward players in proportion to their contribution. When they're confident that a player will play well, they offer a straight salary. But when they cannot predict a player's performance, they offer a performance-based compensation scheme. After joining the Patriots in 2004, running back Corey Dillon's compensation depended heavily on how many yards he gained. After he earned the maximum $2.25 million bonus for running 1,600+ yards and impressed everyone with his maturity and competitiveness, the Patriots happily gave him a large signing bonus and base salaries for 2005 and beyond. Upon taking over the Patriots in 2000, Belichick and Pioli did this in reverse, negotiating with overpaid veterans to reduce their base salaries but add incentives, based on both individual and team performance. Receiver Vincent Brisby, for example, accepted a 50% pay cut[2135] but was given a chance to earn even more. Incentive contracts encourage effort and ensure that success is rewarded. Belichick's own contract included a large bonus for winning a Super Bowl. Similarly, new receiver David Terrell was given a one-year contract with a modest (by NFL veteran standards) $200,000 signing bonus and $700,000 salary for 2005. Had he made the team and performed well, the Patriots would undoubtedly have rewarded him with a richer long-term contract. Instead, they weren't happy enough with his performance to keep him.

Reward schemes must define "success" carefully. To the Patriots, "success" is not stats but whatever helps a team win football games. Since being selected 198th in the 1993 NFL Draft–a pick so low that just making an NFL roster was impressive–Troy Brown has helped his Patriots win many games. Brown is now the longest-serving Patriot. Since he turned 33 before the 2004 season and his "production" fell to only 40 catches in 2003 (down from 83 in 2000, 101 in 2001 and 97 in 2002), many expected the Patriots would save money by insisting Brown cut his multi-million dollar salary. Instead, they guaranteed his $2.25 million salary for 2004.[2136] Why would the Patriots uncharacteristically pay so much for an aging player with diminished "production"? Well, Troy Brown has heart and soul. He's now surrounded by more talented players, so the team is throwing the ball his direction less. But Brown remains one of the gutsiest and smartest Patriots. He caught eight passes in Super Bowl XXXVIII after a Carolina Panther broke his nose early in the contest. And he happily runs back punts, an unpleasant task often involving high-speed collisions with powerful professional football players. Troy Brown has long been a team leader and had been voted by his peers a team captain for three consecutive seasons. He's quiet, but he epitomizes "team." This adds value, even if it's not detectable in official statistics.

Non-monetary rewards

Rewarding success means more than merely throwing money at winners. Rewarding success involves taking time to give honest praise where it's due. Tom Brady was touched when Belichick told him, following the Super Bowl, "I'm glad you're our quarterback."[2137] Rodney Harrison must have been similarly touched after winning the 2003 AFC Championship as he embraced Coach Belichick and Bill told him, "Boy, am I glad we got you!" Belichick also said wonderful things about his outgoing coordinators: "It's been an honor and a privilege for me to have Romeo for the last four years and Charlie for the last five as our coordinators on the offensive and defensive side of the ball. They've both done an outstanding job, and we would not be where we are without them."[2138]

Rewarding success involves acknowledging achievements. Tom Brady doesn't need to park a few steps closer than his teammates but has done so every season because he always works out so religiously and so intensely that he earns one of the special parking spaces reserved for "workout warriors." Guys knock themselves out for those parking spaces because they bring status and bragging rights over their teammates. The Patriots also give a "Hit of the Game" award which, no doubt, encourages aggressive hitting. Every photo hung in the team' facility celebrates team achievements. Belichick says players love showing up in new photos:

> "It can only be pictures from games we've won, and pictures of players making plays, or pictures that show a culmination of success or enthusiasm from that success. All the pictures have to be reflective of winning, or a successful team accomplishment. It's sort of exciting to see the players coming in looking for new pictures."[2139]

A great way to reward success is to give gifts that those who performed well want. Bob Kraft did this with the design of the Patriots' first Super Bowl ring:

> "Kraft explained that, at the request of some of his defensive backs, [the Super Bowl ring] was made of white gold. "What a concept!" [Warren] Sapp said loudly. "An owner who listens to his players. That's a great ring! We (the Bucs) got an old-school ring!"[2140]

The rings were also absolutely huge and appraised at over $15,000 per ring. Kraft joked while handing them out that they were "three-barstool rings": so large they could be seen from three barstools away.

Sapp would have been even more impressed by the "token" of appreciation Kraft bought each player after their 2003 championship. The 2003 rings weigh 3.8 ounces, 33% more than the 2001 rings, have 104 diamonds with total weight of over 5 carats, and appraise at over $20,000 a piece. At the private ring ceremony, Kraft helped players put this in perspective: "The last one, if you put it down on a bar, you could see it from three stools away. This is a six-stool ring."[2141] When Pats fan Lou Schorr stumbled onto a "clunker of a ring" linebacker Tully Banta-Cain had amazingly left behind in a Providence Place Mall bathroom, Schorr said, "This was serious stuff. There were so many diamonds, it was like getting a bolt of lightning in your eyes when you looked at it."[2142]

Players were similarly astonished. Said Tedy Bruschi, "It's the greatest ring in the history of the NFL for one of the greatest teams in the history of the NFL. The first [ring] has sentimental value, but the second one, look at it, it's just so significant."[2143] When Patriots practice squad wide receiver Chas Gessner returned from playing in NFL Europe to pick up his ring, he said, "It's amazing. It's the most ridiculous thing that I have ever seen. I almost passed out when I saw it, I really did."[2144] Safety Rodney Harrison said, "Yeah. Mr. Kraft, he really hooked us up with this one."[2145]

Cornerback Ty Law, who just months earlier said he never wanted to play for the Patriots again, was so moved by the 2003 season ring when he received it in June 2004 that he cautioned owner Bob Kraft not to set the bar too high: "The toughest task now is how are you going to top this because we're going to win another one."[2146] Kraft was thrilled: "They've already challenged me about what would happen if we did it again. I welcome the challenge."[2147]

Kraft didn't disappoint. The 2004 rings weighed 4.06 ounces. The 124 diamonds had a total weight of 4.94 carats. After Romeo Crennel—now head coach in Cleveland—lugged his into the Browns locker room, linebacker Kenard Lang said, "Those diamonds hit me in the eyes from all the way in the back of the room. I thought, I got to get me one."[2148] It's not just a pretty hunk of 14-karat white gold encrusted with 124 diamonds. The design Kraft chose groups 21 diamonds to represent the team's 21-game winning streak. Twenty more diamonds are clustered to symbolize their 20-game home winning streak. Nine diamonds reflect their 9-0 playoff record. And three giant marquis cut diamonds signify their three Super Bowl trophies.

Bob Kraft doesn't just walk around Gillette Stadium handing out rings. He invites the entire team to his house for a lavish event. During the 2004 ring ceremony to receive the 2003 season's rings, ring boxes emerged from a dry ice fog synchronized to music and lasers. Players opened their boxes in unison. A year later,

Tedy Bruschi couldn't stand the suspense and sweet-talked Kraft into seeing his ring long before Kraft presented his players with "the richest dessert" they ever enjoyed. Kraft is a sucker for players with good business skills: "I tried to talk [Bruschi] out of it, but he used good salesmanship."[2149] Kraft greeted every player at the door, including Richard Seymour–who was three days into a holdout–because "He's a terrific guy. We're happy he's here."

After winning his first Super Bowl ring in his first season as a Patriot, Corey Dillon choked up during the ring ceremony: "I put this up there with the birth of my child and my wedding to my beautiful wife." Dillon is now officially on the treadmill: "This one is very nice, but I want another. I want to see what the next one looks like."[2150] Russian president Putin apparently agreed because when Robert Kraft showed him his ring: "After glimpsing the bauble's flashiness, Mr. Putin… placed the ring promptly in his pocket and exited the room."[2151] Kraft left Russia without his ring. Several days later, he issued a statement graciously saying he intended to gift his ring to the Russian president. But that was a face-saving gesture. After viewing Kraft's gorgeous ring, the Russian president could not resist it any more than Gollum could part with "my precious." Kraft ordered himself another and smiles when asked about the incident.[2152]

Rewards can also be small and symbolic. On opening day of 2004 training camp, Belichick allowed players who had successfully completed the team's off-season training program to watch practice without a helmet while those who hadn't accomplished everything expected of them had to practice hard with their chinstraps strapped. This was as much a public shaming as a reward for good behavior.

Perhaps the ultimate in rewarding success is allowing someone who grew and flourished in your organization to "re-pot" himself in a bigger pot after outgrowing your organization. As Robert Kraft said of Romeo Crennel and Charlie Weis' departures: "When you have success, it creates opportunities for the good people in your organization."[2153]

Acknowledge teammates' contributions

"I play with some great players. So I have a lot of help out there, and we've got a great passing game."[2154]
   – *Patriots running back Corey Dillon*

"We have so many other guys like myself who put the team first and sacrifice for this team. The Bruschis, the Vrabels, the McGinests as well as guys like Richard Seymour do that. I'm just a small part of the whole crew."[2155]
   – *Patriots safety Rodney Harrison*

"It all comes [from] the offensive line giving us time to throw and having the receivers run great routes. My job is easy. I just have to find the open guy and let it go, and that's what my guys do for me. There's a tremendous amount of confidence in those guys that are doing those jobs."[2156]
– Tom Brady

"We've got some great linebackers. A lot of real athletic guys. I'll never be accused of being 'athletic.' Every guy brings something so different to the table."[2157]
– Patriots linebacker Ted Johnson

"It's kind of an unacknowledged fraternity in a locker room full of leaders. We feel like every guy in the locker room has a special bond and brings special things to the table. For us, it's a bunch of guys who have been through thick and thin… When you do something like that, you develop the special bond that we have."[2158]
– Patriots linebacker Tedy Bruschi

Patriots players' greatest reward has nothing to do with promotions or raises. It is the praise they receive from teammates and coaches. Patriots players and coaches are constantly acknowledging one another's achievements. On some teams, players care only about their own position. On the Patriots, everyone admires everyone else. Tom Brady says, "I look up to people that do things that I don't think I could do."[2159] Tight end Christian Fauria calls his teammates "lifelong friends" and suspects this might be the Patriots' greatest strength:

"When I first got here, everybody greeted me with open arms. Everybody's in this together, and everyone can make a difference… Some teams, I don't think there's as much concern for your fellow man as there is here. We're all interested in everybody doing well. Maybe it's because you win… because you bond."[2160]

Troy Brown is a wide receiver, but he dishes out love for everyone. He says of offensive linemen, "They don't mind not being known and get in there and dig it out, and get dirty, and hit every play, and guys falling on their legs and ankles and punching them in the stomach, all that good stuff. They do all the dirty [work] and get no glory." Told that Tom Brady called him the ultimate teammate, Brown replied "Tell him I said, 'Thank you.' He is no slouch either."[2161] Corey Dillon enthusiastically embraces the star-less philosophy:

"You should have 53 guys you can count on. It shouldn't have to be one guy's responsibility to go out there and win the game. I can't throw the ball to myself. I can't do any of those things. We rely on other people, and it's refreshing knowing I can just go in there and do my part of the job."[2162]

Asked whether Tedy Bruschi being the Patriots' best linebacker was "fact or fiction," fellow linebacker Mike Vrabel answered, "Fact. Fact." After the *ESPN* interviewer said, "That's so sweet," Vrabel continued: "I know! And I hate [saying] it, but it's the truth. The numbers don't lie."[2163] Embarrassed, Bruschi interrupted: "That's fiction! We've got so many great linebackers. I'm going to go with the two-headed monster of Vrabel and McGinest. And you can just start there. You've got Ted Johnson coming in, Rosevelt Colvin, Phife."[2164]

Asked about his legendary clutch kicks, including two Super Bowl winners, Adam Vinatieri shifted the focus onto his teammates:

> "If I'm not on such a great team... I [wouldn't] have such a great opportunity. My name would never be mentioned unless my team was successful. I guess first and foremost I have to credit my teammates. They have a lot of great players. Tom Brady finds a way to work down the field and gave me an opportunity at the end. [Also, the holder and long-snapper and] the other guys up front blocking. They make my job a lot easier when they do such a good job."[2165]

After special teamer and backup linebacker/safety Don Davis decided to assist the strength and conditioning coaches in the 2005 offseason to prepare for a possible post-football career, Davis' teammates encouraged him: "I loved it. The great part about it was that I got a lot of affirmation from a lot of the players I really respect on the team. They were like 'You're a natural at this type of thing.'"[2166] Patriots players are always supporting one another this way.

Patriots punter Josh Miller jokes that his performance is so dependent on his teammates' performance that taking care of them is obligatory: "My long-snapper is doing well. If he's doing well, I'm doing well... I'm with him 90% of the day. It's very important to have a good rapport. You have to take care of these guys. You have to feed them a bit. At Christmas, you have to get them a gift... As a fan, you never see a bad snap; you just see the bad kick... If he puts [the ball] on my hip, that's one less thing I have to worry about."[2167]

Bill Belichick considers himself a team player too. Like every other team player on the Patriots, Belichick deflects praise onto his teammates. Asked about his creative schemes forcing so many turnovers in playoff games, Belichick insists, "It's more a reflection of the players and they way they execute the defense, the way they play the game. Whatever the results we've gotten and production we've gotten is attributable to them and their performance rather than some scheme."[2168] Asked just before winning his third Vince Lombardi trophy as a head coach whether a trophy might some day bear his name, Belichick answered, "No. No... That trophy represents the team—I mean that word collectively, T-E-A-M—that is able to play the best season for the year that it's engraved."[2169]

Patriots players don't care what the media thinks of them. They care what their teammates–who see all their flaws, feats and foibles–think: "The guys on this football team, we know [how good each of us is]. Maybe to the national media, [our individual player talent] probably is overlooked."[2170] What excites Patriots players is– for example–former offensive coordinator Charlie Weis' visiting 2005 training camp to thank players. According to Troy Brown, "He just told us he was appreciative of all the things we did for him, and he thanked us for helping him get a [head coaching] job. And there weren't even any [swear words]. That was different."[2171]

Incentives must match comprehensive responsibilities

"Measurements present very real problems... Yet precisely because what we measure and how we measure determine what will be considered relevant, and determine thereby not just what we see, but what we–and others–do, measurements are all-important... Objectives are needed in all areas on which the survival of the business depends."[2172]
– Peter Drucker

Catching passes is glamorous. Every receiver and tight end wants to catch 100 passes. Catching passes makes you a star and may get you voted into the Pro Bowl and Hall of Fame. Blocking is thankless, so receivers must be motivated to block for their teammates on the many plays when the quarterback doesn't throw them the ball. Running a pass pattern aggressively when you know the quarterback will hand the ball to a running back or throw to a different receiver is another thankless task that helps your team. Many receivers play hard when there's a chance the ball will be thrown their direction and relax on other plays. Patriots receivers play hard on every play.

One reason Patriots work hard at "thankless" tasks is that their teammates and coaches thank them. When Bill Belichick spotlights players as worthy of emulation, he glosses over the obvious plays that appear in official statistics and emphasizes the oft-overlooked "intangibles" ...which are quite tangible if you watch for them on film. Listen to Belichick praising former Giants tight end Mark Bavaro:

"Mark was special because he was so much of a complete player. He was able to block defensive ends by himself–including Reggie White–which was rare. A lot of tight ends have better receiving numbers, but in my opinion, few had his receiving skill and production combined with his extraordinary blocking ability."[2173]

Bavaro's name didn't appear on even preliminary ballots for the NFL Hall of Fame for five straight years of eligibility, but Bill Belichick ensures that his players appreciate the "thankless" things that differentiate truly great players from statistically great players. Belichick's praise for players like Bavaro spurred Patriots tight end

Daniel Graham to develop into what one NFL scout terms "the best blocking tight end in the league."[2174] Similarly, fullback Patrick Pass' "blocking has improved markedly through the years."[2175] This results from great training, one element of which is showing players examples of what you want and motivating them to achieve that. (Another is running as many blocking drills as pass catching drills, something the Patriots certainly do.)

Countless companies have embraced the seductive management consulting fad *du jour* and suffered after thoughtlessly mis-applying it. One common mistake is "incentivizing" employees in a manner that encourages them to behave selfishly or to ignore job responsibilities for which the company offers no rewards. Rewarding employees for individual achievement can damage collective productivity by encouraging employees to waste time gossiping about and discrediting their colleagues, waste time sucking up to their bosses, claim credit for others' ideas, sabotage others' projects, refuse to help others, work only on whatever is being measured and rewarded to the detriment of all the other job responsibilities that are not being measured and rewarded, *etc*. Individual incentives can produce an uncooperative work environment that devolves–over time–into a poisonous, backstabbing environment.

Employees and teammates should want to do everything in their power to facilitate their team's success. Recognizing the dangers of rewarding individual achievements, Patriots management carefully structures contract incentives to encourage "good" behavior and discourage players from maximizing personal stats to the team's detriment. Explains Patriots "capologist" (salary cap expert) Andy Wasynczuk:

> "If you set [contract incentives] up for, say, interceptions, well, that takes the place of a coach. You don't want your contract being the coach. You want your coach being the coach. We've been very careful in the kind of incentives being built into the contract. …You want it to be grouped with team performance, and at the same time, you want some individual aspect accounted for."[2176]

As an example, after coming off the bench in 2001 when starting quarterback Drew Bledsoe was injured, Tom Brady earned an extra $70,000 in incentives based on playing time.[2177] Playing time is an excellent individual incentive because it motivates players to get onto the field by maximizing their value to their team and by doing whatever the coaches ask of them. You want your players focused on only one statistic: victories. Even as he was impressing the entire world, Tom Brady said, "The only person I care about proving myself to is myself and my coach. Everybody else doesn't matter."[2178] Many Patriots can tell you what percentage of defensive or special teams plays they participated in the previous season. Incenting players based on playing time encourages them to "do the right thing," however their coaches define "the right thing."

The Patriots have included in the rookie contracts of many recent high draftees–including Daniel Graham, Richard Seymour, and Ty Warren–a two-tiered salary structure. Based on the Patriots' assessment–at a prespecified future date–of the player's performance, they can pay the player an "option bonus" to extend that player's contract or–if less pleased–avoid paying the bonus and instead let the player enter free agency sooner. In May 2004, for example, the Patriots decided to pay defensive lineman Ty Warren an optional $3.25 million bonus.

Patriots defensive lineman Ty Warren's rookie contract (excluding 2003)[2179]

	2004	2005	2006	2007	2008
If Patriots do not pay Warren's option bonus	$955,000	$1,145,000	$1,335,000	Free agent	Free agent
If Patriots pay Warren's option bonus	$3,555,000	$495,000	$685,000	$875,000 + up to $3.7 million in individual and team performance bonuses	$1,050,000 + up to $5.6 million in individual and team performance bonuses

Similarly, $12 million of 2004 1st-round draft pick Vince Wilfork's $18 million contract is incentive-based. Wilfork received his $3 million option bonus in 2005 and could receive up to $9 million in potential bonuses if he becomes a "significant player" (though he does not need to become a Pro Bowler),[2180] such as playing in at least 55% of the team's plays.

Like playing time bonuses, "option bonuses" paid at the team's discretion several seasons into a player's contract incent players to work hard and focus on whatever coaches ask. Contracts with option bonuses wisely do not link compensation to particular statistics that might distort the player's incentives away from team success and toward inflating of personal statistics. Another advantage of such contracts is that they are "incentive compatible," meaning that neither side will feel much regret in the future about signing such a contract. If the player plays well, his market value will be higher and he will receive more under the contract. If he plays poorly, his market value will be lower and he will receive less. In either case, neither side feels ripped off. In too many NFL contracts, players locked in to long contracts either: 1) overplay their salaries and feel disgruntled, often to the point of holding out and refusing to play unless the team renegotiates their salary; or, 2) underperform, often to the point that the team cuts the player to dump his inflated salary or demands that he accept a pay cut. And teams often shoot themselves in the foot by agreeing to "voidable contracts" that allow players to void the last season or two of their contracts after achieving contractual milestones, such as having been on the field for a certain percentage of their team's plays. The Patriots avoid voidable contracts, preferring to reward players with higher pay ("option bonuses") rather than early contract termination ("voidable contracts").

NFL teams may find it easier than businesses to use collective performance to incent players. Football players have an obvious stake in their team's on-field success because winning is more fun than losing. People are proud to play on a winning team. And everyone on a football team knows everyone else and enjoys watching their teammates celebrate victory. Although many are proud to work for General Electric or IBM, the relationship between individual and group success is more direct and immediate for players on a football team than for workers at GE or IBM. The Patriots' collective reward strategy can, however, work beautifully for entrepreneurs and small business owners or distinct groups within large corporations.

HOW TO SPEAK BELICHICKIAN

When Bill Belichick arrived in New England in 2000, he brought with him a new language, foreign to all Patriots except holdovers from the 1996 Patriots Super Bowl team whose defense Belichick coordinated. Many 2000 Patriots never learned to speak Belichickian and were released. Old-timers, including Troy Brown, Tedy Bruschi, Ted Johnson, Kevin Faulk, Ty Law, Willie McGinest and Adam Vinatieri, helped their teammates learn the strange language, which linguists and anthropologists report is uniquely reality-based and forward-looking.

Belichickian lacks a past tense, except regarding bad things that might recur unless proactive steps are taken. Belichickian has no 1st person pronoun; it replaces "I" with "we." However, in sentences with negative connotations, there is no 2nd or 3rd person pronoun. You cannot say, for example, "your mistake" or "he blew it." You can only say "my bad" or "I screwed up." Belichickian lacks words for "unfair," "relax," "complacency," "nervous" and "no." Also interestingly, there is no way to express the concepts "give me the damn ball!" "guaranteed win," "moral victory," "totally prepared," "our place in history" or "we *deserved* to win" in Belichickian. In Belichickian culture, pointing one's finger is the ultimate obscenity, except when the finger is pointed at oneself.

The language's trademark is a rhetorical device that uses seemingly meaningless tautologies to convey and emphasize essential facts. The pattern "X is X" occurs constantly in Belichickian. To non-native speakers, this sounds like circular logic. But to those who understand the language, "X is X" is a concise way of saying much with few words, usually that the matter in question is outside of the speaker's control and, therefore, of no concern. Here are examples:

"The way we are is the way we are."[2181]
– Linebacker Tedy Bruschi, explaining that the Patriots will never be the dazzling headline-grabbers the media would love them to be

"The system in place is the system in place."[2182]
– Defensive coordinator Romeo Crennel, explaining it's pointless to waste precious brain cycles on matters one cannot control

"I can only do what I can do… Whatever happens, happens."[2183]
– Patriots receiver Bethel Johnson, on the possibility of being cut in 2005, which he was not

"If we win, then we win."[2184]
– Cornerback/safety Eugene Wilson, explaining his focus on preparing to play as well as he can, not on Vegas betting odds

"If it's not good enough, it's not good enough."[2185]
> *— Troy Brown, saying "I still feel I've got something to give" but that if he's cut in 2005 "There'll be no hard feelings"*

"Players play. Coaches coach. Scouts scout."[2186]
> *— Bill Belichick, explaining that "everybody's got a job to do, and we just try to work hard at it"*

"I can only do what I can do."[2187]
> *— New Patriots linebacker Chad Brown, explaining that "I cannot be Ted [Johnson] or Tedy [Bruschi], but I expect to fulfill that [middle linebacker] role"*

"It is what it is… If we practice indoors, we'll practice indoors."[2188]
> *— Bill Belichick, explaining he has no control over pre-Super Bowl XXXIX practice time weather conditions*

"The game of football is the game of football, no matter what."[2189]
> *— Cornerback Randall Gay*

"Whatever happens happens… If they depend on me throughout the season, then they depend on me throughout the season."[2190]
> *— New Patriots cornerback Duane Starks, explaining that "I'm just taking my role as it comes. It's out of my control. Coach has his hands all over that."*

"He is who he is."[2191]
> *— Linebacker Ted Johnson, explaining that players play, coaches coach and Bill Belichick is Bill Belichick*

"He is what we all know he is."[2192]
> *— Bill Belichick, providing a detailed evaluation of new Patriots receiver Tim Dwight*

"You've got to get the job done or you don't get it done."[2193]
> *— Offensive lineman Stephen Neal, explaining that players who don't do their jobs don't remain in New England long*

"I just do what I need to do."[2194]
> *— Tight end Daniel Graham*

"Whatever we've got to do, we've got to do."[2195]
> *— Linebacker Willie McGinest, in July 2000, on his new coach's toughness*

"Whatever we've accomplished, we've accomplished… It doesn't mean anything."[2196]
> *— Bill Belichick, bragging about all his Super Bowl rings*

"Playing football is playing football."[2197]
> – *Bill Belichick, explaining that "you can't simulate it until you have the other 21 guys out there"*

"What's in the past is in the past."[2198]
> – *New wide receiver David Terrell, explaining that he worries only about catching passes from Tom Brady in a Patriots uniform, not his glory days with Brady in a Michigan uniform*

"Football is football to me."[2199]
> – *Linebacker Tedy Bruschi, explaining how deeply he loves football*

"Coaches are coaches."[2200]
> – *Defensive coordinator Romeo Crennel, explaining that coaches can indeed sometimes overanalyze*

"The rules are the rules."[2201]
> – *Defensive coordinator Romeo Crennel, explaining the folly of wishful thinking*

"If I don't make it, I don't make it."[2202]
> – *Patriots linebacker Wesly Mallard, on the possibility of being cut in 2005, which he was not*

"I am what I am. I do what I do."[2203]
> – *Defensive coordinator Romeo Crennel, asked whether his age was hurting his chances for a head coaching job*

"If he can't play, he can't play. If he can play, he's going to play."[2204]
> – *Defensive tackle Vince Wilfork, asked about Richard Seymour's status*

"Last year was last year."[2205]
> – *Troy Brown, sharing his joy over winning a third Super Bowl*

"Last year is last year."[2206]
> – *Former defensive coordinator Romeo Crennel, explaining the value of his shiny new Super Bowl ring now that he has become the Cleveland Browns' head coach*

"Camp is camp."[2207]
> – *Linebacker Willie McGinest, explaining that training camp is unpleasant but necessary*

"It is what it is."[2208]
> – *Running back Corey Dillon, explaining that he is treating his first Super Bowl as just another game*

"It is what it is."[2209]
> — *Bill Belichick, explaining that he spent exactly zero seconds worrying about having a two-week break before the Super Bowl because it was out of his control*

"Whatever the future holds is what the future holds... If it happens, it happens."[2210]
> — *Patriots nose tackle Vince Wilfork, on whether the Patriots will be able to retain all their great defensive linemen*

APPENDIX

This appendix demonstrates that "high-performance work organizations" exist and look much like Bill Belichick's New England Patriots.

The table below shows this relationship among many employee- and job-related variables, as discussed in the "Motivating" chapter.

I won't bore you with methodological details, but the first column is a variable name, the second column is the question(s) used to calculate the variable, and the numbers in the right-hand column are "1st principal component coefficients." You can think of each coefficient as measuring how correlated that factor is with all the other factors, on a scale of -1 to +1. +1 indicates perfect correlation. -1 indicates perfect negative correlation. 0 indicates no relationship. Almost all of the bivariate correlations (not shown here) are also positive, so my result is "robust": each factor is positively correlated with most every other factor (except "Rules & Regulations" which is negatively correlated with most every factor).

Variable	Example questions	1st P.C.
EDUCATION	Years of education	.108
INTELLIGENCE	Interviewer's assessment of interviewee's intelligence	.133
CREATIVITY	"My job requires that I be creative"	.229
RULES & REGULATIONS	"My job has rules and regulations concerning almost everything I might do or say" "There are procedures for handling everything that comes up"	-.080
DISCRETION	"I have enough authority to do my job" "I have freedom to decide what I do on my job" "It's my own responsibility to decide how my job gets done" "I have a lot of say about what happens on job" "I am given a lot of freedom to decide how I do my own work"	.294
FLEXIBLE WORK	"I decide when I take breaks" "I determine the speed at which I work" "I decide who I work with" "I am given a chance to do the things I do best" "How hard to change particular duties?" (negative)	.288

Variable	Example questions	1ˢᵗ P.C.
REWARD GOOD	"When you do your job well, are you likely to be offered a promotion?" "When you do your job well, are you likely to be praised by superiors?" "When you do your job well, are you likely to get a bonus/pay increase?" "When you do your job well, are you likely to become more secure in your job?" "My employer cares about giving everybody a chance to get ahead"	.248
JOB SECURITY	"The job security is good"	.193
SUPERVISOR FACILITATES	"Supervisor encourages supervisees to develop new ways of doing things" "Supervisor leaves supervisees alone unless they want help" "Supervisor talks things over with people before making decisions about their work" "Supervisor is successful in getting people to work together" "Supervisor is helpful to me in getting my job done"	.251
SUPERVISOR NICE	"Supervisor maintains high standards of performance in own work" "Supervisor treats some supervisees better than others" (negative) "Supervisor is very concerned about the welfare of those under him/her" "Supervisor is friendly"	.234
VARIETY	"I get to do a number of things on my job" "Job requires doing the same things over and over" (negative)	.226
LEARNING	"My job requires that I keep learning new things" "I have an opportunity to develop my own special skills" "How useful & valuable will present job skills be in five years?" "Is there a training or education program you can take to improve your skills?"	.290
PLEASANT SURROUNDINGS	"The physical surroundings are pleasant"	.228

Variable	*Example questions*	*1ˢᵗ P.C.*
LIKE JOB	"The work is interesting" "How satisfied with job?" "Would you recommend this job?" "Would you continue to work if you had the money to live comfortably?" "My main satisfaction in life comes from work" "With hindsight, would you take job again?" "How often does time drag?" (negative) "My main interest in work is to get money" (negative) "I would be happier if I didn't have to work" (negative)	.314
COOPERATIVE	"Coworkers take a personal interest in me" "Coworkers are helpful in getting my job done" "Coworkers are friendly"	.240
MEANINGFUL	"The work I do is meaningful" "Most of the things I do on the job are meaningless" (negative)	.258
PRIDE IN WORK	"When you do your job well, do you get a feeling of accomplishment?" "When you do your job well, do you feel better about yourself?" "I feel personally responsible for the work I do on my job"	.207
EXTRA EFFORT	"How much effort do you put into your job beyond what is required?"	.121
log(HOURLY EARNINGS)	Natural log of hourly earnings	.117
SEE RESULTS	"I can see the results of my work"	.214

Source: James K. Lavin, *Models of Worker-Job Matching, Rules vs. Discretion, and Employee Training vs. Labor Mobility*, Ph.D. dissertation, Stanford University, 2000.

Data come from the *1977 Quality of Employment Survey*.

For the statistically-inclined, there are 768 observations (each an employee at a different firm), the eigenvalue is 6.01–indicating a strong relationship among these variables–and the 1ˢᵗ principal component explains 30.06% of all variation in the dataset.

While studying the Patriots, I suddenly realized the answer to a mystery I encountered while doing my dissertation. I had assumed that rules vs. discretion was a single dimension, a spectrum. The data suggested instead that rules and discretion are correlated but distinct variables. I did not understand why till realizing the Patriots have many rules but also offer great discretion. Rules are inevitable in any business requiring colleagues to coordinate their actions. But smart companies restrict rules to those issues where rules truly facilitate coordination. On all other matters, discretion is preferred because workers desire to control their own destiny.

ACKNOWLEDGEMENTS

I have benefited from the help and encouragement of many in writing Volume 2. I wish to thank:

· The many people who took time to email or call to share with me how much they enjoyed Vol. 1. I heard from Patriots fans, high school and college basketball coaches, managers, college band directors, business owners, football writers… even NBA and Major League Baseball executives. It seems just about everyone who cares about improving their organization shares my fascination with the Patriots. I was overwhelmed by your generous words. Your interest in Vol. 2 inspired me to do my best, and your feedback on what you wanted (esp. more details on *how* the team succeeds) helped guide me. Special thanks to Dr. Paul Buyer, Dave Lash and Barbara Tobin for helpful discussions and to everyone who went out of their way to get my book media attention or tell others about *Management Secrets*.

· *USA Today* sportswriter Jill Lieber and NFL management for arranging media credentials that enabled me to meet Patriots players and coaches during the week leading up to Super Bowl XXXIX! If Jill had not gone out of her way to help an unknown writer, I would not have been able to shoot the player and coach photos on the covers of Volumes 2 and 3, interview players and coaches or meet some of the Patriots reporters I had the pleasure of meeting in Jacksonville.

· Mel Duffey of *ESOP Advisors Group* and Jack Thornton of *PatriotsPlanet.net*, each of whom read–on a tight timeframe–a draft of the entire Vol. 2 manuscript and provided extremely helpful suggestions, insights, corrections and encouragement that greatly improved the final product. If email had speed-dial, Mel would have been on it because I repeatedly asked for his advice and received an outstanding reply every time. Jack knows so much about the Patriots that he pointed out factual errors in several published articles.

· Marquette men's basketball head coach Tom Crean for his interest in my books and for reading Vol. 2 and offering such an enthusiastic endorsement.

· Sportswriters who wrote about my book, quoted me in their articles or emailed to say they enjoyed my book. In alphabetical order: Nick Cafardo of *The Boston Globe*, Ken Castro at *PatriotsInsider.com*, Greg Couch of *The Chicago Sun-Times*, Christopher Cox of *The Boston Herald*, Paul Daugherty of *The Cincinnati Enquirer*, Steve DeCosta of *The Standard-Times*, Gayle Fee ("Inside Track") at *The Boston Herald*, Peter Finney of *The Times-Picayune* (my heart goes out to New Orleans!), Greg Gatlin of *The Boston Herald*, Bob George at *PatsFans.com*, Cindy Krischer Goodman of *The Miami Herald*, Bob Grotz of the *Journal Register News Service*, Reggie Hayes at *The News-Sentinel*, Stan Jaksina at *PatsFans.com,* G. Scott Jones of *Seahawks.NET*, Richard Justice of *The Houston Chronicle*, Chick

Ludwig of *The Dayton Daily News*, Alex Marvez of *The South Florida Sun-Sentinel*, John McClain at *The Houston Chronicle*, Lenny Megliola of *The MetroWest Daily News*, Bob Oates of *The Los Angeles Times*, Marvin Pave of *The Boston Globe*, Dave Perkins of *The Toronto Star*, Dan Pompei of *The Sporting News*, Geoffrey Precort from *Point* magazine, Ron Rapoport of the *Chicago Sun-Times*, Darren Rovell of *ESPN*, Richard Sandomir of *The New York Times*, Skip Sauer at *TheSportsEconomist.com*, Darren Schwandt of *PatsFans.com*, Jon Scott at *PatriotsInsider.com* and Christopher Young of *The Boston Phoenix*. Apologies if I have forgotten to thank you.

· Journalists I met Super Bowl week who were so welcoming. I especially enjoyed talking with Greg Gatlin, Alex Marvez, Lenny Megliola, Dan Pires, Mike Reiss, Darren Rovell, Michael Smith and Steve Solloway.

· Doug Farrar of *Yahoo! Sports* and *Seahawks.NET* for being the first reporter to take an interest in Vol. 1–reading and reviewing it about a week after I published it–and for his continuing interest in my project.

· Dan Pires of *The Standard-Times* for being so encouraging and working his media contacts to help Vol. 1 get noticed.

· Ed Berliner for a fun interview on Comcast TV (CN8)'s *Sports Pulse*, Orlando Magic Sr. VP Pat Williams for having me as a guest on his radio program, Jack Arute for twice having me as a guest on *Sirius' NFL Channel*, Peter Richon at WPTF Raleigh, Mark Lemay at 1490 WCCM and Deb Halperin and Jonah Davis for inviting me to appear on *NECN*'s *New England Business Day* (I was regrettably unable to appear because I was en route to the Super Bowl).

· Patriots fan boards *PatriotsPlanet.net* and *PatsFans.com*. I have learned from you and been directed to interesting articles. Most valuably, *PatriotsPlanet.net* members–including "Annihilus," "dchester," "dreithraider76," "FallingAlice," "Hawg73," "mgoblue," "Ras" and "RoadGrader"–have kept me laughing for months. The inclusive, sarcastic PatriotsPlanet culture reminds me of the Patriots locker room. No one takes her/himself too seriously or attacks people rather than facts.

· Mr. Andre Tippett, Patriots Hall of Famer, current Patriots director of football development and promotions and one of my all-time favorite athletes. I wrote to Mr. Tippett hoping to get a copy of the *Coach's Playbook* the Patriots give participants in their wonderful "coaching academy" for New England area football coaches. The book turned out to be generic football information, not specific to the Patriots, but I appreciate Mr. Tippett's response. And his hand-written note is one of the most treasured pieces of paper I own. Mr. Tippett was a Belichick-type player long before Bill Belichick landed in New England.

- Michael Conrad for pointing me to a Daytona Beach motel with availability Super Bowl week.

- Bob Lavin, my dad, who worked tirelessly to send me relevant *NFL Network* programs unavailable here in Stamford. (Come on, Cablevision! I have twice begged you for *NFL Network*!)

- My brother Eric who sees in his work every day the value of the Patriots' organizational genius. I always learn something about the team talking with Eric.

- Others who have provided help but requested anonymity. Though I cannot thank you here, I appreciate your assistance just as much.

- My marvelous wife Yingmei, for tolerating my quirks for ten fabulous years and sacrificing financially to let me go on and on with this seemingly endless project.

Finally, thanks again to Belichick's Patriots for teaching us about organizational greatness and demonstrating the true sources of personal happiness (concern for others, respect for opponents, humility, sacrifice, friendship, striving for perfection, doing what you love and loving what you do, concern for what's right rather than who's right, *etc.*). You are not merely one of the greatest football teams ever. You are one of the greatest organizations ever, and your accomplishments and methods are inspiring companies, nonprofits, the public sector and teams of all kinds… including your rivals! I echo NFL Commissioner Paul Tagliabue's surprising comment while handing you your latest Lombardi Trophy: "Congratulations. And keep it up!" You are so impressive that even the league commissioner momentarily lost his impartiality.

ENDNOTES

[1] Dave Boling, "Patriot Doctrine now law of land for the Seahawks," *The News Tribune*, 27 March 2005, www.thenewstribune.com/sports/story/4723576p-4359825c.html.

[2] Chris Mortensen, *ESPN*, quoted in: Gregg Easterbrook, "Tough guy predicts exact final score!" 15 February 2005, www.nfl.com/features/tmq/021505.

[3] Ed Reed, star safety of the Baltimore Ravens, quoted in: Kevin McNamara, "Albeit reluctantly, the Ravens have to tip their caps," *Providence Journal*, 29 November 2004, www.projo.com/patriots/content/projo_20041129_29side1.2ee33.html.

[4] Cornerback Otis Smith, quoted in: New England Patriots, "Otis Smith retires as a Patriot," *Patriots.com*, 18 May 2005.

[5] Theo Epstein, Boston Red Sox GM, quoted in: Karen Guregian, "Theo likes Pat hand: GM follows Kraft model," *Boston Herald*, 11 April 2005, http://redsox.bostonherald.com/redSox/view.bg?articleid=77810.

[6] Jimmy Johnson, multi-Super Bowl champion head coach, quoted in: Peter King, "Welcome back to the NFL," *Sports Illustrated*, 27 March 2005, http://sportsillustrated.cnn.com/2005/writers/peter_king/03/27/mmqb.owners.meetings/ and in "Could the Patriots of the 2000's match the Cowboys of the 1990's?" www.dallascowboysfanclub.com/Cowboys_Patriots_Comparison.htm.

[7] Oakland Raiders owner Al Davis, quoted in many sources.

[8] Tom Donohoe, Buffalo Bills general manager, quoted in: Bryan Morry, "Combine Notes: Trying to play catch-up," *Patriots.com*, 25 February 2005, www.patriots.com/news/index.cfm?ac=generalnewsdetail&pcid=41&pid=10872.

[9] Cleveland Indians general manager Mark Shapiro, quoted in: Mike Reiss, "Respect carries from football to baseball," *MetroWest Daily News*, 19 June 2005.

[10] Michael Andretti, whose Andretti Green Racing won the IndyCar championship and eight of 16 Honda car races in 2004, quoted in: Michael Welton, "Andretti Green Racing is team-first operation," *East Valley Tribune*, 18 March 2005, www.eastvalleytribune.com/index.php?sty=38165.

[11] Todd Christensen, former Oakland Raiders tight end, quoted in: Dr. Z, "High anxiety," *Sports Illustrated*, 7 April 2005, http://sportsillustrated.cnn.com/2005/writers/dr_z/04/07/drz.high.draft/index.html.

[12] Baltimore Ravens head coach Brian Billick, quoted in: Tom E. Curran, "Ravens might give Pats one last test," *Providence Journal*, 28 November 2004, www.projo.com/patriots/content/projo_20041128_pat28x.2df4b3.html.

[13] Jason Taylor, Miami Dolphins defensive end, quoted in: "You don't say..." *Providence Journal*, 26 December 2004, www.projo.com/patriots/content/projo_20041226_26quotesx.1d53f6.html.

[14] R.C. Buford, quoted in: David Aldridge, "Spurs, Patriots have formed a winning alliance," *Philadelphia Inquirer*, 26 June 2005.

[15] Don Banks, "Magic act," *Sports Illustrated*, 29 November 2004, http://sportsillustrated.cnn.com/2004/writers/don_banks/11/29/patriots.defense/.

[16] Michael Wilbon, *Washington Post*, quoted in: Gregg Easterbrook, "Tough guy predicts exact final score!" 15 February 2005, www.nfl.com/features/tmq/021505.

[17] Kansas City Chiefs owner Lamar Hunt, quoted in: Randy Covitz, "Kraft crafts a model franchise in New England," *Kansas City Star*, 21 November 2004, www.mercurynews.com/mld/mercurynews/sports/10241108.htm?1c.

[18] Indianapolis Colts GM Bill Polian, quoted in: Mark Gaughan, "Even on links, Polian thinks about Pats," *Buffalo News*, 7 June 2005, www.buffalonews.com/editorial/20050607/1009900.asp.

[19] Boomer Esiason, "Ten things to be thankful for this season," *NFL.com*, 24 November 2004, www.nfl.com/news/story/7924611.

[20] Joe Theismann, "If Pats win, use the D-word," *ESPN Insider*, 17 January 2005.

[21] Kansas City Chiefs coach Dick Vermeil, quoted in: David Aldridge, "Belichick's mantra is in midseason form," *San Jose Mercury News*, 22 March 2005, www.mercurynews.com/sports/11204085.htm.

[22] Paul Zimmerman ("Dr. Z"), "Beware of the Bills," *Sports Illustrated*, 24 November 2004, http://sportsillustrated.cnn.com/2004/writers/dr_z/11/24/power.rankings.part1/index.html.

[23] Mark Starr, "When Reality Trumps Fantasy," Newsweek, 10 February 2005, http://msnbc.msn.com/id/6947534/site/newsweek/.

[24] Indianapolis Colts head coach Tony Dungy, quoted in: Bob Kravitz, "This has to be the year they go all the way, right?" *Indianapolis Star*, 31 July 2005.

[25] Fox Sports analyst and former NFL lineman Brian Baldinger, " Patriots know their job, and they do it," *Fox Sports*, 10 February 2005, http://msn.foxsports.com/nfl/story/3381472.

[26] Jonathan Rand, "Patriots show how to beat the system," *KCChiefs.com*, 8 March 2005, www.kcchiefs.com/news/2005/03/08/rand_patriots_show_how_to_beat_the_system/.

[27] Minnesota Vikings quarterback Daunte Culpepper, quoted in: Mark Craig (*Star Tribune*), "Culpepper wants Vikes to be more like Patriots," Nashua Telegraph, 1 August 2005.

[28] New Patriots kick returner Chad Morton, quoted in: Michael Parente, "Brown in familiar territory at camp," *WoonsocketCall.com*, 5 August 2005.

[29] Tom E. Curran, "There's no second-guessing Pats' strategy," *Providence Journal*, 25 April 2005.

[30] Pittsburgh Steelers head coach Bill Cowher, quoted in: David Aldridge, "Belichick's mantra is in midseason form," *San Jose Mercury News*, 22 March 2005, www.mercurynews.com/mld/mercurynews/sports/11204085.htm.

[31] John Clayton, "Patchwork Patriots triumph again," *ESPN*, 22 November 2004, http://sports.espn.go.com/nfl/columns/story?columnist=clayton_john&id=1929637.

[32] Linebacker Willie McGinest, quoted in: Jackie MacMullan, "Sack leader is a sacrifice leader," *Boston Globe*, 23 January 2005.

[33] Frank Dascenzo, "Back-to-back champions fewer and farther between," *The Herald-Sun*, 12 April 2005, www.herald-sun.com/sports/18-596519.html.

[34] President Bush, "President Congratulates Super Bowl Champion New England Patriots," 13 April 2005, www.whitehouse.gov/news/releases/2005/04/20050413-5.html.

[35] Baltimore Ravens general manager Ozzie Newsome, quoted in: Ken Murray, "Belichick success built on personnel, planning," *Baltimore Sun*, 28 November 2004, www.baltimoresun.com/sports/football/bal-sp.belichick28nov28,1,5358260.print.story?coll=bal-sports-football.

[36] Jeffrey Martin, "Our take on the draft," *York Daily Record*, 21 April 2005, ydr.com/story/sportscolumns/66029/.

[37] Gary Shelton, "Denying dynasty," *St. Petersburg Times*, 7 February 2005.

[38] Patriots receiver David Terrell, "David Terrell Phone Interview," 7 April 2005, www.patriots.com/news/index.cfm?ac=generalnewsdetail&pcid=81&pid=11291.

[39] University of Florida football coach Urban Meyer, quoted in: Randy Beard, "Urban Meyer has Florida's fans revitalized," *Tallahassee Democrat*, 12 May 2005.

[40] Adam Schefter, "Rebuilt Patriots might be even better," *NFL.com*, 13 May 2005.

[41] Romeo Crennel, quoted in: Zac Jackson, "Coach has championship resume," *ClevelandBrowns.com*, 14 February 2005.

[42] Peyton Manning, quoted in: David Aldridge, "For Colts, it's all about the Patriots," *Philadelphia Inquirer*, 28 August 2005.

[43] Jon Gruden, Tampa Bay Buccaneers head coach, on *ESPN*'s "NFL Live," 28 January 2005.

[44] Andrew Perloff, "Tough road ahead," *Sports Illustrated*, 13 April 2005, http://sportsillustrated.cnn.com/2005/writers/andrew_perloff/04/13/toughest.schedules/.

[45] Nat Jackson, "A list of the few things I know for sure," *Yale Daily News*, 21 April 2005, www.yaledailynews.com/article.asp?AID=29378.

[46] John Libby, brigadier general of the National Guard, quoted in: Travis Lazarczyk, "A parade for true Patriots," *Morning Sentinel*, 9 April 2005, http://morningsentinel.mainetoday.com/sports/stories/15277.25.shtml.

[47] New Patriots receiver David Terrell, quoted in: Adam Kilgore, "Terrell catching up with Brady in hurry," *Boston Globe*, 3 August 2005.

[48] Kansas City Chiefs linebacker Scott Fujita, quoted in: AP, "9-1 Patriots make believers out of Chiefs," JournalNow, 24 November 2004, www.journalnow.com/servlet/Satellite?pagename=Common%2FMGArticle%2FPrintVersion&c=MGArticle&cid=1031779320236&image=wsj80x60.gif&oasDN=journalnow.com&oasPN=%21sports%21football.

[49] Richard Oliver, "Let's praise old-school Patriots," *San Antonio Express-News*, 28 November 2004, www.mysanantonio.com/sports/stories/MYSA112804.1C.COL.FBNoliver.9c712fc6.html.

[50] Eric McHugh, "This will be a prove-it season for Belichick," *The Patriot Ledger*, 29 July 2005.

[51] Navy admiral Walter Doran, Pacific Fleet commander, quoted in: Dawn S. Onley, "DOD takes a page from the Patriots' playbook," *Government Computer News*, 9 February 2005.

[52] Michael Lombardo, "If I were a carpenter," *Chargers Update*, 22 June 2005.

[53] Phil Simms, quoted in: Ira Kaufman, "Patriots Players Hold Themselves To A Higher Standard," *Tampa Tribune*, 31 January 2005.

[54] Jacksonville Jaguars head coach Jack Del Rio, quoted in: Len Pasquarelli, "Efficiency key to Patriots' success," *ESPN.com*, 29 August 2005.

[55] Greg Garber, "Patriots might just keep on winning," *ESPN*, 6 February 2005.

[56] Elizabeth A. Sherman, Letter to the Editor, *New York Times*, 16 April 2004, p. A18.

[57] Tom Brady, speaking at William and Mary's Colonial All-Pro Football Camp, quoted in: Dave Johnson, "Road to success often is unpaved," *DailyPress.com*, 28 June 2005.

[58] Bill Belichick, quoted in: Michael Felger, "Off the depth charts: Early positional battles shape up," *Boston Herald*, 10 August 2004, http://patriots.bostonherald.com/patriots/view.bg?articleid=39192.

[59] Jonathan Comey, "'Coach,'" *The Standard-Times*, 5 September 2005.

[60] "John F. Welch Leadership Center," www.ge.com/en/company/companyinfo/welchcenter/welch.htm.

[61] Bill Belichick, quoted in: Tom E. Curran, "Belichick knows sound foundation key to success," *Providence Journal*, 1 May 2005.

[62] Second-year Giants offensive lineman Chris Snee, quoted in: Mike Reiss, "Reiss: Light weighs in," *MetroWest Daily News*, 10 July 2005.

[63] "David Givens," *FootballGaming.com*, 2002, www.football-gaming.com/data/02draft/166.shtml.

[64] Antuan Edwards' agent Brian Levy, quoted in: Mike Reiss, "Safety valve: Patriots sign DB Antuan Edwards," *Boston Herald*, 7 June 2005.

[65] Patriots cornerback Asante Samuel, "Quotes from New England Patriots Press Conference," 2 February 2005.

[66] Patriots offensive lineman Russ Hochstein, quoted in: Russ Charpentier, "Pressure heavily on Hochstein," *Cape Cod Times*, January 2003, www.capecodonline.com/cctimes/sports/russ131.htm.

[67] Bill Belichick, quoted in: Marla Ridenour, "Special Time for Belichick," *Akron Beacon Journal*, 29 May 2002, www.allthingsbillbelichick.com/articles/specialtime.htm.

[68] Charlie Weis, quoted in: Dennis Dodd, "Weis doing his part ... now players must follow," *Sportsline.com*, 12 August 2005.

[69] Bill Belichick, quoted in: Tom E. Curran, "Patriots Notebook: Stronger Brady greets rookies at Gillette Stadium," *Providence Journal*, 1 May 2004, http://www.projo.com/patriots/content/projo_20040501_01patsjo.fbbc0.html.

[70] KC Joyner, The Football Scientist, *Scientific Football 2005* (KC's Football Services, Altamonte Springs, FL, 2005), p. 317.

[71] KC Joyner, The Football Scientist, *Scientific Football 2005* (KC's Football Services, Altamonte Springs, FL, 2005), p. 317.

[72] Bill Belichick, quoted in: Michael Felger, "Dillon is one happy camper," *Boston Herald*, 1 August 2005.

[73] Patriots linebacker Tedy Bruschi, "Quotes from New England Patriots Press Conference," 31 January 2005.

[74] Patriots linebacker Ted Johnson, quoted in: Tom E. Curran, "Bruschi decision eases minds, leaves void," *Providence Journal*, 24 July 2005.

[75] Linebacker Rosevelt Colvin, quoted in: Jerome Solomon, "Winning formula," *Boston Globe*, 26 July 2005.

[76] Patriots running back Corey Dillon, quoted in: Chris Kennedy, "Dillon thrilled to stay with Patriots," *The Republican*, 1 August 2005.

[77] Patriots veteran Mike Vrabel, quoted in: Jackie MacMullan, "Change is their constant," *Boston Globe*, 25 August 2005.

[78] Cleveland Browns fullback Terrelle Smith, quoted in: Steve King, "Camp Crennel yields progress," *ClevelandBrowns.com*, 25 August 2005.

[79] Tom E. Curran, "Belichick knows sound foundation key to success," *Providence Journal*, 1 May 2005.

[80] Patriots kicker Adam Vinatieri, "Quotes from New England Patriots Media Day," 1 February 2005.

[81] Steve Sabol (NFL Films), "Write On: Belichick's Place in History," 12 April 2005, www.allthingsbillbelichick.com/transcripts/writeontranscript.htm.

[82] Patriots owner Robert Kraft, "Quotes from New England Patriots Photo Day," 1 February 2005.

[83] Linebacker Ryan Claridge, 2005 Patriots draftee, "Ryan Claridge Phone Conference," *Patriots.com*, 24 April 2005.

[84] Offensive lineman Nick Kaczur, "Nicholas Kaczur Phone Conference," Patriots.com, 23 April 2005.

[85] Quarterback Matt Cassel, quoted in: Gary Klein, "Cassel Will Take It Slow With Patriots," *L.A. Times*, 30 April 2005, www.latimes.com/sports/la-sp-cassel30apr30,1,4408142.story.

[86] Chad Brown, quoted in: Michael Felger, "Humbling experience: Brown caught in middle," *Boston Herald*, 6 August 2005.

[87] Tom Brady, on: *3 Games to Glory III* DVD, 2005.

[88] Patriots linebacker Ted Johnson, quoted in: Paul Kenyon, "The party is over," *Eagle-Tribune*, 18 July 2000.

[89] Scott Pioli, "Quotes From New England Patriots Press Conference," 1 February 2005.

[90] Philadelphia Eagles offensive coordinator Brad Childress, "Quotes From Philadelphia Eagles Media Day," 1 February 2005.

[91] Patriots safety/cornerback Eugene Wilson, quoted in: Michael Parente, "Pats' Wilson a big hit," Woonsocket Call, 22 September 2004, www.woonsocketcall.com/site/news.cfm?newsid=12976112&BRD=1712&PAG=461&dept_id=106787&rfi=6.

[92] Patriots receiver Deion Branch, "Quotes from New England Patriots Press Conference," January 31, 2005.

[93] Patriots safety Rodney Harrison, "Quotes from New England Patriots Press Conference," January 30, 2005.

[94] Patriots backup quarterback Chris Redman, quoted in: Mike Reiss, "Chris Redman Q&A," *Boston Herald* blog, 13 May 2005.

[95] Patriots center Dan Koppen, quoted in: Adam Kilgore, "Thus far, Mankins is guardedly optimistic," *Boston Globe*, 31 July 2005.

[96] Cornerback Ellis Hobbs, drafted by the Patriots in April 2005, quoted in: Fluto Shinzawa, "Big challenge for Hobbs," *Boston Globe*, 24 April 2005.

[97] Linebacker Willie McGinest, quoted in: Jackie MacMullan, "Sack leader is a sacrifice leader," *Boston Globe*, 23 January 2005.

[98] Tedy Bruschi, "Quotes from New England Media Day," 1 February 2005.

[99] Romeo Crennel, quoted in: Ron Borges, "On top of things," *Boston Globe*, 23 August 2005.

[100] Scott Pioli, quoted in: David Aldridge, "Spurs, Patriots have formed a winning alliance," *Philadelphia Inquirer*, 26 June 2005.

[101] Romeo Crennel, "Quotes from New England Patriots Media Session," 3 February 2005.

[102] Tom Brady, quoted in: Nicholas J. Cotsonika, "Game by game, U-M's Brady strives to achieve perfection," *Detroit Free Press*, 23 September 1998, www.patriotsplanet.com/BB/showthread.php?s=&threadid=6999.

[103] Philadelphia Eagles cornerback Sheldon Brown, "Quotes from Philadelphia Eagles Press Conference," 3 February 2005.

[104] Tom Brady, quoted in: Nicholas J. Cotsonika, "Game by game, U-M's Brady strives to achieve perfection," *Detroit Free Press*, 23 September 1998, www.patriotsplanet.com/BB/showthread.php?s=&threadid=6999.

[105] Tom Brady, quoted in: Jefferey Wank, "Experiences Guide Brady's Michigan Success," Notre Dame Football Program, September 1999, www.patriotsplanet.com/BB/showthread.php?s=&threadid=6999.

[106] Tom Brady, quoted in: Mike Reiss, "Scenes from the Super Bowl ring ceremony," *Boston Herald* blog, 12 June 2005.

[107] Tom Brady, "Tom Brady Post Practice Interview," *Patriots.com*, 4 August 2005.

[108] Tom Brady, quoted in: Jefferey Wank, "Experiences Guide Brady's Michigan Success," Notre Dame Football Program, September 1999, www.patriotsplanet.com/BB/showthread.php?s=&threadid=6999.

[109] Michigan linebacker James Hall, quoted in: Michael Rosenberg, "Brady glad maturity finally came to pass," *Detroit Free Press*, 27 December 1999, www.patriotsplanet.com/BB/showthread.php?s=&threadid=6999.

[110] Tom Brady, quoted in: Nicholas J. Cotsonika, "Game by game, U-M's Brady strives to achieve perfection," *Detroit Free Press*, 23 September 1998, www.patriotsplanet.com/BB/showthread.php?s=&threadid=6999.

[111] University of Michigan head coach Lloyd Carr, quoted in: Michael J. Happy, "Brady comes off the canvas to lead Michigan past Penn State," *SportsLine*, 13 November 1999, www.patriotsplanet.com/BB/showthread.php?s=&threadid=6999.

[112] Pam Rehbein, quoted in: Jackie MacMullen, "Glory tinged with sorrow," *Boston Globe*, 31 January 2005, www.boston.com/sports/football/patriots/superbowl/globe_stories/013102/glory_tinged_with_sorrow+.shtml.

[113] Former Patriot defensive end and Tom Brady housemate Dave Nugent, quoted in: Bill Beuttler, "Tom Brady Avoids the Blitz," *Boston Magazine*, August 2002, www.absolutebrady.com/Articles/BIOBM080102.html.

[114] Patriots nose tackle Vince Wilfork, "Quotes from New England Patriots Press Conference," 3 February 2005.

[115] Patriots quarterback Doug Flutie, quoted in: Nick Cafardo, "Terms of enrichment," *Boston Globe*, 12 June 2005.

[116] Patriots VP of player personnel Scott Pioli, quoted in: Dan Shaughnessy, "The brains behind Belichick," *Boston Globe*, 6 February 2005, www.mercurynews.com/mld/mercurynews/sports/football/nfl/san_francisco_49ers/10826560.htm.

[117] Dr. David Lykken, *Happiness*, New York: St. Martin's Griffin, 1999, p. 105.

[118] Edward L. Gubman, *The Talent Solution*, USA: McGraw-Hill, 1998, p. 134.

[119] L. Cranmer, "Belichick has come a long way," *Chillicothe Gazette*, 7 February 2005, www.chillicothegazette.com/news/stories/20050207/localsports/1963706.html.

[120] New defensive coordinator Eric Mangini, quoted in: Jerome Solomon, "Winning formula," *Boston Globe*, 26 July 2005.

[121] Patriots offensive lineman Joe Andruzzi, "Quotes from New England Patriots Press Conference," 30 January 2005.

[122] Patriots tight end Christian Fauria, quoted in: Damon Hack, "Patriots: Dynasty is at a crossroads," *International Herald Tribune*, 14 January 2005.

[123] Patriots fullback/linebacker Dan Klecko, quoted in: Michael Felger, "Klecko conversion far from complete," *MetroWest Daily News*, 30 March 2005, www.dailynewstribune.com/sportsNews/view.bg?articleid=53191.

[124] Associated Press, "Redskins to troubled Taylor: Stay away," *San Gabriel Valley Tribune*, 6 June 2005.

[125] Washington Redskins safety Sean Taylor, quoted in: Joseph White (AP), "Redskins' Sean Taylor Expresses No Regrets," *SFGate.com*, 1 August 2005.

[126] Richard Oliver, "Bledsoe must stand his ground," *San Antonio Express-News*, 3 June 2005.

[127] Ed Duckworth, "Bucs Mosh Patriots," *South Coast Today*, 17 November 1997, www.southcoasttoday.com/daily/11-97/11-17-97/d03sp117.htm.

[128] Drew Bledsoe, quoted in: Ed Duckworth, "Bucs Mosh Patriots," *South Coast Today*, 17 November 1997, www.southcoasttoday.com/daily/11-97/11-17-97/d03sp117.htm.

[129] Patriots linebacker Ted Johnson, quoted in: Nick Cafardo, "This hobby can be hobbling," *Boston Globe*, 15 May 2005.

[130] Teresa M. Walker (AP), "Notes: Titans RB Brown breaks hand; Dolphins re-sign Boston," *USA Today*, 18 May 2005.

[131] Tony Grossi, "Andre Davis receives the OK to look," *Cleveland Plain Dealer*, 21 August 2005.

[132] Left tackle Matt Light, quoted in: Nick Cafardo, "Patten looks out for No. 1," *Boston Globe*, 26 June 2005.

[133] Patriots tight end Benjamin Watson, quoted in: Jerome Solomon, "They're eager to make amends," *Boston Globe*, 26 May 2005.

[134] Patriots safety Rodney Harrison, "Quotes from New England Patriots Press Conference," 30 January 2005.

[135] Tom Brady, quoted in: Chris Kennedy, "Brady ready for new season," *The Republican*, 10 June 2005.

[136] Bill Belichick, "Quotes from New England Patriots Press Conference," 31 January 2005.

[137] Saints head coach Jim Haslett, quoted in: Kevin Mannix, "Prize was size: Sullivan: 'Roid use was obvious," *Milford Daily News*, 27 March 2005, www.milforddailynews.com/sportsNews/view.bg?articleid=68225.

[138] Linebacker Tedy Bruschi, quoted in: Bryan Morry, "SB Analysis: Light 4-3 gave Pats the edge; SB Notes," *Patriots.com*, 9 February 2005.

[139] Dr. David Lykken, *Happiness*, New York: St. Martin's Griffin, 1999, pp. 82-83.

[140] Patriots safety Rodney Harrison, "Quotes from New England Patriots Press Conference," February 2, 2005.

[141] Dr. David Lykken, *Happiness*, New York: St. Martin's Griffin, 1999, p. 63.

[142] Charlie Nobles, "Dolphins' New Coach Casts a Grimace in the Mold of Shula," *New York Times*, 24 July 2005.

[143] Daniel Goleman, quoted in: Paul Kaihla, "The CEO's Secret Handbook." *Business 2.0*, July 2005, 70.

[144] Hugh Guthrie, quoted in: Peter Coy, "Old. Smart. Productive." *BusinessWeek*, 27 June 2005, p. 86.

[145] Steve Jobs, CEO of Apple and Pixar, speech at Stanford University graduation, reprinted in: "Stay Hungry. Stay Foolish." *Fortune*, 5 September 2005.

[146] "BuzzardBlaster's 2002 NFL Draft Prospect Ratings: Wide Receivers," www.brownsplay.com/offseason/2002/draft2002/2002WR.asp.

[147] Bill Belichick, after drafting receiver Deion Branch, quoted in: "2002 NFL Draft at a glance," www.sandlotshrink.com/fbcollege2002.htm.

[148] San Francisco 49ers coach Mike Nolan, quoted in: Marcia C. Smith, *Orange County Register*, 29 January 2005.

[149] Patriots VP of player personnel Scott Pioli, quoted in: Jeff Legwold, "Safe deposits," *Rocky Mountain News*, 26 February 2005, http://rockymountainnews.com/drmn/broncos/article/0,1299,DRMN_17_3578518,00.html.

[150] Patriots safety Rodney Harrison, quoted in: Jim Trotter, "MVP has double-double," *San Diego Union-Tribune*, 7 February 2005, www.signonsandiego.com/sports/nfl/20050207-9999-1z1x7super4b.html.

[151] Bill Belichick, "Belichick Press Conference," *Patriots.com*, 24 April 2005.

[152] Cornerback Ellis Hobbs, quoted in: Alan Greenberg, "Patriots Just Stick to the Essentials," *Hartford Courant*, 25 April 2005.

[153] Offensive lineman Logan Mankins, "Logan Mankins - Phone Conference," Patriots.com, 23 April 2005.

[154] Matt Light, quoted in: Mike Reiss, "Reiss: Light weighs in," *MetroWest Daily News*, 10 July 2005.

[155] Vince Wilfork's high school football coach Ray Berger, quoted in: Bryan Morry, "PFW: Wilfork rides the wave," *Patriots Football Weekly*, 27 June 2005.

[156] Vince Wilfork's high school football coach Ray Berger, quoted in: Bryan Morry, "PFW: Wilfork rides the wave," *Patriots Football Weekly*, 27 June 2005.

[157] Vince Wilfork's high school football coach Ray Berger, quoted in: Bryan Morry, "PFW: Wilfork rides the wave," *Patriots Football Weekly*, 27 June 2005.

[158] Chris Zorich, quoted in: Jim O'Donnell, "Irish 'Patriots' show Weis they've got game," *Chicago Sun-Times*, 24 April 2005, www.suntimes.com/output/campus/cst-spt-nd24.html.

[159] "bigcheelay" on the *Fresno State Bark Board*, 24 April 2005, http://mb3.scout.com/ffresnostatefrm1.showMessage?topicID=11694.topic.

[160] Linebacker Ryan Claridge, 2005 Patriots draftee, "Ryan Claridge Phone Conference," *Patriots.com*, 24 April 2005.

[161] Dr. Mihaly Csikszentmihalyi, *Flow*, USA: HarperPerennial, 1990, p. 10.

[162] Dr. David Lykken, *Happiness*, New York: St. Martin's Griffin, 1999, pp. 23-24.

[163] Tom Brady, quoted in: Tom E. Curran, "Save for you ladies, no reason to shed tears for Brady," tombradyonline.net/arcnov.html, 30 November 2003.

[164] Patriots receiver David Terrell, quoted in: Mike Lowe, "NFL's model for success? The Patriots," *MaineToday.com*, 12 June 2005.

[165] Notre Dame head coach Charlie Weis, quotedin: Todd D. Burlage, "First spring drills leave Irish with long to-do list," *Journal Gazette*, 30 March 2005, www.fortwayne.com/mld/journalgazette/sports/11266127.htm.

[166] Dr. Mihaly Csikszentmihalyi, *Flow*, USA: HarperPerennial, 1990, pp. 3-4.

[167] Dr. Mihaly Csikszentmihalyi, *Flow*, USA: HarperPerennial, 1990, p. 49.

[168] Patriots offensive lineman Joe Andruzzi, "Quotes from New England Patriots Press Conference," 30 January 2005.

[169] Matthew Boyle, "The Wegmans Way," *Fortune*, 24 January 2005, p. 68.

[170] Bill Belichick, in speech at Bryant University, quoted in: Steve Mazzone, "Belichick keynote speaker at Bryant," *The Herald News*, 1 April 2005, www.zwire.com/site/news.cfm?newsid=14263950.

[171] Ken Hartnett, "In-Vince-a-Bill," *Standard-Times*, 21 July 2002.

[172] Dr. Mihaly Csikszentmihalyi, *Finding Flow*, USA: Basic Books, 1997, pp. 42-43.

[173] 2005 Patriots draftee Andy Stokes, *Patriots Video News*, 4 May 2005.

[174] Daniel Goleman, *Emotional Intelligence*, 1995, quoted in: www.uwsp.edu/education/lwilson/learning/emot.htm.

[175] Patriots linebacker Rosevelt Colvin, quoted in: Bryan Morry, "Patriots provide inside look at Super Bowl XXXIX," 10 March 2005, www.patriots.com/news/index.cfm?ac=latestnewsdetail&pid=11041&pcid=41.

[176] Patriots backup quarterback Chris Redman, quoted in: Mike Reiss, "Chris Redman Q&A," *Boston Herald* blog, 13 May 2005.

[177] Tom Brady, "Quotes from New England Patriots Press Conference," February 2, 2005.

[178] Patriots linebacker Willie McGinest, "NFL Total Access: Week in Review," *NFL Network*, recorded 15 May 2005.

[179] According to data from the University of Chicago's National Opinion Research Center, cited in: Bob Condor, "In Pursuit of Happiness," December 9, 1998, www.evergreenpark.org/departments/teachersites/boersma/files/WhatisHappiness.html.

[180] Patriots linebacker Ted Johnson, "Quotes from New England Patriots Press Conference," 3 February 2005.

[181] See, for example, the review article "Unit Cohesion and the Military Mission," http://psychology.ucdavis.edu/rainbow/html/military_cohesion.html. Also: www.montana.edu/craigs/team%20cohesion.htm and Section IV of www.exercisephysiologists.com/SocialInfluences/.

[182] Daniel Goleman, quoted in: Paul Kaihla, "The CEO's Secret Handbook." *Business 2.0*, July 2005, 70.

[183] Michael Andretti, whose Andretti Green Racing won the IndyCar championship and eight of 16 Honda car races in 2004, quoted in: Michael Welton, "Andretti Green Racing is team-first operation," *East Valley Tribune*, 18 March 2005, www.eastvalleytribune.com/index.php?sty=38165.

[184] See www.watchman.org/cat95.htm, www.factnet.org and www.freedomofmind.com/resourcecenter/groups/.

[185] Patriots center/guard Damien Woody, quoted in: Jackie MacMullan, "Grief channeled to higher goals," *Boston Globe*, 5 February 2002.

[186] Catalyst survey, cited in: Betsy Morris, "How Corporate America is Betraying Women," *Fortune*, 10 January 2005, pp. 70 & 72.

[187] 93,700 vs. 22,000 on 14 July 2005.

[188] "News in brief," 8 February 2005, www.braintypes.com/news_in_brief.htm.

[189] Calculated based on estimates based on inferential statistics using the U.S. population posted at http://en.wikipedia.org/wiki/Myers-Briggs_Type_Indicator.

[190] CEO of SAB Graham Mackay, quoted in: Patricia Sellers, "SAB brews up big trouble for Bud," *Fortune*, 22 August 2005.

[191] Patriot defensive lineman Mike Wright, quoted in: Alan Greenberg, "Wright Creates Spot For Himself On Patriots Roster," *Hartford Courant*, 5 September 2005.

[192] P.K. Sam, quoted in: Jerome Solomon, "Sam and Terrell among Patriots' cuts," *Boston Globe*, 4 September 2005.

[193] Raytheon CEO Bill Swanson, quoted in: Paul Kaihla, "The CEO's Secret Handbook." *Business 2.0*, July 2005, p. 74.

[194] Cornerback Asante Samuel, "Quotes From New England Patriots Press Conference," 2 February 2005.

[195] Former Patriots safety Lawyer Milloy, quoted in: John Hassan, "Inside Belichick's Brain," *ESPN the Magazine*, 9 September 2002.

[196] Patriots safety Rodney Harrison, "Quotes from New England Patriots Press Conference," 30 January 2005.

[197] Tom Brady, "Mini Camp: Day 2," *Patriots Video News*, 10 June 2005.

[198] Bill Belichick, quoted in: Ian M. Clark, "Patriots Notebook: Cassel is out of Heismans' shadow," *Union Leader*, 5 August 2005.

[199] Patriots linebacker Ted Johnson, "Patriots Video News," *Patriots.com*, 30 June 2005.

[200] Patriots linebacker Willie McGinest, "Quotes from New England Patriots Press Session," 2 February 2005.

[201] Patriots safety Rodney Harrison, "Quotes From New England Patriots Media Day," 1 February 2005.

[202] Patriots linebacker Ted Johnson, "Quotes from New England Patriots Press Conference," 3 February 2005.

[203] Bill Belichick, speech to the Big Brothers of Massachusetts Bay, quoted in: Bryan Morry, "Belichick delivers his message to Big Brothers," *Patriots.com*, 20 May 2005.

[204] Bill Belichick, pre-commencement address to Wesleyan Assembly, May 2005, www.wesleyan.edu/newsrel/pressreleases/belichickcomm05.html.

[205] Bill Belichick, speech to the Big Brothers of Massachusetts Bay, quoted in: Bryan Morry, "Belichick delivers his message to Big Brothers," *Patriots.com*, 20 May 2005.

[206] Linebacker Willie McGinest, quoted in: Jackie MacMullan, "Sack leader is a sacrifice leader," *Boston Globe*, 23 January 2005.

[207] New Patriots receiver David Terrell, quoted in: Mike Reiss, "David Terrell Q&A," *Boston Herald* blog, 27 May 2005.

[208] Patriots linebacker Ted Johnson, quoted in: Tom E. Curran, "Bruschi decision eases minds, leaves void," *Providence Journal*, 24 July 2005.

[209] Running back Kory Chapman, quoted in: Mike Reiss, "Chapman in RB mix," *Boston Herald* blog, 18 May 2005.

[210] "Box_O_Rocks" posting on "NFLE: Kory Chapman" thread on *PatsFans.com*, 29 May 2005.

[211] Deion Branch, quoted in: Howard Ulman (AP), "Troy Brown excited to return to Patriots," *LA Times*, 10 August 2005.

[212] Patriots rookie receiver Brandon "Bam" Childress, quoted in: Alan Greenberg, "Childress, Anderson Vie For Spot That May Not Exist," *Hartford Courant*, 15 August 2005.

[213] Rookie offensive lineman Nick Kaczur, "Early Roster Cuts and More," *Patriots Video News*, 29 August 2005.

[214] Bill Belichick, "Quotes from New England Patriots Press Conference," 30 January 2005.

[215] Patriots nose tackle Ethan Kelley, quoted in: Andy Hart, "Opportunity knocks at NT for Kelley," *Patriots.com*, 5 May 2005.

[216] Patriots nose tackle Keith Traylor, "Quotes from New England Patriots Media Day," 3 February 2005.

[217] Buffalo Bills general manager Tom Donahoe, quoted in: Nick Cafardo, "McGinest tackles some topics," *Boston Globe*, 24 July 2005.

[218] Former Patriots and Bills quarterback Drew Bledsoe, quoted in: "A tough drop for Bledsoe," *Boston Globe*, 20 February 2005, www.boston.com/sports/football/articles/2005/02/20/a_tough_drop_for_bledsoe.

[219] Former Patriots and Bills quarterback Drew Bledsoe, quoted in: AP, "Bledsoe gets 3-year deal from Dallas," *Providence Journal*, 24 February 2005, www.projo.com/patriots/content/projo_20050224_24bledsoe.236f585.html.

[220] Patriots cornerback Randall Gay, quoted in: Associated Press, "New England CB reflects on memorable rookie season," *The Dispatch*, 4 August 2005.

[221] Patriots cornerback Duane Starks, quoted in: Mark Farinella, "Starks upbeat," *Sun Chronicle*, 4 August 2005.

[222] New Patriots receiver David Terrell, quoted in: Matt Kalman, "Terrell's new Pat-itude: Team first," *Chicago Sun-Times*, 5 August 2005.

[223] Tedy Bruschi, "Quotes from New England Media Day," 1 February 2005.

[224] Patriots linebacker Ted Johnson, audio recording, 1 February 2005.

[225] Patriots wide receiver David Givens, "Quotes from New England Patriots Press Conference," 31 January 2005.

[226] Patriots receiver P.K. Sam, quoted in: Howard Ulman (AP), "Youngest player drafted last year is maturing," *Tuscaloosa News*, 1 August 2005.

[227] Patriots safety Rodney Harrison, "Quotes From New England Patriots Media Day," 1 February 2005.

[228] Patriots safety Rodney Harrison, "Quotes From New England Patriots Media Day," 1 February 2005.

[229] Safety Eugene Wilson, telephone interview, *ProFootballCentral.com* radio, 9 March 2005.

[230] Patriots cornerback Randall Gay, "Quotes From New England Patriots Press Conference," 2 February 2005.

[231] Cornerback Asante Samuel, "Quotes From New England Patriots Press Conference," 2 February 2005.

[232] Patriots safety Guss Scott, quoted in: Andy Hart, "Scott anxious for '05 action," *Patriots.com*, 3 June 2005.

[233] Patriots safety Rodney Harrison, "Quotes From New England Patriots Press Conference," February 3, 2005.

[234] Bill Belichick, quoted in: Jerome Solomon, "Secondary issues are a priority for Patriots," *Boston Globe*, 11 June 2005.

[235] Patriots tight end Andy Stokes, quoted in: "Stokes pursues spot on Patriots' roster," *The Spectrum* (St. George, UT), 8 July 2005.

[236] David Patten, quoted in: Nick Cafardo, "Patten looks out for No. 1," *Boston Globe*, 26 June 2005.

[237] Patriots linebacker Ted Johnson, "Quotes from New England Patriots Press Conference," 3 February 2005.

[238] 2005 Patriots draftee Andy Stokes, *Patriots Video News*, 4 May 2005.

[239] Patriots linebacker Tedy Bruschi, "Quotes from New England Patriots Press Conference," 31 January 2005.

[240] Phil Simms, "Belichick learns as he goes," *Superbowl.com*, 28 January 2004, www.superbowl.com/news/story/7043711.

[241] New Patriot linebacker Chad Brown, quoted in: Jim Corbett, "Despite key losses, now is no time to count Patriots out," *USA Today*, 17 August 2005.

[242] Patriots wide receiver / nickel back / punt returner Troy Brown, "Quotes from New England Patriots Press Conference," 30 January 2005.

[243] Patriots linebacker Willie McGinest, *21: The Story Behind the NFL's longest winning streak*.

[244] Bill Belichick, *21: The Story Behind the NFL's longest winning streak*.

[245] Jim Thomas, "Rams shake, rattle and roll," *St. Louis Post-Dispatch*, www.ramsfan.us/oldnews/2001/111801-1.htm.

[246] Bill Belichick, "Bill Belichick Press Conf. Transcript 9/5/04," *Patriots.com*, 5 September 2004, www.patriots.com/news/FullArticle.sps?id=30434.

[247] New Patriot receiver Tim Dwight, quoted in: Mike Reiss, "Patriots beat: He's catching on quickly," *MetroWest Daily News*, 28 April 2005.

[248] Don Norford, quoted in: Jackie MacMullan, "Sack leader is a sacrifice leader," *Boston Globe*, 23 January 2005.

[249] Patriots safety Rodney Harrison, "Quotes From New England Patriots Press Conference," 30 January 2005.

[250] www.rotarylombardiaward.com.

[251] Ken Sims, quoted in: Chip Brown (Dallas Morning News), "UT legend Sims at peace with NFL career," WFAA.com, 30 May 2005.

[252] Kevin Elko, sports psychologist to some NFL teams, quoted in: Mike Freeman, *Bloody Sundays*, Perennial Currents: USA, 2003, p. xviii.

[253] Patriots tight end Andy Stokes, quoted in: "Stokes pursues spot on Patriots' roster," *The Spectrum* (St. George, UT), 8 July 2005.

[254] Bill Belichick, quoted in: Harvey Mackay, *We Got Fired!*, New York: Ballantine Books, 2004, p. 67.

[255] Tim Green, *The Dark Side of the Game*, USA: Warner Books, 1996, pp. 75 & 78.

[256] Troy Brown, "Quotes from New England Press Conference," 2 Febuary 2005.

[257] Patriots linebacker Willie McGinest, "Quotes from New England Patriots Press Session," 3 February 2005.

[258] Patriots inside linebackers coach Pepper Johnson, *Won For All*, Chicago: Contemporary Books, 2003, p. 141.

[259] Bill Belichick, quoted in: Hector Longo, "Not your average Joe," *Eagle Tribune*, 1 February 2002, www.eagletribune.com/news/stories/20020201/SP_006.htm.

[260] Quarterback Doug Flutie, quoted in: Mike Reiss, "Flutie ready to provide assistance," *MetroWest Daily News*, 12 May 2005.

[261] 2005 Patriots draft choice, TE Andy Stokes, quoted in: Michael Parente, " Rookies take first steps in Patriots uniforms," *Woonsocket Call*, 30 April 2005.

[262] Scott Pioli, quoted in: Paul Doyle, "Pioli Remains True To His School," *Hartford Courant*, 15 May 2005, www.courant.com/sports/football/patriots/hc-pioli0515.artmay15,0,6021677.print.story.

[263] Bill Belichick, speech at Bryant University, quoted in: Mike Reiss, "Leftovers from Belichick," 31 March 2005, www.bostonherald.com/blogs/reissPieces/index.bg.

[264] Michael Silver, "Pat Answer," *Sports Illustrated*, 11 February 2002, http://sportsillustrated.cnn.com/si_online/news/2002/02/11/pat_answer/.

[265] Inside linebackers coach Pepper Johnson, quoted in: Jay Glazer, "Pats notes: New England defense lays down the Law," *CBS Sportsline*, 4 February 2002, http://cbs.sportsline.com/b/page/pressbox/0,1328,4948780,00.html.

[266] Patriots tight end Christian Fauria, quoted in: Bob Ryan, "No disguise, Fauria is just one of the guys," *Boston Globe*, 2 February 2004, www.boston.com/sports/football/patriots/articles/2004/02/02/no_disguise_fauria_is_just_one_of_the_guys.

[267] Patriots special teams captain Larry Izzo, "Quotes from New England Patriots Press Conference," 30 January 2005.

[268] Patriots quarterback Tom Brady, "Quotes from New England Patriots Press Conference," 30 January 2005.

[269] Patriots quarterback Tom Brady, "Quotes from New England Patriots Press Conference," 30 January 2005.

[270] Patriots special teams captain Larry Izzo, "Quotes from New England Patriots Press Conference," 30 January 2005.

[271] Patriots receiver David Givens, "Quotes from New England Patriots Press Conference," 31 January 2005.

[272] Eagles cornerback Lito Sheppard, "Quotes from Philadelphia Eagles Press Conference," 30 January 2005.

[273] Eagles linebacker Jeremiah Trotter, "Quotes from Philadelphia Eagles Press Conference," 1 February 2005.

[274] Eagles linebacker Mark Simoneau, "Quotes from Philadelphia Eagles Press Conference," 2 February 2005.

[275] Philadelphia Eagles head coach Andy Reid, quoted in: Chris Colston (*USA Today Weekly*), "Philadelphia Eagles Pool Report," 2 February 2005.

[276] Philadelphia Eagles head coach Andy Reid, "Quotes from Philadelphia Eagles Press Conference," 30 January 2005.

[277] Eagles safety Brian Dawkins, "Quotes From Philadelphia Eagles Media Day," 31 January 2005.

[278] Eagles defensive tackle Corey Simon, "Quotes from Philadelphia Eagles Press Conference," 31 January 2005.

[279] Eagles defensive tackle Corey Simon, "Quotes from Philadelphia Eagles Media Day," 1 February 2005.

[280] Eagles center Hank Fraley, "Quotes from Philadelphia Eagles Media Conference," 2 February 2005.

[281] Patriots linebacker Willie McGinest, "Quotes From New England Patriots Media Day," 1 February 2005.

[282] Patriots linebacker Tedy Bruschi, "Quotes from New England Patriots Media Session," 2 February 2005.

[283] Tom Brady, "Quotes from New England Patriots Press Conference," 3 February 2005.

[284] Offensive lineman Joe Andruzzi, "Quotes from New England Patriots Media Day," 1 February 2005.

[285] Patriots left tackle Matt Light, "Quotes from New England Press Conference," 2 Febuary 2005.

[286] Patriots linebacker Tedy Bruschi, "Quotes from New England Patriots Media Session," 2 February 2005.

[287] Patriots receiver Troy Brown, "Quotes from New England Patriots Press Conference," February 2, 2005.

[288] Defensive end Jarvis Green, quoted in: Mike Kiral, "Green says Patriots aren't feeling pressure to win third straight Super Bowl in 2005," *Ascension Citizen*, 27 July 2005.

[289] Patriots receiver Deion Branch, "Quotes From New England Patriots Press Conference," 2 February 2005.

[290] Patriots receiver Deion Branch, quoted in: Eric McHugh, "And now, it's time for Deion to appear," *Patriot Ledger*, 5 September 2005.

[291] Mike Reiss, "Football's end game: The challenge of post-career planning," *Metrowest Daily News*, 30 May 2004, www.metrowestdailynews.com/sportsNews/view.bg?articleid=69553.

[292] Defensive lineman Jarvis Green, quoted in: Larry Weisman, "NFL players work 9-to-5 jobs to get ready for post-football life," *Salt Lake Tribune*, 20 June 2004, www.sltrib.com/2004/Jun/06202004/sports/177026.asp.

[293] Defensive lineman Jarvis Green, quoted in: Mike Reiss, "Football's end game: The challenge of post-career planning," *Metrowest Daily News*, 30 May 2004, www.metrowestdailynews.com/sportsNews/view.bg?articleid=69553.

[294] Jarvis Green, quoted in: Chris Kennedy, "Green's priorities in order," *The Republican*, 2 August 2005.

[295] Patriots defensive lineman Anthony Pleasant, quoted in: Thomas Heath, "Today's smart professional athletes are banking those big paydays," *Washington Post*, 28 June 2004, www.projo.com/business/content/projo_20040628_jock28x.2ecb35.html.

[296] Matt Light, quoted in: Thomas Heath, "Today's smart professional athletes are banking those big paydays," *Washington Post*, 28 June 2004, www.projo.com/business/content/projo_20040628_jock28x.2ecb35.html.

[297] Patriots rookie defensive end Marquise Hill, quoted in: Chris Kennedy, "Patriots' rookie sees future after football," *The Republican*, 20 August 2004, www.masslive.com/patriots/republican/index.ssf?/base/sports-0/1092988103142780.xml.

[298] Patriots rookie defensive end Marquise Hill, quoted in: Chris Kennedy, "Patriots' rookie sees future after football," *The Republican*, 20 August 2004, www.masslive.com/patriots/republican/index.ssf?/base/sports-0/1092988103142780.xml.

[299] Patriots safety Rodney Harrison, quoted in: Brian Fleming, "Harrison seeing life on other side," *Boston Sports Review*, 12 April 2005.

[300] Patriots special teamer Je'Rod Cherry, quoted in: Mike Reiss, "Football's end game: The challenge of post-career planning," *Metrowest Daily News*, 30 May 2004, www.metrowestdailynews.com/sportsNews/view.bg?articleid=69553.

[301] Patriots special teamer Je'Rod Cherry, quoted in: Mike Reiss, "Football's end game: The challenge of post-career planning," *Metrowest Daily News*, 30 May 2004, www.metrowestdailynews.com/sportsNews/view.bg?articleid=69553.

[302] Glen Crevier, Associated Press Sports Editors, June 2000, apse.dallasnews.com/jun2000/19-21crevier.html.

[303] Patriots linebacker Willie McGinest, "Quotes from New England Patriots Press Conference," 30 January 2005.

[304] Bob Socci, "A Friendship Formed By Fate," *Navy Sports*, 28 January 2004, www.navysports.com/sports/football/release.asp?RELEASE_ID=15595.

[305] Patriots fullback Fred McCrary, quoted in: Andy Kent, "NFL: McCrary eyes Pats starting role," *Naples Daily News*, 20 July 2004, www.naplesnews.com/npdn/sports/article/0,2071,NPDN_15000_3049089,00.html.

[306] Patriots director of media relations Stacey James, quoted in: Mike Reiss, "Patriots rookies learn to relate," *Boston Herald*, 5 June 2004.

[307] Bill Belichick: *Patriots Video News*, 12 November 2004, http://cachewww.patriots.com/mediacenter/index.cfm?ac=videonewsdetail&pid=9708&pcid=78.

[308] Tom E. Curran, "Second-rounder Hill gets reported 5-year Pats deal," *Providence Journal*, 24 June 2004, www.projo.com/patriots/content/projo_20040624_24patsjo.a1a78.html.

[309] Patriots rookie Benjamin Watson, quoted in: Chris Kennedy, "Rookie joins teammates," *The Republican*, 17 August 2004, www.masslive.com/sports/republican/index.ssf?/base/sports-2/1092734132304750.xml.

[310] Patriots center Dan Koppen, quoted in: Adam Kilgore, "Mankins's play speaks for itself," *Boston Globe*, 13 August 2005.

[311] Patriots linebacker Ted Johnson, "Quotes from New England Patriots Media Day," February 1, 2005.

[312] Patriots running back Corey Dillon, "Quotes from New England Patriots Media Day," 1 February 2005.

[313] Patriots running back Corey Dillon, "Quotes from New England Patriots Media Day," 1 February 2005.

[314] Patriots linebacker Willie McGinest, "Quotes From New England Patriots Press Session," 2 February 2005.

[315] Patriots linebacker Tedy Bruschi, "Quotes from New England Patriots Press Conference," 31 January 2005.

[316] Patriots linebacker Roman Phifer, "Quotes From New England Patriots Press Conference," 3 February 2005.

[317] Patriots running back Corey Dillon, quoted in: Michael Felger, "Food for thought: Dillon still hungry," *Boston Herald*, 27 May 2005.

[318] Patriots running back Corey Dillon, quoted in: Nick Cafardo, "Dillon rushing to prove there will be no dropoff," *Boston Globe*, 1 August 2005.

[319] Patriots tight end Christian Fauria, quoted in: Karen Guregian, "Mangini in spotlight," *Boston Herald*, 31 August 2005.

[320] Patriots tight end Ted Johnson, "Patriots Video News," *Patriots.com*, 30 June 2005.

[321] Len Pasquarelli, "In Romeo they trust," *ESPN.com*, 3 August 2005.

[322] Cleveland Browns tight end Aaron Shea, quoted in: Steve King, "Camp Crennel yields progress," *ClevelandBrowns.com*, 25 August 2005.

[323] Rick Gosselin, "By power of 3, Patriots defy rules," *Dallas Morning News*, 2 August 2005.

[324] Bill Belichick, quoted in: Cam Inman, "Patriots Provide Model the 49ers Want to Emulate," *Contra Costa Times*, 2 January 2005.

[325] Patriots owner Bob Kraft, quoted in: Monte Burke, "Unlikely Dynasty," *Forbes*, 19 September 2005.

[326] Quarterback Doug Flutie, quoted in: Mike Reiss, "Flutie ready to provide assistance," *MetroWest Daily News*, 12 May 2005.

[327] Tom Brady, quoted in: Alan Greenberg, "Pat-ended process; Belichick can find those keepers," 1 February 2004, p. E1, ProQuest database.

[328] Andy Hart, "Media members walk in players' shoes," *Patriots Football Weekly*, 17 July 2003, www.patriots.com/news/fullarticle.sps?id=24287&type=general&special_section=TrainingCamp2003&bhcp=1.

[329] Bill Belichick, quoted in: Tom E. Curran, "Notebook: Watson signs deal in time for practice," *Providence Journal*, 17 August 2004, www.patriots.com/content/projo_20040817_17patsjo.2d6a6.html.

[330] Tom Brady, quoted in: Alan Greenberg, "Pat-ended process; Belichick can find those keepers," 1 February 2004, p. E1, ProQuest database.

[331] Michael Holley, "Best seat in the house," *Boston Globe*, 7 December 2000, www.allthingsbillbelichick.com/articles/bestseat.htm.

[332] Bill Belichick, "Belichick Press Conference," *Patriots.com*, 9 June 2005.

[333] Bill Belichick, "Belichick Press Conference," *Patriots.com*, 24 April 2005.

[334] Patriots cornerback Ty Law, on WEEI Sports Radio 850 AM, "Ty Law with the Big Show on WEEI," 2 March 2005, www.allthingsbillbelichick.com/transcripts/tylawtranscript.htm.

[335] Bill Belichick, quoted in: Tom E. Curran, "Belichick knows sound foundation key to success," *Providence Journal*, 1 May 2005.

[336] Bill Belichick, "Belichick Press Conference," *Patriots.com*, 24 April 2005.

[337] KC Joyner, The Football Scientist, *Scientific Football 2005* (KC's Football Services, Altamonte Springs, FL, 2005), p. 308.

[338] Patriots receiver Deion Branch, quoted in: Tom King, "Catch him if you can," *Nashua Telegraph*, 6 August 2005.

[339] Patriots inside linebacker Ted Johnson, quoted in: Nick Cafardo, "Solid middle management," *Boston Globe*, 30 November 2004, www.boston.com/sports/football/patriots/articles/2004/11/30/solid_middle_management.

[340] Patriots linebacker Chad Brown, "Mini Camp – Day 1," *Patriots Video News*, *Patriots.com*, 9 June 2005 and AP, "Ex-All-Pro finds it tough to replace Bruschi," MSNBC, 10 June 2005.

[341] New Patriot receiver David Terrell, quoted in: Chris Kennedy, "Patriots suit Terrell," *The Republican*, 11 August 2005.

[342] Tom Brady, quoted in: Vic Carucci, "No worries about Brady's slow start," *NFL.com*, 30 July 2005.

[343] Susan A. Jackson and Mihaly Csikszentmihalyi, *Flow in Sports*, www.humankinetics.com/products/showexcerpt.cfm?excerpt_id=3101.

[344] Coach Bill Belichick, quoted in: Associated Press, "Pats' coach Belichick speaks at college graduation ceremony," 3 May 2004, www.abc6.com/superstar_article.php?ID=5092.

[345] Coach Bill Belichick: "Bill Belichick Press Conf. Transcript 4/25/04," *Patriots.com*, 25 April 2004, www.patriots.com/news/FullArticle.sps?id=28541&type=draft.

[346] Bill Belichick, quoted in: Len Pasquarelli, "Coach, QB rewarded for Super Bowl heroics," *ESPN.com*, 4 February 2002, http://espn.go.com/nfl/playoffs01/columns/pasquarelli_len/1322633.html.

[347] Eagles defensive coordinator Jim Johnson, "Quotes from Philadelphia Eagles Media Day," 1 February 2005.

[348] Tom Brady, quoted in: Shannon Ryan, "For Brady, no time to look back," *Philadelphia Inquirer*, 9 September 20004, www.centredaily.com/mld/centredaily/sports/football/nfl/philadelphia_eagles/9613562.htm.

[349] Bill Belichick, quoted in: Ian M. Clark, "Patriots Notebook: Wilson getting comfortable at safety," *Union Leader*, 8 August 2004, www.theunionleader.com/articles_showa.html?article=41934.

[350] Patriots linebacker Willie McGinest, "Quotes From New England Patriots Press Session," 2 February 2005.

[551] Patriots practice squad offensive lineman Jamil Soriano, quoted in: Tom E. Curran, "Pats' Andruzzi keeps leading by example," *Providence Journal*, 15 September 2004, www.projo.com/patriots/content/projo_20040915_15pats.a329f.html.

[552] Jamil Soriano, quoted in: Andy Hart, "Soriano seeking experience, NFL Europe ring," *Patriots Football Weekly*, 5 May 2004, www.patriots.com/news/FullArticle.sps?id=28665&type=general.

[553] Patriots backup quarterback Rohan Davey, quoted in: Michael Felger, "Davey makes noise with Thunder," *Boston Herald*, 28 April 2004, http://patriots.bostonherald.com/patriots/view.bg?articleid=13896.

[554] Patriots backup quarterback Rohan Davey, quoted in: Mike Reiss, "Time is now for Davey: Third-year QB has chance to solidify backup role," *MetroWest Sports*, 12 August 2004, www.metrowestdailynews.com/sportsNews/view.bg?articleid=75296.

[555] Patriots backup quarterback Rohan Davey, quoted in: Kevin McNamara, "Backup plan at QB is starting to take shape," *Providence Journal*, 18 August 2004, www.projo.com/patriots/content/projo_20040818_18pats.116cc8.html.

[556] Patriots backup quarterback Rohan Davey, quoted in: Mike Reiss, "Time is now for Davey: Third-year QB has chance to solidify backup role," *MetroWest Sports*, 12 August 2004, www.metrowestdailynews.com/sportsNews/view.bg?articleid=75296.

[557] Patriots nose tackle Keith Traylor, "Quotes from New England Patriots Media Day," 3 February 2005.

[558] Patriots cornerback Randall Gay, "Quotes from New England Patriots Press Conference," 2 February 2005.

[559] Linebacker Willie McGinest, quoted in: Jackie MacMullan, "Sack leader is a sacrifice leader," *Boston Globe*, 23 January 2005.

[560] Patriots linebacker Chad Brown, quoted in: Tom E. Curran, "Due to a power shortage, Brown working overtime," *Providence Journal*, 1 August 2005.

[561] Receiver Jamin Elliott, quoted in: Henry Hodgson, "Inside the Huddle... Jamin Elliott," 3 March 2005, www.nfleurope.com/news/story/8248626.

[562] Patriots rookie defensive lineman Vince Wilfork, quoted in: Kevin Mannix, "Traylor, Wilfork look to fill a very big hole: Washington leaves void," *Boston Herald*, 9 September 2004, http://patriots.bostonherald.com/patriots/view.bg?articleid=43417.

[563] Bill Belichick, quoted in: Nick Cafardo, "Belichick is in rare form," *Boston Globe*, 23 October 2004, www.boston.com/sports/football/patriots/articles/2004/10/23/belichick_is_in_rare_form.

[564] Tom Brady, quoted in: Tom E. Curran, "Tom Curran: Brady, Belichick seem perfect for each other," *Providence Journal*, 12 August 2004, www.projo.com/patriots/content/projo_20040812_12currcol.dcb5f.html.

[565] Notre Dame tight end Anthony Fasano, quoted in: Todd D. Burlage, "Irish will hit books to learn Weis way," [Fort Wayne, IN] *Journal Gazette*, 29 March 2005, www.fortwayne.com/mld/journalgazette/sports/colleges/11257101.htm.

[566] Notre Dame offensive lineman Dan Stevenson, quoted in: Jason Kelly, "Irish offense gains ground on learning curve," *South Bend Tribune*, 10 April 2005, www.southbendtribune.com/stories/2005/04/10/sports.20050410-sbt-MICH-D1-Irish_offense.sto.

[567] Former Notre Dame quarterback and acting quarterbacks coach Ron Powlus, quoted in: Jason Kelly, "Irish offense gains ground on learning curve," *South Bend Tribune*, 10 April 2005, www.southbendtribune.com/stories/2005/04/10/sports.20050410-sbt-MICH-D1-Irish_offense.sto.

[568] Bill Belichick, quoted in: Rich Thompson, "Vrabel's FBI file full of information," *Boston Herald*, 9 August 2005.

[569] Patriots defensive tackle Ty Warren, quoted in: Jerome Solomon, "This group could be the Patriots' lifeline," *Boston Globe*, 8 August 2005.

[570] Tom Brady, quoted in: Sam Farmer, "Brady Just Wants to Hang With His Bunch," *AbsoluteBrady.com*, 30 January 2004.

[571] Tedy Bruschi, quoted in: Steve King, "Patriots lament Crennel's departure," *ClevelandBrowns.com*, 8 February 2005.

[572] Patriots offensive lineman Russ Hochstein, quoted in: Randy Dockendorf, "Hochstein Emphasizes Importance Of Faith In Education," *Yankton Daily Press & Dakotan*, 22 March 2005.

[573] Patriots running back Corey Dillon, "Quotes from New England Patriots Press Conference," 31 January 2005.

[574] Patriots offensive lineman Russ Hochstein, "Patriots Video News," 9 March 2005, www.patriots.com/mediacenter/index.cfm?ac=videonewsdetail&pid=11017&pcid=78.

[575] Patriots defensive lineman Ty Warren, quoted in: Michael Felger, "Pats' Warren: Time on mind," *Boston Herald*, 18 May 2005.

[576] Former Ravens quarterback Chris Redman, quoted in: Mike Reiss, "Chris Redman Q&A" *Boston Herald* blog, 13 May 2005.

[577] New Patriots receiver David Terrell, quoted in: Mike Reiss, "David Terrell Q&A," *Boston Herald* blog, 27 May 2005.

[578] Patriots coach Mike Woicik, quoted in: Michael Felger, "Woicik fosters winning conditions," *Boston Herald*, 8 September 2005.

[579] Tom Brady, "Quotes from New England Patriots Press Conference," 3 February 2005.

[580] Tom Brady, "Quotes from New England Patriots Press Conference," 3 February 2005.

[581] Romeo Crennel, audio recording, 2 February 2005.

[582] Patriots linebacker Mike Vrabel, "Quotes from New England Patriots Press Conference," 31 January 2005.

[583] Romeo Crennel, audio recording, 2 February 2005.

[584] Patriots special teams coordinator Brad Seely, quoted in: Dan Pompei, "Inside Pats' Super Bowl Preparations," *Sporting News*, 2 February 2004, www.allthingsbillbelichick.com/articles/insidesbprep.htm.

[585] Linebacker Mike Vrabel, "Quotes from New England Patriots Media Day," 1 February 2005.

[586] Patriots linebacker Mike Vrabel, "Quotes from New England Patriots Media Day," 1 February 2005.

[587] Patriots quarterback Doug Flutie, quoted in: Mike Lowe, "NFL's model for success? The Patriots," *MaineToday.com*, 12 June 2005.

[588] Patriots linebacker Monty Beisel, quoted in: Howard Ulman (AP), "Hard-hitting safety ready to face Moss," *San Jose Mercury News*, 6 September 2005.

[589] Patriots quarterback Tom Brady, "Quotes from New England Patriots Press Conference," 30 January 2005.

[590] Patriots receiver Deion Branch, "Quotes from New England Patriots Press Conference," 31 January 2005.

[591] Patriots punter Josh Miller, "Quotes from New England Press Session," 3 February 2005.

[592] Raiders receiver Tim Brown, quoted in: Eric Retter, "FOOTBALL: Guest coaches relish chance," *The Observer*, 26 April 2005.

[593] Patriots receiver Deion Branch, "Quotes from New England Patriots Press Conference," 31 January 2005 and *ESPN* video 1 February 2005.

[594] Patriots linebacker Ted Johnson, quoted in: Mark Purdy, "Quarterback sets own benchmark," *San Jose Mercury News*, February 2004, on: *AbsoluteBrady.com*.

[595] Tom Brady, quoted in: Tom E. Curran, "Save for you ladies, no reason to shed tears for Brady," tombradyonline.net/arcnov.html, 30 November 2003.

[596] Damon Huard, quoted in: Seth Wickersham, "Pat hand," *ESPN The Magazine*, 19 January 2004.

[597] Tom Brady, quoted in: Tom E. Curran, "Running back Chapman is making a case to stay," *Providence Journal*, 17 August 2005.

[598] Tom Brady's uncle, Brother Christopher Brady, quoted in: Karen Crouse, "Brady a reluctant celebrity," 29 January 2004, http://absolutebrady.com/Archive/January2004.html.

[599] Safety Rodney Harrison, quoted in: Karen Guregian, "Back to pass -- Brady calms nerves with practice throws," *Boston Herald*, 15 August 2005.

[600] Tom Brady, quoted in: Jeff Gluck, "Future continues to be bright for Patriots," February 2004, on: *AbsoluteBrady.com*.

[601] Patriots linebacker Willie McGinest, quoted in: Chris Kenney, "Unfinished business," *AbsoluteBrady.com*, 9 January 2004.

[602] Richard Seymour, quoted in: Hector Longo, "Light makes might," *Eagle-Tribune*, 28 January 2004.

[603] Patriots running back Corey Dillon, "Quotes from New England Patriots Press Conference," 31 January 2005.

[604] Patriots receiver Deion Branch, "Quotes from New England Patriots Press Conference," 31 January 2005.

[605] Patriots backup linebacker Matt Chatham, quoted in: Karen Guregian, "Chatham's making his presence known," *Boston Herald*, 2 August 2005.

[606] Patriots linebacker Ted Johnson, "Patriots Video News," *Patriots.com*, 30 June 2005.

[607] Patriots linebacker Ted Johnson, "Patriots Video News," *Patriots.com*, 30 June 2005.

[608] Patriots linebacker Tully Banta-Cain, quoted in: Mike Reiss, "Pats in bonus time: Green and Vrabel in the money," *Boston Herald*, 7 August 2005.

[609] Patriots linebacker Rosevelt Colvin, quoted in: Chris Kennedy, "Seymour just a happy camper," *The Republican*, 4 August 2005.

[610] Bill Belichick, "Bill Belichick Press Conf. Transcript 8/3/04," 3 August 2004, www.patriots.com/news/fullarticle.sps?id=29867&special_section=TrainingCamp2004&type=training.

[611] Patriots nose tackle Vince Wilfork, quoted in: Jerome Solomon, "Wilfork eager to tackle second season," *Boston Globe*, 27 May 2005.

[612] Indianapolis Colts running back Edgerrin James, in the 2001 offseason, quoted in: Mike Chappell, "Organized workouts part of program," *Indianapolis Star*, 29 May 2005.

[613] Tom Brady, "Quotes from New England Patriots Press Conference," 3 February 2005.

[614] Patriot Jake Schifino, quoted in: Mike Reiss, "Offseason program is no joke," *Boston Herald*, 15 May 2005.

[615] Tom Brady, quoted in: David Kamp, "Tom Brady's Glory Days," *GQ*, September 2005.

[616] Bill Belichick, quoted in: Michael Felger, "Belichick keeps focus," *Boston Herald*, 31 January 2004.

[617] Patriots linebacker Mike Vrabel, quoted in: Chris Kennedy, "Pats open camp," *The Republican*, 30 July 2005.

[618] ItsGood_ItsGood, "A few pointless observations from one morning at training camp," *PatriotsPlanet.net*, 9 August 2005.

[619] New Patriots receiver David Terrell, quoted in: Michael Parente, " Terrell seeks new life with Pats," *Herald News*, 6 August 2005.

[420] New Patriots receiver David Terrell, quoted in: Michael Parente, " Terrell seeks new life with Pats," *Herald News*, 6 August 2005.

[421] New Patriots receiver David Terrell, quoted in: Michael Parente, " Terrell seeks new life with Pats," *Herald News*, 6 August 2005.

[422] Woody Hayes, on: Desmond Wilcox, "Americans: The Football Coach," aired on: *ESPN Classic*, 1 June 2005.

[423] John Madden, "A good crop of NFL teachers," *AllMadden.com*, 27 August 2002.

[424] Patriots defensive end Ty Warren, quoted in: "Quotes from New England Patriots Press Conference," 31 January 2005.

[425] Carolina Panthers offensive coordinator, Dan Henning, quoted in: Phil Barber, "New math: 3-4 is in again in the NFL," *Sporting News*, 7 May 2004, www.foxsports.com/content/view?contentId=2373626.

[426] Philadelphia Eagles receiver Freddie Mitchell, quoted in: John Tomase, "Mitchell's mouth motors on," *Gloucester Daily Times*, 8 April 2005, www.ecnnews.com/cgi-bin/04/g/gstory.pl?fn-tomase_409.

[427] Notre Dame running back Darius Walker, quoted in: Avani Patel, "Weis getting Irish's attention, respect," *ChicagoSports.com (Chicago Tribune)*, 9 April 2005.

[428] Notre Dame quarterback Brady Quinn, quoted in: Avani Patel, "Weis getting Irish's attention, respect," *ChicagoSports.com (Chicago Tribune)*, 9 April 2005.

[429] Michael Smith, "Patriots retain Mangini," *Boston Globe*, 8 February 2004, www.boston.com/sports/football/patriots/articles/2004/02/08/patriots_retain_mangini/.

[430] Patriots linebacker Rosevelt Colvin, quoted in: Jerome Solomon, "Patriots rookies hit ground running at camp," *Boston Globe*, 25 July 2005.

[431] Tim Green, *The Dark Side of the Game*, USA: Warner Books, 1996, p. 187.

[432] Former Cowboys coach Jimmy Johnson, quoted in: Tim Green, *The Dark Side of the Game*, USA: Warner Books, 1996, pp. 185-6.

[433] Nick Cafardo, "Patten looks out for No. 1," *Boston Globe*, 26 June 2005.

[434] Bill Belichick, quoted in: Thomas George, "A Changed Dr. Doom Returns," *New York Times*, 15 September 2002, p. 8.1, ProQuest database.

[435] Buffalo Bills defensive backs coach Steve Szabo, quoted in: Bucky Gleason, "Belichick buddy knows you don't mess with Bill," *Buffalo News*, 29 September 2004, www.buffalonews.com/editorial/20040929/1023679.asp.

[436] Bill Belichick, quoted in: Michael Felger, "Snake-bitten Klemm hurts foot," *Boston Herald*, 2 October 2004, http://patriots.bostonherald.com/patriots/view.bg?articleid=47057.

[437] Bill Belichick, quoted in: Michael Felger, "Snake-bitten Klemm hurts foot," *Boston Herald*, 2 October 2004, http://patriots.bostonherald.com/patriots/view.bg?articleid=47057.

[438] Bill Belichick, quoted in: Joe Burris, "Can Szabo corner the market?" *Boston Globe*, 2 October 2004, www.boston.com/sports/football/patriots/articles/2004/10/02/can_szabo_corner_the_market.

[439] Bill Belichick, quoted in: Michael Felger, "Snake-bitten Klemm hurts foot," *Boston Herald*, 2 October 2004, http://patriots.bostonherald.com/patriots/view.bg?articleid=47057.

[440] Patriots guard/center Damien Woody, quoted in: Michael Holley, *Patriot Reign*, William Morrow, 2004, p. 183.

[441] Bill Belichick, "Bill Belichick Press Conf. Transcript 9/5/04," *Patriots.com*, 5 September 2004, www.patriots.com/news/fullarticle.sps?id=30434.

[442] Former New Orleans Saints general manager Randy Mueller, quoted in: Paul Attner, " Whatever 'It' is, Brady has 'It,'" *Sports Illustrated*, 6 October 2004, http://msn.foxsports.com/story/3059636.

[443] Nick Kaczur, "Mini Camp: Day 2," *Patriots Video News*, 10 June 2005.

[444] Patriots rookie defensive lineman Vince Wilfork, quoted in: Michael Felger, "Patriots start a wild ride by busting Colts: Champions pull out 27-24 victory," *Boston Herald*, 10 September 2004, http://patriots.bostonherald.com/patriots/view.bg?articleid=43642.

[445] Dr. Mihaly Csikszentmihalyi, *Finding Flow*, USA: Basic Books, 1997, p. 106.

[446] Patriots nose tackle Vince Wilfork, quoted in: Dan Pires, "INSIDE THE PATRIOTS: Wilfork feels he's ready to step up," *Standard-Times*, 29 May 2005.

[447] Former New York Giants and Cleveland Browns linebacker Carl Banks, quoted in: Bob Glauber, "Billy Ball," *Newsday*, 25 January 2004, www.allthingsbillbelichick.com/articles/billyball.htm.

[448] Patriots receiver Deion Branch, quoted in: Matt Kalman, "Terrell's new Pat-itude: Team first," *Chicago Sun-Times*, 5 August 2005.

[449] Bill Belichick, quoted in: Tom E. Curran, "Kinda Sticky Here," www.beloblog.com/ProJo_Blogs/PatsBlog/, 3 August 2005.

[450] Offensive coordinator Charlie Weis, quoted in: Hector Longo, "Pats' Belichick passes all tests," *Eagle Tribune*, 13 January 2002, www.eagletribune.com/news/stories/20020113/SP_001.htm.

[451] Mark Gaughan, "Pats riding the crest of a brain wave," *Buffalo News*, 2 October 2004, www.buffalonews.com/editorial/20041002/1003819.asp.

[452] Patriots receiver Deion Branch, quoted in: Michael Felger, "Branch in position to step up," *Boston Herald*, 2 September 2004, http://patriots.bostonherald.com/patriots/view.bg?articleid=42513.

[453] Michael Felger, "New England Patriots," *The Sporting News Pro Football Fantasy Rankings and Tips*, p. 33.

[454] Tom Brady, quoted in: Tom E. Curran, "Patriots Notebook: Still nothing doing on the Watson front," *Providence Journal*, 12 August 2004, www.projo.com/patriots/content/projo_20040812_12patsjo.dca0a.html.

[455] Patriots center Dan Koppen, quoted in: Rich Thompson, "Koppen knows QB at center: Brady keeps offense on toes," *Boston Herald*, 13 September 2004, http://patriots.bostonherald.com/patriots/view.bg?articleid=43944.

[456] Patriots center Dan Koppen, quoted in: Mike Reiss, "From the start to the finish, a very productive run," *Daily News Tribune*, 11 October 2004, www.dailynewstribune.com/sportsNews/view.bg?articleid=42518.

[457] Bill Belichick, "Bill Belichick Press Conf. Transcript 9/5/04," *Patriots.com*, 5 September 2004, www.patriots.com/news/fullarticle.sps?id=30434.

[458] Michelle Conlin, "Take a vacation from your BlackBerry," *BusinessWeek*, 20 December 2004, p. 56.

[459] Stephanie Winston, author of *Organized for Success: Top Executives and CEOs Reveal the Organizing Principles That Helped Them Reach the Top*, quoted in: Anne Fisher, "Get Organized At Work—Painlessly," *Fortune*, 10 January 2005, p. 30.

[460] Charlie Weis, quoted in: Terrance Harris, "Scrimage will show new foundation," *South Bend Tribune*, 23 April 2005.

[461] Bill Belichick, quoted in: Tom Curran, "Sounds like fun," Projo.com *PatsBlog*, 30 July 2005.

[462] Notre Dame head coach Charlie Weis, quoted in: Todd D. Burlage, "First spring drills leave Irish with long to-do list," *Journal Gazette*, 30 March 2005, www.fortwayne.com/mld/journalgazette/sports/11266127.htm.

[463] Marc Narducci, "Back to school: Weis working to revive Irish," *Philadelphia Inquirer*, 10 April 2005, www.philly.com/mld/philly/sports/special_packages/marchmania/11354581.htm.

[464] Notre Dame head coach Charlie Weis, "Quotes From Charlie Weis and Brady Quinn Following The First Spring Practice," 29 March 2005, www.collegesports.com/sports/m-footbl/stories/032905abc.html.

[465] Notre Dame quarterback Brady Quinn, "Quotes From Charlie Weis and Brady Quinn Following The First Spring Practice," 29 March 2005, www.collegesports.com/sports/m-footbl/stories/032905abc.html.

[466] Notre Dame safety Tom Zbikowski, quoted in: Heather VanHoegarden, "CHARLIE WEIS: Family and football," *The Observer*, 22 April 2005.

[467] Patriots safety Rodney Harrison, "Quotes from New England Patriots Press Conference," 30 January 2005.

[468] Patriots wide receiver / nickel back / punt returner Troy Brown, "Quotes from New England Patriots Press Conference," 30 January 2005.

[469] Patriots linebacker Willie McGinest, "NFL Total Access: Week in Review," *NFL Network*, recorded 15 May 2005.

[470] Tom Brady, quoted in: "Tom Brady Post-Game Interview," *Patriots.com*, 17 October 2004, http://originwww.patriots.com/news/index.cfm?ac=LatestNewsDetail&PID=9364&PCID=41.

[471] Tom Brady, quoted in: "Tom Brady Post-Game Interview," *Patriots.com*, 17 October 2004, http://originwww.patriots.com/news/index.cfm?ac=LatestNewsDetail&PID=9364&PCID=41.

[472] Bill Belichick, quoted in: Tom E. Curran, "Dillon's addition gives Weis a whole new bag of tricks," *Providence Journal*, 19 October 2004, www.projo.com/patriots/content/projo_20041019_19pats.d1ad0.html.

[473] Bill Belichick, quoted in: John Tomase, "Built To Win," *Eagle Tribune*, 27 January 2004, www.eagletribune.com/news/stories/20040127/SP_001.htm.

[474] Dean Pees, new Patriots linebackers coach and former Kent State head coach, quoted in: Michael Felger, "Pees: Cues from Belichick," *Boston Herald*, 19 August 2004, http://patriots.bostonherald.com/patriots/view.bg?articleid=40466.

[475] Notre Dame head coach Charlie Weis, quoted in: Adam Rittenberg, "Weis' philosophies take hold at Notre Dame," *The Daily Herald*, 22 April 2005, www.dailyherald.com/search/printstory.asp?id=39514.

[476] Bill Belichick, quoted in: Michael Parente, " Patriots have ups and downs against Saints," *Herald News*, 20 August 2005.

[477] Patriots cornerback Tyrone Poole, quoted in: Steve King, "Patriots lament Crennel's departure," *ClevelandBrowns.com*, 8 February 2005.

[478] Defensive coordinator Romeo Crennel, quoted in: "Q&A With Romeo Crennel," 17 November 2004, www.nflcoaches.com/StoryArchives/Crennel.asp.

[479] Patriots linebacker Chad Brown, quoted in: Jerome Solomon, "He nearly took one Giant step," *Boston Globe*, 1 September 2005.

[480] Patriots linebacker Willie McGinest, quoted in: Michael Parente, " Kick returner needed to replace injured Johnson," *Woonsocket Call*, 31 July 2005.

[481] Bill Belichick, quoted in: Chris Kennedy, "McGinest returns to practice," *The Republican*, 10 August 2005.

[482] Bill Belichick, quoted in: Mark Farinella, "Patriots Notebook," *TheSunChronicle.com*, 1 August 2005.

[483] Patriots linebacker Chad Brown, quoted in: Tom E. Curran, "Due to a power shortage, Brown working overtime," *Providence Journal*, 1 August 2005.

[484] Patriots rookie Dan Klecko, quoted in: Michael Smith, "These rookies class acts," *Boston Globe*, 29 January 2004, www.boston.com/sports/football/patriots/articles/2004/01/29/these_rookies_class_acts/.

[485] New defensive coordinator Eric Mangini, quoted in: Jerome Solomon, "Winning formula," *Boston Globe*, 26 July 2005.

[486] Bill Belichick, quoted in: Tom E. Curran, "Due to a power shortage, Brown working overtime," *Providence Journal*, 1 August 2005.

[487] Patriots running back Cedric Cobbs, quoted in: Andy Hart, "Cobbs looking forward to backing up," *Patriots.com*, 29 June 2005.

[488] Rookie offensive lineman Nick Kaczur, quoted in: "Inside Slant," *USA Today*, 25 June 2005.

[489] I credit this insight to the always impressive Andy Hart, "Ask PFW: You got your Brown back," *Patriots.com*, 24 May 2005.

[490] Tom Brady, "Tom Brady Post Practice Interview," *Patriots.com*, 4 August 2005.

[491] Bill Belichick, "Belichick Press Conference," *Patriots.com*, 24 April 2005.

[492] Bill Russell, quoted in: Paul Kaihla, "The CEO's Secret Handbook," *Business 2.0*, July 2005, web exclusive content.

[493] Patriots receiver Troy Brown, "Quotes from New England Patriots Press Conference," February 2, 2005.

[494] Offensive lineman Joe Andruzzi, "Quotes From New England Patriots Media Day," 1 February, 2005.

[495] Patriots receiver Deion Branch, "Quotes from New England Patriots Press Conference," January 31, 2005.

[496] Patriots receiver David Givens, "Quotes from New England Patriots Media Day," February 1, 2005.

[497] Bill Belichick, speech at Bryant University, quoted in: Mike Reiss, "Leftovers from Belichick," 31 March 2005, www.bostonherald.com/blogs/reissPieces/index.bg.

[498] Bill Belichick, quoted in: Eric Hansen, "Putting the 'O' back in offense," *South Bend Tribune*, 17 August 2005.

[499] Patriots linebacker Willie McGinest, quoted in: AP, "Champs must contend with Moss in opener," *MSNBC*, 7 September 2005.

[500] Bill Belichick, media conference call, 27 August 2005, quoted in: Mike Reiss blog, "Belichick breaks it down," *Boston.com*, 28 August 2005.

[501] Patriots linebacker Monty Beisel, quoted in: Michael Felger, "LBs are slow learners: Brown, Beisel adjust to pace of Pats' system," *Boston Herald*, 1 September 2005.

[502] Patriots receiver Deion Branch, "Quotes from New England Patriots Press Conference," January 31, 2005.

[503] Patriots nose tackle Vince Wilfork, quoted in: Dan Pires, "INSIDE THE PATRIOTS: Wilfork feels he's ready to step up," *Standard-Times*, 29 May 2005.

[504] Bill Belichick, on *21: The Story Behind the NFL's longest winning streak*.

[505] Bill Belichick, on *21: The Story Behind the NFL's longest winning streak*.

[506] For a diagram and description, see Bob Davie, "Football 101: Cover 2," espn.go.com/ncf/columns/davie/1437187.html.

[507] Tim Green, *The Dark Side of the Game*, USA: Warner Books, 1996, pp. 107-8.

[508] Patriots cornerback Duane Starks, quoted in: Michael Felger, "Starks finds fit on Pats' corner," *Boston Herald*, 26 May 2005.

[509] Patriots nose tackle Vince Wilfork, quoted in: Dan Pires, "INSIDE THE PATRIOTS: Wilfork feels he's ready to step up," *Standard-Times*, 29 May 2005.

[510] Patriots cornerback Duane Starks, quoted in: Mike Lowe, "NFL's model for success? The Patriots," *MaineToday.com*, 12 June 2005.

[511] Tedy Bruschi, "Bruschi speaks at ring ceremony," *Patriots.com*, 13 June 2005.

[512] Charlie Weis, quoted by Joe Theismann in: Eric Retter, "FOOTBALL: Guest coaches relish chance," *The Observer*, 26 April 2005.

[513] Running back Kory Chapman, quoted in: Mike Reiss, "Chapman in RB mix," *Boston Herald* blog, 18 May 2005.

[514] Tom Brady, "Tom Brady Post Practice Interview," *Patriots.com*, 4 August 2005.

[515] Bill Belichick, quoted in: Chris Harry, "Patriots rookies fail to impress," *Orlando Sentinel*, 8 May 2005.

[516] Patriots receiver Deion Branch, quoted in: Eric McHugh, "And now, it's time for Deion to appear," *Patriot Ledger*, 5 September 2005.

[517] Charlie Weis, Notre Dame head coach and former Patriots offensive coordinator, quoted in: Terrance Harris, "Weis gives ND 'special' attention," *South Bend Tribune*, 10 April 2005, www.southbendtribune.com/stories/2005/04/10/sports.20050410-sbt-MICH-D1-Weis_gives.sto.

[518] Tom Brady, "Quotes from New England Patriots Press Conference," 2 February 2005.

[519] Patriots safety Rodney Harrison, quoted in: Tom E. Curran and Kevin McNamara, "Gillette's was certainly no field of dreams," *Providence Journal*, 29 November 2004, www.projo.com/patriots/content/projo_20041129_29patsjo.2e340.html.

[520] Rodney Harrison, on *21: The Story Behind the NFL's longest winning streak*.

[521] Tom Brady, "Quotes from New England Patriots Press Conference," 2 February 2005.

[522] Bill Belichick, quoted in: Michael Felger, "Dillon is one happy camper," *Boston Herald*, 1 August 2005.

[523] Patriots punter Josh Miller, quoted in: Mike Reiss, "Miller now has better foothold," *Boston Globe*, 2 September 2005.

[524] Baltimore Ravens punter Matt Stover, quoted in: Tom E. Curran and Kevin McNamara, "Gillette's was certainly no field of dreams," *Providence Journal*, 29 November 2004, www.projo.com/patriots/content/projo_20041129_29patsjo.2e340.html.

[525] Patriots punter Josh Miller, quoted in: Mike Reiss, "Miller now has better foothold," *Boston Globe*, 2 September 2005.

[526] Gary Shelton, "Want a title? Tear the roof off the place," *St. Petersburg Times*, 20 January 2005.

[527] Gary Shelton, "Want a title? Tear the roof off the place," *St. Petersburg Times*, 20 January 2005.

[528] Bill Belichick, quoted in: Hector Longo, " Pats cap 14-2 regular season," *Eagle-Tribune*, 3 January 2005.

[529] Jamil Soriano, quoted in: Andy Hart, "Soriano seeking experience, NFL Europe ring," *Patriots Football Weekly*, 5 May 2004, www.patriots.com/news/FullArticle.sps?id=28665&type=general.

[530] Coach Bill Belichick, quoted in: Alan Greenberg, "Belichick Game Plan For Life," *Hartford Courant*, 3 May 2004, www.ctnow.com/sports/hc-belichick0503.artmay03,1,707205.story.

[531] Patriots linebacker Ted Johnson, quoted in: Michael Felger, "Pats aim to give Bruschi his due," *Boston Herald*, 24 July 2005.

[532] Patriots quarterback Drew Bledsoe, quoted in: Jimmy Golen, "Belichick upset as Patriots open training camp," *SouthCoastToday.com*, 18 July 2000.

[533] Bill Belichick, "Belichick Press Conference," *Patriots.com*, 24 April 2005.

[534] Chad Morton's agent Leigh Steinberg, quoted in: Mike Reiss, "Pats land returner: Morton picks champs," *MetroWest Daily News*, 22 June 2005.

[535] New Patriots linebacker Monty Beisel, quoted in: Tom King, " Hopes are high for Pats' Beisel," *Nashua Telegraph*, 1 August 2005.

[536] Patriots cornerback Duane Starks, quoted in: Len Pasquarelli, "Efficiency key to Patriots' success," *ESPN.com*, 29 August 2005.

[537] Safety Rodney Harrison, quoted in: Jerome Solomon, "Injury report: Read between lines," *Boston Globe*, 7 September 2005.

[538] Patriots owner Robert Kraft, speech to graduating seniors at Foxboro high school, in: Patricia Russell, "Patriots owner tells grads 'Dream big,'" *TownOnline.com*, 17 June 2005.

[539] Patriots linebacker Roman Phifer, "Quotes From New England Patriots Press Conference," 3 February 2005.

[540] Patriots running back Cedric Cobbs, quoted in: (1st half) Michael Felger, "Cobbs eyes backup plan," *Boston Herald*, 5 May 2005 and (2nd half) Andy Hart, "Cobbs looking forward to backing up," *Patriots.com*, 29 June 2005.

[541] Tom Brady, "NFL Films Presents: Super Bowl XXXVI," aired on: *NFL Network*, 18 May 2005.

[542] Patriots running back Corey Dillon, quoted in: AP, "Dillon prepares for another long season," *TuscaloosaNews.com*, 31 July 2005.

[543] Jason Kelly, "Big dreams drive Weis and family," *South Bend Tribune*, 15 March 2005.

[544] Jason Kelly, "Big dreams drive Weis and family," *South Bend Tribune*, 15 March 2005.

[545] Jason Kelly, "Big dreams drive Weis and family," *South Bend Tribune*, 15 March 2005.

[546] Notre Dame head coach Charlie Weis, quoted in: Terry Shields, "Notre Dame offense sharp, different in debut," *Pittsburgh Post-Gazette*, 24 April 2005.

[547] Notre Dame head coach Charlie Weis, quoted in: Adam Rittenberg, "Weis' philosophies take hold at Notre Dame," *The Daily Herald*, 22 April 2005, www.dailyherald.com/search/printstory.asp?id=39514.

[548] Patriots cornerback Randall Gay, quoted in: Associated Press, "New England CB reflects on memorable rookie season," *The Dispatch*, 4 August 2005.

[549] Patriots safety Rodney Harrison, quoted in: Jerome Soloman, "Safety patrol: Harrison tries out officiating job," *Boston Globe*, 9 March 2005.

[550] Martin E.P. Seligman, *Authentic Happiness*, New York: Free Press, 2002, pp. 7-8 & 13.

[551] Patriots wide receiver / nickel back / punt returner Troy Brown, "Quotes from New England Patriots Press Conference," 30 January 2005.

[552] Patriots inside linebacker Ted Johnson, quoted in: Nick Cafardo, "Solid middle management," *Boston Globe*, 30 November 2004, www.boston.com/sports/football/patriots/articles/2004/11/30/solid_middle_management.

[553] Patriots linebacker Ted Johnson, quoted in: Mike Reiss, "Football's end game: The challenge of post-career planning," *Metrowest Daily News*, 30 May 2004, www.metrowestdailynews.com/sportsNews/view.bg?articleid=69553.

[554] Patriots inside linebacker Ted Johnson, quoted in: Nick Cafardo, "Solid middle management," *Boston Globe*, 30 November 2004, www.boston.com/sports/football/patriots/articles/2004/11/30/solid_middle_management.

[555] Patriots linebacker Mike Vrabel, quoted in: "NFL: Ex-pivot learns new position," *Toronto Star*, 2 August 2005.

[556] Patriots tight end Benjamin Watson, quoted in: Jerome Solomon, "They're eager to make amends," *Boston Globe*, 26 May 2005.

[557] Bill Belichick, quoted in: Rich Thompson, "Ram tough: Belichick, Patriots work to solve St. Louis system," *Boston Herald*, 5 November 2004, http://patriots.bostonherald.com/patriots/view.bg?articleid=52667.

[558] Patriots rookie defensive lineman Vince Wilfork, quoted in: Michael Felger, "Wilfork in line for more action," *Boston Herald*, 17 September 2004, http://patriots.bostonherald.com/patriots/view.bg?articleid=44682.

[559] Patriots wide receiver David Terrell, quoted in: Mike Reiss, "Terrell makes a connection," *MetroWest Daily News*, 29 May 2005.

[560] New Patriots receiver David Terrell, quoted in: Michael Parente, " Terrell seeks new life with Pats," *Herald News*, 6 August 2005.

[561] Former GE CEO Jack Welch, "A Conversation With Jack Welch," at Sacred Heart University, Fairfield, CT, 6 May 2005.

[563] Patriots receiver Deion Branch, "Quotes from New England Patriots Press Conference," January 31, 2005.

[564] Patriots safety Guss Scott, quoted in: Michael Parente, "Scott a great safety net," *Herald News*, 2 August 2005.

[565] Charlie Weis, quoted in: Heather VanHoegarden, "CHARLIE WEIS: Family and football," *The Observer*, 22 April 2005.

[566] Charlie Weis, quoted in: Avani Patel, "Weis tries to wake up the echoes - Rockne style," *San Jose Mercury News*, 15 April 2005.

[567] Browns linebacker Ben Taylor, quoted in: "Browns look to Patriots' D for pointers," *Springfield News-Sun*, 18 August 2005.

[568] New Patriots receiver David Terrell, quoted in: Mike Reiss, "David Terrell Q&A," *Boston Herald* blog, 27 May 2005.

[569] David Patten, quoted in: Nick Cafardo, "Patten looks out for No. 1," *Boston Globe*, 26 June 2005.

[570] Patriots safety Guss Scott, quoted in: Jerome Solomon, "They're eager to make amends," *Boston Globe*, 26 May 2005.

[571] Patriots punter Josh Miller, quoted in: Tom E. Curran, "Miller is kicking himself the most over his bad day," *Providence Journal*, 30 November 2004, www.projo.com/patriots/content/projo_20041130_30patsjo.3d761.html.

[572] Patriots punter Josh Miller, quoted in: Tom E. Curran, "Miller is kicking himself the most over his bad day," *Providence Journal*, 30 November 2004, www.projo.com/patriots/content/projo_20041130_30patsjo.3d761.html.

[573] Patriots punter Josh Miller, quoted in: Tom E. Curran, "Miller is kicking himself the most over his bad day," *Providence Journal*, 30 November 2004, www.projo.com/patriots/content/projo_20041130_30patsjo.3d761.html.

[574] Bill Belichick, quoted in: Jerome Solomon, "Mind over matter," *Boston Globe*, 22 April 2005, www.boston.com/sports/football/patriots/articles/2005/04/22/patriots_day.

[575] Bill Belichick, quoted in: Kevin Mannix, "Rookies take off wraps," *MetroWest Daily News*, 30 April 2005.

[576] Patriots tight end Andy Stokes, quoted in: "Stokes pursues spot on Patriots' roster," *The Spectrum* (St. George, UT), 8 July 2005.

[577] Scott Pioli, "Quotes from New England Patriots Press Conference," 2 February 2005.

[578] Kevin Byrne, former Browns VP, quoted in: Mark Craig, " Mangini second to none," *Minneapolis Star Tribune*, 4 February 2005.

[579] Patriots linebacker Tedy Bruschi, "Quotes from New England Patriots Press Conference," 31 January 2005.

[580] Patriots wide receiver David Givens, quoted in: George Kimball, "The art of the game: On the field or in the studio, David Givens has designs on greatness," *Boston Herald*, 10 October 2004, http://patriots.bostonherald.com/patriots/view.bg?articleid=48342.

[581] Bill Belichick, quoted in: Kevin Mannix, "Catching his wind: Sam shapes up just in time," *Boston Herald*, 2 May 2004, http://patriots.bostonherald.com/patriots/view.bg?articleid=17349.

[582] Patriots linebacker Dan Klecko, quoted in: Kevin Mannix, "Bruschi and his shadow: Klecko's journey similar to LB's," *Boston Herald*, 29 January 2004.

[583] Bill Belichick, quoted in: Paul Zimmerman, "While the offense stands pat, a rebuilt defense looks to regain that Super Bowl swagger," *CNNSI.com*, 1 September 2003, http://sportsillustrated.cnn.com/2003/magazine/08/25/patriots/.

[584] Patriot Dan Klecko, quoted in: "Klecko remembers draft week," *Patriots Football Weekly*, 21 April 2005.

[585] Patriots inside linebackers coach Pepper Johnson, *Won For All*, Chicago: Contemporary Books, 2003, p. 33.

[586] Former NFL tight end Mark Bavaro, quoted in: Bill Kipouras, "Advice from a Giants legend," *Eagle Tribune*, 1 August 2003, www.eagletribune.com/news/stories/20030801/SP_003.htm.

[587] Former NFL tight end Mark Bavaro, quoted in: Bill Kipouras, "Advice from a Giants legend," *Eagle Tribune*, 1 August 2003, www.eagletribune.com/news/stories/20030801/SP_003.htm.

[588] Former NFL tight end Mark Bavaro, quoted in: Bill Kipouras, "Advice from a Giants legend," *Eagle Tribune*, 1 August 2003, www.eagletribune.com/news/stories/20030801/SP_003.htm.

[589] Bill Belichick, as recollected by Scott Pioli, quoted in: Mike Sando, "Pioli's timing, persistence pays off in New England," *Tacoma News Tribune*, 29 January 2004, www.sacbee.com/24hour/spec/football/playoffs/story/1133862p-7892957c.html.

[590] Patriots Vice President of Player Personnel Scott Pioli, quoted in: Bill Burt, "More than a coach," *Eagle Tribune*, 25 January 2004, www.eagletribune.com/news/stories/20040125/SP_001.htm.

[591] Patriots Vice President of Player Personnel Scott Pioli, quoted in: Jeff Jacobs, "Class Clown Gets Serious With Patriots," *Hartford Courant*, 3 February 2002, p. A1.

[592] Frank Leonard, former Central Connecticut State University offensive line coach, quoted in: Jeff Jacobs, "Class Clown Gets Serious With Patriots," *Hartford Courant*, 3 February 2002, p. A1.

[593] Patriots VP of player personnel, Scott Pioli, quoted in: Mike Sando, "Pioli's timing, persistence pays off in New England," *Tacoma News Tribune*, 29 January 2004, www.sacbee.com/24hour/spec/football/playoffs/story/1133862p-7892957c.html.

[594] Patriots VP of player personnel Scott Pioli, quoted in: Jeff Jacobs, "Class Clown Gets Serious With Patriots," *Hartford Courant*, 3 February 2002, p. A1.

[595] Eric Mangini, quoted in: Mark Craig, " Mangini second to none," *Minneapolis Star Tribune*, 4 February 2005.

[596] Eric Mangini, quoted in: Jerome Solomon, "Winning formula," *Boston Globe*, 26 July 2005.

[597] Kyle Mangini, quoted in: Jerome Solomon, "Winning formula," *Boston Globe*, 26 July 2005.

[598] New Patriots linebacker Monte Beisel, "Mini Camp – Day 1," *Patriots Video News*, Patriots.com, 9 June 2005.

[599] Patriots defensive end Jarvis Green, "Mini Camp – Day 1," *Patriots Video News*, Patriots.com, 9 June 2005.

[600] Charlie Weis, quoted in: Avani Patel, "Weis tries to wake up the echoes - Rockne style," *San Jose Mercury News*, 15 April 2005.

[601] Charlie Weis, quoted in: Tim Prister, "Armed with a Notre Dame education," bgi.rivals.com, 13 June 2005.

[602] Charlie Weis, quoted in: Tim Prister, "Armed with a Notre Dame education," bgi.rivals.com, 13 June 2005.

[603] Bill Belichick, quoted in: Pete Thamel, "Building Programs Using Belichick's Blueprint," 18 September 2004, www.nytimes.com/2004/09/18/sports/ncaafootball/18college.html.

[604] Bill Belichick, 2003, quoted in: Michael Parente, "Patriots kick-off preseason Friday," *Woonsocket Call*, 10 June 2004, www.zwire.com/site/news.cfm?newsid=11926807&BRD=1712&PAG=461&dept_id=24361&rfi=6.

[605] Patriots wide receiver / nickel back / punt returner Troy Brown, "Quotes from New England Patriots Press Conference," 30 January 2005.

[606] Bill Belichick, "Bill Belichick Press Conf. Transcript - 4/30," *Patriots.com*, 30 April 2004, www.patriots.com/news/FullArticle.sps?id=28597&type=general.

[607] Bill Belichick, "Bill Belichick Press Conf. Transcript - 4/30," *Patriots.com*, 30 April 2004, www.patriots.com/news/FullArticle.sps?id=28597&type=general.

[608] Bill Belichick, quoted in: Don Pierson, "Bad news for Patriots' foes: Backup QB looks good," *Chicago Tribune*, 8 May 2004, www.charlotte.com/mld/charlotte/sports/football/8620926.htm?1c.

[609] Bill Belichick, quoted in: Frank Tadych, "Patriots Notebook: Dillon's status still in doubt," *Patriots.com*, 15 October 2004, http://cachewww.patriots.com/news/index.cfm?ac=LatestNewsDetail&PID=9341&PCID=41.

[610] Bill Belichick, quoted in: Hector Longo, "If you can't beat Kleckos then start drafting them," *Eagle Tribune*, 28 April 2003, www.eagletribune.com/news/stories/20030428/SP_008.htm.

[611] Patriots rookie guard Logan Mankins, quoted in: Adam Kilgore, "Thus far, Mankins is guardedly optimistic," *Boston Globe*, 31 July 2005.

[612] Unnamed NFL general manager, quoted in: Kevin Mannix, "Rivals give Pats' draft a pass," *Boston Herald*, 1 May 2005.

[613] Bill Belichick, quoted in: Jerome Solomon, "Patriots set for learning experience," *Boston Globe*, 9 June 2005.

[614] Bill Belichick, "Mini Camp – Day 1," *Patriots Video News*, Patriots.com, 9 June 2005.

[615] Bill Belichick, "Belichick Press Conference," *Patriots.com*, 9 June 2005.

[616] Bill Belichick, quoted in: Jerome Solomon, "Patriots set for learning experience," *Boston Globe*, 9 June 2005.

[617] VP of player personnel Scott Pioli, quoted in: Rick Braun, "Patriots built with free agents, draft," *Milwaukee Journal Sentinel*, 4 February 2004, www.jsonline.com/packer/rev/feb04/204957.asp.

[618] Patriots offensive coordinator Charlie Weis, "Quotes from New England Patriots Press Conference," 3 February 2005.

[619] Former Patriots quarterback Damon Huard, quoted in: Eric McHugh, "Pats start to adjust to coaching changes," *Patriot Ledger*, 8 June 2005.

[620] Tom Brady, "Quotes From New England Patriots Press Conference," 2 February 2005.

[621] Tom Brady, "Quotes From New England Patriots Press Conference," 2 February 2005.

[622] Jeff Clarke, Dell, quoted in: Andy Serwer, "The Education of Michael Dell," *Fortune*, 7 March 2005, p. 78.

[623] John Giannandrea, quoted in: Adam Lashinsky, "The Birth of the Web," *Fortune*, 25 July 2005, p. 162.

[624] Patriots defensive lineman Ty Warren, quoted in: Pro Football Weekly, "The way we hear it," 29 November 2004, www.profootballweekly.com/PFW/NFL/AFC/AFC+East/New+England/WWH/default.htm.

[625] Patriots receiver Deion Branch, quoted in: Tom E. Curran, "Branch remains steady after season of change," *Providence Journal*, 17 April 2005, www.projo.com/patriots/content/projo_20050417_17branch.202bc6f.html.

[626] Tom E. Curran, "Plenty of knowledge is being absorbed," *Providence Journal*, 4 August 2005.

[627] STATS, Inc. data, cited in: Kevin Pelton, "Dropping Some Knowledge on Seattle," *FootballOutsiders.com*, 26 August 2005.

[628] Patriots receiver Deion Branch, quoted in: Tom E. Curran, "Branch remains steady after season of change," *Providence Journal*, 17 April 2005, www.projo.com/patriots/content/projo_20050417_17branch.202bc6f.html.

[629] STATS, Inc. data, cited in: Kevin Pelton, "Dropping Some Knowledge on Seattle," *FootballOutsiders.com*, 26 August 2005.

[630] Tom Brady, quoted in: Tim Weisberg, "Tom's toolbox gets heavier by the year," *Standard-Times*, 4 September 2005.

[631] Michael Smith, "Small role may produce star," *Boston Globe*, 4 July 2004, www.boston.com/sports/football/patriots/articles/2004/07/04/small_role_may_produce_star.

[632] Bill Belichick, quoted in: Dan Pires, "Patriots Notebook: Success now worry for Wilson," *Standard-Times*, 7 August 2005.

[633] Patriots safety Lawyer Milloy, quoted in: Mike Freeman, "Belichick shows his relaxed side," *New York Times*, 4 April 2000, www.allthingsbillbelichick.com/articles/relaxedside.htm.

[634] Bill Belichick, quoted in: Paul Kenyon, "The party is over," *Eagle-Tribune*, 18 July 2000.

[635] Bill Belichick, on: *21: The Story Behind the NFL's longest winning streak*.

[636] Patriots linebacker Chad Brown, quoted in: AP, "Ex-All-Pro finds it tough to replace Bruschi," MSNBC, 10 June 2005.

[637] Patriots linebacker Chad Brown, quoted in: AP, "Ex-All-Pro finds it tough to replace Bruschi," MSNBC, 10 June 2005.

[638] Patriots linebacker Monty Beisel, quoted in: Michael Parente, "Seymour's absence not a big camp distraction," *Woonsocket Call*, 11 June 2005.

[639] Patriots linebacker Monty Beisel, quoted in: AP, "Ex-All-Pro finds it tough to replace Bruschi," MSNBC, 10 June 2005.

[640] Patriots defensive lineman Ty Warren, quoted in: Tom E. Curran, "2005 salary hike gets Seymour into the camp mix," *Providence Journal*, 3 August 2005.

[641] Bill Belichick, "Quotes from New England Patriots Press Conference," 3 February 2005.

[642] Bill Belichick, "Quotes from New England Patriots Press Conference," 3 February 2005.

[643] Patriots linebacker Eric Alexander, quoted in: Eric McHugh, "LB candidates state their case," *Patriot Ledger*, 2 September 2005.

[644] Dr. Peter F. Drucker, *Management: Tasks, Responsibilities, Practices*, USA: HarperCollins, 1973, p. 199.

[645] Bill Belichick, "An Interview With New England Patriots Head Coach Bill Belichick," 4 February 2005.

[646] Bill Belichick, quoted in: Mike Reiss, "Belichick at Big Brother event," *Boston Herald* blog, 20 May 2005.

[647] Patriots free agent offensive tackle/guard Victor Leyva, quoted in: Mike Reiss, "Passing camp begins," *Boston Herald* blog, 17 May 2005.

[648] Associated Press, "Culpepper scrambles to get diamonds back," *MSNBC.com*, 2 February 2005, http://msnbc.msn.com/id/6903176/.

[649] Tom Brady, quoted in: Tom E. Curran, "Tom Curran: Brady, Belichick seem perfect for each other," *Providence Journal*, 12 August 2004, www.projo.com/patriots/content/projo_20040812_12currcol.dcb5f.html.

[650] Patriots receiver David Givens, "Quotes from New England Patriots Press Conference," 31 January 2005.

[651] Cleveland Browns cornerback Gary Baxter, quoted in: Len Pasquarelli, "In Romeo they trust," *ESPN.com*, 3 August 2005.

[652] Patriots safety Rodney Harrison, "Quotes from New England Patriots Press Conference," 30 January 2005.

[653] Patriots receiver David Givens, "Quotes from New England Patriots Press Conference," 31 January 2005.

[654] Patriots rookie cornerback Ellis Hobbs, quoted in: Jerome Solomon, "Hobbs covering all the angles," *Boston Globe*, 15 August 2005.

[655] Patriots rookie cornerback Ellis Hobbs, quoted in: Jerome Solomon, "Hobbs covering all the angles," *Boston Globe*, 15 August 2005.

[656] Philadelphia Eagles defensive tackle Hollis Thomas, "Quotes from Philadelphia Eagles Press Conference," 3 February 2005.

[657] Former Patriots offensive lineman Damien Woody, quoted in: Mark Gaughan, "Tom Terrific," *AbsoluteBrady.com*, 28 January 2004.

[658] Philadelphia Eagles cornerback Sheldon Brown, "Quotes from Philadelphia Eagles Press Conference," 3 February 2005.

[659] Tom Brady, "Quotes From New England Patriots Press Conference," February 3, 2005.

[660] Tom Brady, "Quotes From New England Patriots Press Conference," February 3, 2005.

[661] New Patriots receiver David Terrell, quoted in: Mike Reiss, "David Terrell Q&A," *Boston Herald* blog, 27 May 2005.

[662] Patriots left tackle Matt Light, "Quotes From New England Patriots Press Conference," February 3, 2005.

[663] Patriots safety Rodney Harrison, "Quotes from New England Patriots Press Conference," 30 January 2005.

[664] Patriots defensive lineman Richard Seymour, quoted in: Michael Parente, " Pats' DL Seymour continues to rise," *New Britain Herald*, 11 August 2004, www.zwire.com/site/news.cfm?newsid=12664369&BRD=1641&PAG=461&dept_id=17739&rfi=6.

[665] New Patriots punter Josh Miller, quoted in: Michael Smith, "No Snap Judgment," *Boston Globe*, 12 August 2004, www.boston.com/sports/football/patriots/articles/2004/08/12/no_snap_judgment.

[666] Former GE CEO Jack Welch, "A Conversation With Jack Welch," at Sacred Heart University, Fairfield, CT, 6 May 2005.

[667] Cornerback Asante Samuel, quoted in: Paul Perillo, "PFW: Samuel looks to shed sub status," *Patriots.com*, 22 June 2005.

[668] President Richard Nixon, oration at funeral of Woody Hayes, 1987, shown on *ESPN Classics*, 1 June 2005.

[669] Tedy Bruschi, audio recording of *ESPN* broadcast on morning of 2 February 2005.

[670] Bill Belichick, *21: The Story Behind the NFL's longest winning streak*.

[671] Woody Hayes, on: Desmond Wilcox, "Americans: The Football Coach," aired on: *ESPN Classic*, 1 June 2005.

[672] Patriots nose tackle Vince Wilfork, quoted in: Scout.com, "PATRIOTS: Concerns In The Middle," 16 August 2005.

[673] Toyota CEO Fujio Cho, quoted in: Clay Chandler, "Full Speed Ahead," *Fortune*, 7 February 2005, p. 84.

[674] New Patriots receiver David Terrell, quoted in: Mike Reiss, "David Terrell Q&A," *Boston Herald* blog, 27 May 2005.

[675] Dr. Peter F. Drucker, *Management: Tasks, Responsibilities, Practices*, 1973, p. 128.

[676] Patriots nose tackle Keith Traylor, "Quotes from New England Patriots Media Day," 3 February 2005.

[677] Miami Dolphins head coach Nick Saban, quoted in: Dan Pompei, "Saban is more than just a Belichick disciple," *Sporting News*, 16 May 2005, www.sportingnews.com/experts/dan-pompei/20050516.html.

[678] Bill Belichick, quoted in: Jay Mariotti, "Patriots build modern sports dynasty," *Chicago Sun-Times*, 11 October 2004, www.suntimes.com/output/mariotti/cst-spt-jay111.html.

[679] Patriots safety Rodney Harrison, quoted in: Don Banks, "By any means necessary," *Sports Illustrated*, 10 October 2004, http://sportsillustrated.cnn.com/2004/writers/don_banks/10/10/patriots.insider/.

[680] Former Patriots defensive lineman Bobby Hamilton, quoted in: Nick Cafardo, "The Buck Stops With Bill," *Boston Globe*, 24 November 2001, www.allthingsbillbelichick.com/articles/buckstops.htm.

[681] Romeo Crennel, "Quotes from New England Patriots Press Conference," 2 February 2005.

[682] Troy Brown, quoted in: Mark Craig, " Mangini second to none," *Minneapolis Star Tribune*, 4 February 2005.

[683] Patriots inside linebackers coach Pepper Johnson, *Won For All*, Chicago: Contemporary Books, 2003, p. 100.

[684] Bill Belichick, quoted in: Bill Burt, "Smith passes, then goes mum," *Eagle Tribune*, 25 July 2003, www.eagletribune.com/news/stories/20030725/SP_008.htm.

[685] Bill Belichick, "Bill Belichick Press Conf. Transcript 8/3/04," 3 August 2004, www.patriots.com/news/fullarticle.sps?id=29867&special_section=TrainingCamp2004&type=training.

[686] Coach Bill Belichick, "FullBelichick Press Conf. Transcript - 4/30," *Patriots.com*, 30 April 2004, www.patriots.com/news/FullArticle.sps?id=28597&type=general.

[687] Ethan J. Skolnick, "Keys to successful draft start at home," *South Florida Sun-Sentinel*, 1 December 2004.

[688] Bill Belichick, quoted in: Glen Farley, "Patriots on the verge of history," *The Enterprise*, 25 July 2005.

[689] Buck Harvey, "The Eagles as favorites? Beli-change," *San Antonio Express-News*, 6 February 2005.

[690] Patriots punter Josh Miller, quoted in: Chuck Finder, "Bill Belichick: The Mastermind of New England," *Pittsburgh Post-Gazette*, 21 January 2005.

[691] Tom Brady, quoted in: Michael Silver, "Cold Blooded," *Sports Illustrated*, 25 January 2004, on: *AbsoluteBrady.com*.

[692] Bill Belichick, "Bill Belichick Press Conf. Transcript 9/5/04," *Patriots.com*, 5 September 2004, www.patriots.com/news/FullArticle.sps?id=30434.

[693] Patriots linebacker Matt Chatham, quoted in: Dan Pires, "Postgame talk ranges from Sapp to streaker," *Standard-Times*, 4 February 2004, www.southcoasttoday.com/daily/02-04/02-04-04/c01sp273.htm.

[694] Patriots owner Robert Kraft, aired on "Dollars and Sports," CNBC September 5, 2005.

[695] Barney Gimbel, "Southwest's New Flight Plan," *Fortune*, 16 May 2005, p. 97.

[696] Nicole Gaouette, "A Diminished FEMA Scrambles to the Rescue," *Los Angeles Times*, 1 September 2005.

[697] Kenneth R. Bazinet, "FEMA packed with W's pals," *New York Daily News*, 7 September 2005.

[698] Matt Stearns and Seth Borenstein, "Head of FEMA has an unlikely background," *Knight Ridder* Washington Bureau, 3 September 2005, www.realcities.com/mld/krwashington/12554964.htm.

[699] Editor & Publisher staff, "Knight Ridder Exposes Horsey Background of FEMA Chief," *Editor & Publisher*, 4 September 2005.

[700] Jefferson Parish president Aaron Broussard, quoted in: Reuters, "Louisiana official haunted by drowned woman," *alertnet.org*, 4 September 2005, www.alertnet.org/thenews/newsdesk/N04620416.htm.

[701] Secretary of Homeland Security Michael Chertoff, quoted in: *CNN*, "Chertoff: Katrina scenario did not exist," 3 September 2005.

[702] President George Bush, quoted in: Maureen Dowd, "United States of Shame," *New York Times*, 3 September 2005.

[703] FEMA director Michael Brown, quoted in: *CNN*, "Chertoff: Katrina scenario did not exist," 3 September 2005.

[704] Fred Kaplan, "$41 Billion, and Not a Penny of Foresight," *Slate*, 2 September 2005, slate.msn.com/id/2125478/.

[705] Regional Red Cross executive director Kay Wilkins, quoted in *New Orleans Times-Picayune* article on 24 July 2005, excerpted in: "Government Policy: We Won't Evacuate the Poor," *Public Journalism Network*, 1 September 2005, www.pjnet.org. Also excerpted in: John Byrne, "July 2005 article reveals New Orleans told poor: 'You're on your own,'" *RawStory.com*, 2 September 2005.

[706] *CNN*, "Chertoff: Katrina scenario did not exist," 3 September 2005.

[707] Homeland Security director Michael Chertoff, quoted in: Jesse Berney, "Chertoff Blames Refugees and the Dead for Their Fate," www.democrats.org/blog.html.

[708] *NBC News* anchor Brian Williams, "NBC Nightly News with Brian Williams" blog, 5 September 2005, 11:57 a.m. EDT, www.msnbc.msn.com/id/9216831/.

[709] Louisiana governor Kathleen Blanco, quoted in: Josh White and Peter Whoriskey, "Planning, Response Are Faulted," *Washington Post*, 2 September 2005.

[710] www.redcross.org/faq/0,1096,0_682_4524,00.html#4524.

[711] Chicago mayor Richard Daley, quoted in: Staff reports, "Daley 'shocked' at federal snub of offers to help," *Chicago Tribune*, 2 September 2005.

[712] KLFY 10 Lafayette, LA, "Boaters turned around," www.klfy.com/Global/story.asp?S=3792283; and: Clark Warner, "FEMA stops a rescue convoy of 500 boats," bellaciao.org/en/article.php3?id_article=8034, 3 September 2005.

[713] Stephen J. Hedges, "Navy ship nearby underused," *Chicago Tribune*, 4 September 2005.

[714] Navy Lt. Cmdr. Sean Kelly, Northern Command spokesman, quoted in: "Military's Northern Command steps up response efforts," *GovExec.com*, 2 September 2005, www.govexec.com/story_page.cfm?articleid=32146&sid=21.

[715] Navy Lt. Cmdr. Sean Kelly, Northern Command spokesman, *BBC World* video posted online at news.globalfreepress.com/movs/katrina/BBC_Katrina.mpg. Also, complete transcript posted at www.democraticunderground.com/discuss/duboard.php?az=show_mesg&forum=104&topic_id=4605183&mesg_id=4605183.

[716] New Orleans' head of emergency operations Terry Ebbert, quoted in: NBC, MSNBC and news services, "Cries for help spread across New Orleans," *MSNBC*, 1 September 2005.

[717] Jefferson Parish president Aaron Broussard, quoted in: "[Meet the Press] Transcript for September 4," 4 September 2005, www.msnbc.msn.com/id/9179790.

[718] LSU hurricane researcher Ivor Van Heerden, quoted in: Lisa Myers, "Was FEMA ready for a disaster like Katrina?" *NBC News*, 2 September 2005, msnbc.msn.com/id/9178501.

[719] FEMA director Michael D. Brown, on CNN with Paula Zahn, quoted in: Eric Lipton and Scott Shane, "Leader of Federal Effort Feels the Heat," *New York Times*, 3 September 2005.

[720] Andrew Martin and Andrew Zajac, "Funding cuts led way to lesser levees," *Chicago Tribune*, 31 August 2005.

[721] Walter Maestri, emergency management chief of Jefferson Parish, quoted in 2004 by the *New Orleans Times-Picayune*, cited in: Seth Borenstein, "Experts blast federal response," *Philadelphia Inquirer*, 1 September 2005.

[722] Mike Parker, former head of the Army Corps of Engineers, quoted in: Jason Vest and Justin Rood, " Ex-Army Corps officials say budget cuts imperiled flood mitigation efforts," *GovExec.com*, 1 September 2005, www.govexec.com/dailyfed/0905/090105jv1.htm.

[723] Marcel Honore, "Alaska trounces Washington in funding special transportation projects," *Seattle Times*, 22 August 2005.

[724] "The Man-Made Disaster," *New York Times*, 2 September 2005.

[725] Jimmy Breslin, "While Bush fiddles, New Orleans dies," *Newsday*, 4 September 2005.

[726] Patriots running back Corey Dillon, "Quotes from New England Patriots Press Conference," 2 February 2005.

[727] Dr. Peter F. Drucker, *Management: Tasks, Responsibilities, Practices*, USA: HarperCollins, 1973, p. 48.

[728] Bill Belichick, "Belichick Press Conference," *Patriots.com*, 24 April 2005.

[729] Patriots special teamer/linebacker/safety Don Davis, quoted in: Tom E. Curran, "Due to a power shortage, Brown working overtime," *Providence Journal*, 1 August 2005.

[730] Bill Belichick, "Belichick Press Conference," *Patriots.com*, 24 April 2005.

[731] Bill Belichick, quoted in: Allen Wilson, "NFL labor negotiations reach a dead end in paradise," *Buffalo News*, 27 March 2005, www.buffalonews.com/editorial/20050327/1030325.asp.

[732] Bill Belichick, quoted in: Rick Gosselin, "Patriots' Belichick focuses on filling the gaps," *Dallas Morning News*, 31 July 2005.

[733] KC Joyner, The Football Scientist, *Scientific Football 2005* (KC's Football Services, Altamonte Springs, FL, 2005), p. 310.

[734] Offensive lineman Damien Woody, quoted in: Michael Smith, "Snowballin'," *Boston Globe*, 8 December 2003, www.boston.com/sports/football/patriots/articles/2003/12/08/snowballin/.

[735] Tom Brady, "Quotes From New England Patriots Press Session," 2 February 2005.

[736] Charlie Weis, quoted in: Eric Hansen, "Putting the 'O' back in offense," *South Bend Tribune*, 17 August 2005.

[737] Bill Belichick, quoted in: Peter King, "Rinse, repeat?" *Sports Illustrated*, 16 May 2002.

[738] Patriots backup linebacker Tully Banta-Cain, quoted in: Andy Hart, "Banta-Cain hoping to make a bigger impact in '05," *Patriots.com*, 27 May 2005.

[739] Troy Brown, quoted in: Howard Ulman (AP), "Troy Brown excited to return to Patriots," *LA Times*, 10 August 2005.

[740] Tom Brady, "Tom Brady Locker Room Interview," *Patriots.com*, 29 August 2005.

[741] Left tackle Matt Light, "Early Roster Cuts and More," *Patriots Video News*, 29 August 2005.

[742] Notre Dame head coach Charlie Weis, quoted in: Todd D. Burlage, "First spring drills leave Irish with long to-do list," *Journal Gazette*, 30 March 2005, www.fortwayne.com/mld/journalgazette/sports/11266127.htm.

[743] Former Patriots offensive coordinator Charlie Weis and new head coach at Notre Dame, quoted in: Pat Leonard, "Weis makes recruiting his first main focus," *Notre Dame and St Mary's Observer*, 16 March 2005, www.ndsmcobserver.com/news/2005/03/16/Sports/Weis-Makes.Recruiting.His.First.Main.Focus-895142.shtml.

[744] Bill Belichick, quoted in: Andy Hart, "Belichick impresses large Bryant University audience," *Patriots.com*, 31 March 2005, www.patriots.com/news/index.cfm?ac=generalnewsdetail&pcid=41&pid=11235.

[745] Special teams captain Larry Izzo, "Quotes from New England Patriots Press Conference," February 2, 2005.

[746] Dr. Peter F. Drucker, *Management: Tasks, Responsibilities, Practices*, USA: HarperCollins, 1973, p. 140.

[747] New Patriot defensive lineman Keith Traylor, quoted in: Michael Felger, "Big man, a big job: Traylor is getting used to new role on defensive line," *Boston Herald*, 13 June 2004, http://patriots.bostonherald.com/patriots/view.bg?articleid=31721.

[748] 2005 draftee Ellis Hobbs, quoted in: Michael Parente, " Rookies take first steps in Patriots uniforms," *Woonsocket Call*, 30 April 2005.

[749] Bill Belichick, quoted in: Tom E. Curran, "For Pats, it'll be hard work defending title," *Providence Journal*, 28 July 2004, www.projo.com/patriots/content/projo_20040728_28pats.5df0.html.

[750] Notre Dame head coach Charlie Weis, quoted in: AP, "Great expectations," 30 March 2005, http://sportsillustrated.cnn.com/2005/football/ncaa/03/30/bc.fbc.irishspring.ap/.

[751] Bill Belichick, quoted in: Dan Pires, "Belichick on the verge of history," *Standard-Times*, 1 February 2004, www.southcoasttoday.com/daily/02-04/02-01-04/c01sp874.htm.

[752] Dan Pompei, "Why Starting Points Often Mean End Results," *Sporting News*, 4 June 2004, www.foxsports.com/content/view?contentId=2428736 .

[753] Tom Brady, quoted in: Judy Battista, "The Patriots Become 20-Game Winners," *New York Times*, 18 October 2004, www.nytimes.com/2004/10/18/sports/football/18patriots.html.

[754] Data from former San Diego Chargers offensive coordinator Geep Chryst, cited in: Dan Pompei, "Why Starting Points Often Mean End Results," *Sporting News*, 4 June 2004, www.foxsports.com/content/view?contentId=2428736.

[755] Elias Sports Bureau statistics, cited in: Bob Oates, "In NFL, Passing Pays Off," *L.A. Times*, 31 August 2005.

[756] Data from former San Diego Chargers offensive coordinator Geep Chryst, cited in: Dan Pompei, "Why Starting Points Often Mean End Results," *Sporting News*, 4 June 2004, www.foxsports.com/content/view?contentId=2428736.

[757] Tom Brady, quoted in: Glen Farley, "Speeding Patriots make a Pitt stop," *The Enterprise*, 31 October 2004, http://enterprise.southofboston.com/articles/2004/10/31/news/sports/sports01.txt.

[758] Stats Inc., cited in: Don Banks, "Blowout Bowl," *Sports Illustrated*, 4 February 2005, http://sportsillustrated.cnn.com/2005/writers/don_banks/02/04/banks.top.10/.

[759] Bill Belichick, quoted in: Tom E. Curran, "Patriots' early execution can't be beat," *Providence Journal*, 26 October 2004, www.projo.com/patriots/content/projo_20041026_26pats.2b168a.html.

[760] Michael Silver, "Pat Answer," *Sports Illustrated*, 11 February 2002, www.absolutebrady.com/SB36.html.

[761] Patriots linebacker Tedy Bruschi, "Patriots Video News," 4 October 2004, http://originwww.patriots.com/MediaCenter/index.cfm?ac=VideoNewsDetail&PID=9160&PCID=78.

[762] Patriot veteran Troy Brown, quoted in: Chris Kennedy, "Brown aims to earn spot," *The Republican*, 31 July 2005.

[763] Patriots center Dan Koppen, "Quotes from New England Patriots Press Conference," 2 February 2005.

[764] Bill Belichick on *The David Letterman Show*, 4 February 2004, www.patriots.com/mediaworld/mediadetail.sps?id=27974.

[765] Tom Brady, quoted in: Mike Lowe, "It's a super way to start the season," *Portland Press Herald*, 8 September 2004, http://pressherald.mainetoday.com/sports/pro/patriots/040908lowecolumn.shtml.

[766] Patriots linebacker Tedy Bruschi, quoted in: Dan Pires, "Woody ready to say his good-byes," *Standard-Times*, 22 February 2004, www.southcoasttoday.com/daily/02-04/02-22-04/c05sp148.htm.

[767] Patriots wide receiver / nickel back / punt returner Troy Brown, "Quotes from New England Patriots Press Conference," 30 January 2005.

[768] Charlie Weis, quoted in: Heather VanHoegarden, "CHARLIE WEIS: Family and football," *The Observer*, 22 April 2005.

[769] Patriots defensive lineman Ty Warren, "Quotes from New England Patriots Press Conference," February 3, 2005.

[770] Charlie Weis, quoted in: Vahe Gregorian, "Notre Dame hopes Weis has healing touch," *St. Louis Today*, 5 May 2005.

[771] Patriots quarterback Tom Brady, "Quotes from New England Patriots Press Conference," 30 January 2005.

[772] Patriots receiver Deion Branch, quoted in: Andy Hart, "Super Bowl MVP Branch remains humble," *Patriots.com*, 30 June 2005.

[773] Patriots wide receiver / nickel back / punt returner Troy Brown, "Quotes from New England Patriots Press Conference," 30 January 2005.

[774] Patriots safety Rodney Harrison, "Quotes From New England Patriots Press Conference," February 3, 2005.

[775] Patriots linebacker Mike Vrabel, quoted in: "Quotes from New England Patriots Press Conference," February 3, 2005.

[776] Patriots cornerback Ty Law, quoted in: "NEW ENGLAND 30, SEATTLE 20," 17 October 2004, http://sportsillustrated.cnn.com/football/nfl/recaps/2004/10/17/1170_recap.html.

[777] Patriots offensive lineman Stephen Neal, quoted in: Michael Vega, "No longer wrestling with job," *Boston Globe*, 8 October 2004, www.boston.com/sports/football/patriots/articles/2004/10/08/no_longer_wrestling_with_job.

[778] Mike Reiss, "Wilfork key to youth movement," *Metrowest Daily News*, 18 July 2004, http://patriots.bostonherald.com/patriots/view.bg?articleid=36086.

[779] Patriots defensive lineman Ty Warren, quoted in: Michael Parente, " Warren, Robertson key for Pats, Jets," *Register Citizen*, 22 October 2004, www.registercitizen.com/site/news.cfm?newsid=13200213&BRD=1652&PAG=461&dept_id=464186&rfi=6.

[780] Patriots safety Rodney Harrison, quoted in: Rich Eisen, "A conversation with Rodney Harrison," *NFL.com*, 19 July 2004, www.nfl.com/nflnetwork/story/7513397.

[781] Patriots punter Josh Miller, quoted in: Mike Reiss, "Miller now has better foothold," *Boston Globe*, 2 September 2005.

[782] Patriots punter Josh Miller, quoted in: Mike Reiss, "Miller now has better foothold," *Boston Globe*, 2 September 2005.

[783] Bill Belichick, "Quotes from New England Patriots Press Conference," 30 January 2005.

[784] Bill Belichick, "Quotes from New England Patriots Press Conference," 30 January 2005.

[785] Miguel de Icaza, quoted in: Steve Hamm, "Linux Inc.," *BusinessWeek*, 31 January 2005, pp. 66-68.

[786] Patriots linebacker Rosevelt Colvin, quoted in: Jerome Solomon, "Multiple choices for biggest question," *Boston Globe*, 24 July 2005.

[787] Patriots safety Rodney Harrison, "Quotes From New England Patriots Press Conference," February 3, 2005.

[788] Patriots right tackle Tom Ashworth, quoted in: Michael Felger, "Ashworth on track to start off right," *Boston Herald*, 25 August 2005.

[789] Bill Belichick, quoted in: Paul Kenyon, "Either way, Scott has right attitude," *Providence Journal*, 25 August 2005.

[790] Bill Belichick, quoted in: Tom E. Curran, "Pack of reasons to pay attention to this exhibition," *Providence Journal*, 26 August 2005.

[791] Troy Brown, quoted in: Ron Borges, "Patriots veteran Brown is leery about cutdown," *Boston Globe*, 29 August 2005.

[792] Patriots linebacker Willie McGinest, "Quotes From New England Patriots Media Day," 1 February 2005.

[793] Safety Rodney Harrison, "Quotes From New England Patriots Press Conference," 3 February 2005.

[794] Patriots safety Rodney Harrison, "Quotes From New England Patriots Press Conference," 2 February 2005.

[795] Rodney Harrison, quoted in: Michael Felger, "Harrison shows another side," Boston Herald, 27 August 2005.

[796] Tedy Bruschi, "Bruschi speaks at ring ceremony," *Patriots.com*, 13 June 2005.

[797] Rodney Harrison, quoted in: Bryan Morry, "Latest ring wows Pats," *Patriots.com*, 13 June 2005.

[798] Rodney Harrison, "Patriots Video News," *Patriots.com*, 15 June 2005.

[799] Ted Johnson, quoted in: Bryan Morry, "Latest ring wows Pats," *Patriots.com*, 13 June 2005.

[800] Patriots tight end Benjamin Watson, quoted in: Jerome Solomon, "They're eager to make amends," *Boston Globe*, 26 May 2005.

[801] Patriots linebacker Mike Vrabel, quoted in: "Quotes from New England Patriots Press Conference," February 3, 2005.

[802] Tom Brady, speaking at William and Mary's Colonial All-Pro Football Camp, quoted in: Dave Johnson, "Road to success often is unpaved," *DailyPress.com*, 28 June 2005.

[803] Bill Belichick, "Quotes from New England Patriots Press Conference," 30 January 2005.

[804] Patriots linebacker Rosevelt Colvin, "Quotes From New England Patriots Press Conference," 3 February 2005.

[805] Bill Belichick, "Quotes from New England Patriots Press Conference," 3 February 2005.

[806] Patriots linebacker Rosevelt Colvin, quoted in: Michael Felger, "Colvin creeps toward 100 percent," *MetroWest Daily News*, 5 August 2005.

[807] Patriots linebacker Rosevelt Colvin, "Quotes From New England Patriots Media Day," 1 February 2005.

[808] Patriots inside linebackers coach Pepper Johnson, *Won For All*, Chicago: Contemporary Books, 2003, p. 133.

[809] Tom Brady, quoted in: Hector Longo, "Walter attempting to redeem himself," *Eagle Tribune*, 18 December 2003, eagletribune.com/news/stories/20031218/SP_005.htm.

[810] Troy Brown, quoted in: Ian Logue, "Pats Improve to 8-5 With a 27-16 Win Over Cleveland," 9 December 2001, www.patsfans.com/story/recap_120901.shtml.

[811] Patriots linebacker Willie McGinest, quoted in: Pete Thamel, "Jets Face Patriots' Resurgent Defense," *New York Times*, 18 September 2004, p. D3, ProQuest database.

[812] Patriots running back Corey Dillon, Bill Finley, "Dillon Relishes Icing Victory for the Patriots," *New York Times*, 25 October 2004, www.nytimes.com/2004/10/25/sports/football/25patriots.html.

[813] Patriots tight end Christian Fauria, quoted in: Jimmy Golen (AP), "Streak over, Patriots back to work," *San Francisco Chronicle*, 1 November 2004, http://sfgate.com/cgi-bin/article.cgi?f=/news/archive/2004/11/01/sports1717EST0282.DTL.

[814] Patriots defensive lineman Richard Seymour, quoted in: Jon Japha, "Patriots beat: Clear class distinctions," *MetroWest Daily News*, 18 October 2004, www.metrowestdailynews.com/sportsNews/view.bg?articleid=80807.

[815] Patriots special teams captain Larry Izzo, quoted in: Chris Kennedy, "Patriots evade Bills, tie record for victories," *The Republican*, 4 October 2004, www.masslive.com/sports/republican/index.ssf?/base/sports-2/1096876146255200.xml.

[816] Bill Belichick, quoted in: Patriots Video News, 21 October 2004, http://cachewww.patriots.com/MediaCenter/index.cfm?ac=VideoNewsDetail&PID=9415&PCID=78.

[817] Bill Belichick, quoted in: John Canzano, "Belichick does just fine by himself," *The Oregonian*, 30 January 2004, www.oregonlive.com/sports/oregonian/john_canzano/index.ssf?/base/exclude/1075468056315520.xml.

[818] Patriots cornerback Ty Law, quoted in: Rob Longley, "Pats D coming up aces," *Toronto Sun*, 25 October 2004, http://slam.canoe.ca/Slam/Football/NFL/2004/10/25/684630.html.

[819] Patriots cornerback Ty Law, quoted in: Jim Litke, "Cool, calm Brady gets it done yet again," *MSNBC.com*, 25 January 2004, http://msnbc.msn.com/id/3995389/.

[820] Patriots linebacker Mike Vrabel, quoted in: Bill Burt, "Ready, willing and Vrabel," *Eagle Tribune*, 27 January 2004, www.eagletribune.com/news/stories/20040127/SP_005.htm.

[821] Bill Belichick, "Bill Belichick Press Conf. Transcript," *Patriots.com*, 22 September 2004, www.patriots.com/Common/PrintThis.sps?id=31304.

[822] Patriots kicker Adam Vinatieri, quoted in: Michael Smith, "Adam Vinatieri," in: *Again!*, Chicago: Triumph Books, 2004, p. 124.

[823] Tight end Christian Fauria, quoted in: Alan Greenberg, "Patriots: Streak? What Streak?" *Hartford Courant*, 26 September 2004, www.ctnow.com/sports/hc-patsstreak0926.artsep26.1,3170251.print.story.

[824] Patriots linebacker Tedy Bruschi, quoted in: Shaun Powell, "Pats Recall Big Blue's Glory Days," *Newsday*, 19 January 2004, www.newsday.com/sports/ny-pow193632305jan19,0,3171907.column?coll=ny-sports-headlines.

[825] Denver Broncos head coach Mike Shanahan, on the 2001 Patriots' Super Bowl victory, quoted in: Will McDonough, "A few musings on a miracle in the Big Easy," *Patriots United*, Canada: Team Power Publishing, 2002, p. 13.

[826] Tom Brady, quoted in: Michael Smith, "Snowballin'," *Boston Globe*, 8 December 2003, www.boston.com/sports/football/patriots/articles/2003/12/08/snowballin/.

[827] Bill Kongsberg, "The Rams Will Win a Blowout," *Outsports.com*, 30 January 2002, www.outsports.com/nfl/2001/superpickbillk.htm.

[828] Rams running back Marshall Faulk, quoted in: Bryan McGovern, "Patriot Day," *The Sports Network*, 3 February 2002, www.sportsnetwork.com/default.asp?c=sportsnetwork&page=nfl/misc/mcgovern/nfl-weekly-020302.htm.

[829] Joe Theismann, "Super Pats were team of destiny," *ESPN.com*, 3 February 2002, http://espn.go.com/nfl/playoffs01/columns/theismann_joe/1322325.html.

[830] Patriots defensive lineman Richard Seymour, quoted in: Gus Martins, "Pats' united front: Defensive line focuses on Panthers RBs," *Boston Herald*, 29 January 2004, http://patriots.bostonherald.com/patriots/view.bg?articleid=14095.

[831] Tennessee Titans defensive coordinator Jim Schwartz, quoted in: Nick Cafardo, "Schwartz's way is stat of the art," *Boston Globe*, 8 January 2004, www.boston.com/sports/football/patriots/articles/2004/01/08/schwartzs_way_is_stat_of_the_art.

[832] Tennessee Titans defensive coordinator Jim Schwartz, quoted in: "Football Outsiders Interview: Jim Schwartz," www.footballoutsiders.com/ramblings.php?p=243&cat=1.

[833] Bill Belichick, quoted in: Alan Greenberg, "Streak Aside, Pats' Losses May Go Beyond 1 Game," *Hartford Courant*, 2 November 2004, www.ctnow.com/sports/football/hc-patriots1102.artnov02,1,3264531.print.story?coll=hc-headlines-football.

[834] Patriots fullback Larry Centers, quoted in: Dan Pires, "Postgame talk ranges from Sapp to streaker," *Standard-Times*, 4 February 2004, www.southcoasttoday.com/daily/02-04/02-04-04/c01sp273.htm.

[835] Bill Belichick, quoted in: Thomas George, "A Changed Dr. Doom Returns," *New York Times*, 15 September 2002, p. 8.1, ProQuest database.

[836] Bill Belichick, "Quotes from New England Patriots Sunday Press Conference," 30 January 2005.

[837] Patriots linebacker Willie McGinest, "Quotes From New England Patriots Media Day," 1 February 2005.

[838] Patriots running back Corey Dillon, "Quotes from New England Patriots Press Conference," 2 February 2005.

[839] Stan Parrish, Tom Brady's positional coach at Michigan, quoted in: Tom Danyluk, "Comparing Brady to Montana is unwarranted," *Pro Football Weekly*, 11 August 2004, www.profootballweekly.com/PFW/NFL/AFC/AFC+East/New+England/Features/2004/danyluk081104.htm.

[840] Former Patriots quarterback Drew Bledsoe, quoted in: Glen Farley, "Bledsoe now in Brady's shadow," *The Enterprise*, 30 September 2004, http://enterprise.southofboston.com/articles/2004/09/30/news/sports/sports01.txt.

[841] Indianapolis Colts quarterback Peyton Manning, quoted in: Nick Cafardo, "Quarterback faceoff a bit of a throwback," *Boston Globe*, 7 September 2004, www.boston.com/sports/football/patriots/articles/2004/09/07/quarterback_faceoff_a_bit_of_a_throwback.

[842] Paul Attner, "Whatever 'It' is, Brady has 'It,'" *Sports Illustrated*, 6 October 2004, http://msn.foxsports.com/story/3059636.

[843] NFL personnel expert Gil Brandt, quoted in: Tom Danyluk, "Comparing Brady to Montana is unwarranted," *Pro Football Weekly*, 11 August 2004, www.profootballweekly.com/PFW/NFL/AFC/AFC+East/New+England/Features/2004/danyluk081104.htm.

[844] Patriots running back J.R. Redmond, in: "Quotes," http://bostonbrat.net/brady/quotes.html.

[845] Patriots wide receiver David Patten, quoted in: Tim Polzer, "Super Bowl XXXVI: New England 20, St. Louis 17," 3 February 2002, www.superbowl.com/history/mvps/game/sbxxxvi.

[846] Patriots wide receiver Troy Brown, quoted in: Len Pasquarelli, "MVP poised, poignant on morning after," *ESPN.com*, 2 February 2004, http://sports.espn.go.com/nfl/playoffs03/columns/story?columnist=pasquarelli_len&id=1725363.

[847] Michigan guard Steve Hutchinson, quoted in: Michael Rosenberg, "Brady glad maturity finally came to pass," *Detroit Free Press*, 27 December 1999, www.patriotsplanet.com/BB/showthread.php?s=&threadid=699.

[848] Patriots cornerback Ty Law, quoted in: Jim Litke, "Cool, calm Brady gets it done yet again," *MSNBC.com*, 25 January 2004, http://msnbc.msn.com/id/3995389/.

[849] Former Patriots assistant coach Steve Szabo, quoted in: Leo Roth, "Can Szabo's secrets help the Bills?" *Democrat and Chronicle*, 28 September 2004, www.democratandchronicle.com/apps/pbcs.dll/article?AID=/20040928/SPORTS03/409280510/1007/SPORTS.

[850] Patriots tight end Christian Fauria, quoted in: Leonard Shapiro, "For Dillon, Patriots, It's a Win-Win," *Washington Post*, 16 October 2004, www.washingtonpost.com/ac2/wp-dyn/A36825-2004Oct15.

[851] Patriots linebacker Tedy Bruschi, "Quotes from New England Patriots Press Conference," 31 January 2005.

[852] *Sports Illustrated*, "SI Players Poll," survey of 354 current and former NFL players, http://sportsillustrated.cnn.com/2004/players/09/14/players.poll/index.html.

[853] Unnamed Giants player, quoted in: Ken Palmer, "Giant outrage," *Yahoo.com*, 17 August 2004, http://ca.sports.yahoo.com/nfl/news?slug=citadel-2_284807_64.

[854] Patriots safety Eugene Wilson, quoted in: Michael Felger, "Wilson punches clock: Pats safety turns out to be big steal," *Milford Daily News*, 29 September 2004, www.milforddailynews.com/sportsNews/view.bg?articleid=56720.

[855] Michael Felger, "Wilson punches clock: Pats safety turns out to be big steal," *Milford Daily News*, 29 September 2004, www.milforddailynews.com/sportsNews/view.bg?articleid=56720.

[856] Patriots safety Eugene Wilson, quoted in: Michael Felger, "Wilson punches clock: Pats safety turns out to be big steal," *Milford Daily News*, 29 September 2004, www.milforddailynews.com/sportsNews/view.bg?articleid=56720.

[857] Patriots Vice President of Player Personnel Scott Pioli, quoted in: Bill Burt, "More than a coach," *Eagle Tribune*, 25 January 2004, www.eagletribune.com/news/stories/20040125/SP_001.htm.

[858] Patriots spokesman Stacey James, quoted in: Gayle Fee and Laura Raposa, "Attire rule change won't suit Belichick," *Boston Herald*, 11 May 2005.

[859] Steve Belichick, quoted in: Terry Pluto, "The Man Behind the Mask," *Akron Beacon Journal*, 18 December 1994, www.allthingsbillbelichick.com/articles/behindthemask.htm.

[860] Gordon Edes, "The flag was raised -- why not salary?" *Boston Globe*, 17 May 2005; Nick Cafardo, "He's a wanted man," *Boston Globe*, 10 February 2005.

[861] Jim Moore, "Dillon's 'questionable' status a misnomer," *Seattle Post-Intelligencer*, 18 October 2004, http://seattlepi.nwsource.com/football/195710_hside18.html.

[862] Former Giants quarterback and CBS analyst Phil Simms, quoted in: Kevin Paul Dupont, "Winner's Circle," *Boston Globe*, 23 January 2004, www.boston.com/sports/football/patriots/articles/2004/01/23/winners_circle/.

[863] Former Giants quarterback and CBS analyst Phil Simms, quoted in: Kevin Paul Dupont, "Winner's Circle," *Boston Globe*, 23 January 2004, www.boston.com/sports/football/patriots/articles/2004/01/23/winners_circle/.

[864] Steve Buckley, "Meet Bill Belichick, Mr. Popular," *Boston Herald*, 17 January 2002, www.allthingsbillbelichick.com/articles/meetbb.htm.

[865] Bill Belichick, "O.K. Champ, Now Comes the Hard Part," *New York Times*, 26 January 2003, www.allthingsbillbelichick.com/articles/okchamp.html.

[866] Bill Belichick conference call, *Steelers.com*, late October 2004, www.steelers.com/article/46622/.

[867] Kevin Mannix, "Top Billing," *Boston Herald*, 31 August 2004, www.allthingsbillbelichick.com/articles/topbilling.htm.

[868] Patriots VP of player personnel Scott Pioli, quoted in: Harvey Araton, "Pioli Prefers the Back Seat In the Patriots' Front Office," *New York Times*, 29 January 2004, www.nytimes.com/2004/01/29/sports/football/29ARAT.html.

[869] Patriots owner Robert Kraft, quoted in: Bud Shaw, "Follow the Belichick highway," *Plain Dealer* (Cleveland), 28 January 2004, www.cleveland.com/sports/plaindealer/index.ssf?/base/sports/1075285922190293.xml.

[870] Patriots owner Robert Kraft, quoted in: Bud Shaw, "Follow the Belichick highway," *Plain Dealer* (Cleveland), 28 January 2004, www.cleveland.com/sports/plaindealer/index.ssf?/base/sports/1075285922190293.xml.

[871] Patriots linebacker Ted Johnson, quoted in: Bill Burt, "Properly Seasoned," *Eagle-Tribune*, 3 January 2005.

[872] Dr. Peter F. Drucker, *Management: Tasks, Responsibilities, Practices*, USA: HarperCollins, 1973, pp. 43-44.

[873] Patriots owner Robert Kraft, "Quotes from New England Patriots Photo Day," 1 February 2005.

[874] Jerry Magee, "Could heist by Patriots become haul for Bills," *San Diego Union-Tribune*, 22 April 2002.

[875] Jerry Magee, "Could heist by Patriots become haul for Bills," *San Diego Union-Tribune*, 22 April 2002.

[876] Patriots owner Robert Kraft, "Quotes from New England Patriots Photo Day," 1 February 2005.

[877] Robert Kraft in 1994, quoted in: Bill Burt, "Properly Seasoned," *Eagle-Tribune*, 3 January 2005.

[878] Stephen Nover, "Bookmakers start putting up NFL over/under win totals," *Covers.com*, 16 May 2005.

[879] Bill Belichick, quoted in: Chris Kennedy, "Arizona changes its tune," *The Republican*, 16 September 2004, www.masslive.com/sports/republican/index.ssf?/base/sports-0/109538370014040.xml.

[880] Robert Kraft, quoted in: Jim Donaldson, "Kraft finally shares his thoughts," *SouthCoast Today*, 24 January 1998, www.southcoasttoday.com/daily/01-98/01-24-98/c03sp116.htm.

[881] Tom Brady, quoted in: "San Diego Chargers down to New England Patriots 26-29," 14 October 2001, http://stats.staugustine.com/football/pro/nfl/2001/recap/153681.shtml.

[882] Patriots offensive coordinator Charlie Weis, "Quotes from New England Patriots Press Conference," 3 February 2005.

[883] Tom E. Curran, "Patriots of 2004 find their identity," *Providence Journal*, 9 November 2004, www.projo.com/patriots/content/projo_20041109_09patanal.94368.html.

[884] Hector Longo, "Bobby Grier's guys are riding out the ridicule," *Eagle-Tribune*, 1 February 2002, www.eagletribune.com/news/stories/20020201/SP_003.htm.

[885] Bill Belichick, "Bill Belichick Press Conf. Transcript - 4/30," *Patriots.com*, 30 April 2004, www.patriots.com/news/FullArticle.sps?id=28597&type=general.

[886] Romeo Crennel, quoted in: Len Pasquarelli, "Chemistry, character heavily considered by Browns," *ESPN*, 15 June 2005.

[887] Drew Bledsoe, Troy Brown, Tedy Bruschi, Kevin Faulk, Terry Glenn, Ted Johnson, Tebucky Jones, Ty Law, Willie McGinest, Lawyer Milloy, Brandon Mitchell, Rod Rutledge, Adam Vinatieri, and Damien Woody.

[888] Troy Brown, Tedy Bruschi, Kevin Faulk, Ted Johnson, Ty Law, Willie McGinest, Adam Vinatieri, and Damien Woody.

[889] Michael Felger, "Pats subject of cheap talk," *Boston Herald*, 4 April 2004, http://patriots.bostonherald.com/patriots/view.bg?articleid=13945.

[890] Kevin Paul Dupont, "Pioli Finding Success With Patriots," *Boston Globe*, 13 January 2002, www.allthingsbillbelichick.com/articles/piolisuccess.htm..

[891] Bill Belichick, quoted in: Ed Duckworth, "Belichick crafts new image," *New England Sports Service*, 6 June 2000, www.standardtimes.com/daily/06-00/06-06-00/c02sp105.htm.

[892] Unnamed Patriots coach, quoted in: Len Pasquarelli, "Belichick Becomes Life of Patriots' Party," *ESPN.com*, 22 December 2001, www.allthingsbillbelichick.com/articles/lifeofparty.htm.

[893] Michael Felger, "Pats subject of cheap talk," *Boston Herald*, 4 April 2004, http://patriots.bostonherald.com/patriots/view.bg?articleid=13945.

[894] Scott Pioli, "Quotes from New England Patriots Press Conference," 3 February 2005.

[895] Rick Braun, "Patriots built with free agents, draft," *Milwaukee Journal-Sentinel*, 4 February 2004.

[896] Michael J. Duberstein, NFL Players Association, "It Happens Every February," March 2002, www.nflpa.org/PDFs/Shared/Media_Misperceptions.pdf.

[897] Bob McGinn, "A priceless collection," *Milwaukee Journal-Sentinel*, 31 January 2002, www.jsonline.com/packer/prev/jan02/16658.asp.

[898] Mike O'Hara, "Compton succeeds as ex-Lion," *Detroit Lions*, 1 February 2002, www.detnews.com/2002/lions/0201/31/g01-403534.htm.

[899] Len Pasquarelli, "Belichick Becomes Life of Patriots' Party," *ESPN.com*, 22 December 2001, www.allthingsbillbelichick.com/articles/lifeofparty.htm.

[900] Bill Belichick, quoted in: Len Pasquarelli, "Patriots hope shopping spree yields bargains," *ESPN*, 9 August 2001, http://espn.go.com/nfl/trainingcamp01/s/010080/patriots.html.

[901] Quarterback Drew Bledsoe, quoted in: Glen Farley (*Pro Football Weekly*), "Revamped Patriots better recognize," *ESPN*, 27 August 2001, http://espn.go.com/nfl/preview01/s/nwe.html.

[902] Bill Belichick, quoted in: Andrew Mason, "Patriots' game: Massaging the market," *NFL.com*, 7 March 2002, www.nfl.com/teams/story/NE/5099329.

[903] Tom E. Curran, "Patriots' Pioli won't be going anywhere fast," *Providence Journal*, 30 December 2003, www.projo.com/patriots/content/projo_20031230_30pats.693b5.html.

[904] St. Louis Rams general manager Charley Armey, quoted in: Bob McGinn, "A priceless collection," *Milwaukee Journal-Sentinel*, 31 January 2002, www.jsonline.com/packer/prev/jan02/16658.asp.

[905] Ron Borges, "Belichick Has a Gifted Touch," *Boston Globe*, 24 December 2001, www.allthingsbillbelichick.com/articles/giftedtouch.htm.

[906] Judy Battista, "Patriots Leave Jets High, Dry And Helpless," *New York Times*, 16 September 2002, p. D1, ProQuest database.

[907] Michael Felger, "Pats subject of cheap talk," *Boston Herald*, 4 April 2004, http://patriots.bostonherald.com/patriots/view.bg?articleid=13945.

[908] Patriots receiver Charles Johnson, quoted in: Len Pasquarelli, "Patriots hope shopping spree yields bargains," *ESPN.com*, 9 August 2001, http://espn.go.com/nfl/trainingcamp01/s/010080/patriots.html.

[909] Patriots owner Robert Kraft, quoted in: Michael Felger, "Pats subject of cheap talk," *Boston Herald*, 4 April 2004, http://patriots.bostonherald.com/patriots/view.bg?articleid=13945.

[910] Bill Belichick, quoted in: John Tomase, "Belichick has a few surprises ready," *Eagle Tribune*, 2 February 2000, www.eagletribune.com/news/stories/20000202/SP_011.htm..

[911] Costco CEO Jim Sinegal, quoted in: Steven Greenhouse, "Is being generous good for business?" *New York Times*, 16 July 2005.

[912] Nick Saban, quoted in Clifton Brown, "Saban's Next Magic Trick: Make the Dolphins Reappear," *New York Times*, 2 May 2005.

[913] Intel's Andy Grove, quoted in: Cliff Edwards, "Supercharging Silicon Valley," *BusinessWeek*, 4 October 2004, p. 18.

[914] Patriots VP of Player Personnel Scott Pioli, quoted in: Kevin Paul Dupont, "Pioli Finding Success With Patriots," *Boston Globe*, 13 January 2002, www.allthingsbillbelichick.com/articles/piolisuccess.htm.

[915] Including: Terry Allen, Bruce Armstrong, Vincent Brisby, Chris Carter, Ben Coates, Chad Eaton, Ed Ellis, Heath Irwin, Steve Israel, Shawn Jefferson, Marty Moore, Zefross Moss, Todd Rucci, Greg Spires, Chris Sullivan, and Larry Whigham.

[916] Scott Pioli, Patriots VP of player personnel, quoted in: Alan Greenberg, "There's No Room For Error; The Deal Maker," *Hartford Courant*, 4 September 2002, p. G3, ProQuest database.

[917] Bill Belichick, quoted in: Judy Battista, "Patriots Adhere to Bottom Line to Stay on Top," *New York Times*, 8 August 2004, www.nytimes.com/2004/08/08/sports/football/08patriots.html.

[918] Robert Kraft, quoted in: Bill Griffith, "Earning double coverage," *Boston Globe*, 19 October 2004, www.boston.com/sports/football/patriots/articles/2004/10/19/earning_double_coverage/.

[919] Patriots owner Robert Kraft, in speech to TIECON 2004, the annual conference of the Boston chapter of The Indus Entrepreneurs, quoted in: Christine Walsh, "Patriots' football - a winning business," *IndUS Business Journal*, 15 June 2004, www.indusbusinessjournal.com/news/2004/06/15/Tie/Patriots.Football.A.Winning.Business-688799.shtml..

[920] Patriots owner Robert Kraft, quoted in: Michael Felger, "Pats subject of cheap talk," *Boston Herald*, 4 April 2004, http://patriots.bostonherald.com/patriots/view.bg?articleid=13945.

[921] NFL commissioner Paul Tagliabue, quoted in: Tom E. Curran, "Pats owner has created a masterpiece," *Providence Journal*, 13 June 2004, www.projo.com/patriots/content/projo_20040613_13kraft.1b891c.html.

[922] Former Packers GM Ron Wolf, quoted in: Paul Attner, "Super Bowl 36: Standing Pat," *The Sporting News*, 4 February 2002, www.a1-sports-odds.com/292.htm.

[923] Bill Belichick, "Bill Belichick Press Conf. Transcript," *Patriots.com*, 22 September 2004, www.patriots.com/Common/PrintThis.sps?id=31304.

[924] Patriots safety/cornerback Eugene Wilson, quoted in: George Kimball, "Klemm takes hold of role," *Boston Herald*, 22 September 2004, http://patriots.bostonherald.com/patriots/view.bg?articleid=45375.

[925] Bill Belichick, speech to the Big Brothers of Massachusetts Bay, quoted in: Bryan Morry, "Belichick delivers his message to Big Brothers," *Patriots.com*, 20 May 2004.

[926] Jonathan Kraft, quoted in: Jerome Solomon, "Mind over matter," *Boston Globe*, 22 April 2005, www.boston.com/sports/football/patriots/articles/2005/04/22/patriots_day.

[927] Bill Belichick, quoted in: Frank Tadych, "Reaction to MNF continues," *Patriots.com*, 18 November 2004, http://cachewww.patriots.com/news/index.cfm?ac=latestnewsdetail&pid=9774&pcid=41.

[928] Linebacker Mike Vrabel, "Quotes from New England Patriots Media Day," 1 February 2005.

[929] Patriots defensive line coach Pepper Johnson, "Quotes from New England Patriots Press Conference," 3 February 2005.

[930] Patriots nose tackle Vince Wilfork, quoted in: Ron Borges, "Their plan of attack was right on the nose," *Boston Globe*, 25 January 2005.

[931] Patriots nose tackle Vince Wilfork, quoted in: Ron Borges, "Their plan of attack was right on the nose," *Boston Globe*, 25 January 2005.

[932] Bill Belichick, "Quotes from New England Patriots Press Conference," 31 January 2005.

[933] Scott Pioli, "Quotes from New England Patriots Press Conference," 2 February 2005.

[934] Michael Felger, "Pats settle, move on: Make most of weak draft and stock picks," *Milford Daily News*, 25 April 2005.

[935] Bill Belichick, "Belichick Press Conference," *Patriots.com*, 24 April 2005.

[936] "2004 Statesmen Football Preview," 11 August 2004, http://statesmen.wmpenn.edu/news.php?id=23.

[937] "2004 Statesmen Football Preview," 11 August 2004, http://statesmen.wmpenn.edu/news.php?id=23.

[938] "2004 Statesmen Football Preview," 11 August 2004, http://statesmen.wmpenn.edu/news.php?id=23.

[939] Unnamed Cleveland Browns scout to Andy Stokes, quoted in: Gordon Monson, "Patriots draft No. 255, Mr. Irrelevant," *Salt Lake Tribune*, 9 May 2005.

[940] Bill Belichick, quoted in: Kevin Mannix, "Last man alive: Mr. Irrelevant has real chance," *Boston Herald*, 1 May 2005.

[941] Patriots Director of College Scouting Tom Dimitroff, Jr., quoted in: Mike Reiss, "Inside look at the Pats' draft preparation," *MetroWest Daily News*, 1 May 2005.

[942] Bill Belichick, "Quotes from New England Patriots Media Day," 1 February 2005.

[943] Patriots defensive lineman Dan Klecko, quoted in: Jimmy Golen (AP), "New England Patriots hope to extend streak one more game in Super Bowl," 30 January 2004, http://ca.sports.yahoo.com/040130/6/wkdt.html.

[944] Patriots special teams captain Larry Izzo, "Quotes from New England Patriots Press Conference," 30 January 2005.

[945] Coach Bill Belichick, quoted in: John Hassan, "Inside Belichick's Brain," *ESPN The Magazine*, 9 September 2002, www.allthingsbillbelichick.com/articles/insidebrain.htm.

[946] Dan Shaughnessy, "Champs again," *Boston Globe*, 2 February 2004, www.boston.com/sports/football/patriots/articles/2004/02/02/champs_again/.

[947] Tom Brady Sr., recalling 2001, quoted in: Ron Kroichick, "Brady's bunch ready for some football Frenzy in San Mateo as Patriots star heads to 2nd Super Bowl," 30 January 2004.

[948] Tom Brady, quoted in: NFL, "Official Super Bowl XXXVI game summary," www.absolutebrady.com/SB36.html.

[949] Patriots tight end Jermaine Wiggins, quoted in: NFL, "Official Super Bowl XXXVI game summary," www.absolutebrady.com/SB36.html.

[950] Patriots offensive coordinator Charlie Weis, quoted in: NFL, "Official Super Bowl XXXVI game summary," www.absolutebrady.com/SB36.html.

[951] Tom Brady, quoted in: Paul Attner, "Super Bowl 38: Red, white and two," *The Sporting News*, 9 February 2004, www.sportingnews.com/archives/superbowl/.

[952] Tom Brady, quoted in: Bryan Morry, "Managing the Moment," *Lindy's 2004 Pro Football*, p. 10.

[953] Dedric Ward, quoted in: Mark Gaughan, "Tom Terrific," *AbsoluteBrady.com*, 28 January 2004.

[954] Pittsburgh Steelers coach Bill Cowher, quoted in: Tony Grossi, "Brows raised mile-high over former Browns," *(Cleveland) Plain Dealer*, 3 April 2005, www.cleveland.com/sports/plaindealer/index.ssf?/base/sports/1112520789272920.xml.

[955] Bill Belichick, quoted in: Mike Reiss, "Multi-purpose Monday," *Boston Herald* blog, 8 November 2004.

[956] Bill Belichick, quoted in: Mike Reiss, "New twist to Beli-flex system aids Patriots' charge," *Milford Daily News*, 9 November 2004.

[957] Troy Brown, "Quotes from New England Patriots Press Conference," 30 January 2005.

[958] Patriots safety Lawyer Milloy, quoted in: John Hassan, "Inside Belichick's Brain," *ESPN The Magazine*, 9 September 2002, www.allthingsbillbelichick.com/articles/insidebrain.htm.

[959] Netscape founder Jim Barksdale, quoted in: Matthew Boyle, "When FedEx Is Flying High," *Fortune*, 1 November 2004, p. 150.

[960] Patriots linebacker Ted Johnson, audio recording, 1 February 2005.

[961] Bill Belichick, quoted in: Paul Perillo, "Belichick rolls with preseason punches; Monday's notes," *Patriots.com*, 9 August 2004, www.patriots.com/news/FullArticle.sps?id=30020&type=general.

[962] Tom Brady, quoted in: Nolan Nawrocki, "Passion transcends the game," *Pro Football Weekly*, 5 February 2002, http://archive.profootballweekly.com/content/archives2001/features_2001/daily_020502.asp.

[963] Patriots safety Lawyer Milloy, quoted in: Michael Holley, "Best-case scenarios," *Boston Globe*, 5 November 2003, www.boston.com/sports/football/patriots/articles/2003/11/05/best_case_scenarios.

[964] Patriots outside linebackers coach Rob Ryan, quoted in: Michael Holley, "A Texas steel-cage match to the finish," *Boston Globe*, 27 September 2004, www.boston.com/sports/football/patriots/articles/2004/09/27/a_texas_steel_cage_match_to_the_finish..

[965] Bill Belichick, live video news conference, streamed online from Patriots.com, 20 October 2004.

[966] Patriots offensive lineman Stephen Neal, "Quotes from New England Patriots Media Day," 1 February 2005.

[967] Patriots safety Rodney Harrison, quoted in: Michael Felger, "Safety fire -- Harrison's intensity sparks Pats," *Boston Herald*, 25 August 2005.

[968] Bill Belichick, quoted in: Patriots Insider, "Patriots: Week 10 Insiders Perspective," 12 November 2004, http://patriots.scout.com/2/318044.html.

[969] Tom Brady, quoted in: *Patriots United*, Canada: Team Power Publishing, 2002, p 95.

[970] Patriots rookie defensive tackle Vince Wilfork, quoted in: Mark Farinella, "Depth of Patriots' defense too much for Miami," *Sun Chronicle*, 11 October 2004, www.thesunchronicle.com/articles/2004/10/11/sports/sports2.txt.

[971] Patriots defensive lineman Marquise Hill, quoted in: Andy Hart, "Hill hopes for greater contribution in '05," *Patriots Football Weekly*, 6 May 2005.

[972] Bill Belichick, quoted in: Joe Burris, "Deep route," *Boston Globe*, 29 October 2004, www.boston.com/sports/football/patriots/articles/2004/10/29/deep_route.

[973] Patriots backup quarterback Rohan Davey, quoted in: Chris Kennedy, "Patriots begin journey," *The Republican*, 12 August 2004, www.masslive.com/sports/republican/index.ssf?/base/sports-0/1092361501223171.xml.

[974] Bill Belichick, quoted in: Michael Felger, "Bruschi works on extension," *Boston Herald*, 12 June 2004, http://patriots.bostonherald.com/patriots/view.bg?articleid=31607.

[975] Bill Belichick, quoted in: Kevin McNamara, "Backup plan at QB is starting to take shape," *Providence Journal*, 18 August 2004, www.projo.com/patriots/content/projo_20040818_18pats.116cc8.html.

[976] Bill Belichick, quoted in: Alan Greenberg, "Last Shot For Some Pats," *Hartford Courant*, 2 September 2004, www.ctnow.com/sports/football/hc-patriots0902.artsep02,1,5230607.print.story.

[977] Tom Brady, audio recording, 2 February 2005.

[978] Tom Brady, quoted in: "New England Patriots Quarterback Tom Brady: Post Practice Interview," email, 16 August 2005.

[979] Tom Brady, "Quotes from New England Patriots Press Conference," 2 February 2005.

[980] Adam Kilgore, "Brady will get started," *Boston Globe*, 16 August 2005.

[981] Tom Brady, "Quotes from New England Patriots Press Conference," 2 February 2005.

[982] Woody Hayes, on: Desmond Wilcox, "Americans: The Football Coach," aired on: *ESPN Classic*, 1 June 2005.

[983] N.D. Kalu, quoted in: Larry O'Rourke, "Eagles regroup, reflect on loss," *The Morning Call*, 15 August 2004, www.mcall.com/sports/all-eaglesaug15,0,2172916.story?coll=all-sports-hed.

[984] Bill Belichick, quoted in: Michael Felger, "Pats unfazed by pain: Injury threat is not big concern," *Boston Herald*, 15 August 2004, http://patriots.bostonherald.com/patriots/view.bg?articleid=39889.

[985] Tom Brady, quoted in: Michael Felger, "Pats unfazed by pain: Injury threat is not big concern," *Boston Herald*, 15 August 2004, http://patriots.bostonherald.com/patriots/view.bg?articleid=39889.

[986] Tom Brady, quoted in: Tom E. Curran, "Patriots aiming to step up a grade tonight," *Providence Journal*, 21 August 2004, www.projo.com/patriots/content/projo_20040821_21patady.166e3b.html.

[987] Patriots safety Rodney Harrison, quoted in: Michael Vega, "He's still a big hit," *Boston Globe*, 30 July 2004, www.boston.com/sports/football/patriots/articles/2004/07/30/hes_still_a_big_hit.

[988] Running back Corey Dillon, quoted in: AP, "As always, Pats come through," *Newsday*, 18 October 2004, www.newsday.com/sports/football/ny-sppats184010887oct18,0,7450495.story.

[989] Safety Eugene Wilson, telephone interview, *ProFootballCentral.com* radio, 9 March 2005.

[990] Patriots linebacker Roman Phifer, quoted in: Mike Lowe, "Nothing very fancy, but the result is simply unique," *Portland Press Herald*, 18 October 2004, http://sports.mainetoday.com/pro/patriots/041018patscolumn.shtml.

[991] Bill Belichick, quoted in: Andrew Bagnato, "Patriots are quietly making a run at league history," *Arizona Republic*, 19 September 2004, www.azcentral.com/arizonarepublic/sports/articles/0919nflsundaycol0919.html.

[992] Bill Belichick, quoted by Boston College hockey coach Jerry York, in: Glen Farley, "Belichick has the magic touch," *The Enterprise*, 14 August 2004, http://enterprise.southofboston.com/articles/2004/08/14/news/sports/sport01.txt.

[993] Patriots cornerback Ty Law, quoted in: Dan Pires, "Belichick on the verge of history," *Standard-Times*, 1 February 2004, www.southcoasttoday.com/daily/02-04/02-01-04/c01sp874.htm.

[994] Multi-Super Bowl winner Bill Walsh, quoted in: Tom Bass, "Section III: Football Skills-Successful Offense,"NFL/NFF Coaching Academy, *2005 Coach's Playbook*, 2005.

[995] Thrice Super Bowl champion and Hall of Fame coach Bill Walsh, quoted in: John Hassan, "Inside Belichick's Brain," *ESPN The Magazine*, 9 September 2002, www.allthingsbillbelichick.com/articles/insidebrain.htm..

[996] Former Buffalo Bills head coach Marv Levy, quoted in: Kevin Paul Dupont, "Winner's Circle," *Boston Globe*, 23 January 2004, www.boston.com/sports/football/patriots/articles/2004/01/23/winners_circle/.

[997] Tedy Bruschi, Kevin Paul Dupont, "Missions are accomplished," *Boston Globe*, 15 November 2004, www.boston.com/sports/football/patriots/articles/2004/11/15/missions_are_accomplished/.

[998] Patriots linebacker Willie McGinest, quoted in: Howard Ulman (AP), "Veteran LB still producing for Patriots," *San Francisco Chronicle*, 20 October 2004, http://sfgate.com/cgi-bin/article.cgi?f=/news/archive/2004/10/20/sports1938EDT0309.DTL.

[999] Tom Brady, quoted in: Michael Felger, "Patriots notebook: Brady feels he can be better," *MetroWest Sports*, 9 August 2004, www.metrowestdailynews.com/sports\ews/view.bg?articleid=75106.

[1000] Bill Belichick, quoted in: Michael Smith, "Camp fires burning," *Boston Globe*, 30 July 2004, www.boston.com/sports/football/patriots/articles/2004/07/30/camp_fires_burning/.

[1001] Tom Brady, quoted in: Dan Pires, "Belichick on the verge of history," *Standard-Times*, 1 February 2004, www.southcoasttoday.com/daily/02-04/02-01-04/c01sp874.htm.

[1002] Patriots linebacker Mike Vrabel, quoted in: John Clayton, "Injured McGinest makes crucial play," *ESPN.com*, 30 November 2003, http://sports.espn.go.com/nfl/columns/story?columnist=clayton_john&id=1674752.

[1003] Peter King, "Wild-card draw," *Sports Illustrated*, 10 November 2003, http://sportsillustrated.cnn.com/2003/writers/peter_king/11/10/mmqb/.

[1004] Bill Belichick, quoted in: Peter King, "Wild-card draw," *Sports Illustrated*, 10 November 2003, http://sportsillustrated.cnn.com/2003/writers/peter_king/11/10/mmqb/.

[1005] Bill Belichick, quoted in: Dan Shaughnessy, "Filling the Bill As Master Motivator," *Boston Globe*, 10 December 2001, www.tiznowpress.com/globe.html.

[1006] Bob George, "Pats Win The December Way: Tough," 9 December 2001, www.patsfans.com/bgeorge/story/121001.shtml.

[1007] Tom Brady, quoted in: Rich Thompson, "If Brady's not mistaken, victories count," *Boston Herald*, 8 December 2003, on: *AbsoluteBrady.com*.

[1008] Dan Pompei, "Inside Pats' Super Bowl Preparations," *Sporting News*, 2 February 2004, www.allthingsbillbelichick.com/articles/insidesbprep.htm.

[1009] Patriots quarterback Tom Brady, "Tom Brady Press Conference Transcript," *Patriots.com*, 6 January 2004, www.patriots.com/games/GamesDetails.sps?matchid=27174&matchreportid=27208.

[1010] Patriots long snapper Lonie Paxton, quoted in: NFL, "Official Super Bowl XXXVI game summary," www.absolutebrady.com/SB36.html.

[1011] Patriots long snapper Lonie Paxton, quoted in: NFL, "Official Super Bowl XXXVI game summary," www.absolutebrady.com/SB36.html.

[1012] Patriots offensive lineman Matt Light, on: *3 Games to Glory III* DVD, 2005.

[1013] Patriots offensive lineman Matt Light, on: *3 Games to Glory III* DVD, 2005.

[1014] Patriots linebacker Ted Johnson, on: *3 Games to Glory III* DVD, 2005.

[1015] Dean Pees, new Patriots linebackers coach and former Kent State head coach, quoted in: Michael Felger, "Pees: Cues from Belichick," *Boston Herald*, 19 August 2004, http://patriots.bostonherald.com/patriots/view.bg?articleid=40466.

[1016] JPEG file with title "The Huddle" and hand-written note saying "Patriots 2003."

[1017] Bill Burt, "By any measure, Patriots QB ranks at the top," *Eagle Tribune*, 9 November 2003, www.eagletribune.com/news/stories/20031109/SP_001.htm.

[1018] New York Jets head coach Herman Edwards, quoted in: Dan Pompei, "Time is now to work on clock management," *SportingNews*, 16 May 2004, www.foxsports.com/content/view?contentId=2390266.

[1019] Rich Cimini, "Father time," *New York Daily News*, 1 August 2004, www.nydailynews.com/sports/story/217825p-187394c.html.

[1020] Patriots linebacker Mike Vrabel, quoted in: Michael Felger, "Adams: Pats' mystery man: Research director invaluable," *Boston Herald*, 30 January 2004, http://patriots.bostonherald.com/patriots/view.bg?articleid=563.

[1021] Patriots offensive coordinator Charlie Weis, quoted in: NFL, "Official Super Bowl XXXVI game summary," www.absolutebrady.com/SB36.html.

[1022] Tom Brady, quoted in: Bryan Morry, "Managing the Moment," *Lindy's 2004 Pro Football*, p. 9.

[1023] Tom Brady, quoted in: Bryan Morry, "Managing the Moment," *Lindy's 2004 Pro Football*, p. 9.

[1024] Bill Belichick, quoted in: Dan Pompei, "Time is now to work on clock management," *SportingNews*, 16 May 2004, www.foxsports.com/content/view?contentId=2390266.

[1025] Bill Belichick, *Patriots Video News*, 11 November 2004, http://originwww.patriots.com/mediacenter/index.cfm?ac=videonewsdetail&pid=9695&pcid=78.

[1026] Patriots linebacker Ted Johnson, quoted in: Tom E. Curran, "Let's count reasons for Pats' success," *Providence Journal*, 9 December 2003, www.projo.com/patriots/content/projo_20031209_09pats.b0805.html.

[1027] Patriots cornerback Asante Samuel, quoted in: Eric McHugh, "Grand Opening," *Patriot Ledger*, 9 September 2005.

[1028] Linebacker Roman Phifer, "Quotes From New England Patriots Media Day," 1 February 2005.

[1029] Patriots linebacker Ted Johnson, "Quotes from New England Patriots Media Day," February 1, 2005.

[1030] Patriots linebacker Willie McGinest, "Quotes from New England Patriots Media Day," 1 February 2005.

[1031] Bill Belichick, "Bill Belichick Pre-Game Press Conf. Transcript," *Patriots.com*, 6 September 2004, www.patriots.com/games/gamedetails.sps?matchreportid=30447&matchid=28318.

[1032] Special teamer and backup linebacker/safety Don Davis, quoted in: Shalise Manza Young, "Players are all ears in Mangini's class," *Providence Journal*, 31 August 2005.

[1033] Tom Brady, quoted in: Ira Kaufman, "Patriots Players Hold Themselves To A Higher Standard," *Tampa Tribune*, 31 January 2005.

[1034] Patriots cornerback Ty Law, quoted in: Chuck Pollock, "POLLOCK: Pats' streak among most impressive," *Times Herald* (Olean, NY), 30 September 2004, www.zwire.com/site/news.cfm?BRD=386&dept_id=444921&newsid=13040313&PAG=461&rfi=9.

[1035] Seth Wickersham, "It's all about Belichick," *ESPN Insider*, 31 August 2005.

[1036] Patriots inside linebackers coach Pepper Johnson, *Won For All*, Chicago: Contemporary Books, 2003, p. 36.

[1037] Patriots scout team coach Pepper Johnson, "Quotes from New England Patriots Press Conference," 3 February 2005.

[1038] Seattle Times news services, "Notebook: Huard's contribution to Patriots on DVD," 13 May 2004, http://seattletimes.nwsource.com/html/seahawks/2001927409_nfl13.html.

[1039] Bill Belichick, quoted in: Frank Tadych, "Patriots Notebook: Practice makes perfect in key series," *Patriots.com*, 25 October 2004, http://originwww.patriots.com/news/index.cfm?ac=generalnewsdetail&pcid=41&pid=9444.

[1040] Bill Belichick, quoted in: Tom E. Curran, "Patriots' early execution can't be beat," *Providence Journal*, 26 October 2004, www.projo.com/patriots/content/projo_20041026_26pats.2b168a.html.

[1041] Patriots linebacker Willie McGinest, "Quotes From New England Patriots Media Day," 1 February 2005.

[1042] Patriots offensive coordinator Charlie Weis, "Quotes From New England Patriots Media Day," 1 February 2005.

[1043] Bill Belichick, quoted in: Tom E. Curran, "Patriots, Colts both know to expect the unexpected," *Providence Journal*, 8 September 2004, www.projo.com/patriots/content/projo_20040908_08pats.5c710.html.

[1044] Jonathan Comey, "Follies in D.C. help show how Patriots shine," *Standard-Times*, 27 April 2005.

[1045] Bill Belichick, quoted in: Jerome Solomon, "Patriots set for learning experience," *Boston Globe*, 9 June 2005.

[1046] Patriots linebacker Don Davis, quoted in: AP, "Challenge for the champs," *Sports Illustrated*, 9 January 2005.

[1047] Tom Brady, quoted in: Sam Farmer, "Brady Just Wants to Hang With His Bunch," *AbsoluteBrady.com*, 30 January 2004.

[1048] Patriots cornerback Asante Samuel, "Quotes from New England Press Conference," 3 Febuary 2005.

[1049] Bill Belichick, "An Interview With New England Patriots Head Coach Bill Belichick," 4 February 2005.

[1050] Bill Belichick, quoted in: Mike Reiss, "Belichick at Big Brother event," *Boston Herald* blog, 20 May 2005.

[1051] Bill Belichick, "Bill Belichick Press Conf.Transcript 7/31/04," 31 July 2004, www.patriots.com/news/fullarticle.sps?id=29754&type=general.

[1052] Bill Belichick, quoted in: Paul Kenyon, "Either way, Scott has right attitude," *Providence Journal*, 25 August 2005.

[1053] Bill Belichick, "Bill Belichick Press Conf. Transcript - 9/14/2004," *Patriots.com*, 14 September 2004, www.patriots.com/Common/PrintThis.sps?id=30535.

[1054] George Kimball, "The art of the game: On the field or in the studio, David Givens has designs on greatness," *Boston Herald*, 10 October 2004, http://patriots.bostonherald.com/patriots/view.bg?articleid=48342.

[1055] Bill Belichick, "Belichick Press Conference," *Patriots.com*, 9 June 2005.

[1056] Bill Belichick, quoted in: Nick Cafardo, "Belichick is in rare form," *Boston Globe*, 23 October 2004, www.boston.com/sports/football/patriots/articles/2004/10/23/belichick_is_in_rare_form.

[1057] Bill Belichick, quoted in: Jim Salisbury, "Patriots' linebackers lead defensive charge," *San Jose Mercury News*, 19 January 2005.

[1058] Bill Belichick, quoted in: Paul Kenyon, "Receivers battling to find best route onto the roster," *Providence Journal*, 14 August 2004, www.projo.com/patriots/content/projo_20040814_14patsid1.2030e3.html.

[1059] Patriots fullback Patrick Pass, quoted in: Rich Thompson, "This Pat has much to do: FB's time comes to Pass," *Boston Herald*, 5 September 2004, http://patriots.bostonherald.com/patriots/view.bg?articleid=42874.

[1060] Bill Belichick, "Bill Belichick Press Conf. Transcript 8/30/04," *Patriots.com*, www.patriots.com/Common/PrintThis.sps?id=30322&keytype=NEWS&type=general.

[1061] Nick Cafardo, "Weaver suddenly in a tight spot," *Boston Globe*, 1 October 2004,
www.boston.com/sports/football/patriots/articles/2004/10/01/weaver_suddenly_in_a_tight_spot.

[1062] Bill Belichick, quoted in: Tom E. Curran, "Patriots Notebook: Signing will add depth," *Providence Journal*, 1 October 2004,
www.projo.com/patriots/content/projo_20041001_01patsjo.1baca9.html.

[1063] Charlie Weis, quoted in: Reggie Hayes, "Montana would be Irish windfall," *Fort Wayne News-Sentinel*, 2 June 2005.

[1064] Bill Belichick, "Bill Belichick Press Conf. Transcript 8/30/04," *Patriots.com*,
www.patriots.com/Common/PrintThis.sps?id=30322&keytype=NEWS&type=general.

[1065] Bill Belichick, quoted in: John Tomase, "Built To Win," *Eagle Tribune*, 27 January 2004, www.eagletribune.com/news/stories/20040127/SP_001.htm.

[1066] Bill Belichick, quoted in: Alex Timiraos, "Pats coach talks leadership at BC," *The Heights*, 9 April 2004, www.bcheights.com/news/2004/04/09/News/Pats-Coach.Talks.Leadership.At.Bc-656659.shtml.

[1067] Patriots executive Jonathan Kraft, quoted in: Bill Burt, "Meehan: I almost picked Terrell," *Eagle Tribune*, 29 April 2001,
www.eagletribune.com/news/stories/20010428/SP_002.htm.

[1068] Bill Belichick, quoted in: Tom E. Curran, "Coach explains how Pats' picks stack up," *Providence Journal*, 11 April 2004,
www.projo.com/patriots/content/projo_20040411_11pats.143a10.html.

[1069] Bill Belichick, quoted in: Tom E. Curran, "Coach explains how Pats' picks stack up," *Providence Journal*, 11 April 2004,
www.projo.com/patriots/content/projo_20040411_11pats.143a10.html.

[1070] Bill Belichick, quoted in: Tom E. Curran, "This time around, Dillon definitely a known commodity," *Providence Journal*, 7 September 2005.

[1071] Mike Reiss, "Dwight toes the line," *Boston Herald* blog, 11 July 2005.

[1072] Ryan Larue or Michael Parente (article has two author lines with different names), "Miller's Uphill Struggle," *Herald News*, 6 August 2004,
www.zwire.com/site/news.cfm?newsid=12632369&BRD=1710&PAG=740&dept_id=353135&rfi=6.

[1073] Bill Belichick, quoted in: Paul Perillo, "Pats already preparing for 2006," *Patriots.com*, 24 April 2005.

[1074] Bill Belichick, quoted in: Tom E. Curran, "Let's count reasons for Pats' success," *Providence Journal*, 9 December 2003,
www.projo.com/patriots/content/projo_20031209_09pats.b0805.html.

[1075] Bill Belichick, "Quotes from New England Patriots Press Conference," 3 February 2005.

[1076] Bill Belichick, quoted in: Phil Richardson, "Opening lines," *Indianapolis Star*, 9 September 2004, www.indystar.com/articles/2/177203-5062-036.html.

[1077] Patriots defensive end Ty Warren, quoted in: Rich Thompson, "Dillon gives Pats a decisive leg up," *Boston Herald*, 28 September 2004,
http://patriots.bostonherald.com/patriots/view.bg?articleid=46336.

[1078] Star running back of the New York Jets, Curtis Martin, quoted in: Andrea Adelson (AP), "The streak continues," *Slam Sports*, 24 October 2004,
http://slam.canoe.ca/Slam/Football/NFL/2004/10/24/683789-ap.html.

[1079] Bill Belichick, quoted in: Jarrett Bell, "Patriots defy odds in face of salary cap, free agency," *USA Today*, 10 September 2004,
www.usatoday.com/sports/football/nfl/patriots/2004-09-09-building-champ_x.htm.

[1080] Colts head coach Tony Dungy, quoted in: Phil Richardson, "Opening lines," *Indianapolis Star*, 9 September 2004, www.indystar.com/articles/2/177203-5062-036.html.

[1081] Patriots receiver Troy Brown, quoted in: Michael Smith, "Swoon over Miami," in: *Again!*, Chicago: Triumph Books, 2004, p. 60.

[1082] Patriots linebacker Ted Johnson, quoted in: Kevin Mannix, "Crunch Bunch: Pats know how to put hammer down when needed," *Boston Herald*, 31 October 2004.

[1083] Colts GM Bill Polian, quoted in: Michael Smith, "Another Indy effort bites the dust," *ESPN.com*, 10 September 2004,
http://sports.espn.go.com/nfl/news/story?id=1878509.

[1084] *ColdHardFootballFacts.com*, "Refs target Patriots," September 16-22, 2004.

[1085] Buffalo Bills head coach Mike Mularky, quoted in: Frank Tadych, "Patriots Notebook: Watson done for season," *Patriots.com*, 29 September 2004,
http://cachewww.patriots.com/news/index.cfm?ac=LatestNewsDetail&PID=9121&PCID=41.

[1086] Buffalo Bills quarterback Drew Bledsoe, quoted in: Mike Reiss, "Mistaken identity: Foes off mark when pinpointing Patriots' success," *Daily News Tribune*, 26 October 2004, www.dailynewstribune.com/sportsNews/view.bg?articleid=43566.

[1087] Miami Dolphins coach Dave Wannstedt, quoted in: Joe Burris, "Mistakes keep surfacing for Dolphins," *Boston Globe*, 11 October 2004,
www.boston.com/sports/football/patriots/articles/2004/10/11/mistakes_keep_surfacing_for_dolphins.

[1088] Seattle Seahawks quarterback Matt Hasselbeck, quoted in: Mike Reiss, "Mistaken identity: Foes off mark when pinpointing Patriots' success," *Daily News Tribune*, 26 October 2004, www.dailynewstribune.com/sportsNews/view.bg?articleid=43566.

[1089] Jets receiver Justin McCareins, quoted in: Dave Anderson, "Unknown Three Years Ago, Brady Is Now Patriots' Difference," *New York Times*, 25 October 2004, www.nytimes.com/2004/10/25/sports/football/25anderson.html.

[1090] Jets head coach Herm Edwards, quoted in: Chris Ruddick, " Jets can't overcome mistakes against Pats," *Sports Network*, 25 October 2004,
www.sportsnetwork.com/default.asp?c=sportsnetwork&page=/nfl/news/ABN3567326.htm.

[1091] New York Jets guard Pete Kendall, quoted in: Don Banks, "Jets cave into Big Game pressure," *Sports Illustrated*, 24 October 2004,
http://sportsillustrated.cnn.com/2004/writers/don_banks/10/24/jets.pats.folo/.

[1092] Rams coach Mike Martz, quoted in: AP, "Held in check," CNNSI.com, 4 February 2002,
http://sportsillustrated.cnn.com/football/2002/playoffs/news/2002/02/03/rams_sidebar1_ap/.

[1093] Joe Theismann, "Super Pats were team of destiny," *ESPN.com*, 3 February 2002, http://espn.go.com/nfl/playoffs01/columns/theismann_joe/1322325.html.

[1094] Don Banks, "AFC Playoff Field: Breakdown of the conference's six teams vying for Super Bowl XXXVIII," *Sports Illustrated*, 29 December 2003,
http://sportsillustrated.cnn.com/2003/writers/don_banks/12/29/playoff.field/.

[1095] *FootballOutsiders.com*, "Super Bowl Preview," www.footballoutsiders.com/superbowl2004.php?view=message&mid=152&showcomment=1&vmid=152.

[1096] Patriots safety Rodney Harrison, quoted in: Rich Eisen, "A conversation with Rodney Harrison," *NFL.com*, 19 July 2004,
www.nfl.com/nflnetwork/story/7513397.

[1097] Patriots safety Rodney Harrison, quoted in: Rich Eisen, "A conversation with Rodney Harrison," *NFL.com*, 19 July 2004,
www.nfl.com/nflnetwork/story/7513397.

[1098] Patriots safety Rodney Harrison, quoted in: Rich Eisen, "A conversation with Rodney Harrison," *NFL.com*, 19 July 2004,
www.nfl.com/nflnetwork/story/7513397.

[1099] Colts tight end Marcus Pollard, quoted in: Peter King, "Patriot predicament," *Sports Illustrated*, 1 August 2005.

[1100] Green Bay Packers offensive coordinator Sherman Lewis, quoted in: Bob McGinn, "Secretary of Defense," *Milwaukee Journal-Sentinel*, 25 January 1997,
www.allthingsbillbelichick.com/articles/secretaryofd.htm.

[1101] Patriots inside linebackers coach Pepper Johnson, *Won For All*, Chicago: Contemporary Books, 2003, p. 182.

[1102] Tom Brady, quoted in: Frank Dell'Apa, "Brady showing he still knows the drill," *Boston Globe*, 25 October 2004,
www.boston.com/sports/football/patriots/articles/2004/10/25/brady_showing_he_still_knows_the_drill.

[1103] Philadelphia Eagles receiver Freddie Mitchell, "Quotes from Philadelphia Eagles Press Conference," 1 February 2005.

[1104] Steve Sabol, "The Look of a Champion," *NFL Films Game of the Week*, February 2005.

[1105] Patriots backup quarterback Rohan Davey, quoted in: Mike Reiss, "Patriots QB Davey plays ball," *Boston Herald*, 4 April 2004,
http://patriots.bostonherald.com/patriots/view.bg?articleid=13944.

[1106] Rams quarterback and league MVP Kurt Warner, quoted in: *BBC*, "Pats' Brady hunch pays off," 4 February 2002,
http://news.bbc.co.uk/sport1/hi/other_sports/us_sport/1799953.stm.

[1107] Jim Fassel, former Denver Broncos offensive coordinator, quoted in: Paul Attner, "Mile High Miracle," *The Sporting News*, 25 January 1998,
www.supernfl.com/SuperBowl/sb32.html.

[1108] Patriots linebacker Mike Vrabel, "Quotes from New England Patriots Press Conference," 31 January 2005.

[1109] AP, "Bunch of success," *CNNSI.com*, 4 February 2002, http://sportsillustrated.cnn.com/football/2002/playoffs/news/2002/02/03/brady_mvp_ap/.

[1110] Patriots running back Antowain Smith, quoted in: Paul Attner, " Whatever 'It' is, Brady has 'It,'" *Sports Illustrated*, 6 October 2004,
http://msn.foxsports.com/story/3059636.

[1111] Gary Shelton, "20 Super Bowls, 20 late-night stories," *St. Petersburg Times*, 31 January 2005.

[1112] Patriots linebacker Rosevelt Colvin, on: *3 Games to Glory III* DVD, 2005.

[1113] Patriots linebacker Roman Phifer, "Quotes From New England Patriots Press Conference," 3 February 2005.

[1114] Eagles quarterback Donovan McNabb, "Quotes from Philadelphia Eagles Media Day," 1 February 2005.

[1115] Patriots receiver David Givens, "Quotes from New England Patriots Media Day," February 1, 2005.

[1116] Patriots safety Rodney Harrison, "Quotes from New England Patriots Press Conference," February 2, 2005.

[1117] Patriots linebacker Mike Vrabel, "Quotes from New England Patriots Media Day," February 1, 2005.

[1118] Patriots linebacker Ted Johnson, "Quotes from New England Patriots Media Day," February 1, 2005.

[1119] Patriots running back Cedric Cobbs, quoted in: Michael Felger, "Cobbs eyes backup plan," *Boston Herald*, 5 May 2005.

[1120] Patriots receiver Deion Branch, "Quotes from New England Patriots Press Conference," 31 January 2005.

[1121] Tom Brady, quoted in: Lynn DeBruin, "Patriots' Tom Terrific," *AbsoluteBrady.com*, 28 January 2004.

[1122] Richard Seymour, quoted in: Hector Longo, "Light makes might," *Eagle-Tribune*, 28 January 2004.

[1123] Michael Felger, "Pats' OL picks have right stuff -- Team learns from mistakes," *Boston Herald*, 26 April 2005.

[1124] Dave Jennings, New York Giants punter in 1978, quoted in: Terry Pluto, "The Man Behind the Mask," *Akron Beacon Journal*, 18 December 1994, www.allthingsbillbelichick.com/articles/behindthemask.htm.

[1125] Bill Belichick, "Bill Belichick Press Conference," 3 November 2004, http://cachewww.patriots.com/mediacenter/index.cfm?ac=audionewsdetail&pid=9555&pcid=85.

[1126] Joe Hatfield, Wal-Mart's Asia CEO, quoted in: "The Great Wal-Mart of China," 25 July 2005, p. 112.

[1127] Bill Belichick, quoted in: Don Banks, "Five Questions with ... Bill Belichick," *Sports Illustrated*, 17 August 2004, http://sportsillustrated.cnn.com/2004/football/nfl/specials/preview/2004/08/17/fivequestion.belichick/.

[1128] Kirk Ferentz, quoted in: Jeff Reynolds, "Belichick paving way for students' success," *Pro Football Weekly*, 1 December 2003, www.profootballweekly.com/PFW/NFL/AFC/AFC+East/New+England/Features/2003/reynolds120103.htm.

[1129] Kirk Ferentz, quoted in: Jeff Reynolds, "Belichick paving way for students' success," *Pro Football Weekly*, 1 December 2003, www.profootballweekly.com/PFW/NFL/AFC/AFC+East/New+England/Features/2003/reynolds120103.htm.

[1130] Michael Felger, "Pats subject of cheap talk," *Boston Herald*, 4 April 2004, http://patriots.bostonherald.com/patriots/view.bg?articleid=13945.

[1131] Scott Pioli, Patriots VP of player personnel, quoted in: Alan Greenberg, "There's No Room For Error; The Deal Maker," *Hartford Courant*, 4 September 2002, p. G3, ProQuest database.

[1132] "Miguel's UNOFFICIAL 2004 Patriots Salary Cap Information Page," www.patscap.com/capfootnotes.html#davis.

[1133] Bill Belichick, "Quotes from New England Patriots Media Day," 1 February 2005.

[1134] Aaron Schatz, "'Tis Better to Have Rushed and Lost than Never to Have Rushed at All," *FootballOutsiders.com*, www.footballoutsiders.com/powerrush011204.php.

[1135] Aaron Schatz, "'Tis Better to Have Rushed and Lost than Never to Have Rushed at All," *FootballOutsiders.com*, www.footballoutsiders.com/powerrush011204.php.

[1136] David Leonhardt, "Incremental Analysis, With Two Yards to Go," *New York Times*, 1 February 2004, www.nytimes.com/2004/02/01/weekinreview/01foot.html.

[1137] John Clayton, "Teams hurt themselves going for two points," *ESPN.com*, 8 December 2003 (not sure of year), http://espn.go.com/nfl/columns/clayton_john/1472283.html.

[1138] 1997 & 1998 data from: Harold Sackrowitz, "Refining the Point(s)-After-Touchdown Decision," *Chance*, vol. 13, no. 3, 2000, www.stat.duke.edu/chance/133.sackrowitz.pdf.

[1139] David Sweet, "To Go Or Not To Go," *Street & Smith's Pro Football 2004 Yearbook*, p. 13.

[1140] Phil Simms, "Abusing the two-point conversion," *NFL.com*, 10 September 2003, www.nfl.com/news/story/6630149.

[1141] It's slightly better. For simplicity, I am ignoring the 2.57% chance of missing one extra point.

[1142] John Clayton, "Teams hurt themselves going for two points," *ESPN.com*, 8 December 2003 (not sure of year), http://espn.go.com/nfl/columns/clayton_john/1472283.html.

[1143] Jim Litke, "Cool, calm Brady gets it done yet again," *MSNBC.com*, 25 January 2004, http://msnbc.msn.com/id/3995389/.

[1144] Professor David Romer, "It's Fourth Down and What Does the Bellman Equation Say? A Dynamic-Programming Analysis of Football Strategy," February 2003 (original version in Summer of 2002), http://emlab.berkeley.edu/users/dromer/papers/nber9024.pdf.

[1145] Professor David Romer, "It's Fourth Down and What Does the Bellman Equation Say? A Dynamic-Programming Analysis of Football Strategy," February 2003 (original version in Summer of 2002), http://emlab.berkeley.edu/users/dromer/papers/nber9024.pdf.

[1146] Michael Gee, "Kicking around new math," *Boston Herald*, 13 September 2002, p. 112.

[1147] Michael Gee, "Kicking around new math," *Boston Herald*, 13 September 2002, p. 112.

[1148] Bill Belichick, quoted in: Michael Gee, "Kicking around new math," *Boston Herald*, 13 September 2002, p. 112.

[1149] David Leonhardt, "Incremental Analysis, With Two Yards to Go," *New York Times*, 1 February 2004, www.nytimes.com/2004/02/01/weekinreview/01foot.html.

[1150] Then-New York Giants head coach Jim Fassel, quoted in: Greg Garber, "Fourth-down analysis met with skepticism," *ESPN.com*, 1 November 2002, http://espn.go.com/nfl/columns/garber_greg/1453717.html.

[1151] Associated Press, "Game of chance," *CNNSI.com*, 1 September 2002, http://sportsillustrated.cnn.com/football/news/2002/09/01/fourth_down_ap/.

[1152] Still Desi, "Tale of Two Coaches," *Stillers.com*, 2 March 2004, www.stillers.com/article_show.asp?ID=1146.

[1153] Bill Belichick, quoted in: Greg Garber, "Fourth-down analysis met with skepticism," *ESPN.com*, 1 November 2002, http://espn.go.com/nfl/columns/garber_greg/1453717.html.

[1154] David Sweet, "To Go Or Not To Go," *Street & Smith's Pro Football 2004 Yearbook*, p. 13.

[1155] Greg Garber, "Fourth-down analysis met with skepticism," *ESPN.com*, 1 November 2002, http://espn.go.com/nfl/columns/garber_greg/1453717.html.

[1156] New defensive coordinator Eric Mangini, quoted in: Jerome Solomon, "Winning formula," *Boston Globe*, 26 July 2005.

[1157] Bill Belichick, quoted in: Ron Borges, "What Makes Belichick Tick," *Boston Globe Magazine*, 10 September 2000, www.allthingsbillbelichick.com/articles/makestick.html.

[1158] Belichick tells this story on pp. 196-7 of Michael Felger, *Tales From the Patriots Sideline*, Sports Publishing, 2004.

[1159] Bill Belichick, quoted in: AP, "Brady, new-look Patriots shut down Steelers," *ESPN*, 9 September 2004, http://sports.espn.go.com/nfl/recap?gameId=220909017.

[1160] Bill Belichick, quoted in: AP, "Brady, new-look Patriots shut down Steelers," *ESPN*, 9 September 2004, http://sports.espn.go.com/nfl/recap?gameId=220909017.

[1161] Many of the preceding facts come from: www.nfl.com/stats/2002/regular and www.nfl.com/stats/2003/regular.

[1162] www.pro-football-reference.com/teams/nwe2003.htm

[1163] Bill Belichick, quoted in: Associated Press, "Pats' Harrison gets back to winning ways," 14 January 2004, http://msnbc.msn.com/id/3960632/.

[1164] "New England 17, Tennessee 14," http://sports.espn.go.com/nfl/boxscore?gameId=240110017.

[1165] Patriots defensive coordinator Romeo Crennel, quoted in: Mike Reiss, "Patriots beat: More NFL teams spread the wealth," *MetroWest Daily News*, 16 May 2004, www.metrowestdailynews.com/sportsColumnists/view.bg?articleid=68425.

[1166] Patriots defensive coordinator Romeo Crennel, quoted in: Mike Reiss, "Patriots beat: More NFL teams spread the wealth," *MetroWest Daily News*, 16 May 2004, www.metrowestdailynews.com/sportsColumnists/view.bg?articleid=68425.

[1167] Tennessee Titans head coach Jeff Fisher, quoted in: Mike Reiss, "Patriots beat: Free-agent forecast," *Metrowest Daily News*, 23 May 2004, www.metrowestdailynews.com/sportsColumnists/view.bg?articleid=69001.

[1168] "The Blotter," *New York Sports Express*, 29 June 2004, www.nysportsexpress.com/2/26/thefront/BLOTTER_v2_i_26.cfm.

[1169] Patriots inside linebackers coach Pepper Johnson, *Won For All*, Chicago: Contemporary Books, 2003, pp. xi-xii.

[1170] Bill Belichick, quoted in: Bob Glauber, "Genius at work," *Newsday*, 24 October 2004, www.newsday.com/sports/football/jets/ny-spsunspec244017947oct24,0,3329835.story.

[1171] Ernie Adams, quoted in: Andy Cline, "Sports Talk: Heeding the Call," *Andover.edu*, Fall 2004.

[1172] Willie McGinest, quoted in: Nick Cafardo, "McGinest tackles some topics," *Boston Globe*, 24 July 2005.

[1173] Fresno State head coach Pat Hill, who worked for four years as tight ends coach on Belichick's Cleveland Browns, quoted in: Billy Witz, "Sideline IQs meet at line of scrimmage," *Los Angeles Daily News*, 1 February 2004, http://extras.berkshireeagle.com/NeTrp/superbowl/2004/superbowl/default.asp?id=article12.

[1174] Alan Greenberg, "Pats Have Plenty Of Work For Bye Week," *Hartford Courant*, 21 September 2004, www.ctnow.com/sports/football/patriots/hc-patriots0921.artsep21,1,4724649.print.story.

[1175] Patriots linebacker Mike Vrabel, quoted in: Nick Cafardo, "Vrabel knows tricks of the trade," *Boston Globe*, 20 September 2004, www.boston.com/sports/football/patriots/articles/2004/09/20/vrabel_knows_tricks_of_the_trade.

[1176] Patriots linebacker Mike Vrabel, quoted in: Tom E. Curran, "Little things have helped these Pats achieve big things," *Providence Journal*, 21 September 2004, www.projo.com/patriots/content/projo_20040921_21patanal.67e28.html.

[1177] Former New York Giants and Cleveland Browns linebacker Carl Banks, quoted in: Bob Glauber, "Billy Ball," *Newsday*, 25 January 2004, www.allthingsbillbelichick.com/articles/billyball.htm.

[1178] Former New York Giants and Cleveland Browns linebacker Carl Banks, quoted in: Bob Glauber, "Billy Ball," *Newsday*, 25 January 2004, www.allthingsbillbelichick.com/articles/billyball.htm.

[1179] Former Cleveland Browns linebacker Carl Banks, quoted in: Bob Glauber, "Billy Ball," *Newsday*, 25 January 2004, www.allthingsbillbelichick.com/articles/billyball.htm.

[1180] Bill Belichick, quoted in: Steve Corkran, "Formula is secret to Patriots' success," *San Jose Mercury News*, 7 September 2005.

[1181] Bill Belichick, quoted in: Michael Holley, "Best seat in the house," *Boston Globe*, 7 December 2000, www.allthingsbillbelichick.com/articles/bestseat.htm.

[1182] Bill Belichick, foreward to: Timothy Gay, *Football Physics*, Rodale Books, 2004.

[1183] Bill Belichick, quoted in: Associated Press, "McGinest making one big play after another," *MSNBC*, 13 January 2004, www.msnbc.msn.com/id/3941840/.

[1184] Patriots linebacker Mike Vrabel, quoted in: Judy Battista, "An Exhibition of Total Football, New England Style," *New York Times*, 12 January 2004, p. D6, ProQuest database.

[1185] Patriots linebacker Tedy Bruschi, quoted in: Alan Greenberg, "Pats Pick It Up In Second Half," *Hartford Courant*, 4 October 2004, www.ctnow.com/sports/football/patriots/hc-patriots1004.artoct04,1,3287450.print.story.

[1186] Patriots linebacker Tedy Bruschi, quoted in: Ron Borges, "Another opponent is left smarting," *Boston Globe*, 4 October 2004, www.boston.com/sports/football/patriots/articles/2004/10/04/another_opponent_is_left_smarting.

[1187] Buffalo Bills quarterback Drew Bledsoe, quoted in: Ron Borges, "Another opponent is left smarting," *Boston Globe*, 4 October 2004, www.boston.com/sports/football/patriots/articles/2004/10/04/another_opponent_is_left_smarting.

[1188] St. Louis Rams safety Aeneas Williams, "NFL Films Presents: Super Bowl XXXVI," aired on: NFL Network, 18 May 2005.

[1189] Patriots rookie Marquise Hill, quoted in: Michael Felger, "Belichick method comes full circle," *Boston Herald*, 3 May 2004, http://patriots.bostonherald.com/patriots/view.bg?articleid=18878.

[1190] Patriots quarterback Tom Brady, quoted in: Marla Ridenourhen, " Human Interests," *Akron Beacon Journal*, 9 December 2001, www.allthingsbillbelichick.com/articles/humaninterests.htm.

[1191] Patriots receiver David Givens, quoted in: Bucky Gleason, "New England plays like champ," *Buffalo News*, 4 October 2004, www.buffalonews.com/editorial/20041004/1012132.asp.

[1192] Buffalo Bills running back Travis Henry, quoted in: Mark Singelais, "Patriots get record-tying win," *Times Union*, 4 October 2004, www.timesunion.com/AspStories/story.asp?storyID=291514&category=SPORTS&BCCode=SPORTS&newsdate=10/4/2004.

[1193] Buffalo Bills running back Travis Henry, quoted in: Rob Longley, "Stum-Bills at it again," *Toronto Sun*, 4 October 2004, http://slam.canoe.ca/Slam/Football/NFL/2004/10/04/655518.html.

[1194] Bills receiver Eric Moulds, quoted in: Rob Longley, "Stum-Bills at it again," *Toronto Sun*, 4 October 2004, http://slam.canoe.ca/Slam/Football/NFL/2004/10/04/655518.html.

[1195] VP of player personnel Scott Pioli, quoted in: Mark Maske, "Time for 49ers to Get Serious About Top Pick," *Washington Post*, 14 April 2005, www.washingtonpost.com/wp-dyn/articles/A52912-2005Apr14.html.

[1196] Patriots linebacker Willie McGinest, quoted in: John Clayton, "Injured McGinest makes crucial play," *ESPN.com*, 30 November 2003, http://sports.espn.go.com/nfl/columns/story?columnist=clayton_john&id=1674752.

[1197] Patriots linebacker Willie McGinest, quoted in: John Clayton, "Injured McGinest makes crucial play," *ESPN.com*, 30 November 2003, http://sports.espn.go.com/nfl/columns/story?columnist=clayton_john&id=1674752.

[1198] Patriots inside linebackers coach Pepper Johnson, *Won For All*, Chicago: Contemporary Books, 2003, p. 72.

[1199] Bill Belichick, quoted in: Bob Glauber, "Genius at work," *Newsday*, 24 October 2004, www.newsday.com/sports/football/jets/ny-spsunspec244017937oct24,0,3329835.story.

[1200] John Clayton, "Injured McGinest makes crucial play," *ESPN.com*, 30 November 2003, http://sports.espn.go.com/nfl/columns/story?columnist=clayton_john&id=1674752.

[1201] Eric Wilbur, "Heat Index," *Boston Globe*, 13 January 2004, www.boston.com/sports/nesn/wilbur/sports_blog/blog/01_12_04?mode=PF.

[1202] Jim McCabe, "It was nothing to kick about," *Boston Globe*, 19 October 2004, www.boston.com/sports/football/patriots/articles/2004/10/19/it_was_nothing_to_kick_about.

[1203] Mark Gaughan, "Even on links, Polian thinks about Pats," *Buffalo News*, 7 June 2005, www.buffalonews.com/editorial/20050607/1009900.asp.

[1204] Indianapolis Colts head coach Tony Dungy, quoted in: Peter King, "Monday Morning QB," *SportsIllustrated.cnn.com*, 21 March 2005.

[1205] Jarrett Bell, "Colts set to tee it up again as Patriot games loom," *USA Today*, 16 August 2005.

[1206] Patriots linebacker Ted Johnson, quoted in: Michael Felger, "Pats aim to give Bruschi his due," *Boston Herald*, 24 July 2005.

[1207] Patriots linebacker Ted Johnson, "Patriots Video News," *Patriots.com*, 30 June 2005.

[1208] Coach Bill Belichick, quoted in: Alan Greenberg, "Patriots' Belichick still cramming for NFL draft," *Miami Herald* (*Hartford Courant*), 14 April 2004, www.miami.com/mld/miamiherald/sports/football/8433415.htm?1c.

[1209] Bill Belichick, quoted in: Hector Longo, "Confident Patriots coach stacks up talent," *Eagle Tribune*, 25 April 2004, www.eagletribune.com/news/stories/20040425/SP_003.htm.

[1210] Unnamed NFC general manager, quoted in: Kevin Mannix, "GMs say Pats hit jackpot: Agree Wilfork was steal with 21st pick," *Boston Herald*, 27 April 2004, http://patriots.bostonherald.com/patriots/view.bg?articleid=13899.

[1211] Unnamed AFC general manager, quoted in: Kevin Mannix, "GMs say Pats hit jackpot: Agree Wilfork was steal with 21st pick," *Boston Herald*, 27 April 2004, http://patriots.bostonherald.com/patriots/view.bg?articleid=13899.

[1212] Patriots defensive end Ty Warren, quoted in: "Quotes from New England Patriots Press Conference," 31 January 2005.

[1213] Patriots cornerback Randall Gay, "Quotes from New England Patriots Press Conference," 2 February 2005.

[1214] Hector Longo, "Belichick, Pioli search for hidden backfield gem," *Eagle Tribune*, 12 February 2004, www.eagletribune.com/news/stories/20040212/SP_002.htm.

[1215] Patriots safety Rodney Harrison, quoted in: Michael Smith, "Fitting acquisition," *Boston Globe*, 9 September 2004, www.boston.com/sports/football/patriots/articles/2004/09/09/fitting_acquisition.

[1216] Michael Smith, "Distance runner," *Boston Globe*, 16 May 2004, www.boston.com/sports/football/patriots/articles/2004/05/16/distance_runner?mode=PF.

[1217] Michael Smith, "Distance runner," *Boston Globe*, 16 May 2004, www.boston.com/sports/football/patriots/articles/2004/05/16/distance_runner?mode=PF.

[1218] *Maxim* magazine, "The Sports Felon Hall of Fame," January 2002, www.maximonline.com/sports/articles/article_4459.html.

[1219] Scott Pioli, "Quotes from New England Patriots Press Conference," 3 February 2005.

[1220] Scott Pioli, "Quotes from New England Patriots Press Conference," 3 February 2005.

[1221] Scott Pioli, "Quotes from New England Patriots Press Conference," 2 February 2005.

[1222] New Patriots running back Corey Dillon, quoted in: "A conversation with Corey Dillon," *NFL.com*, 20 April 2004, www.nfl.com/nflnetwork/story/7271974.

[1223] New Patriots running back Corey Dillon, quoted in: Peter King "No rush to judgment," *Sports Illustrated*, 11 October 2004, http://sportsillustrated.cnn.com/2004/writers/peter_king/10/11/mmqb.pats/.

[1224] Patriots running back Corey Dillon, "Quotes From New England Patriots Media Day," 3 February 2005.

[1225] Michael Felger, "Kraft OK with deal: Has faith in Belichick's judgment," *Boston Globe*, 21 April 2004, http://patriots.bostonherald.com/patriots/view.bg?articleid=13916.

[1226] New Patriots running back Corey Dillon, quoted in: Michael Smith, "Distance runner," *Boston Globe*, 16 May 2004, www.boston.com/sports/football/patriots/articles/2004/05/16/distance_runner?mode=PF.

[1227] New Patriots running back Corey Dillon, quoted in: "A conversation with Corey Dillon," *NFL.com*, 20 April 2004, www.nfl.com/nflnetwork/story/7271974.

[1228] New Patriots running back Corey Dillon, quoted in: Michael Smith, "Distance runner," *Boston Globe*, 16 May 2004, www.boston.com/sports/football/patriots/articles/2004/05/16/distance_runner?mode=PF.

[1229] Bill Belichick, "Quotes from New England Patriots Press Conference," 3 February 2005.

[1230] Patriots tight end Christian Fauria, quoted in: Jim Moore, "Go 2 Guy: Playing Seahawks isn't thrillin' Dillon, or Boston," *Seattle Post-Intelligencer*, 15 October 2004, http://seattlepi.nwsource.com/football/195311_moore15.html.

[1231] Chick Ludwig, "Corey Dillon timeline," *Dayton Daily News*, 20 April 2004, www.daytondailynews.com/sports/content/_sports/bengals/daily/0420timeline.html.

[1232] Bill Belichick, quoted in: Tom E. Curran, "Trying Brown at DB a matter of depth," *Providence Journal*, 15 August 2004, www.projo.com/patriots/content/projo_20040815_15beat.136343.html.

[1233] Patriots linebacker Tedy Bruschi, "Quotes from New England Patriots Press Conference," 31 January 2005.

[1234] Charlie Weis, quoted in: Jay, "Distillery," 8 June 2005, http://bluegraysky.blogspot.com/2005_06_01_bluegraysky_archive.html.

[1235] Bill Belichick, "Quotes from New England Patriots Press Conference," 3 February 2005.

[1236] Bill Belichick, quoted in: Tom E. Curran, "Patriots Notebook: Team is fast out of the gate," *Providence Journal*, 11 June 2004, www.projo.com/patriots/content/projo_20040611_11patsjo.fcc1f.html.

[1237] Former Patriot running back J.R. Redmond, quoted in: "Management gives Pats edge in parity era," *Arizona Republic*, 1 September 2005.

[1238] Patriots linebacker Mike Vrabel, "Quotes from New England Patriots Media Day," 1 February 2005.

[1239] Dr. Peter F. Drucker, *Management: Tasks, Responsibilities, Practices*, USA: HarperCollins, 1973, p. 126.

[1240] Scott Pioli, quoted in: Michael Felger, "Receivers await their fate," *Boston Herald*, 2 September 2005.

[1241] Patriots scout Larry Cook, quoted in: Michael Holley, *Patriot Reign*, William Morrow, 2004, p. 134-5.

[1242] Bill Belichick, quoted in: Don Banks, "Complacent? No way," *Sports Illustrated*, 29 April 2005.

[1243] Bill Belichick, cited in: Don Banks, "Complacent? No way," *Sports Illustrated*, 29 April 2005.

[1244] Bill Belichick, quoted in: Michael Parente, "Patriots address root zone problems," *The Herald News*, 16 August 2004, www.zwire.com/site/news.cfm?newsid=12702554&BRD=1710&PAG=740&dept_id=353135&rfi=6.

[1245] Bill Belichick, quoted in: Alan Greenberg, "Pat-ended process; Belichick can find those keepers," 1 February 2004, p. E1, ProQuest database.

[1246] Bill Belichick, "Bill Belichick Press Conf. Transcript 4/25/04," *Patriots.com*, 25 April 2004, www.patriots.com/news/FullArticle.sps?id=28531&type=draft.

[1247] New Patriots running back Corey Dillon, quoted in: Michael Smith, "Dillon adds weapon to Patriots' offense," *ESPN.com*, 17 October 2004, http://sports.espn.go.com/nfl/columns/story?id=1903876.

[1248] Bill Belichick, "Patriots Video News," 24 August 2004, www.patriots.com/mediaworld/mediadetail.sps?id=30265.

[1249] Bill Belichick, quoted in: Michael Felger, "Bruschi works on extension," *Boston Herald*, 12 June 2004, http://patriots.bostonherald.com/patriots/view.bg?articleid=31607.

[1250] Patriots kicker Adam Vinatieri, quoted in: Glen Farley, "Patriots ready to defend," *The Enterprise*, 25 July 2004, http://enterprise.southofboston.com/articles/2004/07/25/news/sports/sports02.txt.

[1251] Tom Brady, quoted in: Joe Burris, "Fundamental problems," *Boston Globe*, 23 August 2004, www.boston.com/sports/football/patriots/articles/2004/08/23/fundamental_problems.

[1252] Patriots safety Rodney Harrison, quoted in: Michael Felger, "Pats hit on 17 in a struggle with Cards: Winning streak rolls on despite imperfections," *Boston Herald*, 20 September 2004, http://patriots.bostonherald.com/patriots/view.bg?articleid=45106.

[1253] Bill Belichick, quoted in: Kent Somers, "Always a step ahead," *Arizona Republic*, 16 September 2004, www.azcentral.com/arizonarepublic/sports/articles/0916cards0916.html.

[1254] Former Patriots outside linebackers coach Rob Ryan, quoted in: Peter King, "The anti-Ricky," *Sports Illustrated*, 2 August 2004, http://sportsillustrated.cnn.com/2004/writers/peter_king/08/02/king.mmqb/index.html.

[1255] Special teamer and backup linebacker/safety Don Davis, quoted in: Karen Guregian, "Reid, Cobbs get gate," *Boston Herald*, 30 August 2005.

[1256] Patriots rookie Marquise Hill, quoted in: Michael Felger, "Belichick method comes full circle," *Boston Herald*, 3 May 2004, http://patriots.bostonherald.com/patriots/view.bg?articleid=18878.

[1257] Patriots linebacker Mike Vrabel, "Quotes from New England Patriots Press Conference," 31 January 2005.

[1258] Philadelphia Eagles head coach Andy Reid, "Quotes from Philadelphia Eagles Press Conference," 31 January 2005.

[1259] Coach Bill Belichick, quoted in: Alan Greenberg, "Belichick Game Plan For Life," *Hartford Courant*, 3 May 2004, www.ctnow.com/sports/hc-belichick0503.artmay03,1,707205.story.

[1260] Patriots offensive lineman Russ Hochstein, "Patriots Video News," 9 March 2005, www.patriots.com/mediacenter/index.cfm?ac=videonewsdetail&pid=11017&pcid=78.

[1261] Patriots linebacker Ted Johnson, "Patriots Video News," *Patriots.com*, 30 June 2005.

[1262] Bill Belichick, quoted in: Tom Pedulla, "Patriots feel Super with 'extra ingredient' Dillon," *USA Today*, 22 July 2004, www.usatoday.com/sports/football/nfl/patriots/2004-07-22-camp_x.htm.

[1263] Buffalo Bills linebacker Takeo Spikes, quoted in: Len Pasquarelli, "Franchise takes it 'one game at a time,'" *Sports Illustrated*, 6 October 2004, http://sports.espn.go.com/nfl/columns/story?columnist=pasquarelli_len&page=/trend/2004week4.

[1264] Patriots wide receiver / nickel back / punt returner Troy Brown, "Quotes from New England Patriots Press Conference," 30 January 2005.

[1265] Patriots tight end Andy Stokes, quoted in: "Stokes pursues spot on Patriots' roster," *The Spectrum* (St. George, UT), 8 July 2005.

[1266] Bill Belichick, "Bill Belichick Press Conf. Transcript - 4/30," *Patriots.com*, 30 April 2004, www.patriots.com/news/FullArticle.sps?id=28597&type=general.

[1267] Bill Belichick, "Bill Belichick Press Conference," *Patriots.com*, 2 September 2005.

[1268] Patriots nose tackle Vince Wilfork, quoted in: Scout.com, "PATRIOTS: Concerns In The Middle," 16 August 2005.

[1269] Bill Belichick, "Bill Belichick Press Conf. Transcript - 4/30," *Patriots.com*, 30 April 2004, www.patriots.com/news/FullArticle.sps?id=28597&type=general.

[1270] Bill Belichick, "Belichick Press Conference," *Patriots.com*, 24 April 2005.

[1271] Patriots offensive guard Russ Hochstein, quoted in: Michael Smith, "A chip on block," *Boston Globe*, 29 July 2004, www.boston.com/sports/football/patriots/articles/2004/07/29/a_chip_on_block.

[1272] Tom Brady, quoted in: Ken Lechtanski, "A bunch of happy campers report," *The Enterprise*, 30 July 2004, http://enterprise.southofboston.com/articles/2004/07/30/news/sports/sports02.txt.

[1273] Bill Belichick, "Bill Belichick Press Conference," *Patriots.com*, 2 September 2005.

[1274] Former Wesleyan football coach John Biddiscombe, quoted in: Kevin Kernan, "Belichick's Dad Knows Best," *New York Post*, 6 January 2000, www.allthingsbillbelichick.com/articles/dadknows.htm.

[1275] Phil Barber, "New math: 3-4 is in again in the NFL," *Sporting News*, 7 May 2004, www.foxsports.com/content/view?contentId=2373626.

[1276] Former Patriots safety Victor Green, quoted in: Alan Greenberg, "Buckley accepts his role," *Hartford Courant*, 15 September 2002, p. E4, ProQuest database.

[1277] Michael Holley, "Script casts coach in new light," *Boston Globe*, 4 February 2004, www.boston.com/sports/football/patriots/superbowl/globe_stories/020402/script_casts_coach_in_new_light+.shtml.

[1278] Patriots linebacker Willie McGinest, quoted in: John Clayton, "Injured McGinest makes crucial play," *ESPN.com*, 30 November 2003, http://sports.espn.go.com/nfl/columns/story?columnist=clayton_john&id=1674752.

[1279] John Clayton, "Illegal contact enforcement could have huge impact," ESPN, 15 July 2004, http://sports.espn.go.com/espn/print?id=1840261&type=story.

[1280] Former Patriots and current Jets defensive back Terrell Buckley, quoted in: Michael Smith, "Jets trying to follow Pats' mold," *ESPN.com*, 21 October 2004, http://sports.espn.go.com/nfl/columns/story?id=1906485.

[1281] Football broadcaster and former Super Bowl-winning quarterback Phil Simms, quoted in: Mark Maske, "Secrets of Their Success; Wisdom of Defensive Gurus Belichick, Fox Is Reflected on Field," *Washington Post*, 1 February 2004, p. E1, ProQuest database.

[1282] Steelers receiver Hines Ward, quoted in: Chuck Finder, "Bill Belichick: The Mastermind of New England," *Pittsburgh Post-Gazette*, 21 January 2005.

[1283] Jacksonville Jaguars defensive coordinator Mike Smith, quoted in: Jeff Reynolds, "New England refused to play at Peyton's pace," *Pro Football Weekly*, 19 January 2004, www.profootballweekly.com/PFW/NFL/AFC/AFC+East/New+England/Features/2004/reynolds011904.htm.

[1284] Patriots rookie quarterback Matt Cassel, quoted in: interview with Jim Corbett, "Five minutes with Matt Cassel," *USA Today*, 17 August 2005.

[1285] venture capitalist John Doerr, quoted in: Adam Lashinsky, "The Birth of the Web," *Fortune*, 25 July 2005, p. 148.

[1286] Notre Dame head coach Charlie Weis, quoted in: Avani Patel (Chicago Tribune), "In a hurry for success Irish start under new coach this fall," *Pioneer Press*, 14 August 2005.

[1287] Patriots tight end Daniel Graham, quoted in: Mike Lowe, "Graham takes advantage as New England's new option," *Portland Press Herald*, 14 October 2004, http://sports.mainetoday.com/pro/patriots/041014lowecolumn.shtml.

[1288] Tennessee Titans defensive coordinator Jim Schwartz, quoted in: Nick Cafardo, "A defensive realignment for Titans," *Boston Globe*, 15 August 2004, www.boston.com/sports/articles/2004/08/15/a_defensive_realignment_for_titans.

[1289] Patriots offensive lineman Stephen Neal, "Quotes from New England Patriots Media Day," 1 February 2005.

[1290] Philadelphia Eagles special teams coordinator John Harbaugh, "Quotes from Philadelphia Eagles Media Day," 1 February 2005.

[1291] Bill Belichick, "Quotes from New England Patriots Press Conference," 30 January 2005.

[1292] Patriots wide receiver Troy Brown, foreword to: Nick Cafardo, *The Impossible Team*, Triumph Books, 2002, p. ix.

[1293] Philadelphia Eagles special teams coordinator John Harbaugh, "Quotes from Philadelphia Eagles Media Day," 1 February 2005.

[1294] Philadelphia Eagles special teams coordinator John Harbaugh, "Quotes from Philadelphia Eagles Media Day," 1 February 2005.

[1295] Special teams captain Larry Izzo, "Quotes from New England Patriots Press Conference," February 2, 2005.

[1296] Philadelphia Eagles special teams coordinator John Harbaugh, "Quotes from Philadelphia Eagles Media Day," 1 February 2005.

[1297] Patriots linebacker Mike Vrabel, quoted in: "Quotes from New England Patriots Press Conference," February 3, 2005.

[1298] Bill Belichick, quoted in: Karen Guregian, "Pats get no special treatment -- Even stars do dirty work," *Boston Herald*, 16 August 2005.

[1299] Philadelphia Eagles special teams coordinator John Harbaugh, "Quotes from Philadelphia Eagles Media Day," 1 February 2005.

[1300] Bill Belichick, "Quotes from New England Patriots Press Conference," 30 January 2005.

[1301] Bill Belichick, quoted in: Dan Shaughnessy, "Filling the Bill As Master Motivator," *Boston Globe*, 10 December 2001, www.tiznowpress.com/globe.html.

[1302] Peter King, "Let the parity begin," *Sports Illustrated*, 25 July 2005.

[1303] Patriots punter Josh Miller, quoted in: Rich Thompson, "Miller steps right in: Win-win situation for Pats' new punter," *Boston Herald*, 9 September 2004, http://patriots.bostonherald.com/patriots/view.bg?articleid=43420.

[1304] Patriots defensive coordinator Romeo Crennel, quoted in: Mike Holbrook, "'Black Cloud' has lifted," *Pro Football Weekly*, 30 January 2004, www.profootballweekly.com/PFW/NFL/AFC/AFC+East/New+England/Features/2004/phifer013004.htm.

[1305] Patriots leading wide receiver Troy Brown, quoted in: "Patriots headed to Super Bowl XXXVI," 27 January 2002, www.nfl.com/xxxvi/ce/recap/0,3895,NFL_20020127_NE@PIT,00.htm.

[1306] Bob George, "Wacky Draft Alters Patriotic Strategy," *PatsFans.com*, 26 April 2003.

[1307] Patriots veteran backup linebacker Don Davis, quoted in: Alan Greenberg, "Pat-ended process; Belichick can find those keepers," 1 February 2004, p. E1, ProQuest database.

[1308] Ira Schoffel, "Sawyer gunning for Patriot games," *The Osceola*, 15 June 2004, http://floridastate.rivals.com/content.asp?CID=305091.

[1309] Patriots rookie longsnapper Brian Sawyer, quoted in: Ira Schoffel, "Sawyer gunning for Patriot games," *The Osceola*, 15 June 2004, http://floridastate.rivals.com/content.asp?CID=305091.

[1310] Patriots linebacker Ted Johnson, quoted in: Mike Holbrook, "Welcome to 'The Izzone South,'" *Pro Football Weekly*, 28 January 2004, www.profootballweekly.com/PFW/NFL/AFC/AFC+East/New+England/Features/2004/izzo012804.htm.

[1311] Patriots inside linebackers coach Pepper Johnson, *Won For All*, Chicago: Contemporary Books, 2003, p. 236.

[1312] Bill Belichick, "Bill Belichick Press Conference," *Patriots.com*, 15 October 2004, http://originwww.patriots.com/search/index.cfm?ac=SearchDetail&PID=9337&PCID=85.

[1313] Patriots punter Josh Miller, quoted in: Rich Thompson, "Miller steps right in: Win-win situation for Pats' new punter," *Boston Herald*, 9 September 2004, http://patriots.bostonherald.com/patriots/view.bg?articleid=43420.

[1314] Bill Belichick, "Bill Belichick Press Conference," *Patriots.com*, 15 October 2004, http://originwww.patriots.com/search/index.cfm?ac=SearchDetail&PID=9337&PCID=85.

[1315] Rick Gosselin, "NFL Special Teams Rankings," *Dallas Morning News*, 7 February 2004, www.cowboysplus.com/columnists/rgosselin/stories/020804cpsspecialteams.b2905.html.

[1316] Rick Gosselin, "NFL Special Teams Rankings," *Dallas Morning News*, 7 February 2004, www.cowboysplus.com/columnists/rgosselin/stories/020804cpsspecialteams.b2905.html.

[1317] Rick Gosselin, "NFL Special Teams Rankings," *Dallas Morning News*, 7 February 2004, www.cowboysplus.com/columnists/rgosselin/stories/020804cpsspecialteams.b2905.html.

[1318] Buffalo Bills safety Lawyer Milloy, quoted in: Kevin Mannix, "Attack's tough to crack: Patriots offense takes center stage," *Boston Herald*, 15 November 2004, http://patriots.bostonherald.com/patriots/view.bg?articleid=54125.

[1319] Safety Tebucky Jones while he played for the Patriots in 2001, quoted in: *Sports Illustrated*, special commemorative issue, 13 February 2002, p. 37.

[1320] Former NFL great tight end Mark Bavaro, quoted in: Bill Kipouras, "Boxford ex-All-Pro Bavaro likes New England's chances," *Eagle Tribune*, 6 January 2004, www.eagletribune.com/news/stories/20040106/SP_001.htm.

[1321] Bill Belichick, quoted in: Paul Kenyon (Scripps Howard), "Pats out to prove a couple of points against Redskins," *Eagle Tribune*, 11 August 2000, www.eagletribune.com/news/stories/20000811/SP_004.htm.

[1322] Patriots linebacker Bryan Cox, quoted in: Hector Longo, "Patriots have Jets to thank for yesterday's spirited victory," *Eagle Tribune*, 1 October 2001, www.eagletribune.com/news/stories/20011001/SP_002.htm.

[1323] Patriots linebacker Roman Phifer, quoted in: Hector Longo, "Patriots have Jets to thank for yesterday's spirited victory," *Eagle Tribune*, 1 October 2001, www.eagletribune.com/news/stories/20011001/SP_002.htm.

[1324] Patriots defensive lineman Bobby Hamilton, quoted in: Hector Longo, "Patriots have Jets to thank for yesterday's spirited victory," *Eagle Tribune*, 1 October 2001, www.eagletribune.com/news/stories/20011001/SP_002.htm.

[1325] Patriots linebacker Ted Johnson, quoted in: Bill Burt, "What a kick!" *Eagle Tribune*, 4 February 2004, www.eagletribune.com/news/stories/20020204/FP_001.htm.

[1326] Patriots linebacker Roman Phifer, quoted in: Bill Burt, "What a kick!" *Eagle Tribune*, 4 February 2004, www.eagletribune.com/news/stories/20020204/FP_001.htm.

[1327] Patriots safety Lawyer Milloy, quoted in: Bill Burt, "What a kick!" *Eagle Tribune*, 4 February 2004, www.eagletribune.com/news/stories/20020204/FP_001.htm.

[1328] "Jon," a football fan, "A Super Tuesday's Popping Off," *Sports-Point.com*, www.sports-point.com/Jon/TuesdayPopOff/16.htm.

[1329] Marshall Faulk, quoted in: Pete Prisco, "Greatest Show on Turf stubs its toe," *CBS Sportsline*, 4 February 2002, http://cbs.sportsline.com/b/page/pressbox/0,1328,4948953,00.html.

[1330] Patriots linebacker Roman Phifer, quoted in: Karen Guregian, "Patriots groove on Harrison's hits," *Boston Herald*, 29 January 2004, http://patriots.bostonherald.com/patriots/view.bg?articleid=14097.

[1331] Patriots wide receiver Deion Branch, quoted in: Hector Longo, "Belichick may have been a Branch manager," *Eagle Tribune*, 10 September 2002, www.eagletribune.com/news/stories/20020910/SP_004.htm.

[1332] Patriots linebacker Roman Phifer, quoted in: Jimmy Golen (AP), "For Patriots, Vinatieri is Mr. Reliable," *Sacramento Bee*, 23 January 2004, www.sacbee.com/24hour/spec/football/playoffs/story/1128258p-7852341c.html.

[1333] Patriots rookie longsnapper Brian Sawyer, quoted in: Ira Schoffel, "Sawyer gunning for Patriot games," *The Osceola*, 15 June 2004, http://floridastate.rivals.com/content.asp?CID=305091.

[1334] Patriots kicker Adam Vinatieri, quoted in: Judy Battista, "Vinatieri Does His Best During the Last Minute," *New York Times*, 1 February 2004, section 8, p. 7, ProQuest database.

[1335] Troy Brown, "Quotes From New England Patriots Media Day," 1 February 2005.

[1336] Bill Belichick, quoted in: Hector Longo, "Belichick not offering any bulletin-board material for Raiders," *Eagle-Tribune*, 17 January 2002, www.eagletribune.com/news/stories/20020117/SP_012.htm.

[1337] Patriots special teams captain Larry Izzo, quoted in: Jimmy Golen (AP), "For Patriots, Vinatieri is Mr. Reliable," *Sacramento Bee*, 23 January 2004, www.sacbee.com/24hour/spec/football/playoffs/story/1128258p-7852341c.html.

[1338] Bill Belichick, quoted in: Bill Burt, "NFL Preview: Patriots will make the playoffs," *Eagle Tribune*, 27 August 2000, www.eagletribune.com/news/stories/20000827/SP_002.htm.

[1339] Johnny Unitas, quoted in: Josh Tyrangiel, "Magic on Sunday afternoon: Johnny Unitas," *Time*, 30 December 2002, www.time.com/time/personoftheyear/2002/memoriam/munitas.html. Others have given different accounts of Unitas' statement. In an NFL Films show on Unitas, John Steadman quoted Unitas as saying, "If you know what you're doing, you're not really taking a chance." Others quote Unitas as saying, "If I saw a danger… I would have thrown the ball out of bounds. When you know what you're doing, you're not intercepted."

[1340] Patriots owner Robert Kraft, quoted in: Tom E. Curran, "Pats owner has created a masterpiece," *Providence Journal*, 13 June 2004, www.projo.com/patriots/content/projo_20040613_13kraft.1b891c.html.

[1341] Patriots linebacker Tedy Bruschi, quoted in: Jim Donaldson, "New England defense keeps Bills bumbling," *Providence Journal*, 4 October 2004, www.projo.com/patriots/content/projo_20041004_04defense.93dcb.html.

[1342] Tom Brady, quoted in: Tom E. Curran, "For the Patriots, a lot of take and give with the Rams," *Providence Journal*, 5 November 2004, www.projo.com/patriots/content/projo_20041105_05pats.fbf4b.html.

[1343] Bill Belichick, quoted in: Michael Silver, "Pat Answer," *Sports Illustrated*, 11 February 2002, http://sportsillustrated.cnn.com/si_online/news/2002/02/11/pat_answer/.

[1344] Patriots offensive coordinator Charlie Weis, quoted in: NFL, "Official Super Bowl XXXVI game summary," www.absolutebrady.com/SB36.html.

[1345] Patriots offensive coordinator Charlie Weis, quoted in: Kevin Mannix, "Weis thriving in pro game," *Boston Herald*, 31 January 2004, http://patriots.bostonherald.com/patriots/view.bg?articleid=14055.

[1346] Tom E. Curran, "Patriots have talent to match expectations," *Providence Journal*, 4 July 2004, www.projo.com/patriots/content/projo_20040704_04patscol.f0c2c.html.

[1347] Tom Brady, quoted in: NFL, "Official Super Bowl XXXVI game summary," www.absolutebrady.com/SB36.html.

[1348] Patriots offensive coordinator Charlie Weis, quoted in: NFL, "Official Super Bowl XXXVI game summary," www.absolutebrady.com/SB36.html.

[1349] Patriots running back J.R. Redmond, quoted in: NFL, "Official Super Bowl XXXVI game summary," www.absolutebrady.com/SB36.html.

[1350] Tom Brady, quoted in: NFL, "Official Super Bowl XXXVI game summary," www.absolutebrady.com/SB36.html.

[1351] Tom Brady, quoted in: NFL, "Official Super Bowl XXXVI game summary," www.absolutebrady.com/SB36.html.

[1352] Patriots offensive coordinator Charlie Weis, quoted in: NFL, "Official Super Bowl XXXVI game summary," www.absolutebrady.com/SB36.html.

[1353] KC Joyner, The Football Scientist, *Scientific Football 2005* (KC's Football Services, Altamonte Springs, FL, 2005), p. 308.

[1354] Rohan Davey, "Davey NFL Europe diary – Week 5," *Patriots.com*, 29 April 2004, www.patriots.com/news/FullArticle.sps?id=28559&type=general.

[1355] Bill Belichick, quoted in: Tom E. Curran, "Rookie who gambled and lost receives a bit of Belichick's wrath," *Providence Journal*, 23 August 2005.

[1356] Bill Belichick, quoted in: Michael Felger, "Risky corner: Belichick picks on Hobbs' play," *Boston Herald*, 23 August 2005.

[1357] Ellis Hobbs, quoted in: Chris Kennedy, "Hobbs learns from rookie mistakes," *The Republican*, 24 August 2005.

[1358] Patriots cornerback Duane Starks, quoted in: Michael Felger, "Starks finds fit on Pats' corner," *Boston Herald*, 26 May 2005.

[1359] Patriots cornerback Duane Starks, "Mini Camp – Day 2," *Patriots Video News, Patriots.com*, 10 June 2005.

[1360] No author named, "Etc.," *Boston Globe*, 3 July 2005.

[1361] Carlos Ghosn, CEO of Nissan and Renault, quoted in: Alex Taylor III, "Double Duty," *Fortune*, 7 March 2005, p. 108.

[1362] Bill Belichick, quoted in: Nick Cafardo, "The Buck Stops With Bill," *Boston Globe*, 24 November 2001, www.allthingsbillbelichick.com/articles/buckstops.htm.

[1363] Bill Belichick, quoted in: Nick Cafardo, "The Buck Stops With Bill," *Boston Globe*, 24 November 2001, www.allthingsbillbelichick.com/articles/buckstops.htm.

[1364] Patriots safety Lawyer Milloy, quoted in: ESPN.com news services, "Glenn's agent plans legal action against NFL," *ESPN.com*, 14 August 2001, http://espn.go.com/nfl/news/2001/0814/1239630.html.

[1365] Len Pasquarelli, "Belichick Becomes Life of Patriots' Party," *ESPN.com*, 22 December 2001, www.allthingsbillbelichick.com/articles/lifeofparty.htm.

[1366] Bob McGinn, "Might Packers pursue Glenn?" *Milwaukee Journal Sentinel*, 31 January 2002, www.jsonline.com/packer/prev/jan02/16888.asp.

[1367] Bill Burt, "A star is reborn," *Eagle Tribune*, 16 November 2003, www.eagletribune.com/news/stories/20031116/SP_001.htm.

[1368] Howard Ulman (AP), "Injured Brisby can't get going," *SouthCoast Today*, 26 September 1996, www.s-t.com/daily/09-96/09-26-96/d01sp075.htm.

[1369] Dan Pires, "Carroll has holes to fill," *Standard-Times*, 19 July 1998, www.southcoasttoday.com/daily/07-98/07-19-98/d01sp134.htm.

[1370] Dan Pires, "Carroll has holes to fill," *Standard-Times*, 19 July 1998, www.southcoasttoday.com/daily/07-98/07-19-98/d01sp134.htm.

[1371] Bob McGinn, "Might Packers pursue Glenn?" *Milwaukee Journal Sentinel*, 31 January 2002, www.jsonline.com/packer/prev/jan02/16888.asp.

[1372] Former Patriots wide receiver Terry Glenn, quoted in: Ed Duckworth, "Passing the blame around," *SouthCoast Today*, 2 December 1999, www.southcoasttoday.com/daily/12-99/12-02-99/d03sp228.htm.

[1373] Former Patriots wide receiver Shawn Jefferson, quoted in: Ed Duckworth, "Passing the blame around," *SouthCoast Today*, 2 December 1999, www.southcoasttoday.com/daily/12-99/12-02-99/d03sp228.htm.

[1374] Peter King, "Patriots' Carroll gone by midweek," *Sports Illustrated*, 2 January 2004, http://sportsillustrated.cnn.com/inside_game/peter_king/news/2000/01/02/king_insider/.

[1375] Bill Belichick said, "we pretty much put the offense in during the spring and he wasn't here for that, either." Quoted in: Len Pasquarelli, "Pats in no hurry to end Glenn's season," *ESPN.com*, 8 August 2001, http://espn.go.com/nfl/news/2001/0808/1236632.html.

[1376] Len Pasquarelli, "Pats in no hurry to end Glenn's season," *ESPN.com*, 8 August 2001, http://espn.go.com/nfl/news/2001/0808/1236632.html.

[1377] Bill Belichick, quoted in: ESPN.com news services, "Glenn's agent plans legal action against NFL," *ESPN.com*, 14 August 2001, http://espn.go.com/nfl/news/2001/0814/1239630.html.

[1378] Bill Burt, "A star is reborn," *Eagle Tribune*, 16 November 2003, www.eagletribune.com/news/stories/20031116/SP_001.htm.

[1379] Bob McGinn, "Might Packers pursue Glenn?" *Milwaukee Journal Sentinel*, 31 January 2002, www.jsonline.com/packer/prev/jan02/16888.asp.

[1380] Bill Belichick, quoted in: John McClain, "Glenn the X factor in Cowboys-Pats spat," *Houston Chronicle*, 15 November 2003, www.chron.com/cs/CDA/ssistory.mpl/sports/mcclain/2224175.

[1381] Former Patriots wide receiver Terry Glenn, quoted in: John McClain, "Glenn the X factor in Cowboys-Pats spat," *Houston Chronicle*, 15 November 2003, www.chron.com/cs/CDA/ssistory.mpl/sports/mcclain/2224175.

[1382] Scott Pioli, Patriots VP of player personnel, quoted in: Hector Longo, "All the right moves," *Eagle-Tribune*, 30 January 2004, www.eagletribune.com/news/stories/20040130/SP_001.htm.

[1383] Scott Pioli, Patriots VP of player personnel, quoted in: Phil Barber, "NFL off-season: How did your team do?" *Sporting News*, 22 May 2004, www.foxsports.com/content/view?contentId=2408070.

[1384] Scott Pioli, quoted in: John Tomase, "Built To Win," *Eagle Tribune*, 27 January 2004, www.eagletribune.com/news/stories/20040127/SP_001.htm.

[1385] Michael Holley, *Patriot Reign*, William Morrow, 2004, p. 167.

[1386] Scott Pioli, VP of player personnel, quoted in: Rick Braun, "Patriots built with free agents, draft," *Milwaukee Journal Sentinel*, 4 February 2004, www.jsonline.com/packer/rev/feb04/204957.asp.

[1387] Indianapolis Colts general manager Bill Polian, quoted in: Dave Goldberg (AP), "New England and Washington: NFL free agency contrasts," *Yahoo! Canada Sports*, 27 February 2004, http://ca.sports.yahoo.com/040227/6/wxki.html.

[1388] Bill Belichick, quoted in: Nick Cafardo, "The Buck Stops With Bill," *Boston Globe*, 24 November 2001, www.allthingsbillbelichick.com/articles/buckstops.htm.

[1389] Steve Belichick, quoted in: Terry Pluto, "The Man Behind the Mask," *Akron Beacon Journal*, 18 December 1994, www.allthingsbillbelichick.com/articles/behindthemask.htm.

[1390] Autodesk CEO Carol Bartz, quoted in: David Kirkpatrick, "The Reigning Queen of Tech," *Fortune*, 16 May 2005, p. 40.

[1391] Mike Martz as overheard by Patriots players as told by Bill Belichick, reported in: Seth Wickersham, "It's all about Belichick," *ESPN Insider*, 31 August 2005.

[1392] Tom Brady, quoted in: Tim Weisberg, "Tom's toolbox gets heavier by the year," *Standard-Times*, 4 September 2005.

[1393] Betsy Morris, "Charles Schwab's Big Challenge," *Fortune*, 30 May 2005, p. 92.

[1394] Defensive coordinator Romeo Crennel, quoted in: "Q&A With Romeo Crennel," 17 November 2004, www.nflcoaches.com/StoryArchives/Crennel.asp.

[1395] Patriots offensive coordinator Charlie Weis, quoted in: Gordon Edes, "Patriots coach has well-earned reputation for stopping whatever's thrown his way," *Boston Globe*, 2 February 2002, www.boston.com/sports/football/patriots/superbowl/globe_stories/020202/patriots_coach_has_well_earned_reputation_for_stopping_whatever_s_thrown_his_way+.shtml.

[1396] Defensive coordinator Romeo Crennel, quoted in: "Q&A With Romeo Crennel," 17 November 2004, www.nflcoaches.com/StoryArchives/Crennel.asp.

[1397] Ernie Adams, quoted in: Andy Cline, "Sports Talk: Heeding the Call," *Andover.edu*, Fall 2004.

[1398] Chicago Bears head coach Dick Jauron, quoted in: Bill Kipouras, "Swampscott situation disheartens Jauron," *The Salem News*, 27 June 2005.

[1399] Patriots owner Robert Kraft, speech at Harvard Business School, quoted in: Frank Yang, "New England Patriots: Building a Champion Krafts Construct Dynasty, Model Franchise," *Harbus News*, 9 May 2005.

[1400] Bill Belichick, quoted in: "Coach's Corner," *Patriots Football Weekly*, 1 June 2005, reprinted on: www.allthingsbillbelichick.com.

[1401] Dr. Peter F. Drucker, *Management: Tasks, Responsibilities, Practices*, USA: HarperCollins, 1973, p. 39.

[1402] New defensive coordinator Eric Mangini, quoted in: Jerome Solomon, "Winning formula," *Boston Globe*, 26 July 2005.

[1403] Defensive coordinator Romeo Crennel, quoted in: "Q&A With Romeo Crennel," 17 November 2004, www.nflcoaches.com/StoryArchives/Crennel.asp.

[1404] Bill Belichick, quoted in: Associated Press, "Patriots searching for coaches," *tsn.ca*, 11 June 2005.

[1405] Bill Belichick, quoted in: Nick Cafardo, "The Buck Stops With Bill," *Boston Globe*, 24 November 2001, www.allthingsbillbelichick.com/articles/buckstops.htm.

[1406] Bill Belichick, quoted in: Nick Cafardo, "The Buck Stops With Bill," *Boston Globe*, 24 November 2001, www.allthingsbillbelichick.com/articles/buckstops.htm.

[1407] Dr. Peter F. Drucker, *Management: Tasks, Responsibilities, Practices*, USA: HarperCollins, 1973, pp. 281-282.

[1408] Bill Belichick, quoted in: Ernest Hooper, "N.E.'s Belichick now flexible," *St. Petersburg Times*, 1 September 2000, www.sptimes.com/News/090100/Sports/NE_s_Belichick_now_fl.shtml.

[1409] Coach Bill Belichick, quoted in: Greg Garber, "Belichick Gets Second Chance In New England," *ESPN.com*, 20 June 2000, www.allthingsbillbelichick.com/articles/secondchance.htm.

[1410] Bill Belichick, quoted in: Ed Duckworth, "Belichick crafts new image," *New England Sports Service*, 6 June 2000, www.standardtimes.com/daily/06-00/06-06-00/c02sp105.htm.

[1411] Bill Belichick, quoted in: Bill Burt, "Time to see if Belichick can lead," *Eagle Tribune*, 2 February 2001, www.eagletribune.com/news/stories/20010202/SP_001.htm.

[1412] Bill Belichick, quoted in: Bill Burt, "Time to see if Belichick can lead," *Eagle Tribune*, 2 February 2001, www.eagletribune.com/news/stories/20010202/SP_001.htm.

[1413] Bill Belichick, quoted in: Dan Pompei, "Many second-chance coaches deliver first-rate results," *The Sporting News*, 14 January 2003, http://t.tsn.com/voices/dan_pompei/20030114.html.

[1414] Patriots offensive coordinator Charlie Weis, quoted in: Gordon Edes, "Patriots coach has well-earned reputation for stopping whatever's thrown his way," *Boston Globe*, 2 February 2002, www.boston.com/sports/football/patriots/superbowl/globe_stories/020202/patriots_coach_has_well_earned_reputation_for_stopping_whatever_s_thrown_his_way+.shtml.

[1415] Dr. Peter F. Drucker, *Management: Tasks, Responsibilities, Practices*, USA: HarperCollins, 1973, pp. 217-8.

[1416] Patriots defensive lineman Richard Seymour , "Quotes from New England Patriots Press Session," 3 February 2005.

[1417] Patriots defensive end Ty Warren, quoted in: Tom E. Curran, "Rookie who gambled and lost receives a bit of Belichick's wrath," *Providence Journal*, 23 August 2005.

[1418] Patriots defensive lineman Richard Seymour , "Quotes from New England Patriots Press Session," 3 February 2005.

[1419] Patriots receiver Troy Brown, "Quotes from New England Patriots Press Conference," February 2, 2005.

[1420] Bill Belichick, "Quotes from New England Patriots Press Conference," 3 February 2005.

[1421] Patriots owner Robert Kraft, quoted in: Tom E. Curran, "Pats owner has created a masterpiece," *Providence Journal*, 13 June 2004, www.projo.com/patriots/content/projo_20040613_13kraft.1b891c.html.

[1422] Patriots scout Jason Licht, quoted in: Michael Holley, *Patriot Reign*, William Morrow, 2004, p. 153.

[1423] Charles M Elson, quoted in: Joseph Weber, "How the Best Boards Stay Glued In," *BusinessWeek*, 27 June 2005, p. 40.

[1424] Patriots owner Bob Kraft, quoted in: Michael Felger, "Kraft OK with deal: Has faith in Belichick's judgment," *Boston Globe*, 21 April 2004, http://patriots.bostonherald.com/patriots/view.bg?articleid=13916.

[1425] Bill Belichick, quoted in: Nick Cafardo, "The Buck Stops With Bill," *Boston Globe*, 24 November 2001, www.allthingsbillbelichick.com/articles/buckstops.htm.

[1426] Patriots owner Bob Kraft, quoted in: Nick Cafardo, "The Buck Stops With Bill," *Boston Globe*, 24 November 2001, www.allthingsbillbelichick.com/articles/buckstops.htm.

[1427] Patriots owner Bob Kraft, quoted in: Michael Felger, "Kraft OK with deal: Has faith in Belichick's judgment," *Boston Globe*, 21 April 2004, http://patriots.bostonherald.com/patriots/view.bg?articleid=13916.

[1428] Corey Dillon's agent Steven Feldman, quoted in: Greg Bishop, "Dillon winning them over in New England," *Seattle Times*, 15 October 2004, http://seattletimes.nwsource.com/html/sports/2002063922_dillon15.html.

[1429] Joe Slye, Corey Dillon's football coach at Franklin High School, quoted in: Greg Bishop, "Dillon winning them over in New England," *Seattle Times*, 15 October 2004, http://seattletimes.nwsource.com/html/sports/2002063922_dillon15.html.

[1430] Former Patriots head coach Pete Carroll, quoted in: Michael Felger, "Control key for Petey: Didn't have it his way," *Boston Herald*, 8 September 2005.

[1431] Former Patriots head coach Pete Carroll, quoted in: Michael Felger, "Control key for Petey: Didn't have it his way," *Boston Herald*, 8 September 2005.

[1432] Patriots VP of player personnel Scott Pioli, quoted in: Jeff Jacobs, "Class Clown Gets Serious With Patriots," *Hartford Courant*, 3 February 2002, p. A1.

[1433] Patriots owner Bob Kraft, quoted in: Michael Felger, "Pioli helps put it together," *Boston Herald*, 26 January 2004, http://patriots.bostonherald.com/patriots/view.bg?articleid=510.

[1434] Jeff Jacobs, "Class Clown Gets Serious With Patriots," *Hartford Courant*, 3 February 2002, p. A1.

[1435] Bill Belichick, "Quotes from New England Patriots Media Day," 1 February 2005.

[1436] Bill Belichick, quoted in: Michael Holley, *Patriot Reign*, William Morrow, 2004, p. 39.

[1437] Bill Belichick, quoted in: Barry Milner (AP), "Belichick turns down Jets' coaching job and quits," 5 January 2000, http://augustasports.com/stories/010500/pro_124-5202.shtml.

[1438] Bill Belichick, "Quotes from New England Patriots Media Day," 1 February 2005.

[1439] Bill Belichick, quoted in: SportsLine wire reports, "Patriots might not be available to Belichick," 4 January 2000.

[1440] Patriots owner Bob Kraft, quoted in: Monte Burke, "Unlikely Dynasty," *Forbes*, 19 September 2005.

[1441] David Welch, "The Spark Plug Behind the Pistons," *BusinessWeek*, 28 June 2004, p. 54.

[1442] Bill Davidson, quoted in: Tom Walsh, "Low-key works for Pistons' Davidson," *Detroit Free Press*, 29 April 2004, www.freep.com/money/business/walsh29_20040429.htm.

[1443] Tom Walsh, "Low-key works for Pistons' Davidson," *Detroit Free Press*, 29 April 2004, www.freep.com/money/business/walsh29_20040429.htm.

[1444] 81-year-old billionaire businessman William Davidson, quoted in: Thomas Heath, "Bill Davidson, Pistons - Lightening owner doubles his pleasure," *Sports Business News*, 23 June 2004, www.sportsbusinessnews.com/index.asp?story_id=36854.

[1445] Former Detroit Pistons coach Chuck Daly, quoted in: Thomas Heath, "Bill Davidson, Pistons - Lightening owner doubles his pleasure," *Sports Business News*, 23 June 2004, www.sportsbusinessnews.com/index.asp?story_id=36854.

[1446] Wire services, "A trio of titles for Davidson," *St. Petersburg Times*, 16 June 2004, www.sptimes.com/2004/06/16/Sports/A_trio_of_titles_for_.shtml.

[1447] Thomas Heath, "Bill Davidson, Pistons - Lightening owner doubles his pleasure," *Sports Business News*, 23 June 2004, www.sportsbusinessnews.com/index.asp?story_id=36854.

[1448] Patriots VP of player personnel Scott Pioli, who worked for Belichick in Cleveland, quoted in: Mary Kay Cabot, "Belichick's influence reaches far in football," *Plain Dealer*, 31 January 2004, www.cleveland.com/sports/plaindealer/index.ssf?/base/sports/1075545297213372.xml.

[1449] Richard Branson, Virgin CEO, quoted in: A.L., Pick industry. Dive in. Repeat." *Fortune*, 15 November 2004, p. 202.

[1450] Patriots linebacker Tedy Bruschi, quoted in: Gordon Edes, "Patriots coach has well-earned reputation for stopping whatever's thrown his way," *Boston Globe*, 2 February 2002, www.boston.com/sports/football/patriots/superbowl/globe_stories/020202/patriots_coach_has_well_earned_reputation_for_stopping_whatever_s_thrown_his_way+.shtml.

[1451] University of Louisville head basketball coach Rick Pitino, speaking at newsconference aired on *ESPN*, 23 March 2005.

[1452] Phil Simms, "Belichick learns as he goes," *Superbowl.com*, 28 January 2004, www.superbowl.com/news/story/7043711.

[1453] Unnamed Bryant University student, quoted in: Andy Hart, "Belichick impresses large Bryant University audience," *Patriots.com*, 31 March 2005, www.patriots.com/news/index.cfm?ac=generalnewsdetail&pcid=41&pid=11235.

[1454] Bill Belichick, quoted in: Mike Reiss, "Belichick spreads message," *MetroWest Daily News*, 31 March 2005, http://patriots.bostonherald.com/patriots/view.bg?articleid=75811.

[1455] Defensive coordinator Romeo Crennel, quoted in: "Q&A With Romeo Crennel," 17 November 2004, www.nflcoaches.com/StoryArchives/Crennel.asp.

[1456] Rob Ryan, Patriots outside linebackers coach until he accepted the Oakland Raiders' offer to coordinate their entire defense, quoted in: Michael Felger, "Directory assistants: Belichick's staff is full of information," *Boston Herald*, 28 January 2004, http://patriots.bostonherald.com/patriots/view.bg?articleid=540.

[1457] Bill Belichick, quoted in: Tom E. Curran, "Let's count reasons for Pats' success," *Providence Journal*, 9 December 2003, www.projo.com/patriots/content/projo_20031209_09pats.b0805.html.

[1458] Patriots safety Rodney Harrison, quoted in: Karen Guregian, "Mangini in spotlight," *Boston Herald*, 31 August 2005.

[1459] 36-year-old tight ends coach Jeff Davidson, quoted in: Michael Felger, "Directory assistants: Belichick's staff is full of information," *Boston Herald*, 28 January 2004, http://patriots.bostonherald.com/patriots/view.bg?articleid=540.

[1460] Bill Belichick, quoted in: "Line Changes Coming?" *The Insiders*, 15 July 2004, http://story.theinsiders.com/a.z?s=69&p=2&c=274853.

[1461] Patriots guard Joe Andruzzi, quoted in: Judy Battista, "Patriots' Line Coach Thrives With Longevity," *New York Times*, 28 January 2004, p. D4, ProQuest database.

[1462] Bill Belichick, quoted in: Marla Ridenour, "Special Time for Belichick," *Akron Beacon Journal*, 29 May 2002, www.allthingsbillbelichick.com/articles/specialtime.htm.

[1463] Michael Felger, "Pats must be tougher team: Look to continue mastery of Colts," *Boston Herald*, 13 January 2004.

[1464] Tennessee Titans defensive coordinator Jim Schwartz, quoted in: Nick Cafardo, "Schwartz's way is stat of the art," *Boston Globe*, 8 January 2004, www.boston.com/sports/football/patriots/articles/2004/01/08/schwartzs_way_is_stat_of_the_art.

[1465] Tennessee Titans defensive coordinator Jim Schwartz, quoted in: "Football Outsiders Interview: Jim Schwartz," www.footballoutsiders.com/ramblings.php?p=243&cat=1.

[1466] Tennessee Titans defensive coordinator Jim Schwartz, quoted in: Nick Cafardo, "Schwartz's way is stat of the art," *Boston Globe*, 8 January 2004, www.boston.com/sports/football/patriots/articles/2004/01/08/schwartzs_way_is_stat_of_the_art.

[1467] Tennessee Titans defensive coordinator Jim Schwartz, quoted in: Nick Cafardo, "Schwartz's way is stat of the art," *Boston Globe*, 8 January 2004, www.boston.com/sports/football/patriots/articles/2004/01/08/schwartz_way_is_stat_of_the_art.

[1468] Tennessee Titans defensive coordinator Jim Schwartz, quoted in: Nick Cafardo, "Schwartz's way is stat of the art," *Boston Globe*, 8 January 2004, www.boston.com/sports/football/patriots/articles/2004/01/08/schwartz_way_is_stat_of_the_art.

[1469] Ed Bouchette, "Is Adams a genius' genius?" *Pittsburgh Post-Gazette*, 29 January 2004, www.post-gazette.com/pg/04029/266893.stm.

[1470] Steelers video coordinator Bob McCartney, quoted in: Ed Bouchette, "Is Adams a genius' genius?" *Pittsburgh Post-Gazette*, 29 January 2004, www.post-gazette.com/pg/04029/266893.stm.

[1471] San Francisco 49ers director of player personnel Bill Rees, quoted in: Pete Thamel, "Low-Key Adams Makes High Impact on Patriots," *New York Times*, 16 January 2004, p. D7, ProQuest database.

[1472] Bill Belichick, quoted in: Bill Burt, "More than a coach," *Eagle Tribune*, 25 January 2004, www.eagletribune.com/news/stories/20040125/SP_001.htm.

[1473] Patriots linebacker Mike Vrabel, quoted in: Michael Felger, "Adams: Pats' mystery man: Research director invaluable," *Boston Herald*, 30 January 2004, http://patriots.bostonherald.com/patriots/view.bg?articleid=563.

[1474] Patriots punter Josh Miller, quoted in: Chuck Finder, "Bill Belichick: The Mastermind of New England," *Pittsburgh Post-Gazette*, 21 January 2005.

[1475] Patriots secondary coach Eric Mangini, quoted in: Michael Felger, "Adams: Pats' mystery man: Research director invaluable," *Boston Herald*, 30 January 2004, http://patriots.bostonherald.com/patriots/view.bg?articleid=563.

[1476] Patriots special teams coach Brad Seely, quoted in: Michael Felger, "Adams: Pats' mystery man: Research director invaluable," *Boston Herald*, 30 January 2004, http://patriots.bostonherald.com/patriots/view.bg?articleid=563.

[1477] Patriots running backs coach Ivan Fears, quoted in: Michael Felger, "Adams: Pats' mystery man: Research director invaluable," *Boston Herald*, 30 January 2004, http://patriots.bostonherald.com/patriots/view.bg?articleid=563.

[1478] Ernie Adams, quoted in: Andy Cline, "Sports Talk: Heeding the Call," *Andover.edu*, Fall 2004.

[1479] Ernie Adams, quoted in: Pete Thamel, "Low-Key Adams Makes High Impact on Patriots," *New York Times*, 16 January 2004, p. D7, ProQuest database.

[1480] Ernie Adams, quoted in: Pete Thamel, "Low-Key Adams Makes High Impact on Patriots," *New York Times*, 16 January 2004, p. D7, ProQuest database.

[1481] Baltimore Ravens' senior VP Kevin Byrne, quoted in: Ed Bouchette, "Is Adams a genius' genius?" *Pittsburgh Post-Gazette*, 29 January 2004, www.post-gazette.com/pg/04029/266893.stm.

[1482] Tennessee Titans defensive coordinator Jim Schwartz, quoted in: "Football Outsiders Interview: Jim Schwartz," www.footballoutsiders.com/ramblings.php?p=243&cat=1.

[1483] Phil Savage, Cleveland Browns GM and former Belichick assistant, quoted in: Joe Schad, "Saban brings Belichick system to Dolphins draft," *Palm Beach Post*, 17 April 2005, www.palmbeachpost.com/dolphins/content/sports/epaper/2005/04/17/a1b_PBP_FINS_0417.html.

[1484] Nick Saban, Bill Belichick's defensive coordinator, 1991-94, quoted in: Harvey Fialkov, "Saban has draft experience - and now, final say," *South Florida Sun-Sentinel*, 18 April 2005, www.sun-sentinel.com/sports/sfl-saban18apr18,0,1931545.story.

[1485] Rick Gosselin, "Good show: '94 Browns' Brainy Bunch," *Dallas Morning News*, 20 December 2003, www.cowboysplus.com/columnists/rgosselin/stories/122103cpgosselin.a3cd2.html.

[1486] Bill Belichick, quoted in: Pete Thamel, "Building Programs Using Belichick's Blueprint," 18 September 2004, www.nytimes.com/2004/09/18/sports/ncaafootball/18college.html.

[1487] Former Browns offensive line coach Kirk Ferentz, quoted in: Pete Thamel, "Building Programs Using Belichick's Blueprint," 18 September 2004, www.nytimes.com/2004/09/18/sports/ncaafootball/18college.html.

[1488] http://sports.espn.go.com/nfl/columns/story?columnist=pasquarelli_len&id=1703745.

[1489] Charlie Nobles, "Dolphins' New Coach Casts a Grimace in the Mold of Shula," *New York Times*, 24 July 2005.

[1490] Rick Gosselin, "Good show: '94 Browns' Brainy Bunch," *Dallas Morning News*, 20 December 2003, www.cowboysplus.com/columnists/rgosselin/stories/122103cpgosselin.a3cd2.html.

[1491] http://sports.espn.go.com/nfl/statistics/season=2&year=2002.

[1492] Len Pasquarelli, "Packers in no rush to find Favre's replacement," *ESPN*, 8 May 2003, http://espn.go.com/nfl/columns/pasquarelli_len/1548302.html.

[1493] Nick Saban, quoted in: Mary Kay Cabot, "Belichick's influence reaches far in football," *Plain Dealer*, 31 January 2004, www.cleveland.com/sports/plaindealer/index.ssf?/base/sports/1075545297213372.xml.

[1494] Bill Belichick, quoted in: Rick Stroud, "Belichick a big Saban fan," *St. Petersburg Times*, 2 February 2002, www.sptimes.com/2002/02/02/news_pf/Sports/Belichick_a_big_Saban.shtml.

[1495] New Orleans Saints defensive coordinator Rick Venturi, quoted in: Carl Dubois, "Venturi relishes friends' success," *The Advocate* (Baton Rouge, LA), www.2theadvocate.com/stories/012504/col_carlcol001.shtml.

[1496] Fred Smith, quoted in: "Fred Smith on the Birth of FedEx," *BusinessWeek*, 20 September 2004.

[1497] Patriots owner Robert Kraft, in speech to TIECON 2004, the annual conference of the Boston chapter of The Indus Entrepreneurs, quoted in: Christine Walsh, "Patriots' football - a winning business," *IndUS Business Journal*, 15 June 2004, www.indusbusinessjournal.com/news/2004/06/15/Tie/Patriots.Football.A.Winning.Business-688799.shtml.

[1498] Patriots owner Bob Kraft, quoted in: Monte Burke, "Unlikely Dynasty," *Forbes*, 19 September 2005.

[1499] Patriots owner Robert Kraft, quoted in: Michael Gee, "Kraft is Pats' big cheese," *Boston Globe*, 31 January 2004.

[1500] Patriots owner Robert Kraft, speech at Harvard Business School, quoted in: Frank Yang, "New England Patriots: Building a Champion Krafts Construct Dynasty, Model Franchise," *Harbus News*, 9 May 2005.

[1501] Myra Kraft, quoted by Robert Kraft in speech to TIECON 2004, the annual conference of the Boston chapter of The Indus Entrepreneurs, quoted in: Christine Walsh, "Patriots' football - a winning business," *IndUS Business Journal*, 15 June 2004, www.indusbusinessjournal.com/news/2004/06/15/Tie/Patriots.Football.A.Winning.Business-688799.shtml.

[1502] Patriots owner Robert Kraft, "Quotes from New England Patriots Photo Day," 1 February 2005.

[1503] Jonathan Kraft, quoted in: Monte Burke, "Unlikely Dynasty," *Forbes*, 19 September 2005.

[1504] Patriots owner Bob Kraft, quoted in: Felice J. Freyer, "'Don't be afraid to dream big,'" *Providence Journal*, 23 May 2004, www.projo.com/extra/graduation/college/content/projo_20040523_jw23.21c45b.html.

[1505] Dallas Cowboys owner Jerry Jones, cited in: Judy Battista, "Kraft Changes a Heavy Hand Into a Guiding Hand," *New York Times*, 17 January 2004, p. D5, ProQuest database.

[1506] Patriots owner Robert Kraft, quoted in: John Powers, "Mr. Fix-It," *Boston Globe*, 25 January 2004, http://redsoxnation.net/forum/lofiversion/index.php/t1298.html.

[1507] Jonathan Kraft, quoted in: John Powers, "Mr. Fix-It," *Boston Globe*, 25 January 2004, http://redsoxnation.net/forum/lofiversion/index.php/t1298.html.

[1508] Patriots owner Robert Kraft, "Quotes from New England Patriots Photo Day," 1 February 2005.

[1509] *Forbes* estimates reported in: Associated Press, "Texans third on Forbes 'Most valuable team' list," *KHOU.com*, 3 September 2004, www.khou.com/sports/texans/stories/khou040903_mh_texansforbes.c01f8478.html.

[1510] Monte Burke, "Unlikely Dynasty," *Forbes*, 19 September 2005.

[1511] Monte Burke, "Unlikely Dynasty," *Forbes*, 19 September 2005.

[1512] Jonathan Kraft, quoted in: Monte Burke, "Unlikely Dynasty," *Forbes*, 19 September 2005.

[1513] Patriots owner Robert Kraft, aired on "Dollars and Sports," CNBC September 5, 2005.

[1514] Patriots Vice President of Player Personnel Scott Pioli, quoted in: Vincent Pullia, "NFL : The evolution of Bill Belichick," 17 December 2001, www.esportsmediagroup.com/e-sports/articles/0,1090,46-12483--1-2,00.html.

[1515] Judy Battista, "Kraft Changes a Heavy Hand Into a Guiding Hand," *New York Times*, 17 January 2004, p. D5, ProQuest database.

[1516] Patriots owner Bob Kraft, quoted in: Jimmy Golen (AP), "Buying the Bill," *SouthCoast Today*, 28 January 2000, www.s-t.com/daily/01-00/01-28-00/d01sp116.htm.

[1517] Peter King, "Downright dominant," *Sports Illustrated*, 11 November 2004, http://sportsillustrated.cnn.com/2004/writers/peter_king/11/08/king.mmqb/index.html.

[1518] Patriots inside linebackers coach Pepper Johnson, *Won For All*, Chicago: Contemporary Books, 2003, p. 73.

[1519] Patriots inside linebackers coach Pepper Johnson, *Won For All*, Chicago: Contemporary Books, 2003, p. 90.

[1520] Charlie Weis, quoted in: Ian O'Connor, "When boring Bill smiles," *The Journal News*, 6 February 2005.

[1521] Bill Belichick, quoted in: Todd Archer, "Big Bill vs. Little Bill," *Dallas Morning News*, 16 November 2003, www.cowboysplus.com/topstory/stories/111603cpcowlede_29e2b.html.

[1522] Gerald Eskenazi (*New York Times*), "Pats defense built in reverse," *SouthCoast Today*, 22 January 1997, www.s-t.com/daily/01-97/01-22-97/d04sp157.htm.

[1523] Bob Glauber, *Newsday* sports reporter, quoted in: Dan Pires, "The changing face of Bill Belichick," *SouthCoast Today*, 22 December 2001, www.s-t.com/daily/12-01/12-22-01/c01sp071.htm.

[1524] "Drew Has Left the Building," by PatriotPlanet.com's Hawg73, www.patriotsplanet.com/BB/showthread.php?s=&threadid=1722. Reprinted with permission.

[1525] Patriots special teams captain and Pro Bowler Larry Izzo, quoted in: Bill Burt, "Man with the plan Belichick's sure hand guides Patriots back to Super Bowl," *Eagle Tribune*, 19 January 2004, www.eagletribune.com/news/stories/20040119/FP_003.htm.

[1526] Patriots VP of player personnel Scott Pioli, quoted in: Don Pierson, "Expect teams to follow Patriots' formula," *MSNBC.com*, 2 March 2004, http://msnbc.msn.com/id/4415299/.

[1527] Bill Belichick, quoted in: Nick Cafardo, "The Buck Stops With Bill," *Boston Globe*, 24 November 2001, www.allthingsbillbelichick.com/articles/buckstops.htm.

[1528] Bud Shaw, "The classy Belichick is keeping his last laughs to himself," *Plain Dealer* (Cleveland), February 08, 2004, www.cleveland.com/sports/plaindealer/index.ssf?/base/sports/10762362849321.xml.

[1529] Bill Livingston, "Free thinkers pay a price in the NFL," *Cleveland Plain Dealer*, 17 November 2002, www.clevelandbrowns.com/news_room/press/files/127.doc.

[1530] Browns receiver Michael Jackson, quoted in: *Browns News/Illustrated*, 18 October 1993, cited in: www.nflhistory.net/shared/articles.asp?Team=7&Article=96.

[1531] Greg Couch, "Doofus to genius simply a super story," *Sun-Times*, 8 February 2005, http://bears.hosttown.com/lofiversion/index.php/t41470.html and Bill Livingston, "Free thinkers pay a price in the NFL," *Cleveland Plain Dealer*, 17 November 2002, www.clevelandbrowns.com/news_room/press/files/127.doc.

[1532] Former Browns receiver Reggie Langhorne, quoted in: Bob Glauber (*Newsday*), "All Grown Up," *TizNow.com*, 27 January 2002.

[1533] Bill Belichick, on *21: The Story Behind the NFL's longest winning streak.*

[1534] Bill Belichick, quoted in: Jerome Solomon, "Business as usual for Brady," *Boston Globe*, 5 August 2005.

[1535] "Return of a Favored Son," by PatriotPlanet.com's Hawg73, www.patriotsplanet.com/BB/showthread.php?s=&threadid=3936. Reprinted with permission.

[1536] Nick Cafardo, "The Buck Stops With Bill," *Boston Globe*, 24 November 2001, www.allthingsbillbelichick.com/articles/buckstops.htm.

[1537] Glen Farley (*Pro Football Weekly*), "Revamped Patriots better recognize," *ESPN*, 27 August 2001, http://espn.go.com/nfl/preview01/s/nwe.html.

[1538] Ron Borges, "There's a Risk Factor At Work For Belichick," *Boston Globe*, 22 November 2001, www.allthingsbillbelichick.com/articles/riskfactor.htm.

[1539] Ron Borges, "There's a Risk Factor At Work For Belichick," *Boston Globe*, 22 November 2001, www.allthingsbillbelichick.com/articles/riskfactor.htm.

[1540] Ron Borges, "There's a Risk Factor At Work For Belichick," *Boston Globe*, 22 November 2001, www.allthingsbillbelichick.com/articles/riskfactor.htm.

[1541] Bill Belichick, quoted in: Michael Holley, *Patriot Reign*, William Morrow, 2004, p. 47.

[1542] Ron Borges, "There's a Risk Factor At Work For Belichick," *Boston Globe*, 22 November 2001, www.allthingsbillbelichick.com/articles/riskfactor.htm.

[1543] Ron Borges, "There's a Risk Factor At Work For Belichick," *Boston Globe*, 22 November 2001, www.allthingsbillbelichick.com/articles/riskfactor.htm.

[1544] Bill Belichick, "Bill Belichick Press Conference," 5 November 2005.

[1545] Bill Belichick, quoted in: Nick Cafardo, "The Buck Stops With Bill," *Boston Globe*, 24 November 2001, www.allthingsbillbelichick.com/articles/buckstops.htm.

[1546] Bill Belichick, *21: The Story Behind the NFL's longest winning streak.*

[1547] Patriots offensive coordinator Charlie Weis, quoted in: Bill Burt, "New Orleans Drew's last stop," *Eagle Tribune*, 1 February 2002, www.eagletribune.com/news/stories/20020201/SP_002.htm.

[1548] Former Patriots quarterback Michael Bishop, quoted in: Bill Reynolds, "It seems like Brady has come a long way," 22 January 2004, www.absolutebrady.com/Archive/January2004.html.

[1549] Bill Belichick, quoted in: Hector Longo, "Pats' Belichick passes all tests," *Eagle Tribune*, 13 January 2002, www.eagletribune.com/news/stories/20020113/SP_001.htm.

[1550] Bill Belichick, "Bill Belichick Press Conference," 22 January 2002, www.patriots.com/news/FullArticle.sps?id=16686&type=general.

[1551] Patriots inside linebackers coach Pepper Johnson, *Won For All*, Chicago: Contemporary Books, 2003, pp. 125-126.

[1552] Patriots inside linebackers coach Pepper Johnson, *Won For All*, Chicago: Contemporary Books, 2003, p. 199.

[1553] Former Patriots quarterback Drew Bledsoe, "NFL Films Presents: Super Bowl XXXVI," aired on: *NFL Network*, 18 May 2005.

[1554] Drew Bledsoe quoted by Bill Belichick quoted by David Halberstam as reported by Seth Wickersham, "Belichick's Revelations," *ESPN Insider*, 28 August 2005.

[1555] Bob McGinn, "Brady to lead Pats' bunch," *Milwaukee Journal-Sentinel*, 30 January 2002.

[1556] Patriots defensive lineman Richard Seymour, quoted in: Bryan Morry, "Belichick's three F's help Patriots earn A's," *NFL.com*, 21 October 2003, www.nfl.com/news/story/6739641.

[1557] Bill Burt, "New Orleans Drew's last stop," *Eagle Tribune*, 1 February 2002, www.eagletribune.com/news/stories/20020201/SP_002.htm.

[1558] http://scores.nfl.com/scores/2001/week20/gamecenter/NFL_20020127_NE@PIT.html.

[1559] Rodney McKissic, "Bills hope to derail Patriots' express," *Buffalo News*, 28 September 2004, www.buffalonews.com/editorial/20040928/1027154.asp; also: Leo Roth, "Belichick turns up the heat," *Democrat and Chronicle*, 30 September 2004, www.democratandchronicle.com/apps/pbcs.dll/article?AID=/20040930/SPORTS03/409300343/1007/SPORTS.

[1560] Bill Belichick, live video news conference, streamed online from Patriots.com, 20 October 2004.

[1561] Tom Brady, quoted in: Kimberly Jones, "Jets: It isn't personal to Pats' Brady," *Star-Ledger*, 22 October 2004, www.nj.com/sports/ledger/index.ssf?/base/sports-1/1098420619120.xml.

[1562] Dallas Cowboys head coach Bill Parcells, quoted in: Tom E. Curran, "You don't say…" *Providence Journal*, 21 August 2005.

[1563] Offensive coordinator Charlie Weis, quoted in: Paul Attner, "Super Bowl 36: Standing Pat," *The Sporting News*, 4 February 2002, www.a1-sports-odds.com/292.htm.

[1564] Patriots offensive coordinator Charlie Weis, quoted in: Kevin Mannix, "Weis thriving in pro game," *Boston Herald*, 31 January 2004, http://patriots.bostonherald.com/patriots/view.bg?articleid=14055.

[1565] Bill Belichick, quoted in: "Line Changes Coming?" *The Insiders*, 15 July 2004, http://story.theinsiders.com/a.z?s=69&p=2&c=274853.

[1566] Patriots safety Lawyer Milloy, quoted in: Bill Simmons, "Slight sadness amid Boston's big wins," *ESPN*, 23 April 2002, http://espn.go.com/page2/s/simmons/020423.html.

[1567] Drew Bledsoe, quoted in: "NFL quarterbacks are bound for Boise," *Idaho Statesman*, 26 May 2005.

[1568] Tom King, "Patriots late rally falls short," *Portsmouth Herald*, 4 September 2000, www.seacoastonline.com/2000news/9_4_s2.htm.

[1569] Dave Goldberg (AP), "Jets defeat Pats in 'Tuna Helper Bowl' with late 2-TD rally," *Daily Ardmoreite*, 12 September 2000, http://ardmoreite.com/stories/091200/spo_defeat.shtml.

[1570] Steve Grogan & R.R. Marshall, "2000 Grogan's Grade: Week 3 vs Vikings," *PatsFans.com*, September 2000, www.patsfans.com/stories/display_story.php?story_id=2142.

[1571] AP, "Versatile Culpepper guides Vikings," *ESPN*, 17 September 2000, http://espn.go.com/nfl/2000/20000917/recap/minnwe.html.

[1572] *USA Today*, "New England vs. Miami," 24 September 2000, www.usatoday.com/sports/scores100/100268/100268339.htm.

[1573] Tom Brady, quoted in: Bryan Morry, "Managing the Moment," *Lindy's 2004 Pro Football*, p. 9.

[1574] Bill Belichick, quoted in: Bryan Morry, "Managing the Moment," *Lindy's 2004 Pro Football*, p. 10.

[1575] Tom Brady, quoted in: Tom E. Curran, "Tom Curran: Brady, Belichick seem perfect for each other," *Providence Journal*, 12 August 2004, www.projo.com/patriots/content/projo_20040812_12currcol.dcb5f.html.

[1576] Patriots fullback Larry Centers, quoted in: "Tom's Posse, New England Patriots," www.tombradyfan.com/quotes.html.

[1577] Alan Ameche, "Official Vegas Odds 2003," November 8, 2003 (Revised 11/09/03), http://amecheleague.tripod.com/vegas2003.htm.

[1578] Bill Belichick, quoted in: Judy Battista, "Patriots Adhere to Bottom Line to Stay on Top," *New York Times*, 8 August 2004, www.nytimes.com/2004/08/08/sports/football/08patriots.html.

[1579] Bill Belichick, quoted in: Tom E. Curran, "From the start, Brady has remained a genuine superstar," *Providence Journal*, 4 September 2004.

[1580] Bill Belichick, quoted in: Mike Reiss, "Patriots beat: Titanic similarities," *Milford Daily News*, 2 May 2004, www.milforddailynews.com/sportsColumnists/view.bg?articleid=47039.

[1581] Basketball star and Bill Belichick friend Charles Barkley, quoted in: Fran Blinebury, "Belichick, Barkley proof that opposites attract," *Houston Chronicle*, 31 January 2004, www.chron.com/cs/CDA/ssistory.mpl/sports/2379958.

[1582] Bill Burt, "Hey, ex-Pats, stop the whining on the way out," *Eagle Tribune*, 8 March 2004, www.eagletribune.com/news/stories/20040308/SP_005.htm.

[1583] Charlie Weis, quoted in: Dennis Dodd, "Weis doing his part … now players must follow," *Sportsline.com*, 12 August 2005.

[1584] Former Cleveland Browns and Patriots fullback Marc Edwards, quoted in: Marla Ridenourhen, " Human Interests," *Akron Beacon Journal*, 9 December 2001, www.allthingsbillbelichick.com/articles/humaninterests.htm.

[1585] Mike Carlson, "The Unified Gillette Field Theory," *ColdHardFootballFacts.com*, 16 June 2005.

[1586] Bill Belichick, quoted in: Michael Felger, "Vrabel hurt in practice," *Boston Herald*, 13 November 2004.

[1587] Bill Belichick, "Quotes from New England Patriots Media Day," 1 February 2005.

[1588] Ron Borges, Boston Globe, 2001, quoted in: Boston Sports Media, 2 May 2004, www.bostonsportsmedia.com/archives/002088.php.

[1589] "The SeaHawk Boys 2001 Fearless and Stupid 2001 NFL Preview!" www.lunaranomalies.com/2001%20preview.htm.

[1590] Doug Farrar, "Koren Robinson: Countdown to Extinction?" Seahawks.net, 1 June 2005.

[1591] Mike Sando and Sean Robinson, "Robinson in trouble again," TheNewsTribune.com, 1 June 2005.

[1592] Doug Farrar, "Koren Robinson: Countdown to Extinction?" Seahawks.net, 1 June 2005.

[1593] Chris Mihale, "Tampa Bay Buccaneers," Fantasy Football Mastermind, 23 February 2005, www.ffmastermind.com/2005/offseason/reports/eye13.php.

[1594] "2001 redraft pick #3: Cleveland is On The Clock," www.mrfootball.com/forums/showthread.php?p=1627064.

[1595] Bryan Curtis, "Mel Kiper's Rough Draft," Salon.com, 12 April 2001, http://slate.msn.com/id/104163/.

[1596] Rick Gosselin, "2001 NFL Combine report: No perfect QB," Dallas Morning News, 3 March 2001, http://buffzone.big12.net/stories/030301/nfl_03030115606.shtml.

[1597] Bruce Allen, "Bill Belichick and the New England Media," BostonSportsMedia.com, 27 April 2005.

[1598] Bruce Allen, "Bill Belichick and the New England Media," BostonSportsMedia.com, 27 April 2005.

[1599] Kevin Mannix, article in the Boston Herald, quoted in: Bruce Allen, "Bill Belichick and the New England Media," BostonSportsMedia.com, 27 April 2005.

[1600] Andy Hanacek, "What were the Patriots thinking when they cut Milloy loose? Pro Football Weekly, 3 September 2003, www.profootballweekly.com/PFW/NFL/AFC/AFC+East/New+England/Features/2003/hanacek090303.htm.

[1601] "SI Players Poll: Who is the dirtiest player in the NFL?" Sports Illustrated, 12 October 2004, http://sportsillustrated.cnn.com/2004/players/10/12/poll.dirtiest/index.html.

[1602] Patriots safety Rodney Harrison, quoted in: Nick Cafardo and Jim McCabe, "Dillon fights through pain," Boston Globe, 15 November 2004, www.boston.com/sports/football/patriots/articles/2004/11/15/dillon_fights_through_pain/.

[1603] Patriots safety Rodney Harrison, quoted in: Jerome Solomon, "Kelley can't make cut," Boston Globe, 2 August 2005.

[1604] Andy Hanacek, "What were the Patriots thinking when they cut Milloy loose? Pro Football Weekly, 3 September 2003, www.profootballweekly.com/PFW/NFL/AFC/AFC+East/New+England/Features/2003/hanacek090303.htm.

[1605] Nick Cafardo, "A Battle of QBs," Boston Globe, 12 September 2003, www.boston.com/sports/football/patriots/extras/asknick/09_12_03.

[1606] Nick Cafardo, "A Battle of QBs," Boston Globe, 12 September 2003, www.boston.com/sports/football/patriots/extras/asknick/09_12_03.

[1607] Tom E. Curran, "Two Pats deserve to cash in on success," Providence Journal, 12 June 2005.

[1608] Hector Longo, "Bledsoe Bowl I: Patriots' perfect distraction," Eagle Tribune, 31 October 2002, www.eagletribune.com/news/stories/20021031/SP_001.htm.

[1609] Bill Burt, "Patriots tackle a big need," Eagle Tribune, 22 April 2001, www.eagletribune.com/news/stories/20010422/SP_001.htm.

[1610] Congressman Marty Meehan, quoted in: Bill Burt, "Meehan: I almost picked Terrell," Eagle Tribune, 29 April 2001, www.eagletribune.com/news/stories/20010428/SP_002.htm.

[1611] Patriots executive Jonathan Kraft, quoted in: Bill Burt, "Meehan: I almost picked Terrell," Eagle Tribune, 29 April 2001, www.eagletribune.com/news/stories/20010428/SP_002.htm.

[1612] Patriots executive Jonathan Kraft, quoted in: Bill Burt, "Meehan: I almost picked Terrell," Eagle Tribune, 29 April 2001, www.eagletribune.com/news/stories/20010428/SP_002.htm.

[1613] Ron Hobson, "NFL DRAFT 2004: Belichick: Defensive mission complete," Patriot Ledger (Quincy, MA), 26 April 2004, http://ledger.southofboston.com/articles/2004/04/26/sports/sports05.txt.

[1614] May 12-26 poll of 22 NFL personnel directors by USA Today Sports Weekly, cited in: Michael Smith, "Whipping them into shape," Boston Globe, 27 June 2004, www.boston.com/sports/football/patriots/articles/2004/06/27/whipping_them_into_shape.

[1615] Kevin Mannix, "Seymour was right pick for Patriots," NFL Insider, 23 January 2002, www.nfl.com/xxxvi/ce/feature/0,3892,4880669,00.html.

[1616] Tom E. Curran, "Patriots can't pass at WR," 19 April 2004, www.projo.com/patriots/content/projo_20040419_19patswr.1367d9.html.

[1617] Howard Bryant, "Receivers earn respect: New blood revives Pats," Boston Herald, 28 January 2004, http://patriots.bostonherald.com/patriots/view.bg?articleid=14108.

[1618] Bill Belichick, "Bill Belichick Press Conf. Transcript," Patriots.com, 22 September 2004, www.patriots.com/Common/PrintThis.sps?id=31304.

[1619] Bill Belichick, quoted in: Peter King, "Rinse, repeat?" Sports Illustrated, 15 August 2002.

[1620] Fresno State Bulldogs head coach Pat Hill, quoted in: Lamar Lopez, "Mankins now stands Pat," Fresno Bee, 24 April 2005.

[1621] Pete Thamel, "Building Programs Using Belichick's Blueprint," 18 September 2004, www.nytimes.com/2004/09/18/sports/ncaafootball/18college.html.

[1622] John Robinson, UNLV head coach, quoted in: Michael Felger, "Claridge all business," Boston Herald, 28 April 2005.

[1623] Bill Belichick, quoted in: Jeff Goldberg, "Coaching Fraternity," Hartford Courant, 1 October 2004, www.ctnow.com/sports/hc-sidecover1001.artoct01,1,4313054,print.story?coll=hc-headlines-sports.

[1624] Bill Belichick, quoted in: Jeff Goldberg, "Coaching Fraternity," Hartford Courant, 1 October 2004, www.ctnow.com/sports/hc-sidecover1001.artoct01,1,4313054,print.story?coll=hc-headlines-sports.

[1625] Michael Holley, Patriot Reign, William Morrow, 2004, pp. 85-86.

[1626] Former LSU and current Patriot defensive lineman Jarvis Green, quoted in: Sheldon Mickles, "Green, Davey were prepared," The Advocate (Baton Rouge, LA), 31 January 2004, www.2theadvocate.com/stories/013104/col_mickles001.shtml.

[1627] Former LSU and current Patriot defensive lineman Jarvis Green, quoted in: Tom E. Curran, "Pats can pluck good from the bad," Providence Journal, 3 July 2004, www.projo.com/patriots/content/projo_20040703_03green.126f0a.html.

[1628] Dean Pees, new Patriots linebackers coach and former Kent State head coach, quoted in: Michael Felger, "Pees: Cues from Belichick," Boston Herald, 19 August 2004, http://patriots.bostonherald.com/patriots/view.bg?articleid=40466.

[1629] Pete Thamel, "Building Programs Using Belichick's Blueprint," 18 September 2004, www.nytimes.com/2004/09/18/sports/ncaafootball/18college.html.

[1630] LSU head coach Nick Saban, quoted in: Jeff Goldberg, "Coaching Fraternity," Hartford Courant, 1 October 2004, www.ctnow.com/sports/hc-sidecover1001.artoct01,1,4313054,print.story?coll=hc-headlines-sports.

[1631] Bill Belichick, quoted in: Rich Thompson, "LSU's Hill a perfect match," Boston Herald, 27 April 2004, http://patriots.bostonherald.com/patriots/view.bg?articleid=13898.

[1632] Nick Saban, quoted in: Pete Thamel, "Building Programs Using Belichick's Blueprint," 18 September 2004, www.nytimes.com/2004/09/18/sports/ncaafootball/18college.html.

[1633] Bill Belichick, "Bill Belichick Pre-Game Press Conf. Transcript," Patriots.com, 6 September 2004, www.patriots.com/games/gamesdetails.sps?matchreportid=30447&matchid=28318.

[1634] Patriots rookie cornerback Randall Gay, quoted in: Nick Cafardo, "Dillon experiences a whole new feeling," Boston Globe, 10 September 2004, www.boston.com/sports/football/patriots/articles/2004/09/10/dillon_experiences_a_whole_new_feeling.

[1635] John Czarnecki, "CZAR: Dolphins still unsettled at QB," 6 May 2004, www.foxsports.com/content/view?contentId=2376070.

[1636] Bill Belichick, speech to Big Brothers of Massachusetts Bay, quoted in: Bryan Morry, "Patriots have a familiar ring," USA Today, 1 June 2005.

[1637] Bill Belichick, quoted in: Tom E. Curran, "Coach explains how Pats' picks stack up," Providence Journal, 11 April 2004, www.projo.com/patriots/content/projo_20040411_11pats.143a10.html.

[1638] Bill Belichick, quoted in: Judy Battista, "Kraft Changes a Heavy Hand Into a Guiding Hand," New York Times, 17 January 2004, p. D5, ProQuest database.

[1639] Romeo Crennel, audio recording, 2 February 2005.

[1640] Romeo Crennel, "Quotes from New England Patriots Media Session," 3 February 2005.

[1641] Bill Belichick, "Bill Belichick Press Conf. Transcript 9/5/04," Patriots.com, 5 September 2004, www.patriots.com/Common/PrintThis.sps?id=30434.

[1642] Bill Belichick, quoted in: Nick Cafardo, "The Buck Stops With Bill," Boston Globe, 24 November 2001, www.allthingsbillbelichick.com/articles/buckstops.htm.

[1643] Bill Belichick, quoted in: Jarrett Bell, "Piecing the Patriots together," USA Today, 21 April 2005.

[1644] Bill Belichick, quoted in: Len Pasquarelli, "Belichick and Pioli have winning formula," ESPN.com, 27 July 2002, http://espn.go.com/nfl/trainingcamp02/columns/patriots/1410739.html.

[1645] Bill Belichick, quoted in: Jackie MacMullan, "Pioli and Belichick a nice team," Boston Globe, 26 January 2004, www.boston.com/sports/football/patriots/articles/2004/01/26/pioli_and_belichick_a_nice_team/.

[1646] Bill Belichick, quoted in: Jarrett Bell, "Piecing the Patriots together," USA Today, 21 April 2005.

[1647] Patriots VP of player personnel Scott Pioli, quoted in: Jarrett Bell, "Piecing the Patriots together," USA Today, 21 April 2005.

[1648] Scott Pioli, "Quotes from New England Patriots Press Conference," 3 February 2005.

[1649] Patriots VP of player personnel Scott Pioli, quoted in: Len Pasquarelli, "Belichick and Pioli have winning formula," ESPN.com, 27 July 2002, http://espn.go.com/nfl/trainingcamp02/columns/patriots/1410739.html.

[1650] Bill Belichick, quoted in: Mike Reiss, "Patriots beat: Grocery shopping," MetroWest Daily News, 17 October 2004, www.metrowestdailynews.com/sportsNews/view.bg?articleid=80695.

[1651] Bill Belichick, quoted in: Jackie MacMullan, "Pioli and Belichick a nice team," Boston Globe, 26 January 2004, www.boston.com/sports/football/patriots/articles/2004/01/26/pioli_and_belichick_a_nice_team/.

[1652] Dan Pires, "The changing face of Bill Belichick," SouthCoast Today, 22 December 2001, www.s-t.com/daily/12-01/12-22-01/c01sp071.htm.

[1653] Bill Belichick, quoted in: Jackie MacMullan, "Pioli and Belichick a nice team," Boston Globe, 26 January 2004, www.boston.com/sports/football/patriots/articles/2004/01/26/pioli_and_belichick_a_nice_team/.

[1654] Scott Pioli, Patriots VP of player personnel, quoted in: Hector Longo, "All the right moves," Eagle-Tribune, 30 January 2004, www.eagletribune.com/news/stories/20040130/SP_001.htm.

[1655] Hadley Engelhard, agent of Patriots cornerback Tyrone Poole, quoted in: Jackie MacMullan, "Pioli and Belichick a nice team," Boston Globe, 26 January 2004, www.boston.com/sports/football/patriots/articles/2004/01/26/pioli_and_belichick_a_nice_team/.

[1656] Jackie MacMullan, "Pioli and Belichick a nice team," Boston Globe, 26 January 2004, www.boston.com/sports/football/patriots/articles/2004/01/26/pioli_and_belichick_a_nice_team/.

[1657] Robert McNamara, speech at Harvard University titled, "Lessons of the Vietnam War," 3 March 2004, aired on C-SPAN 24 August 2005.

[1658] Bill Belichick, quoted in: Harvey Mackay, We Got Fired!, New York: Ballantine Books, 2004, p. 65.

[1659] Dr. Peter F. Drucker, Management: Tasks, Responsibilities, Practices, USA: HarperCollins, 1973, pp. 35.

[1660] Patriots linebacker Ted Johnson, audio recording, 1 February 2005.

[1661] Pat Fitzmaurice, "Touting the Tuna," Pro Football Weekly, 1998, http://archive.profootballweekly.com/content/archives/features_1998/daily_081998.asp.

[1662] Bill Belichick, quoted in: "Five Questions … with Bill Belichick," Sports Illustrated, 17 August 2004, http://sportsillustrated.cnn.com/2004/football/nfl/specials/preview/2004/08/17/fivequestion.belichick.

[1663] New York Giants head coach Bill Parcells, "NFL Yearbook: 1986 New York Giants," aired on ESPN Classics, 18 April 2005.

[1664] Romeo Crennel, quoted in: Len Pasquarelli, "In Romeo they trust," ESPN.com, 3 August 2005.

[1665] Eric Schmidt, Google CEO, quoted in: Fred Vogelstein, "It's not just business, it's personal," Fortune, 15 November 2004, p. 200.

[1666] Patriots linebacker Willie McGinest, quoted in: Karen Guregian, "Survivors laud Bill," Boston Herald, 8 September 2005.

[1667] Chuck Noll, quoted in: Ira Kaufman, "Patriots Players Hold Themselves To A Higher Standard," Tampa Tribune, 31 January 2005.

[1668] Center Mike Baab, who played on Belichick's Cleveland Browns, quoted in: Terry Pluto, "The Man Behind the Mask," Akron Beacon Journal, 18 December 1994, www.allthingsbillbelichick.com/articles/behindthemask.htm.

[1669] Bill Parcells as told by Bill Belichick to David Halberstam in his forthcoming book, reported in: Seth Wickersham, "It's all about Belichick," ESPN Insider, 31 August 2005.

[1670] Bill Belichick, speech at Big Brothers of Massachusetts Bay, quoted in: Eric McHugh, "Belichick: Brown best leader in NFL," Patriot Ledger, 20 May 2005.

[1671] Charlie Weis, quoted in: Vahe Gregorian, "Notre Dame hopes Weis has healing touch," St. Louis Today, 5 May 2005.

[1672] Patriots receiver Deion Branch, quoted in: Jerome Solomon, "Business as usual for Brady," Boston Globe, 5 August 2005.

[1673] Former New York Giants tight end Mark Bavaro, quoted in: Michael Felger, "One last haul for Bavaro?" Boston Herald, 24 July 2005.

[1674] Dick Hoyt, interview on HBO's Real Sports, aired on HBO 25 August 2005.

[1675] Bill Belichick, quoted in: "Super-Bowl Champion New England Patriots inspired by giant-screen film SHACKLETON'S ANTARCTIC ADVENTURE," http://main.wgbh.org/imax/shackleton/patriots.html.

[1676] Patriots receiver/punt returner Tim Dwight, quoted in: Clark Judge, "Camp tour: Pats take care of business in free agency," Sportsline.com, 25 August 2005.

[1677] Patriots wide receiver / nickel back / punt returner Troy Brown, "Quotes from New England Patriots Press Conference," 30 January 2005.

[1678] Patriots wide receiver / nickel back / punt returner Troy Brown, "Quotes from New England Patriots Press Conference," 3 February 2005.

[1679] Patriots wide receiver / nickel back / punt returner Troy Brown, "Quotes from New England Patriots Press Conference," 30 January 2005.

[1680] Patriots wide receiver / nickel back / punt returner Troy Brown, "Quotes from New England Patriots Press Conference," 3 February 2005.

[1681] Ken Sims, quoted in: Chip Brown (Dallas Morning News), "UT legend Sims at peace with NFL career," WFAA.com, 30 May 2005.

[1682] Ken Sims, quoted in: Chip Brown (Dallas Morning News), "UT legend Sims at peace with NFL career," WFAA.com, 30 May 2005.

[1683] Troy Brown, "Troy Brown Press Conference," Patriots.com, 24 May 2005.

[1684] Patriots cornerback / wide receiver Troy Brown, "Quotes From New England Patriots Press Conference," January 30, 2005.

[1685] Rodney Harrison, quoted in: Howard Ulman (AP), "Troy Brown excited to return to Patriots," LA Times, 10 August 2005.

[1686] New Patriots linebacker Monty Beisel, quoted in: Jerome Solomon, "Beisel lands with Patriots," Boston Globe, 9 April 2005, www.boston.com/sports/football/patriots/articles/2005/04/09/beisel_lands_with_patriots.

[1687] Buffalo Bills head coach Mike Mularkey, quoted in: Bryan Morry, "Combine Notes: Trying to play catch-up," Patriots.com, 25 February 2005, www.patriots.com/news/index.cfm?ac=generalnewsdetail&pcid=41&pid=10872.

[1688] David Neeleman, JetBlue CEO, quoted in: Nadira A. Hira, "Customer Service. In New York. Who Knew?" Fortune, 15 November 2004, p. 198.

[1689] Former Patriots safety Lawyer Milloy, quoted in: John Hassan, "Inside Belichick's Brain," ESPN the Magazine, 9 September 2002.

[1690] Coach Bill Belichick, quoted in: Alan Greenberg, "Belichick Game Plan For Life," Hartford Courant, 3 May 2004, www.ctnow.com/sports/hc-belichick0503.artmay03,1,707205.story.

[1691] Tedy Bruschi, "Quotes from New England Media Day," 1 February 2005.

[1692] Patriots safety Rodney Harrison, quoted in: Howard Ulman (AP), "Hard-hitting safety ready to face Moss," San Jose Mercury News, 6 September 2005.

[1693] Jim Moore, "Go 2 Guy: Tale of a dogged newshound," Seattle Post-Intelligencer, 14 October 2004, http://seattlepi.nwsource.com/football/195099_moore14.html.

[1694] Patriots guard Damien Woody, quoted in: Michael Smith, "A first step," in: Again!, Chicago: Triumph Books, 2004, p. 52.

[1695] Patriots safety Rodney Harrison, quoted in: Michael Smith, "A first step," in: Again!, Chicago: Triumph Books, 2004, p. 52.

[1696] Bill Belichick, quoted in: Pete Thamel, "Belichick Expects Changes In Rematch With the Titans," New York Times, 6 January 2004, p. D3, ProQuest database.

[1697] Coach Bill Belichick quoted in: Ron Borges, "Dismissing Jets could be a trap play," Boston Globe, 16 September 2003, www.boston.com/sports/football/patriots/articles/2003/09/16/dismissing_jets_could_be_a_trap_play/.

[1698] Bill Belichick, quoted in: Nick Cafardo, "Patriots have memory to feel sorry about," Boston Globe, 30 September 2004, www.boston.com/sports/football/patriots/articles/2004/09/30/patriots_have_memory_to_feel_sorry_about.

[1699] Patriots cornerback Ty Law, quoted in: Michael Smith, "Lone Star state," in: Again!, Chicago: Triumph Books, 2004, p. 74.

[1700] Unnamed reporter, quoted in: Mark Cannizzaro, "Patriots Put Pete in Pinch," New York Post, 21 October 2004, www.nypost.com/sports/jets/30775.htm.

[1701] Bill Belichick , quoted in: Mark Cannizzaro, "Patriots Put Pete in Pinch," New York Post, 21 October 2004, www.nypost.com/sports/jets/30775.htm.

[1702] Tom E. Curran, "In Seahawks' case, Beli-hype may actually be true," Providence Journal, 14 October 2004, www.projo.com/patriots/content/projo_20041014_14pats.319f06.html.

[1703] Bill Belichick, "Quotes from New England Patriots Press Conference," 31 January 2005.

[1704] Bill Belichick, quoted in: Tom E. Curran, "Is this Belichick's version of I've Got A Secret?" Providence Journal, 7 September 2004, www.projo.com/patriots/content/projo_20040907_07pats.2c05d.html.

[1705] Tom Brady, quoted in: Tom E. Curran, "Is newest Patriot a prophet or ill-timed voice of doom?" Providence Journal, 1 October 2004, www.projo.com/patriots/content/projo_20041001_01pats.1bb128.html.

[1706] Patriots quarterback Tom Brady, "Quotes from New England Patriots Press Conference," 30 January 2005.

[1707] Defensive end Jarvis Green, quoted in: Mike Kiral, "Green says Patriots aren't feeling pressure to win third straight Super Bowl in 2005," Ascension Citizen, 27 July 2005.

[1708] Ken Hartnett, "In-Vince-a-Bill," Standard-Times, 21 July 2002.

[1709] Patriots nose tackle Vince Wilfork, quoted in: Jerome Solomon, "This group could be the Patriots' lifeline," Boston Globe, 8 August 2005.

[1710] Patriots offensive lineman Russ Hochstein, quoted in: Randy Dockendorf, "Hochstein Emphasizes Importance Of Faith In Education," Yankton Daily Press & Dakotan, 22 March 2005.

[1711] Bill Belichick, quoted in: Alan Greenberg, "Cassel's Strong Debut May Put Davey On Bubble," Hartford Courant, 14 August 2005.

[1712] Then-New York Jets head coach Bill Parcells, quoted in: Phil Simms, Sunday Morning Quarterback, HarperCollins, 2004, p. 149.

[1713] Then-New York Jets head coach Bill Parcells, quoted in: Phil Simms, Sunday Morning Quarterback, HarperCollins, 2004, p. 149.

[1714] Patriots center Dan Koppen, quoted in: Karen Guregian, "Practice far from perfect," Boston Globe, 4 August 2005.

[1715] Notre Dame head coach Charlie Weis, quoted in: AP, "Great expectations," 30 March 2005, http://sportsillustrated.cnn.com/2005/football/ncaa/03/30/bc.fbc.irishspring.ap/.

[1716] Len Pasquarelli, "In Romeo they trust," *ESPN.com*, 3 August 2005.

[1717] Eric Mangini, quoted in: Jerome Solomon, "Winning formula," *Boston Globe*, 26 July 2005.

[1718] Patriots safety Rodney Harrison, quoted in: Ron Indrisano, "Like his hits, Harrison takes the outcome very hard," *Boston Globe*, 19 August 2005.

[1719] Cardinal Health executive VP Anthony J. Rucci, cited in: Keith H. Hammonds, "Why We Hate HR," *Fast Company*, August 2005, 40.

[1720] Keith H. Hammonds, "Why We Hate HR," *Fast Company*, August 2005, 40.

[1721] Troy Brown, "Troy Brown Press Conference," *Patriots.com*, 24 May 2005.

[1722] Patriots special teamer and backup linebacker Matt Chatham, quoted in: Michael Parente, " Chatham says it's his time to shine," *Herald News*, 5 August 2005.

[1723] Patriots owner Robert Kraft, "Quotes from New England Patriots Photo Day," 1 February 2005.

[1724] Patriots linebacker Mike Vrabel, "Quotes from New England Patriots Media Day," 1 February 2005.

[1725] St. Louis Rams head coach Mike Martz, quoted in: Roger Mills, "New England simply the model franchise," *St. Petersburg Times*, 15 October 2004, www.sptimes.com/2004/10/15/Sports/New_England_simply_th.shtml.

[1726] Marcus Pollard, quoted in: Vic Carucci, "Pats' defense already in championship form," *NFL.com*, 18 January 2004.

[1727] Bill Belichick, on: *21: The Story Behind the NFL's longest winning streak*.

[1728] Patriots defensive lineman Richard Seymour, quoted in: Glen Farley, "Pats' Seymour a happy camper," *The Enterprise*, 4 August 2005.

[1729] Patriots special teamer and backup linebacker Matt Chatham, quoted in: Michael Parente, " Chatham says it's his time to shine," *Herald News*, 5 August 2005.

[1730] Patriots linebacker Ted Johnson, "Quotes from New England Press Conference," 3 Febuary 2005.

[1731] Patriots linebacker Ted Johnson, quoted in: Mike Reiss, "Patriots beat: Johnson easy to admire," *MetroWest Daily News*, 29 July 2005.

[1732] Troy Brown, quoted in: Anthony Hanshew, "Humble hero," *Herald-Dispatch*, 27 June 2004, www.herald-dispatch.com/2004/June/27/MUspot.htm.

[1733] Patriots cornerback Asante Samuel, "Quotes from New England Press Conference," 3 Febuary 2005.

[1734] Patriots kicker Adam Vinatieri, "Quotes from New England Media Session," 3 Febuary 2005.

[1735] Bill Belichick, then New York Giants defensive coordinator, "NFL Yearbook: 1986 New York Giants," aired on *ESPN Classics*, 18 April 2005.

[1736] Bill Belichick, on: *3 Games to Glory III* DVD, 2005.

[1737] Patriots running back Corey Dillon, "Quotes from New England Patriots Media Day," 1 February 2005.

[1738] Tom Brady, quoted in: Glen Farley, "No Weis, but Brady wiser," *The Enterprise*, 8 August 2005.

[1739] Tom Brady, quoted in: AP, "The defense rests for Patriots," *MaineToday.com*, 30 July 2005.

[1740] Tom Brady, quoted in: Vic Carucci, "Patriots' resiliency put to test again," *NFL.com*, 29 July 2005.

[1741] Gary Shelton, "History's favor falls on unheralded Pats," *St. Petersburg Times*, 24 January 2005.

[1742] Bill Belichick, "Quotes from New England Patriots Press Conference," 31 January 2005.

[1743] Patriots wide receiver / nickel back / punt returner Troy Brown, "Quotes from New England Patriots Press Conference," 3 February 2005.

[1744] Patriots linebacker Willie McGinest, "Quotes From New England Patriots Press Session," 2 February 2005.

[1745] Patriots linebacker Willie McGinest, "Quotes From New England Patriots Press Session," 2 February 2005.

[1746] Tom Brady, "Quotes From New England Patriots Press Session," 2 February 2005.

[1747] Bill Belichick, "Quotes from New England Patriots Press Conference," 31 January 2005.

[1748] Tom Brady, "Tom Brady Post Practice Interview," *Patriots.com*, 4 August 2005.

[1749] Bill Belichick, quoted in: Dave Goldberg (AP), "Patriots' Branch Still Relatively Unknown," *Los Angeles Times*, 5 August 2005.

[1750] Philadelphia Eagles special teams coordinator John Harbaugh, "Quotes from Philadelphia Eagles Media Day," 1 February 2005.

[1751] Patriots defensive lineman Ty Warren, "Quotes from New England Patriots Press Conference," 31 January 2005.

[1752] New Patriots linebacker Chad Brown, quoted in: Michael Parente, " New LB Brown happy with progress," *Woonsocket Call*, 23 August 2005.

[1753] Patriots running back Corey Dillon, quoted in: Paul Harber, "Dillon more than willing to go extra yard," *Boston Globe*, 25 October 2004, www.boston.com/sports/football/patriots/articles/2004/10/25/dillon_more_than_willing_to_go_extra_yard.

[1754] Patriots owner Bob Kraft, quoted in: Nick Cafardo, *The Impossible Team*, Triumph Books, 2002, p. 13.

[1755] Patriots defensive lineman Richard Seymour, "Camp Daze," in: Bryan Morry, *Patriots United*, Canada: Team Power Publishing, 2002, p. 58.

[1756] Bill Belichick, quoted in: Bill Burt, "Bruschi a true blue Patriot," *Eagle Tribune*, 31 January 2002, www.eagletribune.com/news/stories/20020131/SP_001.htm.

[1757] Bill Belichick, quoted in: Hector Longo, "Belichick not going to reinvent Patriots," *Eagle Tribune*, 27 February 2002, www.eagletribune.com/news/stories/20020227/SP_004.htm.

[1758] Bill Burt, "Ready, willing and Vrabel," *Eagle Tribune*, 27 January 2004, www.eagletribune.com/news/stories/20040127/SP_005.htm.

[1759] Patriots linebacker Mike Vrabel, quoted in: Bill Burt, "Ready, willing and Vrabel," *Eagle Tribune*, 27 January 2004, www.eagletribune.com/news/stories/20040127/SP_005.htm.

[1760] Patriots inside linebackers coach Pepper Johnson, *Won For All*, Chicago: Contemporary Books, 2003, p. 61.

[1761] Linebacker Mike Vrabel, quoted in: Dan Pires, "Belichick on the verge of history," *Standard-Times*, 1 February 2004, www.southcoasttoday.com/daily/02-04/02-01-04/c01sp874.htm.

[1762] Patriots defensive lineman Bobby Hamilton, quoted in: Hector Longo, "Patriots have Jets to thank for yesterday's spirited victory," *Eagle Tribune*, 1 October 2001, www.eagletribune.com/news/stories/20011001/SP_002.htm.

[1763] Bill Belichick, on: *3 Games to Glory III* DVD, 2005.

[1764] Bill Belichick, quoted in: Kevin Mannix, "Bills of Right Stuff," *Boston Herald*, 26 January 2002.

[1765] Tom Brady, quoted in: "Super-Bowl Champion New England Patriots inspired by giant-screen film SHACKLETON'S ANTARCTIC ADVENTURE," http://main.wgbh.org/imax/shackleton/patriots.html.

[1766] Patriots inside linebackers coach Pepper Johnson, *Won For All*, Chicago: Contemporary Books, 2003, p. 84.

[1767] Tiznow owner Michael Cooper, quoted in: "Breeders' Cup Classic," 27 October 2001, www.horse-races.net/library/aa102701cl.htm.

[1768] Kenny Mayne, "From one dark horse to another," *ESPN*, www.tiznowpress.com/espn.html and other sources.

[1769] Bill Belichick, quoted in: Kevin Mannix, "Bills of Right Stuff," *Boston Herald*, 26 January 2002.

[1770] Patriots linebacker Tedy Bruschi, quoted in: Dan Shaughnessy, "Filling the Bill As Master Motivator," *Boston Globe*, 10 December 2001, www.tiznowpress.com/globe.html.

[1771] Rudy Ruettiger, quoted in: Dennis Dodd, "Weis doing his part ... now players must follow," *Sportsline.com*, 12 August 2005.

[1772] Kicker Adam Vinatieri, quoted in: Michael Felger, *Tales From the Patriots Sideline*, Sports Publishing, 2004, p. 170.

[1773] Issam Thamer al-Diwan, a former Iraqi volleyball player, quoted in: Don Yaeger, "Son of Saddam," *Sports Illustrated*, 24 March 2003, http://sportsillustrated.cnn.com/si_online/news/2003/03/24/son_of_saddam/.

[1774] ESPN 2005 NFL Draft coverage. I believe Suzie Colbert said this after talking with Parcells.

[1775] Cowboys tight end Dan Campbell, quoted in: Clarence E. Hill Jr., "Hole seen in free agency safety net," *Star-Telegram*, 3 August 2005.

[1776] Mike Freeman, *Bloody Sundays*, Perennial Currents: USA, 2003, p. 29.

[1777] Bryce Wyatt, free-agent defensive end from LSU , quoted in Clifton Brown, "Saban's Next Magic Trick: Make the Dolphins Reappear," *New York Times*, 2 May 2005.

[1778] AP, "Miami Rookie Manuel Wright Misses Practice," *SFGate.com*, 27 July 2005.

[1779] Associated Press, "Defensive lineman in tears at Dolphins camp," 26 July 2005, http://sports.espn.go.com/nfl/news/story?id=2117413.

[1780] Rookie defensive end Matt Roth, quoted in: Harvey Fialkov, "Wright has a back injury and had an MRI," *San Jose Mercury News*, 27 July 2005.

[1781] Michael Holley, *Patriot Reign*, William Morrow, 2004, p. 15.

[1782] Bill Belichick, quoted in: Michael Holley, *Patriot Reign*, William Morrow, 2004, p. 16.

[1783] Bill Belichick, quoted in: Jerome Solomon, "Hobbs covering all the angles," *Boston Globe*, 15 August 2005.

[1784] Patriots rookie cornerback Ellis Hobbs, quoted in: Jerome Solomon, "Hobbs covering all the angles," *Boston Globe*, 15 August 2005.

[1785] Patriots backup quarterback Damon Huard, quoted in: Jeff Reynolds, "Brady, coordinator share special bond," *Pro Football Weekly*, 31 January 2004, www.profootballweekly.com/PFW/NFL/AFC/AFC+East/New+England/Features/2004/reynolds013104.htm.

[1786] Patriots offensive coordinator Charlie Weis, quoted in: Matt Mosley, "Bill still big among colleagues," *Dallas Morning News*, 28 January 2004, www.cowboysplus.com/columnists/mmosley/stories/012804jcpmosley.5a346955.html.

[1787] Former Patriots defensive coordinator Romeo Crennel, quoted in: Pat McManamon, "Savage, Crennel settle in nicely," 24 March 2005, www.clevelandbrowns.com/news_room/news/arts/4113.0.html.

[1788] Patriots offensive coordinator Charlie Weis, quoted in: Dan Pompei, "Inside Pats' Super Bowl Preparations," *Sporting News*, 2 February 2004, www.allthingsbillbelichick.com/articles/insidesbprep.htm.

[1789] Former Patriots offensive coordinator Charlie Weis, quoted in: Greg '23Blast' Katz , "O/NSO - Quotable edition," 14 March 2005, http://story.scout.com/a.z?s=147&p=2&c=360032.

[1790] Former Patriots offensive coordinator Charlie Weis, quoted in: Dennis Dodd, "Indies preview: Notre Dame getting message from upstairs," *CBS Sportsline*, 12 August 2005.

[1791] Former Patriots offensive coordinator Charlie Weis, quoted in: Jason Kelly, "Big dreams drive Weis and family," *South Bend Tribune*, 15 March 2005.

[1792] Charlie Weis, quoted in: "This is not a recruiting trip, I swear," 19 June 2005, http://bluegraysky.blogspot.com/2005_06_01_bluegraysky_archive.html.

[1793] Notre Dame head coach Charlie Weis, quoted in: Terry Shields, "Notre Dame offense sharp, different in debut," *Pittsburgh Post-Gazette*, 24 April 2005.

[1794] Notre Dame head coach Charlie Weis, quoted in: Avani Patel (Chicago Tribune), "In a hurry for success Irish start under new coach this fall," *Pioneer Press*, 14 August 2005.

[1795] Bill Belichick, quoted in: Michael Holley, *Patriot Reign*, William Morrow, 2004, pp. 87-88.

[1796] Bill Belichick, quoted in: Mark Farinella, "Patriots Notebook," *Sun Chronicle*, 4 August 2005.

[1797] Tedy Bruschi, quoted in: Ira Kaufman, "Patriots Players Hold Themselves To A Higher Standard," *Tampa Tribune*, 31 January 2005.

[1798] Patriots inside linebackers coach Pepper Johnson, *Won For All*, Chicago: Contemporary Books, 2003, p. 140.

[1799] Bill Belichick Press Conf. - 09/05/2002," Patriots.com, www.patriots.com/mediaworld/MediaDetail.sps?ID=20143&keywords=Press+Conference&media=audio&team=0&player=0&game=0&currpgno=27&pageid=2.

[1800] Patriots cornerback Ty Law, quoted in: Associated Press, "Law wants out of New England," TSN.ca, www.tsn.ca/nfl/news_story.asp?id=76289.

[1801] Patriots cornerback Ty Law, quoted in: Associated Press, "Law, once disgruntled, now wants to retire with Patriots," 10 June 2004, http://sfgate.com/cgi-bin/article.cgi?f=/news/archive/2004/06/10/sports1245EDT0296.DTL.

[1802] Patriots cornerback Ty Law, quoted in: Eric McHugh, "New faces spice camp," *Patriot Ledger*, 9 June 2004, http://ledger.southofboston.com/articles/2004/06/09/sports/sports04.txt.

[1803] Patriots cornerback Ty Law, quoted in: Michael Parente, "Law and Belichick 'hash out' problems," *Woonsocket Call*, 11 June 2004, www.zwire.com/site/news.cfm?newsid=11933847&BRD=1712&PAG=461&dept_id=106787&rfi=6.

[1804] Patriots cornerback Ty Law, quoted in: Associated Press, "Law wants out of New England," TSN.ca, www.tsn.ca/nfl/news_story.asp?id=76289.

[1805] Bill Belichick, quoted in: Hector Longo, "Confident Patriots coach stacks up talent," *Eagle Tribune*, 25 April 2004, www.eagletribune.com/news/stories/20040425/SP_003.htm.

[1806] Bill Belichick, quoted in: Tom E. Curran, "Belichick, Berman join forces," *Providence Journal*, 16 April 2004, www.projo.com/patriots/content/projo_20040416_16pats.1b97ba.html.

[1807] Patriots owner Bob Kraft, quoted in: Michael Felger, "Owner still a Law fan; Pats add Burris," *Boston Herald*, 21 April 2004, http://patriots.bostonherald.com/patriots/view.bg?articleid=13917.

[1808] Peter King, "Value proposition," *CNNSI*, 1 March 2004, http://sportsillustrated.cnn.com/2004/writers/peter_king/03/01/mmqb/.

[1809] It might have been PlayStation vs. XBox. I did not tape this "First-and-10" segment with Terry Bradshaw and am relating what I recall two days after the segment aired.

[1810] Elizabeth Fenner, book review of Richard Layard's *Happiness*, Fortune, 21 February 2005.

[1811] Research findings of Laura Tach and Glenn Firebaugh, cited in: Emily Singer, "Happiness in the bank," L.A. Times, 15 August 2005.

[1812] Bill Belichick, quoted in: Michael Felger, "Belichick credits Brown," *Boston Herald*, 20 May 2005.

[1813] Patriots cornerback Ty Law, quoted in: Ian Logue, "Offseason Turmoil Despite A Title For The Patriots," *PatsFans.com*, 24 May 2004, www.patsfans.com/stories/display_story.php?story_id=2438.

[1814] Patriots cornerback Ty Law, quoted in: Ian Logue, "Offseason Turmoil Despite A Title For The Patriots," *PatsFans.com*, 24 May 2004, www.patsfans.com/stories/display_story.php?story_id=2438.

[1815] Patriots cornerback Ty Law, quoted in: Ian Logue, "Offseason Turmoil Despite A Title For The Patriots," *PatsFans.com*, 24 May 2004, www.patsfans.com/stories/display_story.php?story_id=2438.

[1816] Lenny Megliola, "Kraft-ing a model franchise," *MetroWest Daily News*, 29 May 2004, www.metrowestdailynews.com/sportsColumnists/view.bg?articleid=69468.

[1817] Bill Belichick, quoted in: Tom E. Curran, "Pats expect to see Law at mini-camp," *Providence Journal*, 4 June 2004, www.projo.com/patriots/content/projo_20040604_04patsjo_d0677.html.

[1818] Patriots cornerback Ty Law, quoted in: Michael Parente, "Law and Belichick 'hash out' problems," *Woonsocket Call*, 11 June 2004, www.zwire.com/site/news.cfm?newsid=11933847&BRD=1712&PAG=461&dept_id=106787&rfi=6.

[1819] Patriots cornerback Ty Law, quoted in: Michael Felger, "Law reverses field in beef with Pats," *Boston Herald*, 11 June 2004, http://patriots.bostonherald.com/patriots/view.bg?articleid=31492.

[1820] Patriots cornerback Ty Law, quoted in: Associated Press, "Law, once disgruntled, now wants to retire with Patriots," 10 June 2004, http://sfgate.com/cgi-bin/article.cgi?f=/news/archive/2004/06/10/sports1245EDT0296.DTL.

[1821] Patriots cornerback Ty Law, quoted in: Glen Farley, "Patriots' Law changes tune," *The Enterprise*, 11 June 2004, http://enterprise.southofboston.com/articles/2004/06/11/news/sports/sports04.txt.

[1822] Patriots cornerback Ty Law, quoted in: Glen Farley, "Patriots' Law changes tune," *The Enterprise*, 11 June 2004, http://enterprise.southofboston.com/articles/2004/06/11/news/sports/sports04.txt.

[1823] Patriots cornerback Ty Law, quoted in: Glen Farley, "Patriots' Law changes tune," *The Enterprise*, 11 June 2004, http://enterprise.southofboston.com/articles/2004/06/11/news/sports/sports04.txt.

[1824] Bill Belichick, quoted in: Glen Farley, "Patriots' Law changes tune," *The Enterprise*, 11 June 2004, http://enterprise.southofboston.com/articles/2004/06/11/news/sports/sports04.txt.

[1825] Bill Belichick, quoted in: Michael Parente, "Law and Belichick 'hash out' problems," *Woonsocket Call*, 11 June 2004, www.zwire.com/site/news.cfm?newsid=11933847&BRD=1712&PAG=461&dept_id=106787&rfi=6.

[1826] Patriots cornerback Ty Law, quoted in: Glen Farley, "Patriots' Law changes tune," *The Enterprise*, 11 June 2004, http://enterprise.southofboston.com/articles/2004/06/11/news/sports/sports04.txt.

[1827] Patriots cornerback Ty Law, quoted in: Michael Parente, "Law and Belichick 'hash out' problems," *Woonsocket Call*, 11 June 2004, www.zwire.com/site/news.cfm?newsid=11933847&BRD=1712&PAG=461&dept_id=106787&rfi=6.

[1828] Ken Hartnett, "In-Vince-a-Bill," *Standard-Times*, 21 July 2002.

[1829] Bill Belichick, quoted in: Alan Greenberg, "Getting Along Well Belichick Still A Little Grim, But With A Grin," *Hartford Courant*, 3 September 2000, p. E1, ProQuest database.

[1830] Tom Brady, quoted in: Richard Oliver, "Let's praise old-school Patriots," *San Antonio Express-News*, 28 November 2004, www.mysanantonio.com/sports/stories/MYSA112804.1C.COL.FBSoliver.9c712fc6.html.

[1831] Patriots nose tackle Keith Traylor, "Quotes from New England Patriots Media Day," 3 February 2005.

[1832] Dr. Peter F. Drucker, *Management: Tasks, Responsibilities, Practices*, USA: HarperCollins, 1973, p. 188.

[1833] Patriots cornerback Ty Law, quoted in: Jimmy Golen (AP), "Belichick might not be slick, but he makes Pats tick," *Arizona Daily Star*, 20 January 2004, www.dailystar.com/dailystar/relatedarticles/6555.php.

[1834] Cleveland Browns quarterback Trent Dilfer, quoted in: Len Pasquarelli, "In Romeo they trust," *ESPN.com*, 3 August 2005.

[1835] Former Cleveland Browns center Mike Baab, quoted in: Terry Pluto, "The Man Behind the Mask," *Akron Beacon Journal*, 18 December 1994, www.allthingsbillbelichick.com/articles/behindthemask.htm.

[1836] *The David Letterman Show*, 4 February 2004, www.patriots.com/mediaworld/mediadetail.sps?id=27974.

[1837] Jim Litke, "The Heart of an Accountant," *CBS Sportsline*, 4 November 2002, http://golfholidays.sportsline.com/nfl/story/5860596.

[1838] New Patriot receiver David Terrell, quoted in: Pat Kirwan, "Despite changes, Pats ready for another run," *NFL.com*, 31 July 2005.

[1839] Patriots offensive guard Russ Hochstein, quoted in: Michael Smith, "A chip on block," *Boston Globe*, 29 July 2004, www.boston.com/sports/football/patriots/articles/2004/07/29/a_chip_on_block.

[1840] Cornerback Ty Law, quoted in: Charles Stein, "Bill Belichick, CEO," *Boston Globe*, 28 January 2004.

[1841] Greg Garber, "Belichick Gets Second Chance In New England," *ESPN.com*, 20 June 2000, www.allthingsbillbelichick.com/articles/secondchance.htm.

[1842] Former Patriots defensive lineman Bobby Hamilton, quoted in: Nick Cafardo, "The Buck Stops With Bill," *Boston Globe*, 24 November 2001, www.allthingsbillbelichick.com/articles/buckstops.htm.

[1843] Special teamer and backup linebacker/safety Don Davis, quoted in: Shalise Manza Young, "Players are all ears in Mangini's class," *Providence Journal*, 31 August 2005.

[1844] Notre Dame offensive tackle Ryan Harris, quoted in: Colin Burns, "Harris's Goal is Simple: Win," *Scout.com*, 14 August 2005.

[1845] Current Notre Dame quarterback Brady Quinn, quoted in: Terry Shields, "Notre Dame offense sharp, different in debut," *Pittsburgh Post-Gazette*, 24 April 2005.

[1846] Oakland Raiders receiver Tim Brown, quoted in: Associated Press, "Fans get first glimpse of Irish under Weis," MSNBC, 23 April 2005, http://msnbc.msn.com/id/7614024/.

[1847] Bruce Allen, "Tidbits from Ron," *Boston Sports Media Watch*, 10 March 2005, www.bostonsportsmedia.com/archives/002720.php said that "according to a couple readers… [Ron Borges] said the following…"

[1848] Tom E. Curran, "Pats' Weis sets the record straight," *Providence Journal*, 9 June 2004.

[1849] Bob LaMonte, Charlie Weis' agent, quoted in: Tom E. Curran, "Pats' Weis sets the record straight," *Providence Journal*, 9 June 2004.

[1850] Bruce Allen, *Boston Sports Media Watch*, 20 May 2004, www.bostonsportsmedia.com/archives/002123.php.

[1851] Ron Borges, "Weis will be good fit for Notre Dame," *NBCSports.com*, Updated: 25 June 2005, www.msnbc.msn.com/id/6703100/.

[1852] Patriots nose tackle Keith Traylor, "Quotes from New England Patriots Media Day," 3 February 2005.

[1853] Troy Brown, "Troy Brown Press Conference," *Patriots.com*, 24 May 2005.

[1854] Ricky Gervais, the actor who plays David Brent in *The Office*, quoted in: "How to Be the World's Worst Boss," *Business 2.0*, May 2004, p. 36.

[1855] Kicker Adam Vinatieri, quoted in: Michael Felger, *Tales From the Patriots Sideline*, Sports Publishing, 2004, pp. 181-2.

[1856] Unnamed "veteran" Patriot, quoted in: Michael Felger, *Tales From the Patriots Sideline*, Sports Publishing, 2004, p. 181.

[1857] Bill Belichick, quoted in: Alan Greenberg, "A Working Relationship," *Hartford Courant*, 9 September 2004, www.ctnow.com/sports/hc-nflpatsmain0908.artsep09.1,2684889.story.

[1858] Patriots inside linebackers coach Pepper Johnson, *Won For All*, Chicago: Contemporary Books, 2003, p. 27.

[1859] Troy Brown, "Troy Brown Press Conference," *Patriots.com*, 24 May 2005.

[1860] Bill Burt, "Bickering Law, Belichick cut from same cloth," *Eagle Tribune*, 18 March 2004, www.eagletribune.com/news/stories/20040318/SP_001.htm.

[1861] Bill Belichick, quoted in: Jeff Goldberg, "Coaching Fraternity," *Hartford Courant*, 1 October 2004, www.ctnow.com/sports/hc-sidecover1001.artoct01.1,4313054.print.story?coll=hc-headlines-sports.

[1862] Former LSU Tiger and current Patriot cornerback Randall Gay, quoted in: Jeff Goldberg, "Coaching Fraternity," *Hartford Courant*, 1 October 2004, www.ctnow.com/sports/hc-sidecover1001.artoct01.1,4313054.print.story?coll=hc-headlines-sports.

[1863] Patriots linebacker Tedy Bruschi, quoted in: Dan O'Neill, "Belichick's gruff football facade gives way to a serious softy," *St. Louis Post-Dispatch*, 1 February 2002, www.ramsfan.us/oldnews/2002/020102-9.htm.

[1864] Jim Nantz, *NFL Today* host, "Observations from 'The NFL Today' anchor desk," *CBS Sportsline*, 20 January 2004, www.sportsline.com/u/football/nfl/nfltoday/overtime.html.

[1865] Cornerback Ty Law, quoted in: Thomas George, "After Years of Waiting, Crennel Moves to Head of Line," *New York Times*, 23 December 2003, p. D1, ProQuest database.

[1866] Ian Fried, "HP board slams Walter Hewlett," *CNET News*, 18 January 2002.

[1867] Steve Belichick, father of Bill Belichick, quoted in: Bill Burt, "More than a coach," *Eagle Tribune*, 25 January 2004, www.eagletribune.com/news/stories/20040125/SP_001.htm.

[1868] Cleveland Browns defensive lineman Orpheus Roye, quoted in: Viv Bernstein, "Proven Winner Tries to Make Browns Win," *New York Times*, 19 August 2005.

[1869] New Patriots defensive coordinator Eric Mangini, quoted in: Jerome Solomon, "Mangini speaks, a bit defensively," *Boston Globe*, 31 August 2005.

[1870] New Patriots defensive coordinator Eric Mangini, quoted in: Jerome Solomon, "Mangini speaks, a bit defensively," *Boston Globe*, 31 August 2005.

[1871] Bill Belichick, quoted in: Seth Wickersham, "It's all about Belichick," *ESPN Insider*, 31 August 2005.

[1872] Corey Dillon, quoted in: Nick Cafardo, "He felt bad, but Dillon carried on after fumble," *Boston Globe*, 23 November 2004.

[1873] Former Patriots star quarterback Drew Bledsoe, quoted in: Ernest Hooper, "N.E.'s Belichick now flexible," *St. Petersburg Times*, 1 September 2000, www.sptimes.com/News/090100/Sports/NE_s_Belichick_now_fl.shtml.

[1874] Patriots linebacker Tedy Bruschi, quoted in: Kevin Mannix, "Top Billing," *Boston Herald*, 31 August 2000, www.allthingsbillbelichick.com/articles/topbilling.htm.

[1875] Bob Hanna, "No captain in this ship," *Standard-Times*, 3 December 1999, www.s-t.com/daily/12-99/12-03-99/d01sp074.htm.

[1876] Ed Duckworth (*Providence Journal Bulletin*), "Langham joins Pats," *Nashua Telegraph*, 29 April 2000, archive.nashuatelegraph.com/Daily_Sections/Sports/Archives/2000/april/stories/0429w-patriots.htm.

[1877] Patriots inside linebackers coach Pepper Johnson, *Won For All*, Chicago: Contemporary Books, 2003, p. 39.

[1878] Patriots inside linebackers coach Pepper Johnson, *Won For All*, Chicago: Contemporary Books, 2003, 37.

[1879] Patriots scout team coach Pepper Johnson, "Quotes from New England Patriots Press Conference," 3 February 2005.

[1880] Sharp president Katsuhiko Machida, quoted in: Mariko Mikami, "Passing the Screen Test," *Business 2.0*, August 2005, p. 38.

[1881] Patriots receiver Deion Branch, quoted in: Jerome Solomon, "Business as usual for Brady," *Boston Globe*, 5 August 2005.

[1882] Colts coach, possibly offensive coordinator Tom Moore, on *21: The Story Behind the NFL's longest winning streak*.

[1883] Defensive end Jarvis Green, quoted in: Mike Kiral, "Green says Patriots aren't feeling pressure to win third straight Super Bowl in 2005," *Ascension Citizen*, 27 July 2005.

[1884] Lawyer Milloy, quoted in: Peter King, "Much more than money," *Sports Illustrated*, 8 February 2005.

[1885] Patriots linebacker Chad Brown, quoted in: Clark Judge, "Camp tour: Pats take care of business in free agency," *Sportsline.com*, 25 August 2005.

[1886] Patriots linebacker Tedy Bruschi, quoted in: Shalise Manza Young, "Patriots Notebook: Brady knows modesty is name of the game for Pats," *Providence Journal*, 22 January 2005, on: BostonBrat.

[1887] Cornerback Asante Samuel, "Quotes From New England Patriots Press Conference," 2 February 2005.

[1888] New Patriots receiver David Terrell, quoted in: Matt Kalman, "Terrell's new Pat-itude: Team first," *Chicago Sun-Times*, 5 August 2005.

[1889] Tedy Bruschi, quoted in: Ira Kaufman, "Patriots Players Hold Themselves To A Higher Standard," *Tampa Tribune*, 31 January 2005.

[1890] Linebacker Roman Phifer, "Quotes From New England Patriots Media Day," 1 February 2005.

[1891] Defensive lineman Richard Seymour, "Quotes from New England Patriots Press Conference," February 2, 2005.

[1892] Patriots left tackle Matt Light, "Quotes from New England Patriots Press Conference," 2 February 2005.

[1893] Jerome Solomon, "Kaczur gets in the mix," *Boston Globe*, 11 August 2005.

[1894] Patriots running back Corey Dillon, quoted in: Chris Kennedy, "Dillon thrilled to stay with Patriots," *The Republican*, 1 August 2005.

[1895] Tight end Christian Fauria, quoted in: Alan Greenberg, "Fauria May Be Caught Out Of Position," *Hartford Courant*, 17 August 2005.

[1896] Former Netscape employee Mike Homer, quoted in: John Battelle, "Reinventing television," *Business 2.0*, June 2005, p. 118.

[1897] Tom Brady, quoted in: David Kamp, "Tom Brady's Glory Days," *GQ*, September 2005.

[1898] Patriots running back Kevin Faulk, "Quotes from New England Patriots Press Conference," 2 February 2005.

[1899] Patriots wide receiver / nickel back / punt returner Troy Brown, "Quotes from New England Patriots Press Conference," 30 January 2005.

[1900] Patriots safety Rodney Harrison, "Quotes From New England Patriots Press Conference," 2 February 2005.

[1901] Patriots linebacker Willie McGinest, "Quotes from New England Patriots Press Conference," 30 January 2005.

[1902] Patriots linebacker Willie McGinest, "Quotes from New England Patriots Press Conference," 30 January 2005.

[1903] Philadelphia Eagles head coach Andy Reid, "Quotes from Philadelphia Eagles Press Conference," 30 January 2005.

[1904] Patriots linebacker Willie McGinest, "Quotes from New England Patriots Press Conference," 30 January 2005.

[1905] Patriots safety Rodney Harrison, quoted in: Jerome Soloman, "Safety patrol: Harrison tries out officiating job," *Boston Globe*, 9 March 2005.

[1906] Patriots safety Rodney Harrison, quoted in: Jim Trotter, "Harrison can't believe washed-up guy has two picks," *San Diego Union-Tribune*, 7 February 2005, www.signonsandiego.com/sports/nfl/20050207-9999-1s7sbnotes.html.

[1907] Rodney Harrison, on *21: The Story Behind the NFL's longest winning streak*.

[1908] Philadelphia Eagles receiver Freddie Mitchell, "Quotes from Philadelphia Eagles Press Conference," 1 February 2005.

[1909] Philadelphia Eagles receiver Freddie Mitchell, "Quotes from Philadelphia Eagles Press Conference," 1 February 2005.

[1910] Patriots linebacker Willie McGinest, "Quotes from New England Patriots Press Session," 2 February 2005.

[1911] Spoof article, "Team Many Calling the "Greatest Ever" Tired of Being Disrespected," 26 January 2005, www.sportspickle.com/features/volume4/2005-0126-patriots.html.

[1912] Philadelphia Eagles receiver Freddie Mitchell, "Quotes from Philadelphia Eagles Press Conference," 3 February 2005.

[1913] Denver Broncos safety John Lynch, quoted in: Gary Shelton, "Harrison dials up heat until pot boils over," *St. Petersburg Times*, 3 February 2005.

[1914] Eagles safety Brian Dawkins, "Quotes from Philadelphia Eagles Media Day," 1 February 2005.

[1915] Eagles safety Michael Lewis, "Quotes from Philadelphia Eagles Media Day," 1 February 2005.

[1916] Patriots safety Rodney Harrison, "Quotes from New England Patriots Press Conference," 30 January 2005.

[1917] Patriots safety Rodney Harrison, "Quotes from New England Patriots Press Conference," 30 January 2005.

[1918] Philadelphia Eagles receiver Freddie Mitchell, "Quotes from Philadelphia Eagles Press Conference," 1 February 2005.

[1919] Terrell Owens, "Quotes from Philadelphia Eagles Press Conference," 3 February 2005.

[1920] Chad Brown, quoted in: Michael Felger, "Humbling experience: Brown caught in middle," Boston Herald, 6 August 2005.

[1921] Terrell Owens, "Quotes from Philadelphia Eagles Press Conference," 3 February 2005.

[1922] Patriots safety Rodney Harrison, quoted in: Tim Smith, "Rodney has Eagles' number, & they'll remember his," New York Daily, 7 February 2005.

[1923] Patriots cornerback Randall Gay, quoted in: John Clayton, "Playing injured, Owens still a handful," ESPN, 6 February 2005.

[1924] Philadelphia Eagles receiver Freddie Mitchell, quoted in: John Tomase, "Mitchell's stinging words," Centre Daily Times, 9 April 2005, www.centredaily.com/mld/centredaily/sports/football/nfl/philadelphia_eagles/11349940.htm.

[1925] Philadelphia Eagles receiver Freddie Mitchell, quoted in: Bob Ford, "Harvard Business School... welcome Fast Freddie's mouth," San Jose Mercury News, 11 April 2005, www.mercurynews.com/mld/mercurynews/sports/11369724.htm.

[1926] Philadelphia Eagles receiver Freddie Mitchell, quoted in: Bob Ford, "Harvard Business School... welcome Fast Freddie's mouth," San Jose Mercury News, 11 April 2005, www.mercurynews.com/mld/mercurynews/sports/11369724.htm.

[1927] Philadelphia Eagles receiver Freddie Mitchell, the morning after the Super Bowl, quoted in: Bob Grotz, "Mitchell's mouth isn't taking any time off," zwire.com, 10 April 2005.

[1928] Philadelphia Eagles receiver Freddie Mitchell, quoted in: John Tomase, "Mitchell's mouth motors on," Gloucester Daily Times, 8 April 2005, www.ecnnews.com/cgi-bin/04/g/gstory.pl?fn-tomase.409.

[1929] Philadelphia Eagles receiver Freddie Mitchell, quoted in: John Tomase, "Mitchell's mouth motors on," Gloucester Daily Times, 8 April 2005, www.ecnnews.com/cgi-bin/04/g/gstory.pl?fn-tomase.409.

[1930] Philadelphia Eagles receiver Freddie Mitchell, quoted in: John Tomase, "Mitchell's stinging words," Centre Daily Times, 9 April 2005, www.centredaily.com/mld/centredaily/sports/football/nfl/philadelphia_eagles/11349940.htm.

[1931] Philadelphia Eagles receiver Freddie Mitchell, quoted in: John Tomase, "Mitchell's stinging words," Philadelphia Inquirer, 9 April 2005, www.philly.com/mld/philly/sports/11349305.htm.

[1932] Philadelphia Eagles receiver Freddie Mitchell, quoted in: Les Bowen, "Mitchell happy to FredExit," Philadelphia Inquirer, 9 May 2005.

[1933] Philadelphia Eagles quarterback Donovan McNabb, "Quotes from Philadelphia Eagles Press Conference," 30 January 2005.

[1934] Patriots linebacker Willie McGinest, "Quotes from New England Patriots Press Conference," 30 January 2005.

[1935] Patriots cornerback Ty Law, quoted in: WEEI Sports Radio 850 AM, "Ty Law with the Big Show on WEEI," 2 March 2005, www.allthingsbillbelichick.com/transcripts/tylawtranscript.htm.

[1936] Patriots cornerback Ty Law, quoted in: WEEI Sports Radio 850 AM, "Ty Law with the Big Show on WEEI," 2 March 2005, www.allthingsbillbelichick.com/transcripts/tylawtranscript.htm.

[1937] Patriots linebacker Willie McGinest, "Quotes from New England Patriots Press Conference," 30 January 2005.

[1938] Patriots safety Rodney Harrison, quoted in: Karen Guregian, "Rodney still ragin'," Boston Herald, 8 September 2005.

[1939] Patriots left tackle Matt Light, "Quotes from New England Press Conference," 2 Febuary 2005.

[1940] Patriots running back Corey Dillon, "Quotes from New England Patriots Press Conference," 2 February 2005.

[1941] Patriots linebacker Ted Johnson, "Quotes from New England Patriots Press Conference," 3 February 2005.

[1942] Patriots receiver Deion Branch, quoted in: Andy Hart, "Super Bowl MVP Branch remains humble," Patriots.com, 30 June 2005.

[1943] Patriots wide receiver / nickel back / punt returner Troy Brown, "Quotes from New England Patriots Press Conference," 30 January 2005.

[1944] Patriots safety Rodney Harrison, "Quotes from New England Patriots Media Day," 1 February 2005.

[1945] Patriots linebacker Mike Vrabel, quoted in: "Quotes from New England Patriots Press Conference," February 3, 2005.

[1946] Patriots VP of player personnel Scott Pioli, quoted in: Vic Carucci, "Pioli reluctantly ends up in the spotlight again," NFL.com, 22 March 2005.

[1947] Tom Brady, "Tom Brady Post Practice Interview," Patriots.com, 4 August 2005.

[1948] Patriots receiver Deion Branch, "Quotes from New England Patriots Press Conference," January 31, 2005.

[1949] Tampa Bay Bucs coach Jon Gruden, Do You Love Football?, 2003, p. 4.

[1950] Harvard Business School professor Nancy Koehn, quoted in: Joshua Hyatt, "The Real Secrets of Entrepreneurs," Fortune, 15 November 2005, p. 186.

[1951] Patriots defensive lineman Marquise Hill, quoted in: Andy Hart, "Hill hopes for greater contribution in '05," Patriots Football Weekly, 6 May 2005.

[1952] Patriots left tackle Matt Light, "Quotes From New England Patriots Press Conference," February 3, 2005.

[1953] Patriots running back Corey Dillon, "Quotes from New England Patriots Media Day," 3 February 2005.

[1954] Defensive lineman Richard Seymour, "Quotes from New England Patriots Press Conference," February 2, 2005.

[1955] Defensive lineman Richard Seymour, "Quotes from New England Patriots Press Conference," February 2, 2005.

[1956] Patriots kicker Adam Vinatieri, "Quotes from New England Patriots Press Conference," February 2, 2005.

[1957] Patriots kicker Adam Vinatieri, "Quotes from New England Patriots Press Conference," February 2, 2005.

[1958] Patriots kicker Adam Vinatieri, quoted in: Michael Felger, "Woicik fosters winning conditions," Boston Herald, 8 September 2005.

[1959] Patriots nose tackle Vince Wilfork, "Quotes from New England Patriots Press Conference," 3 February 2005.

[1960] Patriots nose tackle Keith Traylor, "Quotes from New England Patriots Media Day," 3 February 2005.

[1961] Patriots nose tackle Vince Wilfork, "Quotes from New England Patriots Press Conference," 3 February 2005.

[1962] Patriots wide receiver Deion Branch, quoted in: Hector Longo, "Patriots grab a Deion in round 2," Eagle-Tribune, 20 April 2002, www.eagletribune.com/news/stories/20020421/SP_017.htm.

[1963] Patriots linebacker Willie McGinest, quoted in: Karen Guregian, "Survivors laud Bill," Boston Herald, 8 September 2005.

[1964] Patriots rookie cornerback Ellis Hobbs, quoted in: Jerome Solomon, "Hobbs covering all the angles," Boston Globe, 15 August 2005.

[1965] Bill Belichick, in speech at Bryant University, quoted in: Steve Mazzone, "Belichick keynote speaker at Bryant," The Herald News, 1 April 2005, www.zwire.com/site/news.cfm?newsid=14263950.

[1966] Patriots inside linebackers coach Pepper Johnson, Won For All, Chicago: Contemporary Books, 2003, p. 91.

[1967] Patriots safety Rodney Harrison, quoted in: Michael Felger, "Safety fire -- Harrison's intensity sparks Pats," Boston Herald, 25 August 2005.

[1968] Patriots offensive lineman Joe Andruzzi, "Quotes from New England Patriots Press Conference," 30 January 2005.

[1969] Patriots linebacker Rosevelt Colvin, "Quotes From New England Patriots Media Day," 1 February 2005.

[1970] Bill Belichick, "Quotes from New England Patriots Press Conference," 30 January 2005.

[1971] Defensive coordinator and former secondary coach Eric Mangini, quoted in: Karen Guregian, "Kraft tries to put lid on Tedy talk," Boston Herald, 2 September 2005.

[1972] Cleveland Browns broadcaster Casey Coleman, quoted in: Terry Pluto, "The Man Behind the Mask," Akron Beacon Journal, 18 December 1994, www.allthingsbillbelichick.com/articles/behindthemask.htm.

[1973] Former Cleveland Browns center Mike Baab, quoted in: Terry Pluto, "The Man Behind the Mask," Akron Beacon Journal, 18 December 1994, www.allthingsbillbelichick.com/articles/behindthemask.htm.

[1974] Bill Belichick, quoted in: Jerome Solomon, "Another round at Oval Office," Boston Globe, 14 April 2005, www.boston.com/sports/football/patriots/articles/2005/04/14/another_round_at_oval_office/.

[1975] Patriots defensive coordinator Romeo Crennel, "Quotes from New England Patriots Media Day," 1 February 2005.

[1976] Patriots defensive coordinator Romeo Crennel, "Quotes from New England Patriots Media Day," 1 February 2005.

[1977] Patriots defensive coordinator Romeo Crennel, "Quotes from New England Patriots Media Day," 1 February 2005.

[1978] Patriots inside linebackers coach Pepper Johnson, Won For All, Chicago: Contemporary Books, 2003, p. 92.

[1979] "Reality TV stint humbles California Pizza Kitchen co-CEOs," PizzaMarketplace.com, www.pizzamarketplace.com/research_18376_127.htm.

[1980] Patriots linebacker Mike Vrabel, "Quotes from New England Patriots Press Conference," 31 January 2005.

[1981] Patriots offensive coordinator Charlie Weis, quoted in: Michael Felger, "Weis sets record straight," 9 June 2004, MetroWest Daily News, www.metrowestdailynews.com/sportsNews/view.bg?articleid=70314.

[1982] Charlie Weis, quoted in: Mark Blaudschun, "Weis gives it the old college try," Boston Globe, 14 August 2005.

[1983] Charlie Weis, quoted in: Colin Burns, "News and Notes 8-15-2005," NotreDame.scout.com, 15 August 2005.

[1984] Charlie Weis, quoted in: Colin Burns, "News and Notes 8-15-2005," NotreDame.scout.com, 15 August 2005.

[1985] Bill Belichick, quoted in: Charles P. Pierce, "Three Days, One Life," Sports Illustrated, 18 October 2004, p. 73.

[1986] Patriots linebacker Rosevelt Colvin, quoted in: Mike Holbrook, "Colvin's increased chatter signals return to pre-injury form," *ProFootballWeekly.com*, 2 August 2005.

[1987] Bill Belichick, "A Special Championship Contribution," in: Bryan Morry, *Patriots United*, Canada: Team Power Publishing, 2002, p. 64.

[1988] Bill Belichick, quoted in: Jim Donaldson, "It's about time to pick the Patriots for a change," *Providence Journal*, 16 September 2002, www.southcoasttoday.com/daily/09-02/09-16-02/c10sp115.htm.

[1989] Patriots offensive lineman Joe Andruzzi, "Quotes from New England Patriots Press Conference," 30 January 2005.

[1990] Romeo Crennel, audio recording, 2 February 2005.

[1991] Woody Hayes, on: Desmond Wilcox, "Americans: The Football Coach," aired on: *ESPN Classic*, 1 June 2005.

[1992] Patriots linebacker Chad Brown, quoted in: David Borges, "Patriots' LBs still a work in progress," *Herald News*, 15 August 2005.

[1993] Patriots linebacker Rosevelt Colvin, quoted in: Adam Kilgore, "With mind at ease, Colvin is now getting ahead," *Boston Globe*, 16 August 2005.

[1994] Patriot linebacker Monty Beisel, quoted in: Jackie MacMullan, "Change is their constant," *Boston Globe*, 25 August 2005.

[1995] Patriots quarterback Doug Flutie, quoted in: Mike Lowe, "NFL's model for success? The Patriots," *MaineToday.com*, 12 June 2005.

[1996] Charlie Weis, quoted in: Ian O'Connor, "When boring Bill smiles," *The Journal News*, 6 February 2005.

[1997] Charlie Nobles, "Dolphins' New Coach Casts a Grimace in the Mold of Shula," *New York Times*, 24 July 2005.

[1998] Defensive lineman Richard Seymour, quoted in: Michael Parente, "Seymour back in action," *Herald News*, 4 August 2005.

[1999] Bill Belichick, quoted in: Karen Guregian, "Pats' future on the line," *Boston Herald*, 7 August 2005.

[2000] Bill Belichick, audio recording, 1 February 2005.

[2001] Patriots linebacker Mike Vrabel, quoted in: "Quotes from New England Patriots Press Conference," February 3, 2005.

[2002] Linebacker Mike Vrabel, "Quotes from New England Patriots Media Day," 1 February 2005.

[2003] Patriots safety Rodney Harrison, quoted in: Alan Greenberg, "Pats Pick It Up In Second Half," *Hartford Courant*, 4 October 2004, www.ctnow.com/sports/football/patriots/hc-patriots1004.artoct04,1,3287450.print.story.

[2004] Defensive lineman Richard Seymour, quoted in: Michael Parente, "Seymour back in action," *Herald News*, 4 August 2005.

[2005] Bill Belichick, "Quotes From New England Patriots Media Day," 1 February 2005.

[2006] Bill Belichick, *21: The Story Behind the NFL's longest winning streak*.

[2007] Patriots offensive lineman Joe Andruzzi, "Quotes from New England Patriots Press Conference," 30 January 2005.

[2008] Massachusetts General Hospital president Peter L. Slavin, quoted in: Charles Stein, "Bill Belichick, CEO," *Boston Globe*, 28 January 2004.

[2009] Notre Dame football head coach and former Patriots offensive coordinator Charlie Weis, quoted in: Associated Press, "Weis not interested in recent struggles," *ChicagoSports.com*, 28 March 2005.

[2010] Steve Belichick, father of Bill Belichick, quoted in: Ian O'Connor, "Invincibility of Belichick enhanced by his invisibility," *USA Today*, 19 January 2004, www.usatoday.com/sports/columnist/oconnor/2004-01-20-oconnor_x.htm.

[2011] Patriots linebacker Rosevelt Colvin, "Quotes From New England Patriots Media Day," 1 February 2005.

[2012] Bill Belichick, "Bill Belichick Press Conf. Transcript - 9/14/2004," *Patriots.com*, 14 September 2004, www.patriots.com/Common/PrintThis.sps?id=30535.

[2013] Patriots linebacker Willie McGinest, "Quotes From New England Patriots Media Day," 1 February 2005.

[2014] Notre Dame head coach Charlie Weis, quoted in: Terry Shields, "Notre Dame offense sharp, different in debut," *Pittsburgh Post-Gazette*, 24 April 2005.

[2015] Patriots cornerback / wide receiver Troy Brown, "Quotes From New England Patriots Press Conference," January 30, 2005.

[2016] Scott Pioli, Patriots VP of player personnel, quoted in: Allen Wilson, "NFL labor negotiations reach a dead end in paradise," *Buffalo News*, 27 March 2005, www.buffalonews.com/editorial/20050327/1030325.asp.

[2017] Patriots inside linebackers coach Pepper Johnson, *Won For All*, Chicago: Contemporary Books, 2003, p. 67.

[2018] Patriots inside linebackers coach Pepper Johnson, *Won For All*, Chicago: Contemporary Books, 2003, p. 101.

[2019] Patriots nose tackle Vince Wilfork, quoted in: Dan Pires, "INSIDE THE PATRIOTS: Wilfork feels he's ready to step up," *Standard-Times*, 29 May 2005.

[2020] Patriots nose tackle Keith Traylor, "Quotes from New England Patriots Media Day," 3 February 2005.

[2021] Bill Belichick, quoted in: Tom E. Curran, "Trying Brown at DB a matter of depth," *Providence Journal*, 15 August 2004, www.projo.com/patriots/content/projo_20040815_15beat.136343.html.

[2022] Patriots inside linebackers coach Pepper Johnson, *Won For All*, Chicago: Contemporary Books, 2003, p. 19.

[2023] Patriots cornerback Duane Starks, quoted in: Eric McHugh, "CASHING IN: Cornerback Gay rewarded for playing time," *Patriot Ledger*, 4 August 2005.

[2024] Jarrett Bell, "NFL weighs ban, policing of 'horse-collar' tackles," *USA Today*, 23 March 2005, www.usatoday.com/sports/football/nfl/2005-03-22-horse-collar-ban_x.htm.

[2025] Quotes retold by Bill Belichick, quoted in: Tom Curran, "Sounds like fun," *Projo.com PatsBlog*, 30 July 2005.

[2026] Patriots linebacker Willie McGinest, quoted in: Howard Bryant, "All together now: Patriots LBs shed the hits, stick to plan," *Boston Herald*, 29 January 2004.

[2027] Patriots kick returner Chad Morton, quoted in: Mark Farinella, "Morton hopes for the big return," *Sun Chronicle*, 11 August 2005.

[2028] Patriots linebacker Ted Johnson, quoted in: Barry Wilner (AP), "Patriots lose another key player as other NFL stars hold out ," *SFGate.com*, 29 July 2005.

[2029] Patriots linebacker Rosevelt Colvin, quoted in: Dan Pires, "Ch-ch-ch-ch-changes at Patriots camp," *Standard-Times*, 30 July 2005.

[2030] Pat Kirwan, "Belichick setting the standard in the NFL," *NFL.com*, 16 September 2002, www.nfl.com/teams/story/NE/5721265.

[2031] Bill Belichick, quoted in: Mark Gaughan, "Pats riding the crest of a brain wave," *Buffalo News*, 2 October 2004, www.buffalonews.com/editorial/20041002/1003819.asp.

[2032] Eagles safety Brian Dawkins, "Quotes from Philadelphia Eagles Media Day," 1 February 2005.

[2033] Patriots inside linebackers coach Pepper Johnson, *Won For All*, Chicago: Contemporary Books, 2003, p. 86-87.

[2034] Eagles cornerback Sheldon Brown, "Quotes from Philadelphia Eagles Press Conference," 2 February 2005.

[2035] Eagles linebacker Dhani Jones, "Quotes from Philadelphia Eagles Press Conference," 2 February 2005.

[2036] Patriots quarterback Tom Brady, quoted in: Tom E. Curran, "Patriots fly better when they spread their wings," *Providence Journal*, 16 September 2003, www.projo.com/patriots/content/projo_20030916_16patscol.c43a9.html.

[2037] Patriots receiver Troy Brown, quoted in: Joe Burris, "Can Szabo corner the market?" *Boston Globe*, 2 October 2004, www.boston.com/sports/football/patriots/articles/2004/10/02/can_szabo_corner_the_market.

[2038] Tom Brady, quoted in: Paul Attner, " Whatever 'It' is, Brady has 'It,'" *Sports Illustrated*, 6 October 2004, http://msn.foxsports.com/story/3059636.

[2039] Tom Brady, "Tom Brady Post Practice Interview," *Patriots.com*, 4 August 2005.

[2040] Eagles cornerback Sheldon Brown, "Quotes from Philadelphia Eagles Press Conference," 2 February 2005.

[2041] KC Joyner, The Football Scientist, *Scientific Football 2005* (KC's Football Services, Altamonte Springs, FL, 2005), p. 308.

[2042] Len Pasquarelli, "Patriots suddenly struggling to address woes," *ESPN*, 31 October 2002, http://espn.go.com/nfl/columns/pasquarelli_len/1453171.html.

[2043] Len Pasquarelli, "Patriots suddenly struggling to address woes," *ESPN*, 31 October 2002, http://espn.go.com/nfl/columns/pasquarelli_len/1453171.html.

[2044] Quarterbacks coach Josh McDaniels, quoted in: Mark Farinella, "Patriots Notebook," *Sun Chronicle*, 5 August 2005.

[2045] Tom Brady, quoted in: Mark Farinella, "Patriots Notebook," *Sun Chronicle*, 5 August 2005.

[2046] Tom Brady, quoted in: "New England Patriots Quarterback Tom Brady: Post Practice Interview," email, 16 August 2005.

[2047] Tom Brady, quoted in: "New England Patriots Quarterback Tom Brady: Post Practice Interview," email, 16 August 2005.

[2048] Pete Thamel, "Building Programs Using Belichick's Blueprint," 18 September 2004, www.nytimes.com/2004/09/18/sports/ncaafootball/18college.html.

[2049] Charlie Weis, quoted in: Heather VanHoegarden, "CHARLIE WEIS: Family and football," *The Observer*, 22 April 2005.

[2050] Maura Weis, quoted in: Cindy Ward, "ND job perfect fit for Weises," *South Bend Tribune*, 1 August 2005.

[2051] Bill Parcells, quoted by Charlie Weis in: Vahe Gregorian, "Notre Dame hopes Weis has healing touch," *St. Louis Today*, 5 May 2005.

[2052] Steve Belichick, father of Bill Belichick, quoted in: Terry Pluto, "The Man Behind the Mask," *Akron Beacon Journal*, 18 December 1994, www.allthingsbillbelichick.com/articles/behindthemask.htm.

[2053] Patriots inside linebackers coach Pepper Johnson, *Won For All*, Chicago: Contemporary Books, 2003, p. 171.

[2054] Former Patriots defensive lineman Chad Eaton, quoted in: Alan Greenberg, "Getting Along Well Belichick Still A Little Grim, But With A Grin," *Hartford Courant*, 3 September 2000, p. E1, ProQuest database.

[2055] Rodney Harrison, quoted in: Ian O'Connor, "When boring Bill smiles," *The Journal News*, 6 February 2005.

[2056] Michael Holley, "Best seat in the house," *Boston Globe*, 7 December 2000, www.allthingsbillbelichick.com/articles/bestseat.htm.

[2057] "The Coach," *60 Minutes*, aired on CBS 19 September 2004.

[2058] Coach Bill Belichick, quoted in: Ethan Butterfield, "Familiar Face In Foxboro," *Inquirer and Mirror*, 17 August 2000, www.allthingsbillbelichick.com/articles/familiarface.htm.

[2059] Bill Belichick, "Lacrosse bonds Belichick, daughter," *NFL Network*, video on *NFL.com*, June 2005.

[2060] "A spy," quoted in: Gayle Fee and Laura Raposa, "Hard-driving Belichick, wife of 28 years separate," *Boston Herald*, 14 July 2005.

[2061] Unnamed NFL executive, cited in: Mike Freeman, *Bloody Sundays*, Perennial Currents: USA, 2003, pp. 7-8.

[2062] Tom Brady, quoted in: Bryan Morry, "Managing the Moment," *Lindy's 2004 Pro Football*, p. 10.

[2063] Tampa Bay Bucs coach Jon Gruden, *Do You Love Football?*, 2003, p. 3.

[2064] Tampa Bay Bucs coach Jon Gruden, *Do You Love Football?*, 2003, p. 63.

[2065] Tampa Bay Bucs coach Jon Gruden, *Do You Love Football?*, 2003, p. 64.

[2066] Tampa Bay Bucs coach Jon Gruden, *Do You Love Football?*, 2003, p. 4.

[2067] Dan Pompei, "Inside Pats' Super Bowl Preparations," *Sporting News*, 2 February 2004, www.allthingsbillbelichick.com/articles/insidesbprep.htm.

[2068] Patriots safety Rodney Harrison, quoted in: Michael Felger, "Safety fire -- Harrison's intensity sparks Pats," *Boston Herald*, 25 August 2005.

[2069] Linebacker Mike Vrabel, quoted in: John MacKenna, "Patriots Camp: Vrabel Thinks Things Will Be Ok," *PatriotsInsider.com*, 1 August 2005.

[2070] Bill Belichick, quoted in: Pat Kirwan, "Despite changes, Pats ready for another run," *NFL.com*, 31 July 2005.

[2071] Bill Belichick, quoted in: Tom E. Curran, "Pack of reasons to pay attention to this exhibition," *Providence Journal*, 26 August 2005.

[2072] Patriots safety Rodney Harrison, quoted in: Jerome Solomon, "Belichick has team focused," *Boston Globe*, 26 August 2005.

[2073] Steve Jobs, CEO of Apple and Pixar, speech at Stanford University graduation, reprinted in: "Stay Hungry. Stay Foolish." *Fortune*, 5 September 2005.

[2074] "A tough drop for Bledsoe," *Boston Globe*, 20 February 2005, www.boston.com/sports/football/articles/2005/02/20/a_tough_drop_for_bledsoe.

[2075] Troy Brown, "Troy Brown Press Conference," *Patriots.com*, 24 May 2005.

[2076] Troy Brown, "Troy Brown Press Conference," *Patriots.com*, 24 May 2005.

[2077] "Pats24Pitt17," posted on the *Boston.com* "Patriots Board," 27 May 2005.

[2078] Patriots linebacker Ted Johnson, quoted in: Tom E. Curran, "Bruschi decision eases minds, leaves void," *Providence Journal*, 24 July 2005.

[2079] New Patriots linebacker Monty Beisel, quoted in: Tom King, " Hopes are high for Pats' Beisel," *Nashua Telegraph*, 1 August 2005.

[2080] Patriots receiver Deion Branch, quoted in: Eric McHugh, "At 5-9, Branch stands tall for Pats," *Patriot Ledger*, 1 September 2005.

[2081] Patriots special teams captain Larry Izzo, "Quotes from New England Patriots Press Conference," 30 January 2005.

[2082] Patriots nose tackle Ted Washington, quoted in: Paul Perillo and Bryan Morry, "Patriots Notebook," *Patriots Football Weekly*, 28 January 2004, www.patriots.com/news/fullarticle.sps?id=27835&type=general&special_section=SuperBowlXXXVIII.

[2083] Patriots offensive lineman Joe Andruzzi, "Quotes from New England Patriots Press Conference," 30 January 2005.

[2084] Patriots wide receiver / nickel back / punt returner Troy Brown, "Quotes from New England Patriots Press Conference," 30 January 2005.

[2085] Patriots offensive coordinator Charlie Weis, quoted in: Avani Patel, "Pro pedigree can only help Irish," *ChicagoSports.com (Chicago Tribune)*, 8 April 2005.

[2086] Patriots wide receiver / nickel back / punt returner Troy Brown, "Quotes from New England Patriots Press Conference," 30 January 2005.

[2087] Patriots special teams captain Larry Izzo, "Quotes from New England Patriots Press Conference," 30 January 2005.

[2088] Patriots owner Robert Kraft, quoted in: Paul Perillo and Bryan Morry, "Patriots Notebook," *Patriots Football Weekly*, 28 January 2004, www.patriots.com/news/fullarticle.sps?id=27835&type=general&special_section=SuperBowlXXXVIII.

[2089] Bill Belichick, quoted in: AP, "Belichick sees improvement in Patriots defense," *Gainesville.com*, 27 August 2005.

[2090] Tennessee Volunteers linebacker Jason Mitchell, quoted in: Elizabeth A. Davis, "Vols Defeat Bulldogs 42-17 On Homecoming," *UTSports.com*, 25 September 2004.

[2091] Tedy Bruschi, quoted in: John McClain, "Former president makes a plug for Houston on the NFL Network," *Houston Chronicle*, 29 January 2004.

[2092] Patriots tight end Christian Fauria, quoted in: Michael Smith, "Pats capitalize on others' mistakes," *ESPN*, 3 October 2004, http://sports.espn.go.com/nfl/columns/story?id=1894443.

[2093] Patriots tight end Christian Fauria, quoted in: Tom E. Curran, "Pats squarely on the mark," *Providence Journal*, 4 October 2004, www.projo.com/patriots/content/projo_20041004_04pats.9472c.html.

[2094] Wide receiver David Givens, quoted in: Michael Smith, "After blocking it all out, offensive line is secure," *Boston Globe*, 2 February 2004, www.boston.com/sports/football/patriots/articles/2004/02/02/after_blocking_it_all_out_offensive_line_is_secure.

[2095] Bill Belichick, quoted in: Frank Tadych and Andy Hart, "Patriots Notebook: Belichick declares run defense a priority," *Patriots.com*, 6 September 2004, www.patriots.com/news/fullarticle.sps?id=30510.

[2096] Willie McGinest, on *21: The Story Behind the NFL's longest winning streak*.

[2097] Charlie Weis, on *21: The Story Behind the NFL's longest winning streak*.

[2098] Patriots receiver Deion Branch, quoted in: Mike Reiss, "Dillon's delight," *Boston Herald* blog, 31 January 2005, www.bostonherald.com/blogs/reissPieces/index.bg.

[2099] Eagles head coach Andy Reid, quoted in: Chris Colston (*USA Today*), "Philadelphia Eagles Pool Report," 3 February 2005.

[2100] Patriots quarterback Tom Brady, "Quotes from New England Patriots Press Conference," 30 January 2005.

[2101] Patriots linebacker Tedy Bruschi, "Quotes from New England Patriots Press Conference," 31 January 2005.

[2102] Patriots linebacker Tedy Bruschi, quoted in: Michael Parente, "Patriots size up playoff opponents," *Taunton Gazette*, 18 January 2004.

[2103] Bill Belichick, quoted in: Harvey Mackay, *We Got Fired!*, New York: Ballantine Books, 2004, p. 63.

[2104] Bill Belichick, "An Interview with New England Patriots Head Coach Bill Belichick," 4 February 2005.

[2105] Patriots cornerback Tyrone Poole, quoted in: Damon Hack, "No-Nonsense Belichick Attracts No-Nonsense Players," *New York Times*, 10 August 2003, section 8, p. 4, ProQuest database.

[2106] Patriots kicker Adam Vinatieri, "Quotes from New England Patriots Media Day," 1 February 2005.

[2107] Bill Belichick, on: *3 Games to Glory III* DVD, 2005.

[2108] Bill Belichick, quoted in: "New England Patriots head coach Bill Belichick: Post-Game Press Conference," email, 18 August 2005.

[2109] Andreas Burzik, M.Ps., "On the Neurophysiology of Flow," 2nd European Conference on Positive Psychology, 5-8 July 2004, www.gallup-europe.be/PositivePsychology/Pos%20Psy/BURZIK%20Andras_Neurophysiology%20of%20Flow.pdf.

[2110] Arizona State professor Debbie Crews, "ASU Researcher Awarded Prize for Best Science in Golf," Arizona State news release, 31 January 2001, http://clasdean.la.asu.edu/news/golfscience.htm.

[2111] Brett N. Steenbarger, Ph.D., " Finding the Zone: New Perspectives on the Mental Game of Trading," *ActionForex.com*,

[2112] Susan A. Jackson and Mihaly Csikszentmihalyi, *Flow in Sports*, www.humankinetics.com/products/showexcerpt.cfm?excerpt_id=3101.

[2113] "A practical intro to staying cool & calm in the clutch," www.competitivedge.com/athletes4.htm.

[2114] Patriots cornerback Duane Starks, quoted in: Michael Parente, "Playoff savvy the calling card for Starks," *Herald News*, 9 August 2005.

[2115] Quotes from Bob Carter, "Unitas surprised them all," *ESPN.com*, http://espn.go.com/sportscentury/features/00016574.html.

[2116] Patriots receiver Deion Branch, "Quotes from New England Patriots Press Conference," 31 January 2005. And *ESPN* video 1 February 2005.

[2117] Patriots receiver Deion Branch, "Quotes from New England Patriots Press Conference," January 31, 2005.

[2118] Cornerback Asante Samuel, "Quotes From New England Patriots Press Conference," 2 February 2005.

[2119] Patriots nose tackle Vince Wilfork, "Quotes from New England Patriots Press Conference," 3 February 2005.

[2120] Jimmy Johnson, endorsement of Susan A. Jackson and Mihaly Csikszentmihalyi, *Flow in Sports*, on: www.humankinetics.com/products/showproduct.cfm?isbn=0880118768.

[2121] T.J. Berka, "Where, when will roller coaster ride end for Michigan?" *Michigan Daily*, 15 November 1999, www.patriotsplanet.com/BB/showthread.php?threadid=11035.

[2122] Michigan fullback Aaron Shea, quoted in: Michael Rosenberg, "Brady glad maturity finally came to pass," *Detroit Free Press*, 27 December 1999, www.patriotsplanet.com/BB/showthread.php?s=&threadid=6999.

[2123] Patriots offensive tackle Matt Light, quoted in: "Patriots Post-Game Quotes," *Patriots.com*, 18 January 2004, http://www.patriots.com/games/GamesDetails.sps?matchreportid=27472&matchid=27282.

[2124] Patriots cornerback Ty Law, quoted in: Mark Gaughan, "Pats riding the crest of a brain wave," *Buffalo News*, 2 October 2004, www.buffalonews.com/editorial/20041002/1003819.asp.

[2125] Tom Brady, quoted in: AP, "Bunch of success," *CNNSI.com*, 4 February 2002, http://sportsillustrated.cnn.com/football/2002/playoffs/news/2002/02/03/brady_mvp_ap/.

[2126] Tom Brady, quoted in: Tim Polzer, "Super Bowl XXXVI: New England 20, St. Louis 17," 3 February 2002, www.superbowl.com/history/mvps/game/sbxxxvi.

[2127] Bill Griffith, quoted in: Bill Griffith, "Belichick analysis gives DVD extra points," *Boston Globe*, 25 April 2004, www.boston.com/sports/football/patriots/articles/2004/04/25/belichick_analysis_gives_dvd_extra_points/.

[2128] Patriots defensive lineman Richard Seymour, quoted in: Michael Felger, "Weis sets record straight," 9 June 2004, *MetroWest Daily News*, www.metrowestdailynews.com/sportsNews/view.bg?articleid=70314.

[2129] Patriots free agent linebacker tryout Grant Steen, quoted in: Michael Felger, "Belichick method comes full circle," *Boston Herald*, 3 May 2004, http://patriots.bostonherald.com/patriots/view.bg?articleid=18878.

[2130] Dr. Peter F. Drucker, *Management: Tasks, Responsibilities, Practices*, USA: HarperCollins, 1973, p. 154.

[2131] Patriots owner Robert Kraft, quoted in: John Wiebusch, "Pats' Kraft has had a year to remember," *NFL Insider*, 9 September 2002, www.nfl.com/insider/story/5688930.

[2132] Patriots VP of Player Personnel Scott Pioli, quoted in: Kevin Paul Dupont, "Pioli Finding Success With Patriots," *Boston Globe*, 13 January 2002, www.allthingsbillbelichick.com/articles/piolisuccess.htm.

[2133] Michael Holley, "More than Xs and Os," in: *Again!*, Chicago: Triumph Books, 2004, p. 101.

[2134] Michael Felger, "Hamilton a tough loss for Pats," *Boston Herald*, 23 May 2004, http://patriots.bostonherald.com/patriots/view.bg?articleid=28994.

[2135] Ed Duckworth, "Belichick gives Brisby the nod," *South Coast Today*, 24 July 2000, www.s-t.com/daily/07-00/07-24-00/c03sp090.htm.

[2136] Michael Felger, "Pats extend Brown through 2005," *Boston Herald*, 25 May 2004, http://patriots.bostonherald.com/patriots/view.bg?articleid=29235.

[2137] Bill Belichick, as recollected by Tom Brady, quoted in: Tom E. Curran, "Tom Curran: Brady, Belichick seem perfect for each other," *Providence Journal*, 12 August 2004, www.projo.com/patriots/content/projo_20040812_12currcol.dcb5f.html.

[2138] Bill Belichick, "Quotes from New England Patriots Press Conference," 30 January 2005.

[2139] Bill Belichick, speech at Bryant University, quoted in: Mike Reiss, "Leftovers from Belichick," 31 March 2005, www.bostonherald.com/blogs/reissPieces/index.bg.

[2140] Gary Shelton, "Story, as usual, is Sapp," *St. Petersburg Times*, 28 January 2004, www.sptimes.com/2004/01/28/Columns/Story_as_usual_is_S.shtml.

[2141] Patriots owner Robert Kraft, quoted in: Chris Kennedy, "Pats: Lords of the Rings," *The Republican*, 14 June 2004, www.masslive.com/sports/republican/index.ssf?/base/sports-0/1087199302168670.xml.

[2142] Pats fan Lou Schorr, quoted in: AP, "Patriots linebacker gets back Super Bowl ring left in mall washroom," 23 June 2004, www.canada.com/sports/football/story.html?id=A5791CC6-CF35-4B11-92C4-E14F43AE1309.

[2143] Patriots linebacker Tedy Bruschi, quoted in: Chris Kennedy, "Pats: Lords of the Rings," *The Republican*, 14 June 2004, www.masslive.com/sports/republican/index.ssf?/base/sports-0/1087199302168670.xml.

[2144] Patriots practice squad wide receiver Chas Gessner, quoted in: Andy Hart, "Gessner looking forward to camp competition," *Patriots Football Weekly*, 28 June 2004, www.patriots.com/news/FullArticle.sps?id=29544.

[2145] Patriots safety Rodney Harrison, quoted in: Rich Eisen, "A conversation with Rodney Harrison," *NFL.com*, 19 July 2004, www.nfl.com/nflnetwork/story/7513397.

[2146] Cornerback Ty Law, quoted in: Mark Pratt, "Patriots receive Super Bowl rings," *Providence Journal*, 14 June 2004, www.projo.com/ap/ne/1087191008.htm.

[2147] Bob Kraft, quoted in: Howard Balzer, "New England rings out the old year," *USA Today*, 24 June 2004, www.usatoday.com/sports/football/columnist/balzer/2004-06-24-super-rings_x.htm.

[2148] Cleveland Browns linebacker Kenard Lang, quoted in: Tom Withers, "Crennel Shows Browns Super Bowl Ring," *SFGate.com*, 14 June 2005.

[2149] Bob Kraft, quoted in: Howard Ulman (AP), "Patriots Get Super Bowl Rings," *Los Angeles Times*, 12 June 2005.

[2150] Corey Dillon quoted in: Bryan Morry, "Latest ring wows Pats," *Patriots.com*, 13 June 2005.

[2151] Jacob Gershman, "Putin Pockets Patriots Ring," *New York Sun*, 28 June 2005.

[2152] Pat Kirwan, "Despite changes, Pats ready for another run," *NFL.com*, 31 July 2005.

[2153] Patriots owner Robert Kraft, quoted in: Jarrett Bell, "Piecing the Patriots together," *USA Today*, 21 April 2005.

[2154] Patriots running back Corey Dillon, "Quotes from New England Patriots Press Conference," 2 February 2005.

[2155] Patriots safety Rodney Harrison, "Quotes From New England Patriots Press Conference," 2 February 2005.

[2156] Tom Brady, on *21: The Story Behind the NFL's longest winning streak*.

[2157] Patriots linebacker Ted Johnson, "Patriots Video News," *Patriots.com*, 30 June 2005.

[2158] Patriots linebacker Tedy Bruschi, "Quotes from New England Patriots Media Session," 2 February 2005.

[2159] Tom Brady, "Quotes from New England Patriots Press Conference," February 2, 2005.

[2160] Tight end Christian Fauria, quoted in: Alan Greenberg, "Fauria May Be Caught Out Of Position," *Hartford Courant*, 17 August 2005.

[2161] Patriots receiver Troy Brown, "Quotes from New England Patriots Press Conference" February 2, 2005.

[2162] Patriots running back Corey Dillon, "Quotes From New England Patriots Media Day," 3 February 2005.

[2163] Mike Vrabel, audio recording of *ESPN* broadcast on morning of 2 February 2005.

[2164] Tedy Bruschi, audio recording of *ESPN* broadcast on morning of 2 February 2005.

[2165] Patriots kicker Adam Vinatieri, "Quotes from New England Media Session," 3 Febuary 2005.

[2166] Special teamer and backup linebacker/safety Don Davis, quoted in: Mike Reiss, "Davis adds to role," *Boston Herald* blog, 8 July 2005.

[2167] Patriots punter Josh Miller, "Quotes from New England Press Session," 3 Febuary 2005.

[2168] Bill Belichick, "An Interview With New England Patriots Head Coach Bill Belichick," 4 February 2005.

[2169] Bill Belichick, "An Interview With New England Patriots Head Coach Bill Belichick," 4 February 2005.

[2170] Patriots defensive lineman Richard Seymour , "Quotes from New England Patriots Press Session," 3 February 2005.

[2171] Patriots receiver Troy Brown, quoted in: Michael Felger, "Weis a camp counselor," *Boston Herald*, 2 August 2005.

[2172] Dr. Peter F. Drucker, *Management: Tasks, Responsibilities, Practices*, USA: HarperCollins, 1973, pp. 128 & 100.

[2173] Bill Belichick, quoted in: Michael Felger, "One last haul for Bavaro?" *Boston Herald*, 24 July 2005.

[2174] Unnamed NFL scout, quoted in: Michael Felger, "Watson catching on: TE could be key for Pats," *Boston Herald*, 25 July 2005.

[2175] Michael Felger, "Backup's for grabs -- Cobbs could spell Dillon," *Boston Herald*, 26 July 2005.

[2176] Patriots "capologist" Andy Wasynczuk, quoted in: Nick Cafardo, The Impossible Team, Triumph Books, 2002, p. 19.

[2177] Nick Cafardo, *The Impossible Team*, Triumph Books, 2002, p. 20.

[2178] Tom Brady, quoted in: Jim Litke, "Cool, calm Brady gets it done yet again," *MSNBC.com*, 25 January 2004, http://msnbc.msn.com/id/3995389/.

[2179] Data from: Michael Smith, "Whipping them into shape," *Boston Globe*, 27 June 2004, www.boston.com/sports/football/patriots/articles/2004/06/27/whipping_them_into_shape.

[2180] Nick Cafardo, "Patriots, top pick agree," *Boston Globe*, 20 July 2004, www.boston.com/sports/football/patriots/articles/2004/07/20/patriots_top_pick_agree.

[2181] Patriots linebacker Tedy Bruschi, "Quotes from New England Media Day," 1 February 2005.

[2182] Patriots defensive coordinator Romeo Crennel, "Quotes from New England Patriots Media Day," 1 February 2005.

[2183] Patriots receiver Bethel Johnson, quoted in: Michael Parente, " Johnson clouds WR picture," *Woonsocket Call*, 2 September 2005.

[2184] Cornerback/safety Eugene Wilson, "Quotes from New England Patriots Press Conference," February 2, 2005.

[2185] Troy Brown, quoted in: Ron Borges, "Patriots veteran Brown is leery about cutdown," *Boston Globe*, 29 August 2005.

[2186] Bill Belichick, quoted in: Steve Corkran, "Formula is secret to Patriots' success," *San Jose Mercury News*, 7 September 2005.

[2187] Patriots linebacker Chad Brown, quoted in: Clark Judge, "Camp tour: Pats take care of business in free agency," *Sportsline.com*, 25 August 2005.

[2188] Bill Belichick, "An Interview With New England Patriots Head Coach Bill Belichick," 4 February 2005.

[2189] Patriots cornerback Randall Gay, "Quotes from New England Patriots Press Conference," 2 February 2005.

[2190] Patriots cornerback Duane Starks, quoted in: Michael Parente, "Playoff savvy the calling card for Starks," *Herald News*, 9 August 2005.

[2191] Patriots linebacker Ted Johnson, audio recording, 1 February 2005.

[2192] Bill Belichick, quoted in: "New England Patriots head coach Bill Belichick: Post-Game Press Conference," email, 18 August 2005.

[2193] Offensive lineman Stephen Neal, quoted in: Jim Trotter, "Neal pins down his new success," *San Diego Union-Tribune*, 20 January 2005.

[2194] Patriots tight end Daniel Graham, "Quotes from New England Patriots Press Conference," 3 February 2005.

[2195] Linebacker Willie McGinest, quoted in: Paul Kenyon, "The party is over," *Eagle-Tribune*, 18 July 2000.

[2196] Bill Belichick, quoted in: Jim Corbett, "Despite key losses, now is no time to count Patriots out," *USA Today*, 17 August 2005.

[2197] Bill Belichick, quoted in: Jerome Solomon, "With a 40 percent raise, Seymour comes to camp," *Boston Globe*, 3 August 2005.

[2198] David Terrell, "Mini Camp: Day 2," *Patriots Video News*, 10 June 2005.

[2199] Tedy Bruschi, "Bruschi speaks at ring ceremony," *Patriots.com*, 13 June 2005.

[2200] Romeo Crennel, audio recording, 2 February 2005.

[2201] Defensive coordinator Romeo Crennel, "Quotes from New England Patriots Media Session," 3 February 2005.

[2202] Patriots linebacker Wesly Mallard, quoted in: Eric McHugh, "LB candidates state their case," *Patriot Ledger*, 2 September 2005.

[2203] Defensive coordinator Romeo Crennel, quoted in: "Q&A With Romeo Crennel," 17 November 2004, www.nflcoaches.com/StoryArchives/Crennel.asp.

[2204] Defensive tackle Vince Wilfork, "Quotes from New England Patriots Press Conference," 3 February 2005.

[2205] Troy Brown, quoted in: Michael Parente, "Brown in familiar territory at camp," *WoonsocketCall.com*, 5 August 2005.

[2206] Romeo Crennel, quoted in: Patrick McManamon, "Shelton impresses Crennel," *Akron Beacon Journal*, 13 June 2005, www.ohio.com/mld/beaconjournal/11886243.htm.

[2207] Linebacker Willie McGinest, quoted in: Shalise Manza Young, "Pats' vets on guard during camp," *Providence Journal*, 15 August 2005.

[2208] Patriots running back Corey Dillon, "Quotes From New England Patriots Media Day," 1 February 2005.

[2209] Bill Belichick, "Quotes From New England Patriots Press Conference," 31 January, 2005.

[2210] Patriots nose tackle Vince Wilfork, quoted in: Eric McHugh, "First-rounders shine on defensive line," *Patriot Ledger*, 1 September 2005.

INDEX

Alphabetical Index

We hope you have enjoyed Volumes 1 and 2 of *Management Secrets of the New England Patriots.*

A third and final volume will cover several additional topics ("Communicating," "Strategizing," *etc.*) and review the 2004 season—that culminated with victory in Super Bowl XXXIX—and the 2005 season. Vol. 3 will not be completed until 2006. We do not have a target release date.

Please visit PointerPress.com or PatriotsBook.com for updates or to request email notification when Vol. 3 becomes available.

Pointer Press

www.PointerPress.com
sales@pointerpress.com
41 Minivale Rd, Stamford, CT 06907
203.355.0677

We thank you for your interest in *Management Secrets of the New England Patriots*!

Management Secrets of the New England Patriots, Vol 1 and *Vol 2* are available for purchase online at PatriotsBook.com, Amazon.com, and BN.com and at select bookstores.

At PatriotsBook.com, single copies of Vol. 1 cost $19.95 + actual mailing cost and single copies of Vol. 2 cost $24.95 + actual mailing cost. Discounts are occasionally available.

Pointer Press charges no additional packaging or handling fee.

Purchases from PatriotsBook.com shipped to Connecticut addresses are subject to a 6% sales tax.

Orders placed on our website of five or more copies of a single title shipped to a single address will receive a 40% discount plus free USPS ground shipping... when offset-printed copies are in stock. This discount is unavailable when we must order copies through print-on-demand (as is normally the case for two months following a new title's release).

All prices and terms subject to change and subject to availability.

Please visit PatriotsBook.com or PointerPress.com for further details.

Printed in the United States
55956LVS00001B/54

9 780976 203988